THE JOURNALS OF
Lewis AND Clark

The American Heritage Library

THE JOURNALS OF
LEWIS AND CLARK

Edited by Bernard DeVoto

Maps by Erwin Raisz

Houghton Mifflin Company · Boston

Library of Congress Catalog Card Number: 53-9244

ISBN 0-395-08380-X (pbk.)

Printed in the United States of America

FFG 13 12 11 10 9 8 7

American Heritage Library is a trademark of
Forbes Inc. All rights reserved

The cover painting is a detail of *The Rocky Mountains*
by Albert Bierstadt, used by permission of The
Metropolitan Museum of Art, New York.

PREFACE

THIS CONDENSATION of the Lewis and Clark journals cannot
be used instead of the original edition for the purposes of
scholarship. It has been edited for the general reader. Many
entries of the original have been omitted. Of those printed here,
perhaps three-quarters have been shortened, many of them considerably shortened.

My edition is based on the first one, *Original Journals of the
Lewis and Clark Expedition*, edited by Reuben Gold Thwaites.
By the kindness of Dodd, Mead & Company I have been able to
regard that edition as a unit and to use whatever I might choose
to of Thwaites's editorial work as well as the text of the journals.

The Thwaites edition, published in 1904–5, runs to seven volumes of text and a volume of maps. (There was also a more expensive edition from the same plates, in which the seven volumes
of text were divided to make fourteen.) The journals themselves
fill five of the seven volumes; typography and format are such that
the five are equivalent to three books the size of this one. I reproduce here, then, about one-third of the original — rather more
than half of the daily log.

It is generally agreed that the journals are an American classic,
and certainly they are by far the most interesting as well as the most
important original narrative of North American exploration.
Nevertheless, few people have read them. The rarity and cost of
the Thwaites edition help to account for this regrettable fact,
but it is due primarily to the presence in the text of much material
essential to the purposes of the expedition but unrelated to the
running narrative and a considerable drag on it. I have made this

condensation, which omits most of the accessory material, in the hope that by means of it a great book will find a wider public than it has had.

I believe that the narrative is retained intact here, except for Clark's journey in 1806 from Traveller's Rest to the mouth of the Yellowstone River. (For which, since it contains nothing of outstanding importance, I have substituted the summary account in my book, *The Course of Empire*.) That is, I have omitted no important event and no incident of more than passing interest. I have included as much as seemed possible of the daily routine and the continuous direct observation of the new country the expedition was traveling. I have also included representative descriptions of the flora and fauna and all important descriptions of Indian life, omitting anthropological details.

As originally printed, the *Journals* include the courses of the rivers traveled every day, except on the return journeys, and sometimes the courses or bearings of the land traverse. In the notebooks a few of these were entered with the daily log at the end of the proper entry, transferred there from the field books in which they were recorded; more often, Thwaites himself transferred them from the field books. I have omitted all these and all astronomical observations and tabulations of temperature and weather. I have omitted most of the detailed scientific descriptions of animals and plants that were made for the eventual use of Jefferson's scientific correspondents, especially Benjamin Smith Barton. Finally, there are some stretches where Thwaites prints both first and final drafts of daily entries and much longer stretches — from the Mandan villages to the Three Forks, down the Columbia, at Fort Clatsop, the return up the Columbia — where entries by both Lewis and Clark cover the same day and the same action, with Clark frequently copying parts of Lewis's entry verbatim. In such places I have reprinted only one draft, usually the final one, and the entry that seemed to me the more interesting or revealing.

This accounts for considerably more than half of the material I have omitted; the remaining deletions are from the text of the daily log. The original has at least one entry for every day the expedition was in the field. I have omitted some days entirely, most freely in the sections between Wood River and the Platte on the upstream journey, at the Great Falls portage, and during the winter at Fort Clatsop. For the rest my deletions consist of paragraphs, consecutive sentences, or at least whole sentences, but I have not hesitated to omit parts of a sentence at times, to preserve continuity or insure clarity.

I have been unable to devise any satisfactory means of indicating these omissions, and I am convinced that none is necessary or even desirable. I have undertaken to produce a straightforward text which could be read without distraction and as if it were the original account, one to which a reader without a specialist's interests need not bring a specialist's preparation. I repeat, therefore, that this edition cannot be used as a substitute for the full version of the journals. Anyone who wants all the data, full information, or assurance that on any given point he has read everything the captains wrote must go to the original.

The nature of the text itself was something else. My job was clearly to preserve Lewis and Clark, not to approximate Nicholas Biddle's *History*. The spellings of the original are a large part of its charm, and I have not changed them at all. For the most part too I have retained the original punctuation; occasionally a deletion I have made has required me to insert or delete or change a mark of punctuation in order to retain the sense. I have omitted a number of irrelevant or inexplicable quotation marks and miscellaneous symbols or abbreviations whose reference is to deleted passages of observation or description. I have repeatedly indented paragraphs, especially in entries by Lewis, where none are set off in the original. I have occasionally inserted commas where there are none in the text and have capitalized a few words which the original prints without initial capitals. Also in two important passages, both by Lewis, who was the more long-winded of the captains, I have set off as separate sentences elements of long discourses that in the original are pinned together by semicolons. No doubt the reader will wish that I had taken such liberties in several other passages.

A word about parenthetical material is called for. When Thwaites published the journals, he was obliged to reproduce them exactly and to supply editorial emendations. He indicated missing letters and words by printing them in brackets; I have retained almost all such emendations. He also inserted in brackets explanatory material of his own, printing it in roman type. I have deleted some of these interpolations, substituted my own bracketed explanations for others, and kept his without acknowledgment where I saw fit to. Thwaites also had to account for interlineations in the manuscripts, many of which were in the handwriting of Nicholas Biddle. When Biddle wrote the account of the expedition that has remained standard ever since,[1] he had the manuscripts, which Clark had turned over to him, and he also had at hand George Shannon, one of the most intelligent members of the party, whom Clark, the surviving principal, sent to him to provide amplification and eyewitness explanation. Thwaites italicized and enclosed in parentheses additions to the manuscript in Biddle's writing (usually the result of Shannon's explanations) and evidently, though he does not say so, some by Shannon. I have retained many of them; since there was no need to identify them, I have not italicized some that read like natural parentheses by the original writer. Thwaites italicized and enclosed in brackets similar emendations in the handwriting of Clark, Elliott Coues, who in 1893 edited a famous edition of Biddle, or others whom he could not identify, but I have retained only a few of them. All the footnotes are mine; I have used none of Thwaites's.

The entry as it appears here has almost always been written up from notes jotted in field books and from other notebooks reserved for courses, bearings, celestial observations, and related data. Evidently most of them were written in the evening of the day whose date they bear but some are several days later than the events they record. Some written at Fort Mandan, the Great Falls, Bitterroot Valley, and the Clearwater, and many written at Fort Clatsop, turn back to much earlier events and observations. In several places where Thwaites has added material not part of a daily entry but obviously belonging with it, I have not interrupted the continuity in order to notify the reader, though of course Thwaites does.[2]

Whether Lewis kept separate journals during the periods for

---

1 *History of the Expedition Under the Command of Captains Lewis and Clark* (Philadelphia, 1814).

2 Coues, who examined the manuscript material and reported on it to the American Philosophical Society, believed that the finished log, the journals as we know them, were not written till after the return to St. Louis. (Thwaites, VII, 422.) He appears to have been wrong and Jefferson's testimony to the contrary (*ibid.*, 394) must be accepted as conclusive.

which only those by Clark survive is not known, except in the
period following the reuniting of all the parties below the mouth
of the Yellowstone on the return journey, when he tells us that he
did not. On the upstream journey to the Mandan villages and
during the winter at Fort Mandan, the daily record is a log kept
mainly by Clark but with occasional entries by Lewis. In this
period the text occasionally suggests that Lewis was keeping a
separate journal of his own, but if he did none has ever been found.

In several passages I have interpolated entries from the journal
of Private Joseph Whitehouse, which is printed in Volume VII of
Thwaites, and from that of Sergeant John Ordway. Biddle made
use of both when writing his *History* but Ordway's had disappeared
from view when Thwaites prepared his edition. It was later discovered among Biddle's private papers and, edited by Milo M.
Quaife, was published in the *Collections* of the State Historical
Society of Wisconsin for 1916. I have also used several passages
from Biddle, taking them from the first edition, not Coues's re-
print.[3]

I have used only one entry from Sergeant Floyd's brief journal,
which is printed in Thwaites, Volume VII, and only a few from
Sergeant Gass's. The latter was put into elegant English by a
West Virginia schoolmaster and published in 1807, less than a year
after the return of the expedition, seven years before Biddle's
History. The earliest authentic account, it became very popular
and has been reprinted many times, but though most useful to
scholars it is wooden and lifeless. Presumably several other members of the party kept journals; the sergeants were ordered and the
enlisted men urged to keep them. If Pryor, the remaining sergeant,
kept one, no one has ever found it, and we know of only one
private besides Whitehouse who did, Robert Frazier. A manuscript prospectus announcing the forthcoming publication of his
journal survives, but there is no evidence that it was published,
nor has the manuscript been found.

For reference and supplementary reading I suggest John Bake-
less, *Lewis & Clark* (New York, 1947), Elijah H. Criswell, *Lewis*

---

[3] We have had no greater editor than Coues but it is well known that he
had a highhanded way with texts, altering them as he saw fit. Even in the
brief passages I use, his edition makes changes in spelling, grammar, and
wording.

and Clark: Linguistic Pioneers (Columbia, Mo., 1940), Bernard DeVoto, *The Course of Empire* (Boston, 1952), Olin D. Wheeler, *The Trail of Lewis and Clark* (New York, 1904). Coues's edition of Biddle is incomparably the best one and the footnotes and other editorial matter are indispensable to students. Note, however, that much has been learned since Coues and Thwaites and that some of their notes, more of Thwaites's than of Coues's, are in error.

BERNARD DeVOTO

Cambridge, Massachusetts
April 15 1953

CONTENTS

LIST OF MAPS

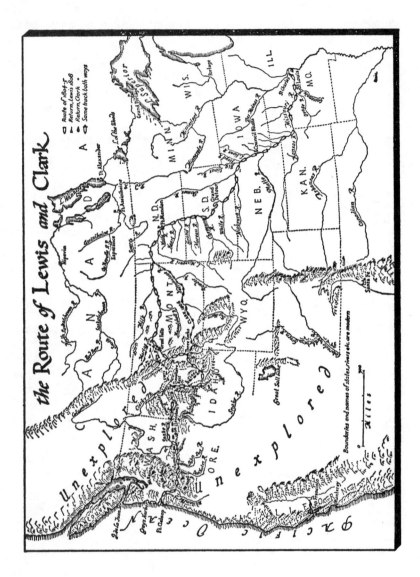

the Route of Lewis and Clark

INTRODUCTION

TOWARD THE END of November 1802, President Thomas Jefferson asked the Spanish minister a carefully unofficial question. Would the Spanish court "take it badly," he inquired, if the United States should send a small expedition to "explore the course of the Missouri River," which lay wholly in the still Spanish territory of Louisiana? The ostensible reason for such an expedition, he went on, would be the advancement of commerce, since Congress had no power to appropriate money for its real object. But "in reality it would have no other view than the advancement of the geography." Louisiana would not continue to be Spanish much longer; it was to be returned to French sovereignty under the Treaty of San Ildefonso, which had been signed in October 1800. But since the transfer had not yet been made, the duty of the minister, the Marqués de Casa Yrujo, was to protect the interests of Spain. He and the Spanish officials in New Orleans and St. Louis had long been afraid of American expansion in Louisiana, and of American and British military expeditions against New Mexico by way of Louisiana. He therefore, with the same scrupulous informality, told the President that "I persuaded myself that an expedition of this nature could not fail to give umbrage to our Government."

"Then he replied to me," Yrujo wrote to his chief, the Commandant of the Interior Provinces at Madrid, "that he did not see the motive why they [the Spanish government] should have the least fear, inasmuch as its object would not be other than to observe the territories which are found between 40° and 60° from the mouth of the Missouri to the Pacific Ocean, and unite the discoveries these men would make with those which the celebrated Makensi [Alexander Mackenzie] made in 1793, and be sure if it were possible in that district to establish a continual communication, or little interrupted, by water as far as the South Sea." Yrujo asserted that there was no need to inquire into this question further than had already been done. He summarized findings of various French, Spanish, Canadian, British, and imaginary explorers in the region proposed. They had demonstrated, he said, that the long sought Northwest Passage did not exist, that "a considerable cordillera" existed between 50° and 60°, that "a very great distance" must be traversed by land, and that Indian tribes had not been able to inform Mackenzie of "any considerable river whatsoever" that flowed from the mountains to the Pacific. In the interest of Spain Yrujo was being a good deal more positive than the state of knowledge justified, was inventing information which no one had, and was actually contradicting some things Mackenzie had said in his book — all of which, of course, Jefferson recognized. But, Yrujo said, "this account of the useless and fruitless attempts, it seems to me calmed his spirit with which he began to talk to me of the subject."

Yrujo had some but not much hope that this would be the end of the proposed expedition. Asking for instructions about it, he ended his dispatch with a comment on Jefferson which expressed the prevailing view of him and his country in the diplomatic corps at Washington. "The President has been all his life a man of letters, very speculative and a lover of glory, and it would be possible he might attempt to perpetuate the fame of his administration not only by the measures of frugality and economy which characterize him, but also by discovering or at least attempting to discover the way by which the Americans may some day extend their population and their influence up to the coasts of the South Sea." He did not need to point out to the colonial minister that the most promising "way" was the one Jefferson had mentioned, the Missouri River, since for ten years the Spanish themselves had been trying to reach the Pacific by ascending it.[1]

---

[1] A. P. Nasatir, ed., *Before Lewis and Clark* (St. Louis, 1952), II, 712–14. For the state of knowledge and explorations of the far Northwest, including Mackenzie and the Spanish efforts from St. Louis, see Nasatir's introduction and Chapters VIII and IX of DeVoto, *The Course of Empire.*

This dispatch of Yrujo's was dated December 2 1802. Two months later, on January 31 1803, he reported that Jefferson "has communicated his design to the Senate, which has already taken a step toward the execution." He understood, however, that the "good judgment of the Senate" could not see in the proposed expedition such advantages as the President claimed for it and was, besides, afraid that "it might offend one of the European nations." Probably therefore, Yrujo concluded, "the project will not proceed." [2]

Modern techniques for leaking to the press the secret proceedings of the Congress of the United States had not yet been developed. Jefferson had sent a secret message to Congress embodying his proposal, on January 18 1803. It had been considered in committees of the whole. The appropriation asked for had promptly been passed by the House and concurred in by the Senate. Thirteen days later a minister is ignorant of the message's content and the action taken on it.

In the message of January 18 Jefferson reversed what he had said to Yrujo. He asked for an appropriation of $2500 to cover the cost of an expedition to ascend the Missouri River to its source and to go on from there to the Pacific Ocean. He suggested that it be made "for the purpose of extending the external commerce of the United States," phraseology which was so general that as the title of a bill it would attract no attention. He would, however, explain the expedition to Spain as "a literary pursuit," that is, as solely an effort to add to geographical and scientific knowledge.

The expedition would indeed accomplish that end but, the message said, its primary purpose was to investigate a commercial opportunity of very great importance to the United States. Certain Indian tribes who lived in the Missouri country were known to "furnish great supplies of furs and peltry to the trade of another nation, carried on in a high latitude through an infinite number of portages and lakes shut up by ice through a long season." A route which would bring this trade down the Missouri to its mouth and then across the United States would be so superior that the established one could "bear no competition with it."

Jefferson went on to tell Congress that the Missouri was understood to traverse country which had "a moderate climate" —

that is, the river did not freeze in winter, or at any rate not for long. It offered "according to the best accounts continued navigation from its source" — that is, there would be no portages at all, as contrasted with the "infinite number" of the northern route. Perhaps indeed, and this was exceedingly important, there need be only "a single portage to the Western Ocean" — that is, trade goods could be carried between the Pacific and the Mississippi with only one transshipment. Then from the Mississippi to American ports on the Atlantic there would be "a choice of channels through the Illinois or Wabash, the (Great) Lakes and Hudson, through the Ohio and Susquehanna, or Potomac or James Rivers, and through the Tennessee and Savannah rivers." [3] The expedition which he desired to send out, the President said, would explore this route and would conduct with the Indians negotiations preparatory to securing to American citizens the trade he envisioned.

The nation he referred to but did not name was Canada, and the route he described was the famous one by which the North West Company transported to Montreal the wealth in beaver it acquired by trade with the Indians west, northwest, and north of Lake Winnipeg. As many entries in the Lewis and Clark journals show, Jefferson believed that by means of the Upper Missouri American traders and carriers could get easy access to the highways of the Canadian fur trade, the Assiniboine, Saskatchewan, and Athabaska

[3] Jefferson was working out a transcontinental route for interoceanic trade, which was the hope that had sustained nearly three centuries of search for the Northwest Passage. He did not need to point out to Congress that some of the routes east of the Mississippi which he named were almost continuous. The one from the mouth of the Missouri to Lake Michigan by way of the Illinois River was interrupted only by the short Chicago Portage; indeed, during the flood season of some years this stretch could be paddled. After the Chicago Portage to Lake Michigan there was no interruption all the way to Oswego on Lake Ontario, and from Oswego a few easy portages led to the Mohawk River. (With equal ease an alternative route led from Lake Erie to the Finger Lakes. Note the relation of both these routes to that of the Erie Canal.) The Great Lakes were not navigable during the winter, however, and a route up the Ohio River would be far preferable — though Jefferson did not say so to New York congressmen. Such a route would necessitate a long interruption for the difficult and costly crossing of the Pennsylvania mountains. Yet in 1803 it was a reasonable expectation that various proposed canals would soon greatly reduce this difficulty, or perhaps even overcome it. In 1802 the Potomac Company, which Washington had helped to organize in 1785, had completed a series of locks round the Great Falls of the Potomac. By 1808 additional locks and short canals provided continuous passage to Harper's Ferry, and eventually, as the Chesapeake and Ohio Canal, the system extended to Cumberland.

Rivers, and to the wealth in furs of the lands they drained. The expedition he now proposed was to establish a basis for opening American trade with Indians along the Missouri — in Louisiana, a province still under Spanish rule though about to be transferred to France. It was also to prepare an early and, so Jefferson believed, very promising effort by American traders to invade, and perhaps eventually to monopolize, the biggest business in Canada.

These were the principal declared purposes of the Lewis and Clark expedition. There were undeclared purposes as well, which will presently be described here. Now, however, it becomes expedient to glance at certain domestic and international matters that were at a critical stage when Jefferson sent his secret message to Congress.

2

THE AREA called Louisiana was the western half of the drainage basin of the Mississippi River, except such parts of it as were acknowledged to have been Spanish before 1762.[4] (Thus excluded is the region south of the Arkansas River, west of the 100th meridian, and east of the Continental Divide.) According to the generally accepted belief, the northern boundary of Louisiana had been established by treaty at the 49th parallel. (Actually it had not been; there was a legal and diplomatic hiatus which permitted the manipulation of many theories and interpretations, one which might well have caused more confusion than in the eventual negotiations with Canada it did.) Jefferson, however, believed that if any portions of the Missouri drainage basin extended north of 49° they were part of Louisiana, and this was in the forefront of his thinking in 1803. The western boundary was the Continental Divide (which was still almost entirely a hypothetical conception), though some people held that, south of 49° and north of the undefined California,

---

4 The fact that the city and "Isle" of New Orleans were east of the Mississippi confused thinking, and therefore negotiation, about the Louisiana Purchase after it was made. Whether the United States had bought "the Isle of Orleans," or part or all of West Florida were questions which provided ample room for honest and dishonest debate and later led to much turmoil, fraud, and even insurrection. The legal question never was directly settled; it was extinguished by the purchase of East Florida and the accompanying concession of West Florida in the Adams-Onís Treaty, signed in 1819.

Louisiana extended all the way to the Pacific. In 1803 Jefferson believed that at least a faint claim to this far-western extension might exist.

Whatever the exact boundaries were, France had ceded Louisiana to Spain in 1762. The cession had a twofold purpose: to win Spain's assent to a peace treaty following the Seven Years' War by compensating her for losses suffered, and to make sure that Great Britain could not acquire Louisiana as well as Canada at the peace conference. Louisiana had therefore been a Spanish possession during the American Revolution and the entire national existence of the United States down to 1800. In October of that year Napoleon, as First Consul, forced Spain to "retrocede" it to France. This cession was made by the Treaty of San Ildefonso, news of which reached the United States in May 1801.

The acquisition of Louisiana was a step in Napoleon's effort to restore the French Empire in North America. In continuation of that effort he assembled two armies. One was sent to San Domingo in January 1802, to recover the island from the Negro dictator Toussaint L'Ouverture. The other, equipped and mobilized with great secrecy, was intended for Louisiana, which it was to secure against the British in the inevitable war whose outbreak would not be long postponed. Also, when reinforced by the one that would reconquer San Domingo, it was to be available for action against Canada — and to awe and if need be invade the United States. As early as April 1802 the State Department learned what its destination was to be.

It never sailed for Louisiana. The army in San Domingo did capture Toussaint but it was wiped out by yellow fever. The regiments that had been mobilized for Louisiana were sent instead to San Domingo, where they too were decimated by the fever and the incessant guerrilla attrition of Toussaint's successors. That Napoleon's great effort in the Western Hemisphere had failed was apparent to Jefferson when he addressed Congress in January 1803, though the full extent of the failure would not be understood till November. In that month the last remnants of the French army surrendered to a blockading British fleet, in order to escape massacre by the blacks.

Spain's cession of Louisiana to France had created a situation of very great danger to the United States. It established on our western boundary, instead of the weak and lethargic government of Spain, the greatest military power that had ever existed, the expanding French Empire under the dictatorship of the man who intended to conquer Europe and so master the world. Unassisted, the United States would be unable to drive the French out except by a total military effort that would require years, and there was little likelihood that under the pressures of war the young republic could hold together for so long a time. "From that moment," Jefferson, a lifelong anglophobe, wrote to our minister at Paris, "from that moment we must marry ourselves to the British fleet and nation." So long as France ruled Louisiana, our hope of safety lay in joint sea power.

That, however, was a long-term problem in foreign relations. The immediate urgency created by the cession was a domestic crisis. The Spanish Intendant took advantage of the impending transfer to reinstitute what he considered the proper trade policy for Louisiana. In October 1802 he withdrew the right of deposit at New Orleans. Together with the right to navigate the Mississippi, the right of deposit (the right to transship cargo from river boats to ocean-going vessels without excise or customs fee) had been granted to the United States for a term of three years by the Treaty of San Lorenzo in 1796, and on the expiration of that term it had been tacitly continued in effect. The withdrawal was a crippling blow to the commerce of the entire United States west of the Appalachian system. Moreover, it was certain that the Mississippi would remain closed after the transfer of Louisiana, for Napoleon's imperial brand of mercantilism would seal it tight against everyone but the French.

Free navigation of the Mississippi and the right of deposit at its mouth, or some other guarantee of free access to the Gulf of Mexico, were economic necessities to the American West. They were therefore political necessities to the United States — and to the administration.

Water transport by way of the Ohio River system and the Mississippi afforded the trans-Alleghany region its only practicable trade outlet. Primarily for that reason the West was but loosely attached to the federal union, which after all in 1801 had been in existence for only twelve years. Throughout the life of the Republic many Westerners had argued and agitated, and some had conspired, for the secession or separation of the West, in order to attach the area to Spain, France, or Great Britain, or to establish an independent republic which could make favorable arrangements with one of these countries. As Washington's Secretary of State, Jefferson had had to deal at alarming length with the possibility that such a separation might occur. Spain had once closed the Mississippi and thereafter, by alternately loosening and tightening control, had repeatedly tried to coerce the United States or detach the West.[5] The treaty of 1796 had quieted both the agitation and the conspiracies but had not killed either of them. All three foreign powers, but most constantly Spain, had given secret encouragement and assistance to Western separatist movements. The attitude toward the West of New England Federalists and the growth of separatist feeling among them following Jefferson's election threatened to intensify such movements.

Moreover, it had always been possible that the impatient Westerners might themselves act to open the Mississippi permanently. They might raise irregular or militia forces and seize New Orleans. (And St. Louis and lesser Louisiana settlements.) That would mean war with Spain, not a dangerous prospect in itself but one that would create a grave, possibly fatal, danger. The world had been on fire since 1792; the wars of the French Revolution were becoming the Napoleonic Wars. In such a world the entrance of the United States into any war would expose it to attack by either France or Great Britain. The outcome might well be destruction.

Jefferson was confident that he could settle both the international and the domestic crises to the advantage of the United States and without war. In the outcome his confidence proved justified. He understood the meaning of events better and estimated the forces at work more accurately than any other statesman of the time. In our entire diplomatic history there has been no greater brilliance or skill than he now displayed.

---

5 The closure was never absolute. The customs house at Natchez and the river patrols ignored some American boats and with even greater frequency granted permission to pass. The uncertainty and the expense combined with the confiscation of many boats and the threat to confiscate every boat, however, were as intolerable as complete closure. Even worse was the flagrant and corrupt favoritism by which the officials, in return for political activity as well as bribes, allowed such agents as Wilkinson the profitable privileges denied the common trade.

Jefferson was entirely clear, as the foreign offices of the other three powers were and long had been, that if the United States entered a war, any war whatever, it would seize not only the mouth of the Mississippi but the rest of Louisiana as well. This fact must be understood, and the further fact that if Louisiana should thus become American only severe defeat could force its return, such a defeat as might involve the military occupation of a large portion of the United States. But it was essential to avoid war. As soon as Jefferson learned that Louisiana was to be ceded to France, he moved to settle the Mississippi question permanently. He directed the American minister to France, Robert R. Livingston, to open negotiations for the purchase of New Orleans,[6] or failing that for the right of deposit or some other means of temporarily saving the situation. Napoleon's foreign minister, Talleyrand, completely frustrated Livingston, refusing to come to grips with his proposals. Yet by October 1802, when the Spanish closed the Mississippi, it was evident that a change in his attitude might soon occur, for the failure of French arms in San Domingo was already far advanced.

The exceedingly sensitive situation became precarious as soon as the closure of the river was announced. It was imperative to prevent the Westerners from taking aggressive action, so that the State Department could continue its work. To convince the West that diplomacy was better than force and that it promised results, Jefferson appointed James Monroe "minister extraordinary and plenipotentiary" to negotiate American rights in the Mississippi. Before Monroe reached Paris, however, Napoleon had accepted the fact that he had failed in San Domingo. Abandoning his plan of attacking the British Empire by way of the Western Hemisphere, he prepared to attack it in the center, by way of Germany and the English Channel. It was certain that on the outbreak of the war he now proposed to make Great Britain, the mistress of the seas, would seize Louisiana. It was primarily to deny her such an enormous increase of wealth and power that Napoleon determined to sell Louisiana to the United States. Empowered to buy a city of seven

---

[6] At various times the size of the area in view varied from a few square miles embracing the city itself, or adjacent to it, on to the entire Isle of Orleans. This was an area of about 2800 square miles, extending to the Gulf of Mexico from the bodies of water lying east of the Mississippi, that actually made an island of the city, Iberville River and Lakes Maurepas and Pontchartrain. As far back as 1790 the United States had tried to buy it from Spain.

thousand inhabitants, Monroe found his colleague Livingston discussing (with the minister of finance, Barbé-Marbois) the purchase of an area somewhat greater than the United States. And since the maximum Livingston had been authorized to offer for New Orleans was only three-quarters of what Napoleon asked, he was haggling over the price.

The Louisiana Purchase was one of the most important events in world history. It was an event of such magnitude that, as Henry Adams said, its results are beyond measurement. Not only did it double the area of the United States, not only did it add to our wealth resources of incalculable value, not only did it provide a potential that was certain to make us a great power, not only did it make equally certain that we would expand beyond the Rockies to the Pacific, and not only did it secure us against foreign victory on any scale conceivable in the nineteenth century — it also provided the centripetal, unifying force that would hold the nation firm against disruptive forces from within. Whether or not the rebellion that became the Civil War was inevitable, the Purchase had made certain that it could not succeed. And there is no aspect of our national life, no part of our social and political structure, and no subsequent event in the main course of our history that it has not affected.

3

A CURIOUS CONVENTION of historiography has long held that the acquisition of all Louisiana was a stunning surprise to Jefferson, and that he believed the area too large to be governed by our political institutions. It is true that he did not expect to obtain all Louisiana at this time and true that he occasionally, though with careful, contingent reservations, faced the hypothesis that a Republic of the West might, at some distant time and in certain eventualities, separate from the old Republic. But to suppose that he did not fully expect the extension of American settlement across Louisiana, or to suppose that he did not expect extension of settlement to produce extension of sovereignty as well, is to ignore the most massive facts about the nation his administration governed. They are all relevant to the Lewis and Clark expedition.

Both as Secretary of State and as President, Jefferson had repeatedly declared that the United States must and would seize Louisiana if war should break out. At an early stage of his negotiations with Talleyrand, Livingston was proposing to buy a large part of Louisiana if not all of it. At the same time Rufus King, our minister to London, was representing to the British that American possession of Louisiana would surely be favorable to their interests. But there was a far weightier fact: if war meant American possession, obviously peace meant it too. The westward progress of settlement that had been filling up the Old West ever since the Revolution was manifestly certain to take the American people across the Mississippi in force, as it had already taken a large number of them by 1803. American sovereignty was manifestly certain to follow them across the river at no very distant date. Early predictions that this would happen, dating back to the adoption of the Constitution or the peace treaty that recognized the independence of the United States, may be dismissed as speculative. (Though the awareness they signalized had also led Great Britain, France, and Spain to endeavor to confine the United States east of the Alleghanies and then, failing that, to detach the West.) But in 1803 the expectation was as logical and as realistic as any on which diplomacy can be based, and discussions of it were routine in the dispatches of all the ministers in Washington. Every chancellery in Europe knew that, unless severely defeated in war, the United States was certain to cross the Mississippi and to advance an unpredictable distance beyond it. Knowledge common to all Europe was not withheld from the American President.

He had, in fact, acted on that knowledge. He was sending, as he had long intended to send, an expedition to explore a water route for American commerce across the territory of a foreign power. He could hardly have believed that the territory was long to remain foreign. The reason why his message was secret was not that the expedition was to be concealed from the three powers, to all of which it would be fully visible and to two of which it was at once formally accredited. Not the expedition but its true purpose was to be concealed. So far as secrecy was possible that purpose had to be concealed, for it had in view the fur trade of Canada, the maritime trade in sea otter and China goods, and the Columbia River, to whose basin the United States had established a valid territorial claim through Captain Robert Gray's discovery of its mouth in

1792. Jefferson's nomination of Monroe to his mission was dated January 11 1803 and Monroe's commission was dated January 13, seven and five days respectively before the secret message; Jefferson had taken up the expedition with the Spanish minister six weeks earlier. That is to say: before Monroe sailed to negotiate for the mouth of the Mississippi, before in fact he was nominated to do so, Jefferson had moved to acquire all Louisiana and, as well, the great expanse that was to be called Oregon. Perhaps it would be just to reverse that order.

The expedition was to be commanded by Captain Meriwether Lewis, First Infantry, U.S.A. He was then on detached duty, serving as Jefferson's private secretary. Jefferson had offered him the position in February 1801, a month before his inauguration. Lewis was a family friend [7] but Jefferson had many friends better qualified by background and education to be secretary to the President. He was, however, uniquely qualified for a project which Jefferson had cherished for many years, the exploration of the Missouri River and the lands west of its source. Obviously, Jefferson entered office determined to carry out the project as soon as possible and took Lewis into his personal and official household for that purpose. Lewis had had a long experience of military command and wilderness life. He was well acquainted with Jefferson's interest in the West and to explore it had long been what he called "a darling project of my heart." And, soliciting Jefferson's help, he had applied to be made a member of André Michaux's attempt to make the exploration in 1793.

Two years as secretary and member of the official family served, as Jefferson said in his instructions,[8] to familiarize Lewis completely with "the objects of my confidential message of Jan. 18, 1803, to the legislature. you have seen the act they passed, which, tho' expressed in general terms, was meant to sanction those objects, and you are appointed to carry them into execution."

The maritime trade of the Northwest coast, which was based on

[7] He had gone to school to the Reverend James Maury, Jefferson's schoolmaster and one of the group of ardent Virginia expansionists who certainly fired his imagination for Western exploration at a very early age. Maury was a conspicuous member of a long line of thinkers who regarded a water route across North America as carrying with it political and commercial domination of the continent. See DeVoto, *op. cit.*, 411 ff.

[8] The instructions are printed as Appendix I.

the value of sea otter furs at Canton, had been opened by the British in 1785. The first American ship that engaged in it was the *Columbia,* on her first voyage, 1787–90, the one before she entered the river to which she gave her name. It was a rich trade and by 1803 the Americans had all but cornered it. The sailing qualities of American ships, the skill of their captains, and American business sagacity had been fundamental in that triumph, but so had the restrictions under which British traders had to operate. Nootka Sound, the original center of the trade, and the adjacent coast were territory in which the South Seas Company held a monopoly charter from the crown; Canton, where the furs were exchanged for China goods, was in the territory of a similar and far more powerful monopoly, the East India Company. The latter had opened the trade but its interests were elsewhere; British traders were forced either to sail under license from it or to find some equally expensive way of circumventing its demands. So that the China trade (comprehending in that term the American commerce with the Orient which did not touch the Northwest coast as well as that which did) had by 1803 become by far the greatest exterior wealth of the United States.

Usually a trading voyage to "the Coast" lasted three years. It was exposed to all the hazards of the Cape Horn route. If the Missouri and the Columbia did indeed provide a water route across North America, as Jefferson believed, the voyage could be shortened, the costs reduced, and the hazards almost eliminated. And there was a further consideration, equally or perhaps even more important in this generation of global warfare. Such a route would be safe from blockade, navies, and privateers.

The discovery of this route would be inestimably valuable to the United States. It is hardly necessary to fill out the syllogism. The route would not be expeditious, cheap, and safe from blockade and attack if the territory it crossed were to remain foreign soil.

These vital considerations grew in exigency as the value of the trade increased and the wars spread. Another compelling circumstance had been intensifying for exactly ten years. The Canadian fur trade east of the Rocky Mountains, much of which Jefferson hoped to divert to American waterways and even to American management, had been endeavoring to establish a base on the Pacific coast.

The development of the trade in the Canadian West and North was primarily the achievement of the North West Company. An organization of remarkably able and daring businessmen, it had become the first large-scale enterprise of the continent and in effect the first trust. It had opened and organized the rich beaver country along the Saskatchewan and Athabaska Rivers, extending its operations to the Arctic on the north, the Rockies on the west, and the Big Bend of the Missouri on the south. By superior skill and enterprise it had won supremacy over its great rival, the cumbersome, conservative Hudson's Bay Company. Yet the English company had an advantage which enabled it to remain in competition and which had grown steadily more important. Like the East India Company it held a monopoly charter from the crown: it alone could use Hudson Bay and the rivers that emptied into it from the west, of which the Hayes was the most important, for access to the beaver country. All the North West Company's goods, supplies, and furs had to be transported to and from Montreal, where deepwater carriage began, along the difficult and almost endless canoe route which Jefferson described to Congress. Every additional mile the North West Company incorporated in its system added to the difficulty and the cost of doing business. Time, distance, logistics, finance, terms and duration of credit had combined to force on the Northwesters an organization remarkably like that of a twentieth-century industrial corporation — all for the purpose of carrying goods from Montreal to the beaver country and carrying furs back to Montreal. Whereas the Hudson's Bay Company, loading its goods at London, could take them direct to Port Nelson, at 92° W. and 57° N. before transshipping them to a river route.

As soon as they reached the far longitudes and high latitudes, the North West Company partners had realized the great desirability of extending their trade network to the Pacific. Deepwater transport to Nootka or some other depot on the coast would neutralize the Hudson's Bay Company's advantage, expediting carriage and enormously lowering the overhead. In 1781, twenty-two years before Jefferson's message, Alexander Henry the elder had proposed to the Royal Society an exploration to discover a water route to the Pacific in the high latitudes. His ideas had been formed by his partner, the crabbed genius Peter Pond. Pond himself trained and inspired the young man who eventually tried to put them into effect. This was Alexander Mackenzie, one of the principal wintering partners, a brilliant geopolitical thinker, and among the most remarkable of American explorers.

In 1789 Mackenzie made an attempt to find the route to the Pacific that Pond had thought must exist north of Lake Athabaska. The venture led him to the river named for him and to the Arctic, not the Pacific. This failure dampened the enthusiasm of the North West Company, but the necessity remained unchanged and the less conservative partners supported Mackenzie's desire to continue the exploration. In 1793, the year of André Michaux's abortive attempt, Mackenzie succeeded in reaching the Pacific after as daring and exciting a journey as any in the annals of discovery. He thus became the first man since Cabeza de Vaca, in 1536, to make a transcontinental crossing north of Mexico. His route involved the Peace River, a stretch of the Fraser River, the Blackwater River, and a long land traverse (the heart of the matter) to the Bella Coola River which led to the sea north of Vancouver Island.

It was a magnificent achievement but commercially futile. To take goods and furs by canoe along this route was impossible. The Rocky Mountains and the kind of rivers that threaded them forbade.

Mackenzie had been led to the Fraser, for which he used an Indian name, Tacoutche Tesse, by Indian reports that it was a big river and emptied into the Pacific. The mouth of the Fraser is just north of 49°, at the city of Vancouver, on the Strait of Georgia, but Mackenzie did not reach the mouth. Unable to take his canoe through the furious water of its upper canyons, he had to abandon it and eventually descended the Bella Coola. When he returned to civilization, he learned that the American Captain Gray had discovered the mouth of a big river at 46°. He assumed that this, the Columbia, must be the river which he had been unable to descend, the Tacoutche Tesse. So, till Lewis and Clark, did everyone else. Meanwhile it remained possible, and in Mackenzie's view likely, that below the place where he had been forced away from it, the Tacoutche Tesse might be navigable and therefore that the North West Company canoes could descend it with their furs. If this were true, the Northwesters must reach it by some route as yet undiscovered — but one that led through British territory.

Mackenzie was now dedicated to getting a Pacific outlet for his company. And now the intensifying urgency that Jefferson felt was communicated to him as well. The Americans had established a claim to the great river part of which, so he thought, he had traveled and which, so he believed, was the solution to the Company's problem. And not only that: the Americans were wresting the maritime trade of the Northwest coast from the British. Mackenzie worked out a plan which foreshadowed the pattern of nineteenth-century British imperialism. But though some North West Company partners supported his ideas, he was frustrated by the hostility, arrogance, and financial conservatism of Simon McTavish, who was the real head of the trust.

In 1799 therefore Mackenzie withdrew from the North West Company and went to England, to try to realize his imperial vision by exterior means. In its final form his plan had three parts:

1. The Hudson's Bay Company must either merge with the North West Company or else grant or lease to it the right to transport goods to the western shore of the Bay and thence to the fur country. If the HBC should refuse to do either, then Parliament must so alter its charter as to enable the Northwesters to use its route. (When it refused, Mackenzie tried to carry the position by financial maneuvers, organizing a syndicate to buy the closely held, immensely valuable HBC stock — it was thus that Lord Selkirk began his fateful career in Canada. In the succeeding years the Northwesters tried to secure the right of transport on the HBC routes by negotiation, by lease or purchase, and by appeal to Parliament.[9] Eventually, following actual guerrilla war between the two companies, Parliament forced precisely the merger that Mackenzie had urged in the beginning.)

2. Either the merger or the North West Company must secure a firm position on the Northwest coast. Thereupon the East India Company must concede it the right to trade at Canton on terms that would make competition with the Americans possible.

3. West of the Continental Divide, British sovereignty must be extended southward far enough to include the Columbia River,

---

[9] British energy and money were absorbed by the Napoleonic Wars or, very likely, Mackenzie's vision would have been acted on by government or by private enterprise. This delay was Napoleon's second gift to American expansion.

which Mackenzie expected to become the route between the beaver country and the Pacific. This, of course, was a problem not for the fur merchants but for the government. In a proposal made after his book was published Mackenzie explained that sovereignty must be supported by a military establishment at Nootka with subsidiary ones at the mouth of the Columbia and elsewhere. He believed that Great Britain had unwisely abandoned her rights east of the Divide when treaties and conventions relating to the Canadian boundary were drawn up, and that the damage thus done must be repaired. He believed, specifically, that Canada was legally and morally entitled to a connection between the Great Lakes and the Mississippi, that it was entitled also to exclusive possession of the great canoe route from Lake Superior to Lake of the Woods, that (west of Lake Superior) British sovereignty extended south to 45°, and that the boundary must be relocated accordingly.[10] If this readjustment could not be made, it was still possible to make the Columbia River securely British and this must be done.

This constituted a blueprint for imperial expansion. At the end of his exposition and analysis Mackenzie says:

By opening this intercourse between the Atlantic and Pacific Oceans, and forming regular establishments through the interior and at both extremes, as well as along the coasts and islands, *the entire command of the fur trade of North America might be obtained from 48° North to the pole, except that portion of it which the Russians have in the Pacific. To this may be added the fishing in both seas and the markets of the four quarters of the globe.* Such would be the field for commercial enterprise and incalculable would be the produce of it,

[10] The boundary ambiguities resulted from ignorance, at the peace treaty following the Revolution, of the source of the Mississippi. Mackenzie's proposal looked to establishing a connection with the Mississippi from the western end of Lake Superior. The St. Louis River would provide the beginning of such a connection but the line must be drawn far enough south to reach the Mississippi at a point where it was navigable by canoes; its extreme upper reach he regarded as "a brook." The 45th parallel is just above Minneapolis; the rectified boundary would run due west from here to intersect a line drawn south from the western shore of Lake of the Woods. It crosses South Dakota, the upper third of which would thus with North Dakota become Canadian, and is the southern boundary of Montana as far as the Continental Divide. Mackenzie's plan allows for the possibility that this equitable and highly desirable relocation might not be secured. But west of the Divide the Columbia *must* be made British and the 45th parallel would effect this; it crosses Oregon just below the latitude of Salem.

when supported by the operations of that credit and capital which Great Britain so pre-eminently possesses. Then would this country begin to be remunerated for the expenses it has sustained in discovering and surveying the coast of the Pacific Ocean, which is at present left to American adventurers. . . . Such adventurers, and many of them, as I have been informed, have been very successful, would instantly disappear before a well-regulated trade. . . . Many *political* reasons, which it is not necessary here to enumerate, must present themselves to the mind of every man acquainted with the enlarged system and capacities of British commerce in support of the Measure which I have very briefly suggested, as promising the most important advantages of the trade of the united kingdoms.

The quoted passage ends Mackenzie's book, *Voyages from Montreal*, which was published late in 1801. Lewis and Clark took a copy of it west with them and it obviously had conclusive force for Jefferson. The President, who already contemplated moving to secure the Columbia to the United States, was thus notified by the most powerful personality in the Canadian fur trade that the fur trust intended to secure the Columbia to Great Britain. The notification, however, only increased his realization that the situation was urgent, for he had long understood the essentials of what Mackenzie set forth.

Following Mackenzie's withdrawal from the North West Company, the despotic McTavish relaxed sufficiently to permit some action on his ideas. For a number of years the fur merchants of St. Louis and the Spanish officials there had known of the company's intention to carry the trade to the Rocky Mountains in Louisiana as it had done in Canada. Now the summer meeting of the North West partners in 1800 voted to send explorers over the Canadian Rockies to the vital area. Duncan M'Gillivray, who was the principal exponent of Mackenzie's ideas, and David Thompson, who was the company's most gifted surveyor, prepared to make the exploration. In the fall of 1800 two of their *engagés* crossed the mountains to prepare a base. Some students have believed that in the next year, 1801, either M'Gillivray or Thompson or both made a quick crossing to the base, but this is not evident and indeed it is unlikely. At least a start had been made toward the execution of Mackenzie's ideas, however, when Jefferson addressed Congress — this in addition to Mackenzie's polemic and his financial efforts in England to get support for them.

These and other efforts continued through the succeeding years. In 1802 Mackenzie returned to Canada and joined the most violent and most successful opposition the North West Company had ever had, a group of former partners and some additional associates usually called the X Y Company in the literature. In 1804 McTavish died and the X Y Company rejoined the North West Company. (News of this reached Lewis and Clark at Fort Mandan; see the journal for March 2 1805.) Immediate resumption of Mackenzie's plan was now possible, and though he was denied participation in field management, Duncan M'Gillivray, who spoke for him, grew steadily in power. Even before tidings of the merger reached the West, François Larocque of the North West Company's Assiniboine Department asked to accompany Lewis and Clark to the Pacific. His request was refused but in the summer of 1805 he made the long contemplated attempt to open the western Louisiana trade, traveling west from the Mandan villages to the Yellowstone River and returning down its valley, while Lewis and Clark were ascending the Missouri. In that same summer, and there can be no doubt that Lewis and Clark were a contributing cause, the partners voted to make a permanent establishment west of the mountains. And Simon Fraser crossed to the Tacoutche Tesse, which in common with everyone else he took to be the Columbia, and built the first trading post on Pacific drainage. He left a party to spend there the same winter that Lewis and Clark spent at Fort Clatsop.

The continuation of this policy may be outlined here. In 1806, the year in which Lewis and Clark made their return journey, Fraser made another extensive exploration farther north, in the country to which he gave the long-memorable name, New Caledonia. He built two other permanent posts there, so that the Northwesters now had three west of the Continental Divide. New Caledonia, however, was in the high latitudes and it offered no water route to the Pacific; it did not satisfy the Northwesters' requirements. In the same year, 1806, therefore, David Thompson sent two men to cut a horse trail across the Canadian Rockies farther south. In 1807, beginning a permanent occupation, he reached the Columbia. He did not recognize it as the Columbia but determined its longitude and realized that it was not the Tacoutche Tesse. (He named it the Kootanae.) The next year,

1808, Thompson moved south of 49° into Idaho. In 1809, provided with information from the first published account of Lewis and Clark, the journal of Patrick Gass, he went still deeper into territory that is now American, the site of Missoula, Montana. But not till 1811 — and there is no satisfactory explanation of his delay — did he descend the Columbia to the sea. He reached it too late by a few months: John Jacob Astor's Pacific Fur Company had got there first and had built Fort Astoria. Meanwhile in 1808 Simon Fraser, triumphing over the ferocious waters that had turned Mackenzie back, had taken a party down the Tacoutche Tesse, now the Fraser, to its mouth. So he had made the shattering discovery that it was not the Columbia after all.

4

UNLESS ALL these forces, pressures, and actions are taken into account, Jefferson's purpose in sending Lewis and Clark up the Missouri and on to the Pacific cannot be understood.[11] (Those mentioned in the last paragraph above were developments of situations already existing in January 1803 when Jefferson asked for the appropriation, and were either foreseen or understood as implicit when he entered office in March 1801.) The "literary" purpose was subsidiary to the others, though it might be of assistance to them. The others can now be stated with assurance.

11 It must be constantly remembered that in 1801 when Jefferson addressed Congress, Louisiana was Spanish territory and destined to become French, and that the United States had a recognized prior claim to the Columbia country, to which Spain had some claim and which both Great Britain (by the Nootka convention) and Russia might also make claim. Thus Jefferson's proposal to establish an American trade route down the Missouri was a proposal to establish American trade in territory from which French law must exclude it. This same route across foreign soil was to be used to give American trade an overland connection with the Columbia. That region, in January 1803, was a legitimate field for American expansion as Louisiana was not. The American prior claim to it was, according to usages of nations, so good that in the same year as Gray's discovery of the Columbia, Vancouver had to take the stand for Great Britain that Gray had never really entered the river, whereas his lieutenant, Broughton, had. This remained the official British stand till the Oregon question was settled.

In January 1803, the attractive force, therefore, was the Columbia region, a detached portion of the American economy, to sovereignty over which the United States had a prior but unadjudicated and untested claim. The tacitly assumed force was the extension of American settlement into Louisiana.

The expedition was to survey in detail the water route up the Missouri and down the Columbia which, so Jefferson supposed, would provide easy transport between the Mississippi and the Pacific. It was to give the United States a direct overland connection with the maritime trade of the Northwest coast. It was to amass the details on which could be laid the groundwork for an American challenge to the North West Company's route of carriage from the beaver country of northwestern Canada, a challenge which might result in just such a trade victory as the sea captains had won at Nootka. Using the standard techniques of negotiating with Indians, it was to prepare the tribes for this challenge, and for the coming of American traders. That is, it was to advertise the superiority of American trade — its superiority to the French-Spanish trade from St. Louis and the British trade of the upper Mississippi and the Assiniboine. It was to establish as much intertribal peace as possible. This much is explicit and another purpose is clearly implied: to buttress the American claim to the Oregon country which rested on the *Columbia*'s discovery by making a land traverse before the British could.

All this in January 1803, when Jefferson addressed Congress and when Louisiana was to remain a French possession. By the middle of June news of Livingston's and Monroe's astonishing triumph reached Washington. The acquisition of Louisiana provided additional duties for the expedition that was to have crossed it as foreign soil. Any fact whatever that could be learned about its far northern fringe would now be welcome, for it might bear on the uncertainties of the boundary and the disputes about them. Also, it was now important to learn as much as possible about the southwestern reaches of Louisiana, the Spanish settlements (which had only an occasional connection with St. Louis), and the topographical, military, and commercial problems associated with them. All the Indian tribes which the expedition would encounter must be notified that the Great Father now lived in Washington and that their allegiance had changed with his residence. In particular the Sioux, about whose hostility to St. Louis traders the administration was well informed, must be impressed by American strength and authority. The British traders who were known to be in the vicinity of the Mandan villages — where their presence was illegal under Spanish law and would have continued to be under French law — must be notified of their accountability as well as their privileges under American jurisdiction. Finally, there was the increased but still deluded hope that the expedition could produce a general prairie peace. It was to induce the tribes to make sacredly binding treaties with one another and it was to persuade delegations of chiefs to travel to Washington, to be impressed by the power and splendor of American civilization.

Two further points. Jefferson's instructions to Lewis say that he need not pay so much attention to the northern affluents of the Missouri River as to the southern ones, for it may be assumed that the British fur companies have pretty well found out whatever should be known about them. This remark is sharply at variance with the behavior of the captains in the field. No other inquiry recorded in the journals is made so persistently as the one about the northern tributaries. At Fort Mandan and beyond it, on both the outward and the return journeys, Lewis and Clark are incessantly preoccupied with the desirability of finding a northern affluent that will lead to the Saskatchewan and the Athabaska. Since this search dovetails with the purpose which Jefferson expressed in his secret message and with his theory about the northern boundary as he phrased it in a memorandum for the ministers to France and Spain, we must conclude that he privately directed Lewis to solve the problem. Finally, the journals contain abundant evidence relating to another purpose that is not specifically stated in either the message to Congress or the instructions to Lewis. The captains repeatedly promise tribes west of the Continental Divide that the Americans will soon open the trade in their country. Two reports by Lewis and one by Clark discuss problems and measures connected with this innovation. The development will require two stages. First, posts will be set up east of the Divide, in American Louisiana, and the tribes will be encouraged to cross the mountains and trade at them. (Protection from the Blackfeet will be provided for them.) Later, when the system has grown in strength, posts will be established west of the Divide, in the home country of the tribes that have become customers during the first stage. No one can suppose that agents of the American government could so confidently promise action of such serious import unless they had directions from the President to do so. Note once more that this trade is to be opened in country that is not American soil when the promises are made.

5

JEFFERSON'S INSTRUCTIONS to Lewis say: "The object of your mission is to explore the Missouri river, & such principal stream of it, as, by it's course & communication with the waters of the Pacific Ocean, may offer the most direct & practicable water communication across this continent, for the purposes of commerce." Ten years earlier, in 1793, speaking for the American Philosophical Society, he had phrased the same objective. André Michaux was "to pursue such of the largest streams of [the Missouri] as shall lead by the shortest way and the lowest latitudes to the Pacific ocean. When, pursuing those streams, you shall find yourself at the point from whence you may get by the shortest and most convenient route to some principal river of the Pacific ocean, you are to proceed to such river and pursue its course to the ocean." When he drafted these instructions for Michaux, the *Columbia* had not yet returned to the States, and so he did not know of Captain Gray's momentous discovery. He reminded Michaux that a large river was supposed to come down to the Pacific somewhere in the vicinity of Nootka, and said that this river would probably prove to be his best route. It was called the Oregon, he said, and its waters "interlocked with the Missouri for a considerable distance." So Jefferson and the sum of geographical knowledge understood. But the Oregon was an entirely hypothetical river, the current embodiment of the imaginary stream, the River of the West, which for more than a century had been believed, deduced, and rumored to cross the part of North America that lay west of the height of land.[12]

---

[12] Rivers that reach the sea must come down to it from a height of land, and on the western coast of a continent the height of land from which they come down must be inland to the east — these axioms behind the theory of the River of the West are entirely sound. The theory, however, had been elaborated from additional axioms which postulated a geographical symmetry at variance with the realities of the North American continent. In its ideal form the theory held that from a fundamental height of land a principal river ran in each of the cardinal directions. The River of the East was the St. Lawrence, which was understood to include the entire chain of the Great Lakes it drained; the River of the South was the Mississippi. The River of the North was hypothetical until the Nelson, which drains Lake Winnipeg, was fairly well understood. By the time the Coppermine and Mackenzie were discovered, the concept of a fundamental height of land had to be abandoned and they could not be assumed to "head" with the Mississippi and the St. Lawrence. By 1793 the River of the West could not head with them, either, but it could with the Missouri.

There *had* to be such a river; the logic of geography, of teleology, and of desire required one. When the Columbia was discovered, it was almost universally accepted as the River of the West. Following Mackenzie's crossing, his Tacoutche Tesse was believed to be the Columbia. The Tacoutche Tesse was the only addition to knowledge of or relating to the vital area which Lewis and Clark must cross, and its relationship was unknown. That area was entirely untraveled by white men: between the Great Bend of the Missouri, in central North Dakota, and the place where the Columbia issued from the Cascade Mountains. Vancouver's Lieutenant Broughton had traveled the Columbia from its mouth almost to that emergence from the Cascades. Mackenzie's crossing had provided no actual knowledge of the area, but it had opened it to additional speculation.

The reader has long since perceived that, in the widest view, the Lewis and Clark expedition belongs to the line of endeavor that had taken Columbus to the New World, the effort to establish a western trade route with the Orient. Specifically, it belongs to the branch of that endeavor which undertook to find direct water communication between the Atlantic and the Pacific, a waterway that led across the land mass of North America. Belief in the existence of such a landlocked Northwest Passage dates back almost to Columbus. Various conceptions of it had existed: as a strait or series of straits leading entirely across the continent at almost any latitude; as such a strait connecting the Pacific with Hudson Bay or the Arctic; as a river route connecting the eastern rivers or the Great Lakes with a body of salt or fresh water in the interior of the continent (the hypothetical or imaginary Western Sea) whence other rivers, or an arm of the sea, would lead on to the Pacific.

By the middle of the eighteenth century, explorations of Hudson Bay had proved that no strait led westward from its far shore, but though this should have destroyed that particular variant of the ancient hope it did not. In 1771 Samuel Hearne of the Hudson's Bay Company went down the Coppermine River to the Arctic. In 1789 Alexander Mackenzie discovered the Mackenzie River and descended it to the Arctic. Meanwhile in 1778 the great James Cook, on his third voyage, had proved that north of Nootka Sound there existed no strait or river which could be the western portal of the Northwest Passage. Gradually the significance of these voyages was realized. When Mackenzie's transcontinental crossing was added to them, that there was no water route to the Pacific in the area of Canada (north of 49°) should have been accepted as proved. For the most part it was so accepted but a few geographical thinkers on both sides of the Atlantic continued to believe that somehow there must be a connection by way of Lake Winnipeg, though the rivers of Lake Winnipeg flow into it from the west. This conception cannot be phrased clearly for it was not precise. But it could convert to the service of wishfulness one hiatus in knowledge that remained following Mackenzie's two voyages. On the first of them he had learned that a mountain barrier extended north all the way to the Arctic. On the second this same barrier, or one to the west of it (and no one, including Mackenzie, had decided which), had prevented him from descending the Tacoutche Tesse to the sea. But how far to the south of his land-crossing did the mountain barrier extend? Yrujo reminded Jefferson that "a very considerable cordillera" existed *between 50° and 60°*. Did it extend below 50° and how continuously? Those who brought Arrowsmith's maps to bear on the problem saw the Rockies as a single chain and knew that this presentation was wholly speculative south of the route ascribed to Peter Fidler, which carried him to 45°. (Actually, Fidler had not reached as far south as 50°.) Northward from New Mexico there was only speculation about the Rockies.

Might there not be a gap in the "cordillera" through which a water route led to the Pacific? There might indeed be a gap, and therefore conceivably (though in retrospect one wonders how) it might somehow connect with Lake Winnipeg. And indeed the best knowledge in St. Louis indicated that there was. On the basis of what St. Louis traders had learned, or thought they had learned, from the Indians, the Missouri River might flow through such a gap — and, in any event, the Missouri could be followed to and into the mountains. And, St. Louis believed, if you ascended the Missouri, which was navigable all the way, it would lead you to within a very short distance of the Pacific, at most a hundred miles.

These various ideas cannot be harmonized — for the simple but adequate reason that they define the state of knowledge, which is always a definition of ignorance as well. But the components of knowledge can never be harmonized until all the relevant facts are in. And the bearing of everything that was known and assumed was clear: the one remaining hope of the water passage from sea to sea was provided by the Missouri River.

Jolliet and Marquette discovered the mouth of the Missouri in 1673. From then on in the ideas that were held of American geography, prismatic with illusion and misconception, the river was supposed to lead near or to the Pacific. No conception of it provided a basis of action, however, and there was no realistic knowledge in the first reasoned proposal to use it as a route to the Pacific, that of the Jesuit Pierre Charlevoix in 1720. Charlevoix had been sent to America by the French government, which was under increasing urgency to reach the Pacific overland, to collect all the existing information about possible routes. He decided that by ascending the Missouri one could reach the Western Sea, which would be found to have some kind of connection with the Northwest Passage. The great explorer Pierre Gaultier de Varennes de la Vérendrye was commissioned to discover the route proposed by Charlevoix. In 1738 he reached the Missouri with his sons, traveling from the Lake Winnipeg region to the Mandan villages below the Great Bend. The Vérendryes were the first white men to see the Upper Missouri (and one of them was the effective discoverer of the other key river of the West, the Saskatchewan) but nothing came of their enterprise.

British thinking about the Missouri route to the Pacific was almost as old, dating back to 1727, when Daniel Coxe concocted the error that was to prove most durable of all, the theorem that only a very short land traverse would be found necessary from Missouri to Pacific waters. Attention was permanently focused on the Missouri route, however, by Robert Rogers, or rather first by his employe Jonathan Carver. In 1765 Rogers proposed to reach the "River Ouragan" from "the head of the Mississippi." It was Carver who, during his journey in Wisconsin and Minnesota, 1766–67, determined that the Missouri was a conceivable route. (And who fixed the spelling of the great name as Oregon.) When Rogers renewed his proposal in 1772, he specified the Missouri, intending to travel it to the source.

Rogers asserted in 1772 that a portage of "about twenty miles" separated navigable waters of the Missouri and the Oregon. Coxe in 1727 had made his hypothetical separation "a ridge of hills" which would prove "passable by horse, foot, or wagon in less than half a day." Jefferson accepted this conception; it defines the "single portage from the Western Ocean" of his message to Congress. It is the basic and crucial conception in his plan, as indeed it had been in all theorems concerning a water route for commerce and (in the Spanish view) for military invasion.

This basic conception, this irreducible minimum, left no room for the Rocky Mountains. Geographical thinking had been unable to imagine them — unable first to imagine their existence and then, when their eastern slope in Canada became familiar, unable to imagine their width or the impossibility of traversing them by canoe. The Spanish knew the southern end of the Rockies in New Mexico and most of the eastern slope in Colorado and in the 1760's they began to travel along the western slope, but did not penetrate them. But the Rockies had been crossed only by Mackenzie's party, and his experience did not give him or suggest to anyone else a realistic conception of the obstacle they were to freight transport by water. In Clark's entry for February 14 1806 Jefferson's "single portage" (Rogers's "twenty miles" and Coxe's "less than half a day") becomes an actual land traverse of 220 miles. That in itself wrecked the expectation of three centuries. And even so, it disregarded the difficulty and expense of water travel on the Missouri above the Great Falls.

In the 1790's Spanish officials and French fur traders in St. Louis had put together from Indian accounts a conception of the Rockies as a single or multiple mountain range that ran parallel to the Pacific coast and a varying distance from it usually less than a hundred miles inland. They believed that the Missouri led up to this range and well into it, or through it by means of a gap or across it by means of a gap and a long and hardly imaginable fall. That vestiges of this idea figured in Jefferson's thinking is evident from his instructions to Lewis and from entries in the captains' journals.

The Missouri was familiar from its mouth to the Mandan villages, some sixty miles upstream from Bismarck, where Lewis and Clark spent the winter of 1804–5. French traders from the Illinois country entered its mouth shortly before 1700. Between 1712 and 1717 Etienne de Bourgmond ranged as far as the mouth of the Platte, perhaps a little farther. The Platte, which was always regarded as the "equator" of the upstream journey, remained the limit of knowledge till shortly before 1790, when somewhat higher ascents were made. Then the Spanish and French of St. Louis undertook to reach the Pacific, both to rescue the Indian trade of upper Louisiana from the British and to secure the route as a military frontier to defend New Mexico. (That New Mexico was considered in danger of invasion by both land and water from Canada shows how ignorant of the land mass they were, how much smaller than it is they conceived it to be.) They got as far as the Mandan villages, but only with great difficulty, and got no farther.[13] They could not finance further exploration nor were they able to compete with the British trade, which had reached the Mandan villages about 1785, coming down from the Assiniboine River and its affluent the Souris.

The tribes between the Platte and the James — Omahas, Otos, and Poncas — harassed and blackmailed the small trading parties that ascended the Missouri from St. Louis. They were less important, however, than the two tribes immediately beyond them, the Arikaras and the Sioux. The former had been till lately a powerful people but they had been weakened by smallpox epidemics and by the Sioux, whose westward migration had reached the Missouri in force. Both tribes sought to establish themselves as middlemen in the upriver trade — the desire of all Indian tribes and a recurrent cause of wars. In this position they could secure the profits of the trade to themselves and could control the supply of guns and powder to their enemies. In effect the two tribes closed the Upper Missouri to St. Louis traders as the Spanish at New Orleans had closed the Mississippi to the Americans. A few years before Lewis and Clark the Sioux had established permanent supremacy over the Arikaras. Among the most warlike of Indians, swaggerers and bullies, bound firmly to the British by the superior goods and cheaper prices of the British trade, incited to opposition by the British who traded with them on the Des Moines and James Rivers, the Sioux were a formidable obstacle to trade, to exploration, and to the exercise of sovereignty over upper Louisiana. That

[13] They supposed themselves then so near to the Pacific that a journey to the coast from the villages, or even from the Platte, and return could be made in a single season. An inexplicable vestige of this naïveté still lingered in Lewis's mind when the expedition started west from the villages in 1805, in spite of the fact that during the winter Clark had worked out an astonishingly accurate table of distances as far as the mountains.

is why so much hung on the meeting of Lewis and Clark with them, which must be regarded as one of the crises of the expedition.

6

IN 1803 MERIWETHER LEWIS was twenty-nine years old. He had joined the militia at the time of the Whiskey Rebellion, at its end he had transferred to the regular army, and he had remained in service ever since. For a short period he had been an ensign in a rifle company commanded by Captain William Clark, and the two had developed an enduring respect for each other. Clark was the youngest brother of George Rogers Clark, who had played the leading role in the actions that saved the trans-Alleghany West for the United States during the Revolution, and whom Jefferson had once proposed to send on an exploring expedition across Louisiana. He was thirty-three years old in 1803. He too had militia service before becoming a regular, and unlike Lewis he saw considerable Indian fighting. He resigned his captaincy in 1796.

Thus both leaders of the expedition had had much experience of command and of wilderness life. Clark was Lewis's choice to share the expedition, and Lewis promised him, on Jefferson's authority, equality of command and a captain's commission. The War Department, however, found bureaucratic reasons to frustrate the President's intention and commissioned Clark a second lieutenant in the Corps of Artillerists. Nevertheless, the journals always refer to him as "Captain Clark" and he signs that rank to orders and other official papers. That the promised equality of command became a fact is evident. But it is also evident that if there had been any occasion to interrupt it, by personality and temperament Lewis was the natural commander and Clark the adjutant. There never was an occasion; the two agreed and worked together with a mutuality unknown elsewhere in the history of exploration and rare in any kind of human association.

Their roles in the expedition are also self-evident in the journals. Lewis was the diplomatic and commercial thinker, Clark the negotiator. Lewis, who went specially to Philadelphia for training in botany, zoology, and celestial navigation, was the scientific specialist, Clark the engineer and geographer as well as the master of frontier crafts. Both were experienced rivermen but Lewis acknowledged that Clark had greater skill and usually left the management of the boats to him. Clark evidently had the greater gift for dealing with Indians. But by chance Lewis was alone at two critical encounters with Indians, the Snakes and the Blackfeet, and he handled them with an expertness that no one could have surpassed. Lewis was better educated than Clark and he had a speculative mind; almost all the abstract ideas and philosophical remarks in the journals are his. He was introverted and mercurial — almost all the bursts of anger and all the depressed moods are his too — whereas Clark was extroverted and even-tempered. Both were men of great intelligence, of distinguished intelligence. The entire previous history of North American exploration contains no one who could be called their intellectual equal.

In fact, intelligence was the principal reason for the success of the expedition, which is also unequaled in American history and hardly surpassed in the history of exploration anywhere. They were masters of every situation and they successfully handled every emergency. Remarkably few emergencies arose, a fact which always defines expert management of wilderness travel. The expedition was of proper, though minimal, size. It was intelligently and adequately equipped, though trade goods ran out and Jefferson was inexplicably negligent in failing to send a ship to the mouth of the Columbia so that the outfit could have been replaced and the supplies replenished.[14] The company was recruited with good judgment and was physically hardened and well disciplined by six months of cantonment life in the winter of 1803–4, on the Illinois shore, opposite the mouth of the Missouri. Only a few infractions of discipline are recorded in the journals and all but one of these occur before the arrival at the Mandans.[15] Moses Reed

14 Obviously, the inventories which Thwaites found and published fail to list the equipment and supplies in full. For instance, in caches at the Three Forks, at the head of the Jefferson, and at Canoe Camp on the Clearwater, almost as much gunpowder is deposited as the inventories show — this on an expedition that had been using gunpowder daily since it left St. Louis and giving sizable amounts of it to Indians. It is equally clear that the original appropriation of $2500 fell short of paying for the expedition but no records of supplementary payments have been found. They could have been made from the Executive's free funds or charged against either the War Department or the State Department.

15 The journals of the captains record the floggings inflicted by sentence of court-martial. Those of Ordway, Gass, and Whitehouse so conspicuously fail to mention them as to suggest that they may have been directed to make no record of them.

deserted in the vicinity of the Platte and so did "La Liberté," a boatman whose connection with the expedition is ambiguous. John Newman was dropped from the permanent party and sent back from the Mandan villages to be discharged, in punishment of an outburst of insubordination. There was no further trouble serious enough to be noted in the journals, and a quarrel between Drewyer and Colter was so unusual an occurrence that it *is* noted. All of which is evidence that cuts two ways: the recruits were sound stock and the captains were remarkable leaders. Unquestionably, military organization and military discipline added effectiveness to the wilderness techniques and so help to explain the success of the expedition, but after the opening weeks of the journals the reader will seldom, if ever, be aware of them.

The only fatality of the expedition, Charles Floyd's death, could not have been prevented. His symptoms suggest a ruptured appendix, which at that period would almost certainly have been fatal anywhere. There was only one serious accident, Cruzatte's wounding of Lewis while they were hunting in the brush. Cruzatte was blind in one eye and the vision of his other eye was impaired, but he nevertheless was one of the expedition's best plainsmen (in the captains' estimation ranking just below Drewyer), as he was its master riverman. And he had been acquitting himself brilliantly as a hunter for two years.

It is the very singularity of these occurrences and certain lesser episodes that makes them stand out so prominently against a background of wilderness travel so expertly conducted that it seems commonplace, to be expected. Indeed, except on the upper stages of the Jefferson, where the labor is enormous, and on the crossing of the Bitterroots where food fails, it seems easy. Yet most of it was exceedingly difficult, recurring portions of it were dangerous in a high degree, and nearly all of it was in country foreign to the wilderness experience of Americans and requiring radically different techniques. Not only the Rocky Mountains, their rivers, and the Cascade Mountains were unprecedented and unimaginable; so were the high plains, the high plateaus, the overwhelming waters of the Columbia, the tremendous forest of the Northwest, and the sodden winter climate there. It added up to a strangeness for which nothing in the previous frontier culture was a preparation. The impact of these new conditions on the frontier consciousness and their strain on the frontier skills were formidable, as the succeeding expeditions by Manuel Lisa and the Astorians amply attest. But there is only a single, momentary lapse in the company's morale, when food fails in the Bitterroots. Running the Columbia rapids in cottonwood dugouts required both skill and courage in the greatest measure, all the more so because not even Cruzatte had ever seen such water, but it is done with entire nonchalance. The same unhesitating confidence in the presence of the unknown and unpredictable can be seen in the decision to strike for the Nez Percé trail when, at Lemhi Pass, they learn that they cannot go down either the Salmon or its banks.

In such episodes certain elements of the wilderness mind reach their highest expression; there are other elements as well. Lewis and Clark exercised a constant but untroubled vigilance. (Nevertheless, they lapsed from it several times, notably at Fort Mandan, when they failed to send with the detail that was to bring in the meat an escort strong enough to keep the Sioux respectful, and when Lewis went to sleep in the presence of the Blackfeet.) Success in a strange country required a curious mixture of open-mindedness and skepticism, capable of adjusting accepted ideas and practices to unfamiliar conditions. It required too both an analytical and an intuitive understanding of geography. Just as Lewis had to amend his disparagement of a grizzly's toughness, so they both had repeatedly to amend their prepossessions and especially their assumptions about the country. The discovery that the Missouri forked at a place where they were not expecting a tributary was a stunning shock. Forthwith they determined that the northern fork, the Marias, was not the Missouri proper, and this determination is a remarkable act of thought, unsurpassed in the annals of exploration in the New World. Yet this analysis of fact, appearance, and evidence, and the empirical demonstration that proved it right, merely confirmed conclusions that both Lewis and Clark reached in the first hour or two. Similarly, Clark knew at once on reaching the main stream of the Clearwater River that it was a part of the same river system as the Salmon River, from whose impassable canyon they had turned back. Lewis clearly ranks with Thompson and Mackenzie as a geographer but Clark had geographical genius.

Ingenuity and resourcefulness in the field are so continuous that a casual reader may not notice them. The portage round the Great

Fall; is a remarkable achievement in all respects, from Clark's survey of the best route to the construction of the crude truck with which the outfit was transported. Perhaps, however, such mastery is to be expected from experienced frontiersmen, who had to be adept at contriving expedients or they did not last to become experienced. What is altogether beyond expectation, and beyond praise too, is the captains' management of the Indians they met. In personal dealings with them they made no mistakes at all. In so much that at the critical points it is impossible to imagine a more successful outcome or a better way of achieving it, whereas it is easy to instance similar occasions when less skillful men failed badly. With the Sioux they were always firm, always clearly incapable of being scared or bluffed, amiable or threatening or defiant to precisely the right degree at precisely the right moments. As a result they won a considerable victory for the international relations of the United States. This triumph served them well with the village tribes farther up the river. But with these tribes, as with those farther west, other qualities as well contributed to their remarkable success. They were obviously unawed and unafraid, but they were also obviously friendly and fair, scrupulously honest, interested, understanding, courteous, and respectful. That last quality must be insisted on, for rare as honesty and fairness were in the white American's dealing with Indians, they were commoner than respect. Lewis and Clark respected the Indians' personal dignity, their rituals, their taboos, their religious thinking, indeed the full content of their thought. They understood that thought so well that they must be ranked among the masters of primitive psychology. Finally there was the simple fact that they, and Clark especially, liked Indians. All this being true, they required a similar attitude from their command.

It paid off. They had no trouble with most tribes, after the Sioux none at all till they reached the decadent, thievish people of the lower Columbia, who had been debauched by the maritime trade, and no difficulty they had with them even threatened to get out of hand.[16] They attached the Nez Percés and the Flatheads to the

16 These tribes had indeed been corrupted by the debauchery, brutality, and terrorism of the Northwest trade, but they were the fringe tribes of their culture group and it seems to be true that they had started on a cultural decline before the arrival of the trade.

American interest permanently. Both tribes were fortunate beyond most others in the missionaries visited on them when the period of Christianizing the Western Indians began,[17] and in the fact that their countries, especially that of the Flatheads, were distant from the area of early settlement. But their loyalty was created by Lewis and Clark. The Flatheads never did commit a hostile act of any consequence, and when one of the most flagrant land-steals in the annals of Indian land-steals was perpetrated, they submitted with bitter fatalism. The Nez Percés accepted great indignity over a long time. When at last an altogether atrocious injustice moved their great man, Chief Joseph, to lead one band of them in a running fight toward a decenter country, he said truthfully that up to that time they not only had never attacked a white man, they had never been offensive to one. (When in the course of the great march Joseph's forces approached the Bitterroot Valley, the Flatheads announced a policy of noninterference, and though they connived at the sale of ammunition to the retreaters they also quietly took measures to protect the white men who had settled in their country and were appropriating it.) The expedition did not win any other tribes so permanently as these, but it established so great a good will as to make the early years of the fur trade era a good deal less violent than they could possibly have been without it.

This climate of approval extended far beyond the tribes which the expedition actually met and it made a kind of culture hero of William Clark. All the Plains and Northwest tribes knew of the Red Headed Chief and came to depend on him for friendship and, if not justice, at least advocacy. He was the white man whose tongue was straight, our elder brother. Miracles were expected of him, indeed he was able to perform miracles on their behalf, but if he had been able to obtain for them any substantial measure of justice it would have been a transcendent miracle. He did what he could; he was able to procure occasional decencies and often able to prevent or moderate indecencies and he accomplished more for the Indians than anyone else in Western history. If a delegation of Indians went to St. Louis, it sought out Clark first of all; if a fur company sent a brigade up the Missouri or into the mountains, it provided itself with a passport in the form of messages and greet-

[17] Henry Spalding and Father de Smet.

ings from Clark. If the U.S. government had to send an embassy to the Indian country it began by trying to get Clark to accompany it, and if Clark consented he was invariably able to get fairer treatment for the Indians and more amenable behavior from them. This subsequent function is a bright strand in a dark history. It has had less attention than it deserves from those who write history; sometime it should be described in detail.

7

CREATING SUCH a predisposition, however insecure, in the Far West must be accounted one of the important results of the Lewis and Clark expedition. Those results were so numerous that little can be said about them in an introduction but they must be characterized. They were of various orders of immediacy and significance.

The first major achievement was the demonstration that the last area of North America in which a commercially practicable water route to the Pacific might exist did not contain one. In the long arc of history this ended the search for the Northwest Passage. And ending that chapter, it closed the volume which opened with the first voyage of Columbus.

Lewis's reluctance to accept the fact which his journey had demonstrated, attested in two of his reports of Jefferson, strikingly signalizes the intensity of the hope. Nevertheless the demonstration was immediately accepted by commercial interests to which an inland water route would have been supremely important. When John Jacob Astor organized a fur company to fulfill the commercial (and incidentally the political) vision of Jefferson, he based the organization solidly on salt-water transport, though he also sent an overland expedition to reconnoiter other areas and to check the results of Lewis and Clark. But unquestioning acceptance of those results was among the reasons why his partisan, Wilson Price Hunt, abandoned the Upper Missouri route and crossed to the south of it.

With the transcontinental water route, Jefferson's hope of engrossing the Canadian fur trade, or at least its carriage, disappeared too. It was not a realistic hope anyway, even if such a route had existed, but on the other hand in the outcome this potential wealth was not missed. Lewis and Clark established that the

American West was a treasury of beaver and its exploitation began at once. The amazing solitary pair of trappers whom they met near the mouth of the Yellowstone in 1806, Dixon and Handcock, were the portents that heralded developments to come. St. Louis capital was behind the venture of Manuel Lisa the next year, 1807. Lisa hired three of the expedition's veterans, Drewyer, Potts, and Wiser, and, meeting Colter on his way downriver from his winter with the forerunners, persuaded him too to return to the fur country. Lisa's first Missouri voyage is the beginning of the Western fur trade, and he was bound for the fields that Lewis and Clark had most highly recommended, the Three Forks and the valley of the Yellowstone. The Western trade, roughly divided between two regions, the Upper Missouri and the Rocky Mountains, was continuous thenceforward and steadily increased in importance till the break in beaver prices toward the end of the 1830's. The "mountain men" whom the trade developed completed the exploration of the West that Lewis and Clark had begun.

It may be that to secure the Columbia country — Oregon — was the earliest as it was certainly the most urgent of Jefferson's purposes. The expedition served it vitally; in fact, one is justified in saying, decisively. The land traverse bolstered the claim established by Robert Gray's discovery and was of equal or greater legal importance; in international polity the two combined to give the United States not only a prior but a paramount claim. More, it was the journey of Lewis and Clark that gave the American people a conviction that Oregon was theirs and this conviction was more important than the claim. And pragmatically, the establishment of Fort Astoria by Astor's party won the British-American race to the Pacific. Astor's American Fur Company and Pacific Fur Company were established not only as a result of the expedition's reports but in exact accordance with Lewis's analysis of the practices required.

Here we may glance at a map. The route of the Western emigration was to be that of the Platte Valley, pioneered in 1824 and 1825 by William Ashley and his subordinates when the Arikaras tried their hand at closing the Missouri. The emigration had to be by land travel; distances and geographical conditions necessitated it. They also made the Platte Valley the route of the Pacific Railroad. Nevertheless, despite the circuitousness of the

Missouri and the hazards and difficulties of traveling it by boat it remained an important route to the West, the Rockies, and the Northwest till the end of the steamboat age. And the railroads which ended that age on the Missouri followed its valley, and beyond it, in great part followed the route of Lewis and Clark to the Northwest. How minutely the expedition pioneered one main course of American economic development a list of names reveals at once: Kansas City, Leavenworth, St. Joseph, Atchison, Omaha, Council Bluffs, Sioux City, Yankton, Pierre, Bismarck, Williston, Miles City, Billings, Bozeman, Fort Benton, Great Falls, Helena, Dillon, Salmon, Missoula, Lewiston, Walla Walla, Portland, Astoria.

A century and a half later, it is still impossible to make a satisfactory statement about the scientific results of the expedition: qualified scientists and historians have not been interested in making the requisite studies. Lewis's untimely death in 1809 [18] prolonged the already serious delay in the issuance of a detailed official account of the expedition. Unquestionably he would have written one if he had lived and he was in a better position to formulate findings than Biddle, who wrote the invaluable *History*. As it is, the only "literary" results that were not indirect are anthropological. The voluminous notes on Indian tribes, mainly by Lewis, which were sent to the War Department from the Mandan villages in 1805, were codified and tabulated and published as "A Statistical View of the Indian Nations Inhabiting the Territory of Louisiana . . ." [19] This report was at once immensely important and, as the first survey of the trans-Mississippi tribes, is permanently important.

The "Statistical View" defines the nature of Biddle's *History*, through which mainly the "literary" purposes of the expedition were fulfilled. Lewis's carefully assembled Indian vocabularies were lost but Biddle worked into narrative an enormous amount

[18] He died in a squalid roadside cabin, used as an ordinary, in frontier Tennessee. He was en route from St. Louis to Washington to cope with snarls of red tape which, from political motives, had brought his official accounts into question. (He was Governor of Louisiana Territory.) The circumstances of the mysterious affair strongly suggest murder but Jefferson, who knew that he was subject to fits of depression, believed that he had committed suicide and it is clear that he was in a very nervous state when he left St. Louis.

[19] *American State Papers*, Indian Affairs, No. 113, 9th Cong., 1st Sess.

of the information about Indians that the journals contained. He also wrote several extended passages of generalization, based not only on the journals but on communications from Clark and discussions with George Shannon, and these too are amazingly sound and useful. The *History* is the first detailed account, and one may add the first reliable account of whatever length, of the Western tribes. It put a valuable bulk of knowledge at the disposal of anyone who had interest in or use for knowledge relating to the Indians of the West. So it has always been a prime source for anthropologists and historians.

But that, of course, is true of much more than anthropology. History is not so divisible as to permit us to say exactly how important the Lewis and Clark expedition was in securing Oregon, as a physical possession, to the United States, though its paramount importance is self-evident. But it gave not only Oregon but the entire West to the American people as something with which the mind could deal. The westering people had crossed the Mississippi with the Louisiana Purchase and by that act had acquired the manifest destiny of going on to the Pacific. But the entire wilderness expanse, more than twice the size of the United States at the beginning of Jefferson's administration, was a blank, not only on the map but in human thought. It was an area of rumor, guess, and fantasy. Now it had been crossed by a large party who came back and told in assimilable and trustworthy detail what a large part of it was. Henceforth the mind could focus on reality. Here were not only the Indians but the land itself and its conditions: river systems, valleys, mountain ranges, climates, flora, fauna, and a rich and varied membrane of detail relating them to one another and to familiar experience. It was the first report on the West, on the United States over the hill and beyond the sunset, on the province of the American future. There has never been another so excellent or so influential. So it was rather as a treasury of knowledge than as a great adventure story that the *History* became a national and international favorite, reprinted, translated, pirated, and counterfeited. It satisfied desire and it created desire: the desire of the westering nation.

That, the increase of our cultural heritage, the beginning of knowledge of the American West, must be accounted the most important result of the Lewis and Clark expedition.

THE JOURNALS OF
Lewis AND Clark

NOTE

THE NAME ENCLOSED in brackets at the beginning of a section is that of the author of the entire section, whether it consists of a single entry or a sequence of entries. Connective passages by the editor of this edition are set in italics.

Explanatory interpolations printed in roman and enclosed in brackets are by Thwaites or the present editor. Those italicized and enclosed in brackets are by Nicholas Biddle, Elliott Coues, or unidentifiable persons. Those italicized and enclosed in marks of parentheses are by Biddle and usually represent explanations by George Shannon.

"L.S." usually means "larboard side" and "S.S." usually means "starboard side"; that is, to the left and the right of the boat. Sometimes, however, they mean the left and the right banks of the river, which on the upstream journey are to the right and the left respectively of the boat, and occasionally "S.S." evidently means the south side of the river, which on a small-scale map may appear to be the east side.

The white pirogue has six oars and as far as the Mandan villages is commanded by Corporal Richard Warfington and rowed by six soldiers who, with him, have been detached from the garrison at St. Louis. The red pirogue, seven oars, is rowed by a party of hired French boatmen whose "patroon" is Baptiste Deschamps (see Appendix II).

CHAPTER I

FROM RIVER DUBOIS TO THE PLATTE

[Biddle]

On the acquisition of Louisiana, in the year 1803, the attention of the Government of the United States was early directed towards exploring and improving the new territory. Accordingly, in the summer of the same year, an expedition was planned by the President for the purpose of discovering the courses and sources of the Missouri and the most convenient water communication thence to the Pacific ocean. His private secretary, captain Meriwether Lewis, and captain William Clarke [Biddle's misspelling], both officers of the army of the United States, were associated in the command of this enterprize. After receiving the requisite instructions, captain Lewis left the seat of government and, being joined by captain Clarke at Louisville, in Kentucky, proceeded to St. Louis, where they arrived in the month of December. Their original intention was to pass the winter at La Charrette, the highest settlement on the Missouri. But the Spanish commandant of the province, not having received an official account of its transfer to the United States, was obliged by the general policy of his government to prevent strangers from passing through the Spanish territory. They therefore encamped at the mouth of Wood River on the eastern side of the Mississippi, out of his jurisdiction, where they passed the winter in disciplining the men and making the necessary preparations for setting out early in the Spring, before which the cession was officially announced.

The party consisted of: nine young men from Kentucky; 14 soldiers of the United States Army, who volunteered their services; two French watermen [Cruzatte, Labiche]; and interpreter and hunter [Drewyer]; and a black servant [York] belonging to captain

1

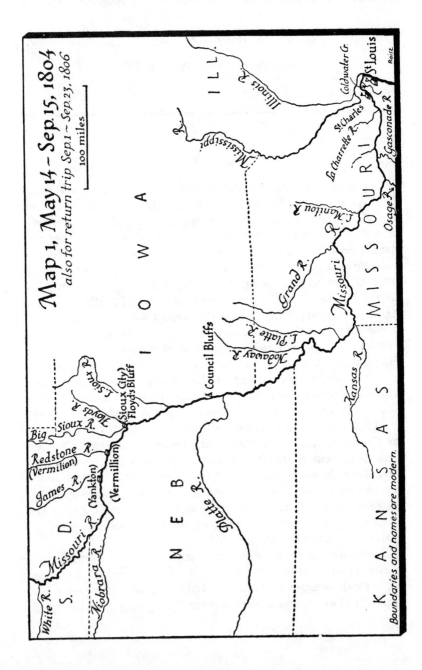

Map 1, May 14 – Sep 15, 1804
also for return trip Sep 1 – Sep 23, 1806
100 miles

Boundaries and names are modern.

Clarke. All these except the last were enlisted to serve as privates during the expedition, and three sergeants appointed from amongst them by the captains [Ordway, Pryor, and Floyd]. In addition to these were engaged a corporal and six soldiers, and nine watermen, to accompany the expedition as far as the Mandan nation, in order to assist in carrying the stores or repelling an attack, which was most to be apprehended between Wood River and that tribe. The party was to embark on board of three boats; the first was a keel-boat fifty-five feet long, drawing three feet of water, carrying one large squaresail and twenty-two oars. A deck of ten feet in the bow and stern formed a forecastle and cabin, while the middle was covered by lockers, which might be raised so as to form a breast-work in case of attack. This was accompanied by two perioques [pirogues] or open boats, one of six and the other of seven oars. Two horses were at the same time to be led along the banks of the river for the purpose of bringing home game or hunting in case of scarcity.

[Clark]   MONDAY MAY 14TH 1804

Rained the fore part of the day   I determined to go as far as St. Charles a french Village 7 Leags. up the Missourie, and wait at that place untill Capt. Lewis could finish the business in which he was obliged to attend to at St. Louis and join me by Land from that place 24 miles

I Set out at 4 oClock P.M, in the presence of many of the neighbouring inhabitents, and proceeded on under a jentle brease up the Missouri to the upper Point of the 1st Island 4 Miles and camped on the Island which is Situated Close on the right (or Starboard) Side, and opposit the mouth of a Small Creek called Cold water,   a heavy rain this after-noon

MAY 15TH TUESDAY —

at 9 oClock Set out and proceeded on 9 miles passed two Islands & incamped on the Starbd. Side at a Mr. Pipers Landing opposet an Island, the Boat run on Logs three times to day, owing her being too heavyly loaded a Sturn,   a fair after noon,   I saw a number of Goslings to day on the Shore, the water excessively rapid, & Banks falling in.

MAY 16TH WEDNESDAY

pass a remarkable Coal Hill on the Larboard Side, Called by the French Carbonere, this hill appear to Contain great quantity of Coal   from this hill the Village of St. Charles may be Seen at 7 miles distance. we arrived at St. Charles at 12 oClock   a number Spectators french & Indians flocked to the bank to See the party. This Village is about one mile in length, Situated on the North Side of the Missourie at the foot of a hill from which it takes its name *Peetiete Coete* or the *Little hill*   This Village Contns. about 100 houses, the most of them small and indefferent and about 450 inhabitents Chiefly French,   those people appear Pore, polite & harmonious.

May 17, Warner and Hall court-martialed and sentenced to 25 lashes for being absent without leave, and Collins to 50 lashes for the same offense aggravated by insubordination. Clark remits sentences of Warner and Hall. Lewis joins the party from St. Louis, May 20.

[Clark]   MAY 21ST 1804 MONDAY —

All the forepart of the Day arranging our party and procureing the different articles necessary for them at this place. Set out at half passed three oClock under three Cheers from the gentlemen on the bank and proceeded on to the head of the Island (which is Situated on the Stbd. Side) 3 Miles   Soon after we Set out to day a hard Wind from the W.SW accompanied with a hard rain, which lasted with Short intervales all night,

MAY 24TH THURSDAY 1804 —

passed a verry bad part of the River Called the Deavels race ground, this is where the Current Sets against some projecting rocks for half a Mile on the Labd. Side, passed between a Isld. and the Lbd. Shore a narrow pass   above this Isld. is a verry bad part of the river,   We attempted to pass up under the Lbd. Bank which was falling in so fast that the evident danger obliged us to cross between the Starbd Side and a Sand bar in the middle of the river,   We *hove* up near the head of the Sand bar, the Same moveing & backing caused us to run on the sand. The Swiftness of the Current Wheeled the boat, Broke our *Toe* rope, and was nearly over Setting the boat,   all hands jumped out on the upper Side and bore on that Side untill the Sand washed from under the boat and Wheeled on the next bank   by the time She wheeled a 3rd Time   got a rope fast to her Stern and by the means of swimmers was Carred to Shore and when her stern was down whilst in the act of Swinging a third time into Deep Water near the Shore,   we returned, to the Island where we Set out and assended under the Bank which I have just mentioned, as falling in,

MAY 25TH FRIDAY 1804 —

Camped at the mouth of a Creek called River a Chouritte [*La Charrette*], above a Small french Village of 7 houses and as many families, settled at this place to be convt. to hunt, & trade with the Indians,   here we met with M. Louisell,[1] imedeately down from the Seeder Isld. Situated in the Country of the Sciox [Sioux] 400 Leagues up   he gave us a good Deel of information [and] Some letters   he informed us that he Saw no Indians on the river below the *Poncrars* [Poncas].

Clark, being the better riverman, is usually on the boat, Lewis usually on shore, hunting and making notes on topography, flora and fauna. The expert Drewyer and from two to five others are usually on shore too, hunting; frequently some of them are away overnight. On May 27 they pass the mouth of the Gasconade

---

1 Régis Loisel, an experienced St. Louis trader who had succeeded to the Missouri Company, the principal effort made during the 1790's to establish trade with the Mandans and explore the Upper Missouri. His first upriver venture, in (probably) 1800, was (probably) frustrated by the Sioux. In 1801 he entered into a kind of partnership with Hugh Heney, whom the expedition will meet later on. In 1802 he built the trading post here alluded to on Cedar Island, just above the Grand Detour. He returned to it in 1803 and during the following winter suffered many indignities and much financial loss at the hands of the Sioux. On starting downriver, he had instructed his principal assistant, Tabeau (of whom the captains had heard in St. Louis), to push on with seven men to the Arikaras.

Though Clark gives no evidence that he was aware of it, Daniel Boone, now seventy years old, was living either at La Charrette or a few miles below it on Femme Osage Creek.

River; also a party of traders returning from the Omahas, another from the Pawnees, and a third from the Osages.

[Clark]   MAY 31ST THURSDAY 1804 —

rained the greater part of last night, the wind from the West raised and blew with great force untill 5 oClock p.m. which obliged us to lay by a *cajaux* [raft] of Bear Skins and pelteries came down from the Grand Osarge [Osage], one french man, one Indian, and a squaw,   they had letters from the man Mr. Choteau Sent to that part of the Osarge nation settled on Arkansa River mentioning that his letter was commited to the flaims,   the Inds. not believing that the Americans had possession of the Countrey they disregard'ed St Louis & their Supplies &c. Several *rats* of Considerable Size was Caught in the woods to day. Capt. Lewis went out to the woods & found many curious Plants & Srubs,   one Deer killed this evening.

JUNE 2ND SATTURDAY

[At the mouth of the Osage River.]

George Drewyer & John Shields who we had sent with the horses by Land on the N. Side joined us this evening much worsted, they being absent Seven Days depending on their gun, the greater part of the time rain,   they were obliged to raft or Swim many Creeks,   those men gave a flattering account of the Countrey Commencing below the first hill on the N Side and extend'g Parrelal with the river for 30 or 40 Ms.   The Two Muddy rivers passing thro. & som fine Springs & Streems   our hunters kill several Deer to day,

JUNE 5TH TUESDAY 1804 —

after Jurking the meet killed yesterday and Crossing the hunting party we Set out at 6 oClock,   at 11 oClock brought too a small Caissee [raft] in which was two french men, from 80 Leagues up the Kansias [Kansas] R. where they wintered, and Cought a great quantity of Beaver, the greater part of which they lost by fire from the Praries,   those men inform that the Kansas Nation are now out in the plains hunting Buffalow, they hunted last winter on this river   Passed a projecting rock on which was painted a figure and a Creek at 2 ms. above Called Little Manitou Creek, from the Painted rock passed a Small Creek on L.S. opposit a verry bad Sand bar of Several Ms. in extent, which we named *Sand C,*   here my Servent York Swam to the Sand bar to geather Greens for our Dinner, and returned with a Sufficent quantity wild *Creases [Cresses]* or Tung grass,   we passed up for 2 ms. on the L. S. of this Sand and was obliged to return, the watr. uncertain the quick Sand moveing   we had a fine wind, but could not make use of it, our Mast being broke, we passed between 2 Small Islands in the Middle of the Current, & round the head of three a rapid Current for one mile and Camped on the S. S. opsd. a large Island in the middle of the river,   one Perogue did not get up for two hours, our Scout discovd. the fresh sign of about 10 Inds.   I expect that those Indians are on their way to war, against the Osages nation probably they are the Saukees [Sauks].

JUNE 7TH THURSDAY 1804 —

a Short distance above the mouth of [a] Creek, is Several Courious paintings and carving on the projecting rock of Limestone inlade with white red & blue flint, of a verry good quallity,   the Indians have taken of this flint great quantities. We landed at this Inscription and found it a Den of Rattle Snakes,   we had not landed 3 Minites before three verry large Snakes was observed in the Crevises of the rocks & killed.

9TH OF JUNE 1804 SATTURDAY —

we got fast on a Snag Soon after we Set out which detained us a Short time   passed the upper Point of the Island,   Several Small Chanels running out of the River below a Bluff & Prarie (Called the Prarie of Arrows) where the river is confined within the width of 300 yds.   opposit the Lower point of the 2d Island on the S. S.   we had like to have Stove our boat, in going round a Snag her Stern Struck a log under water & She Swung round on the Snag, with her broad Side to the Current expd. to the Drifting timber,   by the active exertions of our party we got her off in a fiew Mints. without engerey [injury] and Crossed to the Island where we Campd.   Seeing them and the banks too uncertain to Send her over.

12TH OF JUNE. TUESDAY 1804

at 1 oClock we brought too [to] two Chaussies one loaded with furs & Pelteries, the other with Greece   we purchased 300 lbs of Greese, and finding that old Mr. Durioun [2] was of the party we questioned him untill it was too late to Go further, and Concluded to Camp for the night,   those people inform nothing of much information.

Concluded to take old Durioun back as fur as the Soux nation with a view to get some of their Cheifs to visit the Presdt. of the United S. (This man being a verry confidential friend of those people, he haveing resided with the Nation 20 odd years) and to accompany them on

JUNE 17TH SUNDAY 1804

we Set out early and proceeded on one mile & came too to make oars, & repair our cable & toe rope &c. &c. which was necessary for the Boat & Perogues,   Sent out Sjt. Pryor and Some men to get ash timber for ores, and Set some men to make a Toe Rope out of the Cords of a *Cable* which had been provided by Capt. Lewis at Pittsburg for the Cable of the boat. George Drewyer our hunter and one man came in with 2 Deer & a Bear, also a young Horse, they had found in the Prarie, this horse has been in the Prarie a long time and is fat,   I Suppose, he has been left by Some war party against the *Osage,*   This is a Crossing place for the war parties against that nation from the *Saukees, Aiaouez* [Iowas], & Souix.   The party is much aflicted with *Boils,* and Several have the Deassentary, which I contribute to the water   The Countrey about this place is butifull on the river rich & well timbered on the S. S.   about two miles back a Prarie coms which is rich and interspursed with groves of timber,   the count[r]y rises at 7 or 8 miles Still further back and is rolling. on the L. S. the high lands & Prarie coms. in the bank

2 Pierre Dorion was a St. Louis trader who had many years of experience with the Yankton Sioux on the Des Moines and James Rivers. Competitors accused him of the violence and dishonesty that were commonplace in the fur trade. His marked success with the Sioux rested in his courage: they simply could not bully him. Marrying a Yankton woman, he became the father of Pierre Dorion, Jr., whom the expedition presently meets. The younger Dorion's Iowa wife, Marie Aioë, was to be the heroine of the Astorian expedition.

of the river and and continus back, well watered and abounds in
Deer Elk & Bear   The Ticks & Musquiters are verry troublesome.

*It is full summer on the Missouri, which means ferocious heat
broken by sudden, violent storms. Storms endanger the boats; so
do the many snags past some of which they have to be towed by
handline, an operation made risky by the swiftness of the current.
"Mosquitoes and Ticks are noumerous & bad," but all the diarists
repeatedly remark on the beauty and richness of the land. On
June 26 they reach the mouth of the Kansas River, the future site
of Westport Landing and Kansas City. Here a big bend in the
Missouri changes the direction of travel from predominantly west
to predominantly north. June 29, Hall given 50 lashes for stealing
whiskey and Collins 100 lashes for being drunk on post and for
permitting the theft. July 3, first sign of beaver. July 4 celebrated
by the discharge of a swivel gun [3] and an extra issue of whiskey,
and Joseph Fields bitten by a snake, apparently a rattler. July 7,
the mouth of the Nodaway River; a case of sunstroke — the
extreme heat is affecting many of the party. July 12, Willard given
100 lashes for sleeping on post (in the circumstances a capital
offense).*

[Clark]   July 14th Satturday 1804 —

Some hard Showers of rain this morning prevented our Setting
out untill 7 oClock,   at *half past Seven,* the atmispr. became
Sudenly darkened by a black and dismal looking Cloud,   at the
time we were in a Situation (not to be bettered,) near the upper
point of the Sand Island, on which we lay, and the opposit Shore,
the *bank* was falling in and lined with snags as far as we could
See down,   in this Situation the Storm which passd. over an
open Plain from the N. E. Struck the our boat on the Starbd.
quarter, and would have thrown her up on the Sand Island dashed
to pices in an Instant, had not the party leeped out on the Leward

---

[3] Two Swivels were mounted on the keelboat, bow and stern, and one on
each of the pirogues. They were small guns, perhaps the length of saluting
cannon and somewhat larger of bore, mounted on swivels that enabled them to
be traversed. They were loaded with balls or miscellaneous scrap-iron (langrage).

Side and kept her off with the assistance of the ancker & Cable, untill the *Storm* was over,   the waves washed over her windward Side and she must have filled with water if the *Lockers* which is [had not been] covered with *Tarpoling* & threw of the Water & prevented any quantity getting into Bilge of the Boat   In this Situation we Continued about 40 Minits. when the Storm Sudenly Seased and the river become Instancetaniously as Smoth as Glass.

The two *perogus* dureing this Storm was in a Similar situation with the boat about half a mile above. Several men unwell with *Boils, Felons,* &c. The river falls a little.

JULY 20TH FRIDAY 1804 —

It is worthey of observation to mention that our Party has been much healthier on the Voyage than parties of the same number is in any other Situation. Tumers have been troublesome to them all.

From this evenings encampment a man may walk to the Pani [*Pawnee*] Village on the S bank of the Platt River in two days, and to the *Otteaus* [Otos] in one day,[4] all those Indians are Situated on the South bank of the Platt River,   as those Indians are now out in the Praries following & Hunting the buffalow, I fear we will not see them.

JULY 21st SATTURDAY 1804 —

Set out early under a gentle breeze from the S. E. proceeded on verry well,   passed a willow Island on the L. S. opposit a bad Sand bar,   Some high lands covered with timber L. S. in this hill is limestone and semented rock of shels &c.   in high water the opposit Side is cut thro: by several Small channels, forming Small Islands, a large Sand bar opposit the Hill,   at 7 oClock the wind luled and it Commns'd raining, arrived at the lower Mouth of the Great River *Platt* [Platte] at 10 oClock, (about 3 ms. above the Hill of wood land)   the Same range of High land continus within ¾ of a mile of the Mouth below   This

---

4 Clark is taking these distances from a copy of James Mackay's map. (Later reproduced, in a less detailed version, by Perrin du Lac.) But Drewyer, Cruzatte, and several members of Deschamps' crew were familiar with this area.

Great river being much more rapid than the Missourie forces its Current against the opposit Shore. The Current of this river comes with great velosity roleing its Sands into the Missouri, filling up its Bead & Compelling it to incroach on the S [North] Shore. we found great dificuelty in passing around the Sand at the Mouth of this River. Capt. Lewis and Myself with 6 men in a perogue went up this Great river Platt about 2 [one] Miles, found the Current verry rapid roleing over Sands, passing through different Channels none of them more than five or Six feet deep, about 900 [600] yards Wide at the Mouth,   I am told by one of our Party who wintered two winters on this river, that "it is much wider above, and does not rise more than five or six feet"   Spreds verry wide and from its rapidity & roleing Sands Cannot be navagated with Boats or Perogues. The Indians pass this river in Skin Boats which is flat and will not turn over. The Otteaus a Small nation reside on the South Side 10 Leagues up, the Panies [Pawnees] on the Same Side 5 Leagues higher up. about 10 Leagues up this river on the S. Side a Small river Comes into the Platt Called Salt River, "the water So brackish that it Can't be Drank at Some Seasons,   we proceeded on to get to a good place to Camp and Delay a fiew days and Campd. for the night on the L. S.   a verry hard wind from the N. W.   I went on Shore S. S. and proceeded up one mile thro: high Bottom land open   a great number of wolves about this evening

JULY 22ND SUNDAY 1804 —

Came too and formed a Camp on the S. S. above a Small Willow Island, and opposit the first Hill which aproach the river on the L. S. and covered with timber of Oake Walnut Elm &c. &c.

This being a good Situation and much nearer the Otteaus town than the Mouth of the Platt, we Concluded to delay at this place a fiew days and Send for Some of the Chiefs of that nation, to let them know of the Change of Government the wishes of our government to Cultivate friendship with them, the Objects of our journy and to present them with a flag and Some Small presents.

Some of our Provisions in the French Perogue being wet it became necessary to Dry them a fiew days. wind hard from NW.   five Deer Killed to day. the river rise a little.

CHAPTER II

FROM THE PLATTE TO VERMILION RIVER

[Clark]   MONDAY THE 23D OF JULY 1804 —

A Fair morning   Set a party to look for timber for Ores,
two parties to hunt,   at 11 oClock Sent off George
Drewyer & *Peter Crousett* [Cruzatte] with some tobacco to
invite the Otteaus if at their town and Panies if they saw them,
to come and talk with us at our Camp &c. &c.   (at this Season
the Indians on this river are in the Praries hunting the Buffalow,
but from some signs of hunters, near this place & the Plains being
on fire near their towns induce a belief that they this nation have
returned to get some Green Corn or roasting Ears)   raised a flag
Staff   Sund and Dryed our provisions &c.   I commence
Coppying a Map of the river below to Send to the P. [President]
U. S.   five Deer killed to day   one man with a tumer on
his breast,   Prepared our Camp the men put their arms in order

WHITE CATFISH CAMP 25TH OF JULY WEDNESDAY —

a fair morning   Several hunters out to day,   at 2 oClock
Drewyer & Peter returned from the *Otteau* village, and informs
that no Indians were at their *towns,*   they saw Some fresh Signs
of a Small party But Could not find them.   two Deer killed to
day   1 Turkey Several Grous Seen to day.

CATFISH WHICH IS WHITE CAMP —
26TH OF JULY THURSDAY 1804 —

the wind Blustering and hard from the South all day which
blowed the clouds of Sand in Such a manner that I could not

complete my pan [map] in the tent,   the Boat roled in Such a manner that I could do nothing in that, & was Compessed to go to the woods and combat with the Musquetors,   I opened the Tumer of a man on the left breast, which discharged half a point [pint].

five Beaver Cough[t] near the Camp the flesh of which we made use of.[1] This evening we found verry pleasant. only one Deer killed to day.

White Catfish Camp 10 ms. above Platt
27th of July Friday, —

I took one man R. Fields and walked on Shore with a view of examoning Som Mounds on the L. S. of the river   those Mounds I found to be of Different hight Shape & Size, Some Composed of sand some earth & Sand,   the highest next to the river all of which covered about 200 acres of land, in a circular form,   on the Side from the river a low bottom & small Pond. The Otteaus formerly lived here   I did not get to the boat untill after night.

July the 28th Satturday 1804 —

The flank [guard] came in & informed they heard two Guns to the S. W.   the high land approaches in the 1st bend to the left, we camped on the S. S. below the point of an Island,   G Drewyer brought in a *Missourie Indian* which he met with hunting in the Prarie   This Indian is one of the fiew remaining of that nation, & lives with the Otteauz, his Camp about 4 Miles from the river,   he informs that the 'great gangue' of the Nation were hunting the Buffalow in the Plains. his party was Small Consisting only of about 20 Lodges. Miles further another Camp where there was a french man, who lived in the nation, this Indian appear'd Spritely, and appeared to make use of the Same pronouncation of the Osarge, Calling a Chief *Inea*

---

1 Drewyer was the active trapper.

JULY 29TH SUNDAY 1804 —

Sent a french man *la Liberty* with the Indian to Otteauze Camp to envite the Indians to meet us on the river above. we stoped to Dine under Some high Trees near the high land on the L. S.   in a fiew minits Cought three verry large *Cat fish* one nearly white,   those fish are in great plenty on the Sides of the river and verry fat, a quart of Oile Came out of the surpolous fat of one of those fish   above this high land & on the S. S. passed much falling timber apparently the ravages of a Dreddfull harican which had passed oblequely across the river from N. W. to S. E. about twelve months Since,   many trees were broken off near the ground the trunks of which were sound and four feet in Diameter,

JULY 30TH MONDAY 1804 —

Set out this morning early proceeded on to a clear open Prarie on the L. S. on a rise of about 70 feet higher than the bottom which is also a Prarie (both forming Bluffs to the river) of High Grass & Plumb bush Grapes &c. and situated above high water,   in a small Grove of timber at the foot of the Riseing Ground between those two preraries, and below the Bluffs of the high Prarie we Came too and formed a Camp, intending to waite the return of the frenchman & Indians. the white horse which we found near the Kanzus river, Died Last night

posted out our guard and sent out 4 men, Captn. Lewis & [I] went up the Bank and walked a Short Distance in the high Prarie   this Prarie is Covered with Grass of 10 or 12 inches in hight, Soil of good quality & at the Distance of about a mile still further back the Countrey rises about 80 or 90 feet higher, and is one Continued Plain as fur as Can be seen, from the Bluff on the 2d rise imediately above our Camp, the most butifull prospect of the River up & Down and the Countrey Opsd. presented it Self which I ever beheld;   The River meandering the open and butifull Plains, interspursed with Groves of timber, and each point Covered with Tall timber, Such as Willow Cotton sum Mulberry, Elm, Sucamore Lynn [linden] & ash (The Groves contain Hickory, Walnut, coffee nut & Oake in addition)

Joseph Fields Killed and brought in an Anamale Called by the French *Brarow* [badger] and by the Panies *Cho car tooch*   this Anamale Burrows in the Ground and feeds on Flesh, (Prarie Dogs) Bugs & Vigatables   "his Shape & Size is like that of a Beaver, his head mouth &c. is like a Dogs with Short Ears, his Tail and Hair like that of a Ground Hog, and longer; and lighter. his Interals like the interals of a *Hog*, his Skin, thick and loose, his *Belly* is White and the Hair Short, a white Streek from his nose to his Sholders. The toe nails of his fore feet is one Inch & 3/4 long, & feet large; the nails of his hind feet 3/4 of an Inch long, the hind feet Small and toes Crooked, his legs are short and when he moves Just sufficent to raise his body above the Ground   He is of the Bear Species. We have his skin stuffed.

Jo. & R. Fields did not return this evening,   Several men with verry bad *Boils*. Cat fish is cought in any part of the river   Turkeys Geese & a Beaver Killed & Cought   every thing in prime order men in high Spirits. a fair Still evening Great no. Musquitors this evening

August the 1st 1804 —

a fair morning   Despatched two men after the horses lost yesterday, one man back to the place from which the Messinger was Sent for the *Ottoes* to see if any Indians was or had been there sence our deptr.   he return'd and informed that no person had been there Sence we left it. The Prarie which is situated below our Camp is above the high water leavel and rich covered with Grass from 5 to 8 feet high interspersed with copse of Hazel, Plumbs, Currents (like those of the U. S.) Rasberries & Grapes of Dift. Kinds. also producing a variety of Plants and flowers not common in the United States,

The Indians not yet arrived   we fear Something amiss with our messenger or them.

August 2nd Thursday 1804 —

The Two men Drewyer & Colter returned with the horses loaded with Elk, those horses they found about 12 miles in a Southerly Derection from Camp.

at Sunset Mr. Fairfong [trader resident among the Otos] and a pt. of Otteau & Missourie Nation Came to Camp,   among those Indians 6 were Chiefs, (not the principal Chiefs)   Capt. Lewis & myself met those Indians & informed them we were glad to see them, and would speak to them tomorrow,   Sent them Some rosted meat, Pork flour & meal, in return they sent us Water *millions.* every man on his Guard & ready for any thing.

AUGUST 3RD FRIDAY 1804 —

Mad up a Small preasent for those people in perpotion to their Consiquence, also a package with a Meadle to accompany a Speech for the Grand Chief   after Brackfast we collected those Indians under an owning of our Main Sail, in presence of our Party paraded & Delivered a long Speech to them expressive of our journey the wishes of our Government, Some advice to them and Directions how they were to conduct themselves. The principal Chief for the Nation being absent, we Sent him the Speech flag Meadel & Some Cloathes. after hering what they had to say Delivered a Medal of Second Grade to one for the Ottos & one for the Missourie and present 4 medals of a third Grade to the inferior chiefs two for each tribe. (Those two parts of nations Ottos & Missouries now residing together is about 250 men the Ottoes composeing ⅔d and Missouris ⅓ part)

Those Chiefs all Delivered a Speech, acknowledgeing their approbation to the Speech and promissing two prosue the advice & Derections given them that they wer happy to find that they had fathers which might be depended on &c.

We gave them a Cannister of Powder and a Bottle of Whiskey and delivered a few presents to the whole, after giveing a Br. Cth. [Breech Cloth] some Paint guartering & a Meadell to those we made Chiefs,   after Capt. Lewis's Shooting the air gun a fiew Shots (which astonished those nativs) we Set out and proceeded on five miles on a Direct line   The man *Liberty* whome we Sent for the Ottoes has not Come up   he left the Ottoes Town one Day before the Indians. This man has either tired his horse or, lost himself in the Plains   Some Indians are to hunt for him.

The Situation of our last Camp *Councile Bluff* [2] or Handsom Prarie, (25 Days from this to *Santafee*) appears to be a verry proper place for a Tradeing establishment & fortification   The Soil of the Bluff well adapted for Brick,   Great deel of timber above in the two Points — many other advantages of a small nature. and I am told Senteral to Several nations viz. one Days march from the Ottoe Town, one Day & a half from the great Pania village, 2 days from the Mahar [Omaha] Towns, two ¼ Days from the *Loups* village, & convenient to the Countrey thro: which Bands of the Soux hunt. perhaps no other Situation is as well Calculated for a Tradeing establishment.

The air is pure and helthy so far as we can judge.

AUGUST 4TH SATTURDAY —

proceeded on passed thro between Snags which was quit across the River the Channel confined within 200 yards   one side a Sand pt. the other a Bend, the Banks washing away & trees falling in constantly for 1 mile,   above this place is the rimains of an old Tradeing establishment L. S. where Petr. Crusett one of our hands stayed two years & traded with the Mahars   *Reed* a man who went back to camp for his knife has not joined us.

here the high Land is Some Distance from the river on both Sides, and at this place the High lands are at least 12 or 15 miles a part,   the range of high land on the S. S. appear to contain Some timber. that on the L. S. appear to be intirely clear of any thing but what is common in an open Plain, Some Scattering timber or wood is to be Seen in the reveens, and where the Creeks pass into the Hill. the points and wet lands contain tall timber back of the willows which is generally situated back of a large Sand bar from the Points.

6TH AUGUST, MONDAY 1804 —

Reed has not yet come up. neither has La Liberty the frenchman whome we Sent to the Indian Camps a fiew miles below the *Council Bluffs.*

2 The site was about 25 miles above the city of Council Bluffs, Iowa, but on the Nebraska (eastern) bank. The name came to embrace the whole region near the mouth of the Platte, a natural center for trade.

7TH AUGUST TUESDAY 1804 —

set out late this morning wind from the North. at 1 oClock dispatched George Drewyer, R. Fields, Wm. Bratten & Wm. Labieche back after the Deserter reed with order if he did not give up Peaceibly to put him to Death &c. to go to the Ottoes Village & enquire for La Liberty and bring him to the Mahar Village also with a Speech on the occasion to the Ottoes & Missouries, and derecting a few of their Chiefs to come to the Mahars, & we would make a peace between them & the Mahars and Souex, a String of Wompom & a Carrot of Tobacco. proceeded on and Camped on the S. S.

The expedition proceeds slowly upriver, awaiting word from the parties sent to overtake the deserters and to invite the Otos to a council. Note that whereas Reed was an enlisted man, La Liberté was an employe, a member of Deschamps' boat crew. The Omahas, who now engage the captains' attention, had been driven out of Iowa by the westward migration of the Sioux. They were an active and belligerent tribe and it was they who began the practice of river-piracy on the Upper Missouri. They stopped, plundered, or levied tribute on every trading party that reached their country, which was in northern Nebraska. They had their brief place in the sun under a chief named Blackbird, a notorious thug and pirate, who had learned the use of arsenic and, obtaining it from traders, poisoned such members of his tribe as were disposed to disagree with him. In 1802, however, an epidemic of smallpox that swept this stretch of the river killed Blackbird and reduced the Omahas to about three hundred. (On August 11 Clark records that he visited Blackbird's grave.)

The Poncas, who also had plundered the St. Louis traders and had suffered from the epidemic, were closely related to the Omahas and in fact had once been a part of the tribe.

[Clark]   AUGUST 13TH MONDAY 1804 —

we formed a Camp on a Sand bar on the L. S. & Detached Sergt. Ordeway [Ordway] Peter Crusatt, George Shannon. Werner & Carrn. [Carson] to the Mahar Village with a flag & Some Tobacco to envite the Nation to See & talk with us on tomorrow. we took some Luner observation this evening. the air Pleasant.

14th August Tuesday 1804 —

The men Sent to the Mahar Town last evining has not returned we Conclude to send a Spye to Know the Cause of their delay,   at about 12 oClock the Party returned and informd. us that they Could not find the Indians, nor any fresh Sign, those people have not returned from their Buffalow hunt. Those people haveing no houses no Corn or anything more than the graves of their ansesters to attach them to the old Village, Continue in purseute of the Buffalow longer than others who has greater attachments to their native village. The ravages of the Small Pox (which Swept off 400 men & Womin & children in perpopotion) has reduced this nation not exceeding 300 men and left them to the insults of their weaker neighbours, which before was glad to be on friendly turms with them. I am told when this fatal malady was among them they Carried their franzey to verry extroadinary length, not only of burning their Village, but they put their *wives* & children to *Death* with a view of their all going together to some better Countrey. they burry their Dead on the top of high hills and rais Mounds on the top of them. The cause or way those people took the Small Pox is uncertain, the most Probable, from Some other nation by means of a warparty.

August 15th, Wednesday, 1804.

Camp three Miles N. E. of the Mahar Village

in my absence Capt. Lewis Sent Mr. Durione the Souix interpeter & three men to examine a fire which threw up an emence Smoke from the Praries on the N E. Side of the River and at no great distance from Camp. the Object of this party was to find Some Bands of Seouex which the intptr. thought was near the Smoke and get them to come in. in the evening this Party returned and informed, that the fire arose from Some trees which had been left burning by a small party of Seoux, who had passed Several Days [ago]. the wind Setting from that point, blew the Smoke from that pt. over our Camp. our party all in health and Sperrits.

The men Sent to the Ottoes & in pursute of the Deserter Reed has not yet returned or joined our party.

17TH AUGUST FRIDAY 1804 —

at 6 oClock this evening *Labieche* one of the Party sent to the Ottoes joined, and informed that the Party was behind with one of the Deserters M. B. Reed and the 3 principal Chiefs of the Nations. La Liberty they cought but he decived them and got away. the object of those Chiefs comeing forward is to make a peace with the Mahars thro: us. as the Mahars are not at home this great Object cannot be accomplished at this time. Set the Praries on fire to bring the Mahars & Soues if any were near, this being the useal Signal.

18TH AUGUST, SAT'DAY 1804 —

a fine morning. Wind from the S. E.   in the after part of the Day the Party with the Indians arrivd.   we meet them under a Shade near the Boat and after a Short talk we gave them Provisions to eat & proceeded to the trial of Reed,   he confessed that he "Deserted & stold a public Rifle Shot-pouch Powder & Ball" and requested we would be as favourable with him as we Could consistantly with our Oathes — which we were and only Sentenced him to run the Gantlet four times through the Party & that each man with 9 Swichies Should punish him and for him not to be considered in future as one of the Party. The three principal Chiefs petitioned for Pardin for this man after we explained the injurey such men could doe them by false representations, & explan'g the Customs of our Countrey they were all Satisfied with the propriety of the Sentence & was Witness to the punishment. after which we had Some talk with the Chiefs about the orrigan of the war between them & the Mahars &c &c.   Cap L. Birth day   the evening was closed with an extra gill of whiskey and a Dance untill 11 oClock.

19TH AUGUST SUNDAY 1804 —

the main chief Brackfast with us & beged for a Sun [burning] glass,   those People are all naked, Covered only with Breech Clouts Blankets or Buffalow Roabes, the flesh Side Painted of

Different colours and figures. At 10 oClock we assembled the Chiefs and warriors 9 in number under an owning, and Cap. Lewis explaind the Speech Sent to the Nation from the Council Bluffs by Mr. Faufon. The 3 Chiefs and all the men or warriors made short Speeches approving the advice & Council their great father had Sent them, and concluded by giving themselves some Credit for their acts.

We then brought out the presents and gave all Some Small articles & 8 Carrots of Tobacco,   we gave one Small Meadel to one of the Chiefs and a Sertificate to the others of their good intentions.

one of those Indians after receiving his Certificate delivd. it again to me   the *Big blue eyes* the Chief petitioned for the Ctft. again, we would not give the Certft., but rebuked them verry roughly for haveing in object goods and not peace with their neighbours. this language they did not like at first, but at length all petitioned for us to give back the Certificate to the Big blue eyes   he came forward and made a plausible excuse,   I then gave the Certificate [to] the Great Chief to bestow it to the most Worthy, they gave it to him, we then gave them a Dram and broke up the Council,   we Showed them many Curiosities and the air gun which they were much astonished at. those people beged much for Whiskey. Serjeant Floyd is taken verry bad all at once with a Biliose Chorlick   we attempt to relieve him without success as yet, he gets worst and we are much allarmed at his Situation, all attention to him.[3]

22ND AUGUST FRIDAY 1804 —

at three miles we landed at a Bluff where the two men Sent with the horses were waiting with two Deer,   by examonation this Bluff Contained Alum, Copperas, Cobalt, Pyrites; a Alum Rock Soft & Sand Stone.   Capt. Lewis in proveing the quality of those minerals was Near poisoning himself by the fumes & tast

[3] On July 31, Floyd had written in his journal, "I am verry sick and has ben for Somtime but have Recovered my helth again." This suggests an infected appendix which now becomes acute and perforates. Floyd's death was the only fatality which the expedition suffered. His grave was at the site of Sioux City, Iowa. Private Patrick Gass, who was to live longer than any other member of the expedition, was appointed sergeant in his place.

of the *Cobalt* which had the appearance of Soft Isonglass. Copperas & alum is verry pisen,

Capt. Lewis took a Dost of Salts to work off the effects of the
arsenic,

23RD AUGUST THURSDAY 1804 —

I walked on Shore & Killed a fat Buck. J. Fields Sent out to
hunt   Came to the Boat and informed that he had Killed a
Buffalow in the plain a head. Cap. Lewis took 12 Men and had
the buffalow brought to the boat in the next bend to the S. S.[4]

24TH AUGUST FRIDAY 1804. —

In a northerley derection from the Mouth of this Creek in an
emence Plain a high Hill is Situated, and appears of a Conic form,
and by the different nations of Indians in this quarter is Suppose
to be the residence of Deavels. that they are in human form with
remarkable large heads, and about 18 Inches high, that they are
very watchfull and are arm'd with Sharp arrows with which they
Can Kill at a great distance; they are Said to kill all persons who
are So hardy as to attempt to approach the hill;   they State that
tradition informs them that many Indians have Suffered by these
little people, and among others three *Mahar* Men fell a sacrefise
to their murceless fury not many Years Sence. So Much do the
Maha, Soues, Ottoes and other neighbouring nations believe this
fable, that no Consideration is Suffecient to induce them to approach the hill.

4 The first buffalo they had killed.

CHAPTER III

FROM THE VERMILION TO TETON (BAD) RIVER

[Clark]   25TH AUGUST SATTURDAY 1804. —

Acloudy morning   Capt. Lewis & Myself concluded to go
and See the Mound which was Viewed with Such turror by
all the different Nations in this quarter, we Selected [nine
men to go along]   from the top of this High land the Countrey is
leavel & open as far as can be Seen, except Some few rises at a great
Distance, and the *Mound* which the Indians Call Mountain of *little
people or Spirits,*   at 4 miles we Crossed the Creek 23 yards wide
in an extensive Valley and Contined on at two miles further   our Dog was so Heeted and fatigued we was obliged [to]
Send him back to the Creek,   at 12 oClock we arrived at the
hill   Capt. Lewis much fatigued from heat the day it being
verry hot & he being in a debilitated State from the Precautions he
was obliged to take to prevent the effects of the Cobalt, & Minl
Substance which had like to have poisoned him two days ago,   his
want of water, and Several of the men complaining of Great thirst,
determined us to make for the first water   We proceeded on to
the Place we Campd last night and Stayed all night.

The reagular form of this hill would in Some measure justify a
belief that it owed its orrigion to the hand of man; but as the earth
and loos pebbles and other substances of which it was Composed,
bore an exact resemblance to the Steep Ground which border on
the Creek in its neighbourhood we concluded it was most probably
the production of nature.[1]

The only remarkable Charactoristic of this hill admiting it to be
a natural production is that it is insulated or Seperated a considerable distance from any other, which is verry unusial in the natural order or disposition of the hills.

[1] Spirit Mound near Vermillion, South Dakota.

The Surrounding Plains is open Void of Timber and leavel to a great extent, hence the wind from whatever quarter it may blow, drives with unusial force over the naked Plains and against this hill; the insects of various kinds are thus involuntaryly driven to the Mound by the force of the wind, or fly to its Leeward Side for Shelter; the Small Birds whoes food they are, Consequently resort in great numbers to this place in Surch of them; Perticularly the Small brown Martin of which we saw a vast number hovering on the Leward Side of the hill, when we approached it in the act of catching those insects; they were so gentle that they did not quit the place untill we had arrivd within a fiew feet of them.

One evidence which the Inds give for believeing this place to be the residence of Some unusial Sperits is that they frequently discover a large assemblage of Birds about this Mound is in my opinion a Sufficent proof to produce in the Savage Mind a Confident belief of all the properties which they ascribe it.

from the top of this Mound we beheld a most butifull landscape; Numerous herds of buffalow were Seen feeding in various directions; the Plain to North N. W. & N. E. extends without interuption as far as Can be seen.

the Boat under the Comd of Serjt. Pryor proceeded on in our absence, (after jurking the Elk I killed yesterday) Six Miles and Camped on the Larboard Side   R. Fields brought in five Deer, George Shannon Killed an Elk Buck   Som rain this evening.

We Set the Praries on fire as a signal for the Soues to Come to the River.

On August 27 they pass the mouth of James River and Clark reports that George Shannon is lost. Actually, he was traveling ahead of the boats, thinking he had fallen behind while hunting. Shannon, the best educated of the enlisted men and the one whom Clark was to send to Philadelphia to assist Biddle in preparing his history, was several times separated from the party for long periods. Yet he appears to have been an expert woodsman; he conducted himself with absolute assurance and great skill. On this occasion John Colter, who was to become a celebrated mountain man, was dispatched to find him; he failed to and Shannon did not come in till September 11.

The expedition was now nearing one of its prime objectives, the

Sioux Indians. Recent comers to the Missouri and themselves driven westward by the better-armed Chippewas, the Sioux had terrorized all the neighboring tribes. They had also practically closed the river to St. Louis traders who were trying to reach the Mandan villages where British traders from the Lake Winnipeg region were believed to be doing a prosperous business. They had succeeded in establishing themselves as trade monopolists in this region, extracting a heavy tribute in goods from the occasional traders whom they permitted to pass — Loisel and Heney during the preceding winter, for instance. No doubt they had been encouraged in this brigandage by the British traders on the James and Des Moines Rivers who were their regular source of supply. Their British allegiance was well known in Washington and it had to be broken. The Sioux must be impressed by the power and authority of the United States, and the Missouri must be made safe for American traders. Jefferson also hoped, idly enough, that they could be induced to keep the peace with the other tribes.

The expedition learned that there were some Sioux bands on the James River, whose mouth was reached on August 27, and Dorion was sent with a small escort to invite them to a council. He returned on August 29 with his halfbreed son (also a trader and destined to die on the Astorian expedition) and five chiefs and seventy warriors. They belonged to the Yankton branch of the Sioux nation, which at the moment was much more peaceably disposed than the Teton branch, and to one of two bands which were accustomed to trade with St. Louis, not with the British. They complained about the parsimony of St. Louis traders and regarded the presents which the captains gave them as niggardly. But after stately ceremonies they amiably agreed to make peace with their neighbors (Lewis and Clark were not yet sufficiently acquainted with Plains Indians to realize how worthless the promise was) and to accept American sovereignty. Dorion was left here with a small amount of trade goods for presents, having been engaged to take some of the Yankton chiefs to Washington. Lewis and Clark had been instructed to arrange for such delegations. The purpose was to impress the Indians with the power and wealth of white civilization and to exhort them to keep the peace with one another.

At Council Bluffs Clark had made only perfunctory ethnological notes. Now the expedition sees the culture of the Plains Indians in detail and the notebooks fill with descriptions of Sioux, their costumes, weapons, language, tribal divisions, names, customs and beliefs. Nothing previously written about the Sioux was so accurate, thorough, or permanently valuable.

The true terrorists, however, the Teton Sioux, were still to come. As the expedition moved on toward them, the eroded bluffs beside the river took so regular a form that Clark believed some of them must be fortifications built by people more ancient than the Indians. He measured and described them in detail and made sketches of them. A map they were using, drawn by a St. Louis trader, showed a "volcano," probably a burning seam of lignite, but they could not find it.

They passed the mouth of the Niobrara River, l'Eau Qui Court, on September 4. On the 7th they saw their first prairie dogs (commonly called "barking squirrels" in the journals) and captured one with great difficulty. Clark's description of it, probably a summary of one by Lewis that has not come down, is often but erroneously said to be the first ever written. Wild game, which had been plentiful from the beginning, had now become remarkably abundant. They had seen their first antelope, which they usually called "goats," some time before. "Great numbers of Buffalow & Elk on the hill. . . . I saw Several foxes & Killed a Elk & 2 Deer & Squirrels   the men with me killed an Elk, 2 Deer & a Pelican . . . a great number of Grous & 3 Foxes . . . vast herds of Baffaloe deer Elk and Antilopes were seen feeding in every direction as far as the eye of the observer could reach . . . 8 fallow Deer 5 Common & 3 Buffalow killed to day . . . Muskeetors verry troublesom." Presently they decided that the animals they had been calling foxes were a new, smaller species of wolves; they were, in fact, coyotes.

On September 15 they reached the mouth of the White River and so had passed the long escarpment called Pine Ridge and entered a new geographical province, the Missouri Plateau. Geographically, this is the beginning of the Upper Missouri. For frontiersmen, however, it began at the mouth of the Platte.

[Lewis]   MONDAY SEPTEMBER 17TH. 1804.

Having for many days past confined myself to the boat, I determined to devote this day to amuse myself on shore with my gun and view the interior of the country lying between the river and

100 miles

White Earth R.

Little Missouri R.

Miry R.

Knife R. VILLAGES Ft. Mandan

N O R T H   D A K O T A

Heart R.

Cannonball R.

Missouri R.

Grand R.

Moreau R.

S O U T H   D A K O T A

Cheyenne R.

(Bad) Teton R. Grand Detour

White R.

Map 2, Sep 15, 1804 ~ Apr. 7, 1805
also for return trip   Aug. 12 ~ Sep. 1, 1806

Raisz

the Corvus Creek. accordingly before sunrise I set out with six of my best hunters, two of whom I dispatched to the lower side of Corvus creek, two with orders to hunt the bottoms and woodland on the river, while I retained two others to accompany me in the intermediate country. One quarter of a mile in rear of our camp which was situated in a fine open grove of cotton wood passed a grove of plumb trees loaded with fruit and now ripe,   observed but little difference betwen this fruit and that of a similar kind common to the Atlantic States. the trees are smaller and more thickly set. this forrest of plumb trees garnish a plain about 20 feet more elivated than that on which we were en-camped; this plane extends with the same bredth from the creek below to the distance of near three miles above parrallel with the river, and it is intirely occupied by the burrows of the *barking squiril* heretofore described; this anamal appears here in infinite numbers   and the shortness and virdue of grass gave the plain the appearance throughout it's whole extent of beatifull bowling-green in fine order. it's aspect is S. E.   a great number of wolves of the small kind, halks [hawks] and some pole-cats were to be seen. I presume that those anamals feed on this squirril. found the coun-try in every direction for about three miles intersected with deep revenes and steep irregular hills of 100 to 200 feet high; at the tops of these hills the country breakes of as usual into a fine leavel plain extending as far as the eye can reach. from this plane I had an ex-tensive view of the river below, and the irregular hills which border the opposite sides of the river and creek. the surrounding country had been birnt about a month before and young grass had now sprung up to hight of 4 Inches presenting the live green of the spring   to the West a high range of hills, strech across the country from N. to S. and appeared distant about 20 miles; they are not very extensive as I could plainly observe their rise and termination   no rock appeared on them and the sides were cov-ered with virdue similar to that of the plains   this senery al-ready rich pleasing and beatiful was still farther hightened by im-mence herds of Buffaloe, deer Elk and Antelopes which we saw in every direction feeding on the hills and plains. I do not think I exagerate when I estimate the number of Buffaloe which could be compre[hend]ed at one view to amount to 3000. my object was if possible to kill a female Antelope having already procured a male;

I pursued my rout on this plain to the west flanked by my two hunters untill eight in the morning when I made the signal for them to come to me which they did shortly after. we rested our selves about half an hour, and regailed ourselves on half a bisquit each and some jirks of Elk which we had taken the precaution to put in our pouches in the morning before we set out, and drank of the water of a small pool which had collected on this plain from the rains which had fallen some days before. we had now after various windings in pursuit of several herds of antelopes which we had seen on our way made the distance of about eight miles from our camp. we found the Antelope extreemly shye and watchfull insomuch that we had been unable to get a shot at them; I had this day an opportunity of witnessing the agility and the superior fleetness of this anamal which was to me really astonishing. I had pursued and twice surprised a small herd of seven, in the first instance they did not discover me distinctly and therefore did not run at full speed, tho' they took care before they rested to gain an elivated point where it was impossible to approach them under cover, except in one direction and that happened to be in the direction from which the wind blew towards them; bad as the chance to approach them was, I made the best of my way towards them, freqeuntly peeping over the ridge with which I took care to conceal myself from their view the male, of which there was but one, frequently incircled the summit of the hill on which the females stood in a group, as if to look out for the approach of danger. I got within about 200 paces of them when they smelt me and fled; I gained the top of the eminence on which they stood, as soon as possible from whence I had an extensive view of the country the antilopes which had disappeared in a steep reveene now appeared at the distance of about three miles on the side of a ridge which passed obliquely across me and extended about four miles. so soon had these antelopes gained the distance at which they had again appeared to my view I doubted at ferst that they were the same that I had just surprised, but my doubts soon vanished when I beheld the rapidity of their flight along the ridge before me it appeared reather the rappid flight of birds than the motion of quadrupeds. I think I can safely venture the asscertion that the speed of this anamal is equal if not superior to that of the finest blooded courser.

[Clark]   21ST OF SEPTEMBER FRIDAY 1804 —

at half past one o'clock this morning the Sand bar on which we Camped began to under mind and give way which allarmed the Serjeant on Guard,   the motion of the boat awakened me; I got up & by the light of the moon observed that the Sand had given away both above and below our Camp & was falling in fast I ordered all hands on as quick as possible & pushed off, we had pushed off but a few minits before the bank under which the Boat & perogus lay give way, which would Certainly have Sunk both Perogues,   by the time we made the opsd. Shore our Camp fell in,   we made a 2d Camp for the remainder of the night. & at Daylight proceeded on to the Gouge of this Great bend and Brackfast,   we Sent a man to Measure (step off) the Distance across the gouge, he made it 2,000 yds.,   The distance arround is 30 Mls.   The hills extend thro: the Gouge and is about 200 foot above the water.[2]   in the bend as also the opposit Sides both above and below the bend is a butifull inclined Plain, in which there is great numbers of Buffalow, Elk & Goats in view feeding & scipping on those Plains   Grouse, Larks & the Prarie bird is Common in those Plains.

we Camped at the lower point of the Mock Island on the S. S.   this now Connected with the main land, it has the appearance of once being an Island detached from the main land Covered with tall Cotton Wood. We Saw Some Camps and tracks of the Seaux which appears to be old, three or four weeks ago,   one frenchman I fear has got an abscess on his they [thigh],   he Complains verry much   we are makeing every exertion to reliev him

The Praries in this quarter Contains great qts. of Prickley Pear [opuntia].

                    22ND OF SEPTEMBER SATTURDAY 1804 —

passed a Island Situated nearest the S. S. imediately above the last Called Ceder Island   this Island is about 1½ miles long & nearly as wide Covered with Ceder,   on the South Side of this

2 The Grand Detour, where in the distance Clark states the Missouri twice completely reverses the direction of its flow.

Island Mr. Louiselle a trader from St. Louis built a fort of
Ceder & a good house to trade with the Seaux & Wintered last winter;   about this fort I observed a number of Indian Camps in a
Conecal form. they fed their horses on Cotton limbs as appears.
here our hunters us joined haveing killed 2 Deer & a Beaver,   they
Complain much of the Mineral Substances in the barren hills over
which they passed Distroying their mockessons.

23RD OF SEPTEMBER SUNDAY 1804 —

Set out under a gentle breeze from the S. E.   passed a Small
Island Situated in a bend to the L. S. Called Goat Island, a Short
distance above the upper point a Creek of 12 yards wide Coms in
on the S. S.   we observed a great Smoke to the S. W.   I walked
on Shore & observed Buffalow in great Herds at a distance
    the river is nearly Streight for a great distance wide and
Shoal   passed a Creek on the S. S. 16 yards wide we Call Reuben
Creek, as R. Fields found it. Camped on the S. S. below the mouth
of a Creek on the L. S.   three Souex boys Came to us Swam the
river and informd that the Band of Seauex called the *Tetongues*
[Tetons] of 80 Lodges were Camped at the next Creek above, & 60
Lodges more a Short distance above,   we gave those boys two Car-
rots of Tobacco to Carry to their Chiefs, with directions to tell them
that we would Speak to them tomorrow
    Capt. Lewis walked on Shore this evening,   R. F. [Reuben
Fields] Killed a Doe Goat,

24TH SEPTEMBER MONDAY 1804 —

Set out early   a fair day the wind from the E.   pass the
mouth of Creek on the L. S. Called Creek on high Water, (*High
Water*)   passed a large Island on the L. S. about 2 Miles & ½
long on which Colter had Camped & Killed 4 Elk,   the wind
fair from the S. E.   we prepared Some Clothes and a fiew
Meadels for the Chiefs of the Teton's bands of Seoux which we
expect to See to day at the next river,   observe a great Deel of
Stone on the Sides of the hills on the S. S.   we Saw one Hare, to
day,   prepared all things for Action in Case of necessity,   our
Perogus went to the Island for the Meet,   Soon after the man

on Shore run up the bank and reported that the Indians had
Stolen the horse   We soon after Met 5 Inds. and ankered out
Som distance & Spoke to them   informed them we were friends,
& Wished to Continue So but were not afraid of any In-
dians,   Some of their young men had taken the horse Sent by their
Great father for their Cheif and we would not Speek to them untill
the horse was returned to us again.

passed a Island on the S. S. on which we Saw Several Elk, about
1½ Miles long Called Good humered [*humoured*] Isld.   Came
to about 1½ Miles above off the Mouth of a Small river about 70
yards wide Called by Mr. Evens the Little Mississou [*Missouri*]
River,   The Tribes of the Seauex Called the Teton, is Camped
about 2 Miles up on the N. W. Side, and we Shall Call the River
after that Nation, *Teton* [present-day Bad River]   This river
is 70 yards wide at the mouth of Water, and has a considerable
Current   we anchored off the mouth

the french [boatmen's] Perogue Come up early in the day, the
other did not Get up untill in the evening Soon after we had Come
too. I went & Smoked with the Chiefs who came to See us here
all well,   we prepare to Speek with the Indians tomorrow at
which time we are informed the Indians will be here,   the
French Man who had for Some time been Sick, began to blead
which allarmed him   ⅔ of our party Camped on board the remainder with the Guard on Shore.

CHAPTER IV

From Teton River to the Mandans

September 25 and the succeeding three days marked the first crisis of the expedition and its first climax. At St. Louis the captains had been thoroughly informed about the terrorism which the Upper Missouri Indians, including the Omahas and the Arikaras but most especially the Sioux, had been exercising on French and Spanish traders ever since they first tried to reach the upriver tribes, early in the 1790's. They expected trouble with the Sioux and were prepared for it; they knew, too, that assertion of American authority and sovereignty was absolutely essential to both the domestic and the foreign policy of the United States.

The Teton Sioux had usually stopped upriver trading parties altogether and forced them to dispose of their goods at ruinously low prices which the Sioux themselves set and which amounted to little more than robbery. Occasionally, however, after levying exorbitant tribute, they had permitted parties to go on. The latest of these victims was Régis Loisel, whom the expedition met coming down the river three days out from St. Charles, on May 24. Loisel had suffered extreme humiliation from the same Indians whom the expedition now met, especially the one named The Partisan. When he went back to St. Louis, he sent his clerk, Pierre-Antoine Tabeau (whom the expedition presently meets), on to the Arikara village, where a few months before the arrival of Lewis and Clark he had been viciously bullied and robbed. The Arikaras were themselves victims of the Sioux, a displaced people who had been forced, nine years earlier, to abandon their village (near where the expedition now met the Tetons) and withdraw out of reach farther up the river.

*As the text shows at once, the tactics which had made the French
and Spanish traders from St. Louis impotent did not work with the
Americans. At any time during these four days any willingness to
temporize, any weakness or fright, or any lapse of vigilance would
have produced either fighting or failure or both. But the captains
were prepared and were not afraid. The Sioux perceived this and
understood it: these white men would fight, they could not be made
to yield. So large a band of Indians — they numbered several hundred and additional ones kept coming in — could easily have mas-
sacred the party. A great many of them, however, would have been
killed and such a loss was a price which they would not pay, which
no Indians would pay, even for control of the river and a trade
monopoly. According to the Indian conception of warfare, you did
not attack a well-armed and resolute enemy. You tried bluff,
bluster, and threats. If they did not work you tried diplomacy and
guile, as on the second and third day here. If they did not work,
either, you postponed matters in hope of a more favorable opportunity.*

*Throughout these four days the tension was so great that Clark
did not sleep. It rose to extremity twice. On September 25, in the
first moment of pressure, the young men, always the most belligerent and foolhardy, strung their bows, equivalent to loading and
cocking a rifle. The white man's nerve was intended to fail right
there. It did not. And observe that, with rifles trained on them
from the keelboat, the Sioux did not notch their arrows. Again on
the 28th when an attempt was made to prevent the final departure,
the furious Clark, barely controlling himself, seized "the port fire,"
prepared to discharge the swivel. Indian bluster immediately col-
lapsed and from then on the terrible Tetons were mere beggars.*

*The moral of the episode was that a new breed of white men
had come to the Upper Missouri, one that could not be scared or
bullied. The moral was flashed along the Indian underground
faster than the expedition traveled. It explains why the captains
were received with such solicitous respect by the Arikaras, who had
so recently terrorized Tabeau. It probably explains why, the following summer, the expedition met no Indians between the Mandan villages and the Continental Divide.*

*In fact, the career of the Sioux as river pirates ended here. After
the expedition returned to St. Louis, it was the Arikaras, not the
Sioux, who made trouble for traders bound upriver.*

When Clark speaks of Sioux "soldiers," he is referring to members of the secret, ritualistic military societies. Here they were acting as camp police.

The entries from Ordway's journal fill gaps and clear up ambiguities in Clark's account.

[Clark]   25TH SEPT. —

all well, raised a Flag Staff & made a orning or Shade on a Sand bar in the mouth of Teton River, for the purpose of Speeking with the Indians under,   the Boat Crew on board at 70 yards Distance from the bar   The 5 Indians which we met last night Continued,   about 11 OClock the It & 2d Chief Came we gave them Some of our Provisions to eat, they gave us great Quantitis of Meet Some of which was Spoiled   we feel much at a loss for the want of an interpeter the one we have can Speek but little.

Met in Council at 12 oClock and after Smokeing, agreeable to the useal Custom, Cap. Lewis proceeded to Deliver a Speech which we [were] oblige[d] to Curtail for want of a good interpeter   all our party paraded. gave a Medal to the Grand Chief Calld. in Indian *Un ton gar Sar bar* in French *Beeffe nure* Black Buffalow. Said to be a good Man,   2nd Chief *Torto hon gar* or the *Parti sin* or Partizan *bad*   the 3rd is the Beffe De Medison [Beuffe de Medecine] his name is *Tar ton gar Wa ker*   1st Considerable Man, *War zing go.* 2nd Considerable Man   *Second Bear —* *Mato co que par.*

Envited those Cheifs on board to Show them our boat and such Curiossities as was Strange to them,   we gave them ¼ a glass of whiskey which they appeared to be verry fond of, Sucked the bottle after it was out & Soon began to be troublesom, one the 2d Cheif assumeing Drunkness, as a Cloake for his rascally intentions   I went with those Cheifs *(in one of the Perogues with 5 men — 3 & 2 Inds.)* (which left the boat with great reluctiance) to Shore with a view of reconsileing those men to us,   as Soon as I landed the Perogue three of their young Men Seased the Cable of the Perogue, *(in which we had pressents &c)*   the Chiefs Soldr. Huged the mast, and the 2d Chief was verry insolent both in words & justures *(pretended Drunkenness & staggered up against me)* declareing I should not go on, Stateing he had not receved presents sufficent from us,   his justures were of Such a personal nature I felt My self Compeled to Draw my Sword *(and Made a Signal to the boat to prepare for action)*   at this Motion Capt. Lewis ordered all under arms in the boat,   those with me also Showed a Disposition to Defend themselves and me, the grand Chief then took hold of the roap & ordered the young Warrers away,   I felt My Self warm & Spoke in *verry positive terms.*

Most of the Warriers appeared to have ther Bows strung and took out their arrows from the quiver. as I *(being surrounded)* was not permited to return, I Sent all the men except 2 Inps. [Interpreters] to the boat,   the perogue Soon returned with about 12 of our determined men ready for any event.   this movement caused a no: of the Indians to withdraw at a distance,   Their treatment to me was verry rough & I think justified roughness on my part, they all lift [left] my Perogue, and Councild. with themselves   the result I could not lern and nearly all went off after remaining in this Situation Some time I offered my hand to the 1. & 2. Chiefs who refusd. to receve it. I turned off & went with my men on board the perogue,   I had not prosd. more the [than] 10 paces before the 1st Cheif 3rd & 2 Brave Men Waded in after me. I took them in & went on board

We proceeded on about 1 Mile & anchored out off a Willow Island   placed a guard on Shore to protect the Cooks & a guard in the boat,   fastened the Perogues to the boat,   I call this Island bad humered Island as we were in a bad humer.

[Ordway]   TUESDAY 25TH SEPT. 1804.

a clear and pleasant morning. al things made ready to receive the Band of the Souix nation of Indians, Called the Tribe of Tetons. about 10 o.C. A. M. they Came flocking in from boath Sides of the River. when 30 odd was selected under the american Collours Capt Lewis & Capt Clark went out to Speak and treat with them. Gave the 3 Chiefs 3 niew meddals & 1 american flag Some knives & other Small articles of Goods & Gave the head chief the Black Buffalow a red coat & a cocked hat & feather &.C.   likewise Some Tobacco. We had no good interpreter but the old frenchman could make them understand tollarable well. but they did not appear to talk much untill they had got the goods, and then they wanted more, and Said we must Stop with them or leave one of the pearogues with them as that was what they expected. Capt Lewis Shewed them the air Gun. Shot it several times. then the Captains brought the 3 chiefs and one warrier they had with them. Gave the warrier a Sertifficate. then Shewed the chiefs Some curiousities. Gave them a draghm. they brought a quantity of fat Buffaloe meat and offered us   the Captains accepted of Some of it. & Gave them pork in return. then the Captains told them that we had a great ways to goe & that we did not wish to be detained any longer. they then began to act as if they were Intoxicated   with Some difficulty Capt Clark got them to Shore. they then began to Show Some Signs of Stopping or attempting to Stop us. one of them Stayed on board the pearogue when Capt Clark & the chiefs went out of it. the head chief the Black Buffaloe, Seized hold of the cable of the pearogue and Set down. Capt Clark Spoke to all the party to Stand to their arms   Capt Lewis who was on board ordered every man to his arms. the large Swivel [was] loaded immediately with 16 Musquet Ball in it the 2 other Swivels loaded well with Buck Shot [and] each of them manned. Capt Clark used moderation with them told them that we must and would go on and would go. that we were not Squaws. but warriers. the chief Sayed he had warriers too and if we were to go on they would follow us and kill and take the whole of us by degrees or that he had another party or lodge above this [and] that they were able to destroy us. then Capt Clark told them that we were Sent by their great father the president of the U. S. and that if they misused us that he or Capt Lewis could by writing to him have them all distroyed as it were in a moment. they then requested that their women and children See the Boat as they never Saw Such a one, the Capt told them that we could not go far as the day was far Spent, but we would let them see that they Should not Stop us and that we Should go a Short distance and can Camp for the night. the chief then let go the Cable and Sayed that he was Sorry to have us Go for his women and children were naked and poor and wished to Git Some Goods, but he did not think we were Marchants, nor that we were loaded with Goods, but he was Sorry to have us leave them So Soon — they wished to come on board   Capt Clark took the chief and warriers on bord to Stay all night with them. we then Set off and proceeded on about 1 mile and Camped ankered out. the Guard and cooks on Shore &.C.   the Indians Camped on

s. s.   our Camp was on a willow Isl in the middle of the river,
at our Starbord Side.

[Clark]   26TH OF SEPTEMBER WEDNESDAY 1804 —

Set out early   proceeded on and Came to by the Wish of the
Chiefs for to let their Squars [squaws] & boys see the Boat and
Suffer them to treat us well   great numbers of men womin &
children on the banks viewing us,   these people Shew great
anxiety,   they appear Spritely, Genrally ill looking & not well
made their legs [& arms]Small generally,   they Grese & Black
themselves when they dress make use of a hawks feathers about
their heads. the men [wear] a robe & each a polecats Skin, for to
hold ther *Bawe roley* [1] for Smoking,   fond of Dress & Show badly
armed with fusees, &c.   The Squaws are Chearfull fine look'g
womin not handsom, High Cheeks Dressed in Skins a Peticoat and
roab which foldes back over ther Sholder, with long wool,   do all
their laborious work & I may Say perfect Slaves to the Men, as all
Squars of Nations much at War, or where the Womin are more
noumerous than the men. after Comeing too Capt. Lewis & 5 men
went on Shore with the Cheifs, who appeared disposed to make up
& be friendly,   after Captain Lewis had been on Shore about 3
hours I became uneasy for fear of Deception & Sent a Serjeant to
See him and know his treatment which he reported was friendly,
& they were prepareing for a Dance this evening   The[y] made
frequent Selicitiations for us to remain one night only and let them
Show their good disposition towards us, we deturmined to remain,   after the return of Capt. Lewis, I went on Shore   on
landing I was receved on a elegent painted B.[uffalo] Robe & taken
to the Village by 6 Men & was not permited to touch the ground
untill I was put down in the grand Concill house on a White
dressed Robe. I saw Several Maha Prissners and Spoke to the
Cheifs it was necessary to give those prisoners up & become good
friends with the Mahas if they wished to follow the advice of their
great father   I was in Several Lodges neetly formed as before
mentioned as to the Baureily (*Bois brulé* — Yankton) Tribe. I was

---

1 *Bois roulé:* kinnikinnic — Indian tobacco mixed with any of various leaves
and barks which were used to modify its taste or to eke out the supply; sometimes the substitute for tobacco.

met by about 10 Well Dressd. young Men who took me up in a
roabe Highly adecrated and Set me Down by the Side of their
Chief on a Dressed Robe in a large Council House,   this house
formed a ¾ Circle of Skins Well Dressed and Sown together   under this Shelter about 70 Men Set forming a Circle   in front of
the Cheifs a plac of 6 feet Diameter was Clear and the pipe of peace
raised on Sticks under which there was swans down scattered,   on
each Side of this Circle two Pipes, the *(two)* flags of Spain & the
Flag we gave them in front of the Grand Chief   a large fire was
near in which provisions were Cooking, in the Center about 400
lbs. of excellent Buffalo Beef as a present for us. Soon after they
Set me Down, the Men went for Capt. Lewis   brought him in
the same way and placed him also by the Chief   in a fiew minits
an old man rose & Spoke aproveing what we had done & informing
us of their situation requesting us to take pity on them & which
was answered. The great Chief then rose with great State [speak-
ing] to the Same purpote as far as we Could learn & then with Great
Solemnity took up the pipe of Peace & after pointing it to the
heavins the 4 quarters of the Globe & the earth, he made Some
disertation, lit it and presented the Stem to us to Smoke,   when
the Principal Chief Spoke with the Pipe of Peace he took in one
hand some of the most Delicate parts of the Dog which was prepared for the fiest & made a Sacrefise to the flag. after A Smoke had
taken place, & a Short Harange to his people, we were requested to
take the Meal *(& then put before us the dog which they had been
cooking, & Pemitigon [pemmican] & ground potato*[2] *in Several
platters Pemn. is Buffa meat dried or jerked pounded & mixed with
grease raw. Dog Sioux think great dish used on festivals eat little
of dog — pemn. & pote good.)* We Smoked for an hour *(till)* Dark
& all was Cleared away   a large fire made in the Center, about
10 Musitions playing on tambereens *(made of hoops & Skin
stretched)*, long Sticks with Deer & Goats Hoofs tied so as to make
a gingling noise, and many others of a Similer Kind,   those Men
began to Sing, & Beet on the Tamboren,   the Women Came forward highly Deckerated in their Way, with the Scalps and Tropies

[2] The "prairie turnip," "prairie potato," "prairie apple," or "Indian bread-
fruit": *Psoralea esculenta* and related species of the pea family. The large
turnip-like roots could be eaten raw or cooked; they were usually braided in
strings and dried.

of War of their fathers Husbands Brothers or near Connections &
proceeded to Dance the War Dance which they done with great
Chearfullness untill about 12 oClock when we informed the Cheifs
that they were fatigued &c.   they then retired & we Accompd. by
4 Cheifs returned to our boat, they Stayed with us all night. Those
people have Some brave men which they make use of as Soldiers   those men attend to the police of the Village   Correct
all errors   I saw one of them to day whip 2 Squars, who appeared to have fallen out,   when he approachd. all about appeared to flee with great turrow [terror]. at night they keep two 3,
4 5 men at different Distances walking around Camp Singing the
accurrunces of the night
All the Men on board 100 paces from Shore   Wind from the
S. E. moderate   one man verry sick on board with a Dangerass
Abscess on his Hip. All in [good] Spirits this evening.

In this Tribe I saw 25 Squars and Boys taken 13 days ago in a
battle with the Mahars   in this battle they Destroyd 40 Lodges,
Killed 75 Men, & som boys & Children, & took 48 Prisoners Womin
& boys which they promis both Capt. Lewis and my self Shall be
Delivered up to Mr. Durion at the Bous rulie Tribe,   those are a
retched and Dejected looking people   the Squars appear low &
Corse but this is an unfavourable time to judge of them

We gave our Mahar inteptr. some fiew articles to give those
Squars in his name Such as Alls, needles &c. &c.

I saw & eat Pemitigon the Dog, Groud. potatoe made into a Kind
of homney, which I thought but little inferior. I also Saw a Spoon
Made of a horn of an Animell of the Sheep Kind [Rocky Mountain
sheep] the Spoon will hold 2 quarts.

27TH OF SEPT. THURSDAY 1804 —

I rose early after a bad nights Sleep   found the Chief[s] all up,
and the bank as useal lined with Spectators   we gave the 2 great
Cheifs a Blanket a peace, or rether they took off agreeable to their
Custom the one they lay on and each one Peck of corn. after
Brackfast Capt. Lewis & the Cheifs went on Shore, as a verry large
part of their nation was comeing in, the Disposition of whome I
did not know   one of us being sufficent on Shore, I wrote a letter
to Mr. P. Durion & prepared a meadel & Some Comsns. (*Certifiates*)
& Sent to Cap Lewis   at 2 oClock Capt. Lewis Returned with 4

Chiefs & a Brave Man named *War cha pa* or on his Guard when the friends of those people die they run arrows through their flesh above and below their elbows as a testimony of their Greaf.

after Staying about half an hour, I went with them on Shore, Those men left the boat with reluctience,   I went first to the 2d Cheifs Lodge, where a croud came around   after Speeking on various Subjects I went to a princpal mans lodge from them to the grand Chiefs lodge,   after a fiew minits he invited me to a Lodge within the Circle in which I Stayed with all their principal Men untill the Dance began, which was Similer to the one of last night performed by their women with poles on which Scalps of their enemies were hung, Some with the Guns Spears & War empliments of their husbands in their hands.

Capt. Lewis Came on Shore and we Continued untill we were Sleepy & returned to our boat,   the 2nd Chief & one principal Man accompanied us,   Those two Indians accompanied me on board in the Small Perogue; Capt. Lewis with a guard Still on Shore   the man who Steered not being much acustomed to Steer, passed the bow of the boat & the peroge Came broad Side against the Cable & broke it which obliged me to order in a loud voice all hands up & at their ores,   my preemptry order to the men and the bustle of their getting to their ores allarmd. the Cheifs, together with the appearance of the Men on Shore, as the boat turnd.   The Cheif hollowaed & allarmed the Camp or Town informing them that the Mahars was about attacking us *(them)*. In about 10 minits the bank was lined with men armed the 1st Cheif at their head,   about 200 men appeared and after about ½ hour returned all but about 60 men who continued on the bank all night,   the Cheifs Contd. all night with us. This allarm I as well as Capt. Lewis Considered as the Signal of their intentions (which was to Stop our proceeding on our journey and if Possible rob us)   we were on our Guard all night,   the misfortune of the loss of our Anchor obliged us to Lay under a falling bank much exposd. to the accomplishment of their hostile intentions. P. C. [Cruzatte] our Bowman who cd. Speek Mahar informed us in the night that the Maha Prisoners informed him we were to be Stoped. we Shew as little Sighns of a Knowledge of their intentions as possible   all prepared on board for any thing which might hapen. we kept a Strong guard all night in the boat, no Sleep

[Ordway]   THURSDAY 27TH SEPT 1804.

Sergt Gass informed me as he was at the village to day that he
counted 80 Lodges (of the Teton Tribe) which contain ten persons
each, which were built round with poles about 15 or 20 feet high
& covered with dressed Buffalo hides painted   Some of them
red &.C.   the dance lasted till about 12oClock at night, at which
time the Captains returned to the boat   brought with them 2
Chiefs. the men all returned also. an accident happened as they
came on board by the neglect of the men at the helm of the
pearogue, who Steared hir above the big boat. She Swung round
with the current and She came full force down against the Bow of
the Barge Broke the cable of hir. we found we were all on float.
roused all hands and got Safe to Shore on S.S.   the Indians hearing us, and expected that the Mahars Indians had come to attack us
they all ran to our assistance on the bank of the river & fired
Several guns for an alarm only. I being on duty set up the remainder part of the night, and had all the party on their Guards.

[Clark]   28TH OF SEPTEMBER 1804 FRIDAY —

Made many attemps in different ways to find our anchor, but
Could not, the Sand had Covered it,   from the Misfortune of
last night our boat was laying at Shore in a verry unfavourable
Situation,   after finding that the anchor Could not be found we
deturmined to proceed on,   with great difficuelty got the Chiefs
out of our boat, and when we was about Setting out the Class
Called the Soldiers took possession of the Cable the 1st Cheif which
was Still on board, & intended to go a Short distance up with us.
I told him the men of his nation Set on the Cable,   he went out
& told Capt. Lewis who was at the bow the men Who Set on the
roap was Soldiers, and wanted Tobacco   Capt. Lewis would not
agree to be forced into any thing,   the 2d Chief [The Partisan]
Demanded a flag & Tobacco which we refusd. to Give Stateing
proper reasons to them for it   after much Dificuelty — which
had nearly reduced us to necessity to hostilities I threw a Carrot ot
Tobacco to 1st Chief   took the port fire from the gunner. Spoke
so as to touch his pride   The Chief gave the Tobacco to his
Soldiers & he jurked the rope from them and handed it to the bows-

man we then Set out under a Breeze from the S. E.   about 2
miles up we observed the 3rd Chief on Shore beckining to
us   we took him on board   he informed us the roap was held
by the order of the 2d Chief who was a Double Spoken man,   Soon
after we Saw a man Comeing full Speed, thro: the plains left his
horse & proceeded across a Sand bar near the Shore   we took
him on board & observed that he was the Son of the Chief we had
on board   we Sent by him a talk to the nation Stateint [stating]
the cause of our hoisting the red flag undr. the white,   if they
were for peace Stay at home & do as we had Directed them, if the[y]
were for war or were Deturmined to stop us we were ready to
defend our Selves,   we halted one houre & ½ on the S. S. & made
a Substitute of Stones for a ancher, refreshed our men and proceeded on about 2 Miles higher up & Came to a verry Small Sand
bar in the middle of the river & Stayed all night,   I am verry unwell for want of Sleep   Deturmined to Sleep to night if possible,   the Men Cooked & we rested well.

[Ordway]   FRIDAY 28TH SEPT 1804.

a clear and pleasant morning. Capt Clark went with the
pearogues eairly. this morning to hunt for anker. Searched Some
time with the Boat hook and poles. could not find it. they took a
chord and put Sinks to the middle and took each end to the 2
pearogues and dragged the river diligently a long time but could
not find it. took breakfast about 10 O.Clock the whole lodge of
Indians were waiting on the bank to See us Start. as we intended
if the excident had not of happened last night   we gave up the
Idea of finding our anker. We then were about to Set off. Some
of the chiefs were on bord insisting on our Staying untill the others
came. We told them we could not wait any longer. they then did
not incline to let us go on   they Sayed we might return back
with what we had or remain with them, but we could not go up
the Missouri any further, about 200 Indians were then on the
bank. Some had fire arms. Some had Spears. Some had a kind of
cutlashes, and all the rest had Bows and steel or Iron pointed ar-
rrows. Several of the warries Set by the chord where our boat the big
Barge was tied   the 2 pearogues were tied on the outside of the
Barge. Capt Clark was Speaking to the chiefs in the cabbin. Capt

Lewis asked the chiefs if they were going out of the boat. they did not incline to. then Capt Lewis came out [and] ordered every man to his place ordered the Sail hoisted, then one man went out [and] untied the chord, which the warrier had in his hand, then 2 or 3 more of their warries caught hold of the chord and tyed it faster than before. Capt Lewis then appeared to be angarry, and told [them] to Go out of the Boat and the chief then went out and Sayed we are sorry to have you go. But if you will Give us one carret of tobacco we will be willing for you to go on & will not try to stop you. Capt Lewis Gave it to them. the head chief Sayd then that we must Give him one more carrit of tobacco more for his warries who held the chord and then we might go, boath of our Captains told him that we did not mean to be trifled with. nor would not humer them any more, but would Give him 1 carrit more for the warriers, if he would be a man of his word and Stand to his word like a man. the chief Sayd he was mad too, to See us Stand So much for 1 carrit of tobacco   if we would Give it we might go on. Capt Lewis Gave it to him. he then took the chord in his hand & Gave it to us. we then Set off under a gentle Breeze which happened to be favourable. we proceeded on passd bottom prarie on s. s. high land on N. S.   went 4 miles and halted. we fixed 2 large Stone to our boats to answer as ankers, as we did not inted to Camp on Shore again untill we Got to an other Nation.

[Clark]   29TH OF SEPTR. SATTURDAY 1804. —

    proceeded on   at 9 oClock we observed the 2d Chief & 2 principal Men   one Man & a Squar on Shore,   they wished to go up with us as far as the other part of their band, which they Said was on the river a head not far Distant   we refused Stateing verry Sufficint reasons and was Plain with them on the Subject,

                              30TH OF SEPT. SUNDAY 1804 —

    Set out this morning early   had not proceeded on far before we discovered an Indn. running after us,   he came up with us at 7oClock & requested to come on bord and go up to the *Recorees* [Arikaras]   we refused to take any of that band on board   if he chose to proceed on Shore it was verry Well   Soon after I descovered on the hills at a great distance great numbers of Indians which appeared to be makeing to the river above us, we proceeded on under a Double reafed Sail, & some rain   at 9 oClock observed a large band of Indians the Same which I had before seen on the hills incamping on the bank the L. S.   we Came too on a Sand bar Brackfast & proceeded on & Cast the anchor oppsit their Lodge at about 100 yards distant, and informed the Indians which we found to be a part of the Band we had before Seen, that *(we)* took them by the hand and Sent to each Chief a Carrot of tobacco,

we proceeded on under a verry Stiff Breeze from the S. E.,   the Stern of the boat got fast on a log and the boat turned & was verry near filling before we got her righted, the waves being verry high,   The Chief on board was So fritened at the Motion of the boat which in its rocking Caused Several loose articles to fall on the Deck from the lockers, he ran off and hid himself,   we landed, he got his gun and informed us he wished to return, that all things were cleare for us to go on, we would not see any more Tetons &c. we repeated to him what had been Said before, and advised him to keep his men away, gave him a blanket a Knife & some Tobacco, Smokd. a pipe & he Set out. We also Set Sale and Came to at a Sand bar, & Camped,   a verry Cold evening, all on guard.

Sand bars are So noumerous, that it is impossible to describe them, & think it unnecessary to mention them.

1st of October Monday 1804 —

[They pass the mouth of the Cheyenne River.]

Continued on with the wind imediately a head, and Came too on a large Sand bar in the middle of the river, we Saw a man opposit to our Camp on the L. S. which we discovd. to be a Frenchman,   a little of *(from Shore among)* the Willows we observed a house,   we Call to them to come over, a boy came in a canoe & informed that 2 frenchmen were at the house with good to trade with the Seauex which he expected down from the rickerrees everry day,   Sever'l large parties of Seauex Set out from the *rees* [3] for this place to trade with those men.

---

[3] "Rees" was the common English and American designation of the Arikaras. It never designates the Minnetarees, the neighbors of the Mandans, whom the expedition is about to meet.

This Mr. *Jon Vallie* [4] informs us that he wintered last winter 300 Leagues up the Chien River under the Black mountains, he informs that this river is verry rapid and dificuelt even for Perogues to assend and when riseing the Swels is verry high,   one hundred Leagues up it forks   one fork Comes from the S. the other at 40 Leagues above the forks enters the black Mountain [the Black Hills]. The Countrey from the Missourie to the black mountains is much like the Countrey on the Missourie, less timber. & a great perpotion of Ceder.

The black mountains he Says is verry high, and Some parts of it has Snow on it in the Summer   No beever on Dog [Cheyenne] river,   on the Mountains great numbers of goat, and a kind of anamale with large circular horns,[5] this animale is nearly the Size of an Elk. White bears is also plenty

2ND OF OCTOBER TUESDAY 1804 —

observe great caution this day expecting the Seaux intentions some what hostile towards our progression,   The river not so rapid as below the Chien, its width nearly the same. 12 miles

5TH OF OCTOBER, FRIDAY 1804 —

we Set out early and proceeded on passed a Small Creek on the L. S.   at 7 oClock heard some yels   proceeded on Saw 3 Indians of the Teton band, they called to us to come on Shore, beged Some Tobacco,   we answd. them as useal and proceeded on,   in the evening passed a Small Island Situated close to the L. Side,   at the head of this Isd. a large Creek coms in on the L. S.   saw white Brants, we call this Creek white Brant Creek. I walked on the Isd. found it Covered with wild Rye,   I Shot a Buck, Saw a large gang of Goat on the hills opposit, one Buck killed, also a Prarie wolf this evening. The high Land not so high as below, river about the Same width, the Sand bars as noumerous,

---

4 Jean Vallé of an influential St. Louis fur-trading family. Almost certainly he was associated with, or had been supplied by, Loisel. He could not possibly have been 300 leagues, 750 miles, up the Cheyenne River, and he makes revealing misstatements about it.

5 The bighorn, or Rocky Mountain sheep, *Ovis canadensis.*

the earth Black and many of the Bluffs have the Appearance of being on fire. We came too and camped on a mud bar makeing from the S. S.   the evening is calm and pleasent,   refreshed the men with a glass of whiskey.

7TH OF OCTOBER SUNDAY 1804 —

at the mouth of this [Moreau] river we Saw the Tracks of white [grizzly] bear which was verry large,   I walked up this river a mile. below the mouth of this river is the remains of a Rickorree *Village* or Wintering Camp fortified in a circular form of about 60 Lodges, built in the Same form of those passed yesterday This Camp appears to have been inhabited last winter, many of their willow and Straw mats, Baskets & Buffalow Skin Canoes remain intire within the Camp,

from this river we proceeded on under a gentle Breeze from the S.W.   at 10 oClock we Saw 2 Indians on the S.S. they asked for something to eat, & informed us they were part of the *Beiffs De Medesons* Lodge on their way to the Rickerees   passed a Willow Island in a bend to the S.S.   at 5 Miles passd. a willow Island on the S.S.   Wind hard from the South   in the evening I walked on an Island nearly the middle of the river Called Grous Island,   one of the men killed a Shee Brarow,[6] another man Killed a Black tail Deer, the largest Doe I ever Saw, (Black under her breast)   this Island is nearly 1¼ mls. Squar no timber high and Covered with grass wild rye and contains Great Numbers of Grouse,   we proceeded on a Short distance above the Island and Camped on the S.S.   a fine evening.

8TH OF OCTOBER MONDAY 1804 —

passed the mouth of a River called by the Ricares *We tar hoo* [Grand River] on the L.S.   this river is 120 yards wide, the water of which at this time is Confined within 20 yards, dischargeing but a Small quantity, throwing out mud with Small propotion of Sand, great quantities of the red Berries, ressembling Currents, are on the river in every bend. proceeded on passed the lower pint of an Island close on the L.S.   2 of our men discovered the ricckerree

6 French, *blaireau;* here a female badger, *Taxidea taxus.*

village, about the Center of the Island on the L. Side on the main Shore. this Island is about 3 miles long, Seperated from the L.S. by a Channel of about 60 yards wide verry Deep,   The Isld. is covered with fields, where those People raise their Corn Tobacco Beens &c. &c.   Great numbers of those people came on the Island to See us pass,   we passed above the head of the Island and Capt. Lewis with 2 interpeters & 2 men went to the Village   I formed a Camp of the french [boatmen] & the guard on Shore, with one Sentinal on board of the boat at anchor,   a pleasent evening   all things arranged both for Peace or War,   This Village is Situated about the center of a large Island near the L. Side & near the foot of Some high bald uneaven hills,   Several french men Came up with Capt. Lewis in a Perogue, one of which is a Mr. Gravelin [7] a man well versed in the language of this nation and gave us some information relitive to the Countrey nat[i]on &c.

[Orderly Book; Clark]   ORDERS OCTOBER THE 8TH 1804.

Robert Frazer being regularly inlisted and haveing become one of the *Corps* of *Vollenteers* for *North-Western Discovery*, he is therefore to be viewed & respected accordingly; and will be anexed to Sergeant Gass's mess.

WM. CLARK CPT. &C.
MERIWETHER LEWIS
Capt. 1st U.S. Regt. Infty

RIVER MAROPA 9TH OF OCTOBER 1804. TUESDAY —

a windey rainey night, and cold, So much So we Could not speek with the Indians to day   the three great Chiefs and many others Came to see us to day, we gave them some tobacco and informed them we would Speek on tomorrow, the day continued Cold & windey some rain   Sorry [several] Canoos of Skins passed down from the 2 Villages a Short distance above, and many Came to view us all day,   much astonished at my black Servent, who did not lose the opportunity of [displaying] his powers Strength &c. &c.   this nation never Saw a black man before.

Several hunters Came in with loades of meat,   I observed

[7] Joseph Gravelines, one of Loisel's employes.

Several Canoos made of a Single Buffalow Skin [8] with 3 thre squars
Cross the river to day in waves as high as I ever Saw them on
this river, quite uncomposed   I have a Slite Plursie this evening
verry cold &c. &c.

10TH OF OCTOBER WEDNESDAY 1804.

we prepare all things ready to Speak to the Indians, Mr. Tabo [9]
& Mr. Gravolin came to brackfast with us   at one oClock the
Cheifs all assembled & after Some little Cerremony the council
Commenced,   we informd them what we had told the others
before i. e. Ottoes & Seaux. made 3 Cheif 1 for each Village;   gave them presents. after the Council was over we Shot
the air guns which astonished them much, the[y] then Departed and
we rested Secure all night,   Those Indians wer much astonished
at my Servent, they never Saw a black man before,   all flocked
around him & examind him from top to toe,   he Carried on the
joke and made himself more turribal than we wished him to doe.
Those Indians are not fond of Spirts Licquer. of any kind

11TH OCTOBER THURSDAY 1804 —

at 11 oClock we met the Grand Cheif in Councel and he made a
Short Speech thanking us for what we had given him & his nation
promisseing to attend to the Council we had given him & informed
us the road was open & no one dare Shut it, & we might Departe
at pleasure,   at 1 oClock we Set out for the upper Villages at
1 mile took in the 2d Cheif & Came too off the first [second] Village
Seperated from the 3rd by a Creek after arrangeing all matters we
walked up with the 2d Cheif to his Village, and Set talking on
Various Subjects untill late   we also visited the upper or 3rd
Village each of which gave us Something to eate in their way,
and a fiew bushels of Corn Beens &c. &c.   after being treated
by everry civility by those people who are both pore & Durtey we
returned to our boat at about 10 oClk. P M. informing them before

---

8 A Mandan-type bullboat, circular in form, made by stretching buffalo hides
over a light framework of willow or cottonwood.

9 Loisel's agent, Pierre-Antoine Tabeau.

we Departed that we would Speek to them tomorrow at there Seperate Villages,   Those people gave us to eate bread made of Corn & Beens, also Corn & Beans boild. a large Been which they rob the mice of the Prarie [10] which is rich & verry nurrishing also quashes &c.   all Tranquillity.

12TH OCTOBER FRIDAY 1804 —

we Set Some time before the Councill Commenced   this man Spoke at Some length declareing his dispotion to believe and prosue our Councils, his intention of going to Visit his great father   acknowledged the Satisfaction in receiveing the presents &c. rais'g a Doubt as to the Safty in passing the Nations below particularly the Souex. requested us to take a Chief of their nation and make a good peace with Mandins & nations above.   after answering those parts of the 2d Cheifs Speech which required it, which appeared to give general Satisfaction we went to the Village of the 3rd Chief   This Chief Spoke verry much in the [same] Stile on nearly the Same Subjects of the other Chief who Set by his Side, more Sincear & pleasently,   after we had ansd. his Speech & give them Some account of the Magnitude & power of our Countrey which pleased and astonished them verry much we returned to our boat, the Chiefs accompanied us on board,   we gave them Some Sugar a little Salt and a Sun Glass, & Set 2 on Shore & the third proceeded on with us to the Mandens

The Nation of the Rickerries is about 600 men (Mr. Taboe says, I think 500 men) able to bear arms   a Great perpotion of them have fusees [11]   they appear to be peacefull, their men tall and perpotiend, womin Small and industerous, raise great quantities of Corn Beens Simnins [summer squash] &c. also Tobacco for the men to Smoke   they collect all the wood and do the drugery as Common amongst Savages.

The curruption of the language of [the] different Tribes has So reduced the language that the Different Villages do not under-

---

10 That is, pillaged them from the nests and burrows of the wild (white-footed) mouse and other rodents. This "bean" is *Amphicarpa monoica,* whose seeds were an important food for the tribes of the Upper Missouri. Frontiers-men usually called it the "hog peanut" or "wild peanut."

11 *Fusils,* cheap trade muskets.

stan all the words of the others. Those people are Durtey, Kind, pore, & extravigent. pursessing national pride, not beggarley recive what is given with great pleasure, Live in warm houses, large and built in an oxigon form forming a cone at top which is left open for the smoke to pass,   those houses are Generally 30 or 40 foot Diamiter, Covd. with earth on poles willows & grass to prevent the earths passing thro'. Those people express an inclination to be at peace with all nations. The Seaux who trade the goods which they get of the Britush Traders for their Corn, and great influence over the Rickeres, poison their minds and keep them in perpetial dread.

a curious custom with the Souix as well as the rickeres is to give handsom squars to those whome they wish to Show some acknowledgements to. The Seauex we got clare of without taking their squars, they followed us with Squars two days. The Rickores we put off dureing the time we were at the Towns but 2 [*handsom young*] Squars were Sent by a man to follow us, they came up this evening, and pursisted in their civilities.

Robert Frazier, a member of the squad from Captain Stoddard's company, has been enlisted in the permanent party to fill the vacancy made by Gass's appointment as sergeant. Now John Newman, of the permanent party, is court-martialed for insubordination. sentenced to 75 lashes (the last corporal punishment on the expedition) and denied status — to be returned to St. Louis and discharged from the Army. The Chief alluded to in the next entry is the Arikara who is going as a peace envoy to the Mandans.

[Clark]   14TH OF OCTOBER SUNDAY 1804 —

The punishment of this day allarmd. the Indian Chief verry much, he cried aloud (or effected to cry)   I explained the Cause of the punishment and the necessity (*of it*) which he thought examples were also necessary, & he himself had made them by Death,   his nation never whiped even their Children, from their burth.

15TH OF OCTOBER MONDAY 1804 —

at Sunset we arrived at a Camp of Recares of 10 Lodges on the
S.S.   we came too and camped near them   Capt. Lewis and
my self went with the Chief who accompanis us, to the Huts of
Several of the men all of whome Smoked & gave us something to
eate also Some meat to take away,   those people were kind and
appeared to be much plsd. at the attentioned paid them.
Those people are much pleased with my black Servent. Their
womin verry fond of carressing our men &c.

18TH OF OCTOBER THURSDAY 1804 —

Set out early proceeded on   at 6 mls. passed the mouth of la
Boulet (or Cannon Ball River) about 140 yards wide on the
L.S.   above the mouth of the river Great numbers of Stone
perfectly round with fine Grit are in the Bluff and on the
Shore,   the river takes its name from those Stones which
resemble Cannon Balls. The water of this river is confined within
40 yards. We met 2 frenchmen in a perogue Decending from
hunting, & complained of the Mandans robing them of 4 Traps
their furs & Several other articles. Those men were in the imploy
of our Ricaree interpeter Mr. Gravelin   the[y] turned & followed us.
Saw Great numbers of Goats on the S.S. comeing to the
river   our hunters Killed 4 of them   Some run back and
others crossed & proceded on their journey to the *Court Nou*
[Black Hills]   passed a small creek on the L.S. 1 mile above the
last, and camped on a Sand bar on the L. S.   opposit to us we
Saw a Gangue of Buffalow bulls which we did not think worth
while to kill. our hunters killed 4 Coats [Goats] 6 Deer 4 Elk & a
pelican & informs that they Saw in one gang: 248 Elk,   (I
walked on Shore in the evening with a view to see Some of those
remarkable places mentioned by evins,[12] none of which I could

12 John Evans, the last previous visitor to the Mandans. An employe of
James Mackay, who had made the most formidable effort before Lewis and
Clark to explore the Upper Missouri. He was a young man from Wales who
had come to America to locate the mythical Welsh Indians. For a long time
this myth, the most widespread in American history, had centered on the
Mandans. He had drawn a map of the Missouri and the expedition was using
a copy of it which Jefferson had sent to Lewis.

find). The Countrey in this Quarter is Generally leavel & fine   Some high Short hills, and some ragid ranges of Hills at a Distance

20th of October Satturday 1804 —

Camped on the L.S. above a Bluff containing coal of an inferior quallity, this bank is imediately above the old [deserted] Village of the Mandans. The Countrey is fine, the high hills at a Distance with gradual assents,   I kild. 3 Deer   The Timber confined to the bottoms as useal which is much larger than below. Great numbers of Buffalow Elk & Deer, Goats. our hunters killed 10 Deer & a Goat to day and wounded a white Bear [13]   I saw several fresh tracks of those animals which is 3 times as large as a mans track. The wind hard all Day from the N.E. & East,   great numbers of buffalow Swimming the river   I observe near all large gangues of Buffalow wolves and when the buffalow move those animals follow, and feed on those that are killed by accident or those that are too pore or fat to keep up with the gangue.

22nd October Monday 1804 —

last night at 1 oClock I was violently and Suddenly attacked with the Rhumetism in the neck which was So violent I could not move   Capt. applied a hot Stone raped in flannel, which gave me some temporey ease. We Set out early, the morning Cold   at 7 oClock we came too at a camp of Teton Seaux on the L. S.   those people 12 in number were nackd. [naked] and had the appearance of war,   we have every reason to believe that they are going or have been to Steel Horses from the Mandins,   they tell two Stories,   we gave them nothing   after takeing brackfast proceeded on. my Neck is yet verry painfull at times Spasms.

The hunters killed a buffalow bull,   they Say out of about 300 buffalow which they Saw, they did not, see one Cow. Great Deel of Beever Sign. Several Cought every night.

---

[13] Cruzatte shot it. The expedition had been expecting to meet grizzlies ("grizzled bears," "white bears," etc.) whose ferocity was well known. But, as will be seen later, this one was probably not a grizzly.

24TH OCTOBER WEDNESDAY 1804 —

Set out early   a cloudy day Some little Snow in the morning
I am Something better of the Rhumitism in my neck. a butifull
Countrey on both Sides of the river. the bottoms covd. with
wood,   we have Seen no game on the river to day — a prof of
the Indians hunting in the neighbourhood   passed a Island
on the S. S. made by the river Cutting through a point, by which
the river is Shortened Several miles. on this Isld. we Saw one of
the Grand Chiefs of the Mandins, with five Lodges hunting,   this Chief met the Chief of the *Ricares* who accompanied
us with great Cordiallity & serimony Smoked the pipe & Capt.
Lewis with the Interpeter went with the Chiefs to his Lodges at
1 mile distant,   after his return we admited the Grand Chief &
his brother for a few minits on our boat. proceeded on a Short
distance and camped on the S.S. below the old village of the
Mandins & *ricares*. Soon after our land'g 4 mandins came from
a camp above,   the Ricares Chief went with them to their Camp,

25TH OF OCTOBER THURSDAY 1804 —

a cold morning. Set out early under a gentle Breeze from the
S. E. by E.   proceeded on, passed the 3rd old Village of the
Mandans which has been Desd. for many years,   This village
was situated on an eminance of about 40 foot above the water
on the L. S.   back for Several miles is a butifull Plain at a
Short distance above this old Village on a Continuation of the
same eminance was Situated the Ricares Village which has been
avacuated only Six years,   Several parties of Mandins rode to
the river on the S. S. to view us   indeed they are continuelly in
Sight Satisfying their Curiossities as to our apperance &c.   We
are told that the Seaux has latterly fallen in with & Stole the
horses of the *Big bellies*,[14]   on their way home they fell in with

14 The "Big bellies" are the Gros Ventres, the Minnetarees, called by ethnologists the Hidatsa. Their villages were on Knife River, very near those of the
Mandans, with whom they usually maintained altogether remarkable peace and
friendship. They must not be confused with the Gros Ventres of Canada, a displaced tribe of Arapahos, called by ethnologists the Atsina, who were closely
associated with the Blackfeet.
    The (Canadian) Frenchman whose death is reported was named Ménard. He
was probably the first *engagé* of a British fur company to reach the Mandans —

the Ossiniboin [Assiniboins] who killed them and took the horses. a frenchman has latterly been killed by the Indians on the Track to the tradeing establishment on the Ossinebine R. in the North of this place (or British fort)   This frenchman has lived many years with the Mandins. river full of Sand bars & we are at a great loss to find the channel of the river, frequently run on the Sand bars which Delais us much   passed a verry bad riffle of rocks in the evening by takeing the L. S. of a sand bar and camped on a Sand point on the S. S. opposit a high hill on the L. S.   Several Indians came to see us this evening, amongst others the Sun of the late Great Chief of the Mandins,   this man has his two little fingers off;   on inquireing the cause, was told it was customary for this nation to Show their greaf by some testimony of pain, and that it was not uncommon for them to take off 2 Smaller fingers of the hand (*at the 2nd joints*) and some times more with other marks of Savage effection

R. Fields with the Rhumitism in his neck, P. Crusat with the Same complaint in his Legs — the party other wise is well,   as to my self I feel but slight Simptoms of that disorder at this time,

26th of October Friday 1804 —

proceeded on   saw numbers of the Mandins on Shore,   we set the Ricare Chief on Shore, and we proceeded on to the Camp of two of their Grand Chiefs where we delayed a fiew minits, with the Chiefs and proceeded on takeing two of their Chiefs on board & Some of the heavy articles of his house hold, Such as earthen pots & Corn,   proceeded on,   at this Camp Saw a (*Mr.*) Mc·Cracken Englishmon [15] from the N.W. Company   this man Came nine Days ago to trade for *horses & Buffalow* robes, — one other man came with him. the Indians continued on the banks all day. but little wood on this part of the river, many Sand bars and bad places, water much devided between them

We came too and camped on the L. S. about ½ a mile below

probably in the late 1780's. He went native, living permanently among the Indians and occasionally acting as agent for one of the trading posts on the Assiniboine or the Souris.

[15] Hugh McCracken, an Irishman and former soldier in the British Army, had long been an *engagé* of the North West Company. He first visited the Mandans in 1797 with David Thompson's party.

the 1st Mandin Town on the L. S.   soon after our arrival many men womin & children flocked down to See us, Capt. Lewis walked to the village with the principal Chiefs and our interpters,   my Rhumatic complaint increasing I could not go. I Smoked with the Chiefs who came after. Those people apd. much pleased with the Corn Mill which we were obliged to use, & was fixed in the boat.

CHAPTER V

AMONG THE MANDANS

When the Mandans were first seen by white men — Véren-drye in 1738 — they were living in nine populous villages near the mouth of Heart River. (Mandan and Bismarck, North Dakota, about sixty miles downstream from where Lewis and Clark encountered them.) Cultural decline, the endless war with the Sioux, and especially the smallpox epidemic of 1782 so reduced their strength that they were forced to withdraw upstream, out of the path of the Sioux migration. This removal was made, apparently, about 1790.

Knife River enters the Missouri from the west at Stanton, North Dakota. In this vicinity were located the two villages that were ample to contain the remaining Mandans and three villages of Minnetarees or Gros Ventres. (Rather two villages of Minnetarees and one of their close relatives who maintained a separate tribal organization, the Indians called by Lewis and Clark the Anahaways or Wattersoons.) The first Mandan village was on the right or west bank (Clark calls it the south bank) of the Missouri about four miles below the mouth of Knife River. The captains rendered its name Matootonha and that of its principal chief, Shahaka, Big White; its second chief was Little Raven or Little Crow. The second Mandan village, some three miles farther upstream and on the left or east (Clark's north) bank, was in the captains' spelling Rooptarhe. Its principal chief was Posecopsahe, Black Cat.

A mile beyond Rooptarhe, Knife River entered, and here on the right bank of the Missouri was the small village of the Anaha-ways. Clark rendered its name Maharha and that of its chief,

White Buffalo Robe. Half a mile up Knife River from the mouth was the first Minnetaree village, Metehartan, whose head chief was Black Moccasin. Clark does not give a name for the second Minnetaree village, which was a mile and a half up Knife River from the first one, but calls the head chief Little Wolf's Medicine. These villages, which were surrounded by walled embankments of clay and a ditch, were composed of the earth lodge typical of the Upper Missouri sedentary tribes. The lodges, made of timber, half sunk in the ground, and covered with a thick roof of earth, were large enough to house several families, their best buffalo-horses, and large stocks of food. They were very comfortable dwellings and were entirely safe against marauding Sioux.[1]

The structure of cottonwood logs which the expedition built to winter in and which was called Fort Mandan, was about a mile downstream from the first Mandan town. It was in the river bottom on the opposite, that is, the left, bank.

[Clark]   27TH OF OCTOBER SATTURDAY 1804, MANDANS. —

came too at the Village on the L.S. this village is situated on an eminance of about 50 feet above the Water in a hansom plain   it containes [blank space in MS.] houses in a kind of Picket work,   the houses are round and verry large containing several families, as also their horses which is tied on one Side of the enterance,   I walked up & Smoked a pipe with the Chiefs of the Village   they were anxious that I would stay and eat with them, my indisposition provented my eating which displeased them, untill a full explenation took place,   I returned to the boat and Sent 2 Carrots of Tobacco for them to smoke, and proceeded on,   passed the 2d Village and camped opsd. the Village of the *Weter soon* [or *Ah wah har ways*] which is Situated on an eminance in a plain on the L.S.

we met with a frenchman by the name of *Jessomme*[2] which we

---

[1] Described in Maximilian's *Travels in the Interior of North America* and splendidly pictured by his artist, Charles Bodmer. Bodmer's picture is reproduced as Plate XIV in DeVoto, *Across the Wide Missouri.*

[2] René Jessaume, hired as a Mandan interpreter. He had been coming to the village for more than ten years, sometimes as a free trader, sometimes as an *engagé* of the North West Company or the Hudson's Bay Company. He had led the British party which forced John Evans to return to St. Louis and, according to Evans, had tried to kill him.

imploy as an interpeter. This man has a wife & Children in the
village. Great numbers on both Sides flocked down to the bank
to view us as we passed. we Sent three twists of Tobacco by three
young men, to the three villages above enviting them to come
Down & Council with us tomorrow. many Indians came to view
us Some stayed all night in the Camp of our party. We procured
some information of Mr. Jessomme of the Chiefs of the Different
Nations

SUNDAY. 28TH OF OCTOBER 1804 —

many of the *Grosvantres* (or Big Bellies) and Watersones Came
to See us and hear the Council   the. wind being So violently
hard from the S.W. provented our going into Council, (indeed the
Chiefs of the Mandans from the lower village Could not
Cross,   we made up the presents and entertained Several of the
Curious Chiefs whome, wished to see the Boat which was verry
curious to them viewing it as great medison, as they also Viewed
my black Servent   The Black Cat Grand Chief of the Mandans,
Capt Lewis & myself with an Interpeter walked up the river about
1½ miles   we had Several presents from the woman of Corn
boil'd homney, Soft Corn &c. &c.   I prosent a jar to the Chiefs
wife who receved it with much pleasure. our men verry chearfull
this evening. We Sent the Chiefs of the Gross Vantres to Smoke
a a pipe with the Grand Chef of the Mandans in his Village, &
told them we would Speek tomorrow.

29TH OCTOBER MONDAY 1804 —

a fair fine morning   after Brackfast we were visited by the
old Cheaf of the *Big bellies*   this man was old and had trans-
fired his power to his Sun, who was then out at War against the
Snake Indians who inhabit the Rockey Mountains. we Collected
the Chiefs and Commenced a Councel ounder a orning, and our
Sales Stretched around to keep out as much wind as possible.   we
delivered a long Speech the Substance of which Similer to what
we had Delivered to the nations below. the old Chief of the Gros-
vanters was verry restless before the Speech was half ended observed
that he Could not wait long that his Camp was exposed to the
hostile Indians, &c. &c.   he was rebuked by one of the Chiefs
for his uneasiness at Such a time as the present,   we at the end

of the Speech mentioned the *Recare* who accompanied us to make a firm Peace,   they all Smoked with him (I gave this Cheaf a Dollar of the American Coin as a Meadel with which he was much pleased)   In Councel we prosented him with a certificate of his sinerrity and good Conduct &c.   We also Spoke about the fur which was taken from 2 frenchmen by a Mandan, and informd of our intentions of Sending back the french hands. after the Council we gave the presents with much serimoney, and put the Meadels on the Chiefs we intended to make viz. one for each Town to whome we gave coats hats & flags, one Grand Chief to each nation to whome we gave meadels with the presidents likeness in Council we requested them to give us an answer tomorrow or as Soon as possible to Some Points which required their Deliberation. after the Council was over we Shot the air gun which appeared to astonish the nativs much,   the greater part then retired Soon after.

a Iron or Steel Corn Mill which we gave to the Mandins, was verry thankfully receved. The Prarie was Set on fire (or cought by accident) by a young man of the Mandins,   the fire went with such velocity that it burnt to death a man & woman, who Could not get to any place of Safty, one man a woman & Child much burnt and Several narrowly escaped the flame. a boy half white was saved unhurt in the midst of the flaim, Those ignerent people say this boy was Saved by the Great Medison Speret because he was white. The couse of his being Saved was a Green buffalow Skin was thrown over him by his mother who perhaps had more fore Sight for the pertection of her Son, and [l]ess for herself than those who escaped the flame,   the Fire did not burn under the Skin leaveing the grass round the boy. This fire passed our Camp last [night] about 8 oClock P.M.   it went with great rapitidity and looked Tremendious

We Sent the presents intended for the Grand Chief of the *Mi-ne-tar-re* or Big Belley, and the presents flag and Wompom by the old Chief and those intended for the Chief of the Lower Village by a young Chief.

30TH OCTOBER TUESDAY 1804 —

I took 8 men in a Small perogue and went up the river as fur as the 1st Island about 7 miles to see if a Situation could be got on

it for our Winter quarters,   found the wood on the Isd. as also
on the pt. above so Distant from the water that, I did not think
that we could get a good wintering ground there, and as all the
white men here informed us that wood was scerce, as well as game
above, we Deturmined to drop down a fiew miles near wood and
game

on my return found maney Inds. at our Camp,   gave the
party a dram,   they Danccd as is verry Comn. in the evening
which pleased the Savages much.

[Biddle]   OCTOBER 31st

A second chief arrived this morning with an invitation from the
grand chief of the Mandans to come to his village, where he wished
to present some corn to us and to speak with us. Captain Clarke
walked down to his village; he was first seated with great ceremony
on a robe by the side of the chief, who then threw over his
shoulders another robe handsomely ornamented. The pipe was
then smoked with several of the old men who were seated around
the chief; after some time he began his discourse by observing that
he believed what we had told him, and that they should soon
enjoy peace, which would gratify him as well as his people, because
they could then hunt without fear of being attacked, and the
women might work in the fields without looking every moment
for the enemy, and at night put off their moccasins, a phrase by
which is conveyed the idea of security when the women could
undress at night without fear of attack. As to the Ricaras, he
continued, in order to show you that we wish peace with all
men, that chief, pointing to his second chief, will go with some
warriors back to the Ricaras with their chief now here and smoke
with that nation. When we heard of your coming all the nations
around returned from their hunting to see you, in hopes of receiving large presents; all are disappointed and some discontented; for
his part he was not much so, though his village was. He added
that he would go and see his great father the President. Two of
the steel traps stolen from the Frenchmen were then laid before
Captain Clarke, and the women brought about twelve bushels
of corn. After the chief had finished, Captain Clarke made an
answer to the speech and then returned to the boat.

[Clark]   31ST OF OCTOBER WEDNESDAY 1804 —

the Grand Chief of the Mandans came Dressed in the Clothes
we had given with his 2 small Suns, and requested to See the
men Dance which they verry readily gratified him in,   the wind
blew hard all the after part of the day from the N. E. and continud
all night to blow hard from that point,   in the morning it
Shifted NW.   Capt Lewis wrote to the N. W. Companys agent
on the Orsiniboine River abt. 9 Days march North of this place

                               1ST OF NOVEMBER. THURSDAY 1804 —
Mr. McCrackin a Trader Set out at 7 oClock to the Fort on the
Ossiniboin   by him Send a letter, (inclosing a Copy of the
British Ministers protection) to the principal agent of the Company. at about 10 oClock the Chiefs of the Lower Village came
and after a Short time informed us they wished they would
us to [*i. e.,* that we would] call at their Village & take Some
corn,   [They said] that they would make peace with the *Ricares*   they never made war against them but after the *Rees*
killed their Chiefs they killed them like the birds, and were tired
(*of killing them*) and would Send a Chief and Some brave men
to the Ricares to Smoke with that people.

                               2ND NOVEMBER FRIDAY 1804 —

This Morning at Daylight I went down the river with 4 men
to look for a proper place to winter   proceeded down the river
three miles & found a place well Supld. with wood, & returned,   maney Indians to view us to day

                               3RD OF NOVEMBER SATTERDAY 1804 —

we commence building our Cabins,   Send down in a perogue
6 men to hunt engaged [enlisted] one man,[3]   Set the french who

---

3 Baptiste Lepage, to take the place of Newman; he had been with one of the
Canadian companies, had penetrated the interior as far as the Black Hills, and
had come down from there along the Little Missouri.

intend to return to build a perogue,[4]   Mr. Jessomme with his
Squar & children come down to live, as Interpter,   we receved
(*hired*) a hors for our Service,   the men were indulged with
a Dram, this evening   two Beaver Cought this morning, and
one Trap Lost

4TH NOVEMBER SUNDAY 1804 —

we continued to cut Down trees and raise our houses,   a Mr.
Chaubonie,[5] interpeter for the Gross Ventre nation Came to See
us, and informed that [he] came Down with Several Indians from
a hunting expidition up the river, to here what we had told the
Indians in Council   this man wished to hire as an interpiter,

6TH NOVEMBER TUESDAY 1804 FORT MANDAN —

last night late we wer awoke by the Sergeant of the Guard to
See a Nothern light, which was light, (*but*) not red, and appeared
to Darken and Some times nearly obscured, and open,   many
times appeared in light Streeks, and at other times a great Space
light & containing floating collomns which appeared to approach
each other & retreat leaveing the lighter space   at no time of
the Same appearance

Mr. Jo Gravelin our ricare interpeter Paul *premor, Laguness,*
[Primaut, Lajeunesse] & 2 french Boys, who Came with us, Set out
in a Small perogue, on their return to the recare nation & the
Illinois, Mr. Gravelin has instructions to take on the recares in
the Spring &c.[6]   Continue to build the huts, out of Cotton

[4] Four of Deschamps' boat crew had decided to return to St. Louis now; the
others would spend the winter among the Mandans or at Fort Mandan and
make themselves useful to the expedition. The original intention had been to
send Warfington's squad back before winter too but as early as September 16
it had been decided to keep them through the winter.

[5] Touissant Charbonneau, who was to become one of the most famous members of the expedition because of Sacajawea, one of his Indian wives. An experienced frontiersman, he had been with one or another of the Canadian
companies on the Assiniboine as far back at 1793, if not earlier. He is hired as
interpreter for the Minnetarees, whose language white men found very hard to
learn.

[6] Gravelines was to winter with the Arikaras, then take one of their chiefs to
Washington.

[Cottonwood] Timber, &c. this being the only timber we have,

10TH NOVEMBER SATTURDAY 1804 —

continued to build our fort   numbers of Indians came to See us   a Chief Half Pania [Pawnee] came & brought a Side of a Buffalow, in return We Gave Some fiew small things to himself & wife & Son,   he crossed the river in the Buffalow Skin Canoo & and, the Squar took the Boat (*on her back*) and proceeded on to the Town 3 miles   the Day raw and cold wind from the NW.,   the Gees Continue to pass in gangues as also brant to the South, Some Ducks also pass

11TH NOVEMBER SUNDAY 1804. FORT MANDAN

continued at work at the Fort   Two men cut themselves with an ax,   The large Ducks pass to the South an Indian gave me several roles of parched meat   two Squars [7] of the Rock[y] mountains, purchased from the Indians by a frenchmen came down   The Mandans out hunting the Buffalow

12TH NOVEMBER MONDAY 1804 —

early this morning the Big White princapal Chief of the lower Village of the Mandans came Down, he packd about 100 lb. of fine meet on his squar for us,   3 men Sick with the [blank in M.S.],

The interpeter says that the Mandan nation as they (old men) Say came out of a Small lake (*subterraneous Villages & a lake*) where they had Gardins,   maney years ago they lived in Several Villages on the Missourie low down,   the Small pox destroyed the greater part of the nation and reduced them to one large village and Some Small ones,   all the nations before this mala-dey was affrd. of them,   after they were reduced the Seaux and other Indians waged war, and killed a great maney, and they moved up the Missourie.   those Indians Still continued to wage war, and they moved Still higher, until got in the Countrey of the Panias,   whith this Ntn they lived in friendship maney years,

[7] The younger of these women was Sacajawea.

inhabiting the Same neighbourhood untill that people waged war,   they moved up near the *Watersoons & Winataras* where they now live in peace with those nations,   the Mandans Speake a language peculial to themselves verry much [blank in MS.] they can rase about 350 men the Winataries about 80 and the Big bellies about 600 or 650 men. the Mandans and Seaux have the Same word for water. The *Big bellies* or *Winetaries* & ravin [Crow] Indians Speake nearly the Same language and the presumption is they were origionaly the Same nation   The Ravin Indians have 400 Lodges & about 1200 men, & follow the Buffalow, or hunt for their Subsistance in the plains & on the Court Noi [8] & Rock Mountains, & are at war with the Siaux [and] Snake Indians

The Big bellies & Watersoons are at war with the Snake Indians & Seauex and were at war with the *Ricares* untill we made peace a fiew days passd.   The Mandans are at war with all who make war only, and wish to be at peace with all nations,   Seldom the ogressors [9]

13TH NOV. TUESDAY 1804 —

The Ice began to run in the river ½ past 10 oClock P.M. we rose early & onloaded the boat before brackfast except, the Cabin, & stored away in a Store house   Snow'd all day, the Ice ran thick and air Cold.

16TH NOVEMBER FRIDAY 1804 —

a verry white frost all the trees all covered with ice, cloudy, all the men move into the huts which is not finishd.   The *Ossini-boins* is at the Big bellie Camp,   some trouble like to take place between them from the loss of horses &c. as is Said by an old Indian who visited us with 4 Buffalow robes & corn to trade for a Pistol which we did not let him have,   men imployd untill

8 Côte Noire, the Black Hills, understood by the captains to extend much farther north and south than they do.

9 This is a specimen of the information which Lewis and Clark continued to get all winter long from the Mandans and the Minnetarees. By the time they resumed the journey they had far more and better information about the near-by and distant tribes and about the geography of the West than white men had ever had before.

late in dobing [daubing: chinking spaces between logs with clay]
their huts,   Some horses Sent down to Stay in the woods near
the fort, to prevent the Ossniboins Steeling them.

18TH NOV. SUNDAY 1804 —

the Black Cat, came to see us, he made great inquiries respecting
our fashions,   he also Stated the Situation of their nation, he
mentioned that a Council had been held the day before and it
was thought advisable to put up with the resent insults of the
Ossiniboins & Christinoes [Crees] untill they were convinced that
what had been told them by us,   Mr. Evins [10] had deceived them
& we might also,   he promised to return & furnish them with
guns & amunition,   we advised them to remain at peace & that
they might depend upon Getting Supplies through the Channel
of the Missourie, but it required time to put the trade in opperation. The Ossiniboins &c. have the trade of those [these] nations
in their power and treat them badly, as the Soux does the *Ricarees*,
and they cannot resent, for fear of loseing their trade.

[Biddle]   NOVEMBER 20TH.

We this day moved into our huts which are now completed.
This place which we call Fort Mandan, is situated in a point of
low ground, on the north side of the Missouri, covered with tall
and heavy cottonwood. The works consist of two rows of huts
or sheds, forming an angle where they joined each other; each row
containing four rooms, of 14 feet square and 7 feet high, with
plank cieling, and the roof slanting so as to form a loft above the
rooms, the highest part of which is 18 feet from the ground: the
backs of the huts formed a wall of that height, and opposite the
angle the place of the wall was supplied by picketing: in the area
were two rooms for stores and provisions. The latitude by observation is 47° 21' 47", and the computed distance from the mouth
of the Missouri is sixteen hundred miles.

10 John Evans. Note the concern of Lewis and Clark to get the trade of the
villages into American hands. The Indians are saying that they hope they can
depend on the Americans' promise to supply them with plenty of goods but
they had believed Evans when he made the same promise and he did not keep
it.

In the course of the day several Indians came down to partake of our fresh meat; among the rest, three chiefs of the second Mandan village. They inform us that the Sioux on the Missouri about the Chayenne river, threaten to attack them this winter; that these Sioux are much irritated at the Ricaras for having made peace through our means with the Mandans, and have lately ill-treated three Ricaras who carried the pipe of peace to them, by beating them and taking away their horses. We gave them assurances that we would protect them from all their enemies.

[Clark]   22ND OF NOVEMBER THURSDAY 1804 —

I was allarmed about 10 oClock by the Sentinal, who informed that an Indian was about to kill his wife in the interpeters fire about 60 yards below the works, I went down and Spoke to the fellow about the rash act which he was like to commit and forbid any act of the kind near the fort. Some misunderstanding took place between this man & his fife [wife] about 8 days ago, and she came to this place, & continued with the Squars of the interpeters, *(he might lawfully have killed her for running away)*   2 days ago She returned to the vill'ge. in the evening of the Same day She came to the interpeters fire appearently much beat, & Stabed in 3 places. We Derected that no man of this party have any intercourse with this woman under the penalty of Punishment. he the Husband observed that one of our Serjeants Slept with his wife & if he wanted her he would give her to him,   We derected the Serjeant [Ordway] to give the man Some articles, at which time I told the Indian that I believed not one man of the party had touched his wife except the one he had given the use of her for a nite, in his own bed,   no man of the party Should touch his squar, or the wife of any Indian, nor did I believe they touch a woman if they knew her to be the wife of another man, and advised him to take his squar home and live hapily together in future,

    The Grand Chief continued *(with us)* all day,   a warm Day fair afternoon   many Indian aneckdotes   our Chief & his family stay all night.

27th of November Tuesday 1804 —

Capt. Lewis returned from the Villages with two Chiefs & a considerate [considerable] man with the party who accompanied him, The Menetaries, were allarmed at the tales told them by the Mandans viz: that we intended to join the *Seaux* to Cut off them in the Course of the Winter, many Circumstances Combin'd to give force to those reports i.e. the movements of the interpeters & their families to the *Fort,* the strength of our work &c &c. all those reports was contredicted by Capt. Lewis with a conviction on the minds of the Indians of the falsity of those reports. Seven Traders arrived from the fort on the Ossinoboin from the NW. Company one of which Lafrance took upon himself to speak unfavourably of our intentions &c. the principal Mr. *La Rock* (& Mr. Mc Kensey) was informed of the Conduct of their interpeter & the Consequences if they did not put a Stop to unfavourable & ill founded assursions &c. &c.[11]

The two Chiefs much pleased with ther treatment & the Cherefullness of the party, who Danced to amuse them &c. &c.

The river fall 2 Inches verry Cold and began to Snow at 8 oClock PM and continued all night.

28th Nov. Wednesday 1804 —

river full of floating ice, began to Snow at 7 oClock *a m* and continued all day. at 8 oClock the Black Cat Came to See us, after Showing those Chiefs many thing[s] which was Curiossities to them, and Giveing a fiew presents of Curious Handkerchiefs arm bans & paint with a twist of Tobacco they departed at 1 oClock much pleased, at parting we had Some little talk on the Subject of the British Trader M. Le rock Giveing meadels & Flags, and told those Chiefs to impress it on the minds of their nations that those simbiles were not to be receved by any from

11 The Mandans told the Minnetarees this propaganda lie in order to deter them from visiting Fort Mandan till the Mandans could sew up the expected American trade and become its middlemen. The leader of the North West Company party was François Antoine Larocque; his clerk was Charles Mac-Kenzie, who felt a British superiority to the Americans and called Lewis an anglophobe. This first contact with the Canadian trade from the Lake Winnipeg region was an important event.

them, without they wished [to] incur the displeasure of their Great
American Father. a verry disagreeable day no work done to day

29TH NOVEMBER THURSDAY 1804 —

the detph of the Snow is various in the wood about 13
inches,   The river Closed [frozen over] at the Village
above   Mr. *La Rock* and one of his men Came to visit us, we
informed him what we had herd of his intentions of makeing
Chiefs &c. and forbid him to give Meadels or flags to the Indians,   he Denied haveing any Such intention,   we agreed
that one of our interpeters [Charbonneau] Should Speak for him
on Conditions he did not say any thing more than what tended to
trade alone.
Sergeant Pryor in takeing down the mast put his Sholder out of
Place, we made four trials before we replaced it

30TH OF NOVEMBER FRIDAY 1804 —

This morning at 8 oClock an Indian called from the other Side
and informed that he had Something of Consequence to Communicate, we Sent a perogue for him & he informed us as follows.
Viz: "five men of the Mandan nation out hunting in a S.W. derection about Eight Leagues, was Surprised by a large party of *Seeoux*
& Panies,[12] one man was Killed and two wounded with arrows & 9
Horses taken,   4 of the We ter soon nation was missing, and
they expected to be attacked by the Souex &c. &c.   we thought it
well to Show a Disposition to ade and assist them against their
enemies, and I Deturmined to go to the town with Some men, and
if the Seeoux were comeing to attact the Nation to Collect the
worriers from each Village and meet them,   I crossed the river
in about an hour after the arrival of the Indian express with 23
men including the interpeters and flankd the Town & came up on
the back part. The Indians not expecting to receive Such Strong
aide in So Short a time was much supprised and a littled allarmed
at the formadable appearence of my party. I explained to the
nation the cause of my comeing in this formadable manner to their

12 Here and throughout this period when Clark speaks of the Panias (Pawnees)
he means the Arikaras.

Town, was to assist and Chastise the enemies of our Dutifull Children,   I requested the Grand Cheif to repeat the Circumstancies
as they hapined, which he did as was mentioned by the *express* in
the morning. I then informed them that if they would assemble
their warrers and those of the Different Towns,   I would [go] to
meet the Army of *Souex* &c. chastise them for takeing the blood of
our dutifull Children &c.

after a conversation of a fiew minits amongst themselves, one
Chief. Said they now Saw that what we hade told them was the
trooth, when we expected the enemies of their Nation was Comeing to attact them, or had Spilt their blood [we] were ready to
protect them, and kill those who would not listen to our Good
talk. his people had listened to what we had told them and
cearlessly went out to hunt in Small parties believing themselves
to be Safe from the other nations, and have been killed by the
Panies & Seauex,   "I knew Said he that the Panies were liers,
and told the old Chief who Came with you (to Confirm a piece
with us) that his people were *liers* and bad men and that we killed
them like the Buffalow, when we pleased,   we had made peace
several times and you[r] Nation have always commenced the
war,   we do not want to kill you, and will not Suffer you to kill
us or Steal our horses,   we will make peace with you as our
two fathers have derected, and they Shall See that we will not be
the Ogressors, but we fear the Ricares will not be at peace long.
My father those are the words I spoke to the Ricare in your presents.   you See they have not opened their ears to your good
Councels but have Spuilt our blood. two Ricaries whom we sent
home this day for fear of our peoples killing them in their greaf,
informed us when they came here Several days ago, that two Towns
of the *Ricares* were makeing their Mockersons,[13] and that we had
best take care of our horses &c.   My father the Snow is deep and
it is cold our horses Cannot travel thro the plains, those people
who have Spilt our blood have gone back? if you will go with us in
the Spring after the Snow goes off we will raise the warriers of all
the Towns & Nations around about us, and go with you."

I told this nation that we should be always willing and ready to
defend them from the insults of any nation who would dare to
Come to doe them injury dureing the time we would remain in

---

[13] Preparing for war.

their neighbourhood, and requstd. that they would inform us of any party who may at any time be discovered by their Patroles or Scouts; I was sorry that the snow in the Plains had fallen so Deep Sence the Murder of the young Chief by the Sieoux as prevented their horses from traveling. I wished to meet those Seeoux & all others who will not open their ears, but make war on our dutifull Children, and let you see that the Wariers of your Great father will chastize the enimies of his dutifull Children the Mandans, Wetersoons & Winetarees, who have opend. their ears to his advice. after about two hours conversation on various Subjects all of which tended towards their Situation &c. I informed them I should return to the fort, the Chief said they all thanked me verry much for the fatherly protection which I shewed towards them, that the village had been crying all the night and day for the death of the brave young man, who fell but now they would wipe away their tears, and rejoice in their fathers protection, and cry no more.

I then Paraded & Crossed the river on the ice and Came down on the N. Side, the Snow So Deep, it was verry fatigueing arived at the fort after night,

1ST OF DECEMBER SATTURDAY 1804 —

in the evening a Mr. G Henderson [arrived] in the imploy of the *hudsons bay* Company sent to trade with the *Gros ventre,* or *Big bellies* so called by the french traders

7TH OF DECEMBER FRIDAY 1804 —

the Big White Grand Chief of the 1st Village, came and informed us that a large Drove of Buffalow was near and his people was wating for us to join them in a chase Capt. Lewis took 15 men & went out joined the Indians, who were at the time he got up, Killing the Buffalow on Horseback with arrows which they done with great dexterity, his party killed 10 Buffalow, *five* of which we got to the fort by the assistance of a horse in addition to what the men Packed on their backs. one cow was killed on the ice after drawing her out of a vacancey in the ice in which She had fallen, and Butchered her at the fort. those we did not get in was taken by the indians under a Custom which is established amongst them i e. any person seeing a buffalow lying without an **arrow** Sticking in him, or some purticular mark takes possession, the river Closed opposit the fort last night 1½ inches thick, The Thermometer Stood this Morning at 1 d. below 0. three **men** frost bit badly to day.

8TH DECEMBER SATTURDAY 1804 —

this day being Cold Several men returned a little *frost bit,* one of [the] men with his feet badly frost bit my Servents feet **also** *frosted* & his P —— s a little,

12TH DECEMBER WEDNESDAY 1804 —

the weather is So Cold that we do not think it prudent to turn out to hunt in Such Cold weather, or at least untill our Consts. are prepared to under go this Climate. I measure the river from bank to bank on the ice and make it 500 yards

13TH DECEMBER THURSDAY 1804 —

The Thermometer Stands this morning at 20° below 0, a fine **day.** find it impossible to make an Observation with an arteficial Horrison.

16TH DECEMBER SUNDAY 1804 —

Mr. Henny from the Establishment on River Ossiniboin, with a letter from, Mr. Charles Chaboillez [14] one of the Co arrived in 6 Days, Mr. C. in his letter expressed a great anxiety to Serve **us** in any thing in his power.

a root Discribed by Mr. Henny for the Cure of a Mad Dog

Mr. LeRock a clerk, of the NW. Company and Mr. George Bunch a Clerk of the Hudsons beey Compy accompanied Mr. Henry from the village.

---

14 This Hugh Heney, till recently (and possibly still) a partner of Loisel. Charles Chaboillez commanded on the Assiniboine River for the North West Company and this visit is his first reaction to the news, taken to him by Larocque, that the Americans had arrived at the Mandan villages.

[Gass] SUNDAY 16TH.

Three of the traders from the N.W. Company came to our fort, and brought a letter to our commanding officers. They remained with us all night. The object of the visits we received from the N.W. Company, was to ascertain our motives for visiting that country, and to gain information with respect to the change of government.

[Clark] 17TH DECEMBER MONDAY 1804 —

We found Mr. Henny a Verry intelligent Man from whome we obtained Some Scetches of the Countrey between the Mississippi & Missouri, and Some Sketches from him, which he had obtained from the Indins. to the *West* of this place also the names and charecktors of the Seeaux &c. about 8 oClock P M. the thermometer fell to 74° below the freesing pointe. the Indian Chiefs Sent word that Buffalow was in our Neighbourhood,

18TH DECEMBER TUESDAY 1804 —

Mrs. Haney & La Rocke left us for the Grossventre Camp, Sent out 7 men to hunt for the Buffalow they found the weather too cold & returned, I imploy my Self makeing a Small Map of Connextion &c. Sent Jessomme to the Main Chief of the mandans to know the Cause of his detaining or takeing a horse of *Chabonoe* our big belly interpeter, which we found was thro the rascallity of one Lafrance a trader from the NW. Company,

21ST DECEMBER FRIDAY 1804 —

the Indian whome I stoped from Commiting Murder on his wife, 'thro jellosy of one of our interpeters, Came & brought his two wives and Shewed great anxiety to make up with the man with whome his joulussey Sprung. a Womon brought a Child with an abcess on the lower part of the back, and offered as much Corn as she Could Carry for some Medison, Capt. Lewis administered &c.

22ND DECEMBER SATTURDAY 1804 —

worm. a number of Squars & men Dressed in Squars Clothes [15]
Came with Corn to Sell to the men for little things, We precured
two horns of the animale the french Call the rock Mountain Sheep.

25TH DECEMBER CHRISTMASS TUESDAY —
I was awakened before Day by a discharge of 3 platoons from
the Party and the french [boatmen], the men merrily Disposed,   I
give them all a little Taffia [rum] and permited 3 Cannon fired, at
raising Our flag,   Some Men Went out to hunt & the others to
Danceing and Continued untill 9 oClock P.M. when the frolick
ended &c.

[Ordway]   TUESDAY 25TH DECR 1804, *cloudy.*
we fired the Swivels at day break & each man fired one round.
our officers Gave the party a drink of Taffee. we had the Best to eat
that could be had, & continued firing dancing & frolicking dureing
the whole day. the Savages did not Trouble us as we had requested
them not to come as it was a Great medician day with us. We enjoyed a merry cristmas dureing the day & evening untill nine
oClock — all in peace & quietness.

[15] These are "berdashes," that is, homosexuals; the Indians believed that they
had been directed by a medicine vision to dress and act as women and they
suffered no loss of status.

CHAPTER VI

AMONG THE MANDANS

[Clark] 31ST OF DECEMBER MONDAY 1804 FORT MANDAN —

A number of indians here every Day   our blakSmith Mending their axes hoes &c. &c. for which the Squars bring Corn for payment.

Fort Mandan on the NE bank of the Missouries 1600 Miles up

TUESDAY JANUARY THE 1ST 1805 —

The Day was ushered in by the Descharge of two Cannon, we Suffered 16 men with their Musick[1] to visit the 1st Village for the purpose of Danceing, by as they Said the perticular request of the Chiefs of that Village,   about 11 oClock I with an inturpeter & two men walked up to the Village, (my views were to alay Some little Miss understanding which had taken place thro jelloucy and mortification as to our treatment towards them   I found them much pleased at the Danceing of our men,   I ordered my black Servent to Dance which amused the Croud Verry much, and Somewhat astonished them, that So large a man should be active &c. &c.   a Chief returnd from a Mission on which they had been Sent to meet a large party (150) of *Gross Ventres* who were on their way down from their Camps 10 Miles above to revenge on the *Shoe* tribe an injury which they had received by a Shoe man Steeling a *Gros Ventres Girl,* those Chiefs gave the pipe [and] turned the party back, after Delivering up the Girl, which the Shoe Chief had taken and given to them for that purpose. I returned in the evening, at night the party except 6 returned, with 3 robes, an 13

[1] Ordway: "carried with us a fiddle & a Tambereen & a Sounden horn."

75

Strings of Corn which the indians had given them, The Day was worm, Themtr 34° above 0, Some fiew Drops of rain about Sunset, at Dark it began to Snow, and Snowed the greater part of the night,

5TH OF JANUARY SATTURDAY 1805 —

I imploy my Self Drawing a Connection of the Countrey from what information I have rec[ei]ved. a Buffalow Dance for 3 nights passed [past] in the 1st Village, a curious Custom the old men arrange themselves in a circle & after Smoke[ing] a pipe which is handed them by a young man, Dress[ed] up for the purpose, the young men who have their wives back of the Circle go [each] to one of the old men with a whining tone and request the old man to take his wife (who presents [herself] necked except a robe) and — (or Sleep with her) the Girl then takes the Old Man (who verry often can scarcely walk) and leades him to a convenient place for the business, after which they return to the lodge; if the old man (or a white man) returns to the lodge without gratifying the Man & his wife, he offers her again and again; it is often the Case that after the 2d time without Kissing the Husband throws a new robe over the old man &c. and begs him not to dispise him & his wife (We Sent a man to this Medisan Dance last night, they gave him 4 Girls) all this is to cause the buffalow to Come near So that they may Kill them

9TH OF JANUARY WEDNESDAY 1805

a Cold Day Thermometer at 21° below 0, great numbers of indians go to kill *Cows, (Cp. Clark accd. them with 3 or 4 men killed a number of cows near the fort)* the little Crow Brackft. with us, Several Indians Call at the Fort nearly frosed,

10TH OF JANUARY THURSDAY 1805

last night was excessively Cold the Murckery this morning Stood at 40° below 0 which is 72° below the freesing point, we had one man out last night, who returned about 8 oClock this morning. The Indians of the lower Village turned out to hunt for a man & a boy who had not returnd from the hunt of yesterday, and borrow'd a Slay to bring them in expecting to find them frosed to death about 10 oClock the boy about 13 years of age Came to the fort with his feet frosed and had layed out last night without fire with only a Buffalow Robe to Cover him,   the Dress which he wore was a pr. of Cabra (antelope) Legins, which is verry thin and mockersons   we had his feet put in cold water and they are Comeing too. Soon after the arrival of the Boy, a Man Came in who had also Stayed out without fire, and verry thinly Clothed, this man was not the least injured. Customs & the habits of those people has anured [them] to bare more Cold than I thought it possible for man to endure.

16TH JANUARY WEDNESDAY 1805

one of the 1st War Chiefs of the big bell[i]es nation Came to see us to day with one man and his Squar to wate on him *(requested that she might be used for the night) (his wife handsome)*   We Shot the Air gun, and gave two Shots with the Cannon which pleased them verry much,   4 men of ours who had been hunting returned one frost'd

This War Chief gave us a Chart in his Way of the Missourie, he informed us of his intentions of going to War in the Spring against the Snake Indians   we advised him to look back at the number of Nations who had been distroyed by War, and reflect upon what he was about to do, observing if he wished the happiness of his nation, he would be at peace with all,   by that by being at peace and haveing plenty of goods amongst them & a free intercourse with those defenceless nations, they would get on easy tirms a greater Number of horses, and that Nation would increas,   if he went to War against those Defenceless people, he would displease his great father, and he would not receive that pertection & care from him as other nations who listened to his word. This Chief who is a young man 26 yr. old replied that if his going to war against the Snake indians would be displeasing to us he would not go, he had horses enough.[2]

2 Most of the information about the farther West which the captains had received came, as this does, from the Minnetarees, who raided much farther than the Mandans did. By now they have learned that the Snake Indians, the Shoshones, will be crucially important to them. The great horse herds of the Snakes will provide mounts and pack animals for the land traverse, of uncertain length, which they will have to make to the Columbia watershed. Charbonneau's young wife Sacajawea (possibly only sixteen years old) has thus become unexpectedly important: she is a Snake and can speak their language.

26TH OF JANUARY SATTURDAY 1805

a verry fine worm Day   one man taken violently Bad with the Plurisie, Bleed & apply those remedies Common to that disorder.

27TH OF JANUARY SUNDAY 1805

attempt to Cut our Boat and Canoos out of the Ice, a deficuelt Task I fear as we find water between the Ice,   I bleed the man with the Plurisy to day & Swet him, Capt. Lewis took off the Toes of one foot of the Boy who got frost bit Some time ago,

30TH JANUARY WEDNESDAY 1805

Mr. La Rocke paid us a Visit, & we gave him an answer respecting the request he made when last here of accompanying us on our Journey &c. (*refused*) [3]

[Lewis]   3RD OF FEBRUARY SUNDAY 1805.

the situation of our boat and perogues is now allarming, they are firmly inclosed in the Ice and almost covered with snow — the ice which incloses them lyes in several stratas of unequal thicknesses which are seperated by streams of water. this [is] peculiarly unfortunate because so soon as we cut through the first strata of ice the water rushes up and rises as high as the upper surface of the ice and thus creates such a debth of water as renders it impracticable to cut away the lower strata which appears firmly attached to, and confining the bottom of the vessels. the instruments we have hitherto used has been the ax only, with which, we have made several attempts that proved unsuccessfull. we then determined to attempt freeing them from the ice by means of boiling water which we purposed heating in the vessels by means of hot stones, but this expedient proved also fruitless, as every species of stone which we could procure in the neighbourhood partook so much of the calcarious genus that they burst into small particles on being exposed to the heat of the fire. we now determined as the dernier resort to

[3] A North West Company attempt to learn the purposes of the expedition and to share its results.

prepare a parsel of Iron spikes and attatch them to the end of small poles of convenient length and endeavour by means of them to free the vessels from the ice. we have already prepared a large rope of Elk-skin and a windless by means of which we have no doubt of being able to draw the boat on the bank provided we can free [it] from the ice.

4TH FEBRUARY, MONDAY 1805

Capt Clark set out with a hunting party consisting of sixteen of our command and two frenchmen who together with two others, have established a small hut and resided this winter within the vicinity of Fort Mandane under our protection. our stock of meat which we had procured in the Months of November & December is now nearly exhausted. Capt. Clark therefore determined to continue his rout down the river even as far as the River bullet [Cannonball] unless he should find a plenty of game nearer. the men transported their baggage on a couple of small wooden Slays drawn by themselves, and took with them 3 pack horses. no buffaloe have made their appearance in our neighbourhood for some weeks.

7TH FEBRUARY THURSDAY 1805.

The Sergt. of the guard reported that the Indian women (wives to our interpreters) were in the habit of unbaring the fort gate at any time of night and admitting their Indian visitors, I therefore directed a lock to be put to the gate and ordered that no Indian but those attatched to the garrison should be permitted to remain all night within the fort or admitted during the period which the gate had been previously ordered to be kept shut, which was from sunset untill sunrise.

9TH FEBRUARY SATURDAY 1805

visited by Mr. McKinzey one of the N.W. Company's clerks. this evening a man by the name of Howard whom I had given permission to go [to] the Mandane vilage returned after the gate was shut and reather than call to the guard to have it opened scaled the works   an indian who was looking on shortly after followed his

example. I convinced the Indian of the impropryety of his conduct, and explained to him the risk he had run of being severely
treated,   the fellow appeared much allarmed,   I gave him a
small piece of tobacco and sent him away   Howard I had
comitted to the care of the guard with a determineation to have
him tryed by a Court-martial for this offence. this man is an old
soldier which still hightens this offince.[4]

11TH FEBRUARY MONDAY 1805

about five oClock this evening one of the wives of Charbono
[Sacajawea] was delivered of a fine boy. it is worthy of remark that
this was the first child which this woman had boarn, and as is
common in such cases her labour was tedious and the pain violent;
Mr. Jessome informed me that he had freequently administered a
small portion of the rattle of the rattle-snake, which he assured me
had never failed to produce the desired effect, that of hastening the
birth of the child; having the rattle of a snake by me I gave it to
him and he administered two rings of it to the woman broken in
small pieces with the fingers and added to a small quantity of
water. Whether this medicine was truly the cause or not I shall not
undertake to determine, but I was informed that she had not taken
it more than ten minutes before she brought forth

[Clark]   [FEBRUARY 13TH]

I returned last Night from a hunting party much fatigued, haveing
walked 30 miles on the ice and through Points of wood land in
which the Snow was nearly Knee Deep

15TH OF FEBRUARY FRIDAY 1805

at 10 oClock P M. last night the men that despatched yesterday
for the Meat, returned and informed us that as they were on their
march down at the distance of about 24 miles below the Fort
(G. Drewyer Frasure [Frazier], S Gutterage [Goodrich], & Newmon
with a broken Gun). about 105 Indians which they took to be

4 Howard received a sentence of 50 lashes but Lewis remitted it. From this
time on there were no more courts-martial.

Soues rushed on them and cut their horses from the Slays, *two* of which they carried off in great hast, the 3rd horse was given up to the party by the intersetion of an Indian who assumd. Some authority on the occasion, probably more thro fear of himself or Some of the Indians being killed by our men who were not disposed to be Robed of all they had tamely, they also forced 2 of the mens knives & a tamahauk, the man obliged them to return the tamahawk the knives they ran off with

We dispatched two men to inform the Mandans, and if any of them chose to pursue those robers, to come down in the morning. and join Capt Lewis who intended to Set out with a party of men Verry early, by 12 oClock the Chief of the 2nd Village Big White came down, and Soon after one other Chief and Several men. The Chief observed that all the young men of the 2 Villages were out hunting, and but verry fiew guns were left, Capt. Lewis Set out at Sunrise with 24 men, to meet those *Soues* &c. Several Indians accompanied him Some with Bows & arrows Some with Spears & Battle axes, 2 with fuzees *(fusils).* one Chief of the Mandans returned from Capt Lewises Party nearly blind, this Complaint is as I am informd. Common at this Season of the year and caused by the reflection of the Sun on the ice & Snow, it is cured by jentilley swetting the part affected, by throwing Snow on a hot Stone.

16TH OF FEBRUARY SATTURDAY 1805

at Dusk two of the Indians who wint down with Capt. Lewis returned, Soon after two others and one man (Howard) with his feet frosted, and informed that the Inds. who Commited the roberry of the 2 horses was So far a head that they could not be overtaken, they left a number of pars of Mockersons which, the Mandans knew to be Soues Mockersons,

Capt Lewis & party proceeded on down the meat I left at my last Camp was taken.

21ST FEBRUARY THURSDAY 1805

a Delightfull Day put out our Clothes to Sun. Visited by the big White & Big Man they informed me that Several men of their nation was gone to Consult their Medison Stone about 3 day march to the South West to know what was to be the result of the ensuing year. They have great confidence in this stone, and say that it informs them of every thing which is to happen, & visit it everry Spring & Sometimes in the Summer. They haveing arrived at the Stone give it smoke and proceed to the Wood at Some distance to Sleep   the next morning return to the Stone, and find marks white & raised on the stone representing the peece or War which they are to meet with, and other changes, which they are to meet   This Stone has a leavel Surface of about 20 feet in Surcumfrance, thick and porus, and no doubt has Some mineral quallities effected by the Sun.

Capt Lewis returned with 2 Slays loaded with meat,   after finding that he could not overtake the Soues War party, (who had in their way distroyed all the meat at one Deposit which I had made & Burnt the Lodges) deturmined to proceed on to the lower Deposit which he found had not been observed by the Soues   he hunted two day Killed 36 Deer & 14 Elk, Several of them so meager, that they were unfit for use,   the meet which he killed and that in the lower Deposit amounting to about 3000 lb. was brought up on two Slays   one Drawn by 16 men had about 2400 lb. on it

23RD OF FEBRUARY 1805 SATTURDAY

All hands employed in Cutting the Perogues Loose from the ice, which was nearly even with their top; we found great dificuelty in effecting this work owing to the Different devisions of Ice & water.

The father of the Boy whose feet were frosed near this place, and nearly Cured by us, took him home in a Slay.

25TH OF FEBRUARY MONDAY 1805

We fixed a Windlass and Drew up the two Perogues on the upper bank, and attempted the Boat, but the Roap, which we hade made of Elk skins proved too weak & broke Several times.

26TH FEBRUARY TUESDAY 1805

a fine Day   Commenced verry early in makeing preparations for drawing up the Boat on the bank,   at Sunset by Repeated exertions the whole day, we accomplished this troublesom task, just as we were fixed for hauling the Boat, the ice gave way near us for about 100 yds in length. a number of Indians here to day to See the Boat rise on the Bank.

28th of February Thursday 1805

a fine morning two men of the NW Compy arrive with letters, also a Root and top of a plant, presented by Mr. Haney, for the Cure of Mad Dogs Snakes &c. this root is found on the high lands and asent of hills, the way of useing it is to scarify the part when bitten to chu or pound an inch or more if the root is Small, and applying it to the bitten part renewing it twice a Day. the bitten person is not to chaw nor Swallow any of the Root for it might have contrary effect.

Sent out 16 men to make four Perogus those men returned in the evening and informed that they found trees they thought would answer.

Mr. Gravelin two frenchmen & two Inds. arrive from the Ricara Nation with Letters from Mr. Anty Tabeaux, informing us of the peeceable dispositions of that nation towards the Mandans & Me ne ta rees & their avowed intentions of pursueing our councils & advice, they express a wish to visit the Mandans, & know if it will be agreeable to them to admit the Recaras to Settle near them and join them against their Common Enemy the *Soues*

Mr. Gravelin informs that the *Sisetoons* [Sisseton Sioux] and the 3 upper bands of the *Tetons,* with the Yanktons of the North intend to come to war in a Short time against the nations in this quarter, & will kill everry white man they See. Mr. T. also informs that Mr. Cameron of St Peters [River] has put arms into the hands of the Soues to revenge the death of 3 of his men killed by the Chipaways latterley, and that the Band of tetons which we Saw is desposed to doe as we have advised them, thro the influence of their Chief the Black Buffalow.

Mr. Gravelen further informs that the Party which Robed us of the 2 horses laterly were all Sieoux 106 in number, they Called at the Recaras on their return, the Recares being despleased at their Conduct would not give them any thing to eate, that being the greatest insult they Could peaceably offer them, and upbraded them.

Mr. *LaRocque* a Clerk of the NW Company visit us, he has latterley returned from the Establishments on the Assinniboin River,
with Merchindize to tarade with Indians. Mr. L informs us the
N.W. & XY Companies have joined, & the head of the N.W, Co. is
Dead Mr. Mc Tavish of Montreal.[5]

a Cloudy Cold and windey morning wind from the North. I
walked up to See the Party that is makeing Perogues, about 5 miles
above this, the wind hard and Cold   on my way up I met the
Main Chief of the Ma ne tar res, with four Indians on their way
to see us,   I requested him to proceed on to the fort, where he
would find Capt. Lewis I should be there myself in corse of a fiew
hours,   Sent the interpiter back with him and proceeded on
myself to the Canoes found them nearly finished, the timber verry
bad,   after visiting all the perogues where I found a number of
Indians, I wind to the upper mandan Village & Smoked a pipe
with the Chief and returned. on my return found the Manetarree
Chief about Setting out on his return to his Village, having recived
of Captain M. Lewis a *Medel* Gorget armbans, a *Flag* Shirt, scarlet
&c. &c. &c. for which he was much pleased,   2 guns were fired
for this Great man.[6]

[5] Momentous news. The XY Company, headed by the great Alexander Mackenzie, had been providing the most violent and effective competition the North
West Company had ever had to meet. The merger meant, among other things,
a victory for Mackenzie's ideas of trade imperialism: expansion to the Pacific,
the establishment of trading posts on the Columbia, and exclusion of the United
States from the area north of 45°, which must come under British sovereignty.
The American-British race for the Columbia, which has been already hinted at
in Larocque's request to accompany the expedition West, and which was not to
end till the establishment of Fort Astoria by John Jacob Astor's representatives,
may be said to begin right here.

[6] This is Le Borgne: the One-Eyed Man. He was indeed the head chief of
the Minnetarees, a ferocious, bloodthirsty, tyrannical, and entirely fearless
leader, who had terrorized Tabeau and had forced the Canadian traders to
treat him with the utmost deference. It would appear that his pro-British
sentiment had kept him from visiting Fort Mandan but that he had been unable to prevent the development of a large pro-American faction in his tribe.

[MARCH] 12TH

our Interpeter Shabonah, deturmins on not proceeding with us
as an interpeter under the terms mentioned yesterday,   he will
not agree to work let our Situation be what it may nor Stand a
guard, and if miffed with any man he wishes to return when he
pleases, also have the disposal of as much provisions as he Chuses
to Carry   in admissable and we Suffer him to be off the engagement which was only virbal

[Lewis]   [UNDATED]

Mr. Garrow [Garreau] a Frenchman who has lived many years
with the Ricares & Mandans shewed us the process used by those
Indians to make beads. the discovery of this art these nations are
said to have derived from the Snake Indians who have been taken
prisoners by the Ricaras. the art is kept a secret by the Indians
among themselves and is yet known to but few of them. The Indians are extreemly fond of the large beads formed by this process.
they use them as pendants to their years, or hair and sometimes
wear them about their necks.[7]

[Clark]   17TH OF MARCH SUNDAY —

Mr. Chabonah Sent a frenchman of our party [to say] that he
was Sorry for the foolish part he had acted and if we pleased he
would accompany us agreeabley to the terms we had perposed and
doe every thing we wished him to doe &c. &c.   he had requested
me Some thro our French inturpeter two days ago to excuse his
Simplicity and take him into the cirvice, after he had taken his
things across the River we called him in and Spoke to him on the
Subject,   he agreed to our tirms and we agreed that he might
go on with us &c. &c.

19TH OF MARCH 1805 —

Cold windey Day Cloudy Some little Snow last night visited to
Day by the *big white* & Little Crow, also a man & his wife with a

---

[7] A long description of the process has been omitted from this entry: ordinary
trade beads (of glass) were pulverized, heated to the fusing point, and remolded
into large ones.

Sick Child, I administer for the child   We are told that two parties are gone to war from the Big bellies and one other party going to war Shortly.

20TH MARCH WEDNESDAY 1805.

I with all the men which could be Speared from the Fort went to Canoes,   there I found a number of Indians,   the men carried 4 to the River about 1½ miles thro' the Bottom, I visited the Chief of the Mandans in the Course of the Day and Smoked a pipe with himself and Several old men.

21ST MARCH THURSDAY 1805 —

the men Carried the remaining Canoes to the River, and all except 3 left to take care & complete the Canoes returned to the *fort* with their baggage,[8]   on my return to day to the Fort I came on the points of the high hills,   Saw an emence quantity of Pumice Stone on the Sides & foot of the hills and emence beds of Pumice Stone near the Tops of the[m], with evident marks of the Hills haveing once been on fire,   I Collected Some [of] the different [sorts] i.e. Stone Pumice Stone & a hard earth, and put them into a furnace, the hard earth melted and glazed the others two and the hard Clay became a pumice Stone Glazed.

[8] The "canoes" or "pirogues" (six of them) which the men had been building were cottonwood dugouts. They were to replace the keelboat, which was too big to be used above the villages and was to return to St. Louis.

CHAPTER VII

FROM FORT MANDAN TO THE YELLOWSTONE

I n their intercourse with representatives of the North West
Company and the Hudson's Bay Company, the captains had
carefully asserted American sovereignty over the area they were
traversing and American jurisdiction over the Indians who inhabited it, especially those immediately at hand. They had announced an American trade policy which permitted the British to
go on trading at these villages but would subject them to competition from American companies and to the threat of government
"factories" or trading posts if that competition did not keep prices
in hand. (The British sold goods to the Upper Missouri Indians
at a markup of one hundred per cent above the prices they charged
on the Assiniboine River just to the north.) Also they had notified
their visitors that the posts on the Assiniboine and the Souris were
really south of the boundary, that in fact Louisiana extended as
far north as the Qu'Appelle River, a northern affluent of the Assiniboine. This error resulted from Lewis's incorrect determinations
of latitude, from his belief that the latitudes worked out by the
North West Company's great David Thompson were incorrect, and
from a faulty understanding of the watersheds.

The constant winter occupation, however, was procuring information from the Indians. Most of this was entered not in the daily
log but in notebooks kept separately for that purpose. The analysis
and codification of data about the Indian tribes was principally
the work of Lewis. His voluminous report to Jefferson, which was
sent to the States on the returning keelboat, was the basis of Jefferson's report to Congress which was published as "A Statistical
View of the Indian Nations Inhabiting the Territory of Louisiana,

and the Countries Adjacent to Its Northern and Western Boundaries." Though it contained errors and misconceptions, it was astonishingly accurate and complete, the first and basic document in the anthropology of the Plains tribes. Just as remarkable, perhaps more so, was the compendium of geographical data, principally the work of Clark.

The area they were now about to cross had never been visited by white men and was almost entirely unknown, even in guess and rumor. The information they got about it — as far west as the Continental Divide, that is — was detailed and in the main accurate. Students can examine it in Volume VI of the Journals, *where it appears in the form of tables, digests, and memoranda. Only certain parts of it are relevant to the story of the expedition.*

They were able to form an accurate conception of the Missouri's principal tributary, the Yellowstone, and the principal rivers that flow into it. They seriously misconceived the area of its headwaters, however; none of their Indian informants had visited that region and the error was rooted in the theories which the St. Louis traders had expressed to them. They achieved a clear and reliable conception of the remainder of the Missouri, getting all its courses and big tributaries correct and closely approximating most of the distances. They formed a clear and correct idea of the Great Falls of the Missouri (and were the first white men to do so) and of the nearest ranges of the Rocky Mountains, the ranges from which the river issued. One mistake they made had serious consequences: they misjudged the distance of a northern affluent which the Minnetarees called the River That Scolds All the Others. (Sketching maps on strips of hide or in sand or the fireplace ashes, the Indians would calculate distances in terms of a day's travel, so many "suns" or so many "sleeps.") This error will be manifest when the expedition reaches the mouth of the Marias River.

Also, they misunderstood what the Minnetarees (always their principal informants and here the only ones) told them about the crossing of the Continental Divide — of the Rocky Mountains. The Minnetarees actually described two routes, both of which required a sizable stretch of land travel. Both led to northward-flowing rivers which the captains took to be a previously unsuspected southern fork of the Columbia River, their great objective. One led west from the Great Falls to the Bitterroot River and was short and easy. The other, much longer and incomparably harder travel, continued up the Missouri to the Three Forks, crossed the Divide to the Lemhi River, and went down it to the Salmon River. (With a northward-flowing river west of the Divide the Minnetarees' knowledge of Western geography ended, though they amiably provided a mass of fictitious geography.) For a number of reasons Clark and Lewis failed to understand that they were hearing about two routes. They combined data about both and judged that they all related to the second route.

One more point. Throughout the winter they kept inquiring about a tributary of the Missouri, any navigable tributary, that would enter from the north after coming down from above 49°, the (presumptive) boundary of Canada. After the expedition started west again, they kept looking for one. This inquiry related to one of the basic objectives that Jefferson had set for the expedition. Jefferson had reverted to the original conception of Louisiana: that it included the entire watershed of the Mississippi and therefore the entire watershed of the Missouri. On that basis he argued that the basin of any affluent of the Missouri that extended north of 49° was American and the boundary would have to loop north to include it. Such a river was exceedingly important for Jefferson's plans. He did not know that the Upper Missouri froze over in the winter. He counted on a northern tributary of the Missouri to provide access to the rich fur country of the Canadian Northwest, especially the Saskatchewan River, which was the highway to the richest of all fur countries, the high north. If such a river could be found, then at least the carrying trade in furs could be secured for the United States, if not the whole fur trade. For an American route to the Atlantic seaboard would provide much faster and much cheaper transportation than the Canadian canoe route to Montreal by way of Lake of the Woods, Rainy Lake, the Great Lakes, and the St. Lawrence — a route which was closed by ice throughout a long winter and was made infinitely laborious by many portages. The American route would be open and continuous: the Missouri to the Mississippi, to the Ohio, thence by a choice of rivers to salt-water ports. Furthermore, it would connect with the maritime trade of the Northwest coast (the triangular trade with China based on sea otter and to be reached by the Columbia River) and with the expected rich commerce of Asia. For Jefferson,

*in common with all other geographical thinkers (including, when
they started, Lewis and Clark), believed that there would be only a
single portage, one which would require at most less than a day,
between Missouri and Columbia waters.*

*The Captains believed at the villages that they had learned of
just such a northern tributary of the Missouri as was desired, the
one they called White Earth River. It turned out to be a negligible
creek.*

[Clark]   24TH (23) OF MARCH SATTURDAY 1805 —

after Brackfast Mr. La Rocke and Mr. McKinsey and the Cheifs
& men of the Minetarras leave us. in the fore part in the evening
a little rain & the first this winter.

25TH (24TH) OF MARCH SUNDAY 1805. —

Saw Swans & Wild Gees flying N.E. this evening.

26TH (25TH) OF MARCH MONDAY 1805 —

but fiew Inds. Visit us to day the Ice haveing broken up in Several
places,   The ice began to brake away this evening and was near
destroying our Canoes as they were dec[e]nding to the fort,

30TH (29) OF MARCH SUNDAY (FRIDAY) 1805 —

I observed extrodanary dexterity of the Indians in jumping from
one cake of ice to another, for the purpose of Catching the buffalow
as they float down   many of the cakes of ice which they pass
over are not two feet square. The Plains are on fire in View of the
fort on both Sides of the River,

31ST (30TH) SATURDAY. OF MARCH MONDAY
(SATURDAY) (SUNDAY) 1805 —

all the party in high Sperits   they pass but fiew nights without
amuseing themselves danceing possessing perfect harmony and good
understanding towards each other,   Generally helthy except
Venerials Complaints which is verry Common amongst the natives
and the men Catch it from them

APRIL THE 3RD THURSDAY (WEDNESDAY) 1805 —

Mrs. La Rocke & McKinsey Clerk to the NW. Compy. Visit us. we are all day engaged packing up Sundery articles to be sent to the President of the U.S.[1]

[Lewis]   FORT MANDAN APRIL 7TH. 1805.

Having on this day at 4. P.M. completed every arrangement necessary for our departure, we dismissed the barge and crew with orders to return without loss of time to St. Louis,   a small canoe with two French hunters accompanyed the barge; these men had assended the missouri with us the last year as engages. The barge crew consisted of six soldiers and two [blank space in MS.] Frenchmen; two Frenchmen and a Ricara Indian also take their passage in her as far as the Ricara Vilages, at which place we expect Mr. Tiebeau to embark with his peltry who in that case will make an addition of two, perhaps four men to the crew of the barge.[2] We gave Richard Warfington, a discharged Corpl., the charge of the Barge and crew, and confided to his care likewise our dispatches to the government, letters to our private friends and a number of articles to the President of the United States. One of the Frenchmen by the Name of Gravline an honest discrete man and an excellent boat-man is imployed to conduct the barge as a pilot; we have therefore every hope that the barge and with her our dispatches will arrive safe at St. Louis. Mr. Gravlin who speaks the Ricara language extreemly well, has been imployed to conduct a few of the Recara Chiefs to the seat of government who have

[1] See Appendix III for the "Sundery articles," specimens which had been collected and carefully preserved for the President and the American Philosophical Society. More important, however, were the letters and voluminous reports which were sent with the keelboat.

[2] Four members of Warfington's original squad accompanied him: Boley, Dame, Tuttle, and White. Besides these he had Reed and Newman, who had been sentenced to discharge. The latter had tried hard to regain his lost status; Lewis respected the effort and recommended that he be given a half-share of the land bounty promised all members of the expedition, but was not willing to take into the unknown a man who had been guilty of insubordination. Tabeau and four of his men boarded the boat at the Arikara village. These, with Gravelines and the two former *engagés* of Deschamps, brought the crew to fifteen.

promised us to decend in the barge to St: Liwis with that view.

At the same moment that the Barge departed from Fort Mandan, Capt. Clark emba[r]ked with our party and proceeded up the River. as I had used no exercise for several weeks, I determined to walk on shore as far as our encampment of this evening.

Our vessels consisted of six small canoes, and two large perogues. This little fleet altho' not quite so rispectable as those of Columbus or Capt. Cook, were still viewed by us with as much pleasure as those deservedly famed adventurers ever beheld theirs; and I dare say with quite as much anxiety for their safety and preservation. we were now about to penetrate a country at least two thousand miles in width, on which the foot of civilized man had never trodden; the good or evil it had in store for us was for experiment yet to determine, and these little vessells contained every article by which we were to expect to subsist or defend ourselves. however, as the state of mind in which we are, generally gives the colouring to events, when the immagination is suffered to wander into futurity, the picture which now presented itself to me was a most pleasing one. enterta[in]ing as I do, the most confident hope of succeeding in a voyage which had formed a da[r]ling project of mine for the last ten years, I could but esteem this moment of my departure as among the most happy of my life. The party are in excellent health and sperits, zealously attached to the enterprise, and anxious to proceed; not a whisper of murmur or discontent to be heard among them, but all act in unison, and with the most perfict harmony. Capt. Clark myself the two Interpretters and the woman and child sleep in a tent of dressed skins.[3] this tent is in the Indian stile, formed of a number of dressed Buffaloe skins sewed together with sinues. it is cut in such manner that when foalded double it forms the quarter of a circle, and is left open at one side   here it may be attatched or loosened at pleasure by strings which are sewed to its sides for the purpose.

[Clark]   FORT MANDAN APRIL TH 7TH 1805

Sunday, at 4 oClock PM, the Boat, in which was 6 Soldiers 2 frenchmen & an Indian, all under the command of a corporal who

3 Drewyer, Charbonneau, Sacajawea, and her baby, who was not yet two months old.

had the charge of dispatches, &c. — and a canoe with 2 french men, Set out down the river for St. Louis. at the same time we Sout out on our voyage up the river in 2 perogues and 6 canoes, and proceded on to the 1st villag. of Mandans & camped on the S.S.   our party consisting of Sergts. Nathaniel Pryor, John Ordway, Patrick Gass, Pvts. William Bratton, John Colter, Joseph and Reuben Fields, John Shields, George Gibson, George Shannon, John Potts, John Collins, Joseph Whitehouse, Richard Windsor, Alexander Willard, Hugh Hall, Silas Goodrich, Robert Frazier, Peter Cruzatte, Baptiste Lepage, Francis Labiche, Hugh McNeal, William Werner, Thomas P. Howard, Peter Wiser, John B. Thompson and my servent York, George Drewyer who acts as a hunter & interpreter, Charbonneau and his *Indian Squar* to act as an Interpreter & interpretress for the snake Indians — one Mandan & Charbonneau's infant.[4]

[Lewis]   TUESDAY APRIL 9TH

when we halted for dinner the squaw busied herself in serching for the wild artichokes which the mice collect and deposit in large hoards. this operation she performed by penetrating the earth with a sharp stick about some small collections of drift wood. her labour soon proved successful, and she procured a good quantity of these roots. the flavor of this root resembles that of the Jerusalem Artichoke, and the stalk of the weed which produces it is also similar,

[Clark]   9TH OF APRIL TUESDAY 1805. —

I saw a Musquetor to day   great numbers of Brant flying up the river, the Maple, & Elm has buded & cotton and arrow wood beginning to bud. But fiew resident birds or water fowls which I have Seen as yet   Saw Great numbers of Gees feedin in the Praries on the young grass,   I saw flowers in the praries to day, juniper grows on the Sides of the hills, & runs on the ground

[Lewis]   WEDNESDAY APRIL 10TH 1805.

at the distance of 12 miles from our encampment of last night we arrived at the lower point of a bluff on the Lard side; about 1½

4 These are the correct spellings, not Clark's variants.

miles down this bluff from this point, the bluff is now on fire and throws out considerable quantities of smoke which has a strong sulphurious smell.[5] at 1. P.M. we overtook three french hunters who had set out a few days before us with a view of traping beaver; they had taken 12 since they left Fort Mandan. these people avail themselves of the protection which our numbers will enable us to give them against the Assinniboins who sometimes hunt on the Missouri; and intend ascending with us as far as the mouth of the Yellow stone river and continue there hunt up that river.[6] this is the first essay of a beaver hunter of any discription on this river [above the villages]. the beaver these people have already taken is by far the best I have ever seen.

[Lewis]   SATURDAY APRIL 13TH

The wind was in our favour after 9 A.M. and continued favourable untill three 3. P.M.   we therefore hoisted both the sails in the White Perogue, consisting of a small squar sail, and spritsail, which carried her at a pretty good gate, untill about 2 in the afternoon when a sudden squall of wind struck us and turned the perogue so much on the side as to allarm Sharbono who was steering at the time,   in this state of alarm he threw the perogue with her side to the wind, when the spritsail gibing was as near overseting the perogue as it was possible to have missed. the wind however abating for an instant I ordered Drewyer to the helm and the sails to be taken in, which was instant executed and the perogue being steered before the wind was agin plased in a state of security. this accedent was very near costing us dearly. beleiving this vessell to be the most steady and safe, we had embarked on board of it our instruments, Papers, medicine and the most valuable part of the merchandize which we had still in reserve as presents for the Indians. we had also embarked on board ourselves, with three men who could not swim and the squaw with the young child, all of whom, had the perogue overset, would most probably have perished, as the waves were high, and the perogue upwards of 200 yards from the nearest shore;   just above the entrance of the little Missouri the great Missouri is upwards of a mile in width,

---

5 St. Louis traders had reported such burning lignite as volcanos.

6 The "hunters" — from either Tabeau's or Deschamps' party — stayed with the expedition for only three days.

tho' immediately at the entrance of the former it is not more than 200 yards wide and so shallow that the canoes passed it with seting poles.

we found a number of carcases of the Buffaloe lying along shore, which had been drowned by falling through the ice in winter and lodged on shore by the high water when the river broke up about the first of this month. we saw also many tracks of the white bear of enormous size, along the river shore and about the carcases of the Buffaloe, on which I presume they feed. we have not as yet seen one of these anamals, tho' their tracks are so abundant and recent. the men as well as ourselves are anxious to meet with some of these bear. the Indians give a very formidable account of the strength and ferocity of this anamal, which they never dare to attack but in parties of six eight or ten persons; and are even then frequently defeated with the loss of one or more of their party. the savages attack this anamal with their bows and arrows and the indifferent guns with which the traders furnish them,   with these they shoot with such uncertainty and at so short a distance, that (*unless shot thro' head or heart wound not mortal*) they frequently mis their aim & fall a sacrefice to the bear. this anamall is said more frequently to attack a man on meeting with him, than to flee from him. When the Indians are about to go in quest of the white bear, previous to their departure, they paint themselves and perform all those supersticious rights commonly observed when they are about to make war uppon a neighbouring nation. Oserved more bald eagles on this part of the Missouri than we have previously seen. saw the small hawk, frequently called the sparrow hawk, which is common to most parts of the U. States. great quantities of gees are seen feeding in the praries. saw a large flock of white brant or gees with black wings pass up the river;   there were a number of gray brant with them.

SUNDAY APRIL 14TH 1805.

where the land is level, it is uniformly fertile consisting of a dark loam intermixed with a proportion of fine sand. it is generally covered with a short grass resembling very much the blue grass. the miniral appearances still continue; considerable quantities of bitumenous water, about the colour of strong lye trickles down the sides of the hills; this water partakes of the taste of glauber salts and slightly of allumn. while the party halted to take dinner today Capt. Clark killed a buffaloe bull; it was meagre, and we therefore took the marrow bones and a small proportion of the meat only. passed an Island, above which two small creeks fall in on Lard. side; the upper creek largest, which we called Sharbono's Creek, after our interpreter who encamped several weeks on it with a hunting party of Indians. this was the highest point to which any whiteman had ever ascended, except two Frenchmen (*one of whom Lapage was now with us*) who having lost their way had straggled a few miles further tho' to what place precisely I could not learn.

[Clark]   18TH OF APRIL THURSDAY 1805

after brackfast I assended a hill and observed that the river made a great bend to the South, I concluded to walk thro' the point about 2 miles and take Shabono, with me, he had taken a dost of Salts &c.   his squar followed on with her child,   when I struck the next bend of the [river] could see nothing of the Party, left this man & his wife & child on the river bank and went out to hunt,   Killed a young Buck Elk, & a Deer, the Elk was tolerable meat, the Deer verry pore, Butchered the meat and continued untill near Sunset before Capt Lewis and the party came up,   they were detained by the wind, which rose soon after I left the boat from the NW. & blew verry hard untill verry late in the evening. Saw several old Indian camps,   the game, such as Buffalow Elk, antelopes & Deer verry plenty

19TH OF APRIL FRIDAY 1805

the wind so hard from the N.W. that we were fearfull of ventering our Canoes in the river,   lay by all day on the S. Side in a good harber,   the Praries appear to Green,   the cotton trees bigin to leave,   Saw some plumb bushes in full bloom,   The beaver of this river is much larger than usial,   Great deal of Sign of the large Bear,

20TH OF APRIL SATTURDAY 1805

we set out at 7 oClock proceeded on,   soon after we set out a Bank fell in near one of the canoes which like to have filled her with water,   the wind became hard and waves so rough that we proceeded with our little canoes with much risque,   our situation was such after setting out that we were obliged to pass round the 1st Point or lay exposed to the blustering winds & waves,   in passing round the Point several canoes took in water as also our large Perogue but without injuring our stores &c. much   a short distance below our Camp I saw some rafts on the S. S. near which, an Indian woman was scaffeled in the Indian form of Deposing their Dead and fallen down   She was or had been raised about 6 feet, inclosed in Several robes tightly laced around her, with her dog Slays, her bag of Different coloured earths paint small bones of animals beaver nales and Several other little trinkets, also a blue jay,   her dog was killed and lay near her. Capt. Lewis joined me soon after I landed & informed me he had walked several miles higher, & in his walk killed 2 Deer & wounded an Elk & a Deer, our party shot in the river four beaver & cought two, which were verry fat and much admired by the men,   after we landed they killed 3 Elk 4 Gees & 2 Deer we had some of our Provisions &c. which got a little wet aired, the wind continued so hard that we were compelled to delay all day. Saw several buffalow lodged in the drift wood which had been drouned in the winter in passing the river.

[Lewis]   MONDAY APRIL 22ND 1805.

Set out at an early hour this morning;   proceeded pretty well untill breakfat, when the wind became so hard a head that we proceeded with difficulty even with the assistance of our toe lines. the party halted and Cpt. Clark and myself walked to the white earth river [7] which approaches the Missouri very near at this place, being about 4 miles above it's entrance. we found that it contained more water than streams of it's size generally do at this season. the water is much clearer than that of the Missouri. the banks of the river are steep and not more than ten or twelve feet high; the bed seems to be composed of mud altogether. the salts [alkali] which have been before mentioned as common on the Missouri,

[7] They had passed its mouth the day before. It is the creek now known as the Little Muddy, at Williston, North Dakota. (Not to be confused with another creek actually called the White Earth, farther downstream.) Observe Lewis's conviction that it must lead beyond 49° and provide access to the Saskatchewan River and its rich trade.

appears in great quantities along the banks of this river, which are in many places so thickly covered with it that they appear perfectly white. perhaps it has been from this white appearance of it's banks that the river has derived it's name. this river is said to be navigable nearly to it's source, which is at no great distance from the Saskashawan, and I think from it's size the direction wich it seems to take, and the latitude of it's mouth, that there is very good ground to believe that it extends as far North as latitude 50°   this stream passes through an open country generally.

Coal or carbonated wood pumice stone lava and other mineral apearances still continue. the coal appears to be of better quality; I exposed a specimen of it to the fire and found that it birnt tolerably well, it afforded but little flame or smoke, but produced a hot and lasting fire. I ascsended to the top of the cutt bluff this morning, from whence I had a most delightfull view of the country, the whole of which except the vally formed by the Missouri is void of timber or underbrush, exposing to the first glance of the spectator immence herds of Buffaloe, Elk, deer, & Antelopes feeding in one common and boundless pasture. we saw a number of bever feeding on the bark of the trees alonge the verge of the river, several of which we shot, found them large and fat. walking on shore this evening I met with a buffaloe calf which attatched itself to me and continued to follow close at my heels untill I embarked and left it. it appeared allarmed at my dog which was probably the cause of it's so readily attatching itself to me. Capt Clark informed me that he saw a large drove of buffaloe pursued by wolves today, that they at length caught a calf which was unable to keep up with the herd. the cows only defend their young so long as they are able to keep up with the herd, and seldom return any distance in surch of them.

THURSDAY APRIL 25TH 1805.

the water friezed on the oars this morning as the men rowed. about 10 oclock A.M. the wind began to blow so violently that we were obliged to lye too. my dog had been absent during the last night, and I was fearfull we had lost him altogether, however, much to my satisfaction he joined us at 8 oclock this morning. Knowing that the river was crooked, from the report of the hunters

who were out yesterday, and beleiving that we were at no very
great distance from the Yellow stone River; I determined, in order
as mush as possible to avoid detention, to proceed by land with
a few men to the entrance of that river and make the necessary
observations to determine its position; accordingly I set out at
11 OCk. on the Lard. side, accompanyed by four men. when we
had proceeded about four miles, I ascended the hills from whence
I had a most pleasing view of the country, particularly of the wide
and fertile vallies formed by the missouri and the yellowstone
rivers, which occasionally unmasked by the wood on their borders
disclose their meanderings for many miles in their passage through
these delightfull tracts of country. I determined to encamp on the
bank of the Yellow stone river which made it's appearance about
2 miles South of me. the whol face of the country was covered with
herds of Buffaloe, Elk & Antelopes; deer are also abundant, but
keep themselves more concealed in the woodland. the buffaloe
Elk and Antelope are so gentle that we pass near them while feeding, without appearing to excite any alarm among them; and when
we attract their attention, they frequently approach us more nearly
to discover what we are, and in some instances pursue us a considerable distance apparenly with that view. we encamped on the
bank of the yellow stone river, 2 miles South of it's confluence with
the Missouri.

FRIDAY APRIL 26TH 1805.

This morning I dispatched Joseph Fields up the yellowstone
river with orders to examine it as far as he could conveniently and
return the same evening; while I proceeded down the river with
one man in order to take a view of the confluence of this great
river with the Missouri, which we found to be two miles distant
on a direct line N.W. from our encampment. the bottom land on
the lower side of the yellowstone river near it's mouth, for about
one mile in width appears to be subject to inundation; while that
on the opposite side of the Missouri and the point formed by the
junction of these rivers is of the common elivation, say from twelve
to 18 feet above the level of the water, and of course not liable to
be overflown except in extreem high water, which dose not appear
to be very frequent. there is more timber in the neighbourhood
of the junction of these rivers, and on the Missouri as far below

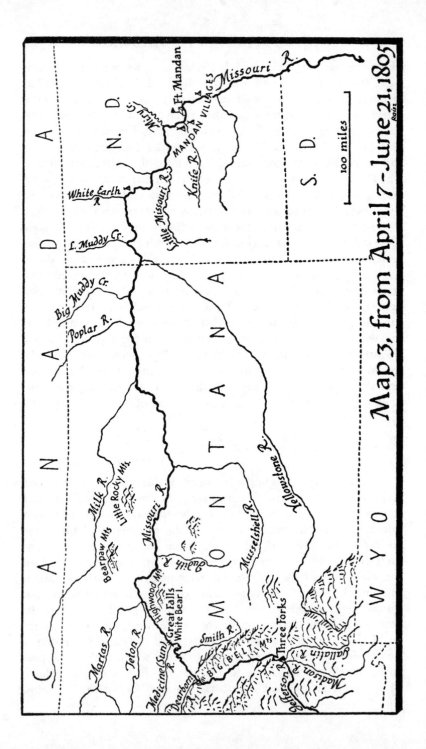

Map 3, from April 7–June 21, 1805

CANADA

N. D.

S. D.

MONTANA

WYO

Missouri R.

Ft. Mandan

MANDAN VILLAGES

Knife R.

Mouse R.

White Earth R.

Little Missouri R.

L. Muddy Cr.

Big Muddy Cr.

Poplar R.

Milk R.

Little Rocky Mts.

Bearpaw Mts

Missouri R.

Marias R.

Teton R.

Highwood Mts

Medicine (Sun) R.

Dearborn R.

Great Falls

White Bear I.

Judith R.

Musselshell R.

Yellowstone R.

Smith R.

BIG BELT Mts

Three Forks

Madison R.

Gallatin R.

Jefferson R.

100 miles

as the White-earth river, than there is on any part of the Missouri above the entrance of the Chyenne river to this place.

about 12 O[c]lock I heard the discharge of several guns at the junction of the rivers, which announced to me the arrival of the pa[r]ty with Capt Clark; I afterwards learnt that they had fired on some buffaloe which they met with at that place, and of which they killed a cow and several Calves; the latter are now fine veal. after I had completed my observations in the evening I walked down and joined the party at their encampment on the point of land formed by the junction of the rivers; found them all in good health, and much pleased at having arrived at this long wished for spot, and in order to add in some measure to the general pleasure which seemed to pervade our little community, we ordered a dram to be issued to each person; this soon produced the fiddle, and they spent the evening with much hilarity, singing & dancing, and seemed as perfectly to forget their past toils, as they appeared regardless of those to come.

Capt Clark measured these rivers just above their confluence; found the bed of the Missouri 520 yards wide, the water occupying 330. it's channel deep. the yellowstone river including it's sandbar, 858 yds. of which, the water occupied 297 yards; the depest part 12 feet; it was falling at this time & appeard to be nearly at it's summer tide. the Indians inform that the yellowstone river is navigable for perogues and canoes nearly to it's source in the Rocky Mountains, and that in it's course near these mountains it passes within less than half a day's march of a navigable part of the Missouri. it's extreem sources are adjacent to those of the Missouri, river platte, and I think probably with some of the South branch of the Columbia river.[8] the water of this river is turbid, tho' dose not possess as much sediment as that of the Missouri.

[8] This information about the headwaters is, of course, erroneous. The first known use of the names Rochejaune or Yellowstone was by James Mackay in 1795. In this same summer, 1805, the North West Company made its first move to open the Far Western trade by sending François Antoine Larocque overland to explore the Yellowstone. He left the Mandan villages in June, traveling with a party of Crows, and reached the Yellowstone near the mouth of the Big Horn. He then traveled slowly down the valley of the Yellowstone, reaching the mouth, where Lewis and Clark now are, at the end of September. It was a fruitless exploration but Larocque did establish (by reliable hearsay) a fact which Clark missed now and on his descent in 1806, the existence of the falls of the Yellowstone.

CHAPTER VIII

FROM THE YELLOWSTONE TO THE MUSSELSHELL

[Lewis]

S et out this morning at an early hour; the wind was favourable and we employed our sails to advantage. Capt Clark walked on shore this morning, and I proceeded with the party. we saw great quantities of game today; consisting of the common and mule deer, Elk, Buffaloe, and Antelopes; also four brown bear, one of which was fired on and wounded by one of the party but we did not get it; the beaver have cut great quantitites of timber; saw a tree nearly 3 feet in diameter that had been felled by them.

MONDAY APRIL 29TH 1805.

I walked on shore with one man. about 8. A.M. we fell in with two brown or yellow bear; [1] both of which we wounded; one of them made his escape, the other after my firing on him pursued me seventy or eighty yards, but fortunately had been so badly wounded that he was unable to pursue me so closely as to prevent my charging my gun; we again repeated our fir and killed him. it was a male not fully grown, we estimated his weight at 300 lbs. not having the means of ascertaining it precisely. The legs of this

---

[1] A grizzly, the first one. Lewis presently loses his easy superiority, the result of the ease with which this one was killed. His erroneous statement that the grizzly's testicles are provided separate individual scrota, which he later repeats, is inexplicable. Though far from being the first description of a grizzly as some texts have said, this is the first detailed one. Henry Kelsey, in 1691, was probably the first white man to see a grizzly.

bear are somewhat longer than those of the black, as are it's tallons and tusks incomparably larger and longer. the testicles, which in the black bear are placed pretty well back between the thyes and contained in one pouch like those of the dog and most quadrupeds, are in the yellow or brown bear placed much further foward, and are suspended in separate pouches from two to four inches asunder;   it's colour is yellowish brown, the eyes small, black, and piercing; the front of the fore legs near the feet is usually black; the fur is finer thicker and deeper than that of the black bear. these are all the particulars in which this anamal appeared to me to differ from the black bear; it is a much more furious and formidable anamal, and will frequently pursue the hunter when wounded. it is asstonishing to see the wounds they will bear before they can be put to death. the Indians may well fear this anamal equiped as they generally are with their bows and arrows or indifferent fuzees, but in the hands of skillfull riflemen they are by no means as formidable or dangerous as they have been represented.

game is still very abundant we can scarcely cast our eyes in any direction without percieving deer Elk Buffaloe or Antelopes. The quantity of wolves appear to increase in the same proportion; they generally hunt in parties of six eight or ten; they kill a great number of the Antelopes at this season; the Antelopes are yet meagre and the females are big with young; the wolves take them most generally in attempting to swim the river; in this manner my dog caught one drowned it and brought it on shore; they are but clumsey swimers, tho' on land when in good order, they are extreemly fleet and dureable. we have frequently seen the wolves in pursuit of the Antelope in the plains; they appear to decoy a single one from a flock, and then pursue it, alturnately relieving each other untill they take it. on joining Capt Clark he informed me that he had seen a female and faun of the bighorned anamal; that they ran for some distance with great aparent ease along the side of the river bluff where it was almost perpendicular; two of the party fired on them while in motion without effect. we took the flesh of the bear on board and proceeded. Capt. Clark walked on shore this evening, killed a deer, and saw several of the big-horned anamals.[2]

[2] The bighorn or Rocky Mountain sheep. Its meat was one of the great delicacies of the West.

[Clark]   MAY 2ND THURSDAY 1805

The wind blew verry hard all the last night,   this morning
about sunrise began to Snow, (The Thermomtr. at 28. abov 0)
and continued untill about 10 oClock, at which time it seased,
the wind continued hard untill about 2 P.M.   the Snow which
fell to day was about 1 In deep,   a verry extraodernarey climate,
to behold the trees Green & flowers spred on the plain, & Snow
an inch deep. we Set out about 3 oClock and proceeded on about
five ½ miles and encamped on the Std Side, the evening verry cold,
Ice freesing to the Ores. I shot a large beaver & Drewyer three in
walking on the bank,   the flesh of those animals the party is
fond of eating &c.

                                       MAY 3RD FRIDAY 1805

we Set out reather later this morning than useal owing to
weather being verry cold, a frost last night and the Thermt. stood
this morning at 26 above 0. which is 6 degrees blow freeseing. the
ice that was on the Kettle left near the fire last night was ¼ of
an inch thick. The snow is all or nearly all off the low bottoms,
the Hills are entireley covered; three of our party found in the
back of a bottom 3 pieces of scarlet [cloth] one brace [3] in each,
which had been left as a sacrifice near one of their swet
houses,   on the L.S. we passed to day a curious collection of
bushes tied up in the shape of *faccene* about 10 feet diamuter,
which must have been left also by the natives as an offering to
their medison which they [are] convinced protected or gave them
relief near the place,   the wind continued to blow hard from
the West, altho' not suffcently so to detain us. Great numbers of
Buffalow, Elk, Deer, antilope, beaver, Procupins, & water fowls
seen to day, such as, Geese, ducks of dift. kinds, & a fiew Swan.

                                       MAY 4TH SATTURDAY 1805

The rudder Irons of our large Perogue broke off last night, the
replaceing of which detained us this morning untill 9 oClock at

[3] A rough measurement of length, from fingertip to fingertip with the arms
stretched out.

which time we set out   The countrey on each side of the Missouri is a rich high and butifull   the bottoms are extencive with a great deal of timber on them   all the fore part of this day the wood land bordered the river on both Sides, in the after part of butifull assending plain on the Std Side   we encamped on the Std. Side a little above. Saw great numbers of anamals of different kinds on the banks,   we have one man Sick. The river has been falling for several days passed; it now begins to rise a little, the rate of rise & fall is from one to 3 inches in 24 hours

5TH OF MAY SUNDAY 1805

We set out verry early and had not proceeded far before the rudder Irons of one of the Perogus broke which detained us a short time   Capt Lewis walked on shore this morning and killed a Deer,   after brackfast I walked on shore Saw great numbers of Buffalow & Elk   Saw also a Den of young wolves, and a number of Grown Wolves in every direction,   The Countrey on both sides is as yesterday handsom & fertile. The river rising & current Strong & in the evening we saw a Brown or Grisley beare on a sand beech,   I went out with one man Geo Drewyer & Killed the bear, which was verry large and a turrible looking animal, which we found verry hard to kill   we Shot ten Balls into him before we killed him, & 5 of those Balls through his lights   This animal is the largest of the carnivorous kind I ever saw

[Lewis]   SUNDAY MAY 5TH 1805

it was a most tremendious looking anamal, and extreemly hard to kill   notwithstanding he had five balls through his lungs and five others in various parts he swam more than half the distance across the river to a sandbar, & it was at least twenty minutes before he died; he did not attempt to attack, but fled and made the most tremendous roaring from the moment he was shot. We had no means of weighing this monster; Capt. Clark thought he would weigh 500 lbs. for my own part I think the estimate too small by 100 lbs.   he measured 8. Feet 7½ Inches from the nose to the extremity of the hind feet, 5 F. 10½ Ins. arround the breast.

1 F. 11. I. arround the middle of the arm, & 3.F. 11.I. arround the neck; his tallons which were five in number on each foot were 4⅜ Inches in length. he was in good order, we therefore divided him among the party and made them boil the oil and put it in a cask for future uce; the oil is as hard as hogs lard when cool, much more so than that of the black bear. this bear differs from the common black bear in several respects; it's tallons are much longer and more blont, it's tale shorter, it's hair which is of a redish or bey brown, is longer thicker and finer than that of the black bear; his liver lungs and heart are much larger even in proportion with his size; the heart particularly was as large as that of a large Ox. his maw was also ten times the size of black bear, and was filled with flesh and fish.

The party killed two Elk and a Buffaloe today, and my dog caught a goat, which he overtook by superior fleetness, the goat it must be understood was with young and extreemly poor.

MONDAY MAY 6TH 1805.

saw a brown [grizzly] bear swim the river above us, he disappeared before we can get in reach of him; I find that the curiossity of our party is pretty well satisfyed with rispect to this anamal,   the formidable appearance of the male bear killed on the 5th added to the difficulty with which they die when even shot through the vital parts, has staggered the resolution [of] several of them, others however seem keen for action with the bear;   I expect these gentlemen will give us some amusement shotly as they [the bears] soon begin now to coppolate. saw a great quantity of game of every species common here. Capt Clark walked on shore and killed two Elk, they were not in very good order, we therefore took a part of the meat only;   it is now only amusement for Capt. C. and myself to kill as much meat as the party can consum.

WEDNESDAY MAY 8TH 1805.

we nooned it just above the entrance of a large river which disimbogues on the Lard. [Starbd] side; I took the advantage of this leasure moment and examined the river about 3 miles;   I have no doubt but it is navigable for boats perogues and canoes, for the latter probably a great distance. from the quantity of water furnished by this river it must water a large extent of country; perhaps this river also might furnish a practicable and advantageous communication with the Saskashiwan river; it is sufficiently large to justify a belief that it might reach to that river if it's direction be such. the water of this river possesses a peculiar whiteness, being about the colour of a cup of tea with the admixture of a tablespoonfull of milk. from the colour of it's water we called it Milk river. we think it possible that this may be the river called by the Minitares *the river which scoalds at all others* [4]   Capt Clark who walked this morning on the Lard. shore ascended a very high point opposite to the mouth of this river; he informed me that he had a perfect view of this river and the country through which it passed for a great distance probably 50 or 60 Miles, that the river from it's mouth bore N.W. for 12 or 15 Miles when it forked, the one taking a direction nearly North, and the other to the West of N. West.

Capt C. could not be certain but thought he saw the smoke and some Indian lodges at a considrable distance up Milk river.

THURSDAY MAY 9TH 1805.

Capt C. killed 2 bucks and 2 buffaloe, I also killed one buffaloe which proved to be the best meat, it was in tolerable order;   we saved the best of the meat, and from the cow I killed we saved the necessary materials for making what our wrighthand cook Charbono calls the *boudin (poudingue) blanc,* and immediately set him about preparing them for supper; this white pudding we all esteem one of the greatest delacies of the forrest, it may not be amiss therefore to give it a place. About 6 feet of the lower extremity of the large gut of the Buffaloe is the first mosel that the cook makes love to,   this he holds fast at one end with the right hand, while with the forefinger and thumb of the left he gently compresses it, and discharges what he says *is not good to eat,*

[4] This identification of the stream here named Milk River as the one which the Indians had called the River That Scolds All the Others was to be responsible for considerable anxiety later on. One result which Lewis does not allude to was to make the expedition believe it was nearer the Three Forks than in fact it was.

but of which in the s[e]quel we get a moderate portion;   the mustle lying underneath the shoulder blade next to the back, and fillets are next saught, these are needed up very fine with a good portion of kidney suit; to this composition is then added a just proportion of pepper and salt and a small quantity of flour;   thus far advanced, our skilfull opporater C——o seizes his recepticle, which has never once touched the water, for that would intirely distroy the regular order of the whole procedure; you will not forget that the side you now see is that covered with a good coat of fat provided the anamal be in good order; the operator sceizes the recepticle I say, and tying it fast at one end turns it inward and begins now with repeated evolutions of the hand and arm, and a brisk motion of the finger and thumb to put in what he says is *bon pour manger;*   thus by stuffing and compressing he soon distends the recepticle to the utmost limmits of it's power of expansion, and in the course of it's longtudinal progress it drives from the other end of the recepticle a much larger portion of the [blank space in MS.] than was prevously discharged by the finger and thumb of the left hand in a former part of the operation; thus when the sides of the recepticle are skilfully exchanged the outer for the iner, and all is compleatly filled with something good to eat, it is tyed at the other end, but not any cut off, for that would make the pattern too scant;   it is then baptised in the missouri with two dips and a flirt, and bobbed into the kettle; from whence, after it be well boiled it is taken and fryed with bears oil untill it becomes brown, when it is ready to esswage the pangs of a keen appetite or such as travelers in the wilderness are seldom at a loss for.

TUESDAY MAY 14TH 1805.

one of the party wounded a brown [grizzly] bear very badly, but being alone did not think proper to pursue him. In the evening the men in two of the rear canoes discovered a large brown bear lying in the open grounds about 300 paces from the river, and six of them went out to attack him, all good hunters; they took the advantage of a small eminence which concealed them and got within 40 paces of him unperceived,   two of them reserved their fires as had been previously conscerted, the four others fired nearly at the same time and put each his bullet through him, two of the balls passed through the bulk of both lobes of his lungs,   in an instant this monster ran at them with open mouth, the two who had reserved their fir[e]s discharged their pieces at him as he came towards them, boath of them struck him, one only slightly and the other fortunately broke his shoulder, this however only retarded his motion for a moment only,   the men unable to reload their guns took to flight, the bear pursued and had very nearly overtaken them before they reached the river; two of the party betook themselves to a canoe and the others seperated an[d] concealed themselves among the willows, reloaded their pieces, each discharged his piece at him as they had an opportunity   they struck him several times again but the guns served only to direct the bear to them,   in this manner he pursued two of them seperately so close that they were obliged to throw aside their guns and pouches and throw themselves into the river altho' the bank was nearly twenty feet perpendicular; so enraged was this anamal that he plunged into the river only a few feet behind the second man he had compelled [to] take refuge in the water, when one of those who still remained on shore shot him through the head and finally killed him;   they then took him on shore and butch[er]ed him when they found eight balls had passed through him in different directions;   the bear being old the flesh was indifferent, they therefore only took the skin and fleece, the latter made us several gallons of oil.

It was after the sun had set before these men come up with us, where we had been halted by an occurence, which I have now to recappitulate, and which altho' happily passed without ruinous injury, I cannot recollect but with the utmost trepidation and horror; this is the upseting and narrow escape of the white perogue. It happened unfortunately for us this evening that Charbono was at the helm of this Perogue, in stead of Drewyer, who had previously steered her; Charbono cannot swim and is perhaps the most timid waterman in the world; perhaps it was equally unluckey that Capt. C. and myself were both on shore at that moment, a circumstance which rarely happened; and tho' we were on the shore opposite to the perogue, were too far distant to be heard or to do more than remain spectators of her fate; in this perogue were embarked, our papers, Instruments, books medicine, a great

part of our merchandize and in short almost every article indispen-
sibly necessary to further the views, or insure the success of the
enterpize in which we are now launched to the distance of 2200
miles. surfice it so say, that the Perogue was under sail when a
sudon squawl of wind struck her obliquely, and turned her considerably,   the steersman allarmed, in stead of puting, her before
the wind, lufted her up into it,   the wind was so violent that
it drew the brace of the squarsail out of the hand of the man who
was attending it, and instantly upset the perogue and would have
turned her completely topsaturva, had it not have been from the
resistance mad by the oarning [awning] against the water. In this
situation Capt. C. and myself both fired our guns to attract the
attention if possible of the crew and ordered the halyards to be
cut and the sail hawled in, but they did not hear us;   such was
their confusion and consternation at this moment, that they suffered the perogue to lye on her side for half a minute before
they took the sail in. The perogue then wrighted but had filled
within an inch of the gunwals;   Charbono still crying to his god
for mercy, had not yet recollected the rudder, nor could the
repeated orders of the Bowsman, Cruzat, bring him to his recollection untill he threatend to shoot him instantly if he did not
take hold of the rudder and do his duty. the waves by this time
were runing very high, but the fortitude resolution and good
conduct of Cruzat saved her; he ordered 2 of the men to throw
out the water with some kettles that fortunately were convenient,
while himself and two others rowed her as[h]ore, where she arrived
scarcely above the water;   we now took every article out of
her and lay them to drane as well as we could for the evening,
baled out the canoe and secured her.

there were two other men beside Charbono on board who could
not swim, and who of course must also have perished had the
perogue gone to the bottom. while the perogue lay on her side,
finding I could not be heard, I for a moment forgot my own situation, and involluntarily droped my gun, threw aside my shot pouch
and was in the act of unbuttoning my coat, before I recollected
the folly of the attempt I was about to make; which was to throw
myself into the river and indevour to swim to the perogue;   the
perogue was three hundred yards distant the waves so high that a
perogue could scarcely live in any situation, the water excessively

could, and the stream rappid; had I undertaken this project therefore, there was a hundred to one but what I should have paid the forfit of my life for the madness of my project, but this had the perogue been lost, I should have valued but little. After having all matters arranged for the evening as well as the nature of the circumstances would permit, we thought it a proper occasion to console ourselves and cheer the sperits of our men and accordingly took a drink of grog and gave each man a gill of sperits.

Thursday May 16th

The morning was fair and the day proved favorable to our operations; by 4 oClock in the evening our Instruments, Medicine, merchandize provision &c, were perfectly dryed, repacked and put on board the perogue. the loss we sustained was not so great as we had at first apprehended; our medicine sustained the greatest injury, several articles of which were intirely spoiled, and many others considerably injured,   the ballance of our losses consisted of some gardin seeds, a small quantity of gunpowder, and a few culinary articles which fell overboard and sunk. the Indian woman to whom I ascribe equal fortitude and resolution, with any person onboard at the time of the accedent, caught and preserved most of the light articles which were washed overboard.

in the early part of the day two of our men fired on a panther, a little below our encampment, and wounded it; they informed us that it was very large, had just killed a deer partly devoured it, and in the act of concealing the ballance as they discovered him. this morning a white bear toar Labuiche's coat which he had left in the plains.

Friday May 17th

we employed the toe line the greater part of the day; the banks were firm and shore boald which favoured the uce of the cord. I find this method of asscending the river, when the shore is such as will permit it, the safest and most expeditious mode of traveling, except with sails in a steady and favourable breze. the great number of large beds of streams perfectly dry which we daily pass indicate a country but badly watered, which I fear is the case with the country through which we have been passing for the last fifteen or twenty days. Capt. Clark walked on shore this evening and killed an Elk; buffaloe are not so abundant as they were some days past. the party with me killed a female brown bear, she was but meagre, and appeared to have suckled young very recently. Capt. Clark narrowly escaped being bitten by a rattlesnake in the course of his walk, the party killed one this evening at our encampment, which he informed me was similar to that he had seen;   this snake is smaller than those common to the middle Atlantic States, being about 2 feet 6 inches long; it is of a yellowish brown colour on the back and sides, variagated with one row of oval spots of a dark brown colour lying transversely over the back from the neck to the tail, and two other rows of small circular spots of the same colour which garnis the sides along the edge of the scuta. it's bely contains 176 [s]cuta on the belly and 17 on the tale. Capt Clark saw an Indian fortifyed camp this evening, which appeared to have been recently occupyed, from which we concluded it was probable that it had been formed by a war party of the Menetares who left their vilage in March last with a view to attack the blackfoot Indians in consequence of their having killed some of their principal warriors the previous autumn. we were roused late at night by the Sergt. of the guard, and warned of the danger we were in from a large tree that had taken fire and which leant immediately over our lodge. we had the loge removed, and a few minutes after a large proportion of the top of the tree fell on the place the lodge had stood; had we been a few minutes later we should have been crushed to attoms. the wind blew so hard, that notwithstanding the lodge was fifty paces distant from the fire it sustained considerable injury from the burning coals which were thrown on it; the party were much harrassed also by this fire which communicated to a collection of fallen timber, and could not be extinguished.

[Clark]   MAY 19TH SUNDAY 1805

a verry cold night, the murckery stood at 38 at 8 oClock this morning,   a heavy *dew* which is the 2d I have seen this spring. The fog (which was the first) was so thick this morning that we could not Set out untill the Sun was about 2 hours up, at which time a small breeze sprung up from the E which cleared off the

fog & we proceeded on by means of the Cord   The hills are high
& rugged the countrey as yesterday. I walked on Shore with two
men we killed a white or grey bear; not withstanding that it was
Shot through the heart it ran at it's usial pace near a quarter of
a mile before it fell. Capt Lewis's dog was badly bitten by a
wounded *beaver* and was near bleading to death,   after killing
the Bear I continued my walk alone, & killed 3 Deer & a
Beaver   finding that the Perogues were below I assended the
highest hill I could see, from the top of which I saw the mouth
of *M. Shell R* & the meanderings of the Missouri for a long distance. I also saw a high mountain in a westerley direction, bearing
S.SW. about 40 or 50 miles distant,   in the evening the river
was verry crooked and much more rapid & containing more sawyers
than any which we have passed above the River Platte Capt Lewis
walked on Shore this after noon & killed an Elk, Buck & a
Beaver,   I kiled three Deer at dinner,   the hunters killed
three other Deer to day several beaver also killed. We camped on
the Stard Side in a bottom of small cotton wood

[Lewis]   MONDAY 20TH 1805.

The hunters returned this evening and informed us that the
country continued much the same in appearance as that we saw
where we were or broken, and that about five miles ab[ov]e the
mouth of shell river a handsome river of about fifty yards in width
discharged itself into the shell river on the Stard. or upper
side;   this stream we called Sâh-câ-ger we-âh or bird woman's
River, after our interpreter the Snake woman.

[Clark]   MAY 20TH MONDAY 1805

a fine morning wind from the N E.   river falling a little we
set out at 7 oClock and proceeded on verry well as usial by the
assistance of the cord   passed some verry swift water, river
narrow and crooked,   at 11 oClock arrived at the mouth of *Shell*
river on the Lard Side and formed a camp for the present, haveing
passed a large creek about 4 miles below on the Ld Side which we
call Blowing fly Creek from the emence quantities of those insects
which geather on our meat in such numbers that we are oblige to
brush them off what we eate. *Muscle Shell* River falls in on Lard

Side 2270 miles up [from the mouth of the Missouri]   contains a greater perportion of water than Rivers of its size below,   I measured it and find it to be 110 yards wide, the water of a Greenish Yellow Colour, and appers to be navagable for Small craft. The *Minetarres* inform us that this river heads in the 1st of the rockey Mountains & passes through a broken Countrey. its head at no great distance from the Yellow Stone River   The Countrey about this river as described yesterday

The Missouri at the mouth of Shell River is 222 yards wide with a smoth current   the Missouri water is not so muddey as below, but retains nearly its usial cholour, and the sand principally confined to the points   I killed two Deer & an Elk, the hunters killed an Elk & several deer mearly for their skins to make Leagins   Sent men out in every derection, the Countrey generally verry broken some leavel plains up the *Shell* river. The bottoms of the *Shell* river is well timbered as also a small river which falls into that river on the upper Side 5 miles above its mouth. The hills on the Lard. contain scattering Pine & cedar

The wind continued to blow so violently hard we did not think it prudent to set out untill it luled a little,   about 10 oClock we set out   the morning cold,   Capt Lewis walked out before dinner & killed a Deer,   I walked out after dinner and assended a but[te] a few miles [off] to view the countrey, which I found roleing & of a verry rich stickey soil producing but little vegetation of any kind except the prickley pear, but little grass & that verry low. a great deal of scattering *Pine* on the Lard Side & Some few on the Stard. Sd.   game not so abundant as below,   the river continues about the same width, fewer Sand bars & current more regular, river falls about an inch a day

We camped on the Stard. Side, earlier than we intend on account of saveing the oil of a bear which the party killed late this afternoon.

Maney of the Creeks which appear to have no water near ther mouths have streams of running water higher up which rise & waste in the sand or gravel. the water of those creeks are so much impregnated with the salt substance that it cannot be Drank with pleasure.

[Clark] MAY 23RD THURSDAY 1805

A severe frost last night, the Thrmotr. stood at the freesing point this morning i. e. 32 a 0. wind S W. the water freezes on the oars Ice on the edge of the river. a mountain which appears to be 60 or 70 miles long bearing E. & W is about 25 miles distant from this river I walked on shore and killed 4 deer & an Elk, & a beaver in the evening we killed a large fat Bear, which we unfortunately lost in the river, after being shot took the water & was carried under a drift passed in course of this day three Islands, two of them covered with tall timber & a 3rd with willows

The after part of this day was worm & the Musquetors troublesome. Saw but five Buffalow a number of Elk & Deer & 5 bear & 2 antilopes to day. the river beginning to rise, and current more rapid than yesterday,

MAY 25TH SATTURDAY 1805

I walked on shore and killed a female *Ibi* or big horn animal in my absence Drewyer & Bratten killed two others, this animal is a species peculiar to this upper part of the Missouri, the head and horns of the male which Drewyer killed to day weighed 27 lbs. it was somewhat larger than the mail of the Common Deer; the body reather thicker deeper and not so long in proportion to it's hight as the common Deer; the head and horns of the male are remarkably large compared with the other parts of the animal; the whole form is much more delicate than that of the common goat, and there is a greater disparity in the size of the

115

mail and female than between those of either the deer or goat. the bone above the Eye is remarkably prominant; the head nostrils and division of the upper lip are precisely in form like the sheep. their legs resemble the sheep more than any other animal with which I am acquainted tho' they are more delicately formed,   like the sheep they stand foward in the knee and the lower joint of the fore leg is smallest where it joins the knee, the hoof is black and large in perpotion, is divided, very open and roundly pointed at the toe; like the sheep; is much hollowed and Sharp on the under edge like the Scotch goat,   has two small Hoofs behind each foot below the ankle as the goat Sheep and Deer have. the belley, iner side of the legs, and the extremity of the rump and buttock's for about two inches ½ around the but of the tail, are white, as is also the tail except just at its extremity on the upper side which is of a dark brown.

the tail is about 3 inches in length covered with short hair, or at least not longer than that of the body; the outer part of the animal are of a duskey brown or reather a lead coloured light brown; the animal is now Sheding its winter coat which is thick not quite as long as that of the Deer and appears to be inter mixt with a considerable quantity of fine fur which lies next to the Skin and concealed by the coarcer hair; the shape of the hair itself is cylindric as that of the Antilope is, but is smaller, shorter and not compressed or flattened as that of the deers winter coat is. I believe this animal only sheds it's hair once a year. it has Eight fore teeth in the under jaw and no canine teeth. The *Horns* are large at their base, and occupy the crown of the head almost entirely, they are compressed, bent backwards and lunated; the surface swelling into wavey rings which incircleing the horn continue to succeed each other from the base to the extremity and becomeing less elivated and more distant as they receed from the head. The horn for about two thirds of its length is filled with a porus bone which is united with the frontal bone   the horns of the *female* are small, but are also compressed and bent backwards and incircled with a succession of wavy rings. the horn is of a light brown colour; when Dressed it is almost white extreamly transparent and very elastic. this horn is used by the natives in constructing their bows; I have no doubt of it's elegance and usefullness in hair combs, and might probably answer as maney valuable purpoces to civilized man, as it does to the native indians, who form their water cups, spoons and platters of it. the females have already brought forth their young, indeed from the size of the young, I suppose that they produce them early in March. they have from one to two at a birth. they feed on grass, but principally on the arramatic herbs which grow on the clifts and inaxcessable hights which they frequent most commonly, and the places they generally collect to lodge is the cranies or cevices of the rocks in the face of inaccessable precepices, where the wolf nor Bear can reach them, and where indeed man himself would in maney instances find a similar deficiency; yet those animals bound from rock to rock and stand apparently in the most careless manner on the Side of precipices of maney hundred feet. they are very shy and quick of both sent and sight.[1]

In my walk of this day I saw mountts on either side of the river at no great distance, those mountains appeared to be detached, and not ranges as laid down by the *Minetarrees,*   I also think I saw a range of high Mounts. at a great distance to the S S W. but am not certain as the horozon was not clear enough to view it with certainty. The appeerence of salts, and bitumun still continue. we saw a *polecat* to day being the first which we have seen for some time past. The Air of this quarter is pure and helthy. the water of the Missouri will tasted not quite so muddy as it is below,   not withstanding the last rains has raised the river a little it is less muddy than it was before the rain.

[Lewis]   Sunday May 26th 1805.

proceeded principally by the toe line, using the oars mearly to pass the river in order to take advantage of the shores. scarcely any bottoms to the river; the hills high and juting in on both sides, to the river in many places. the stone tumbleing from these clifts and brought down by the rivulets became more troublesome today. Capt. Clark walked on shore this morning and ascended to the summit of the river hills   he informed me on his return that he had seen mountains on both sides of the river runing nearly parrallel with it and at no great distance; also an irregular range of mountains on lard. about 50 Mls. distant; the extremities of which boar

[1] In this description of the bighorn, Clark is copying Lewis's journal.

W. and N.W. from his station. he also saw in the course of his walk, some Elk several herds of the Big horn, and the large hare; the latter is common to every part of this open country. scarcely any timber to be seen except the few scattering pine and spruce which crown the high hills, or in some instances grow along their sides.

In the after part of the day I also walked out and ascended the river hills which I found sufficiently fortiegueing. on arriving to the summit [of] one of the highest points in the neighbourhood I thought myself well repaid for my labour; as from this point I beheld the Rocky Mountains for the first time,   I could only discover a few of the most elivated points above the horizon, the most remarkable of which by my pocket compass I found bore N. 65° W. being a little to the N. of the N.W. extremity of the range of broken mountains seen this morning by Capt. C.   these points of the Rocky Mountains were covered with snow and the sun shone on it in such manner as to give me the most plain and satisfactory view.[2] while I viewed these mountains I felt a secret pleasure in finding myself so near the head of the heretofore conceived boundless Missouri; but when I reflected on the difficulties which this snowey barrier would most probably throw in my way to the Pacific, and the sufferings and hardships of myself and party in thim, it in some measure counterballanced the joy I had felt in the first moments in which I gazed on them; but as I have always held it a crime to anticipate evils I will believe it a good comfortable road untill I am compelled to believe differently.

late this evening we passed a very bad rappid which reached quite across the river;   the party had considerable difficulty in ascending it altho' they doubled their crews and used both the rope and the pole. while they were passing this rappid a female Elk and it's fawn swam down through the waves which ran very high, hence the name of Elk rappids which they instantly gave this place,   these are the most considerable rappids which we have yet seen on the missouri and in short the only place where there has appeared to be a suddon decent. This is truly a desert barren country and I feel myself still more convinced of it's being

2 Like many a traveler after him, Lewis mistakes the detached formation now called the Little Rocky Mountains of northern Montana for a chain of the main range.

a continuation of the black hills. we have continued every day to pass more or less old stick lodges of the Indians in the timbered points, there are two even in this little bottom where we lye.

[Clark]   MAY 28TH TUESDAY 1805

a cloudy morning some fiew drops of rain and verry smokey   The shoaley places are verry numerous and some bad to get around   we have to make use of the cord & Poles, and our tow ropes are all except one of Elkskin, & stretch and sometimes brake which indanger the Perogues or canoe, as it imedeately turns and if any rock should chance to be below, the rapidity of the current would turn her over [if] she should chance to strike the rock,   we observe great caution at those places.

I saw great numbers of the Big horned animals, one of which I killed   their fauns are nearly half grown. one of the Party saw a verry large bear,   picked up on the shore a pole which had been made use of by the nativs for lodge poles, & haul'd by dogs   it is new and is a certain sign of the Indians being on the river above   a foot ball and several other articles are also found to substantiate this oppinion. at 1 oClock we had a few drops of rain and some thunder whic is the first thunder we have had since we set out from Fort Mandan,

[Lewis]   WEDNESDAY MAY 29TH 1805

Last night we were all allarmed by a large buffaloe Bull, which swam over from the opposite shore and coming along side of the white perogue, climbed over it to land,   he then allarmed ran up the bank in full speed directly towards the fires, and was within 18 inches of the heads of some of the men who lay sleeping before the centinel could allarm him or make him change his course,   still more alarmed, he now took his direction immediately towards our lodge, passing between 4 fires and within a few inches of the heads of one range of the men as they yet lay sleeping,   when he came near the tent, my dog saved us by causing him to change his course a second time, which he did by turning a little to the right, and was quickly out of sight, leaving us by this time all in an uproar with our guns in o[u]r hands, enquiring of each other the ca[u]se of the alarm, which after a few moments was explained by the centinel: we were happy to find no one hirt. The next morning we found that the buffaloe in passing the perogue had trodden on a rifle, which belonged to Capt. Clark's black man, who had negligently left her in the perogue,   the rifle was much bent, he had also broken the spindle; pivit, and shattered the stock of one of the blunderbushes on board,   with this damage I felt well content, happey indeed, that we had sustaned no further injury,   it appears that the white perogue, which contains our most valuable stores is attended by some evil gennii.

This morning we set out at an early hour and proceded as usual by the Chord. at the distance of 2½ Miles passed a handsome river which discharged itself on the Lard. side,   I walked on shore and acended this river about a mile and a half in order to examine it. the water of this River is clearer much than any we have met with great abundance of the Argalia or Bighorned animals in the high country through which this river passes. Cap. C. who assended this R. much higher than I did has thought proper to call it *Judieths* River.[3] on the Missouri just above the entrance of the *Judith River* I counted the remains of the fires of 126 Indian lodges which appeared to be of very recent date perhaps 12 or 15 days. Capt. Clark also saw a large encamp[m]ent just above the entrance of this river on the Stard. side of reather older date, probably they were the same Indians. The Indian woman with us ex[a]mined the mockersons which we found at these encampments and informed us that they were not of her nation the Snake Indians, but she beleived they were some of the Indians who inhabit the country on this side of [the] Rocky Mountains and North of the Missoury and I think it most probable that they were the Minetaries of Fort de Prarie.[4]

Today we passed on the Stard. side the remains of a vast many mangled carcases of Buffalow which had been driven over a precipice of 120 feet by the Indians and perished; the water appeared to have washed away a part of this immence pile of slaughter and still their remained the fragments of at least a hundred carcases   they created a most horrid stench. in this manner the Indians of the Missouri distroy vast herds of buffaloe at a stroke;   for this pur-

---

[3] For Julia (Judy) Hancock of Virginia, whom Clark later married.
[4] The Fall Indians, the Atsina, who were allied with the Blackfeet.

pose one of the most active and fleet young men is scelected and disguised in a robe of buffaloe skin, having also the skin of the buffaloe's head with the years and horns fastened on his head in form of a cap, thus caparisoned he places himself at a convenient distance between a herd of buffaloe and a precipice proper for the purpose, which happens in many places on this river for miles together; the other indians now surround the herd on the back and flanks and at a signal agreed on all shew themselves at the same time moving forward towards the buffaloe;   the disguised indian or decoy has taken care to place himself sufficiently nigh the buffaloe to be noticed by them when they take to flight and runing before them they follow him in full speede to the precipice, the cattle behind driving those in front over and seeing them go do not look or hesitate about following untill the whole are precipitated down the precepice forming one common mass of dead an[d] mangled carcases: the decoy in the mean time has taken care to secure himself in some cranney or crivice of the clift which he had previously prepared for that purpose. the part of the decoy I am informed is extreamly dangerous, if they are not very fleet runers the buffaloe tread them under foot and crush them to death, and sometimes drive them over the precipice also, where they perish in common with the buffaloe.

we saw a great many wolves in the neighbourhood of these mangled carcases they were fat and extreemly gentle,   Capt. C. who was on shore killed one of them with his espontoon.[5] soon after we landed it began to blow & rain, and as there was no appearance of even wood enough to make our fires for some distance above we determined to remain here untill the next morning, and accordingly fixed our camp and gave each man a small dram. notwithstanding the allowance of sperits we issued did not exceed ½ [jill] pr. man several of them were considerably effected by it; such is the effects of abstaining for some time from the uce of sperituous liquors; they were all very merry.

[Clark]   MAY 30TH THURSDAY 1805

The rain commenced yesterday evining, and continued moderately through the course of the night,   more rain has now

---

[5] The espontoon was a short pike: a staff with a steel lance point at the end.

fallin than we have experienced since the 15th of September last,   the rain continued this morning, and the wind too high for us to proceed, untill about 11 oClock at which time we set out, and proceeded on with great labour,   we were obliged to make use of the Tow rope & the banks were so muddey & slipery that the men could scercely walk   not with standing we proceeded on as well as we could   wind hard from the NW.   in attempting to assend a rapid our toe cord broke & we turned without in-jurey,   those rapids or shoaley points are noumerous and difi-cuelt, one being at the mouth of every drean   Some little rain at times all day   one man assended the high countrey and it was raining & snowing on those hills,   the day has proved to be raw and cold.

We discover in several places old encampments of large bands of Indians, a fiew weeks past and appear to be makeing up the river. Those Indians we believe to be the Blackfoot Inds. or Menitares who inhabit the heads of the Saskashowin & north of this place. and trade a little in the *Fort de Prarie* establishments.

[Lewis]   FRIDAY MAY 31st 1805. —

This morning we proceeded at an early hour with the two perogues leaving the canoes and crews to bring on the meat of the two buffaloe that were killed last evening and which had not been brought in as it was late and a little off the river. soon after we got under way it began to rain and continued untill meridian when it ceased but still remained cloudy through the ballance of the day. The obstructions of rocky points and riffles still continue as yester-day; at those places the men are compelled to be in the water even to their armpits, and the water is yet very could, and so frequent are those point that they are one fourth of their time in the water, added to this the banks and bluffs along which they are obliged to pass are so slippery and the mud so tenacious that they are unable to wear their mockersons, and in that situation draging the heavy burthen of a canoe and walking acasionally for several hundred yards over the sharp fragments of rocks which tumble from the clifts and garnish the borders of the river; in short their labour is incredibly painfull and great, yet those faithfull fellows bear it without a murmur. The toe rope of the white perogue, the only

one indeed of hemp, and that on which we most depended, gave
way today at a bad point, the perogue swung and but slightly
touched a rock; yet was very near overseting; I fear her evil gennii
will play so many pranks with her that she will go to the bottomm
some of those days.

The hills and river Clifts which we passed today exhibit a most
romantic appearance. The bluffs of the river rise to the hight of
from 2 to 300 feet and in most places nearly perpendicular; they
are formed of remarkable white sandstone which is sufficiently soft
to give way readily to the impression of water;   two or thre thin
horizontal stratas of white freestone, on which the rains or water
make no impression, lie imbeded in these clifts of soft stone near
the upper part of them;   the earth on the top of these Clifts is
a dark rich loam, which forming a graduly ascending plain extends
back from ½ a mile to a mile where the hills commence and rise
abruptly to a hight of about 300 feet more. The water in the course
of time in decending from those hills and plains on either side of
the river has trickled down the soft sand clifts and woarn it into
a thousand grotesque figures, which with the help of a little immagination and an oblique view, at a distance are made to represent
eligant ranges of lofty freestone buildings, having their parapets well
stocked with statuary; collumns of various sculpture both grooved
and plain, are also seen supporting long galleries in front of those
buildings;   in other places on a much nearer approach and with
the help of less immagination we see the remains or ruins of eligant buildings; some collumns standing and almost entire with
their pedestals and capitals; others retaining their pedestals but
deprived by time or accident of their capitals, some lying prostrate
an broken othe[r]s in the form of vast pyramids of connic structure bearing a serees of other pyramids on their tops becoming less
as they ascend and finally terminating in a sharp point. nitches
and alcoves of various forms and sizes are seen at different hights
as we pass. the thin stratas of hard freestone intermixed with the
soft sandstone seems to have aided the water in forming this curious
scenery. As we passed on it seemed as if those seens of visionary
inchantment would never have and [an] end; for here it is too that
nature presents to the view of the traveler vast ranges of walls of
tolerable workmanship,   so perfect indeed are those walls that I
should have thought that nature had attempted here to rival the

human art of masonry had I not recollected that she had first began her work. These walls rise to the hight in many places of
100 feet, are perpendicular, with two regular faces and are from
one to 12 feet thick, each wall retains the same thickness at top
which it possesses at bottom.

SUNDAY JUNE 2ND 1805.

The wind blew violently last night and was attended by a slight
shower of rain; the morning was fair and we set out at an early
hour. imployed the chord as usual the greater part of the day. the
courant was strong tho' regular, and the banks afforded us good
toeing. the wind was hard and against us yet we proceeded with
infinitely more ease than the two precedeing days. The river bluffs
still continue to get lower and the plains leveler and more extensive; the timber on the river increases in quantity. Game becomeing more abundant this morning and I thought it best now to
loose no time or suffer an opportunity to escape in providing the
necessary quantity of Elk's skins to cover my leather boat which I
now expect I shall be obliged to use shortly.[6] Accordingly I walked
on shore most of the day with some of the hunters for that purpose
and Killed 6 Elk 2 buffale 2 Mule deer and a bear,   these anamals were all in good order we therefore took as much of the meat
as our canoes and perogues could conveniently carry. the bear
was very near catching Drewyer; it also pursued Charbono who
fired his gun in the air as he ran but fortunately eluded the vigi-
lence of the bear by secreting himself very securely in the bushes
untill Drewyer finally killed it by a shot in the head; the [only]
shot indeed that will conquer the farocity of those tremendious
anamals. we came too on the Lard. side in a handsome bottom of
small cottonwood timber opposite to the entrance of a very considerable river; but it being too late to ex[a]mine these rivers
minutely to night we determined to remain here untill the morning, and as the evening was favourable to make some observations.[7]

6 The expedition was carrying an invention of Lewis's, a collapsible iron
framework for a boat, which he expected to cover with hides and use when the
perogues became impracticable.
7 This is the stream which the Minnetarees had called the River That Scolds
All the Others and which Lewis and Clark supposed they had passed on
May 8. Observe, in the next entry, how it at once creates a crucial problem.

MONDAY JUNE 3RD 1805.

This morning early we passed over and formed a camp on the point formed by the junction of the two large rivers. here in the course of the day I continued my observations. An interesting question was now to be determined; which of these rivers was the Missouri, or that river which the Minnetares call *Amahte Arzzha* or Missouri, and which they had discribed to us as approaching very near to the Columbia river. to mistake the stream at this period of the season, two months of the traveling season having now elapsed, and to ascend such stream to the rocky Mountain or perhaps much further before we could inform ourselves whether it did approach the Columbia or not, and then be obliged to return and take the other stream would not only loose us the whole of this season but would probably so dishearten the party that it might defeat the expedition altogether. convinced we were that the utmost circumspection and caution was necessary in deciding on the stream to be taken. to this end an investigation of both streams was the first thing to be done; to learn their widths, debths, comparative rappidity of their courants and thence the comparitive bodies of water furnished by each; accordingly we dispatched two light canoes with three men in each up those streams; we also sent out several small parties by land with instructions to penetrate the country as far as they conveniently can permitting themselves time to return this evening and indeavour if possible to discover the distant bearing of those rivers by ascending the rising grounds.

between the time of my A. M. and meridian [observations] Capt. C. & myself stroled out to the top of the hights in the fork of these rivers from whence we had an extensive and most inchanting view;   the country in every derection around us was one vast plain in which innumerable herds of Buffalow were seen attended by their shepperds the wolves; the solatary antelope which now had their young were distributed over it's face; some herds of Elk were also seen;   the verdure perfectly cloathed the ground, the weather was pleasant and fair;   to the South we saw a range of lofty mountains which we supposed to be a continuation of the S. Mountains, stretching themselves from S. E. to N. W. terminating abbrubtly about S. West from us; [8] these were partially covered

8 Probably the Highwood Mountains, near Great Falls, Montana.

with snow;   behind these Mountains and at a great distance, a second and more lofty range of mountains appeared to strech across the country in the same direction with the others, reaching from West, to the N of N. W.,[9] where their snowey tops lost themselves beneath the horizon. this last range was perfectly covered with snow. the direction of the rivers could be seen but little way, soon loosing the break of their channels, to our view, in the common plain. on our return to camp we boar a little to the left and discovered a handsome little river falling into the N. fork on Lard. side about 1½ Mls. above our camp. this little river has as much timber in it's bottoms as either of the larger streams.

we took the width of the two rivers, found the left hand or S. fork 372 yards and the N. fork 200. The no[r]th fork is deeper than the other but it's courant not so swift; it's waters run in the same boiling and roling manner which has uniformly characterized the Missouri throughout it's whole course so far; it's waters are of a whitish brown colour very thick and terbid, also characteristic of the Missouri; while the South fork is perfectly transparent runds very rappid but with a smoth unriffled surface it's bottom composed of round and flat smooth stones like most rivers issuing from a mountainous country. the bed of the N. fork composed of some gravel but principally mud; in short the air & character of this river is so precisely that of the missouri below that the party with very few exceptions have already pronounced the N. fork to be the Missouri; myself and Capt. C. not quite so precipitate have not yet decided but if we were to give our opinions I believe we should be in the minority, certain it is that the North fork gives the colouring matter and character which is retained from hence to the gulph of Mexico. I am confident that this river rises in and passes a great distance through an open plain country   I expect that it has some of it's sou[r]ces on the Eastern side of the rocky mountain South of the Saskashawan, but that it dose not penetrate the first range of these Mountains. and that much the greater part of it's sources are in a northwardly direction towards the lower and middle parts of the Saskashawan in the open plains. convinced I am that if it penetrated the Rocky Mountains to any great distance it's waters would be clearer unless it should run an immence distance indeed after leaving those mountains through these level

9 Perhaps the Big Belt Mountains.

plains in order to acquire it's turbid hue. what astonishes us a little is that the Indians who appeared to be so well acquainted with the geography of this country should not have mentioned this river on wright hand if it be not the Missouri; *the river that scolds at all others,* as they call it if there is in reallity such an one, ought agreeably to their account, to have fallen in a considerable distance below, and on the other hand if this right hand or N. fork be the Missouri I am equally astonished at their not mentioning the S. fork which they must have passed in order to get to those large falls which they mention on the Missouri. thus have our cogitating faculties been busily employed all day.

Those who have remained at camp today have been busily engaged in dressing skins for cloathing, notwithstanding that many of them have their feet so mangled and bruised with the stones and rough ground over which they passed barefoot, that they can scarcely walk or stand; at least it is with great pain they do either. for some days past they were unable to wear their mockersons; they have fallen off considerably, but nothwithstanding the difficulties past, or those which seem now to menace us, they still remain perfectly cheerful. In the evening the parties whom we had sent out returned agreeably to instructions. The parties who had been sent up the rivers in canoes informed that they ascended some distance and had then left their canoes and walked up the rivers a considerable distance further barely leaving themselves time to return; the North fork was not so rappid as the other and afforded the easiest navigation of course; six (7) feet appeared to be the shallowest water of the S. Branch and 5 feet that of the N. Their accounts were by no means satisfactory nor did the information we acquired bring us nigher to the decision of our question or determine us which stream to take.

Capt. C. and myself concluded to set out early the next morning with a small party each, and ascend these rivers untill we could perfectly satisfy ourselves of the one, which it would be most expedient for us to take on our main journey to the Pacific. accordingly it was agreed that I should ascend the right hand fork and he the left. I gave orders to Serj. Pryor Drewyer, Shields, Windsor, Cruzatte and La Page to hold themselves in readiness to accompany me in the morning. Capt. Clark also selected Reubin & Joseph Fields, Sergt. Gass, Shannon and his black man York, to accompany him. we agreed to go up those rivers one day and a halfs march or further if it should appear necessary to satisfy us more fully of the point in question. I take my Octant with me also, this I confide [to] La Page.

In accordance with this decision they set off the next day, Lewis to travel up the northern fork and Clark up the southern fork till they can be sure. Clark is sure on June 5, being convinced that the south fork leads to the Mountains.

[Clark]   JUNE 5TH WEDNESDAY 1805

Some little rain & snow last night the mountains to our S E. covered with snow this morning   air verry cold & raining a little,   we saw 8 buffalow opposit, the made 2 attempts to cross, the water being so swift they could not,   about the time we were setting out *three* white bear approached our camp   we killed the three & eate part of one & set out & proceeded on N. 20° W 11 miles   struck the river at maney places in this distance to a ridge on the N. Side from the top of which I could plainly see a mountain to the South & W covered with Snow at a long distance,   The mountains opposit to us to the S.E. is also covered with snow this morning. a high ridge from those mountains approached the river on the S E side forming some clifts of hard dark Stone. From the ridge at which place I struck the river last, I could discover that the river run west of south a long distance, and has a strong rapid current,   as this river continued its width debth & rapidity and the course west of south, going up further would be useless,   I deturmined to return,   marked my name in a tree N. side near the ridge where the little river brakes thro'

Lewis has to travel farther before coming to a conclusion.

[Lewis]   THURSDAY JUNE 6TH 1805.

I now became well convinced that this branch of the Missouri had it's direction too much to the North for our rout to the Pacific, and therefore determined to return the next day after taking an observation of the °'s Meridian Altitude in order to fix the latitude of the place.[10] The forepart of the last evening was fair but in the latter part of the night clouded up and contnued so with short intervals of sunshine untill a little before noon when the whole horizon was overcast, and I of course disappointed in making the observation which I much wished. I had sent Sergt. Pryor and Windsor early this morning with orders to procede up the river to some commanding eminence and take it's bearing as far as possible. in the mean time the four others and myself were busily engaged in making two rafts on which we purposed descending the river; we had just completed this work when Sergt. Pryor and Windsor returned, it being about noon;   they reported that they had proceded from hence S 70. W 6 M. to the summit of a commanding eminence from whence the river on their left was about 2½ miles distant; that a point of it's Lard. bluff, which was visible boar S 80. W. distant about 15 Ms.; that the river on their left bent gradually arround to this point, and from thence seemed to run Northwardly. we now took dinner and embarcked with our plunder and five Elk's skins on the rafts but were soon convinced that this mode of navigation was hazerdous particularly with those rafts they being too small and slender. we wet a part of our baggage and were near loosing one of our guns; I therefore determined to abandon the rafts and return as we had come, by land. I regretted much being obliged to leave my Elk's skins, which I wanted to assist in forming my leather boat; those we had prepared at Fort Mandan being injured in such manner that they would not answer.

FRIDAY JUNE 7TH 1805. —

It continued to rain almost without intermission last night and as I expected we had a most disagreable and wrestless night. Our camp possessing no allurements, we left our watery beads at an early hour and continued our rout down the river. it still continues to rain the wind hard from N. E. and could. the grownd remarkably, slipry, insomuch that we were unable to walk on the sides of the

10 This way would have taken him to Marias Pass.

bluffs where we had passed as we ascended the river. notwithstanding the rain that has now fallen the earth of these bluffs is not wet to a greater debth than 2 inches; in it's present state it is precisely like walking over frozen growned which is thawed to small debth and slips equally as bad. this clay not only appears to require more water to saturate it as I before observed than any earth I ever observed but when saturated it appears on the other hand to yeald it's moisture with equal difficulty.

In passing along the face of one of these bluffs today I sliped at a narrow pass of about 30 yards in length and but for a quick and fortunate recovery by means of my espontoon I should been precipitated into the river down a craggy pricipice of about ninety feet. I had scarcely reached a place on which I could stand with tolerable safety even with the assistance of my espoontoon before I heard a voice behind me cry out god god Capt. what shall I do   on turning about I found it was Windsor who had sliped and fallen abut the center of this narrow pass and was lying prostrate on his belley, with his wright hand arm and leg over the precipice while he was holding on with the left arm and foot as well as he could which appeared to be with much difficulty. I discovered his danger and the trepidation which he was in gave me still further concern for I expected every instant to see him loose his strength and slip off; altho' much allarmed at his situation I disguised my feelings and spoke very calmly to him and assured him that he was in no kind of danger, to take the knife out of his belt behind him with his wright hand and dig a hole with it in the face of the bank to receive his wright foot which he did and then raised himself to his knees;   I then directed him to take off his mockersons and to come forward on his hands and knees holding the knife in one hand and the gun in the other   this he happily effected and escaped. those who were some little distance bhind returned by my orders and waded the river at the foot of the bluff where the water was breast deep.

it was useless we knew to attempt the plains on this part of the river in consequence of the numerous steep ravines which intersected and which were quite as bad as the river bluffs. we therefore continued our rout down the river sometimes in the mud and water of the bottom lands, at others in the river to our breasts and when the water became so deep that we could not wade we cut footsteps in the face of the steep bluffs with our knives and proceded. we continued our disagreeable march th[r]ough the rain mud and water untill late in the evening having traveled only about 18 Miles, and encamped in an old Indian stick lodge which afforded us a dry and comfortable shelter. during the day we had killed six deer some of them in very good order altho' none of them had yet entirely discarded their winter coats. we had reserved and brought with us a good supply of the best peices; we roasted and eat a hearty supper of our venison not having taisted a mosel before during the day; I now laid myself down on some willow boughs to a comfortable nights rest, and felt indeed as if I was fully repaid for the toil and pain of the day, so much will a good shelter, a dry bed, and comfortable supper revive the sperits of the waryed, wet and hungry traveler.

CHAPTER X

FROM MARIA'S RIVER TO THE GREAT FALLS OF THE MISSOURI

[Lewis]   SATURDAY JUNE 8TH 1805. —

The whole of my party to a man except myself were fully pe[r]suaided that this river was the Missouri, but being fully of opinion that it was neither the main stream, nor that which it would be advisable for us to take, I determined to give it a name and in honour of Miss Maria W——d. [Wood] called it Maria's River. it is true that the hue of the waters of this turbulent and troubled stream but illy comport with the pure celestial virtues and amiable qualifications of that lovely fair one; but on the other hand it is a noble river; one destined to become in my opinion an object of contention between the two great powers of America and Great Britin with rispect to the adjustment of the Northwestwardly boundary of the former;   and that it will become one of the most interesting branc[h]es of the Missouri in a commercial point of view, I have but little doubt, as it abounds with anamals of the fur kind, and most probably furnishes a safe and direct communication to that productive country of valuable furs exclusively enjoyed at present by the subjects of his Britanic Majesty; in adition to which it passes through a rich fertile and one of the most beatifully picteresque countries that I ever beheld, through the wide expanse of which, innumerable herds of living anamals are seen, it's borders garnished with one continued garden of roses, while it's lofty and open forrests are the habitation of miriads of the feathered tribes who salute the ear of the passing traveler with their wild and simple, yet s[w]eet and cheerfull melody. I arrived at camp about 5 OClock in the evening much fatiegued, where I found Capt. Clark and the ballance of the party waiting our return with some anxiety for our safety having been absent near two days longer than we had engaged to return.

Capt Clark ploted the courses of the two rivers as far as we had ascended them. I now began more than ever to suspect the varacity of Mr. Fidler [1] or the correctness of his instruments. for I see that Arrasmith in his late map of N. America has laid down a remarkable mountain in the chain of the Rocky mountains called the tooth nearly as far South as Latitude 45°, and this is said to be from the discoveries of Mr. Fidler. we are now within a hundred miles of the Rocky Mountains, and I find from my observation of the 3rd Inst that the latitude of this place is 47° 24' 12".8. the river must therefore turn much to the South between this and the rocky Mountain to have permitted Mr. Fidler to have passed along the Eastern border of these mountains as far S. as nearly 45° without even seeing it. but from hence as far as Capt. C. had ascended the S. fork or Missouri being the distance of 55 Miles it's course is S. 29° W. and it still appeared to bear considerably to the W. of South as far as he could see it. I think therefore that we shall find that the Missouri enters the rocky mountains to the North of 45°   we did take the liberty of placing his discoveries or at least the Southern extremity of them about a degree further N. in the sketh which we sent on to the government this spring mearly from the Indian information of the bearing from Fort Mandan of the entrance of the Missouri into the Rocky Mountains, and I reather suspect that actual observation will take him at least one other degree further North.

Sunday June 9th 1805.

We determined to deposite at this place the large red perogue all the heavy baggage which we could possibly do without and some

1 Peter Fidler was a Hudson's Bay Company surveyor and explorer. In 1791 and 1792 he made a brilliant journey up the south branch of the Saskatchewan River and along the foot of the Canadian Rockies, in Alberta. He was the first white man to penetrate that region but he did not get as far south as 49°, still less 45°. The Hudson's Bay Company turned over many of his data to the London cartographer Aaron Arrowsmith, who made use of them when drawing his famous map of North America, first published in 1795. Lewis and Clark appear to have had with them copies of the 1795 and 1796 editions of the Arrowsmith map: on both of them Fidler's route is, as Lewis's entry indicates, shown far to the south of his actual journey.

provision, salt, tools powder and Lead &c; accordingly we set some hands to diging a hole or cellar for the reception of our stores. these holes in the ground or deposits are called by the engages *cashes (cachés);*   today we examined our maps, and compared the information derived as well from them as [from] the Indians and fully settled in our minds the propryety of addopting the South fork for the Missouri, as that which it would be most expedient for us to take. Those ideas as they occurred to me I indevoured to impress on the minds of the party all of whom except Capt. C. being still firm in the belief that the N. Fork was the Missouri and that which we ought to take;   they said very cheerfully that they were ready to follow us any wher we thought proper to direct but that they still thought that the other was the river and that they were affraid that the South fork would soon termineate in the mountains and leave us at a great distance from the Columbia. finding them so determined in this beleif, and wishing that if we were in an error to be able to detect it and rectify it as soon as possible it was agreed between Capt. C. and myself that one of us should set out with a small party by land up the South fork and continue our rout up it until we found the falls or reached the snowy Mountains by which means we should be enabled to determine this question prety accurately. this expedition I prefered undertaking as Capt. C. [is the] best waterman &c and determined to set out the day after tomorrow;   I wished to make some further observations at this place, and as we had determined to leave our blacksmith's bellows and tools here it was necessary to repare some of our arms, and particularly my Airgun the main spring of which was broken, before we left this place. these and some other preperations will necessarily detain us two perhaps three days. I felt myself very unwell this morning and took a portion of salts from which I feel much relief this evening. most of the men are busily engaged dressing skins for cloathing. In the evening Cruzatte gave us some music on the violin and the men passed the evening dancing singing &c and were extreemly cheerfull.

[Clark]   JUNE 10TH MONDAY 1805

we drew up our large Perogue into the middle of a small Island in the North fork and covered her with bushes after makeing her fast to the trees, branded several trees to prevent the Indians injureing her,   Sahcahgagweâ our Indian woman verry sick   I blead her,   we deturmined to assend the South fork, and Capt Lewis selects 4 men George Drewyer, Gibson, Jo. Fields & S. Gutrich to accompany him & deturmine to set out in the morning. The after noon or night cloudy   some rain,   river riseing a little.

[Lewis]   TUESDAY JUNE 11TH 1805.

at 8 A.M. I swung my pack, and set forward with my little party. proceeded to the point where Rose River a branch [of] Maria's River approaches the Missouri so nearly. from this hight we discovered a herd of Elk on the Missouri just above us to which we desended and soon killed four of them. we butchered them and hung up the meat and skins in view of the river, but before the meal was prepared I was taken with such violent pain in the intestens that I was unable to partake of the feast of marrowbones. my pain still increased and towards evening was attended with a high fever; finding myself unable to march, I determined to prepare a camp of some willow boughs and remain all night. having brought no medicine with me I resolved to try an experiment with some simples; and the Choke cherry which grew abundantly in the bottom first struck my attention; I directed a parsel of the small twigs to be geathered striped of their leaves, cut into pieces of about 2 Inches in length and boiled in water untill a strong black decoction of an astringent bitter tast was produced; at sunset I took a point [pint] of this decoction and abut an hour after repeated the d[o]ze   by 10 in the evening I was entirely releived from pain and in fact every symptom of the disorder forsook me; my fever abated, a gentle perspiration was produced and I had a comfortable and refreshing nights rest. Goodrich who is remarkably fond of fishing caught several douzen fish of two different species.

THURSDAY JUNE 13TH 1805.

we again ascended the hills of the river and gained the level country. the country through which we passed for the first six miles tho' more roling than that we had passed yesterday might still with propryety be deemed a level country; our course as yesterday was generally S.W.   the river from the place we left it appeared to make a considerable bend to the South. from the extremity of this roling country I overlooked a most beatifull and level plain of great extent or at least 50 or sixty miles; in this there were infinitely more buffaloe than I had ever before witnessed at a view. nearly in the direction I had been travling or S.W. two curious mountains presented themselves of square figures, the sides rising perpendicularly to the hight of 250 feet and appeared to be formed of yellow clay; their tops appeared to be level plains;   fearing that the river boar to the South and that I might pass the falls if they existed between this an[d] the snowey mountains I altered my course nea[r]ly to the South leaving those insulated hills to my wright and proceeded through the plain;   I sent Feels on my right and Drewyer and Gibson on my left with orders to kill some meat and join me at the river where I should halt for dinner. I had proceded on this course about two miles with Goodrich at some distance behind me whin my ears were saluted with the agreeable sound of a fall of water and advancing a little further I saw the spray arrise above the plain, like a collumn of smoke which would frequently dispear again in an instant caused I presume by the wind which blew pretty hard from the S.W. I did not however loose my direction to this point which soon began to make a roaring too tremendious to be mistaken for any cause short of the great falls of the Missouri. here I arrived about 12 OClock having traveled by estimate about 15. Miles.

I took my position on the top of some rocks about 20 feet high opposite the center of the falls. this chain of rocks appear once to have formed a part of those over which the waters tumbled, but in the course of time has been seperated from it to the distance of 150 yards lying prarrallel to it and a butment against which the water after falling over the precipice beats with great fury;   this barrier extends on the right to the perpendicular clift which forms that board [border] of the river, but to the distance of 120 yards next to the clift it is but a few feet above the level of the water, and here the water in very high tides appears to pass in a channel of 40 yds. next to the higher part of the ledg of rocks; on the left it extends within 80 or ninty yards of the lard. Clift which is also perpendicular; between this abrupt extremity of the ledge of rocks and the perpendicular bluff the whole body of water passes with incredible swiftness.

immediately at the cascade the river is about 300 yds. wide; about ninty or a hundred yards of this next the Lard. bluff is a smoth even sheet of water falling over a precipice of at least eighty feet,   the remaining part of about 200 yards on my right formes the grandest sight I ever beheld,   the hight of the fall is the same of the other but the irregular and somewhat projecting rocks below receives the water in it's passage down and brakes it into a perfect white foam which assumes a thousand forms in a moment sometimes flying up in jets of sparkling foam to the hight of fifteen or twenty feet and are scarcely formed before large roling bodies of the same beaten and foaming water is thrown over and conceals them. in short the rocks seem to be most happily fixed to present a sheet of the whitest beaten froath for 200 yards in length and about 80 feet perpendicular. the water after decending strikes against the butment before mentioned or that on which I stand and seems to reverberate and being met by the more impetuous courant they roll and swell into half formed billows of great hight which rise and again disappear in an instant. this butment of rock defends a handsome little bottom of about three acres which is deversified and agreeably shaded with some cottonwood trees; in the lower extremity of the bottom there is a very thick grove of the same kind of trees which are small, in this wood there are several Indian lodges formed of sticks. a few small cedar grow near the ledge of rocks where I rest. below the point of these rocks at a small distance the river is divided by a large rock which rises several feet above the water, and extends downwards with the stream for about 20 yards.

about a mile before the water arrives at the pitch it decends very rappidly, and is confined on the Lard. side by a perpendicular clift of about 100 feet,   on Stard. side it is also perpendicular for about three hundred yards above the pitch where it is then broken by the discharge of a small ravine, down which the buffaloe have a large beaten road to the water, for it is but in very few places that these anamals can obtain water near this place owing to the steep and inaccessible banks. about 300 yards below me there is another butment of solid rock with a perpendicular face and abot 60 feet high which projects from the Stard. side at right angles to the distance of 134 yds. and terminates the lower part nearly of the bottom before mentioned; there being a passage arround the end of this butment between it and the river of about 20 yards; here the river again assumes it's usual width soon spreading to near 300 yards but still continues it's rappidity. from the reflection of the sun on the sprey or mist which arrises from these falls is a beautifull rainbow produced which adds not a little to the beauty of this majestically grand senery.

after wrighting this imperfect discription I again viewed the falls and was so much disgusted with the imperfect idea which it conveyed of the scene that I determined to draw my pen across it and begin agin, but then reflected that I could not perhaps succeed better than pening the first impressions of the mind;   I retired to the shade of a tree where I determined to fix my camp for the present and dispatch a man in the morning to inform Capt. C. and the party of my success in finding the falls and settle in their minds all further doubts as to the Missouri. the hunters now arrived loaded with excellent buffaloe meat and informed me that they had killed three very fat cows about ¾ of a mile from hence. I walked down the river about three miles to discover if possible some place to which the canoes might arrive or at which they might be drawn on shore in order to be taken by land above the falls; but returned without effecting either of these objects; the river was one continued sene of rappids and cascades which I readily perceived could not be encountered with our canoes, and the Clifts still retained their perpendicular structure and were from 150 to 200 feet high; in short the river appears here to have woarn a channel in the process of time through a solid rock.

My fare is really sumptuous this evening; buffaloe's humps, tongues and marrowbones, fine trout parched meal pepper and salt, and a good appetite; the last is not considered the least of the luxuries.

FRIDAY JUNE 14TH 1805.

[On this day Lewis reconnoiters the remaining four falls and the intervening rapids which compose the Great Falls, going as far as Sun River, which during the winter they had named Medicine River. He is on the way to the latter as the entry continues.[2]]

I decended the hill and directed my course to the bend of the

---

[2] There are five falls in a ten-mile stretch of the river. The highest one is the farthest upstream and is the one which Lewis here calls the Great Falls. Power installations have entirely destroyed their beauty and spectacle.

Missouri near which there was a herd of at least a thousand buffaloe; here I thought it would be well to kill a buffaloe and leave him untill my return from the river and if I then found that I had not time to get back to camp this evening to remain all night here there being a few sticks of drift wood lying along shore which would answer for my fire, and a few s[c]attering cottonwood trees a few hundred yards below which would afford me at least the semblance of a shelter. under this impression I scelected a fat buffaloe and shot him very well, through the lungs; while I was gazeing attentively on the poor anamal discharging blood in streams from his mouth and nostrils, expecting him to fall every instant, and having entirely forgotten to reload my rifle, a large white, or reather brown bear, had perceived and crept on me within 20 steps before I discovered him;   in the first moment I drew up my gun to shoot, but at the same instant recolected that she was not loaded and that he was too near for me to hope to perform this opperation before he reached me, as he was then briskly advancing on me; it was an open level plain, not a bush within miles nor a tree within less than three hundred yards of me; the river bank was sloping and not more than three feet above the level of the water; in short there was no place by means of which I could conceal myself from this monster untill I could charge my rifle;   in this situation I thought of retreating in a brisk walk as fast as he was advancing untill I could reach a tree about 300 yards below me, but I had no sooner terned myself about but he pitched at me, open mouthed and full speed,   I ran about 80 yards and found he gained on me fast, I then run into the water   the idea struk me to get into the water to such debth that I could stand and he would be obliged to swim, and that I could in that situation defend myself with my espontoon; accordingly I ran haistily into the water about waist deep, and faced about and presented the point of my espontoon,   at this instant he arrived at the edge of the water within about 20 feet of me; the moment I put myself in this attitude of defence he sudonly wheeled about as if frightened, declined to combat on such unequal grounds, and retreated with quite as great precipitation as he had just before pursued me.

As soon as I saw him run in that manner I returned to the shore and charged my gun, which I had still retained in my hand throughout this curious adventure. I saw him run through the level open plain about three miles, till he disappeared in the woods on medecine river; during the whole of this distance he ran at full speed, sometimes appearing to look behind him as if he expected pursuit. I now began to reflect on this novil occurence and indeavoured to account for this sudden retreat of the bear. I at first thought that perhaps he had not smelt me bofore he arrived at the waters edge so near me, but I then reflected that he had pursued me for about 80 or 90 yards before I took the water and on examination saw the grownd toarn with his tallons immediately on the imp[r]ession of my steps; and the cause of his allarm still remains with me misterious and unaccountable. so it was and I felt myself not a little gratifyed that he had declined the combat. my gun reloaded I felt confidence once more in my strength.

in returning through the level bottom of Medecine river and about 200 yards distant from the Missouri, my direction led me directly to an anamal that I at first supposed was a wolf; but on nearer approach or about sixty paces distant I discovered that it was not,   it's colour was a brownish yellow; it was standing near it's burrow, and when I approached it thus nearly, it couched itself down like a cat looking immediately at me as if it designed to spring on me. I took aim at it and fired,   it instantly disap- peared in it's burrow;   I loaded my gun and ex[a]mined the place which was dusty and saw the track from which I am still further convinced that it was of the tiger kind. whether I struck it or not I could not determine, but I am almost confident that I did; my gun is true and I had a steady rest by means of my espontoon, which I have found very serviceable to me in this way in the open plains. It now seemed to me that all the beasts of the neighbourhood had made a league to distroy me, or that some fortune was disposed to amuse herself at my expence, for I had not proceded more than three hundred yards from the bur- row of this tyger cat, before three bull buffaloe, which wer feeding with a large herd about half a mile from me on my left, seperated from the herd and ran full speed towards me,   I thought at least to give them some amusement and altered my direction to meet them; when they arrived within a hundred yards they mad[e] a halt, took a good view of me and retreated with precipitation. I then continued my rout homewards passed the buffaloe which I had killed, but did not think it prudent to remain all night at this place which really from the succession of curious adventures wore the impression on my mind of inchantment; at sometimes for a moment I thought it might be a dream, but the prickley pears which pierced my feet very severely once in a while, particularly after it grew dark, convinced me that I was really awake, and that it was necessary to make the best of my way to camp.

[Clark]   JUNE 14TH FRIDAY 1805

a fine morning   the Indian woman complaining all night & excessively bad this morning. her case is somewhat dangerous. two men with the Tooth ake 2 with Tumers, & one man with a Tumor & a slight fever   passed the camp Capt. Lewis made the 1st night at which place he had left part of two bear their skins &c.   three men with Tumers went on shore and stayed out all night   one of them killed 2 buffalow, a part of which we made use of for brackfast,   the current excesevely rapid more so as we assend   we find great dificuelty in getting the Perogue & canoes up in safety, canoes take in water frequently,   at 4 oClock this evening Jo: Fields returned from Capt. Lewis with a letter for me,   Capt Lewis dates his letter from the Great falls of the Missouri, which Fields informs me is about 20 miles in advance & about 10 miles above the place I left the river the time I was up last week.

JUNE THE 15TH SATTURDAY 1805

we set out at the usial time and proceeded on with great dificuelty as the river is more rapid we can hear the falls this morning verry distinctly. our Indian woman sick & low spirited   I gave her the bark & apply it exteranely to her region which revived her much. the current excessively rapid and dificuelt to assend   great numbers of dangerous places, and the fatigue which we have to encounter is incretiatable   the men in the water from morning untill night hauling the cord & boats walking on sharp rocks and round sliperery stones which alternately cut their feet & throw them down, notwith standing all this dificuelty they go with great chearfulness,　　aded to those dificuelties the rattle snakes inumerable & require great caution to prevent being bitten.

[Lewis]　　　　　　　　　　　　　　　　SUNDAY JUNE 16TH 1805.

at noon the men arrived and shortly after I set out with them to rejoin the party,　　we took with us the dryed meat consisting of about 600 lbs. and several douzen of dryed trout. about 2 P.M. I reached the camp found the Indian woman extreemly ill and much reduced by her indisposition. this gave me some concern as well for the poor object herself, then with a young child in her arms, as from the consideration of her being our only dependence for a friendly negociation with the Snake Indians on whom we depend for horses to assist us in our portage from the Missouri to the columbia river. I now informed Capt. C. of my discoveries with rispect to the most proper side for our portage, and of it's great length, which I could not estimate at less than 16 miles. Capt. C. had already sent two men this morning to examine the country on the S. side of the river; he now passed over with the party to that side and fixed a camp about a mile blow the entrance of a Creek where there was a sufficient quantity of wood for fuel, an article which can be obtained but in few places in this neighbourhood.

after discharging the loads four of the canoes were sent back to me, which by means of strong ropes we hawled above the rappid and passed over to the south side from whence the water not being rappid we can readily convey them into the creek by means of which we hope to get them on the high plain with more ease. one of the small canoes was left below this rappid in order to pass and repass the river for the purpose of hunting as well as to procure the water of the Sulpher spring, the virtues of which I now resolved to try on the Indian woman. Capt. Clark determined to set out in the morning to examine (the country) and survey the portage, and discover the best rout. as the distance was too great to think of transporting the canoes and baggage on the men's shoulders, we scelected six men, and ordered them to look out some timber this evening, and early in the morning to set about making a parsel of truck wheels in order to convey our canoes and baggage over the portage. we determined to leave the white perogue at this place, and substitute the Iron boat, and also to make a further deposit of a part of our stores. I found that two dozes of barks and opium which I had given her [Sacajawea] since my arrival had produced an alteration in her pulse for the better; they were now much fuller and more regular. I caused her to drink the mineral water altogether. she complains principally of the lower region of the abdomen, I therefore continued the cataplasms of barks and laudnumn which had been previously used by my friend Capt. Clark. I beleive her disorder originated principally from an obstruction of the mensis in consequence of taking could.

MONDAY JUNE 17TH 1805.

Capt. Clark set out early this morning with five me[n] to examine the country and survey the river and portage as had been concerted last evening. I set six men at work to p[r]epare four sets of truck wheels with couplings, toungs and bodies, that they might either be used without the bodies for transporting our canoes, or with them in transporting our baggage. we were fortunate enough to find one cottonwood tree just below the entrance of portage creek that was large enough to make our carriage wheels about 22 Inchis in diameter; fortunate I say because I do not beleive that we could find another of the same size perfectly sound within 20 miles of us. the cottonwood which we are obliged to employ in the other parts of the work is extreemly illy calculated for it being soft and brittle. we have made two axeltrees of the mast of the white perogue, which I hope will answer tolerably well tho' it is reather small. The Indian woman much better today; I have still continued the same course of medecine; she is free from pain clear of fever, her pulse regular, and eats as heartily as I am willing to permit her of broiled buffaloe well seasoned with pepper and salt and rich soope of the same meat; I think therefore that there is every rational hope of her recovery.

[Clark]   JUNE 18TH TUESDAY 1805

this evening, one man A. Willard going for a load of meat at 170 yards distance on an Island was attact by a white bear and verry near being caught, prosued within 40 yards of the camp where I was with one man   I collected 3 others of the party and prosued the bear (who had prosued my track from a buffalow I had killed on the Island at about 300 yards distance and chance[d] to meet Willard) for fear of his attacking one man Colter at the lower point of the Island. before we had got down the bear had allarmed the man and prosued him into the water,   at our approach he retreated, and we relieved the man in the water,   I saw the bear but the bushes was so thick that I could not shoot him and it was nearly dark,

JUNE 20TH THURSDAY 1805

I direct stakes to be cut to stick up in the praries to show the way for the party to transport the baggage &c. &c.   we set out early on the portage,   soon after we set out it began to rain and continued a short time   we proceeded on thro' a tolerable leavel plain, and found the hollow of a Deep riveen to obstruct our rout   as it could not be passed with canos & baggage for some distance above the place we struck it. I examined it for some time and finding it late deturmined to strike the river & take its Course & distance to camp which I accordingly did   the wind hard from the S.W.   a fair after noon,   the river on both sides cut with raveens some of which is passes thro steep clifts into the river,   the countrey above the falls & up the Medison river is level, with low banks,   a chain of mountains to the west some part of which particller those to the N W. & S W are covered with snow and appear verry high. I saw a rattle snake in an open plain 2 miles from any creek or woods. When I arrived at camp found all well with quantites of meet,   the canoes Capt Lewis had carried up the Creek 1¾ miles to a good place to assend the land & taken up. Not haveing seen the Snake Indians or knowing in fact whither to calculate on their friendship or hostillity, we have conceived our party sufficiently small, and therefore have concluded not to dispatch a canoe with a part of our men to St. Louis as we have entended early in the Spring.[3]   we fear also that

3 In the report sent to Jefferson from Fort Mandan, the captains had announced their intention of sending another one from the Great Falls. The failure of one to arrive convinced the settlements that the whole party had perished.

such a measure might also discourage those who would in such case remain, and migh possibly hazard the fate of the expedition. We have never hinted to any one of the party that we had such a scheem in contemplation, and all appear perfectly to have made up their minds to Succeed in the expedition or perish in the attempt. We all believe that we are about to enter on the most perilous and dificuelt part of our Voyage, yet I see no one repineing; all appear ready to meet those dificuelties which await us with resolution and becomeing fortitude.

the Mountains to the N.W. and West of us are still entirely covered are white and glitter with the reflection of the sun. I do not believe that the clouds that pervale at this season of the year reach the summits of those lofty mountains; and if they do the probability is that they deposit snow only for there has been no proceptable diminution of the snow which they contain since we first saw them. I have thought it probable that these mountains might have derived their appellation of *Shineing Mountains,* from their glittering appearance when the sun shines in certain directions on the snow which cover them.

Dureing the time of my being on the Plains and above the falls I as also all my party repeatedly heard a nois which proceeded from a Direction a little to the N. of West, a loud [noise] and resembling precisely the discharge of a piece of ordinance of 6 pounds at the distance of 5 or six miles. I was informed of it several times by the men J: Fields particularly before I paid any attention to it, thinking it was thunder most probably which they had mistaken. at length walking in the plains yesterday near the most extreem S. E bend of the River above the falls I heard this *nois* very distinctly, it was perfectly calm clear and not a cloud to be seen, I halted and listened attentively about two hour[s] dureing which time I heard two other discharges, and took the direction of the sound with my pocket compass which was as nearly West from me as I could estimate from the sound. I have no doubt but if I had leasure I could find from whence it issued. I have thought it probable that it might be caused by running water in some of the caverns of those emence mountains, on the principal of the blowing caverns; but in such case the sounds would be periodical and regular, which is not the case with this, being sometimes heard once only and at other times several discharges in quick succession. it is heard also at different times of the **day** and night. I am at a great loss to account for this Phenomenon. I well recollect hereing the Minitarees say that those Rocky mountains make a great noise, but they could not tell me the cause, neither could they inform me of any remarkable substance or situation in these mountains which would autherise a conjecture of a probable cause of this noise.

CHAPTER XI

PORTAGING AROUND THE GREAT FALLS

From June 21 to July 15 the expedition remained at the Great Falls, transporting the equipment across the portage and preparing for the next stage of the journey. It was a period of strenuous labor — the most strenuous so far — and of even more violent weather.

Clark surveyed what he considered the easiest route for the portage. Its upper end was near the base camp they made opposite an island which they called White Bear because it was infested with grizzlies, upstream from the mouth of Medicine (Sun) River. From Portage Creek, where they beached the boats, concealed the remaining pirogue, and laboriously carried the dugouts up the side of the sunken valley, the distance was 18¼ miles. It was a comparatively level stretch but was carpeted with cactus. The party's only footwear by now was moccasins, and they had learned to sew to them double soles of parfleche, buffalo rawhide, as the Plains Indians did. (The moccasins of forest tribes did not have stiff soles.) But no rawhide was thick enough to turn the cactus and everyone had viciously sore feet.

Over this portage they hauled both the dugouts and the equipment on the two crude truck frames which they had made of cottonwood. (When the tongue, hounds, and an axle of one broke, they were replaced with the somewhat tougher wood of willow trees, which grew abundantly along the streams.) After the necessary detachments for hunting and the construction of Lewis's collapsible bullboat had been made, there were just enough men left to haul the trucks. Clark wrote that "the men has to haul with all their strength wate & art, maney times every man all

147

*catching the grass & knobes [tufts? hummocks?] & stones with their
hands to give them more force in drawing on the Canoes & Loads,
and notwithstanding the coolness of the air in high presperation
and every halt, those not employed in reparing the course, are
asleep in a moment, maney limping from the soreness of their
feet some become fa[i]nt for a fiew moments, but no man complains all go chearfully on. to state the fatigues of this party would
take up more of the journal than other notes which I find scarcely
time to set down."*

On his way to the Great Falls Lewis had noted the abundance
of buffalo and grizzlies. One herd of the former, Clark said,
numbered ten thousand, and there were so many of the latter and
they became so "troublesome that I [Lewis] do not think it prudent
to send one man alone on an errand of any kind." One charged
Joseph Fields and he was able to escape only by leaping into the
river and crouching under an overhanging bank. Another chased
Drewyer for a hundred yards after he had shot it through the heart.
But all this game — there were large herds of elk and antelope as
well — meant that the party lived high. After leaving the Missouri,
especially in the Bitterroot Mountains where there was no game
at all and along the Columbia where they had to live on salmon,
they were to remember this area with the longing of hungry men.
The captains were prepared for the short rations to come, having
been told by the Minnetarees that there were no buffalo west of
the mountains.

"I have scarcely experienced a day since my first arrival in this
quarter," Lewis wrote, "without experiencing some novel occurrence among the party or witnessing the appearance of some uncommon object." One unpleasant feature was the sudden storms.
They filled the runoff channels that gullied the portage route and
made the clayey soil an impassable glue. Sometimes the rains were
preceded by hail so fierce that everyone had to take shelter from
it. Once "at Capt. Lewis camp" it was "7 Inches in circumference
& waied 3 ounces, fortunately for us it was not so large [along the
portage route], if it had [been] we should most certainly have
fallen victims to its rage as the men were mostly naked, and but a
few with hats or any covering on their heads." And, "the same
cloud will discharge hail in one part hail and rain in another and
rain only in a third within the space of a few miles." Or a gale

*would blow up and chill everyone; at least once "the men informed
me that they hoisted a sail in the canoe and it had driven her
along on the truck wheels."*

*Everyone was wearing buckskin — rather elkskin — shirts and
breeches now. A supply of them had to be built up in this wonder-
land of game for there was no telling what lay ahead. There was
a brief pause for celebration on July 4 but it had a melancholy
overtone: the grog which the captains issued was the last alcohol
they had.*

*And Lewis's prized bullboat on an iron frame proved a failure.
He kept a detachment working on it steadily and he invented many
expedients, but when it was finally put in the water, it leaked too
badly to be used. He attributed the failure to lack of proper gum
to pay the seams and to the fact that his awls were of the wrong
shape and so the holes they made (through which the sinew that
joined the hides was threaded) could not be filled. It is likely however, that hides could not have been, in any circumstances, satisfactorily attached to a rigid frame. Lewis had been enamored of
his invention and was much depressed. He had expected the boat
to be able to carry at least four tons of lading, and two new dugouts
had to be made to take its place. It was characteristic of this vexa-
tious place that axe helves kept breaking, thirteen of them in one
day. Wild cherry proved to be the best wood to make replace-
ments of.*

*(The text that follows has been much abbreviated. The chapter
runs fifty-one pages in the* Journals.*)*

[Lewis]   WEDNESDAY JUNE 26TH 1805.

The Musquetoes are extreemly troublesome to us. This morning early I dispatched J. Fields and Drewyer in one of the canoes
up the river to hunt Elk. set Frazier at work to sew the skins
together for the covering of the boat. Sheilds and Gas I sent over
the river to surch a small timbered bottom on that side opposite
to the Islands for timber and bark; and myself I assign the duty
of cook as well for those present as for the party which I expect
again to arrive this evening from the lower camp. I collected my
wood and water, boiled a large quantity of excellent dryed buffaloe
meat and made each man a large suet dumpling by way of a treat.

about 4 P.M. Shields and Gass returned with a better supply of timber than they had yet collected tho' not by any means enough. they brought some bark principally of the Cottonwood which I found was too brittle and soft for the purpose; for this article I find my only dependence is the sweet willow which has a tough & strong bark. Shields and Gass had killed seven buffaloe in their absence, the skins of which and a part of the best of the meat they brought with them. if I cannot procure a sufficient quantity of Elk's skins I shall substitute those of the buffaloe. late in the evening the party arrived with two more canoes and another portion of the baggage. Whitehouse one of them much heated and fortiegued on his arrivall d[r]ank a very hearty draught of water and was taken almost instantly extreemly ill. his pulse were full and I therefore bled him plentifully from which he felt great relief. I had no other instrument with which to perform this operation but my penknife, however it answered very well. the wind being from S.E. today and favourable the men made considerable progress by means of their sails.

At the lower Camp. Capt. C. scelected the articles to be deposited in the cash consisting of my desk which I had left for that purpose and in which I had left some books, my specimens of plants minerals &c. collected from fort Mandan to that place. also 2 Kegs of Pork, ½ a Keg of flour 2 blunderbushes, ½ a keg of fixed ammunition and some other small articles belonging to the party which could be dispenced with. deposited the swivel and carriage under the rocks a little above the camp near the river.

THURSDAY JUNE 27TH 1805.

The party returned early this morning for the remaining canoe and baggage; Whitehouse was not quite well this morning I therefore detained him and about 10 A.M. set him at work with Frazier sewing the skins together for the boat; Shields and gass continued the operation of shaving and fiting the horizontall bars of wood in the sections of the boat; the timber is so crooked and indifferent that they make but little progress, for myself I continued to act the part of cook in order to keep all hands employed. some Elk came near our camp and we killed 2 of them. at 1 P.M. a cloud arrose to the S.W. and shortly after came on attended with

violent Thunder Lightning and hail &c.   soon after this storm
was over Drewyer and J. Fields returned. they were about 4 miles
above us during the storm, the hail was of no uncommon size
where they were. They had killed 9 Elk and three bear during
their absence; one of the bear was the largest by far that we have
yet seen; the skin appear[s] to me to be as large as a common ox.
while hunting they saw a thick brushey bottom on the bank of
the river where from the tracks along shore they suspected that
there were bare concealed;   they therefore landed without making any nois and climbed a leaning tree and placed themselves
on it's branches about 20 feet above the ground,   when thus
securely fixed they gave a [w]hoop and this large bear instantly
rushed forward to the place from whence he had heard the human
voice issue, when he arrived at the tree he made a short paus and
Drewyer shot him in the head. it is worthy of remark that these
bear never climb. the fore feet of this bear measured nine inches
across and the hind feet eleven and ¾ in length exclusive of the
tallons and seven inches in width. a bear came within thirty yards
of our camp last night and eat up about thirty weight of buffaloe
suit which was hanging on a pole. my dog seems to be in a
constant state of alarm with these bear and keeps barking all night.

[Clark]   June 29th Satturday 1805

a little rain verry early this morning after[wards] clear, finding
that the Prarie was so wet as to render it impossible to pass on to
the end of the portage, deturmined to send back to the top of the
hill at the creek for the remaining part of the baggage left at that
place yesterday, leaveing one man to take care of the baggage at
this place. I deturmined my self to proceed to the falls and take
the river,   according we all set out,   I took my servent
& one man,   Chabono our Interpreter & his Squar accompanied,   soon after I arrived at the falls, I perceived a cloud
which appeared black and threaten imediate rain,   I looked out
for a shelter but could see no place without being in great danger
of being blown into the river if the wind should prove as turbelant
as it is at some times   about ¼ of a mile above the falls I obsd
a Deep riveen in which was shelveing rocks under which we took
shelter near the river and placed our guns the compass &c. &c.
under a shelving rock on the upper side of the creek, in a place

which was verry secure from rain,   the first shower was moderate
accompanied with a violent wind, the effects of which we did not
feel,   soon after a torrent of rain and hail fell more violent
than ever I saw before,   the rain fell like one voley of water
falling from the heavens and gave us time only to get out of the
way of a torrent of water which was Poreing down the hill in the
River with emence force tareing everything before it takeing with
it large rocks & mud,   I took my gun & shot pouch in my left
hand, and with the right scrambled up the hill pushing the Interpreters wife (who had her child in her arms) before me, the
Interpreter himself makeing attempts to pull up his wife by the
hand much scared and nearly without motion,   we at length
reached the top of the hill safe where I found my servent in
serch of us greatly agitated, for our wellfar. before I got out of
the bottom of the reveen which was a flat dry rock when I entered
it, the water was up to my waste & wet my watch,   I scercely got
out before it raised 10 feet deep with a torrent which [was]
turrouble to behold, and by the time I reached the top of the hill,
at least 15 feet water,

I derected the party to return to the camp at the run as fast as
possible to get to our Lode where Clothes could be got to cover
the child whose clothes were all lost, and the woman who was but
just recovering from a severe indisposition, and was wet and cold,
I was fearfull of a relaps   I caused her as also the others of the
party to take a little spirits, which my servent had in a canteen,
which revived [them] verry much. on arrival at the camp on the
willow run met the party who had returned in great confusion
to the run leaveing their loads in the Plain, the hail & wind being
so large and violent in the plains, and them naked, they were much
brused, and some nearly killed   one knocked down three times,
and others without hats or any thing on their heads bloody &
complained verry much,   I refreshed them with a little grog.
Soon after the run began to rise and rose 6 feet in a fiew minets.
I lost at the river in the torrent the large *compas,* an elegant fusee,
Tomahawk *Humbrallo,* [Umbrella] shot pouch & horn with
powder & Ball, Mockersons, & the woman lost her childs Bear [1] &
Clothes bedding &c.   The Compass, is a serious loss, as we have
no other large one.

[1] The rawhide shoulder pack and cradle in which the child was carried.

[Lewis]   SUNDAY JUNE 30TH 1805.

I begin to be extremely impatient to be off as the season is now
waisting a pace   nearly three months have now elapsed since
we left Fort Mandan and not yet reached the Rocky Mountains   I am therefore fully preswaded that we shall not reach
Fort Mandan again this season if we even return from the ocean
to the Snake Indians.

[Clark]   JUNE 30TH SUNDAY 1805

The two men dispatched in serch of the articles lost yesterday
returned and brought the compass which they found in the mud
& stones near the mouth of the reveen,   no other articles found,
the place I sheltered under filled up with hugh Rocks.

[Lewis]   TUESDAY JULY 9TH 1805

we corked [caulked] the canoes and put them in the water and
also launched the boat; she lay like a perfect cork on the water.
five men would carry her with the greatest ease. I now directed
seats to be fixed in her and oars to be fitted. the men loaded the
canoes in readiness to depart. just at this moment a violent wind
commenced and blew so hard that we were obliged to unload the
canoes again; a part of the baggage in several of them got wet
before it could be taken out. the wind continued violent untill
late in the evening, by which time we discovered that a greater
part of the composition had seperated from the skins and left
the seams of the boat exposed to the water and she leaked in such
manner that she would not answer. I need not add that this
circumstance mortifyed me not a little; and to prevent her leaking
without pi[t]ch was impossible with us, and to obtain this article
was equally impossible, therefore the evil was irraparable   I now
found that the section formed of the buffaloe hides on which some
hair had been left, answered much the best purpose; this leaked
but little and the parts which were well covered with hair about
⅛th of an inch in length retained the composition perfectly and
remained sound and dry. from these circumstances I am preswaided, that had I formed her with buffaloe skins singed not

quite as close as I had done those I employed, that she would have answered even with this composition. but to make any further experiments in our present situation seemed to me madness; the buffaloe had principally dserted us, and the season was now advancing fast. I therefore relinquished all further hope of my favorite boat and ordered her to be sunk in the water, that the skins might become soft in order the better to take her in peices tomorrow and deposited the iron fraim at this place as it could probably be of no further service to us.

FRIDAY JULY 12TH 1805.

Musquetoes extreemly troublesome to me today nor is a large knat less troublesome which does not sting, but attacks the eye in swarms and compells us to brush them off or have our eyes filled with them.

[Clark]   JULY 14TH SUNDAY 1805

a fine morning calm and worm   Musquetors & Knats verry troublesom. The Canoes arrive at 12. oClock & unloade to Dry &c.   finished & Lanced [launched] the 2 Canoes,   Some rain this afternoon. all prepareing to Set out on tomorrow.

CHAPTER XII

FROM THE GREAT FALLS TO THE THREE FORKS

[Lewis]   MONDAY JULY 15TH 1805

We arrose very early this morning, assigned the canoes their loads and had it put on board. we now found our vessels eight in number all heavily laden, notwithstanding our several deposits; tho' it is true we have now a considerable stock of dryed meat and grease. we find it extreemly difficult to keep the baggage of many of our men within reasonable bounds; they will be adding bulky articles of but little uce or value to them. At 10 A.M. we once more saw ourselves fairly under way much to my joy and I beleive that of every individual who compose the party. I walked on shore and killed 2 Elk near one of which the party halted and dined. in order to lighten the burthen of the canoes I continued my walk all the evening and took our only invaledes Potts an La Page with me. we passed the river near where we dined and just above the entrance of a beautifull river 80 yards wide which falls in on the Lard. side   in honour of Mr. Robert Smith the Secretary of the Navy we called Smith's River. Drewyer wo[u]nded a deer which ran into the river   my dog pursued caught it drowned it and brought it to shore at our camp. the prickly pear is now in full blume and forms one of the beauties as well as the greatest pests of the plains. the sunflower is also in blume and is abundant. this plant is common to every part of the Missouri from it's entrance to this place. the lambsquarter, wild coucumber, sand rush and narrow dock are also common here. the river is from 100 to 150 yds. wide. more timber on the river than below the falls for a great distance. on

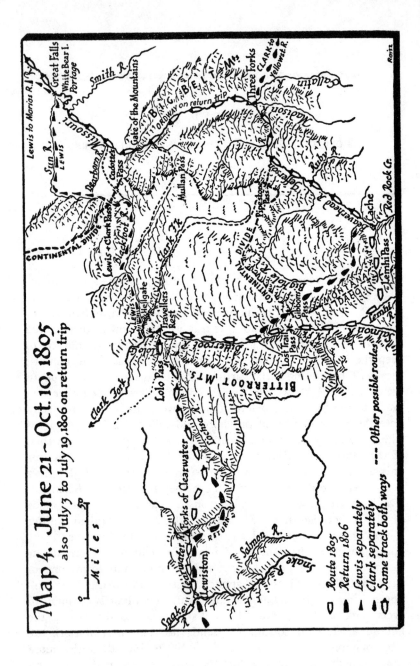

Map 4. June 21 ~ Oct. 10, 1805
also July 3 to July 19, 1806 on return trip

the banks of the river there are many large banks of sand much elivated above the plains on which they ly and appear as if they had been collected in the course of time from the river by the almost incessant S.W. winds; they always appear on the sides of the river opposite to those winds.

TUESDAY JULY 16TH 1805.

Drewyer killed a buffaloe this morning near the river and we halted and breakfasted on it. here for the first time I ate of the small guts of the buffaloe cooked over a blazing fire in the Indian stile without any preperation of washing or other clensing and found them very good. After breakfast I determined to leave Capt. C. and party, and go on to the point where the river enters the Rocky Mountains and make the necessary observations against their arrival; accordingly I set out with the two invalleds Potts and LaPage and Drewyer.

[Clark]   JULY 16TH TUESDAY 1805

a fair morning after a verry cold night, heavy dew,   dispatched one man back for an ax left a fiew miles below, and Set out early   passed about 40 Small Camps, which appeared to be abandoend about 10 or 12 days,   Suppose they were Snake Indians,   a fiew miles above I Saw the poles Standing in their position of a verry large lodge of 60 feet Diameter, & the appearance of a number of Leather Lodges about,   this Sign was old & appeared to have been last fall   great number of buffalow   the river is not So wide as below from 100 to 150 yards wide & Deep Crouded with Islands & Crooked   Some scattering timber on its edge Such as Cotton wood Cotton willow, willow and box elder, the S[h]rubs are arrow wo[o]d red wood, Choke cherry, red berries, Goose beries, Sarvis buries, red & yellow Currents a Sp[e]cie of Shomake &c.

I camped on the head of a Small Island near the Stard. Shore at the Rockey Mountains [1]   this Range of mountains appears to run NW & SE and is about 800 feet higher than the Water in the river faced with a hard black rock   the current of the River

1 At the foot of the Big Belt Mountains.

from the Medison river to the Mountain is gentle, bottoms low and extensive, and its General Course is S. 10° W. about 30 miles on a direct line

JULY 17TH WEDNESDAY 1805

Set out early this morning and crossed the rapid at the Island cald. pine rapid with Some dificuelty,   at this rapid I came up with Capt. Lewis & partey   took a Medn. altitude & we took Some Luner Observations &c. and proceeded on,   the emence high Precipces oblige all the party to pass & repass the river from one point to another [2]   the river confined in maney places in a verry narrow chanel from 70 to 120 yards wide bottoms narrow without timber and maney places the Mountain[s] approach on both Sides,   The river crooked bottoms narrow, Clifts high and Steep,   I assended a Spur of the Mountain, which I found to be highe & dificuelt of axcess, Containing Pitch Pine & Covered with grass   Scercely any game to be seen. The yellow Current now ripe also the fussey [fuzzy] red Choke Cheries getting ripe. Purple Current[s] are also ripe. Saw Several Ibix or mountain rams to day

[Lewis]   THURSDAY JULY 18TH 1805.

previous to our departure saw a large herd of the Bighorned ana-mals on the immencely high and nearly perpendicular clift opposite to us; on the fase of this clift they walked about and bounded from rock to rock with apparent unconcern where it appared to me that no quadruped could have stood, and from which had they made one false step the must have been precipitated at least a 500 feet. this anamal appears to frequent such precepices and clifts where in fact they are perfectly secure from the pursuit of the wolf, bear, or even man himself. at the distance of 2½ miles we passed the en-trance of a considerable river on the Stard. side; about 80 yds wide being nearly as wide as the Missouri at that place. it's current is rapid and water extreamly transparent; the bed is formed of small smooth stones of flat rounded or other figures. it's bottoms are narrow but possess as much timber as the Missouri. the country is

---

2 They are in the long Missouri Canyon.

mountainous and broken through which it passes. it appears as if it might be navigated but to what extent must be conjectural. this handsome bold and clear stream we named in honor of the Secretary of war calling it Dearborn's river.

as we were anxious now to meet with the Sosonees or snake Indians as soon as possible in order to obtain information relative to the geography of the country and also if necessary, some horses we thought it better for one of us either Capt. C. or myself to take a small party & proceed on up the river some distance before the canoes, in order to discover them, should they be on the river before the daily discharge of our guns, which was necessary in procuring subsistence for the party, should allarm and cause them to retreat to the mountains and conceal themselves, supposing us to be their enemies who visit them usually by the way of this river. accordingly Capt. Clark set out this morning after breakfast with Joseph Fields, Pots and his servant York. we proceeded on tolerably well; the current stronger than yesterday; we employ the cord and oars principally tho' sometimes the setting pole.

[Clark]   July 18th Thursday 1805

after brackfast I took J. Fields Potts & my Servent proceeded on. the Country So Hilley that we gained but little of the Canoes untill in the evening I passed over a mountain on an Indian rode by which rout I cut off Several Miles of the Meanderings of the river.   the roade which passes this mountain is wide and appears to have been dug in maney places,   we camped on a Small run of Clear cold water,   musquitors verry troublesom the forepart of the evening   I Saw maney fine Springs & Streams of running water which Sink & rise alternately in the Valies   the water of those Streams are fine,   those streams which run off into the river are damed up by the beaver from near ther mouthes up as high as I could See up them

[Lewis]   Friday July 19th 1805.

this morning we set out early and proceeded on very well tho' the water appears to encrease in volocity as we advance. the current has been strong all day and obstructed with some rapids, tho' these are but little broken by rocks and are perfectly safe. the river deep and from 100 to 150 yds. wide. I walked along shore today and killed an Antelope. wh[en]ever we get a view of the lofty summits of the mountains the snow presents itself, altho' we are almost suffocated in this confined valley with heat. this evening we entered much the most remarkable clifts that we have yet seen. these clifts rise from the waters edge on either side perpendicularly to the hight of 1200 feet. every object here wears a dark and gloomy aspect. the tow[er]ing and projecting rocks in many places seem ready to tumble on us. the river appears to have forced it's way through this immence body of solid rock for the distance of 5¾ Miles and where it makes it's exit below has th[r]own on either side vast collumns of rocks mountains high.

the river appears to have woarn a passage just the width of it's channel or 150 yds.   it is deep from side to side nor is there in the 1st 3 Miles of this distance a spot except one of a few yards in extent on which a man could rest the soal of his foot. several fine springs burst out at the waters edge from the interstices of the rocks. it happens fortunately that altho' the current is strong it is not so much so but what it may be overcome with the oars for there is hear no possibility of using either the cord or Setting pole. it was late in the evening before I entered this place and was obliged to continue my rout untill sometime after dark before I found a place sufficiently large to encamp my small party; at length such an one occurred on the lard. side where we found plenty of lightwood and pich pine. this rock is a black grannite below and appears to be of a much lighter colour above and from the fragments I take it to be flint of a yellowish brown and light creemcoloured yellow. from the singular appearance of this place I called it the *gates of the rocky mounatains.*

[Clark]   JULY 19TH FRYDAY 1805

I proceeded on in an Indian Parth   river verry Crooked passed over two mountains   Saw Several Indians Camps which they have left this Spring. Saw trees Peeled & found poles &c.   at 11 oC. I saw a gange of Elk, as we had no provision Concluded to kill Some. Killd. two and dined being oblige[d] to substitute dry buffalow dung in place of wood,   this evening passed over a

Cream Coloured flint which [has] roled down from the Clifts into the bottoms, the Clifts Contain flint a dark grey Stone & a redish brown intermixed and no one Clift is solid rock,   all the rocks of everry description is in Small pi[e]ces, appears to have been broken by Some Convulsion   my feet is verry much brused & cut walking over the flint, & constantly stuck full [of] Prickley pear thorns,   I puled out 17 by the light of the fire to night   Musqutors verry troublesom.

[Lewis]   SATURDAY 20TH 1805

about 10 A.M. we saw the smoke arrise as if the country had been set on fire up the valley of this creek about 7 Mi. distant   we were at a loss to determine whether it had been set on fire by the natives as a signall among themselves on discovering us, as is their custom or whether it had been set on fire by Capt. C. and party accedentally. the first however proved to be the fact, they had unperceived by us discovered Capt. Clark's party or mine, and had set the plain on fire to allarm the more distant natives (*heard a gun from Cap C's party & fled quite over the mountains, thinking it their enemies Blackfoots.*) and fled themselves further into the interior of the mountains. this evening we found the skin of an Elk and part of the flesh of the anamal which Capt. C. had left near the river at the upper side of the valley where he assended the mountain with a note informing me of his transactions and that he should pass the mounts which lay just above us and wate our arrival at some convenient place on the river. the other elk which Capt. C. had killed we could not find. about 2. in the evening we had passed through a range of low mountains and the country became more open again, tho' still broken and untimbered and the bottoms not very extensive. we encamped on the Lard. side near a spring on a high bank   the prickly pears are so abundant that we could scarcely find room to lye.

SUNDAY JULY 21ST 1805.

Set out early this morning and passed a bad rappid where the river enters the mountain about 1.M. from our camp of last evening   the Clifts high and covered with fragments of broken rocks. the current strong; we employed the toe rope principally; and also the poles as the river is not now so deep but reather wider and much more rapid our progress was therefore slow and laborious. we saw three swans this morning, which like the geese have not yet recovered the feathers of the wing and could not fly   we killed two of them the third escaped by diving and passed down with the current; they had no young ones with them therefore presume they do not breed in this country   these are the first we have seen on the river for a great distance. we daily see great numbers of gees with their young which are perfectly feathered except the wings which are deficient in both young and old. My dog caught several today, as he frequently dose. the young ones are very fine, but the old gees are poor and unfit for uce. saw several of the large brown or sandhill Crain today with their young. the young Crain is as large as a turkey and cannot fly they are of a bright red bey colour or that of the common deer at this season. the grass near the river is lofty and green that of the hill sides and high open grounds is perfectly dry and appears to be scorched by the heat of the sun. the country was rough mountainous & much as that of yesterday untill towards evening when the river entered a beautifull and extensive plain country of about 10 or 12 miles wide which extended upwards further that the eye could reach   this valley is bounded by two nearly parallel ranges of high mountains which have their summits partially covered with snow. below the snowey region pine succeeds and reaches down their sides in some parts to the plain but much the greater portion of their surfaces is uncovered with timber and expose either a barren sterile soil covered with dry parched grass or black and rugged rocks. the river immediately on entering this valley assumes a different aspect and character, it spreads to a mile and upwards in width, crouded with Islands, some of them large; is shallow enough for the use of the seting pole in almost every part and still more rappid than before.

[Clark]   JULY 21ST SUNDAY 1805

a fine morning   our feet So brused and cut that I deturmined to delay for the Canoes, & if possible kill Some meet by the time they arrived,   Small birds are plenty. Some Deer, Elk, Goats, and

Ibex; no buffalow in the Mountains. Those mountains are high
and a great perportion of them rocky: Vallies firtile   I observe on the highest pinecals of some of the Mountains to the West
Snow lying in Spots   Some Still Further North are covered with
Snow and cant be Seen from this point

[Lewis]   MONDAY JULY 22D 1805.

The river being divided into such a number of channels by both
large and small Island[s] that I found it impossible to lay it down
[the courses] correctly following one channel only in a canoe and
therefore walked on shore   I met with great quantities of a smal
onion about the size of a musquit ball and some even larger; they
were white crisp and well flavored   I geathered about half a
bushel of them before the canoes arrived. I halted the party for
breakfast and the men also geathered considerable quantities of
those onions. [In the afternoon] I kiled an otter which sunk to the
bottom on being shot, a circumstance unusual with that anamal.
the water was about 8 feet deep yet so clear that I could see it at
the bottom; I swam in and obtained it by diving. I halted the
party here for dinner;   I placed my thermometer in a good shade
as was my custom about 4. P. M. and after dinner set out without
it and had proceeded near a mile before I recollected it   I sent
Sergt. Ordway back for it, he found it and brought it on. the murcury stood at 80 a. 0   this is the warmest day except one which
we have experienced this summer. The Indian woman recognizes
the country and assures us that this is the river on which her relations live, and that the three forks are at no great distance. this
peice of information has cheered the sperits of the party who now
begin to console themselves with the anticipation of shortly seeing
the head of the missouri yet unknown to the civilized world.

late this evening we arrived at Capt. Carks camp on the stard.
side of the river; we took them on board with the meat they had
collected and proceeded a short distance and encamped on an Island   Capt. Clark's party had killed a deer and an Elk today
and ourselves one deer and an Antelope only. altho' Capt C. was
much fatiegued his feet yet blistered and soar he insisted on pursuing his rout in the morning nor weould he consent willingly to
my releiving him at that time by taking a tour of the same kind.

finding him anxious I readily consented to remain with the
canoes,   he ordered Frazier and Jo. & Reubin Fi[e]lds to hold
themselves in readiness to accompany him in the morning. Sharbono was anxious to accompany him and was accordingly permitted. the musquetoes and knats more than usually troublesome
to us this evening.

TUESDAY JULY 23RD 1805

Capt. Clark left us with his little party of 4 men and continued
his rout on the Stard. side of the river. about 10'OCk. A.M. we
came up with Drewyer who had seperated from us yesterday evening
and lay out all night not being able to find where we had encamped. he had killed 5 deer which we took on board   I ordered
the canoes to hoist their small flags in order that should the indians see us they might discover that we were not Indians, nor
their enemies. we made great uce of our seting poles and cords the
uce of both which the river and banks favored. most of our small
sockets were lost, and the stones were so smooth that the points of
their poles sliped in such manner that it increased the labour of
navigating the canoes very considerably,

[Clark]   JULY 23RD TUESDAY 1805

proceeded on an Indian roade through a wide Vallie which the
Missouri Passes about 25 miles & camped on the bank of the
river,   I saw no fresh Sign of Indians to day   Great number
of antelopes Some Deer & a large Gangue of Elk

[Lewis]   WEDNESDAY JULY 24TH 1805.

the adjacent mountains [3] commonly rise so high as to conceal the
more distant and lofty mountains from our view. I fear every day
that we shall meet with some considerable falls or obstruction in
the river notwithstanding the information of the Indian woman
to the contrary who assures us that the river continues much as we
see it. I can scarcely form an idea of a river runing to great extent

[3] The "adjacent" mountains are the Big Belts to the east and the Bridger
Range to the southeast. To the west is a small range called the Elk Horns.

through such a rough mountainous country without having it's stream intersepted by some difficult and dangerous rappids or falls. we daily pass a great number of small rappids or riffles which decend one to or 3 feet in 150 yards but we are rarely incommoded with fixed or standing rocks and altho' strong rappid water are nevertheless quite practicable & by no means dangerous.

our trio of pests still invade and obstruct us on all occasions, these are the Musquetoes eye knats and prickley pears, equal to any three curses that ever poor Egypt laiboured under, except the *Mahometant yoke*. the men complain of being much fortiegued. their labour is excessively great. I occasionly encourage them by assisting in the labour of navigating the canoes, and have learned to *push a tolerable good pole* in their fraize.

[Clark]   JULY 25TH THURSDAY 1805

a fine morning   we proceeded on a fiew miles to the three forks of the Missouri   those three forks are nearly of a Size, the North fork appears to have the most water and must be Considered as the one best calculated for us to assend [4]   Middle fork is quit as large about 90 yds. wide. The South fork is about 70 yds wide & falls in about 400 yards below the midle fork   those forks appear to be verry rapid & contain some timber in their bottoms which is verry extencive. on the North Side the Indians have latterly Set the Praries on fire, the Cause I can't account for. I saw one horse track going up the river, about four or 5 days past. after Brackfast (which we made on the ribs of a Buck killed yesterday), I wrote a note informing Capt. Lewis the rout I intended to take, and proceeded on up the main North fork thro' a Vallie, the day verry hot,

We Campd on the Same Side   we assended Starboard 20 miles on a direct line up the N. fork. *Shabono* our Interpreter nearly tired [out] one of his ankles falling him. The bottoms are extencive and tolerable land covered with tall grass & prickley pears. The hills & mountains are high Steep & rockey. The river verry much di-

---

[4] Presently to be named Jefferson River. Clark's almost instantaneous decision to ascend is due not only to its greater flow, but to the fact that it leads more directly than the others toward the western mounains. The Three Forks are the beginning of the Missouri River, 2464.4 miles above the mouth.

vided by Islands, Some Elk Bear & Deer and Some small timber on the Islands. Great quantities of Currents red, black, yellow, Purple, also Mountain Currents which grow on the Sides of Clifts, inferior in taste to the others haveing Sweet pineish flaver and are red & yellow, Choke Cheries, Boin roche, and the red buries also abound. Musquetors verry troublesom untill the Mountain breeze sprung up, which was a little after night.

[Lewis] FRIDAY JULY 26TH 1805.

current strong with frequent riffles; employ the cord and seting poles, the oars scarcely ever being used the high lands are thin meagre soil covered with dry low sedge and a species of grass also dry the seeds of which are armed with a long twisted hard beard at the upper extremity while the lower point is a sharp subulate, firm point beset at it's base with little stiff bristles standing with their points in a contrary direction to the subulate point to which they answer as a barb and serve also to pres it forward when onece entered a small distance. these barbed seed penetrate our mockersons and leather legings and give us great pain untill they are removed. my poor dog suffers with them excessively, he is constantly binting and scratching himself as if in a rack of pain.

[Clark] JULY 26TH FRIDAY 1805

I deturmined to leave Shabono & one man who had Sore feet to rest & proceed on with the other two to the top of a mountain 12 miles distant west from thence view the river & vallies a head, we with great dificuelty & much fatigue reached the top at 11 oClock from the top of this mountain I could see the Course of the North fork about 10 miles meandering through a Vallie but could discover no Indians or sign which was fresh. I could also See Some distance up the Small River below, and also the Middle fork. after Satisfying my Self returned to the two me[n] by an old Indian parth, on this parth & in the Mountain we came to a Spring of excessive cold water, which we drank reather freely of as we were almost famished; not with Standing the precautions of wetting my face, hands, & feet I soon felt the effects of the water. We Contind thro a Deep Vallie without a Tree to Shade us scorching with heat to the men who had killed a pore Deer, I was fatigued my feet with Several blisters & Stuck with *prickley pears.* I eate but verry little   deturmined to cross to the Middle fork and examine that. we crossed the Missouri which was divided by a verry large Island   the first Part was knee deep the other waste deep & very rapid,[5]   I felt my Self verry unwell & took up Camp on the little river 3 miles above its mouth & near the place it falls into the bottom   a fiew Drops of rain this evening.

[Lewis]   Saturday July 27th 1805. —

We set out at an early hour and proceeded on but slowly the current still so rapid that the men are in a continual state of their utmost exertion to get on, and they begin to weaken fast from this continual state of violent exertion. at 9. A.M. at the junction of the S.E. fork of the Missouri [6] and the country opens suddonly to extensive and beatifull plains and meadows which appear to be surrounded in every direction with distant and lofty mountains;   supposing this to be the three forks of the Missouri I halted the party on the Lard. shore for breakfast. and walked up the S.E. fork about ½ mile and ascended the point of a high limestone clift from whence I commanded a most perfect view of the neighbouring country. from E. to S. between the S.E. and middle forks a distant range of lofty mountains ran their snow clad tops above the irregular and broken mountains which lie adjacent to this beautifull spot. between the middle and S.E. forks near their junction with the S.W. fork there is a handsome site for a fortification. after making a draught of the connection and meanders of these streams I decended the hill and returned to the party, took breakfast and ascended the S.W. fork 1¾ miles and encamped at a Lard. bend in a handsome level smooth plain just below a bayou, having passed the entrance to the middle fork ½ a mile. here I encamped to wait the return of Capt. Clark and to give the men a little rest which seemed absolutely necessary to them. at the junc-

---

5 From Lewis's summary of Clark's report: "Here Charbono was very near being swept away by the current and cannot swim, Capt. C. however risqued him[self] and saved his life."

6 Lewis's Southeast Fork, which he reaches first because he is coming up the river whereas Clark traveled overland, is Clark's South Fork, the Gallatin.

tion of the S.W. and Middle forks I found a note which had been
left by Capt. Clark informing me of his intended rout, and that he
would rejoin me at this place provided he did not fall in with any
fresh sighn of Indians, in which case he intended to pursue untill
he overtook them calculating on my taking the S. W. fork, which
I most certainly prefer as it's direction is much more promising
than any other.

believing this to be an essential point in the geography of this
western part of the Continent I determined to remain at all events
untill I obtained the necessary data for fixing it's latitude Longitude &c.   after fixing my camp I had the canoes all unloaded
and the baggage stoed away and securely covered on shore, and
then permitted several men to hunt. I walked down to the middle
fork and examined and compared it with the S.W. fork but could
not satisfy myself which was the largest stream of the two, in fact
they appeared as if they had been cast in the same mould there
being no difference in character or size, therefore to call either of
these streams the Missouri would be giving it a preference w[h]ich
it's size dose not warrant as it is not larger then the other. they
are each 90 yds. wide. in these meadows I saw a number of the
duckanmalla[r]d with their young which are now nearly grown.
at 3 P.M. Capt Clark arrived very sick with a high fever on him
and much fatiegued and exhausted. he informed me that he was
very sick all last night had a high fever and frequent chills & constant aking pains in all his mustles. this morning notwithstanding
his indisposition he pursued his intended rout to the middle fork
about 8 miles and finding no recent sign of Indians rested about
an hour and came down the middle fork to this place. Capt. C.
thought himself somewhat bilious and had not had a passage for
several days; I prevailed on him to take a doze of Rushes pills,
which I have always found sovereign in such cases and to bath his
feet in warm water and rest himself. Capt. C's indisposition was
a further inducement for my remaining here a couple of days; I
therefore informed the men of my intention, and they put their
deer skins in the water in order to prepare them for dressing tomorrow.

we begin to feel considerable anxiety with rispect to the Snake
Indians. if we do not find them or some other nation who have
horses I fear the successfull issue of our voyage will be very doubt-

full or at all events much more difficult in it's accomplishment. we are now several hundred miles within the bosom of this wild and mountanous country, where game may rationally be expected shortly to become scarce and subsistence precarious without any information with rispect to the country not knowing how far these mountains continue, or wher to direct our course to pass them to advantage or intersept a navigable branch of the Columbia,   or even were we on such an one the probability is that we should not find any timber within these mountains large enough for canoes if we judge from the portion of them through which we have passed. however I still hope for the best, and intend taking a tramp myself in a few days to find these yellow gentlemen if possible. my two principal consolations are that from our present position it is impossible that the S.W. fork can head with the waters of any other river but the Columbia, and that if any Indians can subsist in the form of a nation in these mountains with the means they have of acquiring food we can also subsist.

[Lewis] SUNDAY JULY 28TH 1805.

Both Capt. C. and myself corrisponded in opinon with rispect to the impropriety of calling either of these streams the Missouri and accordingly agreed to name them after the President of the United States and the Secretaries of the Treasury and state having previously named one river in honour of the Secretaries of War and Navy. In pursuance of this resolution we called the S.W. fork, that which we meant to ascend, Jefferson's River in honor of that illustrious personage Thomas Jefferson. [*the author of our enterprize.*] the Middle fork we called Madison's River in honor of James Madison, and the S.E. Fork we called Gallitin's River in honor of Albert Gallitin [Gallatin]. the two first are 90 yards wide and the last is 70 yards. all of them run with great velocity and th[r]ow out large bodies of water. Gallitin's River is reather more rapid than either of the others, is not quite as deep but from all appearances may be navigated to a considerable distance. Capt. C. who came down Madison's river yesterday and has also seen Jefferson's some distance thinks Madison's reather the most rapid, but it is not as much so by any means as Gallitin's. the beds of all these streams are formed of smooth pebble and gravel, and their waters perfectly transparent; in short they are three noble streams. there is timber enough here to support an establishment, provided it be erected with brick or stone either of which would be much cheaper than wood as all the materials for such a work are immediately at the spot. there are several small sand-bars along the shores at no great distance of very pure sand

and the earth appears as if it would make good brick. I had all our baggage spread out to dry this morning; and the day proving warm, I had a small bower or booth erected for the comfort of Capt. C.   our leather lodge when exposed to the sun is excessively hot. all those who are not hunting altho' much fatiegued are busily engaged in dressing their skins, making mockersons lexing [leggings] &c to make themselves comfortable. the Musquetoes are more than usually troublesome, the knats are not as much so. in the evening about 4 O'Ck the wind blew hard from South West and after some little time brought on a Cloud attended with thunder and Lightning from which we had a fine refreshing shower which cooled the air considerably; the showers continued with short intervals untill after dark. in the evening the hunters all returned they had killed 8 deer and 2 Elk, some of the deer wer in excellent order.

Our present camp is precisely on the spot that the Snake Indians were encamped at the time the Minnetares of the Knife R. first came in sight of them five years since. from hence they retreated about three miles up Jeffersons river and concealed themselves in the woods,   the Minnetares pursued, attacked them, killed 4 men 4 women a number of boys, and mad[e] prisoners of all the females and four boys,   *Sah-cah-gar-we-ah* o[u]r Indian woman was one of the female prisoners taken at that time; tho' I cannot discover that she shews any immotion of sorrow in recollecting this event, or of joy in being restored to her native country; if she has enough to eat and a few trinkets to wear I believe she would be perfectly content anywhere.[1]

TUESDAY JULY 30TH 1805.

Capt. Clark being much better this morning and having completed my observations we reloaded our canoes and set out, ascending Jeffersons river. Sharbono, his woman two invalleds and myself walked through the bottom on the Lard. side of the river about 4½ miles when we again struck it at the place the woman informed us that she was taken prisoner. here we halted untill

[1] Ordway: "She tells us that she was taken in the middle of the River as she was crossing at a Shole place to make hir ascape."

Capt. Clark arrived which was not untill after one P. M. the water being strong and the river extreemly crooked. we dined and again proceeded on; as the river now passed through the woods the invalleds got on board together with Sharbono and the Indian woman; I passed the river and continued my walk on the Stard. side. saw a vast number of beaver in many large dams which they had maid. I directed my course to the high plain to the right which I gained after some time with much difficulty and waiding many beaver dams to my waist in mud and water. I would willingly have joined the canoes but the brush were so thick, the river crooked and bottoms intercepted in such manner by the beaver dams, that I found it uceless to attempt to find them, and therefore proceeded on up the river in order to intersept it where it came near the plain and woult be more collected into one channel.

at length about sunset I arrived at the river only about six miles from my calculation on a direct line from the place I had left the canoes but I thought they were still below me. I found the river was divided where I reached it by an Island and was therefore fearfull that they might pass without my seeing them, and went down to the lower point of the large island;   here I discovered a small Island, close under the shore on which I was;   I passed the narrow channel to the small island and examined the gravly bar along the edge of the river for the tracks of the men, knowing from the appearance of the river at this place that if they had passed they would have used the cord on the side where I was. I saw no tracks and was then fully convinced that they were below me. I fired my gun and hallooed but counld hear nothing of them. by this time it was getting nearly dark and a duck lit on the shore in about 40 steps of me and I killed it; having now secured my supper I looked our for a suitable place to amuse myself in combating the musquetos for the ballance of the evening. I found a parsel of drift wood at the head of the little Island on which I was and immediately set it on fire and collected some willow brush to lye on. I cooked my duck which I found very good and after eating it layed down and should have had a comfortable nights lodge but for the musquetoes which infested me all night. late at night I was awakened by the nois of some animal runing over the stoney bar on which I lay but did not see it; from the weight with which it ran I supposed it to be either an Elk or a brown bear.

WEDNESDAY JULY 31st 1805.

This morning I waited at my camp very impatiently for the arrival of Capt. Clark and party; I observed by my watch t[h]at it was 7 A. M. and they had not come in sight. I now became very uneasy and determined to wait until 8 and if they did not arrive by that time to proceed on up the river taking it as a fact that they had passed my camp some miles last evening. just as I set out to pursue my plan I discovered Charbono walking up shore some distance below me and waited untill [he] arrived   I now learnt that the canoes were behind, they arrived shortly after. their detention had been caused by the rapidity of the water and the circuitous rout of the river. they halted and breakfasted after which we all set out again and I continued my walk on the Stard. shore   the river now becomes more collected the islands tho' numerous ar generally small. the river continues rapid and is from 90 to 120 yds. wide has a considerable quantity of timber in it's bottoms. towards evening the bottoms became much narrower and the timber much more scant.

this evening just before we encamped Drewyer discovered a brown bear enter a small cops of bushes on the Lard. side; we surrounded the place and surched the brush but he had escaped in some manner unperceived but how we could not discover. nothing killed today and our fresh meat is out. when we have a plenty of fresh meat I find it impossible to make the men take any care of it, or use it with the least frugallity. tho' I expect that necessity will shortly teach them this art. the mountiains on both sides of the river at no great distance are very lofty.

We have a lame crew just now, two with tumers or bad boils on various parts of them, one with a bad stone bruise, one with his arm accedently dislocated but fortunately well replaced, and a fifth has streigned his back by slipping and falling backwards on the gunwall of the canoe. the latter is Sergt. Gass. it gives him great pain to work in the canoe in his present situation, but he thinks he can walk with convenience,   I therefore selected him as one of the party to accompany me to-morrow, being determined to go in quest of the Snake Indians. I also directed Drewyer and Charbono to hold themselves in readiness. Charbono thinks that his ankle is sufficiently recovered to stand the march but I entertain my doubts of the fact; he is very anxious to accompany me and I therefore indulge him.

AUGUST 1ST 1805 —

At half after 8 A. M. we halted for breakfast and as had been previously agreed on between Capt. Clark and myself I set out with 3 men in quest of the Snake Indians. the men I took were the two Interpreters Drewyer and Sharbono and Sergt. Gass. the rout we took lay over a rough high range of mountains on the North side of the river. the rive[r] entered these mountains a few miles above where we left it.[2] Capt. Clark recommended this rout to me from a belief that the river as soon as it past the mountains boar to the N. of W. he having a few days before asscended these mountains to a position from which he discovered a large valley passing between the mountains and which boar to the N. West. this however p[r]oved to be the inlet of a large creek which discharged itself into the river just above this range of mountains, the river bearing to the S. W.   we were therefore thrown several miles out of our rout. as soon as we discovered our mistake we directed our course to the river which we at length gained about 2 P. M. much exhausted by the heat of the day the roughness of the road and the want of water.

the mountains are extreemly bare of timber and our rout lay through the steep valleys exposed to the heat of the sun without shade and scarcely a breath of air; and to add to my fatiegue in this walk of about 11 miles I had taken a doze of glauber salts in the morning in consequence of a slight desentary with which I had been afflicted for several days; being weakened by the disorder and the opperation of the medecine I found myself almost exhausted before we reached the river. I felt my sperits much revived on our near approach to the river at the sight of a herd of Elk of which Drewyer and myself killed two. we then hurried to the river and allayed our thirst. I ordered two of the men to skin the Elk and bring the meat to the river while myself and the other prepared a fire and cooked some of the meat for our dinner. we made a comfortable meal of the Elk and left the ballance of the meat on the bank of the river [for] the party with Capt. Clark. this supply was

2 The Tobacco Root Range.

no doubt very acceptable to them as they had had no fresh meat for near two days except one beaver Game being very scarce and shy. we had seen a few deer and some goats but had not been fortunate enough to kill any of them. after dinner we resumed our march and encamped about 6 M. above on the Stard side of the river.

Shortly after I left Capt. Clark this morning he proceed on and passed through the mountains; they formed tremendious clifts of ragged and nearly perpendicular rocks; the lower part of this rock is of the black grannite before mentioned and the upper part a light coloured freestone. these clifts continue for 9 miles and approach the river very closely on either side. he found the current verry strong. Capt. C. killed a big horn on these clifts which himself and party dined on. after passing this range of mountains he entered this beautifull valley in which we also were   just at the upper side of the mountain there is a bad rappid   here the toe line of our canoe broke in the shoot of the rapids and swung on the rocks and had very nearly overset.

Friday August 2ed 1805.

We resumed our march this morning at sunrise. finding that the river still boar to the South I determined to pass it if possible in order to shorten our rout; this we effected by wading the river about 5 miles above our encampment of the last evening. we found the current very rapid waist deep and about 90 yds. wide. bottom smooth pebble with a small mixture of coarse gravel. this is the first time I ever dared to wade the river, tho' there are many places between this and the forks where I presume it might be attempted with equal success. The valley along which we passed today, and through which the river winds it's meandering course is from 6 to 8 miles wide and consists of a bea[u]tifull level plain with but little timber and that confined to the verge of the river; the land is tolerably fertile, and is either black or dark yellow loam, covered with grass from 9 inches to 2 feet high. the plain ascends gradually on either side of the river to the bases of two ranges of high mountains. the tops of these mountains are yet covered partially with snow, while we in the valley are nearly suffocated with the intense heat of the mid-day sun; the nights are so cold that two blankets are not more than sufficient covering.

soon after passing the river this morning Sergt. Gass lost my tommahawk in the thick brush and we were unable to find it, I regret the loss of this usefull implement,   however accedents will happen in the best families, and I consoled myself with the recollection that it was not the only one we had with us. the bones of the buffaloe and their excrement of an old date are to be met with in every part of this valley but we have long since lost all hope of meeting with that animal in these mountains. no recent appearance of Indians. the Indians in this part of the country appear to construct their lodges with the willow boughs and brush; they are small of a conic figure and have a small aperture on one side through which they enter. we continued out rout up this valley on the Lard. side of the river untill sunset, at which time we encamped on the Lard. bank of the river having traveled 24 miles. we had brought with us a good stock of venison of which we eat a hearty supper. I feel myself perfectly recovered of my indisposition, and do not doubt being able to pursue my rout tomorrow with the same comfort I have done today.

Capt. Clark continued his rout early this morning. the rapidity of the current was such that his progress was slow, in short it required the utmost exertion of the men to get on, nor could they resist this current by any other means than that of the cord and pole. in the course of the day they passed some villages of burrowing squirrels, saw a number of beaver dams and the inhabitants of them, many young ducks both of the Duckanmallard and the redheaded fishing duck, gees, several rattle snakes, black woodpeckers, and a large gang of Elk; they found the river much crouded with island both large and small and passed a small creek on Stard. side which we called *birth* Creek.[8] Capt. Clark discovers a tumor rising on the inner side of his ankle this evening which was painfull to him. they incamped in a level bottom on the Lard. side.

SATURDAY AUGUST 3RD 1805.

Set out early this morning, or before sunrise; still continued our march through the level valley on the lard. side of the river. the valley much as yesterday only reather wider; I think it 12 Miles wide, tho' the plains near the mountains rise higher and are more broken with some scattering pine near the mountain. in the

8 Named thus for Clark's birthday (August 1).

leaveler parts of the plain and river bottoms which are very extensive there is no timber except a scant proportion of cottonwood near the river. the Mountains continue high on either side of the valley, and are but scantily supplyed with timber; small pine appears to be the prevalent growth; it is of the pich kind, with a short leaf. at 11 A.M. Drewyer killed a doe and we halted about 2 hours and breakfasted, and then continued our rout untill night without halting, when we arrived at the river in a level bottom which appeared to spread to greater extent than usual. from the appearance of the timber I supposed that the river forked above us and resolved to examine this part of the river minutely to-morrow. this evening we passed through a high plain for about 8 miles covered with prickly pears and bearded grass, tho' we found this even better walking than the wide bottoms of the river, which we passed in the evening. we encamped on the river bank on Lard. side having traveled by estimate 23 Miles.

Capt. Clark set out this morning as usual. he walked on shore a small distance this morning and killed a deer. in the course of his walk he saw a track which he supposed to be that of an Indian from the curcumstance of the large toes turning inward,   he pursued the track and found that the person had ascended a point of a hill from which his camp of the last evening was visible; this circumstance also confirmed the beleif of it's being an Indian who had thus discovered them and ran off. they found the river as usual much crouded with islands, the currant more rapid & much more shallow than usual. in many places they were obliged to double man the canoes and drag them over the stone and gravel. this morning they passed a small creek on Stard. at the entrance of which Reubin Fields killed a large Panther. we called the creek after that animal Panther Creek.[4] they also passed a handsome little stream on Lard. which is form of several large springs which rise in the bottoms and along the base of the mountains with some little rivulets from the melting snows. in the evening they passed a very bad rappid where the bed of the river is formed entrely of solid rock and encamped on an island just above. the men wer

---

[4] Pipestone Creek. Here the expedition passes the last means of access to the better of the two routes which the Minnetarees had recommended (see p. 88). By Pipestone Pass they could have reached Deer Lodge Prairie and then could have gone down the Silverbow and Deer Lodge Rivers — names given to different stretches of the same stream — to the Hellgate River and on to Bitterroot Valley.

compelled to be a great proportion of their time in the water today; they have had a severe days labour and are much fortiegued.

By now the Jefferson is in transition, a plains river becoming a mountain river and as Lewis says: "the river continued to be crouded with Islands, rapid and shoaly. these shoals or riffles succeeded each other every 3 or four hundred yards; at those places they are obliged to drag the canoes over the stone there not being water enough to float them, and between the riffles the current is so strong that they are compelled to have c[r]ecourse to the cord; and being unable to walk on the shore for the brush wade in the river along the shore and hawl them by the cord; this has increased the pain and labour extreemly; their feet soon get tender and soar by wading and walking over the stones. these are also so slipry that they frequently get severe falls. being constantly wet soon makes them feble also."

The party reaches what Lewis describes as the forks of the Jefferson, although the two smaller streams that enter the main one hardly deserve that term. The northerly one, which Lewis personally names Wisdom River, is the Big Hole. The other, Lewis's Philanthropy, is the Ruby of today's maps but the Stinkingwater on earlier ones. Lewis continues to speak of the central fork as the Jefferson, but today the Jefferson ends here and this fork is called the Beaverhead. The labor of pulling the boats up such unnavigable streams steadily increases. "The men were so much fortiegued today that they wished much that navigation was at an end that they might go by land." Clark's infected ankle continues to cripple him. Charbonneau remains lame. Drewyer is almost disabled by a fall.

Lewis and his small party continued to scout ahead of the boats. But they have seen no Indians.

[Lewis]   TUESDAY AUGUST 6TH 1805.

about five miles above the forks I hea[r]d the hooping of the party to my left and changed my rout towards them; on my arrival found that they had taken the rapid fork and learnt from Capt. Clark that he had not found the note which I had left for him at that place and the reasons which had induced him to ascend this stream. it was easeist & more in our direction, and apd. to contain as much water. he had however previously to my comeing up with him, met Drewyer who informed him of the state of the two rivers and was on his return. one of their canoes had just overset and all the baggage wet, the medecine box among other articles and several articles lost a shot pouch and horn with all the implements for one rifle lost and never recovered.

I walked down to the point where I waited their return. on their arrival found that two other canoes had filled with water and wet their cargoes completely. Whitehouse had been thrown out of one of these canoes as she swing in a rapid current and the canoe had rubed him and pressed him to the bottom as she passed over him and had the water been inches shallower must inevitably have crushed him to death. our parched meal, corn, Indian preasents, and a great part of our most valuable stores were wet and much damaged on this ocasion. to examine, dry and arrange our stores was the first object; we therefore passed over to the lard. side opposite to the entrance of the rapid fork where there was a large gravly bar that answered our purposes; wood was also convenient and plenty. here we fixed our camp, and unloaded all our canoes and opened and exposed to dry such articles as had been wet. a part of the load of each canoe consisted of the leaden canestirs of powder which were not in least injured, tho' some of them had remained upwards of an hour under water. about 20 lbs. of powder which we had in a tight Keg or at l[e]ast one which we thought sufficiently so got wet and intirely spoiled. this would have been the case with the other had it not have been for the expedient which I had fallen on of securing the powder by means of the lead having the latter formed into canesters which were filled with the necessary proportion of po[w]der to discharge the lead when used, and those canesters well secured with corks and wax. in this country the air is so pure and dry that any vessel however well seasoned the timber may be will give way or shrink unless it is kept full of some liquid. we found that three deer skins which we had left at a considerable hight on a tree were taken off which we supposed had been done by a panther. we sent out some men to hunt this evening they killed 3 deer and four Elk which gave us a plentifull supply om [of] meat once more.

Shannon had been dispatched up the rapid fork this morning to hunt, by Capt Clark before he met with Drewyer or learnt his mistake in the rivers. when he returned he sent Drewyer in surch of him, but he rejoined us this evening and reported that he had been several miles up the river and could find nothing of him. we had the trumpet sounded and fired several guns but he did not join us this evening. I am fearful he is lost again. this is the same man who was seperated from us 15 days as we came up the Missouri and subsisted 9 days of that time on grapes only. Whitehouse is in much pain this evening with the injury one of his legs sustained from the canoe today at the time it upset and swing over him. Capt Clarks ankle is also very painfull to him. we should have given the party a days rest some where near this place had not this accedent happened, as I had determined to take some observations to fix the Latitude and longitude of these forks. our merchandize medecine &c are not sufficiently dry this evening we covered them securely for the evening.

we believe that the N.W. or rapid fork is the dane [drain] of the melting snows of the mountains, and that it is not as long as the middle fork and dose not at all seasons of the year supply any thing like as much water as the other and that about this season it rises to it's greatest hight. this last appears from the apparent bed of the river which is now overflown and the water in many plases spreads through old channels which have their bottoms covered with grass that has grown this season and is such as appears on the parts of the bottom not innundated. we therefore determined that the middle fork was that which ought of right to bear the name we had given to the lower portion or *River Jefferson,* and called the bold rapid an[d] clear stream *Wisdom,* and the more mild and placid one which flows in from the S.E. *Philanthrophy,* in commemoration of two of those cardinal virtues, which have so eminently marked that deservedly selibrated character through life.

WEDNESDAY AUGUST 7TH 1805

Dispatched Reubin Fields in surch of Shannon. Our stores were now so much exhausted that we found we could proceed with one canoe less, we therefore drew out one of them into a thicket of brush and secured her in such manner that the water could not take her off should the river rise to the hight where she is. my air gun was out of order and her sights had been removed by some accedent   I put her in order and regulated her. she shot again as well as she ever did.

At one oclock all our baggage was dry we therefore packed it up reloaded the canoes and the party proceeded with Capt. Clark up Jefferson's river. I remained with Sergt. Gass to complete the observation of equal altitudes and joined them in the evening at their camp on the Lard. side. we had a shower of rain wich continued about 40 minutes attended with thunder and lightning. this shower wet me perfectly before I reached the camp. the clouds continued during the night in such manner that I was unable to obtain any lunar observations. This evening Drewyer brought in a deer which he had killed. we have not heard any thing from Shannon yet, we expect that he has pursued Wisdom river upwards for som distance probably killed some heavy animal and is waiting our arrival.

THURSDAY AUGUST 8TH 1805.

at Noon Reubin Fields arrived and reported that he had been up Wisdom river some miles above where it entered the mountain and could find nothing of Shannon, he had killed a deer and an Antelope. great quantity of beaver Otter and musk-rats in these rivers. two of the hunters we sent out this morning returned at noon had killed each a deer and an Antelope. we use the seting poles today almost altogether. we encamped on the Lard side where there was but little timber were obliged to use willow brush for fuel; the rosebushes and bryers were very thick. the hunters brought in another deer this evening. t[h]e tumor on Capt. Clarks ankle has discharged a considerable quantity of matter but is still much swolen and inflamed and gives him considerable pain. saw a number of Gees ducks and some Crains today. the former begin to fly. the evening again proved cloudy much to my mortification and prevented my making any lunar observations.

the Indian woman recognized the point of a high plain to our right which she informed us was not very distant from the summer retreat of her nation on a river beyond the mountains which runs to the west. this hill she says her nation calls the beaver's head from a conceived re[se]mblance of it's figure to the head of that animal. she assures us that we shall either find her people on this river or on the river immediately west of it's source; which from it's present size cannot be distant. as it is now all important with us to meet with those people as soon as possible I determined to proceed tomorrow with a small party to the source of the principal stream of this river and pass the mountains to the Columbia; and down that river untill I found the Indians; in short it is my resolusion to find them or some others, who have horses if it should cause me a trip of one month. for without horses we shall be obliged to leave a great part of our stores, of which, it appears to me that we have a stock already sufficiently small for the length of the voyage before us.

Sacajawea has recognized a landmark which tells her that they are not far from the place where her people are accustomed to cross the Bitterroot Mountains (whose crest is here the Continental Divide) to westward-flowing waters. That place is Lemhi Pass. The camp where Lewis makes his decision to go through the Pass in search of the Shoshones is six land miles, fourteen miles by the river, up the Beaverhead from the mouth of the Ruby River, or about twenty miles north of Dillon, Montana.

[Clark]   AUGUST 9TH FRIDAY 1805 —

a fine morning   wind from the N.E.   we proceeded on verry well   rapid places more noumerous than below,   Shannon the man whome we lost on Wisdom River Joined us, haveing returned to the forks & prosued us up after prosueing Wisdom River one day.

Capt Lewis and 3 men [5] Set out after brackft. to examine the river above, find a portage if possible, also the Snake Indians. I Should have taken this trip had I have been able to march, from the rageing fury of a tumer on my anckle musle,   in the evening Clouded up and a fiew drops of rain   Encamped on the Lard Side near a low bluff,   the river to day as yesterday, the three hunters Could kill only two antelopes to day, game of every kind scerce.

[Lewis]   SATURDAY AUGUST 10TH 1805.

after passing a large creek at about 5 miles we fel in with a plain Indian road which led towards the point that the river entered the

[5] Drewyer, Shields, and McNeal.

mountain we therefore pursued the road   I sent Drewyer to the
wright to kill a deer which we saw feeding and halted on the river
under an immencely high perpendicular clift of rocks where it
entered the mountain   here we kindled a fire and waited for
Drewyer. he arrived in about an hour and a half or at noon with
three deer skins and the flesh of one of the best of them; we cooked
and eat a haisty meal and departed, returning a sho[r]t distance to
the Indian road which led us the best way over the mountains,
which are not very high but ar ruggid and approach the river
closely on both sides   from the number of rattle snakes about the
Clifts at which we halted we called them the rattle snake clifts.

the river below the mountains is rapid rocky, very crooked, much
divided by islands and withal shallow. after it enters the mountain
it's bends are not so circuetous and it's general course more direct,
but it is equally shallow les[s] divided more rocky and rapid. we
continued our rout along the Indian road which led us sometimes
over the hills and again in the narrow bottoms of the river till at
the distance of fifteen Ms. from the rattle snake Clifts we arrived
in a ha[n]dsome open and leavel vally where the river divided itself nearly into two equal branches; here I halted and examined
those streams and readily discovered from their size that it would
be vain to attempt the navigation of either any further.[6] here also
the road forked one leading up the vally of each of these streams.
I therefore sent Drewyer on one and Shields on the other to examine these roads for a short distance and to return and compare
their information with respect to the size and apparent plainness
of the roads as I was now determined to pursue that which appeared to have been the most traveled this spring. in the mean

[6] Lewis reaches this momentous decision where Prairie Creek comes down
from the mountains and enters what is now called Red Rock Creek — for in
contemporary usage the Beaverhead ends at Dillon, where it forks into Red
Rock Creek to the west and Blacktail Deer Creek to the east. This is Lewis's
"Forks of the Jefferson" (Coues's "Two Forks of the Jefferson") and by this
decision he makes it the head of navigation. The boats will be sunk in a near-by
pond. Shoshone Cove, which is to be the home camp till August 30, is a high
circular valley reached some five miles up Prairie Creek.

Red Rock Creek flows to this junction from the southeast, from Upper Red
Rock Lake, near the foot of Red Rock Pass, due west of Yellowstone Park. The
lake is near the Continental Divide, which here runs east and west and forms
the Montana-Idaho boundary. It is considered the ultimate source of the
Missouri River, 2714 miles from the junction of the Missouri and the Mississippi.
On the Idaho side of the Divide is Henry Lake, the source of Henry's Fork of
the Snake (Lewis's) River.

time I wrote a note to Capt. Clark informing him of the occurrences which had taken place, recommending it to him to halt
at this place untill my return and enforming him of the rout I had
taken which from the information of the men on their return
seemed to be in favour of the S W or Left hand fork which is
reather the smallest.

accordingly I put up my note on a dry willow pole at the forks,
and set out up the S.E. fork,   after proceeding about 1½ miles
I discovered that the road became so blind that it could not be that
which we had followed to the forks of Jefferson's river; neither
could I find the tracks of the horses which had passed early in the
spring along the other;   I therefore determined to return and
examine the other myself, which I did, and found that the same
horses had passed up the West fork which was reather [the] largest,
and more in the direction that I wished to pursue; I therefore did
not hesitate about changing my rout but determined to take the
western road. I now wrote a second note to Capt C. informing him
of this change and sent Drewyer to put it with the other at the
forks and waited untill he returned. there is scarcely any timber on
the river above the Rt. Snake Clifts, nor is there anything larger
than willow brush in sight of these forks. immediately in the level
plain between the forks and about ½ a mile distance from them
stands a high rocky mountain, the base of which is surrounded by
the level plain; it has a singular appearance. the mountains do
not appear very high in any direction tho' the tops of some of them
are partially covered with snow. this convinces me that we have
ascended to a great hight since we have entered the rocky Mountains, yet the ascent has been so gradual along the vallies that it was
scarcely perceptable by land. I do not beleive that the world can
furnish an example of a river runing to the extent which the
Missouri and Jefferson's rivers do through such a mountainous
country and at the same time so navigable as they are. if the
Columbia furnishes us such another example, a communication
across the continent by water will be practicable and safe. but this
I can scarcely hope from a knowledge of its having in it[s] com-
paritively short course to the ocean the same number of feet to
decend which the Missouri and Mississippi have from this point to
the Gulph of Mexico.

CHAPTER XIV

FROM BEAVER'S HEAD TO THE GREAT DIVIDE

[Lewis]   SUNDAY AUGUST 11TH 1805. —

The track which we had pursued last evening soon disappeared. I therefore resolved to proceed to the narrow pass on the creek about 10 miles West in hopes that I should again find the Indian road at the place,   accordingly I proceeded through the level plain directly to the pass. I now sent Drewyer to keep near the creek to my right and Shields to my left, with orders to surch for the road which if they found they were to notify me by placing a hat in the muzzle of their gun. I kept McNeal with me;   after having marched in this order for about five miles I discovered an Indian on horse back about two miles distant coming down the plain towards us. with my glass I discovered from his dress that he was of a different nation from any that we had yet seen, and was satisfyed of his being a Sosone; his arms were a bow and quiver of arrows, and was mounted on an eligant horse without a saddle, and a small string which was attatched to the under jaw of the horse which answered as a bridle.

I was overjoyed at the sight of this stranger and had no doubt of obtaining a friendly introduction to his nation provided I could get near enough to him to convince him of our being whitemen. I therefore proceeded towards him at my usual pace. when I had arrived within about a mile he mad[e] a halt which I did also and unloosing my blanket from my pack, I mad[e] him the signal of friendship known to the Indians of the Rocky mountains and those of the Missouri, which is by holding the mantle or robe in your hands at two corners and then th[r]owing [it] up in the air higher than the head bringing it to the earth as if in the act of spreading

185

it, thus repeating three times. this signal of the robe has arrisen
from a custom among all those nations of spreading a robe or skin
for ther gests to set on when they are visited. this signal had not
the desired effect, he still kept his position and seemed to view
Drewyer an[d] Shields who were now comiming in sight on either
hand with an air of suspicion,   I wo[u]ld willingly have made
them halt but they were too far distant to hear me and I feared to
make any signal to them least it should increase the suspicion in
the mind of the Indian of our having some unfriendly design upon
him. I therefore haistened to take out of my sack some b[e]ads a
looking glas and a few trinkets which I had brought with me for
this purpose and leaving my gun and pouch with McNeal advanced
unarmed towards him. he remained in the same stedfast poisture
untill I arrived in about 200 paces of him when he turn[ed] his
ho[r]se about and began to move off slowly from me; I now called
to him in as loud a voice as I could command repeating the word
tab-ba-bone, which in their language signifyes *white-man.* but
lo[o]king over his sholder he still kept his eye on Drewyer and
Sheilds who wer still advancing neither of them haveing segacity
enough to recollect the impropriety of advancing when they saw
me thus in parley with the Indian.

I now made a signal to these men to halt, Drewyer obeyed but
Shields who afterwards told me that he did not obse[r]ve the signal
still kept on   the Indian halted again and turned his ho[r]se
about as if to wait for me, and I beleive he would have remained
untill I came up with him had it not been for Shields who still
pressed forward. whe[n] I arrived within about 150 paces I again
repepeated the word tab-ba-bone and held up the trinkits in my
hands and striped up my shirt sleve to give him an opportunity of
seeing the colour of my skin and advanced leasure[ly] towards
him   but he did not remain untill I got nearer than about 100
paces when he suddonly turned his ho[r]se about, gave him the
whip leaped the creek and disapeared in the willow brush in an
instant and with him vanished all my hopes of obtaining horses for
the preasent. I now felt quite as much mortification and disappointment as I had pleasure and expectation at the first sight of
this indian. I fe[l]t soarly chargrined at the conduct of the men
particularly Sheilds to whom I principally attributed this failure
in obtaining an introduction to the natives.

we now set out on the track of the horse hoping by that means to be lead to an indian camp, the trail of inhabitants of which should they abscond we should probably be enabled to pursue to the body of the nation to which they would most probably fly for safety. this rout led us across a large Island framed by nearly an equal division of the creek in this bottom; after passing to the open ground on the N. side of the creek we observed that the track made out toward the high hills about 3 M. distant in that direction. I thought it probable that their camp might probably be among those hills & that they would reconnoiter us from the tops of them, and that if we advanced haistily towards them that they would become allarmed and probably run off; I therefore halted in an elivated situation near the creek had a fire kindled of willow brush cooked and took breakfast. during this leasure I prepared a small assortment of trinkits consisting of some mockkerson awls a few strans of several kinds of b[e]ads some paint a looking glass &c which I attatched to the end of a pole and planted it near our fire in order that should the Indians return in surch of us the[y] might from this token discover that we were friendly and white persons. before we had finis[h]ed our meal a heavy shower of rain came on with some hail wich continued abo[u]t 20 minutes and wet us to the skin,   after this shower we pursued the track of the horse but as the rain had raised the grass which he had trodden down it was with difficulty that we could follow it. we pursued it however about 4 miles it turning up the valley to the left under the foot of the hills. we pas several places where the Indians appeared to have been diging roots today and saw the fresh tracks of 8 or ten horses but they had been wandering about in such a confused manner that we not only lost the track of the hose which we had been pursuing but could make nothing of them. in the head of this valley we passed a large bog covered with tall grass and moss in which were a great number of springs of cold pure water,   we now turned a little to the left along the foot of the high hills and arrived at a small branch on which we encamped for the night,   after meeting with the Indian today I fixed a small flag of the U'.S. to a pole which I made McNeal carry. and planted in the ground where we halted or encamped.

MONDAY AUGUST 12TH 1805.

This morning I sent Drewyer out as soon as it was light, to try and discover what rout the Indians had taken. he followed the track of the horse we had pursued yesterday to the mountain wher it had ascended, and returned to me in about an hour and a half. I now determined to pursue the base of the mountains which form this cove to the S.W. in the expectation of finding some Indian road which lead over the Mountains,   accordingly I sent Drewyer to my right and Shields to my left with orders to look out for a road or the fresh tracks of horses either of which we should first meet with I had determined to pursue. at the distance of about 4 miles we passed 4 small rivulets near each other on which we saw som resent bowers or small conic lodges formed with willow brush. near them the indians had geathered a number of roots from the manner in which they had toarn up the ground; but I could not discover the root which they seemed to be in surch of.

near this place we fell in with a large and plain Indian road which came into the cove from the N.E. and led along the foot of the mountains to the S.W. o[b]liquely approaching the main stream which we had left yesterday. this road we now pursued to the S.W.   at 5 miles it passed a stout stream which is a principal fork of the ma[i]n stream and falls into it just above the narrow pass between the two clifts before mentioned and which we now saw below us. here we halted and breakfasted on the last of our venison, having yet a small peice of pork in reserve. after eating we continued our rout through the low bottom of the main stream along the foot of the mountains   on our right the valley for 5 Mls. further in a S.W. direction was from 2 to 3 miles wide   the main stream now after discarding two stream[s] on the left in this valley turns abruptly to the West through a narrow bottom betwe[e]n the mountains. the road was still plain, I therefore did not dispair of shortly finding a passage over the mountains and of taisting the waters of the great Columbia this evening.

at the distance of 4 miles further the road took us to the most distant fountain of the waters of the Mighty Missouri in surch of which we have spent so many toilsome days and wristless nights. thus far I had accomplished one of those great objects on which my mind has been unalterably fixed for many years, judge then of the pleasure I felt in all[a]ying my thirst with this pure and ice-cold water which issues from the base of a low mountain or hill of a gentle ascent for ½ a mile. the mountains are high on either hand leave this gap at the head of this rivulet through which the road passes. here I halted a few minutes and rested myself. two miles below McNeal had exultingly stood with a foot on each side of this little rivulet and thanked his god that he had lived to bestride the mighty & heretofore deemed endless Missouri. after refreshing ourselves we proceeded on to the top of the dividing ridge from which I discovered immence ranges of high mountains still to the West of us with their tops partially covered with snow. I now decended the mountain about ¾ of a mile which I found much steeper than on the opposite side, to a handsome bold runing Creek of cold Clear water. here I first tasted the water of the great Columbia river.[1] after a short halt of a few minutes we continued our march along the Indian road which lead us over steep hills and deep hollows to a spring on the side of a mountain where we found a sufficient quantity of dry willow brush for fuel,   here we encamped for the night having traveled about 20 Miles. as we had killed nothing during the day we now boiled and eat the remainder of our pork, having yet a little flour and parched meal.

this morning Capt. Clark set out early. found the river shoally, rapid, shallow, and extreemly difficult. the men in the water almost all day. they are geting weak soar and much fortiegued; they complained of the fortiegue to which the navigation subjected them and wished to go by land   Capt. C. engouraged them and passifyed them.

TUESDAY AUGUST 13TH 1805.

at the distance of five miles the road after leading us down a long decending valley for 2 Ms. brought us to a large cheek about 10 yds. wide; this we passed and on rising the hill beyond it had a view of a handsome little valley to our left of about a mile in width through which from the appearance of the timber I conjectured that a river passed. we had proceeded about four miles through a wavy plain parallel to the valley or river bottom when at the distance of about a mile we saw two women, a man and some dogs on an eminence immediately before us. they appeared to v[i]ew us with attention and two of them after a few minutes set down as if to wait our arrival   we continued our usual pace to-

1 Lewis has crossed the Continental Divide by way of Lemhi Pass, due west of Armstead, Montana. The rivulet from which he drinks is one of the headwater streams of the small Lemhi River.

wards them. when we had arrived within half a mile of them I
directed the party to halt and leaving my pack and rifle I took the
flag which I unfurled and a[d]vanced singly towards them   the
women soon disappeared behind the hill, the man continued untill
I arrived within a hundred yards of him and then likewise ab-
sconded. tho' I frequently repeated the word *tab-ba-bone* sufficiently loud for him to have heard it.

I now haistened to the top of the hill where they had stood but
could see nothing of them. the dogs were less shye than their
masters   they came about me pretty close   I therefore thought
of tying a handkerchief about one of their necks with some beads
and other trinkets and then let them loose to surch their fugitive
owners thinking by this means to convince them of our pacific disposition towards them but the dogs would not suffer me to take
hold of them; they also soon disappeared. I now made a signal fror
the men to come on, they joined me and we pursued the the back
track of these Indians which lead us along the same road which
we had been traveling. the road was dusty and appeared to have
been much traveled lately both by men and horses.

we had not continued our rout more than a mile when we were
so fortunate as to meet with three female savages. the short and
steep ravines which we passed concealed us from each other untill
we arrived within 30 paces. a young woman immediately took to
flight, an Elderly woman and a girl of about 12 years old remained.
I instantly laid by my gun and advanced towards them. they appeared much allarmed but saw that we were to near for them to
escape by flight   they therefore seated themselves on the ground,
holding down their heads as if reconciled to die which the[y] expected no doubt would be their fate;   I took the elderly woman
by the hand and raised her up repeated the word *tab-ba-bone* and
strip[ped] up my shirt sleve to s[h]ew her my skin; to prove to her
the truth of the ascertion that I was a white man for my face and
ha[n]ds which have been constantly exposed to the sun were quite
as dark as their own. they appeared instantly reconciled, and the
men coming up I gave these women some beads a few mockerson
awls some pewter looking-glasses and a little paint.

I directed Drewyer to request the old woman to recall the young
woman who had run off to some distance by this time fearing she
might allarm the camp before we approached and might. so exas-

perate the natives that they would perhaps attack us without enquiring who we were.[2] the old woman did as she was requested and
the fugitive soon returned almost out of breath. I bestoed an
equ[i]volent portion of trinket on her with the others. I now
painted their tawny cheeks with some vermillion which with this
nation is emblematic of peace. after they had become composed I
enformed them by signs that I wished them to conduct us to their
camp that we wer anxious to become acquainted with the chiefs
and warriors of their nation. they readily obeyed and we set out,
still pursuing the road down the river. we had marched about 2
miles when we met a party of about 60 warriors mounted on excellent horses who came in nearly full speed,   when they arrived I advanced towards them with the flag leaving my gun with
the party about 50 paces behi[n]d me. the chief and two others
who were a little in advance of the main body spoke to the women,
and they informed them who we were and exultingly shewed the
presents which had been given them   these men then advanced
and embraced me very affectionately in their way which is by
puting their left arm over you[r] wright sholder clasping your
back, while they apply their left cheek to yours and frequently
vociforate the word *âh-hi-e, âh-hi-e* that is, I am much pleased, I
am much rejoiced. bothe parties now advanced and we wer all
carresed and besmeared with their grease and paint till I was
heartily tired of the national hug. I now had the pipe lit and gave
them smoke; they seated themselves in a circle around us and
pulled of[f] their mockersons before they would receive or smoke
the pipe. this is a custom among them as I afterwards learned
indicative of a sacred obligation of sincerity in their profession of
friendship given by the act of receiving and smoking the pipe of a
stranger. or which is as much as to say that they wish they may
always go bearfoot if they are not sincere; a pretty heavy penalty if
they are to march through the plains of their country.

after smoking a few pipes with them I distributed some trifles
among them, with which they seemed much pleased particularly
with the blue beads and vermillion. I now informed the chief
that the object of our visit was a friendly one, that after we should
reach his camp I would undertake to explain to him fully those

2 Drewyer is, of course, addressing the old woman in sign language, the Espe-
ranto of the Plains tribes.

objects, who we wer, from whence we had come and w[h]ither we were going; that in the mean time I did not care how soon we were in motion, as the sun was very warm and no water at hand. they now put on their mockersons, and the principal chief Ca-me-âh-wait made a short speach to the warriors. I gave him the flag which I informed him was an emblem of peace among whitemen and now that it had been received by him it was to be respected as the bond of union between us. I desired him to march on, which [he] did and we followed him; the dragoons moved on in squadron in our rear. after we had marched about a mile in this order he halted them and gave a second harang; after which six or eight of the young men road forward to their encampment and no further regularity was observed in the order of march. I afterwards understood that the Indians we had first seen this morning had returned and allarmed the camp; these men had come out armed cap a pe for action expecting to meet with their enimies the Minnetares of Fort de Prarie whome they Call Pâh'-kees. they were armed with b[o]ws arrow and Shields except three whom I observed with small pieces such as the N.W. Company furnish the natives with which they had obtained from the Rocky Mountain Indians on the Yellow stone river with whom they are at peace. on our arrival at their encampmen[t] on the river in a handsome level and fertile bottom at the distance of 4 Ms. from where we had first met them they introduced us to a londge made of willow brush and an old leather lodge which had been prepared for our reception by the young men which the chief had dispatched for that purpose.

Here we were seated on green boughs and the skins of Antelopes. one of the warriors then pulled up the grass in the center of the lodge forming a smal[l] circle of about 2 feet in diameter   the chief next produced his pipe and native tobacco and began a long cerimony of the pipe when we were requested to take of[f] our mockersons, the Chief having previously taken off his as well as all the warriors present. this we complyed with; the Chief then lit his pipe at the fire kindled in this little magic circle, and standing on the oposite side of the circle uttered a speach of several minutes in length at the conclusion of which he pointed the stem to the four cardinal points of the heavens first begining at the East and ending with the North. he now presented the pipe to me as if desirous that I should smoke, but when I reached my hand to receive it, he drew it back and repeated the same c[e]remony three times, after which he pointed the stem first to the heavens then to the center of the magic circle smoked himself with three whifs and held the pipe untill I took as many as I thought proper; he then held it to each of the white persons and then gave it to be consumed by his warriors.

I now explained to them the objects of our journey &c.   all the women and children of the camp were shortly collected about the lodge to indulge themselves with looking at us, we being the first white persons they had ever seen. after the cerimony of the pipe was over I distributed the remainder of the small articles I had brought with me among the women and children. by this time it was late in the evening and we had not taisted any food since the evening before. the Chief informed us that they had nothing but berries to eat and gave us some cakes of serviceberries and Choke cherries which had been dryed in the sun; of these I made a hearty meal, and then walked to the river, which I found about 40 yards wide very rapid clear and about 3 feet deep.[3] Cameahwait informed me that this stream discharged itself into another doubly as large at the distance of half a days march which came from the S.W.   but he added on further enquiry that there was but little more timber below the junction of those rivers than I saw here, and that the river was confined between inaccessable mountains, was very rapid and rocky insomuch that it was impossible for us to pass either by land or water down this river to the great lake where the white men lived as he had been informed. this was unwelcome information but I still hoped that this account had been exagerated with a view to detain us among them. as to timber I could discover not any that would answer the purpose of constructing canoes or in short more than was bearly necessary for fuel.

these people had been attacked by the Minetares of Fort de prarie [4] this spring and about 20 of them killed and taken prisoners. on this occasion they lost a great part of their horses and all their lodges except that which they had erected for our accomodation; they were now living in lodges of a conic figure made of

[3] Lemhi River. It flows northward to the main fork of Salmon River. So it corresponds to the information which the Minnetarees had given him at Fort Mandan.

[4] The Fall Indians, the Atsina, not the Minnetarees.

willow brush. I still observe a great number of horses feeding in every direction around their camp and therefore entertain but little doubt but we shall be enable[d] to furnish ourselves with an adiquate number to transport our stores even if we are compelled to travel by land over these mountains. on my return to my lodge an indian called me in to his bower and gave me a small morsel of the flesh of an antelope boiled and a piece of a fresh salmon roasted; both which I eat with a very good relish. this was the first salmon I had seen and perfectly convinced me that we were on the waters of the Pacific Ocean.

This evening the Indians entertained us with their dancing nearly all night. at 12 O'Ck. I grew sleepy and retired to rest leaving the men to amuse themselves with the Indians. I observe no essential difference between the music and manner of dancing among this nation and those of the Missouri. I was several times awoke in the course of the night by their yells but was too much fortiegued to be deprived of a tolerable sound night's repose.

In order to give Capt. Clark time to reach the forks of Jefferson's river I concluded to spend this day at the Shoshone Camp and obtain what information I could with rispect to the country. as we had nothing but a little flour and parched meal to eat except the berries with which the Indians furnished us I directed Drewyer and Shields to hunt a few hours and try to kill something,   the Indians furnished them with horses and most of their young men also turned out to hunt. I was very much entertained with a view of this indian chase; it was after a herd of about 10 Antelope and about 20 hunters. it lasted about 2 hours and considerable part of the chase in view from my tent. about 1.A.M. the hunters returned had not killed a single Antelope, and their horses foaming with sweat. my hunters returned soon after and had been equally unsuccessfull. I now directed McNeal to make me a little paist with the flour and added some berries to it which I found very pallatable.

The means I had of communicating with these people was by way of Drewyer who understood perfectly the common language of jesticulation or signs which seems to be universally understood by all the Nations we have yet seen. it is true that this language is imperfect and liable to error but is much less so than would be expected. the strong parts of the ideas are seldom mistaken.

I now told Cameahwait that I wished him to speak to his people and engage them to go with me tomorrow to the forks of Jeffersons river where our baggage was by this time arrived with another Chief and a large party of whitemen who would wait my return at that place. that I wish them to take with them about 30 spare horses to transport our baggage to this place where we would then remain sometime among them and trade with them for horses, and finally concert our future plans for getting on to the ocean and of the traid which would be extended to them after our return to our homes. he complyed with my request and made a lengthey harrangue to his village. he returned in about an hour and a half and informed me that they would be ready to accompany me in the morning. I promised to reward them for their trouble. Drewyer who had had a good view of their horses estimated them at 400. most of them are fine horses. indeed many of them would make a figure on the South side of James River or the land of fine horses. I saw several with spanish brands on them, and some mules which they informed me that they had also obtained from the Spaniards. I also saw a bridle bit of spanish manufactary, and sundry other articles which I have no doubt were obtained from the same source. notwithstanding the extreem poverty of those poor people they are very merry they danced again this evening untill midnight. each warrior keep[s] one or more horses tyed by a cord to a stake near his lodge both day and night and are always prepared for action at a moments warning. they fight on horseback altogether. I observe that the large flies are extreemly troublesome to the horses as well as ourselves.

Thursday August 15th 1805.

This morning I arrose very early and as hungary as a wolf. I had eat nothing yesterday except one scant meal of the flour and berries except the dryed cakes of berries which did not appear to satisfy my appetite as they appeared to do those of my Indian friends. I found on enquiry of McNeal that we had only about two pounds of flour remaining. this I directed him to divide into two equal parts and to cook the one half this morning in a kind of pudding with the burries as he had done yesterday and reserve the ballance for the evening. on this new fashoned pudding four of us break·

fasted, giving a pretty good allowance also to the Chief who declared it the best thing he had taisted for a long time. he took a little of the flour in his hand, taisted and examined [it] very scrutinously and asked me if we made it of roots. I explained to him the manner in which it grew. I hurried the departure of the Indians. the Chief addressed them several times before they would move   they seemed very reluctant to accompany me. I at length asked the reason and he told me that some foolish persons among them had suggested the idea we were in league with the Pahkees and had come on in order to decoy them into an ambuscade where their enimies were waiting to receive them. but that for his part he did not believe it. I readily perceived that our situation was not enterely free from danger as the transicion from suspicion to the confermation of the fact would not be very difficult in the minds of these ignorant people who have been accustomed from their infancy to view every stranger as an enimy.

I told Cameahwait that I was sorry to find that they had put so little confidence in us, that I knew they were not acquainted with whitemen and therefore could forgive them. that among whitemen it was considered disgracefull to lye or entrap an enimy by falsehood. I told him if they continued to think thus meanly of us that they might rely on it that no whitemen would ever come to trade with them or bring them arms and amunition and that if the bulk of his nation still entertained this opinion I still hoped that there were some among them that were not affraid to die, that were men and would go with me and convince themselves of the truth of what I had asscerted. that there was a party of whitemen waiting my return either at the forks of Jefferson's river or a little below coming on to that place in canoes loaded with provisions and merchandize. he told me for his own part he was determined to go, that he was not affraid to die. I soon found that I had touched him on the right string; to doubt the bravery of a savage is at once to put him on his metal. he now mounted his horse and haranged his village a third time; the perport of which as he afterwards told me was to inform them that he would go with us and convince himself of the truth or falsity of what we had told him if he was sertain he should be killed, that he hoped there were some of them who heard him were not affraid to die with him and if there was to let him see them mount their horses and prepare to set out. shortly after this harange he was joined by six or eight only and with these

I smoked a pipe and directed the men to put on their packs being determined to set out with them while I had them in the humour   at half after 12 we set out,   several of the old women were crying and imploring the great sperit to protect their warriors as if they were going to inevitable distruction.

we had not proceeded far before our party was augmented by ten or twelve more, and before we reached the Creek which we had passed in the morning of the 13th it appeared to me that we had all the men of the village and a number of women with us. this may serve in some measure to ilustrate the capricious disposition of those people, who never act but from the impulse of the moment. they were now very cheerfull and gay, and two hours ago they looked as sirly as so many imps of satturn. when we arrived at the spring on the side of the mountain where we had encamped on the 12th the Chief insi[s]ted on halting to let the horses graize with which I complyed and gave the Indians smoke. they are excessively fond of the pipe; but have it not much in their power to indulge themselves with even their native tobacco as they do not cultivate it themselves. after remaining about an hour we again set out, and by engaging to make compensation to four of them for their trouble obtained the previlege of riding with an indian myself and a similar situation for each of my party. I soon found it more tiresome riding without [s]tirrups than walking and of course chose the latter making the Indian carry my pack. about sunset we reached the upper part of the level valley of the Cove which [we] now called Shoshone Cove. the grass being birned on the North side of the river we passed over to the south and encamped near some willow brush about 4 miles above the narrow pass between the hills noticed as I came up this cove. the river was here about six yards wide, and frequently damed up by the beaver. I had sent Drewyer forward this evening before we halted to kill some meat but he was unsuccessfull and did not rejoin us untill after dark   I now cooked and [divided] among six of us [to] eat the remaining pound of flour stired in a little boiling water.

Friday August 16th 1805.

I sent Drewyer and Shields before this morning in order to kill some meat as neither the Indians nor ourselves had any thing to eat. I informed the C[h]ief of my view in this measure, and requested that he would keep his young men with us lest by their hooping and noise they should allarm the game and we should get nothing to eat, but so strongly were there suspicions exited by this measure that two parties of discovery immediately set out one on e[a]ch side of the valley to watch the hunters as I beleive to see whether they had not been sent to give information of their approach to an enemy that they still preswaided themselves were lying in wait for them. I saw that any further effort to prevent their going would only add strength to their suspicions and therefore said no more. after the hunters had been gone about an hour we set out. we had just passed through the narrows when we saw one of the spies comeing up the level plain under whip, the chief pawsed a little and seemed somewhat concerned,   I felt a good deel so myself and began to suspect that by some unfortunate accedent that perhaps some of there enimies had straggled hither at this unlucky moment; but we were all agreeably disappointed on the arrival of the young man to learn that he had come to inform us that one of the whitemen had killed a deer.

in an instant they all gave their horses the whip and I was taken nearly a mile before I could learn what were the tidings; as I was without [s]tirrups and an Indian behind me the jostling was disageeable   I therefore reigned up my horse and forbid the indian to whip him who had given him the lash at every jum[p] for a mile fearing he should loose a part of the feast. the fellow was so uneasy that he left me the horse dismounted and ran on foot at full speed I am confident a mile. when they arrived where the deer was which was in view of me they dismounted and ran in tumbling over each other like a parcel of famished dogs each seizing and tearing away a part of the intestens which had been previously thrown out by Drewyer who killed it; the seen was such when I arrived that had I not have had a pretty keen appetite myself I am confident I should not have taisted any part of the venison shortly. each one had a peice of some discription and all eating most ravenously. some were eating the kidnies the melt [spleen] and liver and the blood runing from the corners of their mouths, others were in a similar situation with the paunch and guts but the exuding substance in this case from their lips was of a different discription. one of the last who att[r]acted my attention on particularly had been fortunate in his allotment or reather active in the division, he had provided himself with about nine feet of the small guts one end of which he was chewing on while with his hands he was squezzing the contents out at the other. I really did not untill now think that human nature ever presented itself in a shape so nearly allyed to the brute creation.

I viewed these poor starved divils with pity and compassion   I directed McNeal to skin the deer and reserved a quarter, the ballance I gave the Chief to be divided among his people; they devoured the whole of it nearly without cooking.

I now boar obliquely to the left in order to interscept the creek where there was some brush to make a fire, and arrived at this stream where Drewyer had killed a second deer; here nearly the same seene was encared [enacted]. a fire being kindled we cooked and eat and gave the ballance of the two deer to the Indians who eat the whole of them even to the soft parts of the hoofs. Drewyer joined us at breakfast with a third deer. of this I reserved a quarter and gave the ballance to the Indians. they all appeared now to have filled themselves and were in a good humour. this morning early soon after the hunters set out a considerable part of our escort became allarmed and returned 28 men and three women only continued with us. after eating and suffering the horses to graize about 2 hours we renued our march and towa[r]ds evening arrived at the lower part of the cove   Shields killed an Antelope on the way a part of which we took and gave the remainder to the Indians.

being now informed of the place at which I expected to meat Capt. C. and the party they insisted on making a halt, which was complyed with. we now dismounted and the Chief with much cerimony put tippets about our necks such as they t[h]emselves woar I redily perceived that this was to disguise us and owed it's origine to the same cause already mentioned. to give them further confidence I put my cocked hat with feather on the chief and my over shirt being of the Indian form my hair deshivled and skin well browned with the sun I wanted no further addition to make me a complete Indian in appearance the men followed my example and we were so[o]n completely metamorphosed. I again repeated to them the possibility of the party not having arrived at the place which I expected they were, but assured them they could not be far below, lest by not finding them at the forks their suspicions might arrise to such hight as to induce them to return precipitately. we now set out and rode briskly within sight of the forks making one of the Indians carry the flag that our own party should know who we were. when we arrived in sight at the distance of about 2 miles I discovered to my mortification that the party had not arrived, and the Indians slackened their pace. I now scarcely new what to do and feared every moment when they would halt altogether,   I now determined to restore their confidence cost what it might and therefore gave the Chief my gun and told him that if his enimies were in those bushes before him that he could defend himself with that gun, that for my own part I was not affraid to die and if I deceived him he might make what uce of the gun he thought proper or in other words that he might shoot me. the men also gave their guns to other indians which seemed to inspire them with more confidence; they sent their spies before them at some distance and when I drew near the place I thought of the notes which I had left and directed Drewyer to go with an Indian man and bring them to me which he did. the indian seeing him take the notes from the stake on which they had been placed.

I now had recourse to a stratagem in which I thought myself justifyed by the occasion, but which I must confess set a little awkward. it had it's desired effect. after reading the notes which were the same I had left I told the Chief that when I had left my brother Chief with the party below where the river entered the mountain that we both agreed not to bring the canoes higher up than the next forks of the river above us wherever this might happen, that there he was to wait my return, should he arrive first, and that in the event of his not being able to travel as fast as usual from the difficulty of the water, that he was to send up to the first forks above him and leave a note informing me where he was,   that this note was left here today and that he informed me that he was just below the mountains and was coming slowly up, and added that I should wait here for him, but if they did not believe me that I should send a man at any rate to the Chief and they might also send one of their young men with him, that myself and two others would remain with them at this place. this plan was readily adopted and one of the young men offered his services; I promised him a knife and some beads as a reward for his confidence in us. most of them seemed satisfyed but there were several that complained of the Chief's exposing them to danger unnecessarily and said that we told different stories, in short a few were much dissatisfyed. I wrote a note to Capt. Clark by the light of some willow brush and directed Drewyer to set out early being confident that there was not a moment to spare. the chief and five or six others slept about my fire and the others hid themselves in various parts of the willow brush to avoid the enimy whom they were fearfull would attack tham in the course of the night. I now entertained various conjectures myself with rispect to the cause of Capt. Clarks detention and was even fearfull that he had found the river so difficult that he had halted below the Rattlesnake bluffs. I knew that if these people left me that they would immediately disperse and secrete themselves in the mountains where it would be impossible to find them or at least in vain to pursue them and that they would spread the allarm to all other bands within our reach & of course we should be disappointed in obtaining horses, which would vastly retard and increase the labour of our voyage and I feared might so discourage the men as to defeat the expedition altogether.

my mind was in reallity quite as gloomy all this evening as the most affrighted indian but I affected cheerfullness to keep the Indians so who were about me. we finally laid down and the Chief placed himself by the side of my musquetoe bier. I slept but little as might be well expected, my mind dwelling on the state of the expedition which I have ever held in equal estimation with my own existence, and the fait of which appeared at this moment to depend in a great measure upon the caprice of a few savages who are ever as fickle as the wind. I had mentioned to the chief several times that we had with us a woman of his nation who had been taken prisoner by the Minnetares, and that by means of her I hoped to explain myself more fully than I could do signs. some of the party had also told the Indians that we had a man with us who was black and had short curling hair,   this had excited their curiossity very much. and they seemed quite as anxious to see this monster as they wer[e] the merchandize which we had to barter for their horses.

CHAPTER XV

CROSSING THE GREAT DIVIDE

[Biddle] SATURDAY, AUGUST 17TH, 1805.

Captain Lewis rose very early and despatched Drewyer and the Indian down the river in quest of the boats. Shields was sent out at the same time to hunt, while M'Neal prepared a breakfast out of the remainder of the meat. Drewyer had been gone about two hours, and the Indians were all anxiously waiting for some news, when an Indian who had straggled a short distance down the river, returned with a report that he had seen the white men, who were only a short distance below, and were coming on. the Indians were all transported with joy, and the chief in the warmth of his satisfaction renewed his embrace to Capt. Lewis, who was quite as much delighted as the Indians themselves; the report proved most agreeably true.

On setting out at seven o'clock, Captain Clarke with Chaboneau and his wife walked on shore, but they had not gone more than a mile before Clarke saw Sacajawea, who was with her husband 100 yards ahead, began to dance and show every mark of the most extravagant joy, turning round him and pointing to several Indians, whom he now saw advancing on horseback, sucking her fingers at the same time to indicate that they were of her native tribe. As they advanced, Captain Clarke discovered among them Drewyer dressed like an Indian, from whom he learnt the situation of the party. While the boats were performing the circuit, he went towards the forks with the Indians, who as they went along, sang aloud with the greatest appearance of delight.

We soon drew near to the camp, and just as we approached it a woman made her way through the croud towards Sacajawea, and recognising each other, they embraced with the most tender affection. The meeting of these two young women had in it something peculiarly touching, not only in the ardent manner in which their feelings were expressed, but from the real interest of their situation. They had been companions in childhood, in the war with the Minnetarees they had both been taken prisoners in the same battle, they had shared and softened the rigours of their captivity, till one of them had escaped from the Minnetarees, with scarce a hope of ever seeing her friend relieved from the hands of her enemies. While Sacajawea was renewing among the women the friendships of former days, Captain Clarke went on, and was received by Captain Lewis and the chief, who after the first embraces and salutations were over, conducted him to a sort of circular tent or shade of willows. Here he was seated on a white robe; and the chief immediately tied in his hair six small shells resembling pearls, an ornament highly valued by these people, who procure them in the course of trade from the sea-coast. The moccasins of the whole party were then taken off, and after much ceremony the smoking began. After this the conference was to be opened, and glad of an opportunity of being able to converse more intelligibly, Sacajawea was sent for; she came into the tent, sat down, and was beginning to interpret, when in the person of Cameahwait she recognised her brother: She instantly jummped up, and ran and embraced him, throwing over him her blanket and weeping profusely: The chief was himself moved, though not in the same degree. After some conversation between them she resumed her seat, and attempted to interpret for us, but her new situation seemed to overpower her, and she was frequently interrupted by her tears. After the council was finished the unfortunate woman learnt that all her family were dead except two brothers, one of whom was absent, and a son of her eldest sister, a small boy, who was immediately adopted by her.

[Lewis]   SATURDAY AUGUST 17TH 1805. —

we made them [the Indians] sensible of their dependance on the will of our government for every species of merchandize as well for their defence & comfort; and apprized them of the strength of our government and it's friendly dispositions towards them. we also gave them as a reason why we wished to pe[ne]trate the country as far as the ocean to the west of them was to examine and find out a more direct way to bring merchandize to them. that as no trade could be carryed on with them before our return to our homes that it was mutually advantageous to them as well as to ourselves that they should render us such aids as they had in their power to furnish in order to haisten our voyage and of course our return home. that such were their horses to transport our baggage without which we could not subsist, and that a pilot to conduct us through the mountains was also necessary if we could not decend the river by water. but that we did not ask either their horses or their services without giving a satisfactory compensation in return. that at present we wished them to collect as many horses as were necessary to transport our baggage to their village on the Columbia where we would then trade with them at our leasure for such horses as they could spare us.

the chief thanked us for friendship towards himself and nation & declared his wish to serve us in every rispect. that he was sorry to find that it must yet be some time before they could be furnished with firearms but said they could live as they had done heretofore untill we brought them as we had promised. he said they had not horses enough with them at present to remove our baggage to their village over the mountain, but that he would return tomorrow and encourage his people to come over with their horses and that he would bring his own and assist us. this was complying with all we wished at present.

we next enquired who were chiefs among them. Cameahwait pointed out two others whom he said were Chiefs. we gave him a medal of the small size with the likeness of Mr. Jefferson the President of the U' States in releif on one side and clasp hands with a pipe and tomahawk in the other,   to the other Chiefs we gave each a small medal which were struck in the Presidency of George Washing[ton] Esqr.   we also gave small medals of the last discription to two young men whom the 1st Chief informed us wer good young men and much rispected among them. we gave the 1st Chief an uniform coat shirt a pair of scarlet legings a carrot of tobacco and some small articles   to each of the others we gave a shi[r]t leging[s] handkerchief a knife some tobacco and a few small articles   we also distributed a good quantity paint mock-

erson awles knives beads looking-glasses &c among the other Indians and gave them a plentifull meal of lyed corn which was the
first they had ever eaten in their lives. they were much pleased
with it. every article about us appeared to excite astonishment in
ther minds; the appearance of the men, their arms, the canoes, our
manner of working them, the b[l]ack man york and the sagacity of
my dog were equally objects of admiration. I also shot my air-gun
which was so perfectly incomprehensible that they immediately denominated it the great medicine.

Capt. Clark and myself now concerted measures for our future
operations, and it was mutually agreed that he should set out tomorrow morning with eleven men furnished with axes and other
necessary tools for making canoes, their arms accoutrements and
as much of their baggage as they could carry. also to take the indians, C[h]arbono and the indian woman with him; that on his
arrival at the Shoshone camp he was to leave Charbono and the
Indian woman to haisten the return of the Indians with their
horses to this place, and to proceede himself with the eleven men
down the Columbia in order to examine the river and if he found
it navigable and could obtain timber to set about making canoes
immediately. In the mean time I was to bring the party and baggage to the Shoshone Camp, calculating that by the time I should
reach that place that he would have sufficiently informed himself
with rispect to the state of the river &c. as to determine us whether
to prosicute our journey from thence by land or water. in the
former case we should want all the horses which we could perchase.
and in the latter only to hire the Indians to transport our baggage
to the place at which we made the canoes.

SUNDAY AUGUST 18TH 1805.

This morning while Capt Clark was busily engaged in preparing for his rout, I exposed some articles to barter with the Indians
for horses as I wished a few at this moment to releive the men who
were going with Capt Clark from the labour of carrying their baggage, and also one to keep here in order to pack the meat to camp
which the hunters might kill. I soon obtained three very good
horses. for which I gave an uniform coat, a pair of legings, a few
handkerchiefs, three knives and some other small articles the whole

of which did not cost more than about 20$ in the U' States. the Indians seemed quite as well pleased with their bargin as I was. the men also purchased one for an old checked shirt a pair of old legings and a knife. two of those I purchased Capt. C. took on with him. at 10 A.M. Capt. Clark departed with his detachment and all the Indians except 2 men and 2 women who remained with us.

after there departure this morning I had all the stores and baggage of every discription opened and aired. and began the operation of forming the packages in proper parsels for the purpose of transporting them on horseback. the rain in the evening compelled me to desist from my operations. I had the raw hides put in the water in order to cut them in throngs proper for lashing the packages and forming the necessary geer for pack horses, a business which I fortunately had not to learn on this occasion. I had the net arranged and set this evening to catch some trout which we could see in great abundance at the bottom of the river.

This day I completed my thirty first year, and conceived that I had in all human probability now existed about half the period which I am to remain in this Sublunary world. I reflected that I had as yet done but little, very little, indeed, to further the hapiness of the human race or to advance the information of the succeeding generation. I viewed with regret the many hours I have spent in indolence, and now soarly feel the want of that information which those hours would have given me had they been judiciously expended. but since they are past and cannot be recalled, I dash from me the gloomy thought, and resolved in future, to redouble my exertions and at least indeavour to promote those two primary objects of human existence, by giving them the aid of that portion of talents which nature and fortune have bestoed on me; or in future, to live for *mankind,* as I have heretofore lived *for myself.*

[Clark]   AUGUST 18TH SUNDAY 1805

at 10 oClock I set out accompanied by the Indians except 3 the interpreter and wife,   the fore part of the day worm,   at 12 oClock it became hasey with a mist of rain   wind hard from the S.W. and cold which increased untill night   the rain Seased in about two hours. We proceeded on thro' a wide leavel vallie without wood except willows & Srubs for 15 miles and Encamped at a place the high lands approach within 200 yards in 2 points   the River here only 10 yards wide   Several Small Streams branching out on each Side below. all the Indians proceeded on except the 3 Chiefs & two young men.

[Lewis]   MONDAY AUGUST 19TH 1805

The Shoshonees may be estimated at about 100 warriors, and about three times that number of woomen and children.[1] they have more children among them than I expected to have seen among a people who procure subsistence with such difficulty. there are but few very old persons, nor did they appear to treat those with much tenderness or rispect. The man is the sole propryetor of his wives and daughters, and can barter or dispose of either as he thinks proper. a plurality of wives is common among them, but these are not generally sisters as with the Minnitares & Mandans but are purchased of different fathers. The father frequently disposes of his infant daughters in marriage to men who are grown or to men who have sons for whom they think proper to provide wives. the compensation given in such cases usually consists of horses or mules which the father receives at the time of contract and converts to his own uce. the girl remains with her parents untill she is conceived to have obtained the age of puberty which with them is considered to be about the age of 13 or 14 years. the female at this age is surrendered to her soveriegn lord and husband agreeably to contract, and with her is frequently restored by the father quite as much as he received in the first instance in payment for his daughter; but this is discretionary with the father. Sah-car-gar-we-ah had been thus disposed of before she was taken by the Minnetares, or had arrived to the years of puberty. the husband was yet living with this band. he was more than double her age and had two other wives. he claimed her as his wife but said that as she had had a child by another man, who was Charbono, that he did not want her.

They seldom correct their children particularly the boys who soon become masters of their own acts. they give as a reason that it cows and breaks the sperit of the boy to whip him, and that he never recovers his independence of mind after he is grown. They

[1] Lewis's figures refer to this band only.

treat their women but with little rispect, and compel them to perform every species of drudgery. they collect the wild fruits and roots, attend to the horses or assist in that duty, cook, dress the skins and make all their apparel, collect wood and make their fires, arrange and form their lodges, and when they travel pack the horses and take charge of all the baggage; in short the man dose little else except attend his horses hunt and fish. the man considers himself degraded if he is compelled to walk any distance; and if he is so unfortunately poor as only to possess two horses he rides the best himself and leavs the woman or women if he has more than one, to transport their baggage and children on the other, and to walk if the horse is unable to carry the additional weight of their persons. the chastity of their women is not held in high estimation, and the husband will for a trifle barter the companion of his bead for a night or longer if he conceives the reward adiquate; tho' they are not so importunate that we should caress their women as the siouxs were. and some of their women appear to be held more sacred than in any nation we have seen. I have requested the men to give them no cause of jealousy by having connection with their women without their knowledge, which with them, strange as it may seem is considered as disgracefull to the husband as clandestine connections of a similar kind are among civilized nations. to prevent this mutual exchange of good officies altogether I know it impossible to effect, particularly on the part of our young men whom some months abstanence have made very polite to those tawney damsels. no evil has yet resulted and I hope will not from these connections.

notwithstanding the late loss of horses which this people sustained by the Minnetares the stock of the band may be very safely estimated at seven hundred of which they are perhaps about 40 coalts and half that number of mules. their arms offensive and defensive consist in the bow and arrows shield, some, lances, and a weapon called by the Cippeways who formerly used it, the poggar'-mag-gon' [war club]. in fishing they employ wairs, gigs, and fishing hooks. the salmon is the principal object of their pursuit. they snair wolves and foxes.

I was anxious to learn whether these people had the venerial, and made the enquiry through the intrepreter and his wife; the information was that they sometimes had it but I could not learn their remedy; they most usually die with it's effects. this seems a strong proof that these disorders bothe ganaræhah and Louis Veneræ are native disorders of America. tho' these people have suffered mu'ch by the small pox which is known to be imported and perhaps those other disorders might have been contracted from other indian tribes who by a round of communications might have obtained from the Europeans since it was introduced into that quarter of the globe. but so much detatched on the other ha[n]d from all communication with the whites that I think it most probable that those disorders are original with them.

from the middle of May to the first of September these people reside on the waters of the Columbia where they consider themselves in perfect security from their enimies as they have not as yet ever found their way to this retreat; during this season the salmon furnish the principal part of their subsistence and as this fish either perishes or returns about the 1st of September they are compelled at this season in surch of subsistence to resort to the Missouri, in the vallies of which, there is more game even [than] within the mountains. here they move slowly down the river in order to collect and join other bands either of their own nation or the Flatheads, and having become sufficiently strong as they conceive venture on the Eastern side of the Rockey mountains into the plains, where the buffaloe abound. but they never leave the interior of the mountains while they can obtain a scanty subsistence, and always return as soon as they have acquired a good stock of dryed meat in the plains; when this stock is consumed they venture again into the plains; thus alternately obtaining their food at the risk of their lives and retiring to the mountains, while they consume it. These people are now on the eve of their departure for the Missouri, and inform us that they expect to be joined at or about the three forks by several bands of their own nation, and a band of the Flatheads.

[Clark] AUGUST 19TH MONDAY 1805.

A verry Cold morning Frost to be seen   we Set out at 7 oClock and proceeded on thro a wide leavel Vallie   this Vallie Continues 5 miles & then becoms narrow,   we proceeded on up the main branch with a gradial assent to the head and passed over a low mountain and Decended a Steep Decent to a butifull Stream, passed over a Second hill of a verry Steep assent & thro' a hilley Countrey for 8 miles an[d] Encamped on a Small Stream, the Indians with us we wer oblige[d] to feed. one man met me with a mule & Spanish Saddle to ride, I gave him a westcoat   a mule is considered of great value among those people   we proceeded on over a verry mountainous Countrey across the head of hollows & Springs

[Lewis]   TUESDAY AUGUST 20TH 1805.

I walked down the river about ¾ of a mile and selected a place near the river bank unperceived by the Indians for a cash [cache], which I set three men to make, and directed the centinel to discharge his gun if he perceived any of the Indians going down in that direction which was to be the signal for the men at work on the cash, to desist and seperate, least these people should discover our deposit and rob us of the baggage we intend leaving here. by evening the cash was completed unperceived by the Indians, and all our packages made up. the Pack-saddles and harnes is not yet complete. in this operation we find ourselves at a loss for nails and boards; for the first we substitute throngs of raw hide which answer verry well, and for the last [had] to cut off the blades of our oars and use the plank of some boxes which have heretofore held other articles and put those articles into sacks of raw hide which I have had made for the purpose. by this means I have obtained as many boards as will make 20 saddles which I suppose will be sufficient for our present exegencies. I made up a small assortment of medicines, together with the specemines of plants, minerals, seeds &c, which, I have collected betwen this place and the falls of the Missouri which I shall deposit here.

I now prevailed on the Chief to instruct me with rispect to the geography of his country. this he undertook very cheerfully, by delineating the rivers on the ground. but I soon found that his information fell far short of my expectation or wishes. he drew the river on which we now are [the Lemhi] to which he placed two branches just above us, which he shewed me from the openings of the mountains were in view; he next made it discharge itself into a large river which flowed from the S.W. about ten miles below us [the Salmon], then continued this joint stream in the same direction of this valley or N.W. for one days march and then enclined it to the West for 2 more days march. here he placed a number of heaps of sand on each side which he informed me represented the vast mountains of rock eternally covered with snow through which the river passed. that the perpendicular and even juting rocks so closely hemned in the river that there was no possibil[it]y of passing along the shore; that the bed of the river was obstructed by sharp pointed rocks and the rapidity of the stream such that the whole surface of the river was beat into perfect foam as far as the eye could reach. that the mountains were also inaccessible to man or horse. he said that this being the state of the country in that direction that himself nor none of his nation had ever been further down the river than these mountains.

I then enquired the state of the country on either side of the river but he could not inform me. he said there was an old man of his nation a days march below who could probably give me some information of the country to the N.W. and refered me to an old man then present for that to the S.W.   the Chief further informed me that he had understood from the persed nosed [Nez Percé] Indians who inhabit this river below the rocky mountains that it ran a great way toward the seting sun and finally lost itself in a great lake of water which was illy taisted, and where the white men lived. I next commenced my enquiries of the old man to whom I had been refered for information relative the country SW. of us. this he depicted with horrors and obstructions scarcely inferior to that just mentioned.[2] he informed me that the band of this nation to which he belonged resided at the distance of 20 days march from hence not far from the white people with whom they traded for horses mules cloth metal beads and the shells which they woar as orniment being those of a species of perl oister. that the course to his relations was a little to the West of South. that in order to get to his relations the first seven days we should be obliged to climb over steep and rocky mountains where we could find no game to kill nor anything but roots such as a ferce and

2 From here on the old man's information is unreliable. Almost all of what he says is hearsay and guess. His own errors and misconceptions and Lewis's misunderstanding and geographical preconceptions unite to produce a fantastic picture of the country west and southwest of Lemhi Pass. The passage is analyzed in DeVoto, *The Course of Empire*, Chap. XII.

warlike nation lived on whom he called the broken mockersons or mockersons with holes, and said inhabited those mountains and lived like the bear of other countries among the rocks and fed on roots or the flesh of such horses as they could take or steel from those who passed through their country. that in passing this country the feet of our horses would be so much wounded with the stones many of them would give out. the next part of the rout was about 10 days through a dry and parched sandy desert in which [there is] no food at this season for either man or horse, and in which we must suffer if not perish for the want of water.[3] that the sun had now dryed up the little pools of water which exist through this desert plain in the spring season and had also scorched all the grass. that no animal inhabited this plain on which we could hope to subsist. that about the center of this plain a large river passed from S.E. to N.W. which was navigable but afforded neither Salmon nor timber. that beyond this plain th[r]ee or four days march his relations lived in a country tolerable fertile and partially covered with timber on another large river which ran in the same direction of the former. that this last discharged itself into a large river on which many numerous nations lived with whom his relations were at war but whether this last discharged itself into the great lake or not he did not know. that from his relations it was yet a great distance to the great or stinking lake as they call the Ocean. that the way which such of his nation as had been to the Stinking lake traveled was up the river on which they lived and over to that on which the white people lived which last they knew discharged itself into the Ocean, and that this was the way which he would advise me to travel if I was determined to proceed to the Ocean but would advise me to put off the journey untill the next spring when he would conduct me. I thanked him for his information and advise and gave him a knife with which he appeared to be much gratifyed.

from this narrative I was convinced that the streams of which he had spoken as runing through the plains and that on which his relations lived were southern branches of the Columbia, heading with the rivers Apostles and Collorado, and that the rout he had pointed out was to the Vermillion Sea or gulph of Callifornia.[4] I

---

[3] The lava plains of southern and southwestern Idaho, along the Snake River.
[4] A crucial misconception of the headwaters. (The River of the Apostles was mythical.)

therefore told him that this rout was more to the South than I wished to travel, and requested to know if there was no rout on the left of this river on which we now are, by means of which, I could intercept it below the mountains through which it passes; but he could not inform me of any except that of the barren plain which he said joined the mountain on that side and through which it was impossible for us to pass at this season even if we were fortunate enough to escape from the broken mockerson Indians. I now asked Cameahwait by what rout the Pierced nosed indians, who he informed me inhabited this river below the mountains, came over to the Missouri; this he informed me was to the north, but added that the road was a very bad one as he had been informed by them and that they had suffered excessively with hunger on the rout being obliged to subsist for many days on berries alone as there was no game in that part of the mountains which were broken rockey and so thickly covered with timber that they could scarcely pass. [5] however knowing that Indians had passed, and did pass, at this season on that side of this river to the same below the mountains, my rout was instantly settled in my own mind, p[r]ovided the account of this river should prove true on an investigation of it, which I was determined should be made before we would undertake the rout by land in any direction. I felt perfectly satisfyed, that if the Indians could pass these mountains with their women and Children, that we could also pass them; and that if the nations on this river below the mountains were as numerous as they were stated to be that they must have some means of subsistence which it would be equally in our power to procure in the same country. they informed me that there was no buffaloe on the West side of these mountains; that the game consisted of a few Elk deer and Antelopes, and that the natives subsisted on fish and roots principally.

in this manner I spent the day smoking with them and acquiring what information I could with respect to their country. they informed me that they could pass to the Spaniards by the way of the yellowstone river in 10 days. I can discover that these people are by no means friendly to the Spaniards. their complaint is, that the Spaniards will not let them have fire arms and amunition, that they put them off by telling them that if they suffer them to have guns they will kill each other, thus leaving them defenceless and

[5] This is vital information and it is correct.

an easy prey to their bloodthirsty neighbours to the East of them, who being in possession of fire arms hunt them up and murder them without rispect to sex or age and plunder them of their horses on all occasions. they told me that to avoid their enemies who were eternally harrassing them that they were obliged to remain in the interior of these mountains at least two thirds of the year where the[y] suffered as we then saw great heardships for the want of food sometimes living for weeks without meat and only a little fish roots and berries. but this added Câmeahwait, with his ferce eyes and lank jaws grown meager for the want of food, would not be the case if we had guns, we could then live in the country of buffaloe and eat as our enimies do and not be compelled to hide ourselves in these mountains and live on roots and berries as the bear do. we do not fear our enimies when placed on an equal footing with them. I told them that the Minnetares Mandans & recares of the Missouri had promised us to desist from making war on them & that we would indevour to find the means of making the Minnetares of fort d[e] Prarie or as they call them Pahkees desist from waging war against them also. that after our finally returning to our homes towards the rising sun whitemen would come to them with an abundance of guns and every other article necesssary to their defence and comfort, and that they would be enabled to supply themselves with these articles on reasonable terms in exchange for the skins of the beaver Otter and Ermin so abundant in their country. they expressed great pleasure at this information and said they had been long anxious to see the whitemen that traded guns; and that we might rest assured of their friendship and that they would do whatever we wished them.

[Clark]   AUGUST 20TH TUESDAY 1805
                            "SO-SO-NE" THE SNAKE INDIANS

    Set out at half past 6 oClock and proceeded on (met maney parties of Indians) thro' a hilley Countrey to the Camp of the Indians on a branch of the Columbia River,   before we entered this Camp a Serimonious hault was requested by the Chief and I smoked with all that Came around, for Several pipes,   we then proceeded on to the Camp & I was introduced into the only Lodge they had which was pitched in the Center for my party   all the other Lodges made of bushes, after a fiew Indian Seremonies I informed the Indians the object of our journey our good intentions towards them my Consirn for their distressed Situation, what we had done for them in makeing a piece with the *Minitarras Mandans Rickara* &c. for them. and requested them all to take over their horses & assist Capt Lewis across &c. also informing them the object of my journey down the river, and requested a guide to accompany me, all of which was repeited by the Chief to the whole village.

Those pore people Could only raise a Sammon & a little dried Choke Cherries for us half the men of the tribe with the Chief turned out to hunt the antilopes, at 3 oClock after giveing a fiew Small articles as presents I set out accompanied by an old man as a Guide I endevered to procure as much information from thos people as possible without much Suckcess they being but little acquainted or effecting to be So. I left one man to purchase a horse and overtake me and proceeded on thro a wide rich bottom on a beaten Roade 8 miles Crossed the river and encamped on a Small run, I left our interpreter & his woman to accompany the Indians to Capt Lewis tomorrow the Day they informed me they would Set out.

CHAPTER XVI

SEARCHING FOR NAVIGABLE WATERS

[Lewis]   WEDNESDAY AUGUST 21ST 1805.

This morning was very cold. the ice ¼ of an inch thick on the water which stood in the vessels exposed to the air. some wet deerskins that had been spread on the grass last evening are stiffly frozen. the ink f[r]eizes in my pen. the bottoms are perfectly covered with frost, insomuch that they appear to be covered with snow. This morning early I dispatched two hunters to kill some meat if possible before the Indians arrive; Drewyer I sent with the horse into the cove for that purpose. The party pursued their several occupations as yesterday. by evening I had all the baggage, saddles, and harness completely ready for a march. after dark, I made the men take the baggage to the cash and deposit it. I believe we have been unperceived by the Indians in this movement. notwithstanding the coldness of the last night the day has proved excessively warm. neither of the hunters returned this evening and I was obliged to issue pork and corn.

The mockersons of both sexes are usually the same and are made of deer Elk or buffaloe skin dressed without the hair. sometimes in the winter they make them of buffaloe skin dressed with the hair on and turn the hair inwards as the Mandans Minetares and most of the nations do who inhabit the buffaloe country. the mockerson is formed with one seem on the outer edge of the foot is cut open at the instep to admit the foot and sewed up behind. in this rispect they are the same with the Mandans. they sometimes ornament their mockersons with various figures wrought with the quills of the Porcupine.

some of the dressey young men orniment the tops of their mock-

ersons with the skins of polecats and trale the tail of that animal
on the ground at their heels as they walk. the robe of the woman
is generally smaller than that of the man but is woarn in the same
manner over the sholders. the Chemise is roomy and comes down
below the middle of the leg the upper part of this garment is
formed much like the shirt of the men except the sholder strap
which is never used with the Chemise. in woman who give suck,
they are left open at the sides nearly as low as the waist, in others,
close as high as the sleeve. the sleeve underneath as low as the
elbow is open, that part being left very full. the sides tail and
upper part of the sleeves are deeply fringed and sometimes ornimented in a similar manner with the shirts of the men with the
addition of little patches of red cloth about the tail edged around
with beads. the breast is usually ornamentd with various figures of
party colours rought with the quills of the Porcupine. it is on this
part of the garment that they appear to exert their greatest engenuity. a girdle of dressed leather confines the Chemise around
the waist. the legings of the women reach as high as the knee and
are confined with a garter below. the mockerson covers and con-
fins it's lower extremity. they are neither fringed nor ornamented.
these legings are made of the skins of the antelope and the Chemise
usually of those of the large deer Bighorn and the smallest elk.

the warriors or such as esteem themselves brave men wear collars
made of the claws of the brown bear which are also esteemed of
great value and are preserved with great care. these claws are
ornamented with beads about the thick end near which they are
peirced through their sides and strung on a throng of dressed
leather and tyed about the neck commonly with the upper edge of
the tallon next the breast or neck but sometimes are reversed. it is
esteemed by them an act of equal celebrity the killing one of these
bear or an enimy, and with the means they have of killing this
animal it must really be a serious undertaking.

[Clark]   AUGUST 21ST WEDNESDAY 1805

I entered a lodge and after smokeing with all who Came about
me I went to see the place those people take the fish, a wear [weir]
across the Creek in which there is Stuk baskets Set in different
derections So as to take the fish either decending or assending   Their method of takeing fish with a *gig* or bone is with a

long pole,   about a foot from one End is a Strong String attached to the pole, this String is a little more than a foot long and is tied to the middle of a bone from 4 to 6 inches long, one end Sharp the other with a whole to fasten on the end of the pole with a beard [barb] to the large end,   the[y] fasten this bone on one end & with the other, feel for the fish & turn and Strike them So hard that the bone passes through and Catches on the opposit Side, Slips off the End of the pole and holds the Center of the bone

Those Indians are mild in their disposition, appear Sincere in their friendship, punctial, and decided. kind with what they have, to spare. They are excessive pore, nothing but horses   there Enemies which are noumerous on account of there horses & Defenceless Situation, have deprived them of tents and all the Small Conveniances of life. They have only a few indifferent Knives, no ax, make use of Elk's horn Sharpened to Sp[l]it ther wood, no clothes except a Short Legins & robes of different animals, Beaver, Bear, Buffalow, wolf Panther, Ibex (Sheep), Deer, but most commonly the antilope Skins which they ware loosely about them. The women are held more sacred among them than any nation we have seen and appear to have an equal Shere in all conversation, which is not the Case in any other nation I have seen. their boys & girls are also admited to speak except in Councels,   the women doe all the drugery except fishing and takeing care of the horses, which the men apr. to take upon themselves. the most sacred of all the orniments of this nation is the Sea Shells of various Sizes and Shapes and colours, of the bassterd perl kind, which they inform us they get from the Indians to the South on the other Side of a large fork of this river in passing to which they have to pass thro: Sandy & barron open plains without water to which place they can travel in 15 or 20 days. The men who passed by the forks informed me that the S W. fork was double the Size of the one I came down, and I observed that it was a handsom river at my camp   I shall in justice to Capt. Lewis who was the first white man ever on this fork of the Columbia Call this Louis's river.[1]

---

[1] There are three principal forks of the Salmon River. The one into which the Lemhi enters is recognized as the main fork. It flows north before turning west, shortly after the entrance of the north fork. Some distance beyond this entrance comes the first of the precipitous canyons whose steep side and swift boulder-filled rapids forced Clark to decide that the expedition could not travel it. From here on it is in no sense a navigable river, although specially built craft occasionally descend it for sport. So far as the editor knows no one

[Lewis]   Thursday August 22ed 1805.

This morning early I sent a couple of men to complete the covering of the cash which could not be done well last night in the dark,   they soon accomplished their work and returned. late last night Drewyer returned with a fawn he had killed and a considerable quantity of Indian plunder. the anecdote with rispect to the latter is perhaps worthy of relation. he informed me that while hunting in the Cove yesterday about 12˙ OCk. he came suddonly upon an Indian Camp, at which there were a young man an Old man and a boy and three women, that they seemed but little supprised at seeing him and he rode up to them and dismounted turning [his] horse out to graize.   these people had just finished their repast on some roots,   he entered into conversation with them by signs, and after 20 minutes one of the women spoke to the others of the party and they all went immediately and collected their horses brought them to camp and saddled them   at this moment he thought he would also set out and continue his hunt, and accordingly walked to catch his horse at some little distance and neglected to take up his gun which he left at camp. the Indians perceiving him at the distance of fifty paces immediately mounted their horses, the young man took the gun, and the whole of them left their baggage and laid whip to their horses directing their course to the pass of the mountains. finding himself deprived of his gun he immediately mounted his horse and pursued; after runing them about 10 miles the horses of two of the women nearly gave out and the young fellow with the gun from their frequent crys slackened his pace and being on a very fleet horse road around the women at a little distance   at length Drewer overtook the women and by signs convinced them that he did not wish to hirt them   they then halted and the young fellow approached still nearer, he asked him for his gun but the only part of the answer which he could understand was pahkee which he knew to be the name by which they called their enimies. watch-

has ever ascended it by boat; locally it is called the River of No Return. After passing through these canyons, and crossing the whole width of Idaho, it empties into the Snake River about fifty miles upstream from the mouth of the Clearwater River, by which the expedition was to reach the Snake.

The expedition traveled beside the north fork of the Salmon upstream, for some distance on its way to Lost Trail Pass.

ing his opportunity when the fellow was off his guard he suddonly rode along side of him seized his gun and wrest her out of his hands. the fellow finding Drewyer too strong for him and discovering that he must yeald the gun had p[r]esents of mind to open the pan and cast the priming before he let the gun escape from his hands; now finding himself devested of the gun he turned his horse about and laid whip leaving the women to follow him as well as they could.

at 11.A.M. Charbono, the Indian Woman, Cameahwait and about 50 men with a number of women and children arrived. they encamped near us. after they had turned out their horses and arranged their camp I called the Cheifs and warriors together and addressed them a second time; gave them some further presents, particularly the second and third Cheifs who it appeared had agreeably to their promise exerted themselves in my favour,   having no fresh meat and these poor devils half starved I had previously prepared a good meal for them all of boiled corn and beans which I gave them as soon as the council was over and I had distributed the presents. this was thankfully received by them. the Cheif wished that his nation could live in a country where they could provide such food. I told him that it would not be many years before the whitemen would put it in the power of his nation to live in the country below the mountains where they might cultivate corn beans and squashes. he appeared much pleased with the information. I gave him a few dryed squashes which we had brought from the Mandans   he had them boiled and declared them to be the best thing he had ever tasted except sugar, a small lump of which it seems his sister Sah-cah-gar Wea had given him. late in the evening I made the men form a bush drag, and with it in about 2 hours they caught 528 very good fish, most of them large trout. among them I now for the first time saw ten or a douzen of a white speceis of trout. they are of a silvery colour except on the back and head, where they are of a bluish cast. the scales are much larger than the speckled trout, but in their form position of their fins teeth mouth &c they are precisely like them. they are not generally quite as large but equally well flavored. I distributed much the greater portion of the fish among the Indians. I purchased five good horses of them very reasonably, or at least for about the value of six dollars a peice in merchandize. the Indians are very orderly and do not croud about our camp nor attempt to disterb any article they see lying about. they borrow knives kettles &c from the men and always carefully return them.

[Clark]   AUGUST 22D THURSDAY 1805.

We Set out early   passed a Small Creek on the right at 1 mile and the points of four mountains verry Steup high & rockey,   the assent of three was So Steup that it is incredeable to describe   the rocks in maney places loose & Sliped from those mountains and is a Solid bed of rugid loose white and dark brown loose rock for miles. the Indian horses pass over those Clifts hills beds & rocks as fast as a man, the three horses with me do not detain me any on account of those dificulties,   passed two bold rung. Streams on the right and a Small river at the mouth of which Several families of Indians were encamped and had Several Scaffolds of fish & buries drying [2]   we allarmed them verry much as they knew nothing of a white man being in their Countrey, and at the time we approached their lodges which was in a thick place of bushes   my guides were behind. They offered every thing they possessed (which was verry little) to us, Some run off and hid in the bushes   The first offer of theirs were Elks tushes from around their childrens necks, Sammon &c.   my guide attempted [to] passify those people and they Set before me berri[e]s, & fish to eate,   I gave a fiew Small articles to those fritened people which added verry much to their pasification but not entirely as some of the women & Childn. Cried dureing my Stay of an hour at this place,   I proceeded on the Side of a verry Steep & rockey mountain for 3 miles and Encamped on the lower pt. of an Island   we attempted to gig fish without Suckcess   caught but one Small one. The last Creek or Small river is on the right Side and a road passes up it & over to the Missouri (to Wisdom) [3]

2 Clark has been descending the main fork of the Salmon River. The "Small river," which comes in from the north, is the North Fork of the Salmon, about twenty-five miles north (downstream) of the town of Salmon, Idaho. Here the river turns west and the going becomes increasingly difficult.

3 This trail would have led over the Divide by Gibbon's Pass.

[Lewis]   FRIDAY AUGUST 23RD 1805.

I wished to have set out this morning but the cheif requested that I would wait untill another party of his nation arrived which he expected today,   to this I consented from necessity. I laid up the canoes this morning in a pond near the forks; sunk them in the water and weighted them down with stone, after taking out the plugs of the gage holes in their bottoms; hoping by this means to guard against both the effects of high water, and that of the fire which is frequently kindled in these plains by the natives. the Indians have promised to do them no intentional injury and [I] beleive they are too laizy at any rate to give themselves the trouble to raise them from their present situation in order to cut or birn them.

The metal which we found in possession of these people consited of a few indifferent knives, a few brass kettles some arm bands of iron and brass, a few buttons, woarn as ornaments in their hair, a spear or two of a foot in length and some iron and brass arrow points which they informed me they obtained in exchange for horses from the Crow or Rocky Mountain Indians on the yellowstone River. the bridlebits and stirreps they obtained from the Spaniards, tho these were but few. many of them made use of flint for knives, and with this instrument, skined the animals they killed, dressed their fish and made their arrows; in short they used it for every purpose to which the knife is applyed. this flint is of no regular form, and if they can only obtain a part of it, an inch or two in length that will cut they are satisfyed. they renew the edge by flecking off the flint by means of the point of an Elk's or deer's horn. with the point of a deer or Elk's horn they also form their arrow points of the flint, with a quickness and neatness that is really astonishing. we found no axes nor hatchets among them; what wood they cut was done either with stone or Elk's horn. the latter they use always to rive or split their wood. their culinary eutensils exclusive of the brass kettle before mentioned consist of pots in the form of a jar made either of earth, or of a white soft stone which becomes black and very hard by birning, and is found in the hills near the three forks of the Missouri between Madison's and Gallitin's rivers. they have also spoons made of the Buffaloe's horn and those of the Bighorn.

they sometimes make bows of the Elk's horn and those also of the bighorn. those of the Elk's horn are made of a single peice and covered on the back with glue and sinues like those made of wood, and are frequently ornamented with a stran[d] wrought [of] porcupine quills and sinues raped around them for some distance at both extremities. the bows of the bighorn are formed of small peices laid flat and cemented with gleue, and rolled with siniws, after which, they are also covered on the back with sinews and glew, and highly ornamented as they are much prized.

forming the sheild is a cerimony of great importance among them, this implement would in their minds be devested of much of its protecting power were it not inspired with those virtues by their older men and jugglers [medicine priests]. their method of preparing it is thus, an entire skin of a bull buffaloe two years old is first provided; a feast is next prepared and all the warriors old men and jugglers invited to partake. a hole is sunk in the ground about the same in diameter with the intended sheild and about 18 inches deep. a parcel of stones are now made red hot and thrown into the hole   water is next thrown in and the hot stones cause it to emit a very strong hot steem, over this they spread the green skin which must not have been suffered to dry after taken off the beast. the flesh side is laid next to the groround and as many of the workmen as can reach it take hold on it's edges and extend it in every direction. as the skin becomes heated, the hair seperates and is taken of with the fingers, and the skin continues to contract untill the who[l]e is drawn within the compas designed for the shield,   it is then taken off and laid on a parchment hide where they pound it with their heels when barefoot. this operation of pounding continues for several days or as long as the feast lasts when it is delivered to the propryeter and declared by the jugglers and old men to be a sufficient defence against the arrows of their enimies or even bullets if feast has been a satisfactory one. many of them beleive implisitly that a ball cannot penitrate their sheilds, in consequence of certain superna[t]ural powers with which they have been inspired by their jugglers.

The Poggâmoggon is an instrument with a handle of wood covered with dressed leather about the size of a whip handle and 22 inches long; a round stone of 2 pounds weight is also covered with leather and strongly united to the leather of the handle by a throng of 2 inches long; a loop of leather united to the handle passes arond the wrist. a very heavy blow may be given with this instrument. They have also a kind of armor which they form with many foalds of dressed a[n]telope's skin, unite with glue and sand. with this they cover their own bodies and those of their horses. these are sufficient against the effects of the arrow. their impliments for making fire is nothing more than a blunt arrow and a peice of well seasoned soft spongey wood such as the willow or cottonwood. the point of this arrow they apply to this dry stick so near one edge of it that the particles of wood which are seperated from it by the friction of the arrow falls down by it's side in a little pile. the arrow is held between the palms of the hand with the fingers extended, and being pressed as much as possible against the peice is briskly rolled between the palms of the hands backwards and forwards by pressing the arrow downwards   the hands of course in rolling [the] arrow so decend; they bring them back with a quick motion and repeat the operation till the dust by the friction takes fire; the peice and arrow are then removed and some dry grass or dooted [rotted] wood is added. in less than a minute they will produce fire.

[Clark]   AUGUST 23RD FRIDAY 1805

   proceed on with great dificuelty as the rocks were So sharp large and unsettled and the hill sides Steep that the horses could with the greatest risque and dificulty get on,   at 4 miles we came to a place the horses Could not pass without going into the river,   we passed one mile to a very bad riffle the water confined in a narrow Channel & beeting against the left Shore,   as we have no parth further and the Mounts. jut So close as to prevent the possibility of horses proceeding down, I Deturmined to delay the party here and with my guide and three men proceed on down to examine if the river continued bad or was practi[c]able,   I set out with three men directing those left to hunt and fish untill my return. I proceeded on. Sometimes in a Small wolf parth & at other times Climing over the rocks for 12 miles to a large Creek on the right Side   above the mouth of this Creek for a Short distance is a narrow bottom & the first, below the place I left my party. The River from the place I left my party to this Creek is almost one continued rapid, five verry considerable rapids   the passage of either with Canoes is entirely impossible, as the water is Confined between huge Rocks & the Current beeting from one against another for Some distance below &c. &c.   at one of those rapids the mountains close so Clost as to prevent a possibility of a portage with [out] great labour in cutting down the Side of the hill removeing large rocks &c. &c.   all the others may be passed by takeing every thing over slipery rocks, and the Smaller ones Passed by letting down the Canoes empty with Cords, as running them would certainly be productive of the loss of Some Canoes,   those dificulties and necessary precautions would delay us an emence time in which provisions would be necessary.

below this Creek the lofty Pine is thick in the bottom hill Sides on the mountains & up the runs. The river has much the resemblance of that above   bends Shorter and no passing after a few miles between the river & the mountains & the Current so Strong that [it] is dangerous crossing the river, and to proceed down it would rend. it necessary to Cross almost at every bend   this river is about 100 yards wide and can be forded but in a few places. below my guide and maney other Indians tell me that the Mountains Close and is a perpendicular Clift on each Side, and Continues for a great distance and that the water runs with great violence from one rock to the other on each Side foaming & roreing thro rocks in every direction, So as to render the passage of any thing impossible. those rapids which I had Seen he said was Small & trifleing in comparrison to the rocks & rapids below, at no great distance & The Hills or mountains were not like those I had Seen but like the Side of a tree Streight up. we proceeded on a well beeten Indian parth up this creak (Berry Creek) about 6 miles and passed over a ridge 1 mile to the river in a Small vally through which we passed and assended a Spur of the Mountain from which place my guide Shew[ed] me the river for about 20 miles lower & pointed out the dificulties.

[Lewis]   SATURDAY AUGUST 24TH 1805.

As the Indians who were on their way down the Missouri had a number of spare ho[r]ses with them I thought it probable that I could obtain some of them and therefore desired the Cheif to speak to them and inform me whether they would trade. they gave no positive answer but requested to see the goods which I was willing to give in exchange. I now produced some battle axes which I had made at Fort Mandan with which they were much pleased. knives also seemed in great demand among them. I soon purchased three horses and a mule. for each horse I gave an ax a knife handkercheif and a little paint; & for the mule the addition of a knife a shirt handkercheif and a pair of legings; at this price which was quite double that given for the horses, the fellow who sold him made a merit of having bestoed [on] me one of his mules. I consider this mule a great acquisition. these Indians soon told me that they had no more horses for sale and I directed the party to prepare to set out. I had now nine horses and a mule, and two which I had hired made twelve these I had loaded and the Indian women took the ballance of the baggage. I had given the Interpreter some articles with which to purchase a horse for the woman which he had obtained.

at twelve Oclock we set out and passed the river below the forks, directing our rout towards the cove along the track formerly mentioned.[4] most of the horses were heavily laden, and it appears to me that it will require at least 25 horses to convey our baggage along such roads as I expect we shall be obliged to pass in the mountains. I had now the inexpressible satisfaction to find myself once more under way with all my baggage and party. an Indian had the politeness to offer me one of his horses to ride which I accepted with cheerfullness as it enabled me to attend better to the march of the party. I had reached the lower part of the cove when an Indian rode up and informed me that one of my men was very sick and unable to come on. I directed the party to halt at a small run which falls into the creek on Lard. at the lower part of the Cove and rode back about 2 Miles where I found Wiser very ill with a fit of the cholic. I sent Sergt. Ordway who had remained with him for some water and gave him a doze of the essence of Peppermint and laudinum which in the course of half an hour so far recovered him that he was enabled to ride my horse and I proceeded on foot and rejoined the party. the sun was yet an hour high

4 Lewis is beginning to transport the outfit across the Divide. His route will lead from the mouth of Prairie Creek to Shoshone Cove, through Lemhi Pass, and down to Lemhi River.

but the Indians who had for some time impatiently waited my return at length unloaded and turned out their horses and my party had followed there example. as it was so late and the Indians had prepared their camp for the night I thought it best to acquiess and determined also to remain. we had traveled only about six miles.

The few guns which the Shoshones have are reserved for war almost exclusively and the bow and arrows are used in hunting. I have seen a few skins among these people which have almost every appearance of the common sheep. they inform me that they finde this animal on the high mountains to the West and S. W. of them. it is about the size of the common sheep, the wool is reather shorter and more intermixed with long hairs particularly on the upper part of the neck. these skins have been so much woarn that I could not form a just Idea of the animal or it's colour. the Indians however inform me that it is white and that it's horns are lunated comprest twisted and bent backward as those of the common sheep.[5] the texture of the skin appears to be that of the sheep. I am now perfectly convinced that the sheep as well as the Bighorn exist in these mountains.

[Clark]   AUGUST 24TH SATTURDAY 1805

I wrote a letter to Capt Lewis informing him of the prospects before us and information rec[ei]ved of my guide which I thought favourable &c. & Stating two plans one of which for us to pursue &c. and despatched one man & horse and directed the party to get ready to march back,   every man appeared disheartened from the prospects of the river, and nothing to eate,   I Set out late and Camped 2 miles above, nothing to eate but Choke Cherries & red haws, which act in different ways So as to make us Sick,   dew verr heavy, my beding wet   in passing around a rock the horses were obliged to go deep into the water.

The plan I stated to Capt Lewis if he agrees with me we shall adopt it. to procure as many horses (one for each man) if possible and to hire my present guide who I sent on to him to interigate thro' the Intptr. and proceed on by land to Some navagable part of the *Columbia* River, or to the *Ocean,* depending on what provisions we can procure by the gun aded to the Small Stock we have on hand depending on our horses as the last resort.

5 The Rocky Mountain goat, *Oreamnos montanus.*

a second plan to divide the party one part to attempt this deficuelte river with what provisions we had, and the remainde[r] to pass by Land on ho[r]se back Depending on our gun &c. for Provisions &c. and come together occasionally on the river. the 1st of which I would be most pleased with &c.   I saw Several trees which would make Small Canoes and by putting 2 together would make a Siseable one, all below the last Indian Camp Several miles

[Lewis]   SUNDAY AUGUST 25TH 1805.

This morning loaded our horses and set out a little after sunrise; a few only of the Indians unengaged in assisting us went on as I had yesterday proposed to the cheif. the others flanked us on each side and started some Antelope which they pursued for several hours but killed none of them. we proceeded within 2 Ms. of the narrow pass or seven miles from our camp of last evening and halted for dinner. Our hunters joined us at noon with three deer the greater part of which I gave the indians. sometime after we had halted, Charbono mentioned to me with apparent unconcern that he expected to meet all the Indians from the camp on the Columbia tomorrow on their way to the Missouri. allarmed at this information I asked why he expected to meet them. he then informed me that the 1st Chief had dispatched some of his young men this morning to this camp requesting the Indians to meet tomorrow and that himself and those with him would go on with them down the Missouri, and consequently leave me and my baggage on the mountain or thereabouts. I was out of patience with the folly of Charbono who had not sufficient sagacity to see the consequencies which would inevitably flow from such a movement of the indians, and altho' he had been in possession of this information since early in the morning when it had been communicated to him by his Indian woman yet he never mentioned it untill the after noon. I could not forbear speaking to him with some degree of asperity on this occasion. I saw that there was no time to be lost in having those orders countermanded, or that we should not in all probability obtain any more horses or even get my baggage to the waters of the Columbia.

I therefore Called the three Cheifs together and having smoked a pipe with them, I asked them if they were men of their words and whether I could depent on the promises they had made me;

they readily answered in the affirmative; I then asked them if they had not promised to assist me with my baggage to their camp on the other side of the mountains, or to the place at which Capt. Clark might build the canoes, should I wish it. they acknowledged that they had. I then asked them why they had requested their people on the other side of the mountain to meet them tomorrow on the mountain where there would be no possibility of our remaining together for the purpose of trading for their horses as they had also promised. that if they had not promised to have given me their assistance in transporting my baggage to the waters on the other side of the mountain that I should not have attempted to pass the mountains but would have returned down the river and that in that case they would never have seen anymore white men in their country. that if they wished the white men to be their friends and to assist them against their enemies by furnishing them with arms and keeping their enemies from attacking them that they must never promis us anything which they did not mean to perform. that when I had first seen them they had doubted what I told them about the arrival of the party of whitemen in canoes, that they had been convinced that what I told them on that occasion was true, why then would they doubt what I said on any other point. I told them that they had witnessed my liberality in dividing the meat which my hunters killed with them; and that I should continue to give such of them as assisted me a part of whatever we had ourselves to eat. and finally concluded by telling them if they intended to keep the promises they had made me to dispatch one of their young men immediately with orders to their people to remain where they were untill our arrival.

the two inferior cheifs said that they wished to assist me and be as good as their word, and that they had not sent for their people, that it was the first Cheif who had done so, and they did not approve of the measure. Cameahwait remained silent for some time, at length he told me that he knew he had done wrong but that he had been induced to that measure from seeing all his people hungry, but as he had promised to give me his assistance he would not in future be worse than his word. I then desired him to send immediately and countermand his orders; accordingly a young man was sent for this purpose and I gave him a handkerchief to engage him in my interest.

MONDAY AUGUST 26TH 1805.

we collected our horses and set out at sunrise. we soon arrived at the extreem source of the Missouri; here I halted a few minutes, the men drank of the water and consoled themselves with the idea of having at length arrived at this long wished for point. from hence we proceeded to a fine spring on the side of the mountain where I had lain the evening before I first arrived at the Shoshone Camp. here I halted to dine and graize our horses, there being fine green grass on that part of the hillside which was moistened by the water of the spring while the grass on the other parts was perfectly dry and parched with the sun. I directed a pint of corn to be given each Indian who was engaged in transporting our baggage and about the same quantity to each of the men which they parched pounded and made into supe. one of the women who had been assisting in the transportation of the baggage halted at a little run about a mile behind us, and sent on the two pack horses which she had been conducting by one of her female friends. I enquired of Cameahwait the cause of her detention, and was informed by him in an unconcerned manner that she had halted to bring fourth a child and would soon overtake us; in about an hour the woman arrived with her newborn babe and passed us on her way to the camp apparently as well as she ever was. It appears to me that the facility and ease with which the women of the aborigines of North America bring fourth their children is reather a gift of nature than depending as some have supposed on the habitude of carrying heavy burthens on their backs while in a state of pregnacy.

Cameahwait requested that we would discharge our guns when we arrived in sight of the Village, accordingly when I arrived on an eminence above the village in the plain I drew up the party at open order in a single rank and gave them a runing fire discharging two rounds. they appeared much gratifyed with this exhibition. we then proceeded to the village or encampment of brush lodges 32 in number. we were conducted to a large lodge which had been prepared for me in the center of their encampment which was situated in a beautifull level smooth and extensive bottom near the river about 3 miles above the place I had first found them encamped. here we arrived at 6 in the evening arranged our baggage

near my tent and placed those of the men on either side of the
baggage facing outwards. I found Colter here who had just arrived
with a letter from Capt. Clark in which Capt. C.. had given me an
account of his perigrination and the description of the river and
country as before detailed   from this view of the subject I found
it a folly to think of attemp[t]ing to decend this river in canoes and
therefore determined to commence the purchase of horses in the
morning from the indians in order to carry into execution the design we had formed of passing the rocky Mountains. I now informed Cameahwait of my intended expedition overland to the
great river which lay in the plains beyond the mountains and told
him that I wished to purchase 20 horses of himself and his people
to convey our baggage. he observed that the Minnetares had stolen
a great number of their horses this spring but hoped his people
would spear me the number I wished. I also asked a (another)
guide, he observed that he had no doubt but the old man who
was with Capt. C. would accompany us if we wished him and that
he was better informed of the country than any of them. matters
being thus far arranged I directed the fiddle to be played and the
party danced very merily much to the amusement and gratification
of the natives, though I must confess that the state of my own mind
at this moment did not well accord with the prevailing mirth as
I somewhat feared that the caprice of the indians might suddenly
induce them to withhold their horses from us without which my
hopes of prosicuting my voyage to advantage was lost.

CHAPTER XVII

DOWN THE LOLO TRAIL

The party moved down the small Lemhi River to the main fork of the Salmon River and about ten miles down that to the mouth of Tower Creek, some fifteen miles above the mouth of the North Fork of the Salmon. It turned up the precipitous canyon of the North Fork, heading northeast toward the (Bitterroot) valley where it would find the trail by which, as both captains had been told, the Nez Percés crossed the mountains to the buffalo plains. Some of the Shoshones accompanied the party for a while but by September 1 all had turned back except "Toby," the old man who had been hired as a guide, and his son. They had been able to buy 29 horses, for packing and, as Clark added, to "Eate if necessary."

[Clark]   SEPTEMBER 2ND MONDAY 1805

we Set out early and proceeded on up the Creek,[1] Crossed a large fork from the right and one from the left; and at 8 miles left the roade on which we were pursuing and which leads over to the Missouri, and proceeded up a West fork without a roade   proceded on thro' thickets in which we were obliged to Cut a road, over rockey hill Sides where our horses were in [per]peteal danger of Slipping to their certain distruction & up & Down Steep hills, where Several horses fell, Some turned over, and others Sliped down Steep hill Sides, one horse Crippeled & 2 gave out. with the greatest dificuelty risque &c. we made five miles & Encamped.

[1] The North Fork of the Salmon River, and "the West fork without a roade" is the main stream.

SEPTEMBER 3RD TUESDAY 1805 —

hills high & rockey on each Side,   in the after part of the day
the high mountains closed the Creek on each Side and obliged us
to take on the Steep Sides of those Mountains, So Steep that the
horses could Scur[ce]ly keep from Slipping down,   Several sliped
& Injured themselves verry much,   with great dificuelty we made
[blank space in MS.] miles & Encamped on a branch of the Creek
we assended after crossing Several Steep points & one mountain,   but little to eate   at dusk it began to Snow, at 3 oClock
Some rain. The mountains to the East Covered with Snow. we
met with a great misfortune, in haveing our last Th[er]mometer
broken, by accident   This day we passed over emence hils and
Some of the worst roads that ever horses passed,   our horses frequently fell   Snow about 2 inches deep when it began to rain
which termonated in a Sleet[storm]

SEPTEMBER 4TH WEDNESDAY 1805 —

Groun[d] covered with Snow,   we assended a mountain & took
a Divideing ridge [2] which we kept for Several Miles & fell on the
head of a Creek which appeared to run the Course we wished to
go,   prosued our Course down the Creek to the forks about 5
miles where we met a part[y] of the Tushepau [Flathead] nation,
of 33 Lodges   about 80 men 400 Total and at least 500
horses,   those people rec[e]ved us friendly, threw white robes
over our Sholders & Smoked in the pipes of peace,   we Encamped with them & found them friendly,   The Chief ha-
rangued untill late at night, Smoked in our pipe and appeared
Satisfied. I was the first white man who ever wer on the waters of
this river.

SEPTEMBER 5TH TUESDAY 1805

we assembled the Chiefs & warriers and Spoke to them (with
much dificuel[t]y as what we Said had to pass through Several

[2] One of the ridges of the Bitterroot Mountains. Probably they crossed by
Lost Trail Pass.

They are still west of the Continental Divide but only a few miles to the
south is Gibbon's Pass, which crosses it to Big Hole Basin.

languages before it got into theirs, which is a gugling kind of language Spoken much thro the throught [throat]   in the Course of the day I purchased 11 horses & exchanged 7 for which we gave a fiew articles of merchandise,   those people possess ellegant horses.

[Whitehouse]   THURSDAY 5TH [AND 6TH] SEPT. 1805.

these Savages has the Strangest language of any we have ever Seen. they appear to us to have an Empediment in their Speech or a brogue or bur on their tongue but they are the likelyest and honestst Savages we have ever yet Seen. . . . we take these Savages to be the Welch Indians if their be any Such from the Language. So Capt. Lewis took down the names of everry thing in their Language, in order that it may be found out whether they are or whether they Sprang or origenated first from the welch or not.

[Ordway]   THURSDAY 5TH SEPT 1805.

these natives have the Stranges language of any we have ever yet seen. they appear to us as though they had an Impedement in their Speech or brogue on their tongue. we think perhaps that they are the welch Indians, &. C.[3]

[Clark]   SEPTEMBER 6TH FRIDAY 1805 —

Crossed a Small river from the right we call (*this was the main river or Clarks*)[4] Soon after Setting out, also a Small Creek from

[3] See footnote, p. 52, entry for October 18, 1804. A belief that there was a tribe of Welsh Indians was the most widespread and most durable myth in American history — in fact, it reappears occasionally even today. It made its first printed appearance in 1583. It has many variants but the basic story relates that in A.D. 1170 a Welsh prince named Madoc sailed across the Atlantic and discovered America. He returned to Wales, raised a large company for coloni-zation, and planted them in the New World. The descendants of this colony lived on somewhere in the western wilderness. They had white skins and spoke Welsh. Some variants of the myth held that they were otherwise indistinguish-able from other Indians. Other versions, however, asserted that they main-tained their European culture intact. The myth is discussed in DeVoto, *The Course of Empire*, Chap. II. See also Chaps. IX, XI, and XII.

[4] Apparently Ross's Fork, and they probably reached it in Ross's Hole. Wheeler, however, says it was Camp Creek and Thwaites concurs.

the North all three forks Comeing together below our Camp at which place the Mountains Close on each Side of the river, We proceeded on N 30 W.   Crossed a Mountain and Struck the river Several miles down, at which place the Indians had Encamped two days before,   we Proceeded on down the River which is 30 yds. wide Shallow & Stoney Crossing it Several times & Encamped in a Small bottom on the right side. rained this evening nothing to eate but berries, our flour out, and but little Corn,

[Lewis]   MONDAY SEPTEMBER 9TH 1805.

the country in the valley of this river is generally a prarie and from five to 6 miles wide. at 12 we halted on a small branch which falls into the river on the E. side, where we breakfasted on a scant proportion of meat which we had reserved from the hunt of yesterday added to three geese which one of our hunters killed this morning. we continued our rout down the valley about 4 miles and crossed the river; it is hear a handsome stream about 100 yards wide and affords a considerable quantity of very clear water, the banks are low and it's bed entirely gravel.[5] the stream appears navigable, but from the circumstance of their being no sammon in it I believe that there must be a considerable fall in it below. our guide could not inform us where this river discharged itself into the columbia river,   he informed us that it continues it's course along the mountains to the N. as far as he knew it and that not very distant from where we then were it formed a junction with a stream nearly as large as itself which took it's rise in the mountains near the Missouri to the East of us and passed through an extensive valley generally open prarie which forms an excellent pass to the Missouri. the point of the Missouri where this Indian pass intersects it, is about 30 miles above the *gates of the rocky Mountain,* or the place where the valley of the Missouri first widens into an extensive plain after entering the rockey Mountains. the guide

5 They are now in Bitterroot Valley, traveling down the Bitterroot River, which they had first called Clark's River and later the Flathead. (It must not be confused with the Flathead River of today.) Observe that they now receive unmistakable information about a route west to the Bitterroot Valley from the Gate of the Mountains. The informant says this route requires four days; they themselves had required 52 days to get here by the route they had taken from the Gate of the Mountains. The camp which they call Traveller's Rest was at the mouth of Lolo Creek.

informed us that a man might pass to the missouri from hence by that rout in four days. we continued our rout down the W. side of the river about 5 miles further and encamped on a large creek which falls in on the West. as our guide inform me that we should leave the river at this place and the weather appearing settled and fair I determined to halt the next day rest our horses and take som scelestial Observations. we called this Creek *Travellers rest.*

TUESDAY SEPTEMBER 10TH 1805

The morning being fair I sent out all the hunters, and directed two of them to procede down the river as far as it's junction with the Eastern fork which heads near the missouri,[6] and return this evening. this fork of the river we determined to name the Valley plain river. (we called the Eastern fork of Clarkes river.) I think it most probable that this river continues it's course along the rocky Mts. Northwardly as far or perhaps beyond the scources of Medecine river and then turning to the West falls into the Tacootchetessee.[7] The Minetares informed us that there wass a large river west of, and at no great distance from the sources of Medicine river, which passed along the Rocky Mountains from S. to N.   this evening one of our hunters returned accompanyed by three men of the Flathead nation whom he had met in his excurtion up *travellers rest* Creek. on first meeting him the Indians were alarmed and prepared for battle with their bows and arrows, but he soon relieved their fears by laying down his gun and advancing towards them. the Indians were mounted on very fine horses of which the Flatheads have a great abundance; that is, each man in the nation possesses from 20 to a hundred head. our guide could not speake the language of these people but soon engaged them in conversation by signs or jesticulation, the common language of all the Aborigines of North America,   it is one understood by all of them and appears to be sufficiently copious to convey with a degree of certainty the outlines of what they wish to communicate. in this

6 Officially Clark's Fork and spelled Clarksfork, this is the river locally called the Missoula and, in its upper stretches, the Hellgate and the Blackfoot. The Bitterroot flows into it at Missoula, Montana.

7 Lewis takes this name from Alexander Mackenzie's map, supposing it to be the Columbia River in its upper reaches, as Mackenzie did when he tried but failed to follow it to the sea in 1793. Actually it was the Fraser River.

manner we learnt from these people that two men which they supposed to be of the Snake nation had stolen 23 horses from them
and that they were in pursuit of the theaves. they told us they were
in great hast, we gave them some boiled venison, of which
the[y] eat sparingly. the sun was now set, two of them departed
after receiving a few small articles which we gave them, and the
third remained having agreed to continue with us as a guide, and
to introduce us to his relations whom he informed us were numerous and resided in the plain below the mountains on the columbia
river, from whence he said the water was good and capable of
being navigated to the sea; that some of his relation[s] were at the
sea last fall and saw an old whiteman who resided there by himself
and who had given them some handkerchiefs such as he saw in our
possession. he said it would require five sleeps

[Clark] SEPTEMBER 11TH WEDNESDAY 1805 —

The loss of 2 of our horses detained us unl. 3 oClock P.M. our
Flat head Indian being restless thought proper to leave us and
proceed on alone, Sent out the hunters to hunt in advance as
usial. we proceeded on up the Creek [*Travelers rest*] on the right
Side thro a narrow valie and good road for 7 miles and Encamped
at Some old Indian Lodges,[8] nothing killed this evening hills
on the right high & ruged, the mountains on the left high &
Covered with Snow. The day Verry worm

SEPTEMBER 12TH THURSDAY 1805.

The road through this hilley Countrey is verry bad passing over
hills & thro' Steep hollows, over falling timber &c. &c. continued
on & passed Some most intolerable road on the Sides of the Steep
Stoney mountains, which might be avoided by keeping up the
Creek which is thickly covered with under groth & falling timber,[9] Crossed a Mountain 8 miles with out water & encamped

8 The Nez Percé trail to the buffalo country, of which they had heard and
which they had come to Bitterroot Valley to find, came down Lolo Creek. The
expedition follows it west up the creek.
9 The Nez Percé "buffalo road" followed the ridges, not the valleys. At Lolo
Pass its elevation was more than 7000 feet and it frequently approximates that
height, or exceeded it, thereafter.

on a hill Side on the Creek after Decending a long Steep mountain, Some of our Party did not get up untill 10 oClock PM. Party and horses much fatigued.

SEPTEMBER 13TH WEDNESDAY (FRIDAY) 1805 —

at 2 miles passed Several Springs which I observed the Deer Elk &c. had made roads to, and below one of the Indians had made a whole to bathe, I tasted this water and found it hot & not bad tasted in further examanation I found this water nearly boiling hot at the places it Spouted from the rocks I put my finger in the water, at first could not bare it in a Second. my guide took a wrong road and took us out of our rout 3 miles through [an] intolerable rout, after falling into the right road I proceeded on thro [a] tolerable rout for abt. 4 or 5 miles and halted to let our horses graze as well as wate for Capt Lewis who has not yet come up, we proceeded over a mountain to the head of the Creek which we left to our left and at 6 miles from the place I nooned it, we fell on a Small Creek from the left which Passed through open glades Some of which [were] ½ a mile wide; we proceeded down this Creek about 2 miles to where the mountains Closed on either Side & Encamped.[10]

One Deer & Some Pheasants killed this morning, I shot 4 Pheasents of the Common Kind except the tale was black. The road over the last mountain was thick Steep & Stoney as usuial, after passing the head of Travelers rest Creek, the road was verry fine leavel open & firm Some mountains in view to the SE & SW Covered with Snow.

SEPTEMBER 14TH THURSDAY (SATURDAY) 1805

in the Valies it rained and hailed, on the top of the mountains Some Snow fell we Set out early and Crossed a high mountain on the right of the Creek for 6 miles to the forks of the Glade Creek (*one of the heads of the Koos koos kee*) [11] we crossed to the left Side at the forks, and crossd a verry high Steep mountain for 9 miles to a large fork from the left which appears to head in the

10 The party has crossed Lolo Pass and is encamped on a stream of the Clearwater watershed.
11 The Clearwater River.

Snow toped mountains Southerley and S.E.   I could see no fish,
and the grass entirely eaten out by the horses,   we proceeded on
2 miles & Encamped opposit a Small Island at the mouth of a
branch on the right side of the river which is at this place 80 yards
wide, Swift and Stoney,   here we were compelled to kill a Colt
for our men & Selves to eat for the want of meat & we named the
South fork Colt killed Creek,   the flat head name is Koos Koos
ke   The Mountains which we passed to day much worst than
yesterday the last excessively bad & thickly Strowed with falling
timber & Pine Spruce fur Hackmatak & Tamerack, Steep &
Stoney   our men and horses much fatigued,

Wednesday (Sunday) Septr. 15th 1805

proceeded on Down the right Side of (*koos koos kee*) River over
Steep points rockey & buschey as usial for 4 miles to an old Indian
fishing place, here the road leaves the river to the left and assends
a *mountain* winding in every direction to get up the Steep assents
& to pass the emence quantity of falling timber which had [been]
falling from dift. causes i e fire & wind and has deprived the greater
part of the Southerly Sides of this mountain of its green timber,   Several horses Sliped and roled down Steep hills which
hurt them verry much   the one which Carried my desk & Small
trunk Turned over & roled down a mountain for 40 yards & lodged
against a tree, broke the Desk the horse escaped and appeared but
little hurt   after two hours delay we proceeded on up the mountain Steep & ruged as usial, more timber near the top,   when we
arrived at the top As we Conceved, we could find no water and
Concluded to Camp and make use of the Snow we found on the
top to cook the remns. of our Colt & make our Supe,   evening
verry cold and cloudy. Two of our horses gave out, pore and too
much hurt to proceed on and left in the rear. nothing killed to day
except 2 Phests.
From this mountain I could observe high ruged mountains in
every direction as far as I could see.

Saturday (Monday) Septr. 16th 1805

began to Snow about 3 hours before Day and continued all
day   the Snow in the morning 4 inches deep on the old Snow,
and by night we found it from 6 to 8 inches deep,   I walked in

front to keep the road and found great dificuelty in keeping it as maney places the Snow had entirely filled up the track, and obliged me to hunt Several minits for the track,　　at 12 oClock we halted on the top of the mountain to worm & dry our Selves a little as well as to let our horses rest and graze a little on Some long grass which I observed,　　I have been wet and as cold in every part as I ever was in my life, indeed I was at one time fearfull my feet would freeze in the thin Mockirsons which I wore,　　after a Short Delay in the middle of the Day, I took one man and proceeded on as fast as I could about 6 miles to a Small branch passing to the right, halted and built fires for the party agains[t] their arrival which was at Dusk, verry cold and much fatigued,　　Killed a Second Colt which we all Suped hartily on and thought it fine meat.

I saw 4 Deer to day and what is singular Snaped 7 times at a large buck. it is singular as my gun has a Steel fuzee and never Snaped 7 times before,　　in examining her found the flint loose. to describe the road of this day would be a repitition of yesterday except the Snow which made it much worse

The high mountains required only one more day. The country into which the expedition emerged remained difficult, however. There were lesser peaks and ridges, high hills, heavy timber. Except for a few "pheasants" (grouse) there was no game. On September 18 Clark pushed ahead with six hunters. On the 19th his group met a stray horse, killed and butchered it, and after breakfasting on it hung the rest on a tree for the main party. Its presence meant that there were Indians in the vicinity and on the 20th he met two small wandering villages of them. They were Nez Percés (pronounced "nezz purses") and though he could talk with them only in sign language they proved friendly and hospitable. They supplied his advance party with their two staples, dried salmon and flour made from the camass (Camassia quamash) root. He attributed his illness that night to overeating, but that it was due to some other cause was promptly established by the experience of the main party. Buying a pack load of salmon and cams, he sent Reuben Fields with it to Lewis. Then he continued on to lower country along the Clearwater, to a large village of Nez Percés presided over by the chief whose name they rendered Twisted Hair and with whom they developed a strong friendship.

Meanwhile short rations were undermining the strength and to some extent the morale of the main party under Lewis. They eked out their small stock of horse meat with some "portable soup" (an army experimental iron ration which nobody liked), an occasional grouse, a coyote, and even a crow. When they caught up with Clark, at a neighboring village, some of them were sick and nearly everyone soon became so.

The trouble was dysentery, in Clark's words a universal "Lax & heaviness at the stomack." It may have been due to bacteria in the dried salmon but the Nez Percés did not suffer from it and since they could hardly have developed immunity to amoebic dysentery, probably the camass was responsible. They had changed from an exclusively meat diet to a cereal one, after being to some extent weakened by a period of cold following the intense heat of the plains. As they move down to the forks of the Clearwater River, accompanied by the Nez Percés, Clark's journal is practically a hospital daybook. "Capt. Lewis scercely able to ride on a jentle horse which was furnished by the Chief,   Several men So unwell that they were Compelled to lie on the Side of the road [trail] for Some time others obliged to be put on horses. . . . 3 parts of Party sick   Capt. Lewis verry sick. . . . most of the Party Complaining. . . . I am a little unwell . . . Several taken Sick at work . . . Drewyer sick . . . Our men nearly all Complaining of their bowels." Clark attacked the illness forthrightly with "Rush's pills," a powerful charge consisting of ten grains of calomel and ten grains of jalap. It was not powerful enough to satisfy him and he supplemented with large doses of Glauber's salts and of emetics.

The Nez Percés navigated the Clearwater in dugouts. Obviously the expedition could resume water travel. They moved down to the forks and began to make dugouts from large pines, probably the Ponderosa or Western yellow pine, "burning out the holler of our canoes."

They continued to get information about the route ahead, and less dependable information about the country that lay to the south and southwest.

[Clark]   (Friday) Sunday 29th Septr. 1805

a cool morning   wind from the S. W.   men Sick as usial, all the men *(that are)* able to *(at)* work, at the Canoes   Drewyer killed 2 Deer Colter killed 1 Deer, the after part of this day worm *(Capt Lewis very Sick, and most of the men Compla[in]-ing very much of their bowels & Stomach)*

OCTOBER 1ST MONDAY (TUESDAY) 1805 —

had Examined and dried all our Clothes and other articles, and laid out a Small assortment of such articles as those Indians were fond of to trade with them for Some provisions (they are remark-ably fond of Beeds) nothin to eate except a little dried fish which they men complain of as working of them as *(as much as)* a dost of Salts. Capt Lewis getting much better. Several Indians visit us from the different tribes below. Some from the main South fork. our hunters killed nothing to day worm evening

OCTOBER 4TH (FRIDAY) 1805 —

a cool wind from off the Eastern mountains, I displeased an Indian by refuseing him a pice of Tobacco which he tooke the liberty to take out of our Sack. Three Indians visit us from the Great River South of us. The two men Frasure and Guterich re-turn late from the Village with Fish roots &c. which they pur-chased as our horse is eaten we have nothing to eate except dried fish & roots which disagree with us verry much. The after part of this day verry worm. *(Capt Lewis Still Sick but able to walk about a little.)*

OCTOBER 5TH FRIDAY SATY. 1805

had all our horses 38 in number Collected and branded [12] Cut off their fore top and delivered them to the 2 brothers and one son of one of the Chiefs who intends to accompany us down the river to each of those men I gave a Knife & Some Small articles &c.

Nothing to eate except dried fish & roots. Capt Lewis & myself eate a Supper of roots boiled, which Swelled us in Such a manner that we were Scercely able to breath for Several hours. finished and

---

[12] The Nez Percés had agreed to take care of the horse herd till the return of the expedition.

lanced (*launched*) 2 of our canoes this evening which proved to be verry good   our hunters with every diligence Could kill nothing. The hills high and ruged and woods too dry to hunt the deer which is the only game in our neighbourhood.

October 6th Saturday [Sunday] 1805

had all our Saddles Collected a whole dug and in the night buried them, also a Canister of powder and a bag of Balls at the place the Canoe which Shields made was cut from the body of the tree. The Saddles were buried on the Side of a bend about ½ a mile below. all the Canoes finished this evening ready to be put into the water. I am taken verry unwell with a pain in the bowels & Stomach, which is certainly the effects of my diet which last all night.

The river below this forks is Called *Kos-kos-kee*   it is Clear rapid with Shoals or Swift places

The open Countrey Commences a fiew miles below this on each side of the river, on the Lard Side below the 1st Creek. with a few trees Scattered near the river.

October 7th Monday 1805 —

I continue verry unwell but obliged to attend every thing all the Canoes put into the water and loaded, fixed our Canoes as well as possible and Set out   as we were about to Set out we missd. both of the Chiefs who promised to accompany us, I also missed my Pipe Tomahawk which could not be found.

The after part of the day cloudy   proceeded on passed 10 rapids which wer dangerous   the Canoe in which I was Struck a rock and Sprung a leak in the 3rd rapid,   a Short distance from the river at 2 feet 4 Inches N. of a dead toped pine Tree had buried 2 Lead Canisters of Powder

Had the Canoes unloaded examined and mended a Small leake which we discovered in a thin place in her Side   passed Several Camps of Indians to day

October 8th Tuesday 1805 —

passed 15 rapids four Islands and a Creek on the Stard. Side at 16 miles just below which one canoe in which Sergt. Gass was Stearing and was nearle turning over,   she Sprung a leak or Split open on one side and Bottom filled with water & Sunk on the rapid, the men, Several of which Could not Swim hung on to the Canoe, I had one of the other Canoes unloaded & with the assistance of our Small Canoe and one Indian Canoe took out every thing & toed the empty Canoe on Shore, one man Tompson a little hurt, every thing wet particularly the greater part of our Small Stock of Merchandize, had every thing opened, and two Sentinels put over them to keep off the Indians, who are enclined to theave haveing Stole Several Small articles those people appeared disposed to give us every assistance in their power during our distress. We passed Several Encampments of Indians on the Islands and those near the rapids in which places they took the Salmon, at one of those Camps we found our two Chiefs who had promised to accompany us, we took them on board after the Serimony of Smokeing.

OCTOBER 9TH WEDNESDAY 1805 —

In examoning our Canoe found that by putting Knees & Strong peces pined to her Sides and bottom &c. She could be made fit for Service in by the time the goods dried, Set 4 men to work at her, Serjs. Pryor & Gass, Jo Fields & Gibson, others to collect rosin, at 1 oClock she was finished stronger than ever The wet articles not sufficiently dried to pack up obliged us to delay another night dureing the time one man was tradeing for fish for our voyage, at Dark we were informed that our old guide [13] & his son had left us and had been Seen running up the river Several miles above, we could not account for the cause of his leaveing us at this time, without receiving his pay for the services he had rendered us, or letting us know anything of his intention.

we requested the Chief [14] to Send a horseman after our old guide to come back and receive his pay &c. which he advised us not to do as his nation would take his things from him before he passed their camps. The Indians and our party were verry mery this after noon a woman faind madness &c. &c. Singular acts of this

---

[13] "Toby," the Shoshone.

[14] The older of the two Nez Percés who accompanied the expedition to the Columbia was named Twisted Hair, the other, whose name is not translated, Tetoharsky.

woman in giveing in small po[r]tions all she had & if they were not received She would Scarrify her self in a horid manner &c.   Capt Lewis recovering fast.

[Ordway]   WEDNESDAY 9TH OCT 1805.

. . . She began Singing Indian and to giving all around hir Some commass roots, and brasslets which hung about hir   one of our party refused to take them from hir. She then appeared angry threw them in the fire. took a Sharp flint from hir husband and cut both hir arms in Sundry places So that the blood gushed out. She Scraped the blood in hir hand and eat it, and So continued in this way about half an hour then fainted or went in to a fit Some time then came too by thier puting water on hir.

[Clark]   OCTOBER 10TH WEDNESDAY (THURSDAY)

at 8½ miles lower we arrived at the heade of a verry bad riffle at which place we landed near 8 lodges of Indians [Nez Percés] on the Lard Side to view the *riffle,* haveing passed two Islands & Six rapids Several of them verry bad   after viewg. this riffle two Canoes were taken over verry well; the third stuck on a rock which took us an hour to get her off which was effected without her receving a greater injurey than a Small Split in her Side which was repaired in a Short time,   we purchased fish & dogs of those people, dined and proceeded on. here we met with an Indian from the falls at which place he Sais he saw white people, and expressd an inclination to accompany us,   we passd. a few miles above this riffle 2 Lodges and an Indian batheing in a hot bath made by hot stones thrown into a pon[d] of water. at five miles lower and Sixty miles below the forks arived at a large southerly fork which is the one we were on with the *Snake* or *So-So-nee* nation.[15] This

---

[15] A remarkable example of geographical intelligence. Clark understands at once that they have again reached the watershed which they first touched at the Lemhi, and have reached it downstream from the junction of Lewis's River with its large southern fork, of whose existence they had learned from the Snakes. That is basically correct. The "southern fork" was in fact the main stream of the Snake River, and the stream whose precipitous canyons turned them back was its principal tributary, the Salmon River. The Salmon flows into the Snake 50 miles above the mouth of the Clearwater

South fork or [of] *Lewis's River* which has two forks which fall into it on the South   The Countrey about the forks [16] is an open Plain on either Side. I can observe at a distance on the lower Lard. Side a high ridge of Thinly timbered Countrey the water of the South fork is a greenish blue, the north as clear as cristial

Imediately in the point is an Indian Cabin & in the South fork a Small Island,   we came to on the Stard. Side below with a view to make some luner observations,   the night proved cloudy and we were disapointed. The Indians Came down all the Cou[r]ses of this river on each side on horses to view us as we were decending. worthey of remark that not one stick of timber on the river near the forks and but a fiew trees for a great distance up the River we decended   I think Lewis's [Snake] River is about 250 yards wide, the *Koos koos ke* River about 150 yards wide and the river below the forks about 300 yards wide   a miss understanding took place between Shabono one of our interpreters and Jo & R Fields which appears to have originated in just [jest]. our diet extremely bad haveing nothing but roots and dried fish to eate,   all the Party have greatly the advantage of me, in as much as they all relish the flesh of the dogs, Several of which we purchased of the nativs for to add to our store of fish and roots &c. &c. —

The *Cho-pun-nish* or Pierced nose Indians are Stout likely men, handsom women, and verry dressey in their way,   the dress of the men are a White Buffalow robe or Elk Skin dressed with Beeds which are generally white, Sea Shells & the Mother of Pirl hung to the[i]r hair & on a piece of otter skin about their necks   hair Ceewed in two parsels hanging forward over their Sholders, feathers, and different Coloured Paints which they find in their Countrey Generally white, Green & light Blue. Some fiew were a Shirt of Dressed Skins and long legins & Mockersons Painted, which appear to be their winters dress, with a plat of twisted grass about their Necks.

The women dress in a Shirt of Ibex or Goat [bighorn] Skins which reach quite down to their anckles with a girdle,   their heads are not ornemented. their Shirts are ornemented with quilled Brass, Small peces of Brass Cut into different forms, Beeds, Shells

---

[16] That is, at the junction of the Clearwater and the Snake at Lewiston, Idaho.

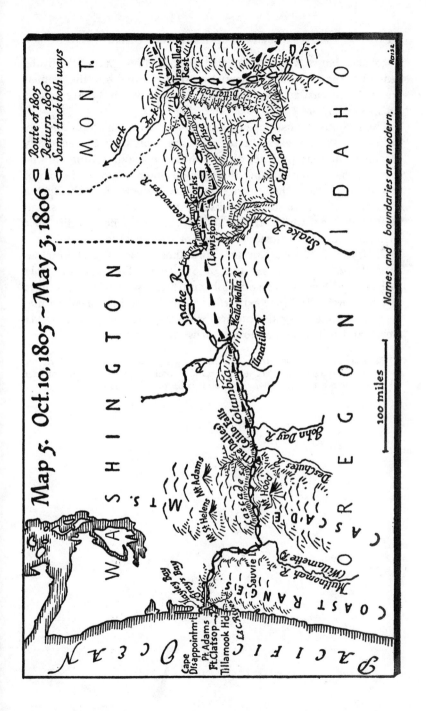

Map 5. Oct. 10, 1805 – May 3, 1806

Route of 1805
Return 1806
Same track both ways

MONT.

Clark Fork
Traveller's Rest
Bitterroot R.
Lochsa R.
Clearwater R.
Forks
Salmon R.
Snake R.
(Lewiston)

Snake R.
Walla Walla R.
Umatilla R.

IDAHO

WASHINGTON

OREGON

Columbia
The Dalles
Celilo Falls
John Day R.
Deschutes

CASCADES
Mt. Adams
Mt. St. Helens
Mt. Hood
Cascades

COAST RANGES
Multnomah R. (Willamette)
Sauvie I.

Baker's Bay
Chinook Bay
Cape Disappointm't
Pt. Adams
Ft. Clatsop
Tillamook Hd.
CLATSOPS

PACIFIC OCEAN

100 miles

Names and boundaries are modern.

Raisz

& curious bones &c.   The men expose those parts which are generally kept from few [view] by other nations but the women are more perticular than any other nation which I have passed [*in s[e]creting the parts*]

Their amusements appear but fiew   as their Situation requires the utmost exertion to pr[o]cure food they are generally employed in that pursute, all the Summer & fall fishing for the Salmon, the winter hunting the deer on Snow Shoes in the plains and takeing care of ther emence numbers of horses, & in the Spring cross the mountains to the Missouri to get Buffalow robes and meet &c.   at which time they frequent[ly] meet with their enemies & lose their horses & maney of their people.

Their disorders are but fiew and those fiew of a s[c]rofelous nature.   they make great use of Swetting.   The hot and cold bathes,   They are verry Selfish and Stingey of what they have to eate or ware, and they expect in return Something for everything give[n] as presents or the survices whic they doe let it be however Small, and fail to make those returns on their part.[17]

---

[17] This seems an unjust stricture, considering the hospitality with which the Nez Percés had received them, and eventually both captains were to consider them the most generous and most likable tribe they had met.

T*he Snake is a big river and from the mouth of the Clearwater most of the way to the Columbia it flows through a series of canyons. The party reached it in the season of low water, which meant that the rapids were at their least dangerous. Even so, "we should make more portages," Clark writes, "if the season was not so far advanced and time precious with us."*

Twisted Hair and Tetoharsky continued as guides, and a small, chattering, and daily changing group of Nez Percés from the Clearwater region moved companionably along the banks, afoot or on horseback. These and local groups, still of either the Nez Percés or the Flathead families, helped or actually piloted them through the rapids. Even so, on October 14, one dugout (in charge of Drewyer) struck a rock and overturned. Some of the small and diminished stock of trade goods sank beyond recovery, a serious loss since this was the currency that paid for food, labor, information, and the services of the trail. The rest of the lading suffered only a wetting. On the 16th Pryor's dugout grounded in still more violent water and its cargo was thoroughly drenched. No one was drowned in this turbulent stretch, although some of the party could not swim.

Everywhere the party saw evidence of the salmon economy, around which the life of these river tribes was organized: weirs, spears, nets (made of fiber), caches of dried fish, etc. Everybody was heartily bored by living on fish; on October 14 Clark wrote, "for the first time for three weeks past I had a good dinner of Blue wing Teel." There were a lot of Indians but they remained amiable; Clark attributed their friendliness to the presence of Sacajawea, which "we find reconsiles all the Indians as to our friendly intentions   a woman with a party of men is a token of peace."

There was little game and less firewood. They were obliged to buy wood from the Indians. They left the canyons but not the rapids behind, coming out to a wide sagebrush plain. Considering that the Columbia was the great objective of their journey, the log records very little emotion when they reach it on October 16, the first white men who ever saw it east of the Cascade Mountains.

[Clark]   OCTOBER 16TH WEDNESDAY 1805

A cool morning,   deturmined to run the rapids,   put our Indian guide in front our Small Canoe next and the other four following each other,   the canoes all passed over Safe except the rear Canoe which run fast on a rock at the lower part of the Rapids,   with the early assistance of the other Canoes & the Indians, who was extreamly ellert every thing was taken out and the Canoe got off without any enjorie further than the articles [with] which it was loaded [getting] all wet. at 14 miles passed a bad rapid at which place we unloaded and made a portage of ¾ of a mile haveing passd 4 Smaller rapids, three Islands and the parts of a house above,   I Saw Indians & Horses on the South Side below   five Indians came up the river in great haste, we Smoked with them and gave them a piece of tobacco to Smoke with their people and sent them back, they Set out in a run & continued to go as fast as they could run as far as we could see them. after getting Safely over the rapid and haveing taken Diner Set out and proceeded on Seven miles to the junction of this river and the Columbia which joins from the N. W. In every direction from the junction of those rivers the countrey is one continued plain low and rises from the water gradually, except a range of high Countrey on the opposit Side about 2 miles distant from the Collumbia.

We halted above the point on the river Kimooenim [1] to smoke with the Indians who had collected there in great numbers to view us,   here we met our 2 Chiefs who left us two days ago and proceeded on to this place to inform those bands of our approach and friendly intentions towards all nations &c.   we also met the 2 men who had passed us Several days ago on horsback, one of

[1] The Snake.

them we observed was a man of great influence with those Indians, harranged them; after Smokeing with the Indians who had collected to view us we formed a camp at the point near which place I saw a fiew pieces of Drift wood   after we had our camp fixed and fires made, a Chief came from this camp which was about ¼ of a mile up the Columbia river at the head of about 200 men singing and beeting on their drums Stick and keeping time to the musik they formed a half circle around us and Sung for Some time, we gave them all Smoke, and Spoke to their Chief as well as we could by signs informing them of our friendly disposition to all nations, and our joy in Seeing those of our Children around us,   Gave the principal chief a large Medal, Shirt and Handkf.   a 2nd Chief a Meadel of Small size, and to the Cheif who came down from the upper villages a Small *Medal* & Handkerchief.

The Chiefs then returned with the men to their camp; Soon after we purchased for our Provisions *Seven* Dogs,   Some fiew of those people made us presents of fish and Several returned and delayed with us untill bedtime. The 2 old chiefs who accompanied us from the head of the river precured us Some fuil Such as the Stalks of weed[s] or plant[s] and willow bushes. one man made me a present of about 20 lb. of verry fat Dried horse meat.

OCTOBER 17TH THURSDAY 1805

Several men and woman offered Dogs and fish to Sell, we purchased all the dogs we could, the fish being out of season and dieing in great numbers in the river, we did not think proper to use them,   send out Hunters to shute the Prarie Cock a large fowl which I have only Seen on this river,   Capt. Lewis took a Vocabelary of the Language of those people who call themselves *Sokulk*,[2] and also one of the language of a nation resideing on a Westerly fork of the Columbia which mouthes a fiew miles above this place who Call themselves *Chim-nâ-pum*   Some fiew of this nation reside with the *Sokulks* nation.

I took *two* men in a Small canoe and assended the Columbia river 10 miles to an Island near the Stard. Shore on which two

[2] Closely related to the Nez Percés, as their language shows, they were prob- ably Yakimas.

large Mat Lodges of Indians were drying Salmon,   The number
of dead Salmon on the Shores & floating in the river is incrediable
to say — and at this Season they have only to collect the fish Split
them open and dry them on their Scaffolds on which they have
great numbers,   how far they have to raft their timber they
make their scaffolds of I could not lern; but there is no timber of any sort except Small willow bushes in sight in any direction.
from this Island the natives showed me the enterance of a large
Westerly fork which they Call *Tâpetêtt* at about 8 miles distant,   the evening being late I deturmined to return to the forks,
at which place I reached at Dark. passed a Island in the middle of
the river at 5 miles at the head of which is a rapid, not dangerous   on the Lard. Side opposit ot this rapid is a fishing place 3
Mat Lodges, and great quants. of Salmon on scaffolds drying. Saw
great numbers of Dead Salmon on the Shores and floating in the
water, great numbers of Indians on the banks viewing me and 18
canoes accompanied me from the point. The waters of this river
is clear, and a Salmon may be seen at the deabth of 15 or 20 feet.
West 4 miles to the lower point of a large Island near the Stard.
Side at 2 Lodges, passed three large lodges on the Star. Side near
which great number of Salmon was drying on scaffolds   one of
those Mat lodges I entered   found it crouded with men women
and children and near the enterance of those houses I saw maney
squars engaged [in] splitting and drying Salmon. I was furnished
with a mat to set on, and one man set about preparing me something to eate,   first he brought in a piece of a Drift log of pine
and with a wedge of the elks horn, and a malet of Stone curioesly
carved he Split the log into Small pieces and lay'd it open on the
fire on which he put round Stones,   a woman handed him a
basket of water and a large Salmon about half Dried,   when the
Stones were hot he put them into the basket of water with the fish
which was soon sufficiently boiled for use   it was then taken out
put on a platter of rushes neetly made, and set before me   they
boiled a Salmon for each of the men with me,   dureing those
preparations, I smoked, with those about me who chose to smoke
which was but fiew, this being a custom those people are but little
accustomed to and only Smok thro: form. after eateing the boiled
fish which was delicious, I set out & halted or come too on the
Island at the two Lodges,   Several fish was given to me, in return

for Which I gave Small pieces of ribbond   on my return found
Great numbs. of the nativs with Capt. Lewis, men all employ[e]d
in dressing ther skins mending their clothes and putting their arms
in the best order the latter being always a matter of attention with
us. The Dress of those natives differ but little from those on the
Koskoskia and Lewis's rivers, except the women who dress verry
different, in as much as those above ware long leather Shirts which
[are] highly orniminted with beeds shells &c. &c. and those on the
main Columbia river only ware a truss or pece of leather tied
around them at their hips and drawn tite between their legs and
fastened before So as bar[e]ly to hide those parts which are so
sacredly hid & s[e]cured by our women. Those women are more
inclined to Co[r]pulency than any we have yet Seen,   their eyes
are of a Duskey black, their hair of a corse black without orniments
of any kind braded as above

   Those people appears to live in a State of comparitive happiness:
they take a great[er] share [in the] labor of the woman, than is
common among Savage tribes, and as I am informed [are] content
with one wife   Those people respect the aged with Veneration.
I observed an old woman in one of the Lodges which I entered,
She was entirely blind as I was informed by signs, had lived more
than 100 winters, She occupied the best position in the house, and
when She Spoke great attention was paid to what she Said. Those
people as also those of the *flat heads* which we had passed on the
Koskoske and Lewis's rivers are subject to sore eyes, and many are
blind of one and Some of both eyes. this misfortune must be owing
to the reflections of the sun &c. on the waters in which they are
continually fishing during the Spring Summer & fall, & the snows
dureing the winter Seasons, in this open country where the eye has
no rest. I have observed amongst those, as well in all other tribes
which I have passed on these waters who live on fish maney of different sectes who have lost their teeth about middle age, Some have
their teeth worn to the gums, perticelar[ly] those of the upper jaw,
and the tribes generally have bad teeth

   The Houses or Lodges of the tribes of the main Columbia river
is of large Mats made of rushes,[3]   those houses are from 15 to 60

---

[3] The skin tipi has been left behind and so has practically all the rest of
the Plains culture, except that some of these people have horses. The culture
of these river Indians is basically that of the Northwest coast tribes.

feet in length generally of an Oblong squar form, Supported by poles on forks in the in[n]er Side, Six feet high,   the top is covered also with mats leaveing a Seperation in the whole length of about 12 or 15 inches wide, left for the purpose of admitting light and for the Smok of the fire to pass which is made in the middle of the house.

Those people appeare of a mild disposition and friendly disposed. They have in their huts independant of their nets gigs & fishing tackling each bows & large quivers or arrows on which they use flint Spikes.

OCTOBER 18TH FRIDAY 1805

The fish being very bad those which was offerd to us we had every reason to believe was taken up on the shore dead we thought proper not to purchase any,   we purchased forty dogs for which we gave articles of little value, such as beeds, bells & thimbles, of which they appeared verry fond,   at 4 oClock we set out down the Great Columbia accompanied by our two old Chiefs,   one young man wished to accompany us, but we had no room for more, & he could be of no service to us.

we landed a few minits to view a rapid,   passd. this rapid which was verry bad, between 2 Small Islands, two Still Smaller near the Lard. Side, at this rapid on the Stard. Side is 2 Lodges of Indians Drying fish,   at 2½ miles lower passed an Island Close under the Stard. Side on which was 2 Lodges of Indians drying fish on Scaffolds   at 16 miles the river passes into the range of high Countrey, at which place the rocks project into the river from the high clifts which is on the Lard. Side about ⅓ of the way across and those of the Stard. Side about the same distance, the countrey rises here about 200 feet above the water and is bordered with black rugid rocks,   at the Commencement of this high countrey on Lard. Side a Small riverlet falls in which appears to [have] passed under the high county. in its whole co[ur]se. saw a mountain bearing S. W. conocal form Covered with Snow.[4]   passed 4 Islands, at

4 The "riverlet" is the Walla Walla River. Just beyond it the Columbia bends sharply to the east and, a mighty and uproarious river, enters the first of the long series of canyons and gorges from which it does not emerge till it hurtles through the Cascade Mountains. The conical mountain, which Clark does not identify from his maps, is Mount Hood. In this stretch of the river it is only occasionally visible.

the upper point of the 3rd is a rapid,   on this Island is *two*
Lodges of Indians, drying fish, on the fourth Island close under
the Stard. Side is *nine* large Lodges of Indians Drying fish on
scaffolds as above   at this place we were called to to land,   as
it was near night, and no appearance of wood, we proceeded on
about 2 miles lower to Some Willows, at which place we observed
a drift log   formed a camp on the Lard. Side under a high hill
nearly opposit to five Lodges of Indians;

OCTOBER 19TH SATURDAY 1805

The great chief *Yel-lep-pit* two other chiefs, and a chief of [a]
Band below presented themselves to us verry early this morning.
Yelleppit is a bold handsom Indian, with a dignified countenance
about 35 years of age, about 5 feet 8 inches high and well perpo-
tiond. he requested us to delay untill the Middle of the day, that
his people might come down and see us,   we excused our Selves
and promised to stay with him one or 2 days on our return which
appeared to Satisfy him;   great numbers of Indians came down
in Canoes to view us before we Set out which was not untill 9
oClock A. M.   we proceeded on passed a Island, close under the
Lard. Side about six miles in length   about four miles below
this Island we arrived at the head of a verry bad rapid,[5] we came
too on the Lard. Side to view the rapid before we would venter to
run it,   as the Chanel appeared to be close under the oppd.
Shore, and it would be necessary to liten our canoe, I deturmined to
walk down on the Lard. Side, with the 2 chiefs the interpreter &
his woman, and derected the Small canoe to pr[o]cede down on the
Lard. Side to the foot of the rapid which was about 2 miles in
length   I assended a high clift about 200 feet above the water;
from this place I descovered a high mountain of emence hight
covered with Snow,   this must be one of the mountains laid
down by Vancouver, as seen from the mouth of the Columbia
River, from the course which it bears which is *West* I take it to be
Mt. St. Helens, destant about 120 miles   a range of mountains
in the Derection crossing a conical mountain S. W. toped with
snow,[6]   I delayed at the foot of the rapid about 2 hours for the

[5] Near the mouth of the Umatilla River.
[6] Mount St. Helens, the perfect cone, would not be visible from where Clark
was. Wheeler identifies this as Mount Adams.

canoes which I could see met with much dificuelty in passing down
the rapid on the opposit Side   maney places the men were obliged
to get into the water and haul the canoes over sholes   I observed a
great number of Lodges on the opposit Side at some distance below,
and Several Indians on the opposit bank passing up to where Capt.
Lewis was with the Canoes,   others I saw on a knob nearly opposit to me at which place they delayed but a Short time, before
they returned to their Lodges as fast as they could run,

I was fearfull that those people might not be informed of
us,   I deturmined to take the little canoe which was with me
and proceed with the three men in it to the Lodges,   on my
aproach not one person was to be seen except three men off in the
plains, and they sheared off as I saw approached near the
Shore,   I landed in front of five Lodges which was at no great
distance from each other, Saw no person   the enterance or Dores
of the Lodges wer Shut with the Same materials of which they were
built a Mat,   I approached one with a pipe in my hand entered a
lodge which was the nearest to me   found 32 persons men,
women and a few children Setting permiscuisly in the Lodge, in the
greatest agutation, Some crying and ringing there hands, others
hanging their heads. I gave my hand to them all and made Signs
of my friendly dispo[si]tion and offered the men my pipe to Smok
and distributed a fiew Small articles which I had in my pock-
ets,   this measure passified those distressed people verry
much,   I then sent one man into each lodge and entered a
Second myself the inhabitants of which I found more fritened than
those of the first lodge   I destributed Sundrey Small articles
amongst them, and Smoked with the men,   I then Set my self
on a rock and made signs to the men to come and Smoke with
me   not one come out untill the canoes arrived with the 2 chiefs,
one of whom spoke aloud, and as was their custom to all we had
passed. the Indians came out & Set by me and smoked   They
said we came from the clouds &c. &c. and were not men &c.
&c.   this time Capt. Lewis came down with the canoes in which
the Indian[s were],   as Soon as they Saw the Squar wife of the
interperter they pointed to her and informed those who continued
yet in the Same position I first found them,   they imediately all
came out and appeared to assume new life,   the sight of This
Indian woman, wife to one of our interprs. confirmed those people

of our friendly intentions, as no woman ever accompanies a war party of Indians in this quarter. Dined, and proceeded on passed a Small rapid and 15 Lodges below the five, and Encamped below an Island close under the Lard. Side, nearly opposit to 24 Lodges on an Island near the middle of the river, and the Main Stard. Shore Soon after we landed which was at a fiew willow trees about 100 Indians came from the different Lodges, and a number of them brought wood which they gave us, we Smoked with all of them, and two of our Party Peter Crusat & Gibson played on the *violin* which delighted them greatly, their Dress are Similar to those at the fork except their robes are smaller and do not reach lower than the waste ¾ of them have scercely any robes at all, the women have only a Small pece of a robe which covers their Sholders neck and reaching down behind to their wastes, with a tite piece of leather about the waste, the brests are large and hang down verry low illy Shaped, high Cheeks flattened heads, & have but fiew orniments.

OCTOBER 20TH SUNDAY 1805

we Set out leaveing about 200 of the nativs at our Encampment, passed a rapid at seven miles one at a Short distance below we passed a verry bad rapid, a chane of rocks makeing from the Stard. Side and nearly chokeing the river up entirely with hugh black rocks, an Island below close under the Stard. Side on which was *four* Lodges of Indians drying fish, here I saw a great number of Pelicons on the wing, and black Comerants. at one oClock we landed on the lower point of an Island, on the upper part of this Island we discovered an Indian Vault, our curiosity induced us to examine the method those nativs practiced in depos[it]eing the dead, the vau[l]t was made by broad poads [boards] and pieces of Canoes leaning on a ridge pole which was Suported by 2 forks Set in the ground six feet in hight in an easterly and westerly direction and about 60 feet in length, and 12 feet wide, in it I observed great numbers of humane bones of every description perticularly in a pile near the center of the vault, on the East End 21 Scul bomes forming a circle on Mats; in the westerley part of the *Vault* appeared to be appropriated for those of more resent death, as many of the bodies of the deceased *raped* up in leather robes, lay [*in rows*] on board[s] covered with mats, &c we observed, independant of the canoes which served as covering, fishing nets of various kinds, Baskets of different Sizes, wooden boles, robes Skins, trenchers, and various kind of trinkets, in and suspended on the ends of the pieces forming the vault; we also Saw the Skeletons of Several Horses at the vault a great number of bones about it, which convinced me that those animals were Sacrefised as well as the above articles to the Deceased. after diner we proceeded on to a bad rapid at the lower point of a Small Island on which four Lodges of Indians were Situated drying fish; here the high countrey commences again on the Stard. Side leaveing a vallie of 40 miles in width, from the mustle shel rapid. examined and passed this rapid close to the Island at 8 miles lower passed a large Island near the middle of the river, a brook on the Stard. Side and 11 Islds. all in view of each other below, a riverlit falls in on the Lard. Side behind a Small Island a Small rapid below, The Star Side is high rugid hills, the Lard. Side a low plain and not a tree to be Seen in any Direction except a fiew Small willow bushes which are scattered partially on the Sides of the bank

The river to day is about ¼ of a mile in width, this evening the countrey on the Lard. Side rises to the hight of that on the Starboard Side, and is wavering we made 42 miles to day; the current much more uniform than yesterday or the day before. Killed 2 Speckle guls severl. ducks of a delicious flavour.

CHAPTER XIX

DESCENDING THE COLUMBIA TO THE RAPIDS

[Clark]   OCTOBER 21ST MONDAY 1805

Passd. a Small Island at 5½ miles a large one 8 miles in the middle of the river, some rapid water at the head and Eight Lodges of nativs opposit its Lower point on the Stard. Side, we came too at those lodges, bought some wood and brackfast, Those people recived us with great kindness, and examined us with much attention, their employments customs, Dress and appearance Similar to those above, Speak the Same language, here we Saw two scarlet and a blue cloth blankets, also a Salors Jacket. [1]

we got from those people a fiew pounded roo[t]s fish and *Acorns* of white oake, those Acorns they make use of as food raw & roasted and inform us they precure them of the natives who live near the falls below which place they all discribe by the term *Timm* at 2 miles lower passed a rapid large rocks stringing into the river of large Size, opposit to this rapid on the Stard. Shore is Situated *two* Lodges of the Nativs drying fish here we halted a fiew minits to examine the rapid before we entered it which was our Constant Custom, and at all that was verry dangerous put out all who Could not Swim to walk around, after passing this rapid we proceeded on passed anoother rapid at 5 miles lower down, above this rapid maney large rocks on each Side at Some distance from Shore, a little below is a bad rapid which is bad crouded with hugh [huge] rocks scattered in every Direction which renders the passage verry Difficult a little above this rapid on

---

[1] These are the first goods of the Northwest trade that the expedition has actually seen.

the Lard. Side emence piles of rocks appears as if Sliped from the clifts under which they lay, passed great number of rocks in every direction scattered in the river. 5 Lodges a little below on the Stard. Side, and one lodge on an Island near the Stard. Shore opposit to which is a verry bad rapid, thro which we found much dificuelty in passing, the river is crouded with rocks in every direction, after Passing this dificult rapid [we came] to the mouth of a Small river on the Larboard Side.[2]

imediately above & below this little river commences a rapid which is crouded with large rocks in every direction, the passage both crooked and dificuelt, we halted at a Lodge to examine those noumerous Islands of rock which apd. to extend maney miles below, great numbs. of Indians came in canoes to View us at this place, after passing this rapid which we accomplished without loss; winding through between the hugh rocks for about 2 miles. proceeded on about two miles lower and landed and encamped near *five* Lodges of nativs, drying fish those are the relations of those at the *great falls* [Celilo Falls], they are pore and have but little wood which they bring up the river from the falls as they Say, we purchased a little wood to cook our Dog meat and fish; those people did not receive us at first with the same cordiality of those above, they appeare to be the Same nation Speak the Same language with a little curruption of maney words Dress and fish in the same way, all of whome have *pierced noses* and the men when Dressed ware a long taper'd piece of Shell or beed put through the nose.

one of the Old Chiefs who accompanies us pointed out a place on the Lard. Side where they had a great battle, not maney years ago, in which maney were killed on both Sides, One of our party J. Collins presented us with verry good *beer* made of the *Pa-shi-co-quar-mash* [camass] bread, which bread is the remains of what was laid in as a part of our Stores of Provisions, at the first flat heads or Cho-pun-nish Nation at the head of the *Kosskoske* river which by being frequently wet molded & sowered &c.

OCTOBER 22D TUESDAY 1805

A fine morning calm and fare we set out at 9 oClock passed a verry bad rapid at the head of an Island close under the Stard.

[2] John Day River.

side   above this rapid on the Stard. side is six Lodges of nativs
Drying fish,   at 9 mls. passed a bad rapid at the head of a large
Island of high & uneaven [rocks], jutting over the water,   a Small
Island in a Stard. Bend opposit the upper point, on which I
counted 20 parcels of dryed and pounded fish; on the main Stand.
Shore opposit to this Island *five* Lodges of Indians are Situated,
Several Indians in canoes killing fish with gigs &c.   opposit the
center of this Island of rocks which is about 4 miles long we discovered the enterence of a large river on the Lard. Side which appeared to come from the S. E.   we landed at some distance above
the mouth of this river and Capt. Lewis and my Self set out to
view this river above its mouth, [3]

we proceeded on pass[ed] the mouth of this river at which place
it appears to discharge ¼ as much water as runs down the Columbia. at *two* miles below this River passed Eight Lodges on the
Lower point of the Rock Island   below this Island on the main
Stard. Shore is 16 Lodges of nativs,   here we landed a fiew minits
to Smoke, the lower point of one Island opposit which heads in the
mouth of *Towornehiooks* [Des Chutes] River which I did not observe untill after passing these lodges   about ½ a mile lower
passed 6 more Lodges on the Same Side and 6 miles below the upper mouth of *Towornehiooks* River the commencement of the
pitch of the great falls,[4] opposit on the Stard. Side is 17 Lodges of
the nativs   we landed and walked down accompanied by an
old man to view the falls, and the best rout for to make a portage
which we Soon discovered was much nearest on the Stard. Side, and
the distance 1200 yards one third of the way on a rock, about 200
yards over a loose Sand collected in a hollar blown by the winds
from the bottoms below which was disagreeable to pass, as it was
steep and loose. at the lower part of those rapids we arrived at 5
Lod[g]es of nativs drying and prepareing fish for market,

we returned droped down to the head of the rapids and took
every article except the Canoes across the portag[e] where I had
formed a camp on [an] ellegable Situation for the protection of our
Stores from thieft, which we were more fearfull of, than their arrows. we despatched two men to examine the river on the opposit
Side, and [they] reported that the canoes could be taken down a

[3] The Des Chutes River.
[4] Celilo Falls: the expedition is approaching the Narrows of the Columbia.

narrow Chanel on the opposit Side after a Short portage at the head of the falls, at which place the Indians take over their Canoes. Indians assisted us over the portage with our heavy articles on their horses, the waters is divided into Several narrow chanels which pass through a hard black rock forming Islands of rocks at this Stage of the water,   on those Islands of rocks as well as at and about their Lodges I observe great numbers of Stacks of pounded Salmon neetly preserved in the following manner, i. e. after [being] suffi[ci]ently Dried it is pounded between two Stones fine, and put into a speces of basket neetly made of grass and rushes better than two feet long and one foot Diamiter, which basket is lined with the Skin of Salmon Stretched and dried for the purpose,   in this it is pressed down as hard as is possible, when full they Secure the open part with the fish Skins across which they fasten th[r]o. the loops of the basket that part very securely, and then on a Dry Situation they Set those baskets the corded part up,   their common custome is to Set 7 as close as they can Stand and 5 on the top of them, and secure them with mats which is raped around them and made fast with cords and covered also with mats,   those 12 baskets of from 90 to 100lbs. each form a Stack. thus preserved those fish may be kept Sound and sweet Several years, as those people inform me,   Great quantities as they inform us are sold to the whites people who visit the mouth of this river as well as to the nativs below.

OCTOBER 23D WEDNESDAY 1805

I with the greater part of the men crossed in the canoes to opposit side above the falls and hauled them across the portage of 457 yards which is on the Lard. Side and certainly the best side to pass the canoes,   I then decended through a narrow chanel of about 150 yards wide forming a kind of half circle in it[s] course of a mile to a pitch of 8 feet in which the chanel is divided by 2 large rocks,   at this place we were obliged to let the Canoes down by strong ropes of Elk Skin which we had for the purpose,   one Canoe in passing this place got loose by the cords breaking, and was cought by the Indians below. I accomplished this necessary business and landed Safe with all the canoes at our Camp below the falls by 3 oClock P. M.   nearly covered with flees which were so thick amongst the Straw and fish Skins at the upper part of the portage at which place the nativs had been Camped not long since; that every man of the party was obliged to strip naked dureing the time of takeing over the canoes, that they might have an oppertunity of brushing the flees of[f] their legs and bodies. Great numbers of *Sea Otters* in the river below the falls, I shot one in the narrow chanel to day which I could not get.[5] Great numbers of Indians visit us both from above and below. one of the old Chiefs who had accompanied us from the head of the river, informed us that he herd the Indians Say that the nation below intended to kill us. we examined all the arms &c. complete the amunition to 100 rounds. The nativs leave us earlyer this evening than usial, which gives a Shadow of confermation to the information of our old Chief,   as we are at all times & places on our guard, are under no greater apprehention than is common.

I observed on the beach near the Indian Lodges two butifull canoes of different Shape & Size to what we had Seen above wide in the midd[l]e and tapering to each end, on the bow curious figures were cut in the wood &c.   Capt. Lewis went up to the Lodges to See those Canoes and exchanged our Smallest canoe for one of them by giveing a Hatchet & few trinkets to the owner who informed that he purchased it of a white man below for a horse,   these canoes are neeter made than any I have ever Seen and calculated to ride the waves, and carry emence burthens,   they are dug thin and are suported by cross pieces of about 1 inch diamieter tied with Strong bark thro' holes in the Sides.

October 24th Thursday 1805

our two old chiefs expressed a desire to return to their band from this place, Saying "that they could be of no further Service to us, as their nation extended no further down the river than those falls, *(they could no longer understand the language of these below the falls, till then not much difference in the vocabs.)* and as the nation below had expressed hostile intentions against us, would certainly kill them; perticularly as they had been at war with each

[5] The sea otter was the basis of the triangular Northwest trade and its appearance here is additional evidence that the party is nearing its destination. So is the large coastal canoe of the next paragraph.

other;" we requested them to Stay with us *two* nights longer, our views were to detain those Chiefs with us, untill we should pass the next falls, which we were told were very bad, and at no great distance below, that they might inform us of any designs of the nativs, and if possible to bring about a peace between them and the tribes below.

The first pitch of this falls is 20 feet perpendecular, then passing thro' a narrow chanel for 1 mile to rapid of about 8 feet fall below which the water has no perceptable fall but verry rapid Capt. Lewis and three men crossed the river and on the opposit Side to view the falls which he had not yet taken a full view of. At 9 oClock a. m. I Set out with the party and proceeded on down a rapid Stream of about 400 yards wide at 2–½ miles the river widened into a large bason to the Stard. Side on which there is five Lodges of Indians. here a tremendious black rock Presented itself high and Steep appearing to choke up the river; nor could I See where the water passed further than the current was drawn with great velocity to the Lard. Side of this rock at which place I heard a great roreing. I landed at the Lodges and the natives went with me to the top of this rock which makes from the Stard. Side, from the top of which I could See the dificuelties we had to pass for Several miles below; at this place the water of this great river is compressed into a chanel between two rocks not exceeding *forty five* yards wide and continues for a ¼ of a mile when it again widens to 200 yards and continues this width for about 2 miles when it is again intersepted by rocks. The whole of the Current of this great river must at all Stages pass thro' this narrow chanel of 45 yards wide.[6]

as the portage of our canoes over this high rock would be impossible with our Strength, and the only danger in passing thro those narrows was the whorls and swills [swells] arriseing from the Compression of the water, and which I thought (as also our principal watermen Peter Crusat) by good Stearing we could pass down Safe, accordingly I deturmined to pass through this place notwithstanding the horrid appearance of this agitated gut swelling, boiling & whorling in every direction, which from the top of the rock did not appear as bad as when I was in it; however we passed Safe to the astonishment of all the Inds. of the last Lodges

6 The Short Narrows, or The Dalles proper.

who viewed us from the top of the rock. passed one Lodge below
this rock, and halted on the Stard. Side to view a very bad place,
the current divided by 2 Islands of rocks the lower of them large
and in the midal of the river,   this place being verry bad I sent
by land all the men who could not Swim and such articles as was
most valuable to us such as papers Guns & amunition, and proceeded down with the canoes two at a time to a village of 20 wood
houses in a Deep bend to the Stard. Side below which [was] a rugid
black rock

The nativs of this village re[ce]ived me verry kindly, one of
whome envited me into his house, which I found to be large and
comodious, and the first wooden houses in which Indians have
lived Since we left those in the vicinity of the Illinois,   they are
scattered permiscuisly on a elivated Situation near a mound of
about 30 feet above the Common leavel, which mound has Some
remains of houses and has every appearance of being artificial. one
half of those houses is apropriated for the storeing away Dried &
pounded fish which is the principal food, the other part next the
dore is the part occupied by the nativs who have beds raised on
either side, with a fire place in the center of this Space   each
house appeared to be occupied by about three families; that part
which is apropriated for fish was crouded with that article, and a
fiew baskets of burries.

I dispatched a Sufficent number of the good Swimers back for
the 2 canoes above the last rapid, and with 2 men walked down
three miles to examine the river Over a bed of rocks, which the
water at verry high fluds passes over,   on those rocks I Saw Several
large scaffols on which the Indians dry fish,   as this is out of
Season the poles on which they dry those fish are tied up verry
Securely in large bundles and put upon the scaffolds,   I counted
107 stacks of dried pounded fish in different places on those rocks
which must have contained 10.000 lb of neet fish,   The evening
being late I could not examine the river to my Satisfaction,   I returned through a rockey open countrey infested with pole-cats to the
village;   here we formed a camp near the village,   The principal chief from the nation below with Several of his men visited us,
and afforded a favourable oppertunity of bringing about a Piece and
good understanding between this chief and his people and the two
chiefs who accompanied us, Peter Crusat played on the *violin* and

the men danced which delighted the nativs, who Shew every civility towards us. we Smoked with those people untill late at night, when every one retired to rest.

Capt. Lewis and my Self walked down to See the place the Indians pointed out as the worst place in passing through the gut, which we found difficuelt of passing without great danger, but as the portage was impracti[c]able with our large canoes, we concluded to Make a portage of our most valuable articles and run the canoes thro.[7] accordingly on our return divided the party Some to take over the Canoes, and others to take our Stores across a portage of a mile to a place on the chanel below this bad whorl & Suck, with Some others I had fixed on the Chanel with roapes to throw out to any who Should unfortunately meet with difficuelty in passing through; great number of Indians viewing us from the high rocks under which we had to pass,   the 3 fir[s]t canoes passed thro very well, the 4th nearly filled with water, the last passed through by takeing in a little water,   thus Safely below what I conceved to be the worst part of this chanel felt my self extreamly gratified and pleased.

We loaded the Canoes & set out, and had not proceeded more than 2 mile[s] before the unfortunate Canoe which filled crossing the bad place above, run against a rock and was in great danger of being lost;   this Chanel is through a hard rough black rock, from 50 to 100 yards wide, swelling and boiling in a most tremendious maner; we passed through a deep bason to the Stard. Side of 1 mile below which the River narrows and [is] divided by a rock   the curent we found quit[e] gentle, here we met with our two old chiefs who had been to a village below to smoke a friendly pipe and at this place they met the Chief & party from the village above on his return from hunting all of whome were then crossing over their horses,   we landed to Smoke a pipe with this Chief whome we found to be a bold pleasing looking man of about 50 years of age dressd. in a war jacket a cap Legins & mockesons. he gave us some meat of which he had but little and informed us he in his rout met with a war party of Snake Indians

7 Entrance of the Long Narrows.

from the great river of the S. E. which falls in a few miles above
and had a fight. we gave this Chief a Medal, &c. [had] a parting
Smoke with our two faithful friends the chiefs who accompanied us
from the head of the river, (who had purchased a horse each with
2 rob[e]s and intended to return on horseback)[8]

we proceeded on down   the water fine, rocks in every derection for a fiew miles when the river widens and becoms a butifull
jentle Stream of about half a mile wide,   Great numbers of the
Sea orter [or Seals] about those narrows and both below and above.
we came too, under a high point of rocks on the Lard. Side below
a creek of 20 yards wide and much water,   as it was necessary to
make Some Selestial observations we formed our camp on the top
of a high point of rocks, which forms a kind of fortification in the
Point between the river & creek, with a boat guard,

*The expedition remains in camp for the next two days, making
observations, hunting, and repairing the dugouts.*

[Clark]   OCTOBER 28TH MONDAY 1805

A cool windey morning   we loaded our canoes and Set out at
9 oClock, a. m.   as we were about to set out 3 canoes from above
and 2 from below came to view us   in one of those canoes I observed an Indian with round hat Jacket & wore his hair
cued   we proceeded on   at four miles we landed at a Village
of 8 houses on the Stard. Side under some rugid rocks,   I entered one of the houses in which I saw a British musket, a cutlash
and Several brass Tea kittles of which they appeared verry
fond   Saw them boiling fish in baskets with Stones,   here we
purchased five Small Dogs, Some dried buries, & white bread made
of roots,   the wind rose and we were obliged to lie by all day
at 1 mile below on the Lard Side. we had not been long on Shore
before a Canoe came up with a man woman & 2 children, who had
a fiew roots to Sell,   Soon after maney others joined them from
above,   The wind which is the cause of our delay, does not retard the motions of those people at all, as their canoes are calculated to ride the highest waves,   they are built of white cedar or
Pine verry light wide in the middle and tapers at each end, with

8 The two Nez Percés, who here take the back trail.

aperns, and heads of animals carved on the bow, which is generally raised. wind blew hard accompanied with rain all the evening, our Situation not a verry good one for an encampment, but such as it is we are obliged to put up with, the harbor is a Safe one, we encamped on the Sand, wet and disagreeable

OCTOBER 29TH TUESDAY 1805

A cloudy morning wind from the west but not hard,   we Set out at day light, and proceeded on about *five* miles   came too on the Stard. Side at a village of 7 houses built in the Same form and materials of those above,   I observed in the lodge of the chief sundery articles which must have been precured from the white people, Such [as] a Scarlet & blue cloth Sword Jacket & hat. I also observed two wide Split boards w[i]th images on them cut and painted in emitation of a man;   The Chief directed his wife to hand him his medison bag which he opened and Showed us 14 fingers which he said was the fingers of his enemies which he had taken in war,   this is the first Instance I ever knew of the Indians takeing any other trofea of their exploits off the dead bodies of their Enimies except the Scalp. The chief painted those fingers with Several other articles which was in his bag red and securely put them back, haveing first mad[e] a short harrang which I suppose was bragging of what he had done in war. we purchased 12 Dogs and 4 Sacks of fish, & some fiew ascid berries,   after brackfast we proceeded on, ·   the mountains are high on each side, containing scattering pine white Oake & under groth, hill Sides Steep and rockey;   at 4 miles lower we observed a small river falling in with great rapidity on the Stard. Side below which is a village of 11 houses,   here we landed to Smoke a pipe with the nativs

we purchased 4 dogs and set out. (this village is the of the Same nation of the one we last passed) and proceeded on. The countrey on each side begin[s] to be thicker timbered with Pine and low white oake; verry rockey and broken. passed three large rocks in the river   the middle rock is large long and has Several Squar vaults on it, we call this rockey Island the Sepulchar. The last river we passed we shall call the *Cataract* River from the number of falls which the Indians say is on it,   passed 2 Lodges of Indians a short distance below the sepulchor Island on the Stard. Side.

river wide, at 4 mile passed 2 houses on the Stard. Side, six miles lower passed 4 houses above the mouth of a Small river 40 yards wide on the Lard. Side a thick timbered bottom above & back of those houses, those are the first houses which we have seen on the South Side of the Columbia River, (and the axess to those dificuelt) for fear of the approach of their common enemies the Snake Indians,[9]

OCTOBER 30TH WEDNESDAY 1805

A cool morning, a moderate rain all the last night, after eating a partial brackfast of venison we Set out, Saw 4 Cascades caused by Small Streams falling from the mountains on the Lard. Side, Some rain, we landed above the mouth of a Small river on the Stard. Side and Dined, J. Shields Killed a Buck & Labeash 3 Ducks, here the river widens to about one mile large Sand bar in the middle, a great [rock] both in and out of the water, large Stones or rocks are also permiscuisly scattered about in the river, The day proved cloudy dark and disagreeable with some rain all day which kept us wet. The countary a high mountain on each side thickly covered with timber, such as Spruce, Pine, Cedar, oake Cotton &c. &c. I took two men and walked down three miles to examine the Shute [10] and river below proceeded along an old Indian path, passd. an old village at 1 mile on an ellevated Situation, Capt. L. Saw one gun and Several articles which must have been precured from the white people. a wet disagreeable evening, the only wood we could get to burn on this little Island on which we have encamped is the newly discovered *Ash,* which makes a tolerable fire.

OCTOBER 31ST THURSDAY 1805

A cloudy rainey disagreeable morning I proceeded down the river to view with more attention [*the rapids*] we had to pass on the river below, the two men with me. Jo. Fields & Peter Crusat proceeded down to examine the rapids the Great Shute which commenced at the Island on which we encamped continued with

---

[9] The "Snake Indians" reported on this stretch of the Columbia were probably the Bannocks.

[10] The beginning of the ferocious rapids called the Cascades, which were to become notorious in the years of the Oregon immigration. They are now covered by the water backed up by Bonneville Dam.

great rapidity and force thro a narrow chanel much compressd. and interspersed with large rocks for ½ a mile, at a mile lower is a verry considerable rapid at which place the waves are remarkably high,   and proceeded on in a old Indian parth 2–½ miles by land thro a thick wood & hill Side, to the river where the Indians make a portage,   from this place I Dispatched Peter Crusat (our principal waterman) back to follow the river and examine the practibility of the canoes passing, as the rapids appeared to continue down below as far as I could See,   I with Jo Fields proceeded on,

the mountain which is but low on the Stard. Side, leave[s] the river, and a leavel stoney open bottom suckceeds on the Said Std. Side for a great Distance down,   the mountains high and rugid on the Lard. Side   this open bottom is about 2 miles   a Short distance below this village is a bad Stoney rapid and appears to be the last in view   I observed at this lower rapid the remains of a large and antient Village which I could plainly trace by the Sinks in which they had formed their houses, as also those in which they had buried their fish. from this rapid to the lower end of the portage the river is crouded with rocks of various sises between which the water passes with great velociety createing in many places large waves,   an Island which is Situated near the Lard. Side occupies about half the distance the lower point of which is at this rapid. immediately below this rapid the high water passes through a narrow chanel through the Stard. Bottom forming an Island of 3 miles Long & one wide; I walked through this Island which I found to be verry rich land, and had every appearance of haveing been at some distant period cultivated   at this time it is covered with grass intersperced with strawberry vines,   I could not see any rapids below in the extent of my view which was for a long distance down the river, which from the last rapids widened and had everry appearance of being effected by the tide [*this was in fact the first tide water*] I deturmind to return to camp 10 miles distant,   a remarkable high detached rock Stands in a bottom on the Stard. Side near the lower point of this Island on the Stard. Side about 800 feet high and 400 paces around, we calle the *Beaten* [*Beacon*] *rock.*[11]

One of the men shot a goose above this Great Shute, which was floating into the Shute, when an Indian observed it, plunged! into

11 Castle Rock

the water & swam to the Goose and brought in on shore, at the head of the Suck, [*great danger, rapids bad, a descent close by him (150 feet off,) of all Columbia River, current dashed among rocks, if he had got in the Suck — lost*]   as this Indian richly earned the goose I suffered him to keep it which he about half picked and Spited it up with the guts in it to roste.

This Great Shute or falls is about ½ a mile, with the water of this great river compressed within the space of 150 paces in which there is great numbers of both large and Small rocks, water passing with great velocity forming [foaming] & boiling in a most horriable manner, with a fall of about 20 feet,   below it widens to about 200 paces and current gentle for a Short distance.

November 1st Friday 1805

A verry cool morning wind hard from the N. E. The Indians who arrived last evening took their Canoes on ther Sholders and carried them below the Great Shute,   we Set about takeing our Small canoe and all the baggage by land 940 yards of bad slippery and rockey way. The Indians we discovered took ther loading the whole length of the portage 2–½ miles, to avoid a second Shute which appears verry bad to pass, and thro' which they passed with their empty canoes. Great numbers of Sea Otters, they are so cautious that I with dificuelty got a Shot at one today, which I must have killed, but could not get him as he Sunk.

We got all our baggage over the Portage of 940 yards, after which we got the 4 large canoes over by slipping them over the rocks on poles placed across from one rock to another, and at some places along partial Streams of the river. in passing those canoes over the rocks &c. three of them rec[ei]ved injuries which obliged us to delay to have them repared. Several Indian Canoes arrived at the head of the portage, Some of the men accompanied by those from the village come down to Smoke with us,   they appear to Speak the same language with a little different axcent

I cannot lern certainly as to the traffick those Inds. carry on below, if white people or the indians who trade with the whites who are either settled or visit the mouth of this river. I believe mostly with the latter as their knowledge of the white people appears to be verry imperfect, and the articles which they appear to trade mostly i. e. Pounded fish, Beargrass, and roots; cannot be an object of comerce with furin merchants. however they git in return for those articles Blue and white *beeds* copper Kettles, brass arm bands, some scarlet and blue robes and a fiew articles of old clothes,   they prefer beeds to any thing, and will part with the last mouthfull or articles of clothing they have for a fiew of those beeds,   those beeds the[y] trafick with Indians Still higher up this river for roabs, Skins, cha-pel-el [biscuitroot] bread, beargrass &c. who in their turn trafick with those under the rockey mountains for Beargrass, *quarmash* roots & robes &c.

The nativs of the waters of the Columbia appear helthy, Some have tumers on different parts of their bodies. and Sore and weak Eyes are common,   maney have lost their Sight entirely, great numbers with one eye out and frequently the other verry weak,   This misfortune I must again asscribe to the water &c. They have bad teeth, which is not common with indians, maney have worn their teeth down and Some quite into their gums, this I cannot satisfactorily account for it,   do ascribe it in some measure to their method of eateing, their food, roots pert[i]cularly, which they make use of as they are taken out of the earth frequently nearly covered with sand, I have not Seen any of their long roots offered for Sale clear of sand. They are rether below the Common Size high cheeks womin Small and homely, and have Swelled legs and thighs, and their knees remarkably large which I ascribe to the method in which they sit on their hams   go nearly necked wareing only a piece of leather tied about their breast which falls down nearly as low as the waste, a small roabe about 3 feet square, and a piece of leather tied about their breach,   They [*womin*] have all flat heads in this quarter both men and women. They are dirty in the extream, both in their person and cookery. ware their hare loose hanging in every direction. They ask high prices for what they Sell and Say that the white people below give great prices for every thing &c.

The noses are all pierced and when they are dressed they have a long tapered piece of white shell or wampum put through the nose, those Shells are about 2 inches in length. I observed in maney of the villeages which I have passed, the heads of the female children in the press for the purpose of compressing their heads in their infancy into a certain form, between two boards

The expedition camps before running the lower half of the Cascades.

CHAPTER XX

FROM THE RAPIDS TO THE SEA

NOVEMBER 2ND SATURDAY 1805

Examined the rapid below us more pert[i]celarly   the danger appearing too great to Hazzard our Canoes loaded, dispatched all the men who could not Swim with loads to the end of the portage below,   I also walked to the end of the portage with the carriers where I delayed untill everry articles was brought over and canoes arrived Safe. here we brackfast and took a Meridn. altitude. about the time we were Setting out 7 Squars came over loaded with Dried fish, and bear grass neetly buldled up,   Soon after 4 Indian men came down over the rapid in a large canoe. passed a rapid at 2 miles & 1 at 4 miles opposit the lower point of a high Island on the Lard. Side, and a little below 4 Houses on the Stard. Bank,   a Small creek on the Lard. Side opposit Strawberry Island, which heads below the last rapid,   opposit the lower point of this Island passed three Islands covered with tall timber opposit the Beaten rock,   Those Islands are nearest the Starboard Side; imediately below on the Stard. Side passed a village of nine houses, which is Situated between 2 Small creeks, and are of the Same construction of those above;   here the river widens to near a mile, and the bottoms are more extensive and thickly timbered, as also the high mountains on each Side, with Pine, Spruce pine, cotton wood, a Species of ash, and alder. at 17 miles passed a rock near the middle of the river, about 100 feet high and 80 feet Diameeter,   proceed on down a smoth gentle Stream of about 2 miles wide, in which the tide has its effect as high as the Beaten rock or the Last rapids at

273

Strawberry Island,   saw great numbers of waterfowl of Different kinds, such as Swan, Geese, white & grey brants, ducks of various kinds, Guls. & Pleaver. Labiesh killed 14 brant Joseph Fields 3 & Collins one. we encamped under a high projecting rock on the Lard. Side,   here the mountains leave the river on each Side, which from the great Shute to this place is high and rugid; thickly covered with timber principalley of the Pine Species.[1] The bottoms below appear extensive and thickly covered with wood. river here about 2-½ miles wide. Seven Indians in a canoe on their way down to trade with the nativs below, encamp with us,   those we left at the portage passed us this evening and proceeded on down. The ebb tide rose here about 9 Inches, the flood tide must rise here much higher.

NOVEMBER 3D SUNDAY 1805

The Fog so thick this morning that we could not see a man 50 Steps off,   this fog detained us untill 10 oClock at which time we Set out, accompanied by our Indian friends who are from a village near the great falis,

A Mountain which we Suppose to be Mt. Hood, is S. 85° E about 47 miles distant. This Mtn. is covered with Snow and in the range of mountains which we have passed through and is of a conical form but rugid. proceeded on to the center of a large Island in the middle of the river which we call Dimond Island from its appearance,   here we met 15 Indn. men in 2 canoes from below,   they informed us they Saw 3 vestles below &c. &c.   we landed on the North side of this Dimond Island and Encamped,   a canoe arrived from the village below the last rapid with a man his wife and 3 children, and a woman whome had been taken prisoner from the Snake Inds. on Clarks River   I sent the Interpreters wife who is a *So so ne* or Snake Indian of the Missouri, to Speake to this squar,   they could not understand each other Sufficiently to converse.[2] This family and the Inds. we met from below continued with us. Capt. Lewis borrowed a Small canoe of those Indians & 4 men took her across to a Small lake in the

1 They have emerged from the gorge of the Columbia, leaving the Cascade Mountains behind.
2 The captive squaw was probably a Bannock.

Isld. he killed a Swan and Several Ducks, which made our number of fowls this evening 3 Swan, 8 brant and 5 Ducks, on which we made a Sumpteous supper. We gave the Indian who lent the Canoe a brant, and some meat to the others. one of those Indians, the man from the village near the Lower Rapids has a gun with a brass barrel & cock of which he prises highly — Note the mountain we saw from near the forks proves to be Mount *Hood*

November 4th Monday 1805

Shannon set out early to walk on the Island to kill something, he joined us at the lower point with a Buck. (Tide rose last night 18 inches perpendicular at Camp) near the lower point of this dimond Island is the head of a large Island Seperated from a Small one by a narrow chanel, and both Situated nearest the Lard. Side, on the Main Lard. Shore a Short distance below the last Island we landed at a village of *25 houses*: 24 of those houses we[re] thached with Straw, and covered with bark, the other House is built of boards in the form of those above, except that it is above ground and about 50 feet in length [*and covered with broad split boards*] This village contains about 200 Men of the *Skilloot* nation I counted 52 canoes on the bank in front of this village maney of them verry large and raised in bow. we recognized the man who over took us last night, (*our pilot who came in his canoe*) he invited us to a lodge in which he had Some part and gave us a roundish roots about the Size of a Small Irish potato which they roasted in the embers until they became Soft, This root they call *Wap-pa-to* the *Bulb* of which the Chinese cultivate in great quantities called the *Sa-git ti folia* or common arrow head, (*we believe it to be the Same*) it has an agreeable taste and answers verry well in place of bread. we purchased about 4 bushels of this root and divided it to our party,

at 7 miles below this village passed the upper point of a large Island nearest the Lard. Side, a Small Prarie in which there is a pond opposit on the Stard. here I landed and walked on Shore, about 3 miles a fine open Prarie for about 1 mile, back of which the countrey rises gradually and wood land comencies Saw Some Elk and Deer Sign, and joined Capt. Lewis at a place he had landed with the party for Diner. Soon after Several canoes of Indians from the village above came down, dressed for the purpose as I supposed of Paying us a friendly visit,   they had scarlet & blue blankets Salor Jackets, overalls, Shirts and hats independant of their usial dress;   the most of them had either [*war axes Spears or Bows Sprung with quivers of arrows,*] Muskets or pistols and tin flasks to hold their powder,   Those fellows we found assumeing and disagreeable, however we Smoked with them and treated them with every attention & friendship.

dureing the time we were at dinner those fellows Stold my pipe Tomahawk which they were Smoking with,   I imediately serched every man and the canoes, but could find nothing of my Tomahawk,   while Serching for the Tomahawk one of those Scoundals Stole a cappoe [capote] of one of our interperters, which was found Stufed under the root of a tree, near the place they Sat,   we became much displeased with those fellows, which they discovered and moved off on their return home to their village, except 2 canoes which had passed on down. we proceeded on met a large & a Small canoe from below with 12 men   the large canoe was orniminted with *Images* carved in wood the figures of a Bear in front & a man in Stern, Painted & fixed verry netely on the canoe, rising to near the hight of a man   two Indians verry finely Dressed & with hats on was in this canoe   passed the lower point of the Island which is *nine* miles in length [3] haveing passed 2 Islands on the Stard. Side of this large Island, three Small Islands at its lower point. the Indians make Signs that a village is Situated back of those Islands on the Lard. Side. and I believe that a chanel is Still on the Lrd. Side as a canoe passed in between the Small Islands, and made Signs that way, probably to traffick with some of the nativs liveing on another chanel.

at 3 miles lower, and 12 Leagues below quick sand river passed a village of four large houses on the Lard. Side, near which we had a full view of *Mt. Helien* [St. Helens] which is perhaps the highest pinical in America   it bears N. 25°. E. about 90 miles. This is the mountain I saw from the Muscle Shell rapid on the 19th of October last [4] covered with Snow, it rises Something in the form of a Sugar lofe   about a mile lower passed a Single house on the

---

[3] Sauvie Island. It masks the mouth of the great Willamette River, whose existence Clark does not yet suspect.

[4] Clark is wrong on both counts. Mount St. Helens is one of the lesser Cascade peaks (alt. 9671 ft.) and, as has been noted, the one he saw on October 19 was probably Mount Adams.

Lard. Side, and one on the Stard. Side,   passed a village on each side and camped near a house on the Stard. Side we proceeded on untill one hour after dark with a view to get clear of the nativs who was constantly about us, and troublesom,   finding that we could not get Shut of those people for one night, we landed and Encamped on the Stard. Side   Soon after 2 canoes came to us loaded with Indians, we purchased a fiew roots of them.

The Indians which we have passd to day (*in their boats were of*) of the *Scil-loot* nation (*going up to the falls — differ a little*) in their language from those near & about the long narrows   their dress differ but little, except they have more of the articles precured from the white traders,   they all have flatened heads both men and women, live principally on fish and *Wap pa too* roots,   They are thievishly inclined as we have experienced.

NOVEMBER 5TH TUESDAY 1805

Rained all the after part of last night, rain continues this morning,   I [s]lept but verry little last night for the noise Kept [up] dureing the whole of the night by the Swans, Geese, white & Grey Brant Ducks &c. on a Small Sand Island close under the Lard. Side; they were emensely noumerous, and their noise horid. We met 4 Canoes of Indians from below, in which there is 26 Indians,   one of those canoes is large, and ornimented with *Images* on the bow & Stern. That in the Bow [is] the likeness of a Bear, and in the Stern the picture of a man. The day proved cloudy with rain the greater part of it, we are all wet cold and disagreeable — I killed a grouse which was verry fat, and larger than common. This is the first night which we have been entirely clear of Indians since our arrival on the waters of the Columbia River.

NOVEMBER 6TH WEDNESDAY 1805

A cool wet raney morning   we Set out early   the Indians of the 2 Lodges we passed to day came in their canoes with Sundery articles to Sell,   we purchased of them *Wap-pa-too roots, salmon-trout,* and I purchased 2 beaver Skins for which I gave 5 small fish hooks. we over took two Canoes of Indians going down [5] to trade, one of the Indians Spoke a fiew words of english and Said that the

[5] Down to the coast to find some ship that was engaged in the Northwest trade.

principal man who traded with them was Mr. Haley, and that he had a woman in his Canoe who Mr. Haley was fond of &c.   he Showed us a Bow of Iron and Several other things which he Said Mr. Haley gave him.

we came too to Dine on [a] long narrow Island   found the woods so thick with under groth that the hunters could not get any distance into the Isld. the red wood, and Green bryers interwoven, and mixed with pine, alder, a Speci[e]s of Beech, ash &c.   we killed nothing to day. The Indians leave us in the evening, river about one mile wide hills high and Steep on the Std.   No place for Several Miles suff[i]cently large and leavil for our camp,   we at length Landed at a place which by moveing the stones we made a place Sufficently large for the party to lie leavil on the Smaller Stones clear of the *Tide*. Cloudy with rain all day   we are all wet and disagreeable, had large fires made on the Stone and dried our bedding and kill the flees which collected in our blankets at every old village we encamped near

NOVEMBER 7TH THURSDAY 1805

A cloudy foggey morning Some rain. we Set out early proceeded under the Stard. Side under a high rugid hills with Steep assent the Shore boalt and rockey, the fog so thick we could not See across the river,   two cano[e]s of Indians met and returned with us to their vilIage,   they gave us to eate Some fish, and Sold us, fish, *Wap pa to* roots three *dogs* and 2 otter skins for which we gave fish hooks principally of which they were verry fond.

Those people call themselves *War-ci-á-cum* and Speake a language different from the nativs above with whome they trade for the *Wapato* roots of which they make great use of as food. their houses differently built, raised entirely above ground eaves about 5 feet from the ground Supported and covered in the same way of those above,   dores about the Same size but in the Side of the house in one corner, one fire place and that near the opposit end, around which they have their beads raised about 4 feet from the flore which is of earth,   under their beads they Store away baskets of dried fish Berries & *Wappato,* over the fire they hang the fiesh as they take them and [of] which they do not make immediate use. Their Canoes are of the Same form of those above.

after delaying at this village one hour and a half we Set out piloted by an Indian dressed in a Salors dress, to the Main Chanel of the river,   the tide being in we should have found much dificuelty in passing into the main Chanel from behind those islands, without a pilot,   here we see a great numbers of water fowls about those Marshey Islands;   here the high mountanious Countrey approaches the river on the Lard Side, a high Mountn. to the S. W. about 20 miles, the high mountans. countrey continue on the Stard. Side,   about 14 miles below the last village we landed at a village of the same nation. it contains 7 indifferent houses built in the same form of those above,   here we purchased a Dog some fish, *wap pa to,* roots and I purchased 2 beaver Skins for the purpose of makeing me a *roab,* as the robe I have is rotten and good for nothing. opposit to this village the high mountaneous countrey leave[s] the river on the Lard. Side below which the river widens into a kind of Bay & is crouded with low Islands Subject to be covered by the tides. We proceeded on about 12 miles below the Village under a high mountaneous Countrey on the Stard. Side, Shore boald and rockey and Encamped under a high hill on the Stard. Side opposit to a rock Situated half a mile from the shore, about 50 feet high and 20 Deamieter;   we with dificuelty found a place clear of the tide and Sufficiently large to lie on and the only place we could get was on round stones on which we lay our mats   rain continud. moderately all day & Two Indians accompanied us from the last village,   they we detected in Stealing a knife and returned,

Great joy in camp we are in *view* of the *Ocian,* this great Pacific Octean which we been so long anxious to See.[6] and the roreing or noise made by the waves brakeing on the rockey Shores (as I suppose) may be heard disti[n]ctly

NOVEMBER 8TH FRIDAY 1805

A cloudy morning Some rain,   we did not Set out untill 9 oClock, haveing changed our Clothing. three Indians in a Canoe overtook us, with salmon to Sell,   we came too at the remains of an old village at the bottom of this nitch and dined, here we Saw great numbers of fowl,   Sent out 2 men and they killed a Goose and two *canves back* Ducks   here we found great numbers of

---

6 In the notebook which he kept on his knee to record courses and bearings, Clark had written *"Ocian in view! O! the joy."* He was mistaken. Tonight's camp is near Pillar Rock and the ocean cannot be seen from there.

flees which we treated with the greatest caution and distance;   after Diner the Indians left us and we took the advantage of a returning tide and proceeded on to the Second point
on the Std.   here we found the Swells or Waves so high that we
thought it imprudent to proceed; we landed unloaded and drew
up our Canoes.[7]

Some rain all day at intervales, we are all wet and disagreeable,
as we have been for Several days past, and our present Situation a
verry disagreeable one in as much as we have not leavel land
Sufficient for an encampment and for our baggage to lie cleare of
the tide, the High hills jutting in so close and steep that we cannot retreat back, and the water of the river too Salt to be
used,   added to this the waves are increasing to Such a hight
that we cannot move from this place,   in this Situation we are
compelled to form our camp between the hite of the Ebb and flood
tides, and rase our baggage on logs. We are not certain as yet if
the white people who trade with those people or from whome they
precure their goods are Stationary at the mouth, or visit this quarter at stated times for the purpose of trafick &c.   I believe the
latter to be the most probably conjecture. The Seas roled and
tossed the Canoes in such a manner this evening that Several of
our party were Sea sick.

NOVEMBER 9TH SATURDAY 1805

The tide of last night did not rise Sufficiently high to come into
our camp, but the Canoes which was exposed to the mercy of the
waves &c. which accompanied the returning tide, they all filled,
and with great attention we Saved them untill the tide left them
dry. wind Hard from the South, and rained hard all the fore part
of the day,   at 2 oClock P M the flood tide came in accompanied
with emence waves and heavy winds, floated the trees and Drift
which was on the point on which we Camped and tossed them
about in such a manner as to endanger the canoes verry
much,   with every exertion and the Strictest attention by every
individual of the party was scercely sufficient to Save our Canoes
from being crushed by those monsterous trees maney of them
nearly 200 feet long and from 4 to 7 feet through. our camp entirely
under water dureing the hight of the *tide,* every man as wet as

---

[7] In the wide indentation on the north (Washington) bank known as Gray's
Bay. (Not to be confused with Gray's Harbor.)

water could make them all the last night and to day all day as the rain continued all day,   at 4 oClock P M the wind Shifted about to the S. W. and blew with great violence imediately from the Ocean for about two hours,   notwithstanding the disagreeable Situation of our party all wet and cold (and one which they have experienced for Several days past) they are chearfull and anxious to See further into the Ocian,   The Water of the river being too Salt to use we are obliged to make use of rain water. Some of the party not accustomed to Salt water has made too free a use of it   on them it acts as a pergitive.

At this dismal point we must Spend another night as the wind & waves are too high to proceed.

November 10th Sunday 1805

rained verry hard the greater part of the last night & continues this morning,   the wind has layed and the swells are fallen. we loaded our canoes and proceeded on,

The wind rose from the N W. and the swells became so high, we were compelled to return about 2 miles to a place where we could unld. our canoes, which was in a small Bay on Driftwood on which we had also to make our fires to dry our selves as well as we could, the shore being either a clift of Purpendicular rocks or steep assents to the hight of 4 or 500 feet,   we continued on this drift wood untill about 3 oClock when the evening appearing favourable we loaded & set out in hopes to turn the Point below and get into a better harber, but finding the *waves & swells* continue to rage with great fury below, we got a safe place for our stores & a much beter one for the canoes to lie and formed a campment on Drift logs in the same little Bay under a high hill at the enterence of a small drean, which we found very convt. on account of its water, as that of the river is Brackish. The logs on which we lie is all on flote every high tide. The rain continues all day. we are all wet also our bedding and maney other articles. we are all employed untill late drying our bedding. nothing to eate but Pounded fish.

November 11th Monday 1805

A hard rain all the last night,   dureing the last tide the logs on which we lay was all on float,   Sent out Jo Fields to hunt, he Soon returned and informed us that the hills was So high & Steep,

& thick with undergroth and fallen Timber that he could not get out any distance; about 12 oClock 5 Indians came down in a canoe, the wind verry high from the S. W. with most tremendous waves brakeing with great violence against the Shores, rain falling in torrents, we are all wet as usial — and our Situation is truly a disagreeable one; the great quantites of rain which has loosened the Stones on the hill Sides; and the Small stones fall down upon us, our canoes at one place at the mercy of the waves, our baggage in another; and our selves and party Scattered on floating logs and Such dry Spots as can be found on the hill sides, and crivicies of the rocks. we purchased of the Indians 13 red charr which we found to be an excellent fish. they are badly clad & illy made, Small and Speak a language much resembling the last nation, one of those men had on a Salors Jacket and Pantiloons. and made Signs that he got those clothes from the white people who lived below the point &c. those people left us and crossed the river (which is about 5 miles wide at this place) through the highest waves I ever Saw a Small vestles ride. Those Indians are certainly the best Canoe navigaters I ever Saw. rained all day.

NOVEMBER 12TH TUESDAY 1805

A Tremendious wind from the S. W. about 3 oClock this morning with Lightineng and hard claps of Thunder, and Hail which Continued untill 6 oClock a. m. when it became light for a Short time, then the heavens became sudenly darkened by a black cloud from the S. W. and rained with great violence untill 12 oClock, the waves tremendious brakeing with great fury against the rocks and trees on which we were encamped. our Situation is dangerous. we took the advantage of a low *tide* and moved our camp around a point to a Small wet bottom, at the Mouth of a Brook, which we had not observed when we came to this cove; from its being verry thick and obscured by drift trees and thick bushes. It would be distressing to See our Situation, all wet and colde our bedding also wet, (and the robes of the party which compose half the bedding is rotten and we are not in a Situation to supply their places) in a wet bottom scercely large enough to contain us our baggage half a mile from us, and Canoes at the mercy of the waves, altho Secured as well as possible, Sunk with emence parcels of Stone to wate them down to prevent their dashing to pecies against the rocks; one got loose last night and was left on a rock a Short distance below, without rec[ei]ving more damage than a Split in her bottom. Fortunately for us our men are healthy. 3 men Gibson Bratten & Willard attempted to go arou[n]d the point below in our Indian Canoe, much Such a canoe as the Indians visited us in yesterday, they proceeded to the point from which they were oblige[d] to return, the waves tossing them about at will. I walked up the branch and giged 3 Salmon trout.

November 13th Wednesday 1805

Some intervals of fair weather last night, rain continue[d] this morning. I walked up the Brook & assended the first Spur of the mountain with much fatigue, the distance about 3 miles, through an intolerable thickets of Small pine, a groth much resembling arrow wood on the Stem of which there is thorns this groth about 12 or 15 feet high interlockd. into each other and scattered over the high fern & fallen timber, added to this the hills were so steep that I was compelled to draw my Self up by the assistance of those bushes. The Timber on those hills are of the pine species large and tall maney of them more than 200 feet high & from 8 to 10 feet through at the Stump the rain continuing and weather proved So cloudy that I could not See any distance. on my return we dispatched 3 men Colter, Willard and Shannon in the Indian canoe to get around the point if possible and examine the river, and the Bay below for a go[o]d harber for our canoes to lie in Safty &c. The tide at every floot tide came in [*with great swells brakeing against the rocks and Drift trees*] with great fury. The rain continue all day. nothing to eate but pounded fish which we Keep as a reserve and use in Situations of this kind.

November 14th Thursday 1805

rained all the last night without intermition, and this morning. wind blows verry hard, but our situation is Such that we cannot tell from what point it comes. one of our canoes is much broken by the waves dashing it against the rocks. 5 Indians came up in a canoe, thro' the waves which is verry high and role with great fury. They made Signs to us that they saw 3 men we Sent down yesterday. only 3 of those Indians landed, the other 2 which was women played off in the waves, which induced me to Suspect that they had taken Something from our men below,   at this time one of the men Colter returnd. by land and informed us that those Indians had taken his Gigg & basket,   I called to the Squars to land and give back the gigg, which they would not doe untill a man run with a gun, as if he intended to Shute them when they landed, and Colter got his gig & basket

Colter informed us that it was but a Short distance from where we lay around the point to a butifull Sand beech which continued for a long ways, that he had found a good harber in the mouth of a creek near 2 Indian Lodges — that he had proceeded in the canoe as far as he could for the waves, the other two men Willard & Shannon had proceeded on down

Capt. Lewis concluded to proceed on by land & find if possible the white people the Indians say is below and examine if a Bay is Situated near the mouth of this river as laid down by Vancouver in which we expect, if there is white traders to find them &c.   at 3 oClock he Set out with 4 men Drewyer Jos. & Ru. Fields & R. Frasure, in one of our large canoes and 5 men to set them around the point on the Sand beech. this canoe returned nearly filled with water at Dark which it receved by the waves dashing into it on its return, haveing landed Capt. Lewis & his party Safe on the Sand beech. The rain &c. which has continued without a longer itermition than 2 hours at a time for ten days past has distroyd. the robes and rotted nearly one half of the fiew clothes the party has, perticularley the leather clothes   if we have cold weather before we can kill & Dress Skins for clothing the bulk of the party will Suffer verry much.

NOVEMBER 15TH FRIDAY 1805

Rained all the last night at intervales of sometimes of 2 hours,   This morning it became cold & fair,   I prepared to set out at which time the wind sprung up from the S. E. and blew down the River & in a fiew minits raised such swells and waves brakeing on the Rocks at the Point as to render it unsafe to proceed. I went to the point in an empty canoe and found it would be dangerous to proceed even in an empty *canoe* The sun shown untill 1 oClock P. M. which gave an oppertunity for us to dry some of our bedding & examine our baggage, the greater Part of which I found wet. some of our Pounded fish spoiled I had all the arms put in order & amunition examined.

The rainey weather continued without a longer intermition than 2 hours at a time, from the 5th in the morng. untill the 16th is *eleven* days rain, and the most disagreeable time I have experenced confined on a tempiest coast wet, where I can neither git out to hunt, return to a better situation, or proceed on: in this situation have we been for Six days past. fortunately the wind lay about 3 oClock we loaded in great haste and set out passed the bluster-ing Point below which is a sand beech, with a small marshey bottom for 3 miles on the Stard. Side, on which is a large village of 36 houses deserted by the Inds & in full possession of the flees, a small creek fall[s] in at this village, which waters the Country for a few miles back; Shannon & 5 Indians met me here, Shannon informed me he met Capt. Lewis some distance below & he took Willard with him & sent him to meet me, the Inds. with him wer rogues, they had the night before stold both his and Willards guns from under their heads,[8] Capt. Lewis & party arrived at the camp of those Indians at so timely a period that the Inds. were allarmed & delivered up the guns &c.

The tide meeting of me and the emence swells from the Main Ocian (imedeately in front of us) raised to such a hite that I con-cluded to form a camp on the highest spot I could find in the marshey bottom, and proceed no further by water as the Coaste becomes verry [dangerous] for crafts of the size of our Canoes, and as the Ocian is imedeately in front and gives us an extensive view of it from Cape disapointment to Point addams, except 3 small Islands off the mouth and S W of us. my situation is in the upper part of Haleys Bay

4 Indians in a canoe came down with *papto* [wapatoo] roots to sell for which they asked blankets or robes, both of which we could not spare I informed those Indians all of which under-stood some English that if they stole our guns &c the men would certainly shute them, I treated them with great distance, & the sentinal which was over our Baggage allarmed them verry much, they all Promised not to take any things, and if any

---

[8] From a later draft of this entry: "I told those Indians who accompanied Shannon that they should not come near us, and if any one of their nation Stold anything from us, I would have him Shot, which they understoot verry well."

thing was taken by the squars & bad boys to return them &c.   the waves became verry high   Evening fare & pleasent,   our men all comfortable in the camps they have made of the boards they found at the Town above

NOVEMBER 17TH SUNDAY 1805

A fair cool morning wind from the East. The tide rises at this place 8 feet 6 inches and comes in with great waves brakeing on the Sand beech on which we lay with great fury   Six hunters out this morning in serch of Deer & fowl.

At half past 10 Clock Capt. Lewis returned haveing travesed Haley Bay to Cape Disapointment and the *Sea* coast to the North for Some distance. Several *Chinnook* Indians followed Capt. L —, and a Canoe came up with roots mats &c. to Sell. those Chinnooks made us a present of a rute boiled much resembling the common liquorice in taste and Size: in return for this root we gave more than double the value to Satisfy their craveing dispostn. It is a bad practice to receive a present from those Indians as they are never satisfied for what they recive in return if ten times the value of the articles they gave. This *Chinnook* Nation is about 400 Souls inhabid the countrey on the Small rivers which run into the bay below us and on the Ponds to the N. W. of us, live principally on fish and roots,   they are well armed with fusees and Sometimes kill Elk Deer and fowl. our hunters killed to day 3 deer, 4 brant and 2 Ducks, and inform me they Saw Some Elk Sign. I directed all the men who wished to see more of the main *Ocian* to prepare themselves to Set out with me early on tomorrow morning. The principal chief of the Chinnooks & his family came up to See us this evening.

NOVEMBER 18TH MONDAY 1805

I set out with 10 men and my man York to the Ocian by land. i. e. Serjt. Ordway & Pryor, Jos. & Ru Fields, Go. Shannon, W. Brattin, J. Colter, P. Wiser, W. Labieche & P. Shabono one of our interpreters & York. I set out at Day light and proceeded on a Sandy beech

after dinner to a Small rock island in a deep nitch passed a nitch in which there is a dreen from Some ponds back; the land low opposite this nitch   a bluff of yellow clay and Soft Stone from the river to the commencement of this nitch. below the countrey rises to high hills of about 80 or 90 feet above the water. at 3 miles passed a nitch. this rock Island is Small and at the South of a deep bend in which the nativs inform us the Ships anchor, and from whence they receive their goods in return for their peltries and Elk skins &c.   this appears to be a very good harber for large Ships. here I found Capt. Lewis name on a tree. I also engraved my name, & by land the day of the month and year, as also Several of the men.

to the iner extremity of *Cape Disapointment* passing a nitch in which there is a Small rock island,   a Small Stream falls into this nitch from a pond which is imediately on the Sea coast passing through a low isthmus. this Cape is an ellivated circlier [cir-] cular] point covered with thick timber on the iner Side and open grassey exposure next to the Sea and rises with a Steep assent to the hight of about 150 or 160 feet above the leavel of the water   this cape as also the Shore both on the Bay & Sea coast is a dark brown rock. I crossed the neck of Land low and ½ of a mile wide to the main Ocian, at the foot of a high open hill pro- jecting into the ocian, and about one mile in Si[r]cumfrance. I assefided this hill which is covered with high corse grass. decended to the N. of it and camped. [walked] 19 Miles [to-day].

from Cape Disapointment to a high point of a Mountn. which we shall call [*Clarke's Point of View*] beares S. 20° W. about 40 [25] miles,   point adams is verry low and is Situated within the derection between those two high points of land,   the water ap- pears verry Shole from off the mouth of the river for a great dis- tance, and I cannot assertain the direction of the deepest chanel,   the Indians point nearest the opposit Side. the waves appear to brake with tremendious force in every direction quite across   a large Sand bar lies within the mouth nearest to point Adams which is nearly covered at high tide. men appear much Satisfied with their trip beholding with estonishment the high waves dashing against the rocks & this emence Ocian

Cape Disapointment at the Enterance of the Columbia River into the Great South Sea or Pacific Ocean.

Tuesday November the 19th 1805.

I arose early this morning from under a Wet blanket caused by a Shower of rain which fell in the latter part of the last night, and

Sent two men on a head with directions to proceed on near the
Sea Coast and Kill Something for brackfast and that I should follow my self in about half an hour. after drying our blankets a
little I set out with a view to proceed near the Coast the direction
of which induced me to conclude that at the distance of 8 or 10
miles, the Bay was at no great distance across. I overtook the
hunters at about 3 miles,   they had killed a Small Deer on which
we brackfast[ed],   it Comen[c]ed raining and continued moderately untill 11 oClock A M.

after takeing a Sumptious brackfast of Venison which was rosted
on Stiks exposed to the fire, I proceeded on through ruged Country of high hills and Steep hollers to the commencement of a Sandy
coast which extended to a point of high land distant near 20 miles.
this point I have taken the Liberty of Calling after my particular
friend Lewis. at the commencement of this Sand beech the high
lands leave the Sea Coast in a Direction to Chinnook river, and
does not touch the Sea Coast again below point Lewis leaveing a
low pondey Countrey, maney places open with small ponds in
which there is great numbr. of fowl   I am informed that the
Chinnook Nation inhabit this low countrey and live in large wood
houses on a river which passes through this bottom Parrilal to the
Sea coast and falls into the Bay

I proceeded on the sandy coast and marked my name on a Small
pine, the Day of the month & year, &c. and returned to the foot of
the hill,   I saw a Sturgeon which had been thrown on Shore and
left by the tide 10 feet in length, and Several joints of the back
bone of a Whale, which must have foundered on this part of the
Coast. after Dineing on the remains of our Small Deer I proceeded to
the bay distance about 2 miles, thence up to the mouth of Chinnook
river 2 miles, crossed this little river in the Canoe we left at its
mouth and Encamped on the upper Side in an open sandy bottom.

WEDNESDAY NOVEMBER THE 20TH 1805

Some rain last night   dispatched Labeech to kill some fowl for
our brackfast   he returned in about 2 hourse with 8 large Ducks
on which we brackfast   I proceeded on to the enterance of a
Creek near a Cabin. No person being at this Cabin and 2 Canoes
laying on the opposit Shore from us, I determined to have a raft

made and Send a man over for a canoe,   a Small raft was Soon made, and Reuben Fields crossed and brought over a Canoe. This Creek which is the outlet of a number of ponds, is at this time (high tide) 300 yds. wide. I proceeded on up the Beech and was overtaken by three Indians one of them gave me Some dried Sturgeon and a fiew Wappato roots, I employ[e]d those Indians to take up one of our Canoes which had been left by the first party that Came down, for which Service I gave them each a fishing hook of a large Size. on my way up I met Several parties of Chinnooks which I had not before Seen,   they were on their return from our Camp. all those people appeared to know my deturmonation of keeping every individual of their nation at a proper distance, as they were guarded and resurved in my presence &c.   found maney of the *Chin nooks* with Capt. Lewis of whome there was 2 Cheifs *Com com mo ly* & *Chil-lar-la-wil* to whome we gave Medals and to one a flag.   one of the Indians had on a roab made of 2 Sea Otter Skins   the fur of them were more butifull than any fur I had ever Seen   both Capt. Lewis & my self endeavored to purchase the *roab* with different articles   at length we precured it for a belt of blue beeds which the Squar-wife of our interpreter Shabono wore around her waste. in my absence the hunters had killed Several Deer and fowl of different kinds.

THURSDAY NOVEMBER 21st 1805

A cloudy morning   most of the Chinnooks leave our camp and return home,   the Wind blew hard from the S. E. which with the addition of the flood tide raised verry high waves which broke with great violence against the shore throwing water into our camp   the forepart of this day Cloudy at 12 oClock it began to rain and continud all day moderately,   Several Indians Visit us to day of different nations or Bands Some of the *Chiltz* Nation who reside on the Sea Coast near Point Lewis, Several of the *Clatsops* who reside on the Opposit Side of the Columbia imediately opposit to us, and a Cheif from the Grand rapid to whome we gave a Medal.

An old woman & Wife to a Cheif of the *Chunnooks* came and made a Camp near ours. She brought with her 6 young Squars (*her daughters & nieces*) I believe for the purpose of Gratifying the passions of the men of our party and receving for those indulgiences Such Small [presents] as She (the old woman) thought proper to accept of.

Those people appear to View Sensuality as a Necessary evel, and do not appear to abhor it as a Crime in the unmarried State. The young females are fond of the attention of our men and appear to meet the sincere approbation of their friends and connections, for thus obtaining their favours,   the Womin of the Chinnoook Nation have handsom faces low and badly made with large legs & thighs which are generally Swelled from a Stopage of the circulation in the feet (which are Small) by maney Strands of Beeds or curious Strings which are drawn tight around the leg above the ankle,   their legs are also picked [tattooed] with defferent figures,   I saw on the left arm of a Squar the following letters *J. Bowman,*   all those are considered by the natives of this quarter as handsom deckerations, and a woman without those deckorations is Considered as among the lower Class   they ware their hair lose hanging over their back and Sholders   maney have blue beeds threaded & hung from different parts of their *ears* and about ther neck and around their wrists,   their dress otherwise is prosisely like that of the Nation of *War ci a cum* as already discribed.

Maney of the men have blankets of red blue or Spotted Cloth or the common three & 2½ point [9] blankets, and Salors old Clothes which they appear to prise highly, they also have robes of *SeaOtter,* Beaver, Elk, Deer, fox and cat common to this Countrey, which I have never Seen in the U States. they also precure a roabe from the nativs above, which is made of the Skins of a Small animal about the Size of a cat, which is light and dureable and highly prized by those people. the greater numbers of the men of the Chinnooks have Guns and powder and Ball. The Men are low homely and badly made, Small crooked legs large feet, and all of both Sects have flattened heads. maney of the Chinnooks appear to have Venerious and pustelus disorders. one woman whome I saw at the Creek appeared all over in Scabs and ulsers &c.

[9] "Points" were lines woven into blankets to denote their size, from one to four. A four-point Mackinaw measured 72 × 90 inches. The Hudson's Bay Company four-point today is the full double blanket, 144 inches long. At one period the blanket cost one beaver pelt per point.

We gave to the men each a pece of ribin.[10] We purchased cramberies Mats verry netely made of flags and rushes, Some roots, Salmon and I purchased a hat made of Splits & Strong grass, which is made in the fashion which was common in the U States two years ago also small baskets to hold Water made of Split and Straw, for those articles we gave high prices.

[10] From an earlier draft of the entry: "to bestow on their favorite Lasses, this plan to save the knives & more valueable articles."

CHAPTER XXI

AT FORT CLATSOP

[Clark]   FRIDAY NOVEMBER 22ND 1805.

A moderate rain all the last night with wind, a little before Day light the wind which was from the S.S.E. blew with Such Violence that we wer almost overwhelmed with water blown from the river, this Storm did not sease at day but blew with nearly equal violence throughout the whole day accompan[i]ed with rain. O! how horriable is the day waves brakeing with great violence against the Shore throwing the Water into our Camp &c. all wet and confind to our Shelters, Several Indian men and women crouding about the mens shelters to day, we purchased a fiew Wappato roots for which we gave Armban[d]s, & rings to the old Squar, those roots are equal to the Irish potato, and is a tolerable substitute for bread

The threat which I made to the men of this nation whome I first Saw, and an indifference towards them, is: I am fully convinced the cause of their conducting themselves with great propriety towards ourselves & Party.

SATURDAY NOVEMBER 22[3]RD 1805.

A calm Cloudy morning, a moderate rain the greater part of the last night, Capt. Lewis Branded a tree with his name Date &c. I marked my name the Day & year on a alder tree, the party all Cut the first letters of their names on different trees in the bottom.

in the evening Seven indians of the *Clot sop* [Clatsop] Nation came over in a Canoe, they brought with them 2 Sea otter Skins for which they asked blue beads &c. and Such high pricies that we were unable to purchase them without reducing our Small Stock of Merchendize, on which we depended for Subcistance on our return up this river. mearly to try the Indian who had one of those Skins, I offered him my Watch, handkerchief a bunch of red beads and a dollar of the American coin, all of which he refused and demanded *"ti-á-co-mo-shack"* which is *Chief beads* and the most common blue beads, but fiew of which we have at this time

The two entries above sound themes that were to be repeated monotonously through the winter, the rainy season of the Northwest coast and the decadent tribes who lived near the mouth of the Columbia.

The expedition was encamped on the northern branch of the river, the Washington shore, which proved to be an acutely unfavorable region. There was little game and the thought of living on dried fish and flour made from the arrowhead root was abhorrent, even if there had been enough trade goods to buy them with. Furthermore, prolonged dampness had rotted the party's clothes, moccasins, and the robes which were used as blankets, and hides were needed to replace them. Where should the winter post be built? Clark disliked the seacoast — "salt water I view as an evil in as much as it is not helthy" and would have liked to go back up the Columbia to The Dalles. That was out of the question, however, for they must not forfeit whatever chance there was of encountering a ship that was engaged in the Northwest trade. From such a ship they could replenish their supplies and equipment and could secure a stock of trade goods for the eastward journey.

(One ship came into the Columbia and passed their campsite on the Washington shore soon after they abandoned it. The Indians who visited the new post carefully refrained from telling them of its presence and did not tell the ship's captain that the expedition was in the vicinity. Jefferson's failure to send a ship to the mouth of the Columbia is inexplicable.)

Visiting Indians reported that game, especially elk, was more plentiful on the southern shore. Lewis took a squad to reconnoiter it, finding it a swampy lowland covered with brush and veined with

tidal creeks. There were occasional stands of timber, however, and so many elk that it was clear there would be no danger of short rations. He selected a site some miles up a creek he called Netul River — now Lewis and Clark River — which wandered through the universal bog. It was "in a thick groth of pine . . . on a rise about 30 feet higher than the high tides leavel." The main party moved to it on December 7, Clark very glad to leave the coast where "the sea which is imedeately in front roars like a repeeted roling thunder and have rored in that way ever since our arrival in its borders which is now 24 days since we arrived in sight of the Great Western Ocian, I cant say Pasific as since I have seen it, it has been the reverse." Before leaving he carved, on a large pine tree, his famous legend, "William Clark December 3rd 1805. By Land from the U.States in 1804 & 1805."

Here, south of the Columbia and inland from the coast, they built the post which they named Fort Clatsop for the nearest neighboring tribe. It was a log stockade fifty feet square, a row of three cabins facing another one of four, with a parade ground twenty feet wide between them. It was completed on January 1. There were showers or steady rain every day while it was being built.

[Clark]   CHRISTMAS WEDNESDAY 25TH DECEMBER 1805

at day light this morning we we[re] awoke by the discharge of the fire arm[s] of all our party & a Selute, Shouts and a Song which the whole party joined in under our windows, after which they retired to their rooms   were chearfull all the morning. after brackfast we divided our Tobacco which amounted to 12 carrots one half of which we gave to the men of the party who used to-bacco,[1] and to those who doe not use it we make a present of a handkerchief,   The Indians leave us in the evening   all the party Snugly fixed in their huts. I recved a pres[e]nt of Capt. L. of a fleece hosrie [hosiery] Shirt Draws and Socks, a pr. Mockersons of Whitehouse a Small Indian basket of Gutherich, two Dozen white weazils tails of the Indian woman, & some black root of the Indians before their departure. Drewyer informs me that he saw a Snake

---

[1] The rest was saved for trading purposes on the return trip. Ordway notes lugubriously, "we have no ardent Spirits."

pass across the parth to day. The day proved Showerey wet and disagreeable.

we would have Spent this day the nativity of Christ in feasting, had we any thing either to raise our Sperits or even gratify our appetites, our Diner concisted of pore Elk, so much Spoiled that we eate it thro' mear necessity, Some Spoiled pounded fish and a fiew roots.

DECEMBER 26TH THURSDAY 1805

rained and blew hard last night, some hard Thunder,   The rain continued as usial all day and wind blew hard from the S.E.   Joseph Fields finish a Table & 2 seats for us. we dry our wet articles and have the blankets fleed,   The flees are so troublesom that I have slept but little for 2 night past and we have regularly to kill them out of our blankets every day for several past. maney of the men have ther Powder wet by the horns being repeatedly wet,   hut smoke[s] verry bad.

DECEMBER 27TH FRIDAY 1805

rained last night as usial and the greater part of this day, the men complete Chimneys & Bunks to day,   in the evening a Chief and 4 men come of the *Clotsop* nation chief *Co-ma-wool*   we sent out R. Fields & Collins to hunt and order Drewyer, Shannon & Labiach to set out early to morrow to hunt,   Jo Fields, Bratten, & Gibson to make salt at Point Addams,[2] Willard & Wiser, to assist them in carrying the Kittles &c. to the Ocian, and all the others to finish the Pickets and gates. worm weather I saw a Musquetor which I showed Capt. Lewis   Those Indians gave is [us], a black root they call *Shan-na-tâh-que* a kind of Licquirish which they rost in embers and call *Cul-ho-mo*, a black berry the size of a Cherry & Dried which they call *Shel-well* — all of which they prise highly and make use of as food to live on,   for which Capt Lewis gave the chief a cap of sheep skin and I his Son, ear bobs, Pice of riben, a pice of brass, and 2 small fishing hooks, of which they were much pleased,   Those roots & berres, are greatfull to our Stomcks as we have nothing to eate but Pore Elk meet,

---

[2] The camp of the salt-makers was at the bold headland called Tillamook Head, more than twenty miles down the coast from Point Adams.

nearly spoiled; & this accident of spoiled meet, is owing to warmth & the repeeted rains, which cause the meet to tante before we can get it from the woods. Musquetors troublesom

[Lewis]   FORT CLATSOP. 1806.
                        JANUARY 1ST TUESDAY. [WEDNESDAY]
This morning I was awoke at an early hour by the discharge of a volley of small arms, which were fired by our party in front of our quarters to usher in the new year; this was the only mark of rispect which we had it in our power to pay this celebrated day. our repast of this day tho' better than that of Christmass, consisted principally in the anticipation of the 1st day of January 1807, when in the bosom of our friends we hope to participate in the mirth and hilarity of the day, and when with the zest given by the recollection of the present, we shall completely, both mentally and corporally, enjoy the repast which the hand of civilization has prepared for us. at present we were content with eating our boiled Elk and wappetoe, and solacing our thirst with our only beverage *pure water*. two of our hunters who set out this morning reterned in the evening having killed two bucks elk; they presented Capt. Clark and myself each a marrow-bone and tonge, on which we suped. visited today by a few of the Clatsops who brought some roots and burries for the purpose of trading with us. we were uneasy with rispect to two of our men, Willard and Wiser, who were dispatched on the 28th ult. with the salt-makers, and were directed to return immediately; their not having returned induces us to believe it probable that they have missed their way. our fourtification being now completed we isssued an order for the more exact and uniform discipline and government of the garrison.

[Clark]   JANUARY 1ST 1806
A List of the names of Sundery persons, who visit this part of the Coast for the purpose of trade &c. &c. in large Vestles; all of which speake the English language &c. as the Indians inform us

Moore   Visit them in a large 4 masted ship,
                             they expect him in 2 moons to
                             trade.

1 Eyd[one-eyed]Skellie	in a large ship, long time gorn.
Youin	In a large Ship, and they expect him in 1 moon to trade with them.
Swepeton	In a Ship, they expect him in 3 month back to trade
Mackey	In a Ship, they expect him back in 1 or 2 Moons to trade with them.
Meship	In a Ship, the[y] expect him 2 moons to trade.
Jackson	Visit them in a Ship and they expect him back in 3 months to trade.
Balch	In a Ship and they expect him in 3 months to trade.
Mr. Haley	Visits them in a Ship & they expect him back to trade with them in 3 Moons to trade. he is the favourite of the Indians (from the number of Presents he gives) and has the trade principally with all the tribes.
Washilton	In a Skooner, they expect him in 3 months to return and trade with them — a favourite.
Lemon	In a Slupe, and they expect him in 3 moons to trade with them.
Davidson	Visits this part of the coast and river in a Brig for the purpose of Hunting the Elk returns when he pleases he does not trade any, kills a great many Elk &c. &c.
Fallawan	In a Ship with guns he fired on & killed several Indians, he does not trade now and they doe not know when he will return, well done

Fort Clatsop was named for a small Chinookan tribe in whose territory it was located. The Chinooks proper, whose country was also south of the Columbia, and two other small Chinook-speaking tribes, the Cowlitzes and the Chehalises, whose country was north of it, were also frequent visitors. All four were fringe tribes of the Northwest Coast culture, which flourished far more vigorously north of Puget Sound. They flattened their heads, lived in houses made of wooden planks, were expert watermen, and had an economy in which the salmon was less central than it was in that of their northern relatives. They were also less warlike but were very skillful thieves. They seem to have been declining culturally before white men first saw them but the decline was accelerated by contact with the new culture. Venereal and other new diseases had decimated them, and the maritime traders had treated them with appalling brutality. Lewis and Clark thought much more highly of the Clatsops than of their neighbors and became very friendly with the chief whose name they rendered Comowool.

[Clark]   FRIDAY THE 3RD JANUARY 1806

At 11 A. M. we were visited by our near neighbour Chief or *tiá Co mo wool* alias *Conia (Cóoné)* and six Clatsops. they brought for Sale Some roots berries and 3 Dogs also a Small quantity of fresh blubber. this blubber they informed us they had obtained from their neighbours the *Cal lá mox* who inhabit the coast to the S.E.   near one of their Villages a Whale had recently perished. this blubber the Indians eat and esteem it excellent food. our party from necescity have been obliged to Subsist some length of time on dogs have now become extreamly fond of their flesh; it is worthey of remark that while we lived principally on the flesh of this animal we wer much more helthy strong and more fleshey then we have been Sence we left the Buffalow Country. as for my own part I have not become reconsiled to the taste of this animal as yet.[3] Send Sarjt. Gass and G. Shannon to the Salt makers who are on the Sea Coast to the S.W. of us, to enquire after Willard & Wiser who have not yet returned. R. Field, potts & Collins the hunters who Set out on the 28th ulto., returned this evening after dark. they reported that they had been about 15 miles up the river which falls into Merewethers Bay to the East of us, and had hunted the country a considerable distance to East, and had proved unsucksesfull haveing killed one Deer and a fiew fowls, bearly as much as Subsisted them. this reminded us of the necessity of take-

[3] But Lewis: "I have become so perfectly reconciled to the dog that I think it an agreeable food and would prefer it vastly to lean Venison or Elk."

ing time by the forelock, and keep out Several parties while we
have yet a little meat beforehand. Capt. Lewis gave the Cheif
Cania a par of Sattin breechies with which he appeared much
pleased.[4]

[Lewis]   SATURDAY JANUARY 4TH 1806.

Comowooll and the Clatsops who visited us yesterday left us in
the evening. These people the Chinnooks and others residing in
this neighbourhood and Speaking the Same language have been
very friendly to us; they appear to be a mild inoffensive people but
will pilfer if they have an opportunity to do so where they conceive themselves not liable to detection. they are great higlers in
trade and if they conceive you anxious to purchase will be a whole
day bargaining for a handfull of roots; this I should have thought
proceeded from their want of knowledge of the comparitive value
of articles of merchandize and the fear of being cheated, did I not
find that they invariably refuse the price first offered them and
afterwards very frequently accept a smaller quantity of the same
article; in order to satisfy myself on this subject I once offered a
Chinnook my watch two knives and a considerable quantity of
beads for a small inferior sea Otter's skin which I did not much
want,   he immediately conceived it of great value, and refused
to barter except I would double the quantity of beads; the next
day with a great deal of importunity on his part I received the skin
in exchange for a few strans of the same beads he had refused the
day before. I therefore believe this trait in their character proceeds
from an avaricious all grasping disposition. in this rispect they
differ from all Indians I ever became acquainted with, for their
dispositions invariably lead them to give whatever they are possessed off no matter how usefull or valuable, for a bauble which
pleases their fancy, without consulting it's usefullness or value.
nothing interesting occured today, or more so, than our wappetoe
being all exhausted.

                                        SUNDAY JANUARY 5TH 1806.

   At 5. P.M. Willard and Wiser returned,   they had not been
lost as we apprehended. they informed us that it was not untill the

   [4] For a considerable time hereafter Clark's journal is based on Lewis's whose
phraseology it frequently reproduces.

fifth day after leaving the Fort that they could find a convenient
place for making salt; that they had at length established themselves on the coast about 15 Miles S.W. from this, near the lodge of
some Killamuck families; that the Indians were very friendly and
had given them a considerable quantity of the blubber of a whale
which perished on the coast some distance S.E. of them; part of
this blubber they brought with them, it was white & not unlike the
fat of Poork, tho' the texture was more spongey and somewhat
coarser. I had a part of it cooked and found it very pallitable and
tender, it resembled the beaver or the dog in flavour. it may appear somewhat extraordinary tho' it is a fact that the flesh of the
beaver and dog possess a very great affinity in point of flavour.

These lads also informed us that J. Fields, Bratten and Gibson
(the Salt Makers) had with their assistance erected a comfortable
camp killed an Elk and several deer and secured a good stock of
meat; they commenced the making of salt and found that they
could obtain from 3 quarts to a gallon a day; they brought with
them a specemine of the salt of about a gallon, we found it excellent, fine, strong, & white; this was a great treat to myself and
most of the party, having not had any since the 20th Ultmo.; I say
most of the party, for my friend Capt. Clark declares it to be a
mear matter of indifference with him whether he uses it or not;
for myself I must confess I felt a considerable inconvenience from
the want of it; the want of bread I consider as trivial provided, I
get fat meat, for as to the species of meat I am not very particular,
the flesh of the dog the horse the wolf, having from habit become
equally formiliar with any other, and I have learned to think that
if the chord be sufficiently strong, which binds the soul and boddy
together, it dose not so much matter about the materials which
compose it. Capt. Clark determined this evening to set out early
tomorrow with two canoes and 12 men in quest of the whale, or at
all events to purchase from the Indians a parcel of the blubber,   for this purpose he prepared a small assortment of merchandize to take with him.

MONDAY JANUARY 6TH 1806.

Capt Clark set out after an early breakfast with the party in two
canoes as had been concerted the last evening;   Charbono and

his Indian woman were also of the party; the Indian woman was very impo[r]tunate to be permited to go, and was therefore indulged; she observed that she had traveled a long way with us to see the great waters, and that now that monstrous fish was also to be seen, she thought it very hard she could not be permitted to see either (she had never yet been to the Ocean).

The Clatsops, Chinnooks, Killamucks &c. are very loquacious and inquisitive; they possess good memories and have repeated to us the names capasities of the vessels &c of many traders and others who have visited the mouth of this river; they are generally low in stature, proportionably small, reather lighter complected and much more illy formed than the Indians of the Missouri and those of our frontier;   they are generally cheerfull but never gay. with us their conversation generally turns upon the subjects of trade, smoking, eating or their women; about the latter they speak without reserve in their presents, of their every part, and of the most formiliar connection. they do not hold the virtue of their women in high estimation, and will even prostitute their wives and daughters for a fishinghook or a stran of beads.[5] in common with other savage nations they make their women perform every species of domestic drudgery. but in almost every species of this drudgery the men also participate,   their women are also compelled to geather roots, and assist them in taking fish, which articles form much the greatest part of their subsistance; notwithstanding the survile manner in which they treat their women they pay much more rispect to their judgment and oppinions in many rispects than most indian nations; their women are permitted to speak freely before them, and sometimes appear to command with a tone of authority; they generally consult them in their traffic and act in conformity to their opinions.

I think it may be established as a general maxim that those nations treat their old people and women with most differrence [deference] and rispect where they subsist principally on such articles that these can participate with the men in obtaining them; and that, that part of the community are treated with least attention, when the act of procuring subsistence devolves entirely on the men in the vigor of life. It appears to me that nature has been much more deficient in her filial tie than in any other of the strong

[5] Clark: "The *Chin-nook* womin are lude and carry on sport publickly."

affections of the human heart, and therefore think, our old men equally with our women indebted to civilization for their ease and comfort. Among the Siouxs, Assinniboins and others on the Missouri who subsist by hunting it is a custom when a person of either sex becomes so old and infurm that they are unable to travel on foot from camp to camp as they rome in surch of subsistance, for the children or near relations of such person to leave them without compunction or remo[r]se;   on those occasions they usually place within their reach a small peace of meat and a platter of water, telling the poor old superannuated wretch for his consolation, that he or she had lived long enough, that it was time they should dye and go to their relations who can afford to take care of them much better than they could. I am informed that this custom prevails even among the Minetares Arwaharmays and Recares when attended by their old people on their hunting excurtions; but in justice to these people I must observe that it appeared to me at their vilages, that they provided tolerably well for their aged persons, and several of their feasts appear to have principally for their object a contribution for their aged and infirm persons.

This day I overhalled our merchandize and dryed it by the fire, found it all damp; we have not been able to keep anything dry for many days together since we arrived in this neighbourhood, the humidity of the air has been so excessively great. our merchandize is reduced to a mear handfull, and our comfort during our return the next year much depends on it, it is therefore almost unnecessary to add that we much regret the reduced state of this fund.

CHAPTER XXII

AT FORT CLATSOP

[Lewis]   MONDAY (TUESDAY) JANUARY 7TH 1806.

Last evening Drewyer visited his traps and caught a beaver and an otter; the beaver was large and fat we have therefore fared sumptuously today; this we consider a great prize for another reason, it being a full grown beaver was well supplyed with the materials for making bate with which to catch others. To prepare beaver bate, the castor or bark stone is taken as the base, this is gently pressed out of the bladderlike bag which contains it, into a phiol of 4 ounces with a wide mouth; if you have them you will put from four to six stone in a phiol of that capacity,   to this you will add half a nutmeg, a douzen or 15 grains of cloves and thirty grains of cinimon finely pulverized, stir them well together and then add as much ardent sperits to the composition as will reduce it the consistency [of] mustard prepared for the table; when thus prepared it resembles mustard precisely to all appearance. when you cannot procure a phiol a bottle made of horn or a tight earthen vessel will answer, in all cases it must be excluded from the air or it will soon loose it's virtue;   it is fit for uce immediately it is prepared but becomes much stronger and better in about four or five days and will keep for months provided it be perfectly secluded from the air. when cloves are not to be had use double the quantity of Allspice, and when no spice can be obtained the bark of the root of sausafras. it appears to me that the principal uce of the spices is only to give a variety to the scent of the bark stone and if so the mace vineller [vanilla] and other sweet-smelling spices might be employed with equal advantage.

303

The male beaver has six stones, two [of] which contain a substance much like finely pulvarized bark of a pale yellow colour and not unlike tanner's ooz in smell, these are called the *bark stones* or castors; two others, which like the bark stone resemble small bladders, containe a pure oil of a strong rank disagreeable smell, and not unlike train oil, these are called the *oil stones;* and 2 others of generation. the Barkstones are about two inc[h]es in length, the others somewhat smaller   all are of a long oval form, and lye in a bunch together between the skin and the root of the tail, beneath or behind the fundament with which they are closely connected and seem to communicate. the pride of the female lyes on the inner side much like those of the hog. they have no further parts of generation that I can perceive and therefore beleive that like the birds they copulate with the extremity of the gut. The female have from two to four young ones at a birth and bring fourth once a year only, which usually happens about the latter end of may and begining of June. at this stage she is said to drive the male from the lodge, who would otherwise destroy the young. dryed our lodge and had it put away under shelter; this is the first day during which we have had no rain since we arrived at this place.

[Clark]   TUESDAY 7TH OF JANUARY 1806

Near the base of [a] high Mountain I found our Salt makers, and with them Sergt. Gass, Geo. Shannon was out in the woods assisting Jo Field and gibson to kill Some Meat,   the Salt Makers had made a Neet close camp, convenient to wood Salt water and the fresh water of the Clâtsop river which at this place was within 100 paces of the Ocian. they wer also Situated near 4 houses of Clatsops & Killamox, who they informed me had been verry kind and attentive to them. I hired a young Indian to pilot me to the whale for which Service I gave him a file in hand and promised Several other small articles on my return,   left Sergt. gass and one man of my party Werner to make Salt & permited Bratten to accompany me,   we proceeded on the round Slipery Stones under a high hill which projected into the ocian about 4 miles further than the direction of the Coast.[1] after walking for 2½ miles on the Stones,

1 Tillamook Head.

my guide made a Sudin halt, pointed to the top of the mountain and uttered the word *Pe shack* which means bad, and made signs that we could not proceed any further on the rocks, but must pass over that mountain, I hesitated a moment & view this emence mountain the top of which was obscured in the clouds, and the assent appeard. to be almost perpindecular; as the small Indian parth allong which they had brought emence loads but a fiew hours before, led up this mountain and appeared to assend in a Sideling direction, I thought more than probable that the assent might be torerably easy and therefore proceeded on, I soon found that the [path] become much worst as I assended, and at one place we were obliged to Support and draw our selves up by the bushes & roots for near 100 feet, and after about 2 hours labour and fatigue we reached the top of this high mountain, from the top of which I looked down with estonishment to behold the hight which we had assended, which appeared to be 10 or 12 hundred feet up a mountain which appeared to be almost perpindicular, here we met 14 Indians men and women loaded with the Oil and Blubber of the whale. In the face of this tremendeous precipic[e] imediately below us, there is a stra*(tar)* of white earth (which my guide informed me) the neighbouring indians use to paint themselves, and which appears to me to resemble the earth of which the French Porcelain is made;

[Lewis] TUESDAY (WEDNESDAY) JANUARY 8TH 1806.

The Clatsops Chinnooks and others inhabiting the coast and country in this neighbourhood, are excessively fond of smoking tobacco. in the act of smoking they appear to swallow it as they draw it from the pipe, and for many draughts together you will not perceive the smoke which they take from the pipe; in the same manner also they inhale it in their lungs untill they become surcharged with this vapour when they puff it out to a great distance through their nost[r]ils and mouth; I have no doubt the smoke of the tobacco in this manner becomes much more intoxicating and that they do possess themselves of all it's virtues in their fullest extent; they freequently give us sounding proofs of it's creating a dismorallity of order in the abdomen, nor are those light matters thought indelicate in either sex, but all take the liberty of obeying the dictates of nature without reserve. these people do not appear to know the uce of sperituous liquors, they never having once asked us for it; I presume therefore that the traders who visit them have never indulged them with the uce of it; from what ever cause this may proceede, it is a very fortunate occurrence, as well for the natives themselves, as for the quiet and safety of thos whites who visit them.

[Clark]   WEDNESDAY 8TH JANUARY 1806

we arived on a butifull Sand Shore,   found only the Skelleton of this Monster on the Sand; the Whale was already pillaged of every Valuable part by the Kilamox Inds. in the Vecinity of whose village's it lay on the Strand where the waves and tide had driven up & left it. this Skeleton measured 105 feet. I returned to the Village of 5 Cabins on the creek, found the nativs busily engaged boiling the blubber, which they performed in a large Squar wooden trought by means of hot stones;   the oil when extracted was secured in bladders and the Guts of the whale; the blubber from which the oil was only partially extracted by this process, was laid by in their cabins in large flickes [flitches] for use; those flickes they usially expose to the fire on a wooden Spit untill it is prutty well wormed through and then eate it either alone or with roots of the rush, Diped in the oil. The *Kil a mox* although they possessed large quantities of this blubber and oil were so prenurious that they disposed of it with great reluctiance and in small quantities only; insomuch that my utmost exertion aided by the party with the Small Stock of merchindize I had taken with me were not able to precure more blubber than about 300 lb. and a fiew gallons of oil;   Small as this stock is I prise it highly; and thank providence for directing the whale to us; and think him much more kind to us than he was to jonah, having Sent this Monster to be *Swallowed by us* in Sted of *Swallowing of us* as jonah's did.

[Lewis]   FRIDAY (THURSDAY) JANUARY 9TH 1806.

The persons who usually visit the entrance of this river for the purpose of traffic or hunting I believe are either English or Americans; the Indians inform us that they speak the same language with ourselves, and give us proofs of their varacity by repeating many words of English, as musquit, powder, shot, [k]nife, file, damned rascal, sun of a bitch &c. whether these traders are from Nootka sound, from some other late establishement on this coast, or immediately from the U'States or Great Brittain, I am at a loss to determine, nor can the Indians inform us. the Indians whom I have asked in what direction the traders go when they depart from hence, or arrive here, always point to the S.W. from which it is presumeable that Nootka cannot be their destination; and as from Indian information a majority of these traders annually visit them about the beginning of April and remain with them six or seven Months, they cannot come immediately from Great Britain or the U'States, the distance being too great for them to go and return in the ballance of the year. from this circumstance I am sometimes induced to believe that there is some other establishment on the coast of America south West of this place of which little is but yet known to the world, or it may be perhaps on some Island in the pacific ocean between the Continents of Asia and America to the South West of us.[2] This traffic on the part of the whites consists in vending, guns, (principally old british or American musquits) powder, balls and shot, Copper and brass kettles, brass teakettles and coffee pots, blankets from two to three point, scarlet and blue Cloth (coarse), plates and strips and sheet copper and brass, large brass wire, knives, beads and tobacco with fishinghooks buttons and some other small articles; also a considerable quantity of Sailor's cloaths, as hats coats, trowsers and shirts. for these they receive in return from the natives, dressed and undressed Elk-skins, skins of the sea Otter, common Otter, beaver, common fox, spuck, and tiger cat; also dryed and pounded sammon in baskets, and a kind of buisquit, which the natives make of roots called by them shappel- ell. The natives are extravegantly fond of the most common cheap blue and white beads, of moderate size, or such that from 50. to 70.

2 From time to time there were temporary trading establishments at Nootka Sound or near by. But there was nothing like a permanent settlement or post between Baranov's station on Kodiak Island and the Spanish mission at San Francisco Bay. This is the only occasion in the *Journals* when either of the captains indulges in speculative creation of settlements so common with other early explorers. It is an inexplicable lapse for Lewis was thoroughly familiar with the triangular Northwest trade and knew that many ships engaged in it touched at the Sandwich (Hawaiian) Islands. His speculation that there might be a "late [recent] establishement" represents a strong anxiety that the British might have erected a post on which they might base a claim to the Columbia region.

will weigh one penneyweight. the blue is usually p[r]efered to the white; these beads constitute the principal circulating medium with all the indian tribes on this river; for these beads they will dispose [of] any article they possess. the beads are strung on strans of a fathom in length and in that manner sold by the bredth or yard.

[Clark]   THURSDAY 9TH OF JANUARY 1806

   last night about 10 oClock while Smokeing with the nativ's I was alarmed by a loud Srill voice from the cabins on the opposite side,   the Indians all run immediately across to the village,   my guide who continued with me made Signs that Some one's throat was Cut,   by enquiry I found that one man McNeal was absent,   I imediately Sent off Sergt. N. Pryor & 4 men in quest of McNeal who' they met comeing across the Creak in great hast, and informed me that the people were alarmed on the opposit side at Something but what he could not tell,   a Man had verry friendly envited him to go and eate in his lodge, that the Indian had locked armes with him and went to a lodge in which a woman give him Some blubber, that the man envited him to another lodge to get Something better, and the woman [*Knowing his design*] held him [*McNeal*] by the blanket which he had around him (*He not knowing her object freed himself & was going off, when* [*This woman a Chinnook an old friend of McNeals*] and another ran out and hollow'd and his pretended friend disapeared. I emediately ordered every man to hold themselves in a State of rediness and Sent Sergt. Pryor & 4 men to know the cause of the alarm which was found to be a premeditated plan of the pretended friend of McNeal to ass[ass]anate [him] for his Blanket and what fiew articles he had about him, which was found out by a Chinnook woman who allarmed the men of the village who were with me in time to prevent the horred act. this man was of another band at Some distance and ran off as soon as he was discovered.

                          SUNDAY THE 12TH JANUARY 1806

   This morning Sent out Drewyer and one man to hunt, they returned in the evening Drewyer haveing killed 7 Elk; I scercely

know how we Should Subsist, I beleive but badly if it was not for
the exertions of this excellent hunter; maney others also exert themselves, but not being accquainted with the best method of finding
and killing the elk and no other wild animals is to be found in this
quarter, they are unsucksessfull in their exertions. at 2 P.M. Sergt.
Gass and the men I left to assist the salt makers in carrying in their
meat arrived also the hunters which I directed to hunt in the point,
they killed nothing. We have heretofore devided the Meat when
first killed among the four messes, into which we have divided our
party, leaveing to each the care of preserving and distribution of
useing it; but we find that they make such prodigal use of it when
they happen to have a tolerable Stock on hand, that we are determined to adopt a Different System with our present stock of
Seven Elk; this is to jurk it and issue it to them in Small quantities.

[Lewis]   TUESDAY (MONDAY) JANUARY 13TH 1806.

   this evening we exhausted the last of our candles, but fortunately
had taken the precaution to bring with us moulds and wick, by
means of which and some Elk's tallow in our possession we do not
yet consider oursleves destitute of this necessary article; the Elk we
have killed have a very small portion of tallow.

                     WEDNESDAY (TUESDAY) JANUARY 14TH 1806.

   From the best estimate we were able to make as we d[e]scended
the Columbia we conceived that the natives inhabiting that noble
stream, for some miles above the great falls to the grand rappids
inclusive annually prepare about 30,000 lbs. of pounded sammon
for market. but whether this fish is an article of commerce with the
whites or is exclusively sold to, and consumed by the natives of the
sea Coast, we are at a loss to determine. the first of those positions
I am disposed to credit most, but, still I must confess that I cannot
imagine what the white merchant's object can be in purchasing
this fish, or where they dispose of it. and on the other hand the
Indians in this neighbourhood as well as the Skillutes have an
abundance of dryed sammon which they take in the creeks and
inlets, and I have never seen any of this pounded fish in their
lodges, which I presume would have been the case if they purchased this pounded fish for their own consumption. the Indians

who prepared this dryed and pounded fish, informed us that it was to trade with the whites, and shewed us many articles of European manufacture which they obtained for it. it is true they obtain those articles principally for their fish but they trade with the Skillutes for them and not immediately with the whites; the intermediate merchants and carryers, the Skillutes, may possibly consume a part of this fish themselves and dispose of the ballance of it [to] the natives of the sea coast, and from them obtain such articles as they again trade with the whites.

FRIDAY (THURSDAY) JANUARY 16TH 1806.

we have plenty of Elk beef for the present and a little salt, our houses dry and comfortable, and having made up our minds to remain until the 1st of April, every one appears content with his situation and his fare. it is true that we could even travel now on our return as far as the timbered country reaches, or to the falls of the river; but further it would be madness for us to attempt to proceede untill April, as the indians inform us that the snows lye knee deep in the plains of Columbia during the winter, and in these plains we could scarcely get as much fuel of any kind as would cook our provision as we descended the river; and even were we happyly over these plains and again in the woody country at the foot of the Rocky Mountains we could not possibly pass that immence barrier of mountains on which the snows ly in winter to the debth in many places of 20 feet;   in short the Indians [3] inform us that they are impracticable untill about the 1st of June, at which time even there is an abundance of snow but a scanty subsistence may be obtained for the horses. we should not therefore forward ourselves on our homeward journey by reaching the rocky mountains. early than the 1st of June, which we can easily effect by seting out from hence on the 1st of April.

TUESDAY (MONDAY) JANUARY 20TH 1806.

Visited this morning by three Clatsops who remained with us all day; the object of their visit is mearly to smoke the pipe. on the morning of the eighteenth we issued 6 lbs. of jirked Elk pr. man,

[3] That is, the Nez Percés.

this evening the Sergt. reported that it was all exhausted; the six lbs. have therefore lasted two days and a half only. at this rate our seven Elk will last us only 3 days longer, yet no one seems much concerned about the state of the stores; so much for habit. we have latterly so frequently had our stock of provisions reduced to a minimum and sometimes taken a small touch of fasting that three days full allowance excites no concern. In those cases our skill as hunters afford us some consolation, for if there is any game of any discription in our neighbourhood we can track it up and kill it. most of the party have become very expert with the rifle. The Indians who visited us today understood us sufficiently to inform us that the whites did not barter for the pounded fish; that it was purchased and consumed by the Clatsops, Chinnooks, Cathlahmahs and Skillutes. The native roots which furnish a considerable proportion of the subsistence of the indians in our neighbourhood are those of a species of Thistle, fern, and rush; the Liquorice, and a small celindric root the top of which I have not yet seen, this last resembles the sweet pittatoe very much in it's flavor and consistency.

CHAPTER XXIII

At Fort Clatsop

N ot any occurences today worthy of notice." The sentence appears repeatedly in the daily log through January, February, and the first half of March 1806. It signalizes the monotony of life at Fort Clatsop.

Bad weather was continuous. At the end of the winter Clark noted that there had been only twelve days without rain and only six with sunshine. The garrison settled down to a routine in which the most exciting activity was the periodic changing of the detachment that was making salt on the beach at Tillamook Head. Hunting details were sent out nearly every day; some of them remained away for several days at a time. These parties provided the staple diet, elk meat, with which everyone became achingly bored. Occasionally it was varied with other game and with fresh and dried fish and roots or berries bought from Indians. There were usually Indians at the fort but their visits became as tiresome as the diet. The sign language remained the basis of communication but nearly everyone learned a little Chinook, which was the lingua franca of the maritime trade. And obviously someone, probably Clark or Drewyer, learned to speak it fairly well.

However hard put to it the captains were to find chores that would keep their command busy, they themselves were never without occupation. They devoted the winter to writing up their notes. The results constitute the bulk of this chapter, which in Volume IV of the Journals runs one hundred and seventy-nine pages. Almost all of it is Lewis's composition — usually Clark's journal is confined to summarizing or repeating what Lewis had written in his. Lewis's disquisitions are zoological, botanical, and anthropological

312

— *describing the fauna, the flora, and the Indians they had seen. He begins with the immediate locale, the Northwest Coast and the Columbia River. Finishing that he systematizes and amplifies the observations he had made since leaving Fort Mandan. The botanical and zoological notes, many of which describe new species or variations proved valuable to science following the return of the expedition. The anthropological notes have been permanently important; they are a rich treasury for ethnologists and historians today.*

Meanwhile Clark was reviewing, codifying, and criticizing his geographical data. (His tables and summaries are in Volume VI of the Journals.) He also drew many small-scale maps of various localities west of the Great Falls and worked on a series of master maps. (Many of the former are reproduced in the Atlas Volume of the Journals.) This activity produced the most important decision of the winter. Primarily as a result of Clark's study, the captains decided that the route they had taken west of the Great Falls was neither the shortest nor the best one — that they should have traveled overland and due west to Bitterroot Valley, avoiding the long, difficult detour to the Three Forks, Lemhi Pass, and the Salmon River. They decided that when they reached Traveller's Rest (in Bitterroot Valley) on the return journey they would divide the party. From there Lewis would explore the country which they believed would provide a better route, going eastward up Hellgate River and down to the Great Falls by Dearborn or Sun River. Clark would go down the Yellowstone River, because it too might provide a better route to Bitterroot Valley and because it was the principal tributary of the Missouri and the terrain it crossed must be important.

(Representative passages of botanical, zoological, anthropological, and geographical observation and discussion are printed in the text that follows.)

The inescapable dampness gave nearly everyone colds or rheumatism. A number of the men had acquired venereal infections, which Lewis treated vigorously. The most interesting illness, however, was Private Bratton's. He was reported "very unwell" on February 10, while at the salt-makers' camp, and was permitted to return to the fort but was so weak that he had to be carried there in a litter. He "appears much reduced with his late indisposition but is now recovering fast." On February 15, however, "Bratton is still very weak and complains of a pain in the lower part of the back when he moves which I supposed proceeds from dability." (That pain seems the most significant symptom.) On the 19th Clark gave him "6 of Scotts pills [1] *which did not work him   he is very weak and complains of his back." The next day he "has an obstenate cough and pain in his back and still appears to be geting weaker." On the 21st Lewis gave him another dose of Scott's pills and on the 22nd considered him "on the recovery." But on March 6 (Clark), "Bratten is now weaker than any of the convalessants and complains verry much of his back, all of them recovering slowly in consequence of the want of proper diet, which we have not in our power to procure." On March 7 (Lewis), "Bratton is much wo[r]se today, he complains of a violent pain in the small of his back and is unable in consequence to set up. we gave him one of our flanel shirts, applyed a bandage of flannel to the part and bathed and rubed it well with some vollatile linniment which I prepared with sperits of wine, camphor, castile soap and a little laudinum. he felt himself better in the evening." On the 8th "Bratton is much better today, his back gives him but little pain" but the next day he "complains of his back being very painfull to him today; I conceive this pain to be something of the rheumatism. we still apply the linniment and flannel; in the evening he was much better." Nothing would cure the ailment, however, and after the start of the return journey Bratton grew much worse. Eventually he was to be cured with dramatic suddenness. The symptoms and the nature of the cure suggest an inflammation or a sprain of the sacroiliac joint.* [2]

[Lewis]   FRIDAY (THURSDAY) JANUARY 23RD 1806.

This morning dispatched Howard and Warner to the Camp of the Salt-make[r]s for a supply of salt. The men of the garrison are still busily employed in dressing Elk's skins for cloathing, they

---

[1] This medicine is not listed in any of the expedition's inventories and I have been unable to determine what it was. We may confidently assume, however, that it was a strong purge.

[2] One of the medical men I have consulted rejects this diagnosis, however, and suggests that Bratton's weakness and backache resulted from a severe abdominal infection suffered at the camp of the salt-makers.

find great difficulty for the want of branes; [3] we have not soap to supply the deficiency, nor can we we procure ashes to make the lye; none of the pines which we use for fuel affords any ashes; extrawdinary as it may seem, the greene wood is consoomed without leaving the residium of a particle of ashes.

Saturday (Friday) January 24th 1806.

Drewyer and Baptiest La Paage returned this morning in a large Canoe with Comowooll and six Clatsops. they brought two deer and the flesh of three Elk & one Elk's skin, having given the flesh of one other Elk which they killed and three Elk's skins to the Indians as the price of their asssitance in transporting the ballance of the meat to the Fort; these Elk and deer were killed near point Adams and the Indians carried them on their backs about six miles, before the waves were sufficiently low to permit their being taken on board their canoes. the Indians remained with us all day. The Indians witnessed Drewyer's shooting some of those Elk, which has given them a very exalted opinion of us as marksmen and the superior excellence of our rifles compared with their guns; this may probably be of service to us, as it will deter them from any acts of hostility if they have ever meditated any such. My Air-gun also astonishes them very much; they cannot comprehend it's shooting so often and without powder; and think that it is *great medicine* which comprehends every thing that is to them incomprehensible.

Tuesday (Monday) January 27th 1806.

Goodrich has recovered from the Louis Veneri which he contracted from an amorous contact with a Chinnook damsel, I cured him as I did Gibson last winter by the uce of mercury. I cannot learn that the Indians have any simples which are sovereign specifics in the cure of this disease; and indeed I doubt very much whet[h]er any of them have any means of effecting a perfect cure. when once this disorder is contracted by them it continues with

[3] The brains of animals from whose hides robes or clothing were to be made were used in the tanning process. They were painstakingly rubbed and worked into the flesh side of the pelt to make it soft and pliable. Other greasy substances could be substituted, including soap as Lewis suggests. Lye was used to remove the fur and undercoat.

them during life; but always ends in dec[r]ipitude, death, or prema-
ture old age; tho' from the uce of certain simples together with their
diet, they support this disorder with but little inconvenience for
many years, and even enjoy a tolerable share of health; particularly
so among the Chippeways who I believe to be better skilled in the
uce of those simples than any nation of Savages in North America.
The Chippeways use a decoction of the Lobelia, and that of a
species of sumac common to the Atlantic states and to this country
near and on the Western side of the Rocky Mountains. this is the
smallest species of the sumac, readily distinguished by it's winged
rib, or common footstalk, which supports it's oppositely pinnate
leaves. these decoctions are drank freely and without limitation.
the same decoctions are used in cases of the gonnærea and are ef-
fecatious and sovereign. notwithstanding that this disorder dose
exist among the Indians on the Columbia yet it is witnessed in but
few individuals, at least the males who are always sufficiently exposed to the observations or inspection of the phisician. in my
whole rout down this river I did not see more than two or three
with the gonnærea and about double that number with the pox.

THURSDAY (WEDNESDAY) JANUARY 29TH 1806.

Nothing worthy of notice occurred today. our fare is the flesh
of lean elk boiled with pure water, and a little salt. the whale
blubber which we have used very sparingly is now exhausted. on
this food I do not feel strong, but enjoy the most perfect
health;   a keen appetite supplys in a great degree the want of
more luxurious sauses or dishes, and still renders my ordinary meals
not uninteresting to me, for I find myself sometimes enquiring of
the cook whether dinner or breakfast is ready.

SATURDAY FEBRUARY 1ST 1806.

They [the Indians of the Northwest] have but few axes among
them, and the only tool usually imployed in felling the trees or
forming the canoe, carving &c is a chissel formed of an old file
about an Inch or an Inch and a half broad. this chissel has sometimes a large block of wood for a handle; they grasp the chissel just
b[e]low the block with the right hand holding the edge down while

with the left they take hold of the top of the block and strike back-
handed against the wood with the edge of the chissel. a person
would suppose that the forming of a large canoe with an instrument like this was the work of several years; but these people make
them in a few weeks. they prize their canoes very highly; we have
been anxious to obtain some of them, for our journey up the river
but have not been able to obtain one as yet from the natives in this
neighbourhood.

today we opened and examined all our ammunition, which had
been secured in leaden canesters. we found twenty seven of the
best rifle powder, 4 of common rifle, th[r]ee of glaized and one of
the musqu[e]t powder in good order, perfectly as dry as when first
put in the canesters, altho' the whole of it from various accedents
has been for hours under the water. these cannesters contain four
lbs. of powder each and 8 of lead. had it not have been for that
happy expedient which I devised of securing the powder by means
of the lead, we should not have had a single charge of powder at
this time. three of the canesters which had been accedentally
bruized and cracked, one [of] which was carelessly stoped, and a
fifth that had been penetrated with a nail, were a little dammaged;
these we gave to the men to make dry; however exclusive of those
five we have an abundant stock to last us back; and we always take
care to put a proportion of it in each canoe, to the end that should
one can[o]e or more be lost we should still not be entirely bereft of
ammunition, which is now our only hope for subsistence and defence in a rout of 4000 Miles through a country exclusively inhabited by savages.

TUESDAY FEBRUARY 4TH 1806.

There are s[e]veral species of fir in this neighbourhood which I
shall discribe as well as my slender botanical skil wil enable me and
for the convenience of comparison with each other shal number
them. (No.1.) a species which grows to immence size; very commonly 27 feet in the girth six feet above the surface of the earth,
and in several instances we have found them as much as 36 feet in the
girth or 12 feet diameter perfectly solid and entire. they frequently
rise to the hight of 230 feet, and one hundred and twenty or 30 of
that hight without a limb. this timber is white and soft throughout

and rives better than any other species we have tryed. the bark shales off in irregula[r] rounded flakes and is of a redish brown colour particularly of the younger growth. the stem of this tree is simple branching, ascending, not very defuse, and proliferous. the leaf of this tree is acerose, ⅒th of an Inh in width, and ¾ of an Inch in length; is firm, stif and accuminate; they are triangular, a little declining, thickly scattered on all sides of the bough, but rispect the three uppersides only and are also sessile growing from little triangular pedestals of soft spungy elastic bark. at the junction of the boughs, the bud-scales continued to incircle their rispective twigs for several year[s]; at least three yea[r]s is common and I have counted as many as the growth of four years beyond these scales. this tree affords but little rosin. it's cone I have not yet had an opportunity to discover altho' I have sought it frequently; the trees of this kind which we have felled have had no cones on them.[4]

WEDNESDAY FEBRUARY 5TH 1806.

Fir No. 2 is next in dignity in point of size. it is much the most common species, it may be sa[i]d to constitute at least one half of the timber in this neighbourhood. it appears to be of the spruse kind. it rises to the hight of 160 to 180 feet very commonly and is from 4 to 6 feet in diameter, very streight round and regularly tapering. the bark is thin of a dark colour, and much divided with small longitudinal intersticies; that of the boughs and young trees is somewhat smoth but not so much so as the balsom fir nor that of the white pine of our country. the wood is white throughout and reather soft but very tough, and difficult to rive. The trunk of this tree is a simple branching diffused stem and not proliferous as the pines & firs usially are but like most other trees it puts forth buds from the sides of the small boughs as well as their extremities. the stem usually terminates in a very slender pointed top like the cedar. The leaves are petiolate, the footstalk small short and oppressed; acerose reather more than half a line in width and very unequal in length, the greatest length being little more than half an inch, while others intermixed on every part of the bough are not more than a ¼ in length. flat with a small longitudinal channel in the

4 The Sitka spruce, *Picea sitchensis.*

upper disk which is of a deep green and glossy, while the u[n]der disk is of a whiteish green only; two ranked, obtusely pointed, soft and flexable. this tree affords but little rosin. the cone is remarkably small not larger than the end of a man's thumb soft, flexable and of an ovate form, produced at the ends of the small twigs.[5]

Friday February 7th 1806.

This evening we had what I call an excellent supper it consisted of a marrowbone a piece and a brisket of boiled Elk that had the appearance of a little fat on it. this for Fort Clatsop is living in high stile.

In this neighbourhood I observe the honeysuckle common in our country   I first met with it on the waters of the Kooskooske near the Chopunnish nation, and again below the grand rappids In the Columbian Valley on tide-water. The Elder also common to our country grows in great abundance in the rich woodlands on this side of the rocky Mountains; tho' it differs here in the colour of it's berry, this being of a pale sky blue while that of the U' States is a deep perple. The seven bark or nine bark as it is called in the U'States is also common in this quarter. There is a species of huckleberry common to the piny lands from the commencement of the Columbian valley to the seacoast; it rises to the hight of 6 or 8 feet. is a simple branching somewhat defuse stem; the main body or trunk is cilindric and of a dark brown, while the colateral branches are green smooth, squar, and put forth a number of alternate branches of the same colour and form from the two horizontal sides only. the fruit is a small deep perple berry which the natives inform us is very good. the leaf is thin of a pale green and small being ¾ of an inch in length and ⅜ in width; oval terminateing more accutely at the apex than near the insertion of the footstalk which is at the base; [veined, nearly] entire, serrate but so slightly so that it is scarcely perceptible; footstalk short and there position with rispect to each other is alternate and two ranked, proceeding from the horizontal sides of the bough only.

The small pox has distroyed a great number of the natives in this quarter. it prevailed about 4 years since among the Clatsops and destroy[ed] several hundred of them, four of their chiefs fell victyms

[5] The mountain nemlock, *Tsuga mertensiana.*

to it's ravages. those Clatsops are deposited in their canoes on the bay a few miles below us. I think the late ravages of the small pox may well account for the number of remains of vilages which we find deserted on the river and Sea coast in this quarter.

WEDNESDAY FEBRUARY 12TH 1806.

This morning we were visited by a Clatsop man who brought with him three dogs as a remuneration for the Elk which himself and nation had stolen from us some little time since,   however the dogs took alarm and ran off; we suffered him to remain in the fort all night.

THURSDAY FEBRUARY 13TH 1806

yesterday we completed the operation of drying the meat, and think we have a sufficient stock to last us this month. the Indians inform us that we shall have great abundance of a small fish in March which from their discription must be the herring. these people have also informed us that one [Captain] *More* who sometimes touches at this place and trades with the natives of this coast, had on board of his vessel three Cows, and that when he left them he continued his course along the N.W. coast. I think this strong circumstancial proof that there is a stettlement of white persons at Nootka sound or some point to the N.W. of us on the coast.

[Clark]   FRIDAY FEBRUARY 14TH 1806

I compleated a *map* of the Countrey through which we have been passing from the Mississippi at the Mouth of Missouri to this place. In the Map the Missouri Jefferson's river the S.E. branch of the Columbia or Lewis's river, Koos-koos-ke and Columbia from the enterance of the S.E. fork to the pacific Ocian, as well as a part of Clark's river [the Bitterroot] and our track across the Rocky Mountains are laid down by celestial observations and survey. the rivers are also conected at their sources with other rivers agreeably to the information of the nativs and the most probable conjecture arrising from their capacities and the relative positions of their respective enterances which last have with but fiew exceptions been established by celestial observations.

We now discover that we have found the most practicable and

navigable passage across the Continent of North America; it is that which we have traveled with the exception of that part of our rout from the foot of the Falls of the Missouri, or in neighbourhood of the enterance of the Rocky Mountains untill we arive on Clarks river at the enterence of *Travelers-rest* Creek; the distance between those two points would be traveled more advantagiously by land as the navigation of the Missouri above the *Falls* is crooked laborious and 521 miles distant, by which no advantage is gained as the rout which we are compelled to travel by land from the source of Jeffersons River to the enterance of *Travellers rest* Creek is 220 miles, being further by abt 600 miles than that from the Falls of the Missourie to the last mentioned point (Travellers rest Creek) and a much worse rout if indian information is to be relied on which is from the *Sosonee* or Snake Indians, and the Flatheads of the Columbia West of the rocky mountains.[6]

from the same information Clarks river like that of the S. E. branch of the Columbia which heads with Jefferson's and Maddisons river's can not be navagated thro' the rocky mountains in consequence of falls and rapids, and as a confirmation of the fact, we discovered that there were no salmon in Clark's river, which is not the case in the S.E. branch of the Columbia altho it is not navigable. added to this, the Indians of different quarte[r]s further inform us, that Clark's river runs in the direction of the Rocky Mountains for a great distance to the north before it discharges itself into the Columbia river. from the same information the Columbia from the enterance of the S. E. branch to the enterance of Clark's river is obstructed with a great number of deficuelt and dangerous rapids (and the place Clark's river comes out of the Rocky Mountains is a tremendious fall &c which there is no possibility of passing the mountains either by land or water.) considering therefore the dangers and deficuelties attending the navigation of the Columbia in this part, as well as the circuitous and distant rout formed by itself and that of Clark's River we conceive that even admitting that Clarks river contrary to information to be as navagable as the Columbia below its enterance, that the tract by land over the Rocky Mountains usually traveled by the nativs from the enterance of Travellers-rest Creek to the Forks of the Kooskooske is preferable; the same being a distance of 184 miles.

[6] They met one band of Salishan (Flathead) people west of the mountains, but Clark probably means Nez Percés here.

The inferrence therefore deduced from these premises are, that the best and most practicable rout across the Continent is by way of the Missouri to the *Falls;* thence to *Clarks* river at the enterance of Travellers rest Creek, from thence up travillers rest Creek to the forks, from whence you prosue a range of mountains which divides the waters of the two forks of this Creek, and which still Continues it's westwardly course on the Mountains which divides the waters of the two forks of the Kookooske river to their junction; from thence to decend this river to the S. E. branch of the Columbia, thence down that river to the Columbia, and down the Latter to the *Pacific Ocian.* There is a large river which falls into the Columbia on its south side at what point we could not lern; which passes thro those extencive Columbian Plains from the South East, and as the Indians inform us head in the Mountains South of the head of Jefferson River and at no great distance from the Spanish settlements, Multnomah and that that fork which heads with the River Rajhone and waters of the Missouri passes through those extensive plains in which there is no wood, and the river crowded with rapids & falls many of which are impassable.[7] the other or westerly fork passes near a range of mountains and is the fork [on] which [live] great numbers of Indian Bands of the *Sosone* or Snake Indians   this fork most probably heads with North River or the waters of Callifornia. this River may afford a practicable land communication with New Mexico by means of its western fork. This river cannot be navagable as an impracticable rapid is within one mile of its enterance into the Columbia, and we are fully purswaded that a rout by this river if practicable at all, would lengthen the distance greatly and incounter the same dificulties in passing the Rocky Mountains with the rout by way of Travellers rest Creek & Clarks river.

[Lewis]   SATURDAY FEBRUARY 15TH 1806.

The quadrupeds of this country from the Rocky Mountains to the pacific Ocean are 1st the *domestic animals,* consisting of the

---

[7] He has learned about the Willamette River since passing its mouth. He has assimilated to it some data which actually relate to the main stream of the Snake River. The "other or westerly fork" mentioned in the next sentence comes close to describing the Willamette, though it does not reach "the waters of Callifornia." That either the Snake or the Willamette provides access to the New Mexican settlements is a gross error. These misconceptions fastened on American cartography for fifty years a nonexistent river called the Multnomah.

horse and the dog only; 2edly the *native wild animals,* consisting of
the Brown white or grizly bear, (which I beleive to be the same
family with a mearly accedental difference in point of colour) the
black bear, the common red deer, the black tailed fallow deer, the
Mule deer, Elk, the large brown wolf, the small woolf of the plains,
the large wolf of the plains, the tiger cat, the common red fox,
black fox or fisher, silver fox, large red fox of the plains, small fox
of the plains or kit fox, Antelope, sheep, beaver, common otter, sea
Otter, mink, spuck, seal, racoon, large grey squirrel, small brown
squirrel, small grey squirrel, ground squirrel, *sewelel,* Braro, rat,
mouse, mole, Panther, hare, rabbit, and polecat or skunk. all of
which shall be severally noticed in the order in which they occur
as well as shuch others as I learn do exist and which [have] not been
here recapitulated.

The horse is confined principally to the nations inhabiting the
great plains of Columbia extending from Latitude 40° to 50° N.
and occupying the tract of country lying between the rocky Mountains and a range [Cascade] of Mountains which pass the Columbia
river about the great falls or from Longitude 116 to 121 West. in
this exte[n]sive tract of principally untimbered country so far as
we have lea[r]nt the following natives reside (viz) the Sosone or
snake Indians, the Chopunnish, Sokulks, Cutssahnims, Chym-
napums, E[c]helutes, Eneshuh & Chilluckkittequaws. all of whom
enjoy the bennefit of that docile, generous and valuable anamal the
horse, and all of them except the three last have immence numbers
of them. Their horses appear to be of an excellent race; they are
lofty eligantly formed active and durable; in short many of them
look like the fine English coarsers and would make a figure in any
country. some of those horses are pided [pied] with large spots of
white irregularly scattered and intermixed with the black brown
bey or some other dark colour, but much the larger portion are of
an uniform colour with stars snips and white feet, or in this rispect
marked much like our best blooded horses in virginia, which they
resemble as well in fleetness and bottom as in form and colours. the
natives suffer them to run at large in the plains, the grass of which
furnishes them with the only subsistence their masters taking no
trouble to lay in a winters store for them, but they even keep fat if
not much used on the dry grass of the plains during the winter.
no rain scarcely ever falls in these plains and the grass is short and
but thin. The natives *(except those near the R. Monts)* appear to

take no pains in scelecting their male horses from which they breed, in short those of that discription which I have noticed appeared much the most indifferent.

whether the horse was orrigeonally a native of this country or not it is out of my power to determine as we cannot understand the language of the natives sufficiently to ask the question. at all events the country and climate appears well adapted to this anamal. horses are said to be found wild in many parts of this extensive plain country. the several tribes of Sosones who reside towards Mexico on the waters of [the Multnomah] river or particularly one of them called *Shâ-bo-bó-ah* have also a great number of mules, which among the Indians I find are much more highly prized than horses. an eligant horse may be purchased of the natives in this country for a few beads or other paltry trinkets which in the U'States would not cost more than one or two dollars. This abundance and cheapness of horses will be extremely advantageous to those who may hereafter attem[p]t the fir trade to the East Indies by way of the Columbia river and the Pacific Ocean. the mules in the possession of the Indians are principally stolen from the Spaniards of Mexeco; they appear to be large and fine such as we have seen. Among the Sosones of the upper part of the S. E. fork of the Columbia we saw several horses with spanish brands on them which we supposed had been stolen from the inhabitants of Mexeco.

THURSDAY FEBRUARY 20TH 1806.

This forenoon we were visited by *Tâh-cum* a principal Chief of the Chinnooks and 25 men of his nation. we had never seen this cheif before   he is a good looking man of about 50 years of age reather larger in statu[r]e than most of his nation; as he came on a friendly visit we gave himself and party something to eat and plyed them plentifully with smoke. we gave this cheif a small medal with which he seemed much gratifyed. in the evening at sunset we desired them to depart as is our custom and closed our gates. we never suffer parties of such number to remain within the fort all night; for notwithstanding their apparent friendly disposition, their great averice and hope of plunder might induce them to be treacherous. at all events we determined allways to be on our guard as much as the nature of our situation will permit us, and never place ourselves at the mercy of any savages. we well know, that the treachery of the aborigenes of America and the too great confidence of our countrymen in their sincerity and friendship, has caused the distruction of many hundreds of us. so long have our men been accustomed to a friendly intercourse with the natives, that we find it difficult to impress on their minds the necessity of always being on their guard with rispect to them. this confidence on our part, we know to be the effect of a series of uninterupted friendly intercou[r]se, but the well known treachery of the natives by no means entitle them to such confidence, and we must check it's growth in our own minds, as well as those of our men, by recollecting ourselves, and repeating to our men that our preservation depends on never loosing sight of this trait in their character, and being always prepared to meet it in whatever shape it may present itself.

SATURDAY FEBRUARY 22ED 1806.

We were visited today by two Clatsop women and two boys who brought a parsel of excellent hats made of Cedar bark and ornamented with beargrass. two of these hats had been made by measures which Capt. Clark and myself had give one of the women some time since with a request to make each of us a hat; they fit us very well, and are in the form we desired them. we purchased all their hats and distributed them among the party. the woodwork and sculpture of these people as well as these hats and their waterproof baskets evince an ingenuity by no means common among the Aborigenes of America. in the evening they returned to their village and Drewyer accompanied them in their canoe in order to get the dogs which the Clatsops have agreed to give us in payment for the Elk they stole from us some weeks since. these women informed us that the small fish began to run which we suppose to be herring from their discription. they also informed us that their Chief Conia or Comowooll, had gone up the Columbia to the valley in order to purchase wappetoe, a part of which he intended trading with us on his return.

one of our canoes brake the cord by which it was attatched and was going off with the tide this evening; we sent Sergt. Pryor and a party after her who recovered and brought her back. our sick consisting of Gibson, Bratton, Sergt. Ordway, Willard and McNeal are all on the recovery. we have not had as ma[n]y sick at any one time since we left Wood River. the general complaint seams to be colds and fevers, something I believe of the influenza.

SUNDAY FEBRUARY 23RD 1806.

The Sea Otter is found on the sea coast and in the salt water. this anamal when fully grown is as large as a common mastive dog. the ears and eyes are remarkab[l]y small, particularly the former which is not an inch in length thick fleshey and pointed covered with short hair. the tail is about 10 inches in length thick where it joins the body and tapering to a very sharp point; in common with the body it is covered with a deep fur particularly on the under part the fur is not so long. the legs are remarkably short and the feet which have five toes each are broad large and webbed. the legs are covered with fur and the feet with short hair. the body of this animal is long and nearly of the same thickness throughout. from the extremity of the tail to that of the nose they will measure 5 feet or upwards. the colour is a uniform dark brown and when in good order and season perfectly black and glossey. it is the riches[t] and I think the most delicious fur in the world at least I cannot form an idea of any more so. it is deep thick silkey in the extreem and strong. the inner part of the fur when opened is lighter than the surface in it's natural position. there are some fine black and shining hairs intermixed with the fur which are reather longer and add much to it's beauty. the nose, about the eyes ears and forehead in some of these otter is of a lighter colour, sometimes a light brown. those parts in the young sucking Otter of this species is sometimes of a cream coloured white, but always much lighter than the other parts. the fur of the infant Otter is much inferior in point of colour and texture to that of the full grown otter, or even after it has been weaned. there is so great a difference that I have for some time supposed it a different animal; the Indians called the infant Otter *Spuck,* and the full grow[n] or such as had obtained a coat of good fur, *E-luck'-ke.* this still further confirmed the opinion of their being distinct species; but I have since learned that the Spuck is the young Otter. the colour of the neck, body, legs and tail is a dark lead brown.

[Clark]   TUESDAY FEBRUARY 25TH 1806

I purchased of the Clatsops this morning about half a bushel of small fish which they had cought about 40 miles up the Columbia in their scooping nets. the rays of the fins are boney but not sharp tho' somewhat pointed. the small fin on the back next to the tail has no rays of bone being a thin membranous pellicle. the fins next to the gills have eleven rays each. those of the abdomen have Eight each, those of the pinna ani are 20 and 2 half formed in front. that of the back has eleven rays. all the fins are of a white colour. the back is of a blueish duskey colour and that of the lower part of the sides and belly is of a silvery white. no spots on any part. the first gills next behind the eye is of a blueish cast, and the second of a light gold colour nearly white. the puple of the eye is black and the iris of a silver white. the under jaw exceeds the upper; and the mouth opens to a great extent folding like that of the Herring. it has no teeth. the abdomen is obtuse and smooth, in this differing from the herring, shad, anchovey &c. of the Malacapterygious order and class clupea, to which however I think it more nearly allyed than to any other altho' it has not their accute and serrate abdomen and the under jaw exceeding the upper. the scales of this little fish are so small and thin that without manute inspection you would suppose they had none. they are filled with roes of a pure white colour and have scercely any perceptable alimentary duct.

I found them best when cooked in Indian stile, which is by rosting a number of them together on a wooden spit without any previous preparation whatever. they are so fat that they require no aditional sauce, and I think them superior to any fish I ever tasted, even more delicate and lussious than the white fish of the Lakes which have heretofore formed my standard of excellence among the fishes. I have herd the fresh anchovey much extoll'd but I hope I shall be pardoned for believing this quite as good. the bones are so soft and fine that they form no obstruction in eating this fish. [8]

TUESDAY 11TH OF MARCH 1806

The *Mule Deer* we have never found except in rough country; they prefer the Open Grounds and are seldom found in the wood

[8] This is the candlefish or eulachon *(Thaleichthys pacificus)*, second only to the salmon in the economy of the Northwest Indians.

lands near the river; when they are met with in the wood lands or
river boottoms and pursued, they imediately run to the hills or
open country as the Elk do, the contrary happens with the common
Deer. there are several differences between the Mule and common
deer as well as in form as in habits. they are fully a third larger
in general, and the male is particularly large; think there is somewhat greater disparity of size between the Male and the female of
this Species than there is between the male and female fallow
Deer;   I am convinced I have seen a Buck of this species twice
the volume [of] a Buck of the common Deer. the Ears are peculiarly large, I measured those of a large Buck which I found to be
eleven inches long and 3½ in width at the widest part; they are
not so delicately formed, their hair in winter is thicker longer and
of a much darker grey, in Summer the hair is still coarser longer
and of a paler red, more like that of the Elk, in winter they also
have a considerable quantity of very fine wool intermixed with the
hair and lying next to the skin as the Antelope has. the long hair
which grows on the outer side of the first joint of the hind legs,
and which in the common Deer do not usially occupy more than 2
inches in them occupy from 6 to 8; their horns also differ, those
in the common deer consist of two main beams gradually deminish-
ing as the points proceed from it,   with the Mule deer the horns
consist of two beams which at the distance of 4 or 6 inches from the
head divide themselves into two equal branches which again either
divide into two other equal branches or terminate in a smaller, and
two equal ones; haveing either 2, 4 or 6 points on a beam; the
horn is not so rough about the base as the common deer, and are
invariably of a much darker colour. the most striking difference
of all, is the white rump and tail. from the root of the tail as a
center there is a circular spot perfectly white of about 3½ inches
radius, which occupy a part of the rump and the extremities of
buttocks and joins the white of the belley underneath; the tail
which is usially from 8 to 9 inches long for the first 4 or 5 inches
from its upper extremity is covered with short white hairs, much
shorter indeed than those hairs of the body; from hence for about
one inch further, the hair is still white but gradually becoms
longer the tail then termonates in a tissue of Black hair of about 3
inches long. from this black hair of the tail they have obtained
among the French engages the appelation of the *black tailed Deer*,

but this I conceive by no means characteristic of the Animal as much the larger portion of the tail is white. the Ears and the tail of this Animale when compared with those of the Common Deer, so well comported with those of the *Mule* when compared with the Horse, that we have by way of distinction adapted the appellation of the Mule Deer which I think much more appropriate. on the inner corner of each eye there is a drane (like the Elk) or large recepticle which seams to answer as a drane to the eye which gives it the appearance of weeping,   this in the Common Deer of the Atlantic States is scercely proceptable but becoms more conspicious in the fallow Deer, and still more so in the Elk; this recepticle in the Elk is larger than any of the Pecora order with which I am acquainted.

[Lewis]   Saturday March 15th 1806.

This morning at 11.OCk. the hunters arrived, having killed four Elk only. Labuish it seems was the only hunter who fell in with the Elk and having by some accedent lost the fore sight of his gun shot a great number of times but killed only the number mentioned. as the elk were scattered we sent two parties for them, they returned in the evening with four skins and the flesh of three Elk, that of one of them having become putrid from the liver and pluck haveing been carelessly left in the animal all night.

we were visited this afternoon by Delashshelwilt a Chinnook Chief his wife and six women of his nation which the old baud his wife had brought for market. this was the same party that had communicated the venerial to so many of our party in November last, and of which they have finally recovered. I therefore gave the men a particular charge with rispect to them which they promised me to observe. late this evening we were also visited by Catel a Clatsop man and his family. he brought a canoe and a Sea Otter Skin for sale neither of which we purchased this evening. The Clatsops who had brought a canoe for sale last evening left us early this morning.

Sunday March 16th 1806.

Drewyer and party did not return from the Cathlahmahs this evening as we expected. we suppose he was detained by the hard winds of today. the Indians remained with us all day, but would not dispose of their canoes at a price which it was in our power to give consistently with the state of our Stock of Merchandize. two handkerchiefs would now contain all the small articles of merchandize which we possess; the ballance of the stock consists of 6 blue robes one scarlet do. one uniform artillerist's coat and hat. five robes made of our large flag, and a few old cloaths trimed with ribbon. on this stock we have wholy to depend for the purchase of horses and such portion of our subsistence from the Indians as it will be in our powers to obtain.

MONDAY MARCH 17TH 1806.

Old Delashelwilt and his women still remain   they have formed a ca[m]p near the fort and seem to be determined to lay close s[i]ege to us but I believe notwithstanding every effort of their wining graces, the men have preserved their constancy to the vow of celibacy which they made on this occasion to Capt. C. and myself. we have had our perogues prepared for our departure, and shal set out as soon as the weather will permit. the weather is so precarious that we fear by waiting untill the first of April that we might be detained several days longer before we could get from this to the Cathlahmahs as it must be calm or we cannot accomplish that part of our rout. Drewyer returned late this evening from the Cathlahmahs with our canoe which Sergt. Pryor had left some days since, and also a canoe which he had purchased from those people. for this canoe he gave my uniform laced coat and nearly half a carrot of tobacco. it seems that nothing excep[t] this coat would induce them to dispose of a canoe which in their mode of traffic is an article of the greatest val[u]e except a wife, with whom it is equal, and is generally given in exchange to the father for his daughter. I think the U'States are indebted to me another Uniform coat for that of which I have disposed on this occasion was but little woarn. we yet want another canoe, and as the Clatsops will not sell us one at a price which we can afford to give we will take one from them in lue of the six Elk which they stole from us in the winter.

CHAPTER XXIV

The Start for Home

[Lewis]   Tuesday March 18th 1806.

D
rewyer was taken last night with a violent pain in his side.
Capt. Clark blead him. several of the men are complaining of being unwell. it is truly unfortunate that they
should be sick at the moment of our departure. we directed Sergt.
Pryor to prepare the two Canoes which Drewyer brought last evening for his mess. they wanted some knees to strengthen them and
several cracks corked and payed. he completed them except the
latter operation which the frequent showers in the course of the
day prevented as the canoes could not be made sufficiently dry even
with the assistance of fire. Comowooll and two Cathlahmahs visited
us today; we suffered them to remain all night. this morning we
gave Delashelwilt a certificate of his good deportment &c. and also
a list of our names, after which we dispatched him to his village
with his female band. These lists of our names we have given to
several of the natives and also paisted up a copy in our room. the
object of these lists we stated in the preamble of the same as follows (viz) "The object of this list is, that through the medium of
some civilized person who may see the same, it may be made known
to the informed world, that the party consisting of the persons
whose names are hereunto annexed, and who were sent out by the
government of the U'States in May 1804. to explore the interior of
the Continent of North America, did penetrate the same by way of
the Missouri and Columbia Rivers, to the discharge of the latter
into the Pacific Ocean, where they arrived on the 14th of November
1805, and from whence they departed the [blank space in MS.] day

of March 1806 on their return to the United States by the same rout they had come out." on the back of some of these lists we added a sketch of the connection of the upper branches of the Missouri with those of the Columbia, particularly of it's main S.E. branch, on which we also delineated the track we had come and that we meant to pursue on our return where the same happened to vary. There seemed so may chances against our government ever obtaining a regular report, through the medium of the savages and the traders of this coast that we declined making any. our party are also too small to think of leaving any of them to return to the U'States by sea, particularly as we shall be necessarily divided into three or four parties on our return in order to accomplish the objects we have in view; and at any rate we shall reach the United States in all human probability much earlier than a man could who must in the event of his being left here depend for his passage to the United States on the traders of the coast who may not return immediately to the U'States or if they should, might probably spend the next summer in trading with the natives before they would set out on their return. this evening Drewyer went in quest of his traps, and took an Otter.

WEDNESDAY MARCH 19TH 1806.

It continued to rain and hail today in such manner that nothing further could be done to the canoes. The Killamucks, Clatsops, Chinnooks, Cathlahmahs and Wâc-ki-a-cums resemble each other as well in their persons and dress as in their habits and manners. their complexion is not remarkable, being the usual copper brown of most of the tribes of North America. they are low in statu[r]e reather diminutive, and illy shapen; poss[ess]ing thick broad flat feet, thick ankles, crooked legs wide mouths thick lips, nose moderately large, fleshey, wide at the extremity with large nostrils, black eyes and black coarse hair. their eyes are sometimes of a dark yellowish brown the puple black. the most remarkable trait in their physiognomy is the peculiar flatness and width of forehead which they artificially obtain by compressing the head between two boards while in a state of infancy and from which it never afterwards perfectly recovers. this is a custom among all the nations we have met with West of the Rocky mountains. I have observed the heads of many infants, after this singular bandage had been dismissed, or about the age of 10 or eleven months, that were not more than two inches thick about the upper edge of the forehead and reather thiner still higher. from the top of the head to the extremity of the nose is one streight line. this is done in order to give a greater width to the forehead, which they much admire. this process seems to be continued longer with their female than their mail children, and neither appear to suffer any pain from the operation. it is from this peculiar form of the head that the nations East of the Rocky mountains, call all the nations on this side, except the Aliohtans or snake Indians, by the generic name of Flatheads.

the large or apparently swolen legs particularly observable in the women are obtained in a great measure by tying a cord tight around the ankle. their method of squating or resting themselves on their hams which they seem from habit to prefer to siting, no doubt contributes much to this deformity of the legs by preventing free circulation of the blood.

the dress of the man consists of a smal robe, which reaches about as low as the middle of the thye and is attached with a string across the breast and is at pleasure turned from side to side as they may have occasion to disencumber the right or left arm from the robe entirely, or when they have occasion for both hands,   the fixture of the robe is in front with it's corners loosly hanging over their arms. a mat is sometimes temperarily thrown over the sholders to protect them from rain. they have no other article of cloathing whatever neither winter nor summer. and every part except the sholders and back is exposed to view. they are very fond of the dress of the whites, which they wear in a similar manner when they can obtain them, except the shoe which I have never seen woarn by any of them.

The dress of the women consists of a robe, tissue, and sometimes when the weather is uncommonly cold, a vest. their robe is much smaller than that of the men, never reaching lower than the waist nor extending in front sufficiently for to cover the body. it is like that of the men confined across the breast with a string and hangs loosly over the sholders and back. the most esteemed and valuable of these robes are made of strips of the skins of the Sea Otter net together with the bark of the white cedar or silk-grass. these strips are first twisted and laid parallel with each other a little distance assunder, and then net or wove together in such a manner that the fur appears equally on both sides, and unites between the strands. it make[s] a warm and soft covering. other robes are formed in a similar manner of the skin of the Rackoon, beaver &c.   at other times the skin is dressed in the hair and woarn without any further preperation. the vest is always formed in the manner first discribed of their robes and covers the body from the armpits to the waist, and is confined behind, and destitute of straps over the sholder to keep it up. when this vest is woarn the breast of the woman is concealed. but without it which is almost always the case, they are exposed, and from the habit of remaining loose and unsuspended grow to great length, particularly in aged women in many of whom I have seen the bubby reach as low as the waist. The garment which occupys the waist, and from thence as low as nearly to the knee before and the ham, behind, cannot properly be denominated a petticoat, in the common acceptation of that term; it is a tissue of white cedar bark, bruised or broken into small shreds, which are interwoven in the middle by means of several cords of the same materials, which serve as well for a girdle as to hold in place the shreds of bark which form the tissue, and which shreds confined in the middle hang with their ends pendulous from the waist, the whole being of sufficient thickness when the female stands erect to conceal those parts usually covered from formiliar view, but when she stoops or places herself in many other attitudes, this battery of Venus is not altogether impervious to the inquisitive and pene-trating eye of the amorite.

The favorite ornament of both sexes are the common coarse blue and white beads which the men wear tightly wound aro[u]nd their wrists and ankles many times untill they obtain the width of three or more inches. they also wear them in large rolls loosly arond the neck, or pendulous from the cartelage of the nose or rims of the ears which are purforated for the purpose. the women wear them in a similiar manner except in the nose which they never purforate. they are also fond of a species of wampum which is furnished them by a trader whom they call Swipton. it seems to be the native form of the shell without any preperation. the men sometimes wear collars of bears claws, and the women and children the tusks of the Elk variously arranged on their necks arms &c.   both males and females wear braslets on their wrists of copper brass or Iron in vari-ous forms.

THURSDAY MARCH 20TH 1806.

It continued to rain and blow so violently today that nothing could be done towards forwarding our departure. we intended to have Dispatched Drewyer and the two Fieldses to hunt near the bay on this side of the Cathlahmahs untill we jounded [joined] them from hence, but the rain rendered our departure so uncertain that we declined this measure for the present. nothing remarkable happened during the day. we have yet several days provision on hand, which we hope will be sufficient to subsist us during the time we are compelled by the weather to remain at this place.

Atho' we have not fared sumptuously this winter and spring at Fort Clatsop, we have lived quite as comfortably as we had any reason to expect we should; and have accomplished every object which induced our remaining at this place except that of meeting with the traders who visit the entrance of this river. our salt will be very sufficient to last us to the Missouri where we have a stock in store. it would have been very fortunate for us had some of those traders arrived previous to our departure from hence, as we should then have had it in our power to obtain an addition to our stock of merchandize which would have made our homeward bound journey much more comfortable. many of our men are still complaining of being unwell; Willard and Bratton remain weak, principally I believe for the want of proper food. I expect when we get under way we shall be much more healthy. it has always had that effect on us heretofore. The guns of Drewyer and Sergt. Pryor were both out of order. the first was repared with a new lock, the old one having become unfit for uce; the second had the cock screw broken which was replaced by a duplicate which had been prepared for the lock at Harpers ferry where she was manufactured. but for the precaution taken in bringing on those extra locks, and parts of locks, in addition to the ingenuity of John Shields, most of our guns would at this moment [have] been untirely unfit for use; but fortunately for us I have it in my power here to record that they are all in good order.

FRIDAY MARCH 21ST 1806.

our sick men Willard and bratton do not seem to recover: the former was taken with a violent pain in his leg and thye last night.

Bratton is now so much reduced that I am somewhat uneasy with rispect to his recovery; the pain of which he complains most seems to be seated in the small of his back and remains obstinate. I beleive that it is the rheumatism with which they are both afflicted.

[Clark]   SUNDAY 23RD MARCH 1806

This morning proved so raney and uncertain that we were undetermined for some time whether we had best set out & risque the [tide] which appeared to be riseing or not. the rained seased and it became fair about Meridian, at which time we loaded our canoes & at 1 P. M. left Fort Clatsop on our homeward bound journey. at this place we had wintered and remained from the 7th of Decr. 1805 to this day and have lived as well as we had any right to expect, and we can say that we were never one day without 3 meals of some kind a day either pore Elk meat or roots, notwithstanding the repeated fall of rain which has fallen almost constantly since we passed the long narrows   Soon after we had set out from Fort Clatsop we were met by Delashelwilt & 8 men of the Chinnook and Delashelwilts wife the old boud and his six Girls,   they had, a canoe, a sea otter skin, dried fish and hats for sale, we purchased a sea otter skin, and proceeded on, thro' Meriwethers Bay,   there was a stiff breese from the S.W. which raised considerable swells around Meriwethers point which was as much as our canoes could ride. above point William we came too at the camp of Drewyer & the 2 Field's. here we encamped for the night having made 16 miles.

The daily rain continued. The winds that accompanied it raised great waves on the Columbia, which added to the difficulty of rowing the dugouts against the current. They hugged the Oregon shore, having usually held to the other one on the descent. Shore parties explored it and hunters ranged ahead, bringing in the interminable elk and an occasional deer.

Indians swarmed about them, some of them acquaintances of the winter or last fall. Mostly they were a wretched lot. The village of one band was "the dirtiest and stinkingest place I ever saw in any shape whatever. and the inhabitants partake of the carrestick [char-

acteristic] of the village." They had food to sell — roots, dogs, sturgeon, dried salmon, seal meat — but they charged prices so high that frequently the captains could not, or would not, buy. The refusal of one group to sell food for anything but tobacco reveals that "we are now obliged to deny the uce of this article" to the party and that they "suffer much for the want of it. they substitute the bark of the wild crab [apple] which they chew; it is very bitter, and they assure me they find it a good substitute for tobacco.   the smokers substitute the inner bark of the red willow and the sacacommis." All of the bands they met were expert thieves but most of them were friendly; the hostile tribes were farther up the river. The captains continued to record ethnological observations and worked out the complex intertribal trading system of the Columbia. In this trade their late neighbors the Clatsops were carriers and middlemen.

They also continued to inquire about the geography. As they neared Sauvie Island, they decided that "there must be some other considerable river which flowed into the columbia on it's south side below us which we have not yet seen, as the extensive valley on that side of the river lying between the mountainous country of the Coast [Range] and the Western [Cascade] mountains must be watered by some stream." It is indeed: by the Willamette.

Now they got important information bearing on their plans.

[Lewis]   TUESDAY APRIL 1ST 1806.

We were visited by several canoes of natives in the course of the day; most of whom were decending the river with their women and children. they informed us that they resided at the great rapids [The Dalles] and that their relations at that place were much streightened at that place for want of food; that they had consumed their winter store of dryed fish and that those of the present season had not yet arrived. I could not learn wheather they took the sturgeon but presume if they do it is in but small quantities as they complained much of the scarcity of food among them. they informed us that the nations above them were in the same situation & that they did not expect the Salmon to arrive untill the full of the next moon which happens on the 2d of May. we did not doubt the varacity of these people who seemed to be on their way with their families and effects in surch of subsistence which they find it easy to procure in this fertile valley.

This information gave us much uneasiness with rispect to our future means of susbsistence. above [the] falls or through the plains from thence to the Chopunnish [Nez Percés] there are no deer Antelope nor Elk on which we can depend for subsistence; their horses are very poor most probably at this season, and if they have no fish their dogs must be in the same situation. under these circumstances there seems to be but a gloomy prospect for subsistence on any terms; we therefore took it into serious consideration what measures we were to pursue on this occasion; it was at once deemed inexpedient to wait the arrival of the salmon as that would detain us so large a portion of the season that it is probable we should not reach the United States before the ice would close the Missouri; or at all events would hazard our horses which we left in charge of the Chopunnish who informed us they intended passing the rocky mountains to the Missouri as early as the season would permit them w[h]ich is as we believe about the begining of May.[1] should these people leave their situation near kooskooske before our arrival we may probably find much difficulty in recovering our horses; without which there will be little possibility of repassing the mountains; we are therefore determined to loose as little time as possible in geting to the Chopunnish Village.

I purchased a canoe from an Indian to day for which I gave him six fathoms of wampum beads; he seemed satisfyed with his bar-· gain and departed in another canoe but shortly after returned and canceled the bargain, took his canoe and returned the beads. this is frequently the case in their method of traiding and is deemed fair by them.

Wednesday April 2ed 1806.

This morning we came to a resolution to remain at our present encampment or some where in this neighbourhood untill we had obtained as much dryed meat as would be necessary for our voyage as far as the Chopunnish. to exchange our perogues for canoes with the natives on our way to the great falls of the columbia or purchase such canoes from them for Elk-skins and Merchandize as would answer our purposes. these canoes we intend exchanging with the natives of the plains for horses as we proceed untill we

1 This, as will appear, was an error.

obtain as many as will enable us to travel altogether by land. at
some convenient point, perhaps at the entrence of the S.E. branch
of the Columbia, we purpose sending a party of four or five men a
head to collect our horses that they may be in readiness for us by
our arrival at the Chopunnish; calculating by thus acquiring a
large stock of horses we shall not only secure the means of transporting our baggage over the mountains but that we will also have
provided the means of subsisting; for we now view the horses as
our only certain resource for food, nor do we look forward to it
with any detestation or horrow [horror], so soon is the mind which
is occupied with any interesting object, reconciled to it's situation.
we now enformed the party of our intention of laying in a store of
meat at this place, and immediately dispatched two parteis consisting of nine men to the opposite side of the river. we also sent
out three others on this side, and those who remained in camp
were employed in collecting wood making a scaffoald and cutting
up the meat in order to dry it.

about this time several canoes of the natives arrived at our camp
and among others one from below which had on board eight men
of the Shah-ha-la nation   these men informed us that 2 young
men whom they pointed out were Cash-hooks and resided at the
falls of a large river which discharges itself into the Columbia on
it's South side some miles below us. we readily prevailed on them
to give us a sketch of this river which they drew on a mat with a
coal. it appeared that this river which they called Mult-no-mâh [2]
discharged itself behind the Island which we called the image
canoe Island and as we had left this island to the S. both in ascending and decending the river we had never seen it. they informed
us that it was a large river and run a considerable distance to the
South between the mountains. Capt. Clark determined to return
and examine this river accordingly he took a party of seven men
and one of the perogues and set out ½ after 11 A.M.,   he hired
one of the Cashhooks, for a birning glass, to pilot him to the entrance of the Multnomah river and took him on board with him.

[Clark]   WEDNESDAY APRIL 2ND 1806

I had not proceeded far eer I saw 4 large canoes at some distance
above decending and bending their course towards our Camp

2 The Willamette.

which at this time is very weak Capt. Lewis haveing only 10 men
with him. I hesitated for a moment whether it would not be advisable for me to return and delay untill a part of our hunters
should return to add more strength to our Camp. but on a second
reflection and reverting to the precautions always taken by my
friend Capt Lewis on those occasions banished all apprehensions
and I proceeded on down. at 8 miles passed a village on the South
side   at this place my Pilot informed me he resided and that the
name of the tribe is *Ne-cha-co-lee,*   I proceeded on without landing. at 3 P. M. I landed at a large double house of the *Ne-er-che-
ki-oo* tribe of the *Shah-ha-la* Nation. on the bank at different places
I observed small canoes which the women make use of to gather
wappato & roots in the Slashes. those canoes are from 10 to 14 feet
long and from 18 to 23 inches wide in the widest part tapering from
the center to both ends and about 9 inches deep and so light that a
woman may with one hand haul them with ease, and they are
sufficient to carry a woman an[d] some loading. I think 100 of these
canoes were piled up and scattered in different directions about in
the woods, in the vicinity of this house,   the pilot informed me
that those canoes were the property of the inhabitents of the Grand
rapids who used them ocasionally to gather roots.

I entered one of the rooms of this house and offered several articles to the nativs in exchange for wappato. they were sulkey and
they positively refused to sell any. I had a small pece of port fire
match [fuse] in my pocket, off of which I cut a pece one inch in
length & put it into the fire and took out my pocket compas and set
myself down on a mat on one side of the fire, and [also showed] a
magnet which was in the top of my ink stand   the port fire
cought and burned vehemently, which changed the colour of the
fire; with the magnit I turned the needle of the compas about very
briskly; which astonished and alarmed these nativs and they laid
several parsles of wappato at my feet, & begged of me to take out
the bad fire; to this I consented; at this moment the match being
exhausted was of course extinguished and I put up the magnet
&c.   this measure alarmed them so much that the womin and
children took shelter in their beads and behind the men,   all
this time a very old blind man was speaking with great vehemunce,
appearently imploring his god. I lit my pipe and gave them smoke,
& gave the womin the full amount [value] of the roots which they

had put at my feet. they appeared somewhat passified and I left
them and proceeded on. on the south side of Image Canoe Island
which I found to be two Islands, hid from the opposit side by one
near the center of the river. the lower point of the upper and the
upper point of the lower cannot be seen from the North Side of
the Columbia on which we had passed both decending and ascending and had not observed the apperture between those islands.

at the distance of 13 miles below the last village and at the place
I had supposed was the lower point of the image canoe island, I
entered this river which the nativs had informed us of, called *Multnomah* River so called by the nativs from a nation who reside on
Wappato Island a little below the enterance of this river. Multnomah discharges itself in the Columbia on the S.E. and may be
justly said to be ¼ the size of that noble river. Multnomah had
fallen 18 inches from its greatest annual height. three small Islands
are situated in it's mouth which hides the river from view from the
Columbia. from the enterance of this river, I can plainly see Mt.
Jefferson which is high and covered with snow S.E. Mt. Hood East,
Mt. St. Helians [and] a high humped mountain [Mount Adams] to
the East of Mt. St. Helians.

THURSDAY APRIL 3RD 1806

The water had fallen in the course of last night five inches. I
set out and proceeded up a short distance and attempted a second
time to fathom the river with my cord of 5 fathom but could find
no bottom. the mist was so thick that I could see but a short distance up this river. When I left it, it was bending to the East of
S.E.   being perfectly satisfyed of the size and magnitude of this
great river which must water that vast tract of Country between the
western range of mountains and those on the sea coast and as far S.
as the Waters of Callifornia about Latd. 37. North. I deturmined
to return. at 7 oClock A. M. set out on my return. the men exirted
themselves and we arived at the Neerchokioo house in which the
nativs were so illy disposed yesterday at 11 A. M.

I observe the wreck of 5 house remaining of a very large village,
the houses of which had been built in the form of those we first
saw at the long narrows of the *E-lute* Nation with whome those
people are connected. I indeavored to obtain from those people of

the situation of their nation, if scattered or what had become of the nativs who must have peopled this great town. an old man who appeared of some note among them and father to my guide brought foward a woman who was badly marked with the Small Pox and made signs that they all died with the disorder which marked her face, and which she was verry near dieing with when a girl. from the age of this woman this Distructive disorder I judge must have been about 28 or 30 years past, and about the time the Clatsops inform us that this disorder raged in their towns and distroyed their nation. Those people speak a different language from those below tho' in their dress habits and manners &c. they differ but little from the Quathlahpohtles. their women ware the *truss* as those do of all the nations residing from the Quathlahpohtle to the enterance of Lewis's river and on the Columbia above for some distance. those people have some words the same with those below but the air of their language is entirely different, their men are stouter and much better made, and their womin ware larger & longer robes than those do below; those are most commonly made of Deer skins dressed with the hair on them. they pay great attention to their aged severall men and women whom I observed in this village had arived at a great age, and appeared to be helthy tho' blind. I provailed on an old man to draw me a sketch of the Multnomar River and give me the names of the nations resideing on it which he readily done, and gave me the names of 4 nations who reside on this river two of them very noumerous.

The enterance of Multnomah river is 142 miles up the Columbia river from its enterance into the Pacific Ocean.

CHAPTER XXV

From Sandy River to The Dalles of the Columbia

The party remained in camp on Sauvie Island, hunting and drying meat. They hoped to amass a sufficient quantity to last them till they reached the Nez Percés. Since the rain was almost continuous, they had to dry it over fires. Overcast skies prevented them from making celestial observations and gales lashed the river to turbulence. In the wide river below the mouth of the Willamette, they had not realized how much the spring flood was adding to the difficulty of their progress.

[Lewis]   SUNDAY APRIL 6TH 1806.

This morning we had the dryed meat secured in skins and the canoes loaded;   we took breakfast and departed at 9 A.M. we continued up the N. side of the river nearly to the place at which we had encamped on the 3rd of Nov. when we passed the river to the south side in quest of the hunters we had sent up yesterday and the day before. from the appearance of a rock near which we were encamped on the 3rd of November last I could judge better of the rise of the water than I could at any point below. I think the flood of this spring has been about 12 feet higher than it was at that time; the river is here about 1½ miles wide; it's general width from the beacon rock which may be esteemed the head of tide water, to the marshey islands is from one to 2 miles tho' in many places it is still wider. it is only in the fall of the year when the river is low that the tides are persceptable as high as the beacon rock. this remarkable rock which stands on the North shore of the river is unconnected with the hills and rises to the hight of seven hundred

343

feet; it has some pine or reather fir timber on it's no[r]thern side, the southern is a precipice of it's whole hight. it rises to a very sharp point and is visible for 20 miles below on the river.

[Clark]   TUESDAY APRIL 8TH 1806

This morning about day light I heard a considerable roreing like wind at a distance and in the course of a short time wavs rose very high which appeared to come across the river and in the course of an hour became so high that we were obliged to unload the canoes,   at 7 oClock A.M. the winds swelded and blew so hard and raised the waves so emensely high from the N.E. and tossed our canoes against the shore in such a manner as to render it necessary to haul them up on the bank. finding from the appearance of the winds that it is probable that we may be detained all day, we sent out Drewyer, Shannon, Colter & Collins to hunt with derections to return if the wind should lul, if not to continue the hunt all day except they killed Elk or bear sooner &c.   John Shields cut out my small rifle & brought hir to shoot very well. the party ows much to the injinuity of this man, by whome their guns are repared when they get out of order which is very often.

I observed an Indian woman who visited us yesterday blind of an eye, and a man who was nearly blind of both eyes. the loss of sight I have observed to be more common among all the nations inhabiting this river than among any people I ever observed. they have almost invariably sore eyes at all stages of life. the loss of an eye is very common among them; blindness in persons of middle age is by no means uncommon, and it is almost invariably a concammitant of old age. I know not to what cause to attribute this prevalent dificientcy of the eye except it be their exposure to the reflection of the sun on the water to which they are constantly exposed in the occupation of fishing.

about 1 P M Collins Shannon and Colter returned. Collins saw 2 bear but could not get a shot at them. neither Shannon nor Colter saw anything worth shooting. Soon after Drewyer returned haveing only a Summer Duck. the Elk is gone to the mountains as the hunters Suppose. in the evening late an old man his Son & Grand Son and their wives &c. came down dureing the time the waves raged with great fury. the wife of the grandson is a woman of difference appearance from any we have seen on this river, [s]he has a very round head and pierceing black eyes. Soon after those people arived the old man was detected in stealing a spoon and he was ordered away,   at about 200 yards below our camp they built themselves a fire and did not return to our fires after.

The wind continued violently hard all day, and threw our canoes with such force against the shore that one of them split before we could get it out

Wednesday April 9th 1806

last night at a late hour the old amsiated [emaciated?] Indian who was detected in stealing a Spoon yesterday, crept upon his belley with his hands and feet, with a view as I suppose to take some of our baggage which was in several defferent parcels on the bank. the Sentinal observed the motions of this old amcinated retch untill he got with[in] a fiew feet of the baggage at [that] he hailed him and approached with his gun in a possion [position] as if going to shoote which allarmed the old retch in such a manner that he ran with all his powers tumbleing over brush and every thing in his way.

at 7 A. M. we set out and proceeded on to the camp of Joseph & Reubin Fields. they had killed nothing. here we did not delay but proceeded on to *Wah-clel-lah* Village on the North side and brackfast   here one of the men Colter observed the Tomahawk which was stolen from [me] on the 4th of Novr. last as we decended the Columbia,   he took the tomahawk   the natives attempted to wrest it from him, he held fast the Tomahawk. Those people attempted to excuse themselves from odium of stealing it, by makeing signs that they had purchased the Tomahawk, but their n[e]ighbours informed me otherwise and made signs that they had taken it. This village appears to be the wintering station of two bands of the *Shah-ha-la* Nation. One band has already moved [to] the Falls of the Multnomah which is the place they take their Salmon. The other band is now moveing a fiew miles above to the foot of the first rapid on this river, at which place they take their salmon. they take with them in their canoes independent of all their household effects the bark of their houses, and boards. those people were not hospita[b]l[e] and with some dificuelty we precured 5 dogs and a fiew Wappato of them.

at 2 oClock P. M. we set out and passed under the Beacon rock on the North Side of two small Islds. situated nearest the N. side. at 4 P. M. we arived at the first rapid at the head of Strawberry island at which place on the N W. Side of the Columbia [1] here we found the nativs from the last village rebuilding their habitations of the bark of their old village 16 Huts are already compleated and appear only temporrary it is most probable that they only reside here dureing the season of the Salmon. as we could not pass with the large canoes up the N.W. Side for the rocks, the wind high and a rainey disagreeable evining. our smallest canoe being too low to cross through the high waves, we sent her up on the N W. Side with Drewyer and the two Fields and after purchaseing 2 dogs crossed and into the sluce of a large high Island seperated from the S.E. Side by a narrow chanel. in this chanel we found a good harbor and encamped on the lower side. evening wet & disagreeable

THURSDAY APRIL 10TH 1806

at 6 A M we set out and proceeded to the lower point of the Island from whence we were compelled to draw our canoes up a rapid for about ¼ mile which we soon performed. in crossing the river which at this place is not more than 400 yards wide we fell down a great distance owing to the rapidity of the current. We continued up on the N. Side of the river which [with] great dificuelty in consequence of the rapidity of the current and the large rocks which forms this shore; the South Side of the river is impassable. As we had but one sufficent toe roap and were obliged to employ the cord in getting on our canoes the greater part of the way we could only take them one at a time which retarded our pregress very much. by evening we arived at the portage on the N. Side where we landed and conveyed our baggage to the top of the hill about 200 paces distant where we formed a camp. We had the canoes drawn on shore and secured. the small canoe got loose from the hunters and went adrift with a tin cup & a tomahawk in her; the Indians caught her at the last village and brought her up this evening for which we gave them two knives; the canoe overset and lost the articles which were in her.

[1] The lowest rapid at the foot of the Cascades. They have entered the Gorge of the Columbia.

[Lewis]   Friday April 11th 1806.

As the tents and skins which covered both our men and baggage
were wet with the rain which fell last evening, and as it continued
still raining this morning we concluded to take our canoes first to
the head of the rapids, hoping that by evening the rain would
cease and afford us a fair afternoon to take our baggage over the
portage. this portage is two thousand eight hundred yards along
a narrow rough and slipery road. the duty of getting the canoes
above the rapid was by mutual consent confided to my friend Capt.
C. who took with him for that purpose all the party except Bratton
who is yet so weak he is unable to work, three others who were
lamed by various accedents and one other to cook for the party.
a few men were absolutely necessary at any rate to guard our baggage from the War-clel-lars who crouded about our camp in considerable numbers. these are the greates[t] thieves and scoundrels
we have met with. by the evening Capt. C. took 4 of our canoes
above the rapids tho' with much difficulty and labour. the canoes were
much damaged by being driven against the rocks in dispite of
every precaution which could be taken to prevent t. the men complained of being so much fatiegued in the evening that we posponed taking up our 5th canoe untill tomorrow. these rapids are
much worse than they were [in the] fall when we passed them,   at
that time there were only three difficult points within seven miles,
at present the whole distance is extreemly difficult of ascent, and it
would be impracticable to decend except by leting down the empty
vessels by a cord and then even the wrisk would be greater than in
taking them up by the same means. the water appears to be (considerably) upwards of 20 feet higher than when we decended the
river.

many of the natives crouded about the bank of the river where
the men were engaged in taking up the canoes; one of them had
the insolence to cast stones down the bank at two of the men who
happened to be a little detatched from the party at the time. on
the return of the party in the evening from the head of the rapids
they met with many of the natives on the road, who seemed but
illy disposed; two of these fellows met with John Sheilds who had
delayed some time in purchasing a dog and was a considerable
distance behind the party on their return with Capt. C. they at-

tempted to take the dog from him and pushed him out of the road. he had nothing to defend himself with except a large knife which he drew with an intention of puting one or both of them to death before they could get themselves in readiness to use their arrows, but discovering his design they declined the combat and instantly fled through the woods. three of this same tribe of villains the Wah-clel-lars, stole my dog this evening, and took him towards their village; I was shortly afterwards informed of this transaction by an indian who spoke the Clatsop language, *(some of which we had learnt from them during the winter)* and sent three men in pursuit of the theives with orders if they made the least resistence or difficulty in surrendering the dog to fire on them; they overtook these fellows or reather came within sight of them at the distance of about 2 miles; the indians discovering the party in pursuit of them left the dog and fled. they also stole an ax from us,   but scarcely had it in their possession before Thompson detected them and wrest[ed] it from them. we ordered the centinel to keep them out of camp, and informed them by signs that if they made any further attempts to steal our property or insulted our men we should put them to instant death. a cheif of the Clah-clel-lah tribe informed us that there were two very bad men among the Wah-clel-lahs who had been the principal actors in these scenes of outradge of which we complained, and that it was not the wish of the nation by any means to displease us. we told him that we hoped it might be the case, but we should certainly be as good as our words if they persisted in their insolence. I am convinced that no other consideration but our number at this moment protects us.

The Cheif had in his possession a very good pipe tomahawk which he informed us he had received as a present from a trader who visited him last winter over land pointing to the N.W., whome he called Swippeton; he was pleased with the tommahawk of Capt. C. in consequence of it's having a brass bowl [2] and Capt. C. gratified him by an exchange. as a further proof of his being esteemed by this white trader, he gave us a well baked Saylor's bisquit which he also informed us he had received from Swippeton. from these evidences I have no doubt but the traders who winter in some of the inlets to the N. of us visit this part of the Columbia by land at certain seasons, most probably when they are confined to their

[2] Clark's hatchet was a pipe-tomahawk.

winter harbour. and if so some of those inlets are probably at no great distance from this place, as there seems to be but little inducement to intice the trader hither from any considerable distance particularly as the difficulty in traveling on the borders of this mountainous country must be great at that season as the natives informed me their snows were frequently breast deep. I observe snow-shoes in all the lodges of the natives above the Columbean vally. I hope that the friendly interposition of this chief may prevent our being compelled to use some violence with these people; our men seem well disposed to kill a few of them. we keep ourselves perefectly on our guard.

Saturday April 12th 1806.

It rained the greater part of last night and still continued to rain this morning. I therefore determined to take up the remaining perogue this morning for which purpose I took with me every man that could be of any service. a small distance above our camp there is one of the most difficult parts of the rapid. at this place the current sets with great violence against a projecting rock. in hawling the perogue arround this point the bow unfortunately took the current at too great a distance from the rock, she turned her side to the stream and the utmost exertions of all the party were unable to resist the forse with which she was driven by the current, they were compelled to let loose the cord and of course both perogue and cord went adrift with the stream. the loss of this perogue will I fear compell us to purchase one or more canoes of the indians at an extravegant price. after breakfast all hands were employed in taking our baggage over the portage. we caused all the men who had short rifles to carry them, in order to be prepared for the natives should they make any attempts to rob or injure them. I went up to the head of the rapids and left Capt. C. below. by 5 P.M. we had brought up all our baggage and Capt. C. joined me from the lower camp with the Clahclellah cheif. I employed Sergt. Pryor the greater part of the day in reparing and corking the perogue and canoes. it continued to rain by showers all day. as the evening was rainy cold and far advanced and ourselves wet we determined to remain all night. the mountains are high steep and rocky. the rock is principally black. they are covered with fir of several speceis and the white cedar. near the river we find the Cottonwood, sweet willow, broad leafed ash, a species of maple, the purple haw, a small speceis of cherry; purple currant, goosberry, red willow, vining and whiteburry honeysuckle, huckleburry, sacacommis, two speceis of mountain holley, & common ash. for the three last days this inclusive we have made only 7 miles.

SUNDAY APRIL 13TH 1806.

The loss of one of our perogues rendered it necessary to distribute her crew and cargo among the 2 remaining perogues and 2 canoes,[3] which being done we loaded and set out [at] 8 A.M. we passed the village immediately above the rapids where only one house at present remains entire, the other 8 having been taken down and removed to the oposite side of the river as before mentioned. we found the additional laiding which we had been compelled to put on board rendered our vessels extreemly inconvenient to mannage and in short reather unsafe in the event of high winds; I therefore left Capt. C. with the two perogues to proceede up the river on the N. side, and with the two canoes and some additional hands passed over the river above the rapids to the Y-eh-huh village in order to purchase one or more canoes. I found the village consisting of 11 houses crouded with inhabitants; it appeared to me that they could have mustered about 60 fighting men then present. they appeared very friendly disposed, and I soon obtained two small canoes from them for which I gave two robes and four elkskins. I also purchased four paddles and three dogs from them with deerskins. the dog now constitutes a considerable part of our subsistence and with most of the party has become a favorite food; certain I am that it is a healthy strong diet, and from habit it has become by no means disagreeable to me, I prefer it to lean venison or Elk, and it is very far superior to the horse in any state. after remaining about 2 hours at this Village I departed and continued my rout with the four canoes along the S. side of the river the wind being too high to pass over to the entrance of Cruzatts [Wind]

[3] By "perogues" Lewis means the two large canoes they had bought from the Indians, one on the downstream voyage, one during the winter. His "canoes" are the remaining dugouts; they had been made at Canoe Camp in the Clearwater. Clark calls all four canoes.

river where I expected to have overtaken Capt. C. not seing the perogues on the opposite side I ascended the river untill one oclock or about 5 ms. above the entrance of Cruzat's river. being convinced that the perogues were behind I halted and directed the men to dress the dogs and cook one of them for dinner; a little before we had completed our meal Capt. C. arrived with the perogues and landed opposite to us. after dinner I passed the river to the perogues and found that Capt. C. had halted for the evening and was himself hunting with three of the party.[4]

MONDAY APRIL 14TH 1806.

at 1 P.M. we arrived at a large village situated in a narrow bottom on the N. side. their houses are reather detached and extent[d] for several miles. they are about 20 in number. These people differ but litt[l]e in appea[ra]nce dress &c. from those of the rapids. they have some good horses of which we saw ten or a douzen. these are the fi[r]st horses we have met with since we left this neighbourhood last fall, in short the country below this place will not permit the uce of this valuable animal except in the Columbian vally and there the present inhabitants have no uce for them as they reside immediately on the river and the country is too thickly timbered to admit them to run the game with horses if they had them. we halted at this village and dined. purchased five dogs, some roots, shappalell, filberds and dryed burries of the inhabitants. these people appeared very friendly. some of them informed us that they had lately returned from a war excurtion against the snake indians who inhabit the upper part of the Multnomah river to the S.E. of them. that they had been fortunate in their expedition and had taken from their enimies most of the horses which we saw in their possession. after dinner we pursued our voyage to the entrance of a small run on N. side a little below a large village on the same side opposite the sepulchre rock.

TUESDAY APRIL 15TH 1806.

We delayed this morning untill after breakfast in order to purchase some horses of the Indians; accordingly we exposed some

4 Clark: "the wind rose and raised the wavs to such a hight that I could not proceed any further."

articles in exchange for horses   the natives were unwilling to barter, we therefore put up our merchandize and at 8 A.M. we set out. we halted a few minutes at the sepulchre rock, and examined the deposits of the ded at that place. there were thirteen sepulchres on this rock which stands near the center of the river and has a surface of about 2 acres above high water mark. from hence we returned to the no[r]thern shore and continued up it about four miles to another village of the same nation with whom we remained last night. here we halted and informed the natives of our wish to purchase horses; the[y] produced us several for sale but would not take the articles which we had in exchange for them. they wanted an instrument which the Northwest traders call an eye-dag *(a sort of war hatchet)* which we had not. we procured two dogs of them and departed.

[Clark]   WEDNESDAY APRIL 16TH 1806

About 8 oClock this morning I passed the river with the two interpreters,[5] and nine men in order to trade with the nativs for their horses, for which purpose I took with me a good part of our stock of merchindize. Capt L. sent out the hunters and set several men at work makeing pack saddles. twelve horses will be sufficient to transport our baggage and some pounded fish with our dried Elk, which we intend takeing with us as a reserved store for the plains & rocky mountains. I formed a Camp on the N. Side and sent Drewyer & Goodrich to the Skillute Village, and Shabono & Frazer down to the Chilluckkitequaw Village with derections to inform the nativs that I had crossed the river for the purpose of purchaseing horses, and if they had horses to sell us to bring them to my camp. Great numbers of Indians came from both villages and delayed the greater part of the day without tradeing a single horse. Drewyer returned with the principal Chief of the Skillutes who was lame and could not walk. after his arival some horses were offered for sale, but they asked nearly half the merchindize I had with me for one horse. this price I could not think of giveing.

the Chief informed me if I would go to his town with him, his people would sell me horses. I therefore concluded to accompany him to his village 7 miles distant. we set out and arrived at the

[5] And Sacajawea, in the hope that this band might understand Shoshone.

village at Sunset. after some serimony I entered the house of the Chief. I then informed them that I would trade with them for their horses in the morning for which I would give for each horse the articles which I had offered yesterd[ay]. The Chief set before me a large platter of onions which had been sweeted [sweated]. I gave a part of those onions to all my party and we all eate of them,   in this state the root is very sweet and the tops tender. the nativs requested the party to dance which they very readily consented and Peter Cruzat played on the violin and the men danced several dances & retired to rest in the houses of the 1st and second Chief. this village is moved about 300 yards below the spot it stood last fall at the time we passed down. We observed maney stacks of fish remaining untouched on either side of the river. This is the great mart of all this country. ten different tribes visit those people for the purpose of purchaseing their fish, and the Indians on the Columbia and Lewis's river quite to the Chopunnish Nation visit them for the purpose of tradeing horses buffalow robes for beeds, and such articles as they have not. The Skillutes precure the most of their cloth knivs axes & beeds from the Indians from the North of them who trade with white people who come into the inlets to the North at no great distance from the Tapteet. their horses of which I saw great numbers, they precure from the Indians who reside on the banks of the Columbia above, and what fiew they take from the Towarnihiooks or Snake Indians. I smoked with all the principal men of this nation in the house of their great Chief and lay my self down on a mat to sleep but was prevented by the mice and vermin with which this house abounded and which was very troublesom to me.

Thursday 17th of April 1806

I rose early after [a] bad nights rest, and took my merchindize to a rock which afforded an eligable situation for my purpose, and at a short distance from the houses, and divided the articles of merchindize into parsels of such articles as I thought best calculated to pleas the Indians. and in each parcel I put as many articles as we could afford to give. and thus exposed them to view, informing the Indians that each parcel was intended for a horse. they tanterlised me the greater part of the day, saying that they had sent out for their horses and would trade as soon as they came. Several parcels of merchindize was laid by for which they told me they would bring horses. I made a bargin with the chief for 2 horses, about an hour after he canseled the bargin and we again bargained for 3 horses which were brought forward,   only one of the 3 could be possibly used the other two had such intolerable backs as to render them entirely unfit for service. I refused to take two of them which displeased him and he refused to part with the 3rd.

I then packed up the articles and was about setting out for the village above when a man came and sold me two horses, and another man sold me one horse, and several others informed me that they would trade with me if I would continue untill their horses could be drove up. this induced me to continue at this village another day. Maney of the nativs from different villages on the Columbia above offered to trade, but asked such things as we had not and double as much of the articles which I had as we could afford to give. this was a very unfavourable circumstance as my dependance for precureing a sufficiency of horses rested on the suckcess above where I had reasons to believe there were a greater abundance of those animals, and was in hopes of getting them on better terms. before precureing the 3 horses I dispatched Crusat, Willard & McNeal and Peter Wiser to Capt Lewis at the Rock fort Camp with a note informing him of my ill suckcess in precureing horses, and advised him to proceed on to this place as soon as possible. that I would in the mean time proceed on to the Enesher Nation above the Great [Celilo] falls and try to purchase some horses of that people. Soon after I had dispatched this party the Chief of the Enesher's and 15 or 20 of his people visited me and appeared to be anxious to see the articles I offered for the horses. several of them agreed to let me have horses if I would add sundery articles to those I offered which I agreed to do, and they lay'd those bundles by and informed me they would deliver me the horses in the morning. the chief informed me that their horses were all in the plains with their womin gathering roots. they would Send out and bring the horses to this place tomorrow. this intelligence was flattering, tho' I doubted the sincerity of those people who had several times disapointed me in a similar way. however I deturmined to continue untill tomorrow. Shabono purchased a verry fine mare for which he gave Hurmen [Ermine], Elks Teeth, a belt and some other articles of no great value. no other purchase was made in the course of this day. in the evening I rec[ei]ved a note from Capt L. by Shannon informing me that he should set out early on tomorrow morning and should proceed up to the bason 2 miles below the Skillute Village. and adviseing me to give double the prices which we had first agreed on for each horse. I was envited into the house of the 2nd Chief where concluded to sleep. this man was pore nothing to eat but dried fish, and no wood to burn. altho' the night was cold they could not rase as much wood as would make a fire.

CHAPTER XXVI

From The Dalles of the Columbia to Walla Walla River

Early this morning I was awoke by an indian man of the Chopunnish Nation [the Nez Percés] who informed me that he lived in the neighbourhood of our horses. this man delivered me a bag of powder and ball which he had picked up this morning at the place the goods were exposed yesterday. I had a fire made of some poles purchased of the nativs a short distance from the houses and the articles exposed as yesterday. Collected the 4 horses purchased yesterday and sent Frazier and Shabono with them to the bason where I expected they would meet Cap L—s and commence the portage of the baggage on those horses. about 10 A. M. the Indians came down from the Eneesher Villages and I expected would take the articles which they had laid by yesterday. but to my estonishment not one would make the exchange to day. two other parcels of goods were laid by, and the horses promised at 2 P.M. I payed but little attention to this bargain, however suffered the bundles to lye.

I dressed the sores of the principal Chief gave some small things to his children and promised the chief some Medicine for to cure his sores. his wife who I found to be a sulky Bitch and was somewhat efflicted with pains in her back. this I thought a good oppertunity to get her on my side giveing her something for her back. I rubed a little camphere on her temples and back, and applyed worm flannel to her back which she thought had nearly restored her to her former feelings. this I thought a favourable time to trade with the chief who had more horses than all the nation be-

356

sides. I accordingly made him an offer which he excepted and sold me two horses. Great numbers of Indians from defferent derections visited me at this place to day. none of them appeared willing to part with their horses, but told me that several were comeing from the plains this evening.

at 3 P.M. Sergt. Ordway & three men arived from Cap Lewis they brought with them several Elk skins, two of my coats and 4 robes of the party to add to the stores I had with me for the purchase of horses. Sgt. O. informed me that Cap L. had arived with all the canoes into the bason 2 miles below and wished some dogs to eate. I had 3 dogs purchased and sent down. at 5 P. M. Capt. Lewis came up. he informed me that he had [passed] the river to the bason [1] with much dificuelty and danger, haveing made one portage. as I had not slept but very little for the two nights past on account of mice & Virmen with which those indian houses abounded, and haveing no blanket with me, and the means of keeping a fire sufficent to keep me worm out [of doors] was too expensive I deturmined to proceed with Capt. L. down to camp at the bason. I left the articles of Merchendize &c. with Drewyer, Werner. Shannon & Goodrich untill the morning. at the bason we cut up two of our Canoes for fire wood, verry much to the sagreen [chagrin] of the nativs notwithstanding they would give us nothing for them. Capt. L. had 12 pack saddles completed and strings prepared of the Elk skins for Lashing the loads.

SATURDAY 19TH APRIL 1806.

We deturmined to make the portage to the head of the long narrows, the 2 large canoes we could take no further and therefore cut them up for fuel. we had our small canoes drawn up very early and employed all hands in transporting our baggage on their backs and by means of 4 pack horses, over the portage. This labour we had accomplished by 3. P. M. and established our camp a little above the present Skillute village. I left Capt L. at the bason and proceeded to the village early this morning with a view to receive the horses which were promised to be brought this morning for articles laid by last evining. in the course of this day I purchased four horses at the Village, and Capt Lewis one at the bason before

1 Below the Long Narrows.

he left it. after the baggage was all safely landed above the portage, all hands brought over the canoes at 2 lodes which was accomplished by 5 P. M. as we had not a sufficiency of horses to transport our baggage we agreed that I should proceed on to the Enesher Villages at the great falls of the Columbia and if possible purchase as maney horses as would transport the baggage from that place, and rid us of the trouble and dificuelty of takeing our canoes further.[2] I set out with Serjt Pryor, Geo. Shannon Peter Crusat & Labiech at half past 5 P. M. for the Enesher village at which place I arrived at 8 P.M. Several showers of rain in the after part of to day, and the S W wind very high.

there was great joy with the nativs last night in consequence of the arrival of the Salmon; one of those fish was cought, this was the harbenger of good news to them. They informed us that those fish would arive in great quantities in the course of about 5 days. this fish was dressed and being divided into small pieces was given to each child in the village. this custom is founded on a supersticious opinion that it will hasten the arrival of the Salmon. We were oblige[d] to dispence with two of our kittles in order to acquire two of the horses purchased to day. we have now only one small kittle to a mess of 8 men. These people are very fa[i]thless in contracts; they frequently recive the merchindize in exchange for their horses and after some hours insist on some additional article being given them or revoke the exchange.

The long narrows are much more formidable than they were when we decended them last fall, there would be no possibility of passing either up or down them in any vessle at this time.

[Lewis] SUNDAY APRIL 20TH 1806.

This morning I was informed that the natives had pilfered six tommahawks and a knife from the party in the course of the last night. I spoke to the cheif on this subject. he appeared angry with his people and addressed them but the property was not restored. one horse which I had purchased and paid for yesterday and which could not be found when I ordered the horses into close confinement yesterday I was now informed had been gambled away by the rascal who had sold it to me and had been taken away by a man

---

[2] A momentous decision. Another long stretch of the water route has been found impracticable.

of another nation. I therefore took the goods back from this fellow. I purchased a gun from the cheif for which I gave him 2 Elkskins. in the course of the day I obtained two other indifferent horses for which I gave an extravigant price. I found that I should get no more horses and therefore resolved to proceed tomorrow morning with those which I had and to convey the baggage in two small canoes that the horses could not carry. for this purpose I had a load made up for seven horses, the eighth Bratton was compelled to ride as he was yet unable to walk. I bart[er]ed my Elkskins old irons and 2 canoes for beads. one of the canoes for which they would give us but little I had cut up for fuel. I had the horses graized untill evening and then picquited and hubbled within the limits of our camp. I ordered the indians from our camp this evening and informed them that if I caught them attempting to perloin any article from us I would beat them severely. they went off in reather a bad humour and I directed the party to examine their arms and be on their guard. they stole two spoons from us in the course of the day.

[Clark]   SUNDAY 20TH APRIL 1806

I shewed the Eneshers the articles I had to give for their horses. they without hezitation informed me that they would not sell me any for the articles I had, if I would give them Kittles they would let me have horses, and not without that their horses were at a long ways off in the planes and they would not send for them &c.   My offer was a blue robe, a calleco Shirt, a Silk handkerchief, 5 parcels of paint, a knife, a Wampom moon, 8 yards of ribon, several pieces of Brass, a Mockerson awl and 6 braces of yellow beeds; and to that amount for each horse which is more than double what we gave either the Sohsohne or first flatheads we met with on Clarks river I also offered my large blue blanket, my coat sword & plume none of which seamed to entice those people to sell their horses. notwithstanding every exertion not a single horse could be precured of those people in the course of the day.

[Lewis]   MONDAY APRIL 21ST 1806.

Notwithstanding all the precautions I had taken with rispect to the horses one of them had broken his cord of 5 strands of Elskin and had gone off spanseled. I sent several men in surch of the horse with orders to return at 10 A.M. with or without the horse being determined to remain no longer with these villains. they stole another tomahawk from us this morning I surched many of them but could not find it. I ordered all the spare poles, paddles and the ballance of our canoe put on the fire as the morning was cold and also that not a particle should be left for the benefit of the indians. I detected a fellow in stealing an iron socket of a canoe pole and gave him several severe blows and mad[e] the men kick him out of camp. I now informed the indians that I would shoot the first of them that attempted to steal an article from us. that we were not affraid to fight them, that I had it in my power at that moment to kill them all and set fire to their houses, but it was not my wish to treat them with severity provided they would let my property alone. that I would take their horses if I could find out the persons who had stolen the tommahawks, but that I had reather loose the property altogether than take the ho[r]se of an inosent person. the chiefs [who] were present hung their heads and said nothing. at 9 A.M. Windsor returned with the lost horse, the others who were in surch of the horse soon after returned also. the Indian who promised to accompany me as far as the Chopunnish country produced me two horses one of which he politely gave me the liberty of packing.[3] we took breakfast and departed a few minutes after 10 OClock. having nine horses loaded and one which Bratton rode not being able as yet to march; the two canoes I had dispatched early this morning. at 1 P.M. I arrived at the Enesher Village where I found Capt. Clark and party; he had not purchased a single horse.

[Clark]   Monday 21st April 1806

I found it useless to make any further attempts to trade horses with those unfriendly people who only crowded about me to view and make their remarks and smoke, the latter I did not indulge them with to day. at 12 oClock Capt Lewis and party came up from the Skillutes Village with 9 horses packed and one which bratten who was yet to weak to walk, rode, and soon after the two small canoes also loaded with the residue of the baggage which

---

[3] This "guide" is the Nez Percé who woke Clark on April 18.

could not be taken on horses. we had every thing imediately taken above the falls. in the mean time purchased 2 Dogs on which the party dined. whilst I remained at the Enesher Village I subsisted on 2 platters of roots, some pounded fish and sun flower seed pounded which an old man had the politeness to give me in return for which I gave him several small articles.

The man who we had reason to believe had stolen the horse he had given for the Kittle we thretened a little and he produced a very good horse in the place of that one which we cheerfully receved. After dinner we proceeded on about 4 miles to a village of 9 Mat Lodges of the Enesher: one of the canoes joined us, the other not haveing observed us halt continued on. We obtained 2 Dogs and a small quantity of fuel of those people for which we were obliged to give a higher price than usial,   our guide continued with us, he appears to be an honest fellow. he tels us that the indians above will treat us with much more hospitallity than those we are now with. we purchased another horse this evening but his back is in such a horrid state that we can put but little on him; we obtained him for a triffle, at least for articles which·might be precured in the U. States for 10/ Virga. currency.

[Lewis]   TUESDAY APRIL 22ED 1806.

we had not arrived at the top of a hill over which the road leads opposite the village before Charbono's horse threw his load, and taking fright at the saddle and robe which still adhered, ran at full speed down the hill,   near the village he disengaged himself from the saddle and robe, an indian hid the robe in his lodge. I sent our guide and one man who was with me in the rear to assist Charbono in retaking his horse which having done they returned to the village on the track of the horse in surch of the lost articles   they found the saddle but could see nothing of the robe the indians denyed having seen it; they then continued on the track of the horse to the place from whence he had set out with the same success. being now confident that the indians had taken it I sent the Indian woman on to request Capt. C. to halt the party and send back some of the men to my assistance being determined either to make the indians deliver the robe or birn their houses. they have vexed me in such a manner by such repeated acts of villany that I am quite disposed to treat them with every severyty, their defenseless state pleads forgivness so far as rispects their lives. with this resolution I returned to their village which I had just reached as Labuish met me with the robe which he informed me he found in an Indian lodg hid behind their baggage. I now returned and joined Capt. Clark who was waiting my arrival with the party.

we now made the following regulations as to our future order of march (viz) that Capt. C. & myself should devide the men who were disencumbered by horses and march alternately each day the one in front and the other in rear. haveing divided the party agreeably to this arrangement, we proceeded on through an open plain country about 8 miles to a village of 6 houses of the Eneshur nation,   here we observed our 2 canoes passing up on the opposite side; the wind being too high for them to pass the river they continued on. we halted at a small run just above the village where we dined on some dogs which we purchased of the inhabitants and suffered our horses to graize about three hours. after dinner we proceeded on up the river about 4 miles to a village of 7 mat lodges of the last mentioned nation. here our Chopunnish guide informed us that the next village was at a considerable distance and that we could not reach it tonight. a man b[e]longing to the next village above proposed exchanging a horse for one of our canoes, just at this moment one of our canoes was passing. we hailed them and ordered them to come over but the wind continued so high that they could not join us untill after sunset and the Indian who wished to exchange his horse for the canoe had gone on. we obtained 4 dogs and as much wood as answered our purposes on moderate terms. we can only afford ourselves one fire, and are obliged to lie without shelter,   the nights are cold and days warm.

WEDNESDAY APRIL 23RD 1806.

At day light this morning we were informed that the two horses of our Interpreter Charbono were absent; on enquiry it appeared that he had neglected to confine them to picqu[i]ts as had been directed last evening. we immediately dispatched Reubin Feilds and Labuish to assist Charbono in recovering his horses. one of them was found at no great distance and the other was given over as lost.

we continued our march along a narrow rocky bottom on the N. side of the river about 12 miles to the Wah-how-pum Village of 12 temperary mat lodges near the Rock rapid. these people appeared much pleased to see us, sold us 4 dogs and some wood for our small articles which we had previously prepared as our only resource to obtain fuel and food through those plains. these articles con[s]isted of pewter buttons, strips of tin iron and brass, twisted wire &c. here we met with a Chopunnish [Nez Percé] man on his return up the river with his family and about 13 head of horses most of them young and unbroken. he offered to hire us some of them to pack as far [as] his nation, but we prefer bying as by hireing his horses we shal have the whole of his family most probably to mentain. at a little distance below this village we passed five lodges of the same people who like those were waiting the arrival of the salmon.

after we had arranged our camp we caused all the old and brave men to set arround and smoke with us. we had the violin played and some of the men danced; after which the natives entertained us with a dance after their method. this dance differed from any I have yet seen. they formed a circle and all sung as well the spectators as the dancers who performed within the circle. these placed their sholders together with their robes tightly drawn about them and danced in a line from side to side, several parties of from 4 to seven will be performing within the circle at the same time. the whole concluded with a premiscuous dance in which most of them sung and danced. these people speak a language very similar to the Chopunnish whome they also resemble in their dress after the dance was ended the indians retired at our request and we retired to rest. we had all our horses side hubbled and turned out to graize; the river is by no means as rapid as when we decended or at least not obstructed with those dangerous rapids the water at present covers most of the rocks in the bed of the river. the natives promised to barter their horses with us in the morning we therefore entertained a hope that we shall be enabled to proceede by land from hence with the whole of our party and baggage.

[Clark]   THURSDAY 24TH APRIL 1806

rose early this morning and sent out after the horses all of which were found except McNeals which I hired an Indian to find and gave him a Tomahawk   had 4 pack saddles made ready to pack the horses which we may purchase. we purchased 3 horses, and hired 3 others of the Chopunnish man who accompanies us with his family, and at 1 P.M. set out and proceeded on through a open countrey rugid & sandy between some high lands and the river to a village of 5 Lodges of the Met-cow-we band haveing passed 4 Lodges at 4 miles and 2 Lodges at 6 miles. Great numbers of the nativs pass us on hors back   maney meet us and continued with us to the Lodges. we purchased 3 dogs which were pore, but the fattest we could precure, and cooked them with straw and dry willow. we sold our canoes for a fiew strands of beeds.[4] the nativs had tantelized us with an exchange of horses for our canoes in the first instance, but when they found that we had made our arrangements to travel by land they would give us nothing for them. we sent Drewyer to cut them up,   he struck one and split her they discovered that we were deturmined to destroy the canoes and offered us several strans of beeds which were accepted   most of the party complain of their feet and legs this evening being very sore. it is no doubt caused by walking over the rough stone and deep sand after being accustomed to a soft soil. my legs and feet give me much pain. I bathed them in cold water from which I experienced considerable relief. we directed that the 3 horses purchased yesterday should be hobbled and confined to pickquets and that the others should be hobbled & spanceled, and strictly attended to by the guard   made 12 miles to day.

[Lewis]   SUNDAY APRIL 27TH 1806.

This morning we were detained untill 9 A.M. in consequence of the absence of one of Charbono's horses. the horse at length being recovered we set out and at the distance of fifteen miles passed through a country similar to that of yesterday; the hills at the extremity of this distance again approach the river and are rocky abrupt and 300 feet high. we ascended the hill and marched through a high plain 9 miles when we again returned to the

---

4 From here on travel is by land: to the Nez Percé villages on the Clearwater River, beyond them to Traveller's Rest in the Bitterroot Valley and on to where the dugouts are hidden at the forks of the Jefferson. They detour Celilo Falls, traveling on the high land above the canyon.

river,   I now thought it best to halt as the horses and men were
much fatiegued altho we had not reached the Wallahwollah village
as we had been led to beleive by our guide who informed us that
the village was at the place we should next return to the river, and
the consideration of our having but little provision had been our
inducement to make the march we had máde this morning. we
collected some of the dry stalks of weeds and the stems of a shrub
which resembles the southernwood; made a small fire and boiled
a small quantity of our jerked meat on which we dined; while here
the principal Cheif of the Wallahwallahs joined us with six men
of his nation. this Cheif by name *Yel-lept!* had visited us on the
morning of the 19 October at our encampment a little below this
place; we gave him at that time a small medal, and promised him a
larger one on our return. he appeared much gratifyed at seeing us
return, invited us to remain at his village three or four days and
assured us that we should be furnished with a plenty of such food
as they had themselves, and some horses to assist us on our journey.

after our scanty repast we continued our march accompanyed by
Yellept and his party to the village which we found at the distance
of six miles situated on the N. side of the river at the lower side
of the low country about 12 ms. below the entrance of Lewis's
river. This Cheif is a man of much influence not only in his own
nation but also among the neighbouring tribes and nations. This
Village consists of 15 large mat lodges. at present they seem to
subsist principally on a speceis of mullet which weigh from one
to three lbs. and roots of various discriptions which these plains
furnish them in great abundance. they also take a few salmon
trout of the white kind. Yellept haranged his village in our favour
intreated them to furnish us with fuel and provision and set the
example himself by bringing us an armfull of wood and a platter
of 3 roasted mullets. the others soon followed his example with
rispect to fuel and we soon found ourselves in possession of an ample stock. they birn the stems of the shrubs in the plains there being no timber in their neighbourhood of any discription. we purchased four dogs of these people on which the party suped heartily
having been on short allowance for near two days. the indians retired when we requested them this evening and behaved themselves
in every rispect extreemly well. the indians informed us that there
was a good road which passed from the columbia opposite to this

village to the entrance of the Kooskooske on the S. side of Lewis's river; they also informed us, that there were a plenty of deer and antelopes on the road, with good water and grass. we knew that a road in that direction if the country would permit it would shorten our rout at least 80 miles.

the indians also informed us that the country was level and the road good, under these circumstances we did not hesitate in pursuing the rout recommended by our guide whos information was corroberated by Yellept and others.

[Clark]   MONDAY APRIL 28TH 1806

This morning early the Great Chief Yelleppet brought a very eligant white horse to our camp and presented him to me, signifying his wish to get a kittle but being informed that we had already disposed of every kittle we could possibly spare he said he was content with whatever I thought proper to give him. I gave him my *Swoard*, 100 balls & powder and some small articles of which he appeared perfectly satisfied. it was necessary before we entered on our rout through the plains where we were to meet with no lodges or resident Indians that we should lay in a stock of provisions and not depend altogether on the gun. we derected R. Frazer to whome we have intrusted the duty of makeing the purchases. to lay in as maney fat dogs as he could procure; he soon obtained 10, being anxious to depart we requested the Chief to furnish us with canoes to pass the river, but he insisted on our remaining with him this day at least, that he would be much pleased if we would consent to remain two or 3 days, but he would not let us have canoes to leave him this day. that he had sent for the *Chim-na-pums* his neighbours to come down and join his people this evening and dance for us. We urged the necessity of our proceeding on imediately in order that we might the sooner return to them, with the articles which they wished brought to them but this had no effect, he said that the time he asked could not make any considerable difference. at length urged that there was no wind blowing and that the river was consequently in good order to pass our horses and if he would furnish us with canoes for that purpose we would remain all night at our present encampment,   to this proposition he assented and soon produced a canoe. I saw a man who had his knee contracted who had previously applyed to me for some medisene, that if he would fournish another canoe I would give him some medisene. he readily consented and went himself with his canoe by means of which we passed our horses over the river safely and hobbled them as usial.

We found a *Sho-sho-ne* woman, prisoner among those people by means of whome and *Sah-cah-gah-weah,* Shabono's wife we found means of converceing with the *Wallahwallârs.* we conversed with them for several hours and fully satisfy all their enquiries with respect to our Selves and the Objects of our pursute. they were much pleased. they brought several disordered persons to us for whome they requested some medical aid. to all of whome we administered much to the gratification of those pore wretches, we gave them some eye water which I believe will render them more essential sirvice than any other article in the medical way which we had it in our power to bestow on them sore eyes seam to be a universal complaint among those people; I have no doubt but the fine sands of those plains and the river contribute much to the disorder. [A] man who had his arm broken had it loosely bound in a piece of leather without any thing to surport it. I dressed the arm which was broken short above the wrist & supported it with broad sticks to keep it in place, put [it] in a sling and furnished him with some lint bandages &c. to Dress it in future. a little before sun set the Chimnahpoms arrived; they were about 100 men and a fiew women; they joined the Wallahwallahs who were about 150 men and formed a half circle arround our camp where they waited verry patiently to see our party dance. the fiddle was played and the men amused themselves with danceing about an hour. we then requested the Indians to dance which they very chearfully complyed with; they continued their dance untill 10 at night. the whole assemblage of Indians about 350 men women and children sung and danced at the same time. Most of them danced in the same place they stood and mearly jumped up to the time of their musick. Some of the men who were esteemed most brave entered the space around which the main body were formed in solid column and danced in a circular manner side wise. at 10 P M. the dance ended and the nativs retired; they were much gratified in seeing some of our party join them in their dance. one of their party who made himself the most conspicious charecter in the dance and songs, we were told was a medesene man & could foretell things. that he had told of our comeing into their country and was now about to consult his God the Moon if what we said was the truth &c &c.

TUESDAY APRIL 29TH 1806

This morning Yelleppit furnished us with 2 canoes, and We began to transport our baggage over the river; we also sent a party of the men over to collect our horses. we purchased some deer [dogs] and chappellell this morning. we had now a store of 12 dogs for our voyage through the plains. by 11 A. M. we had passed the river with our party and baggage but were detained several hours in consequence of not being able to collect our horses. our guide now informed us that it was too late in the evening to reach an eligible place to encamp; that we could not reach any water before night. we therefore thought it best to remain on the Wallahwallah river about a mile from the Columbia untill the morning. The Wallahwallah River discharges it's self into the Columbia on it's South Side 15 miles below tue enterance of Lewis's River, or the S. E. branch. this is a handsom Stream about 4½ feet deep and 50 yards wide. the Indians inform us that it has it's source in the range of Mountains in view of us to the E. and S. E.[5] The Snake indian prisoner informed us that at some distance in the large plains to the South of those Mountains there was a large river running to the N.W. which was as wide as the Columbia at this place,[6] which is nearly 1 mile. this account is no doubt somewhat exagurated but it serves to evince the certainty of the Multnomah being a very large river and that it's waters are seperated from the Columbia by those mountains, and that with the aid of a Southwardly branch of Lewis's river which pass around the Eastern extremity of those mountains, it must water that vast tract of country extending from those mountains to the Waters of the Gulf of California and no doubt it heads with the Rochejhone and Del Nord.

there are 12 other Lodges of the Wallahwallah Nation on this river a short distance below our Camp. those people as well as the Chymnapoms are very well disposed, much more so particular[ly]

5 The Blue Mountains.
6 The Snake River but Clark does not recognize it as such. So he compounds his misconception of the unexplored country to the southwest.

their women than they were when we decended the river last fall.
Most of them have long shirts and leggins, good robes and mockersons. their women were the truss when they cannot precure the
shirt, but very fiew are seen with the former at the present. I
prosume the suckcess of their winters hunt has produced this
change in their attire. they insisted on our danceing this evening,
but it rained a little the wind blew hard and the weather was cold,
we therefore did not indulge them. Several applyed to me to day
for medical aide, one a broken arm another inward fevers and several with pains across their loins, and sore eyes. I administered as
well as I could to all. in the evening a man brought his wife and
a horse both up to me. the horse he gave me as a present and his
wife who was verry unwell the effects of violent coalds was placed
before me. I did not think her case a bad one and gave such medesene as would keep her body open and raped her in flannel. left
some simple medesin to be taken. we also gave some Eye water.

Wednesday April. 30th 1806

This morning we had some dificuelty in collecting our horses
notwithstanding we had hobbled & Picqueted those we obtained
of those people. We purchased two other horses this morning and
4 dogs. we exchanged one of our most indiferent horses for a very
good one with the Choponnish man who has his family with him.
this man has a doughter now arrived at the age of puberty who being a certain situation, is not permited to acoiate with the family
but sleeps at a distance from her father's camp, and when traveling
follows at some distance behind. in this state I am informed that
the female is not permited to eat, nor to touch any article of a culinary nature or manly occupation. at 10 A.M. we had collected
all our horses except the white horse which *Yelleppit* the Great
Chief had given me. the whole of the men haveing returned without being able to find this hors, I informed the Chief and he
mounted Capt Lewis's horse and went in serch of the horse himself.
about half an hour after the Chopunnish man brought my horse.
we deturmined to proceed on with the party leaving one man to
bring up Capt L.—s horse when *Yellepit* should return. We took
leave of those honest friendly people the Wallahwallahs and departed at 11 A.M. accompa'nied by our guide and the Chopunnish
man and family.

CHAPTER XXVII

FROM WALLA WALLA RIVER TO LAWYER'S CAÑON CREEK

*T*he overland route which the expedition followed was a series
of well-worn Indian trails that paralleled the Columbia for
a time, though on the highlands above the canyons, then
struck almost due east across the arid plains of southeastern Washington. This leg of the journey was without incident.

[Clark]   SATURDAY 3RD MAY 1806

This morning we set out at 7 A. M.   we met with the *We ark
koomt* whome we have usially distinguished by the name of the
big horn Chief from the circumstance of his always wareing a horn
of that animal suspended by a cord to his left arm. he is a 1st. chief
of a large band of the Chopunnish Nation. he had ten of his young
men with him. this man went down Lewis's river by Land as we
decended it by water last fall quite to the Columbia, and I believe
was very instrumental in precureing us a hospita[b]l[e] and friendly
reception among the nativs. he had now come a considerable distance to meet us. it rained, hailed, snowed & blowed with Great
Violence the greater portion of the day. it was fortunate for us that
this storm was from the S.W. and of course on our backs. the air
was very cold. we devided the last of our dried meat at dinner
when it was consumed as well as the ballance of our dogs
nearly   we made but a scant supper, and had not any thing for
tomorrow; however We-ark-koomt consoled us with the information that there was an Indian Lodge on the river at no great distance where we might supply ourselves with provisions tomorrow.

[Lewis]   SUNDAY MAY 4TH 1806.

Collected our horses and set out early; the morning was cold and disagreeable. we ascended through a high level plain to a ravine which forms the source of a small creek, thence down this creek to it's entrance into Lewis's river 7½ ms. below the entrance of the Kooskooske [Clearwater]. on the river a little above this creek we arrived at a lodge of 6 families of which We-ark-koomt had spoken. we halted here for breakfast and with much difficulty purchase[d] 2 lean dogs. the inhabitants were miserably poor. we obtained a few large cakes of half cured bread made of a root which resembles the sweet potatoe, with these we made some soope and took breakfast. a great portion of the Chopunnish we are informed are now distributed in small vilages through this plain collecting the quawmash and cows; [1] the salmon not yet having arrived to call them to the river.

the hills of the creek which we decended this morning are high and in most parts rocky and abrupt. one of our packhorses sliped from one of those hights and fell into the creek with it's load consisting principally of ammunition but fortunately neith[er] the horse nor load suffered any material injury. the amunition being secured in canisters the water did not effect it. after dinner we continued our rout up the West side of the river 3 Ms. opposite to 2 lodges the one containing 3 and the other 2 families of the Chopunnish nation; here we met with *Te-toh-ar-sky,* the youngest of the two cheifs who accompanied us last fall [to] the great falls of the Columbia we also met with our pilot who decended the river with us as far as the Columbia. these indians recommended our passing the river at this place and ascending the Kooskooske on the N.E. side. they said it was nearer and a better rout to the forkes of that river where the *twisted hair* resided in whose charge we had left our horses; thither they promised to conduct us. we determined to take the advice of the indians and immediately prepared to pass the river which with the assistance of three indian canoes we effected in the course of the evening, purchased a little wood and some bread of cows from the natives and encamped having traveled 15

---

1 The "quawmash" is, of course, the Western camass. The "cows" (usually "couse" or "Kouse" in future literature) is the cowas or biscuitroot (*Lomatium geyeri*). It was the commonest edible root in this locality and, unlike most, could be eaten raw.

Ms. only today. the evening was cold and disagreeable, and the natives crouded about our fire in great numbers insomuch that we could scarcely cook or keep ourselves warm. at all these lodges of the Chopunnish I observe an appendage of a small lodg with one fire which seems to be the retreat of their women in a certain situation   the men are not permitted to approach this lodge within a certain distance and if they have anything to convey to the occupants of this little hospital they stand at the distance of 50 or 60 paces and throw it towards them as far as they can and retire.

[Clark]   MONDAY MAY 5TH 1806

Collected our horses and set out at 7 A. M. at 4½ ms. we arived at the enterance of Kooskooske, up the N E Side of which we continued our march 12 miles to a large lodge of 10 families haveing passed two other large Mat Lodges the one at 5 and the other at 8 miles from the Mouth of the Kosskooske, but not being able to obtain provisions at either of those Lodges continued our march to the 3rd where we arived at 1 P. M. and with much dificuelty obtained 2 dogs and a small quantity of bread and dryed roots. at the second Lodge of Eight families Capt L. & myself both entered smoked with a man who appeared to be a principal man. as we were about to leave his lodge and proceed on our journey, he brought forward a very eligant Gray mare and gave her to me, requesting some eye water. I gave him a phial of Eye water a handkerchief and some small articles of which he appeared much pleased. while we were encamped last fall at the enterance of Chopunnish river, I gave an Indian man some Volitile liniment to rub his knee and thye for a pain of which he complained, the fellow soon after recovered and have never seased to extol the virtue of our medicines. near the enterance of the Kooskooske, as we decended last fall I met with a man, who could not walk with a tumure on his thye,   this had been very bad and recovering fast. I gave this man a jentle pirge cleaned & dressed his sore and left him some casteel soap to wash the sore which soon got well. this man also assigned the restoration of his leg to me. those two cures has raised my reputation and given those nativs an exolted oppinion of my skill as a phi[si]cian.[2] I have already received maney applications. in our present situation I think it pardonable to continue this deception for they will not give us any provisions without com-

2 Lewis: "my friend Capt. C. is their favorite phisician."

pensation in merchendize, and our stock is now reduced to a mear handfull. We take care to give them no article which can possibly injure them, and in maney cases can administer & give such medicine & sirgical aid as will effectually restore in simple cases &c. the Indians brought my horse which was left at the place we made canoes, from the opposit side and delivered him to me while here. this horse had by some accident seperated from our other horses above, and agreeably to indian information had been in this neighbourhood some weeks.[3]

while at dinner an indian fellow very impertinently threw a half starved puppy nearly into the plate of Capt. Lewis by way of derision for our eating dogs and laughed very hartily at his own impertinence; Capt. L. — was so provoked at the insolence that he cought the puppy and threw it with great violence at him and struck him in the breast and face, seazed his tomahawk, and shewed him by sign that if he repeeted his insolence that he would tomahawk him, the fellow withdrew apparently much mortified and we continued our Dinner without further molestation.

after dinner we continued our rout 4 miles to the enterance of Colter's Creek about ½ a mile above the rapid where we sunk the 1st canoe as we deceded the river last fall. We encamped on the lower side of this creek a little distance from two Lodges of the Chopunnish nation haveing traviled 20½ miles to day one of those Lodges contained 8 families, the other was much the largest we have yet seen. it is 156 feet long and about 15 feet wide built of Mats and straw, in the form of the roof of a house haveing a number of small dores on each side, is closed at the ends and without divisions in the intermediate space. this lodges at least 30 families. their fires are kindled in a row in the center of the Lodge and about 10 feet assunder. we arrived here extreemly hungary and much fatigued, but no articles of merchindize in our possession would induce them to let us have any article of Provisions except a small quantity of bread of *Cows* and some of those roots dryed. We had several applications to assist their sick which we refused unless they would let us have some dogs or horses to eat. a man whose wife had an abcess formed on the small of her back promised a horse in the

[3] Gass: "The old chief who is now with us says that the Snake Guide who deserted us last fall stole and took two of our horses with him." So Toby, who left without collecting his wages, received at least some compensation from the United States.

morning provided we would administer to her,　　I examined the abcess and found it was too far advanced to be cured. I told them her case was desperate. agreeably to their request I opened the abcess. I then introduced a tent and dressed it with bisilican; and prepared some dozes of the flour of sulpher and creem of tarter which were given with directions to be taken on each morning. a little girl and sundery other patients were brought to me for cure but we posponed our opperations untill the morning; they procured us several dogs but they were so pore that they were unfit to eat.

TUESDAY MAY 6TH 1806

　　This morning the husband of the sick woman was as good as his word. he produced us a young horse in tolerable order which we imediately had killed and butchered. the inhabitents seemed more accommodating this morning,　　they sold us some bread. we received a second horse for medecine & pro[s]cription to a little girl with the rhumitism whome I had bathed in worm water, and anointed her a little with balsom capivia. I dressed the woman again this morning who declared that she had rested better last night than she had since she had been sick. I was busily imployed for several hours this morning in administering eye water to a crowd of applicants. we once more obtained a plentiful meal, much to the comfort of all the party. Capt Lewis exchanged horses with *We ark koomt* and gave him a small flag with which he was much pleased and gratifyed. the sorrel which Cap L. obtained is a strong active well broke horse.

　　The Kooskooske river may be safely navigated at present　　all the rocks of the sholes and rapids are perfectly covered; the current is strong, the water clear and cold. this river is riseing fast. The timber of this river which consists principally of the long leafed pine which commences about 2 miles below our present encampment on Colters Creek.

　　it was 2 P M. this evening before we could collect our horses. at 3. P. M. we set out accompanied by the brother of the twisted hair and We-ark-koomt. we derected the horse which I had obtained for the purpose of eateing to be led as it was unbroke, in performing this duty a quarrel ensued between Drewyer and Colter. We continued our march along the river on its North Side 9. miles to a lodge of 6 families built of sticks mats and dryed Hay, of the same form of those heretofore discribed. We passed a Lodge of 3 families at 4ms. on the river, no provisions of any discription was to be obtained of these people. a little after dark our young horse broke the rope by which he was confined and made his escape much to the chagrin of all who recollected the keenness of their appetites last evening. the brother of the twisted hair & *Wearkkoomt* with 10 others encamped with us this evening. The nativs have a considerable Salmon fishery up Colters Creek.

WEDNESDAY MAY 7TH 1806

This morning we collected our horses and set out early accompanied by the brother of the twisted hair as a guide; Wearkkoomt and his party left us. we proceeded up the river 4 miles to a lodge of 6 families just below the enterance of a small Creek, here our guide recommended our passing the river, he informed us that the road was better on the South Side, and that game was more abundant also on that side near the enterance of Chopunnish river. we deturmined to pursue the rout recommended by the guide, and accordingly unloaded our horses and prepared to pass the river which we effected by means of one canoe in the course of 4 hours. a man of this lodge produced us two canisters of Powder which he informed us he had found by means of his dog where they had been berried in the bottom near the river a fiew miles above. they were the same which we had berried as we decended the river last fall. as he had kept them safe and had honisty enough to return them to us, we gave him a fire Steel by way of compensation.

The spurs of the rocky mountains which were in view from the high plain to day were perfectly covered with snow. The Indians inform us that the snow is yet so deep on the mountains that we shall not be able to pass them untill after the next full moon or about the first of June. others set the time at a more distant period. this [is] unwelcom intiligence to men confirmed to a diet of horse-beef and roots, and who are as anxious as we are to return to the fat plains of the Missouri, and thence to our native homes.

I observed in all the Lodges which we have passed since we crossed Lewis's river decoys, or stocking [stalking] heads as they are sometimes called. these decoys are for the deer and is formed of the skin of the head and upper portion of the neck of that animale extended in the nateral shape by means of a fiew little sticks placed within. the hunter when he sees a deer conseals himself and with his hand givs to the decoy the action of a deer at feed, and this induces the deer within arrowshot; in this mode the Indians near the woody country hunt on foot in such places where they cannot pursue the deer with horses which is their favourite method when the grounds will permit.

The orniments worn by the Chopunnish are, in their nose a single shell of Wampom, the pirl & beeds are suspended from the ears. beads are worn arround their wrists, neck and over their sholders crosswise in the form of a double sash. the hair of the men is cewed in two rolls which hang on each side in front of the body. Collars of bears claws are also common; but the article of dress on which they appear to bestow most pains and orniments is a kind of collar or brestplate; this is most commonly a strip of otter skins of about six inches wide taken out of the center of the skin it's whole length including the head. this is dressed with the hair on. this is tied around the neck & hangs in front of the body the tail frequently reaching below their knees; on this skin in front is attatched pieces of pirl, beeds, wampom, pices of red cloth and in short whatever they conceive most valuable or ornamental.

THURSDAY 8TH OF MAY 1806.

Drewyer & P. Crusat brought in a Deer each & Collins wounded one which our Dog caught near our camp. Total of our stock of provisions 4 deer & some horse flesh. on the small creek which passes our Camp, the nativs have lately encamped and as we are informed have been much distressed for provisions, they have fallen a number of small pine in the vicinity of this Encampment for the Seed which is in the bur of which they eate. we are informed that they were compelled to collect the moss of the pine boil & eate it in the latter part of the last winter. on the creek near our camp I observed a kind of trap which was made with great panes to catch the small fish which pass down with the stream. This was a dam formed of stone so as to collect the water in a narrow part not exceeding 3 feet wide from which place the water shot with great force and scattered through some small willows closely connected and fastened with bark,   this mat of willow switches was about 4 feet wide and 6 long lying in a horozontal position, fastened at the extremety. the small fish which fell on those willows was washed on the Willows where they [lie] untill taken off &c.   I cought or took off those willows 9 small trout from 3 to 7 Inches in length.   Soon after I returned from the fishery an Indian came from a fishery of a similar kind a little above with 12 small fish which he offered me which I declined axcepting as I found from his signs that his house was a short distance above, and that those fisheries afforded the principal part of the food for his children.

The great Chief of the Bands below who has a cut nose joined us this morning.   we gave the interals with 4 young fauns which was in two of the deer killed to day to the Indians also some of our deer & horse flesh.   the paunch of the deer they eate without any preperation further than washing them a little.   the fauns they boiled and eate every part of them even the Skins with the hair. The Snake Indian was much displeased that he was not furnished with as much Deer as he could eate.   he refused to speake to the wife of Shabono, through whome we could understand the nativs. we did not indulge him and in the after part of the day he came too and spoke very well.   we loaded up and set on on the roade leading as we were informed to the lodge of the twisted hair, the Chief in whoes care we had left our horses.   we were accompanied by the Cut nose Chief our old Chief who had accompanied us down the river and several men.   we assended the hills which was steep and emencely high to a leavel rich country thinly timbered with pine.   we had not proceeded more than 4 miles before we met the *twisted hair* and several men meeting of us.   we were verry coolly receved by the twisted hair.   he spoke aloud and was answered by the Cut nose.   we could not learn what they said, but plainly discovered that a missunderstanding had taken place between them. we made signs to them that we should proceed on to the next water and encamp.   accordingly I set out and they all followed.   we had not proceeded far before the road crossed a small handsom stream on which we encamped.   The parties of those two Chiefs took different positions at some distance from each other and all appeared sulkey.

after we had formed our camp we sent Drewyer with a pipe to smoke with the twisted hair and lern the cause of the dispute between him and the Cut nose, and also to invite him to our fire to smoke with us.   The twisted hair came to our fire to smoke   we then sent drewyer to the Cut Noses fire with the same directions.

he returned and informed us that the Cut nose said he would join us in a fiew minits. it appears that the cause of the quarrel between those two men is about our horses and we cannot lern the particulars of this quarrel which probably originated through jelousy on the part of the Cut nose who blames the twisted hair for suffer[ing] our horses to be rode, and want water dureing the winter &c.   twisted hair says the horses were taken from him &c.   The Cut nose joined us in a short time   We smoked with all the party of both Chiefs, and told them that we were sorry to find them at varience with each other   the cut nose said that the twisted hair was a bad man and wore two faces, that he had not taken care of our horses as was expected, that himself an the broken arm had caused our horses to be watered in the winter and had them drove together, and that if we would proceed on to the village of the great chief [for] whome we had left a flag last fall the broken arm he would send for our horses, that he had himself three of them. he also informed us that the great Chief hereing of our distressed situation had sent his son and 4 men to meet us and have furnished on the way &c.   that the young men had missed us and could never over take us untill this time. that the great Chief had 2 bad horses for us and expected us to go to his lodge which was near the river and about half a days march above &c.   The *twisted hair* told us that he wished to smoke with us at his lodge which was on the road leading to the Great Chiefs lodge, and but a fiew miles ahead. if we would delay at his lodge tomorrow he would go after our saddles and horses which was near the place we made our canoes last fall. accordingly we informed the Indians of our intentions. we all smoked and conversed untill about 10 P M. the Indians retired and we lay down. Derected 5 hunters to turn out early in the morning to hunt and meet us at the twisted hair's lodge.

FRIDAY 9TH MAY 1806

We were detained untill 9 A.M. for our horses which were much scattered at which time we collected our horses and set out and proceeded on through a butifull open rich country for 6 miles to the camp of the twisted hair. this Campment is formed of two Lodges built in the usial form of mats and straw. the largest and principal Lodge is calculated for 2 fires only. the Second lodge is

small & appears to be intended for the sick women who always retire to a seperate lodge when they have the [blank space in
MS.]   before 2 P M all our hunters joined us haveing killed only
one deer which was lost in the river and a pheasent. Soon after we
halted at the lodge of the twisted hair he set out with two boys and
Willard with a pack horse down to the river near the place we
made the canoes for our saddles and a cannister of powder and
some lead buried there, also a part of our horses which resorted
near that place. late in the evening they returned with 21 of our
horse[s] and about half of our saddles with the powder and ball.
The greater part of the horses were in fine order, tho' five of them
had been rode & worsted in such a manner last fall by the Inds.
that they had not recovered and are in very low order, and 3 with
sore backs. we had all the recovered horses cought & hobbled. we
precured some pounded roots of which a supe was made thick on
which we suped. the wind blew hard from the S.W. accompanied
with rain untill from 7 oClock untill 9 P.M. when it began to snow
and continued all night.

Saturday 10th of May 1806

the air keen and cold the snow 8 inches deep on the plain. we
collected our horses and set out for the village of the Chief with a
flag, and proceeded on through an open plain. the road was slipry
and the snow cloged and caused the horses to trip very frequently.
the mud at heads of the streams which we passed was deep and
well supplied with the *Carmash* [camass]. at 4 P M we arrived at
the village of *Tin nach e moo toolt* the Chief whome We had left
a flag. this flag was hoisted on a pole   under[r] the flag the Chief
met me and conducted me to a spot near a small run about 80
paces from his Lodges where he requested me to halt which I did.
Soon after Cap Lewis who was in the rear came up and we smoked
with and told this Chief our situation in respect to provisions.

they brought forward about 2 bushels of quawmash 4 cakes of
bread made of roots and a dried fish. we informed the Chief that
our party was not accustomed to eate roots without flesh & proposed
to exchange some of our oald horses for young ones to eate. they
said that they would not exchange horses, but would furnish us
with such as we wished, and produced 2 one of which we killed and
informd. them that we did not wish to kill the other at this time.

We gave medals to the broken arm or *Tin-nach-e-moo-tolt* and *Hoh-hâst-ill-pilp* two principal Chiefs of the Chopunnish Nation and was informed that there was one other Great Chief (in all 4) who had but one eye. he would be here tomorrow. a large Lodge of Leather was pitched and Capt. Lewis and my self was envited into it. we entered and the Chief and principal men came into the lodge and formed a circle a parcel of wood was collected and laid at the dore and a fire made in this conic lodge before we entered it. the Chief requested that we might make the Lodge our homes while we remained with him. here after we had taken a repast on roots & horse beef we resumed our council with the indians which together with smokeing took up the ballance of the evening. as those people had been liberal I directed the men not to crowd their Lodges in serch of food the manner hunger has compelled them to do, at most lodges we have passed, and which the *Twisted Hair* had informed us was disagreeable to the nativs. but their previous want of hospitality had enduced us to consult their enclinations but little and suffer our men to obtain provisions from them on the best terms they could.

The Village of the *broken Arm* consists of one house or Lodge only which is 150 feet in length built in the usial form of sticks, Mats and dry grass. it contains 24 fires and about double that number of families. from appearance I prosume they could raise 100 fighting men. the noise of their women pounding the cows roots [biscuitroot] remind me of a nail factory. The Indians appear well pleased, and I am confident that they are not more so than our men who have their stomach once more well filled with horse beef and the bread of cows. Those people has shewn much greater acts of hospitallity than we have witnessed from any nation or tribe since we have passed the rocky Mountains. in short be it spoken to their immortal honor it is the only act which diserves the appelation of hospitallity which we have witnessed in this quarter.

SUNDAY 11TH MAY 1806

we were crouded in the Lodge with Indians who continued all night and this morning Great numbers were around us. The One Eyed Chief arived and we gave him a medal of the small size and spoke to the Indians through a Snake boy Shabono and his wife. we informed them who we were, where we came from & our intentions towards them, which pleased them very much. a young man son to the great Chief who was killed not long sence by the Indians from the N.E. brought an elegant mare and coalt and Gave us, and said he had opened his ears to what we had said and his heart was glad: and requested us to take this mare and coalt as a token of his deturmination to pursue our Councels &c. The twisted hair brough[t] six of our horses all in fine order. Great numbers of Indians apply to us for medical aid which we gave them cherfully so far as our skill and store of Medicine would enable us. schrofla, ulsers, rhumitism, sore eyes, and the loss of the use of their Limbs are the most common cases among them. the latter case is not very common but We have seen 3 instances of it among the Chopunnish. a very extroadinery compl[ai]nt. about 3 P. M. Geo. drewyer arived with 2 deer which he had killed. he informed us that the snow still continued to cover the plains.

We are now pretty well informed [about] the principal Chiefs of the Chopunnish Nation; as all those chiefs were present in our lodge we thought it a favourable time to repeet what had been said and to enter more minutely into the views of our government with respect to the inhabitants of this Western part of the Continent, their intentions of establishing tradeing houses for their relief, their wish to restore peace and harmony among the nativs, the strength welth and powers of our nation &c. to this end we drew a map of the country with a coal on a mat in their way, and by the assistance of the Snake boy and our interpreters were enabled to make ourselves understood by them altho' it had to pass through French, Minnetare, Shoshone and Chopunnish languages. the interpretation being tegious it occupied the greater part of the day, before we had communicated to them what we wished. they appeared highly pleased. after this council was over we amused ourselves with shewing them the power of magnetism, the spye glass, compass, watch, *air gun* and sundery other articles equally novel and incomprehensible to them. they informed us that after we left the Menetares last spring that 3 of their people had visited that nation, and that they had informed them of us, and had told them that we had such things in our possession but that they could not place confidence in the information untill they had now witnessed it themselves.

In the evening a man was brought in a robe by four Indians and laid down near me. they informed me that this man was a Chief of considerable note who has been in the situation I see him for 5 years. this man is incapable of moveing a single limb but lies like a corps in whatever position he is placed, yet he eats hartily, dejests his food perfectly, enjoys his understanding. his pulse are good, and has retained his flesh almost perfectly; in short were it not that he appears a little pale from having been so long in the shade, he might well be taken for a man in good health. I suspect that their confinement to a diet of roots may give rise to all the disorde[r]s of the nativs of this quarter except the Rhumitism & Sore eyes, and to the latter of those, the state of debility incident to a vegitable diet may measureably contribute. The Chopunnish not withstanding they live in the crouded manner before mentioned are much more clenly in their persons and habitations than any nation we have seen sence we left the Illiniois.

MONDAY 12TH MAY 1806

after brackfast I began to administer eye water and in a fiew minits had near 40 applicants with sore eyes, and maney others with other complaints most common Rhumatic disorders & weaknesses in the back and loins perticularly the womin. the Indians had a grand Council this morning after which we were presented each with a horse by two young men at the instance of the nation. we caused the chiefs to be seated and gave them each a flag a pint of Powder and 50 balls to the two young men who had presented the horses we also gave powder and ball. The broken arm pulled off his leather shirt and gave me. In return gave him a shirt. We retired into the Lodge and the natives spoke to the following purpote, i.e. they had listened to our advice and that the whole nation were deturmined to follow it, that they had only one heart and one tongue on this subject. they wished to be at peace with all nations &c. Some of their men would accompany us to the Missouri &c. &c. as a great number of men women & children were wateing and requesting medical assistance maney of them with the most simple complaints which could be easily releived, independent of maney with disorders intirely out of the power of Medison ah requesting something, we agreed that I should administer and Capt L to here and answer the Indians. I was closely employed untill 2 P.M. administering eye water to about 40 grown persons. some simple cooling medicenes to the disabled Chief, to several women with rhumatic effections & a man who had a swelled hip. &c. &c. in the evening three of our horses were brought all in fine order. we have now only Six remaining out. Those people are much affraid of the blackfoot indians, and the Big bellies of *Fort de prarie* establishment. those indians kill great numbers of this nation whenever they pass over to hunt on the Missouri. one of our men bought a horse for a fiew small articles of an Indian. The Indians brought up a fat horse and requested us to kill and eate it as they had nothing else to offer us to eate. The Cut Nose made a present of a horse to Drewyer at the same time the two horses were offered to Capt. Lewis & my self. The horses of those people are large well formed and active. Generally in fine order. sore backs caused by rideing them either with out saddles, or with pads which does not prevent the wate of the rider pressing imediately on the back bone, and weathers [withers] of the horse. the Indians formed two parti[e]s and plaied for their beeds. we gave the twisted hair a gun, powder & 100 ball in part for takeing care of our horses &c. and wish him to camp near us untill we crossed the mountains which he agreed to do, and was much pleased   we have turned our attentions towards the *twisted hair* who has several sons grown who are well acquainted as well as himself with the various roads through the rocky Mountains and will answer very well as guides to us through those mountains.

In the council to day the father of Hohâstillpilp said the Chopunnish were fully convinced of the advantages of peace and ardently wished to cultivate peace with their neighbors. early last Summer 3 of their brave men were sent with a pipe to the Shoshones on the S E. fork of Lewis's river in the Plains of Columbia,   their pipe was disregarded and their 3 men murdered, which had given rise to the War expedition against that nation last fall; that their warriers had fallen in with and killed 42 of the Shoshones with the loss of 3 men only on their part; that this had satisfied the blood of the deceased friends and they would never again make war against the Shoshones, but were willing to receve them as friends. That as we had not seen the Indians towards *Fort de Prarie* they did not think it safe to venture over to the Plains of the Missouri, where they would fondly go provided those nations would not kill them. I gave a vial of eye water to the Broken arm for to wash the eyes of all who applied to him and told him when it was out we would replenish it again.

CHAPTER XXVIII

ENCAMPED ON THE UPPER KOOSKOOSKE

[Clark]   TUESDAY 13TH OF MAY 1806.

A fine morning I administered to the sick and gave directions. we collected all our horses and set out at 1 P.M. and proceeded down the Creek to the *Flat head* [Clearwater] River a short distance below the enterance of the Creek. at this place we expected to have met the Canoe which was promised to be furnished us, and for which an indian set out very early this morning. we halted at the River unloaded our horses and turned them out to feed. Several Indians accompanied us to the river and continued untill evening. The man who set out early this morning to the forks of this river for a canoe did not arive untill after sunset we remained all night; in the evening we tried the speed of several of our horses. these horses are strong active and well formed. Those people have emence numbers of them 50 or 60 or a Hundred head is not unusial for an individual to possess.

The Chopunnish are in general stout well formed active men. they have high noses and maney of them on the acqueline order with chearfull and agreeable countinances; their complexious are not remarkable. in common with other Indian Nations of America they extract their beard, but the men do not uniformly extract their hair below, this is more particularly confined to the females. they appear to be cheerfull but not gay, they are fond of gambling and of their amusements which consists principally in shooting their arrows at a targit made of willow bark, and in rideing and exersiseing themselves on horseback, raceing &c. they are expirt marks men & good riders. they do not appear to be so much devoted to

384

baubles as most of the nations we have met with, but seem anxious always to riceve articles of utility, such as knives, axes, Kittles, blankets & mockerson awls. blue beeds however may form an exception to this remark; This article among all the nations of this country may be justly compared to gold and silver among civilized nations. They are generally well clothed in their stile. their dress consists of a long shirt which reaches to the middle of the leg, long legins which reach as high as the waist, mockersons & robe. those are formed of various skins and are in all respects like those of the Shoshone. Their orniments sonsists of beeds, shells and pieces of brass variously attached to their dress, to their ears arround their necks wrists arms &c. a band of some kind usially serounds the head, this is most frequently the skin of some fir animal as the fox otter &c. I observed a tippet worn by Hohâstillpilp, which was formed of Humane scalps and ornemented with the thumbs and fingers of several men which he had slain in battle. they also were a coller or breastplate of otter skin orniminted with shells beeds & quills. the women brade their hair in two tresses which hang in the same position of those of the men, which ar[e] cewed and hang over each sholder &c.

Wednesday 14th of May 1806

we had all our horses collected by 10 a.m. dureing the time we had all our baggage crossed over the River which is rapid and about 150 yards wide. after the baggage was over to the North Side we crossed our hors[e]s without much trouble and hobbled them in the bottom after which we moved a short distance below to a convenient situation and formed a camp around a very conveniant spot for defence   this situation we concluded would be sufficently convenient to hunt the wood lands for bear & Deer and for the salmon fish which we were told would be here in a fiew days, and also a good situation for our horses. the hills to the E. & N. of us are high broken & but partially timbered; the soil rich and affords fine grass. in short as we are compelled to reside a while in this neighbourhood I feel perfectly satisfied with our position.

imediately after we had crossed the river the Chief called the broken arm [and] another principal Chief arived on the opposite side and began to sing. we sent the canoe over and those chiefs, the son of the broken arm and the son of a Great Chief who was killed last year by the Big bellies of Saskasshewin river. those two young men were the two whome gave Capt Lewis and myself each a horse with great serimony in behalf of the nation a fiew days ago, and the latter a most elligant mare & colt the morning after we arived at the village. Hohâstillpilp with much serimoney presented Capt Lewis with an elegant Gray horse which he had brought for that purpose. Capt Lewis gave him in return a Handkerchief two hundred balls and four pounds of powder, with which he appeared perfectly satisfied, and appeared much pleased. we made several attempts to exchange our Stalions for Geldin[g]s or mar[e]s without success   we even offered two for one. those horses are troublesom and cut each other very much and as we can't exchange them we think it best to *castrate* them and began the opperation this evening   one of the indians present offered his services on this occasion. he cut them without tying the string of the stone as is usial. he [s]craped it very clean & seperate it before he cut it.

about Meridian Shannon came in with two Grows [grouse] & 2 Squireles common to this country. his mockersons worn out obliged to come in early. Collins returned in the evening with the two bears which he had killed in the morning one of them an old hee was in fine order, the other a female with Cubs was meagure. we gave the Indians about us 15 in number two sholders and a ham of the bear to eate which they cooked in the following manner. towit on a brisk fire of dryed wood they threw a parcel of small stones from the river, when the fire had burnt down and heated the stone, they placed them level and laid on a parsel of pine boughs, on those they laid the flesh of the bear in flitches, placeing boughs between each course of meat and then coveing it thickly with pine boughs; after this they poared on a small quantity of water, and covered the whole over with earth to the debth of 4 inches. in this situation they suffered it to remain about 3 hours when they took it out fit for use. This nation esteem the Killing of one of those tremendeous animals equally great with that of an enemy in the field of action. we gave the claws of those bear which Collins had killed to Hohâstillpilp.

THURSDAY 15TH OF MAY 1806

Reubin Fields went out to hunt his horse very early and saw a large bear and no great distance from Camp. Several men went in pursute of the bear, and prosued his trail some time without gitting sight of this monster. Shannon went out with Labeach to

hunt and continued out 3 days, Gibson and Hall accompanied
them for the meat Labeech killed yesterday which they brought in
by 11 A M. this morning the female [bear] was black with
white hares intermixed and a white spot on the breast the Cubs
were about the size of a dog also pore. one of them very black and
the other a light redish brown or bey colour. These bear give me
a stronger evidence of the various coloured bear of this country
being one specie only, than any I have heretofore had. Several
other colours have been seen.

Frazur Jo. Fields and Peter Wizer complain of a violent pain in
their heads. Howard and York with violent cholicks. the cause of
those disorders we are unable to account for. their diet and the
sudin change of climate must contribute. The broken arm and 12
of the young men of his nation left us to day about 11 oClock and
crossed the river to his Village Hoh-hâst-ill-pilt and 3 old men
continued with us untill about 5 P.M. when they left us and returned to their village. a party of 14 Indians passed our camp
about 1 P M on their way to the leavel uplands to run and kill the
deer with their horses and Bows and arrows. Some of them were
also provided with deers heads cased for the purpose of decoying
the deer. those men continued with us but a fiew minits and proceeded on. Those people hunt most commonly on horse back
seround the Deer or Goat which they find in the open plains & kill
them with their arrows, tho' they sometimes hunt the deer on foot
& decoy them. we had all of our horses drove together to day with
a view to fermilurize them to each other. those that were cut
yesterday are stiff and several of them much swelled. we had all
our baggage secured and covered with a rouf of straw. our little
fortification also completely secured with brush around which our
camp is formed. the Greater part of our security from the rains &c.
is the grass which is formed in a kind of ruff so as to turn the rain
completely and is much the best tents we have. as the days are
worm &c. we have a bowry made to write under which we find not
only comfortable but necessary, to keep off the intence heet of the
sun which has great effect in this low bottom. on the high plains off
the river the climate is entirely different cool, some snow on the
north hill sides near the top and vegetation near 3 weeks later than
in the river bottoms, and the rocky Mountains imediately in view
covered several say 4 & 5 feet deep with snow. here I behold three
different climats within a fiew miles

Friday 16th May 1806

The Indians of this country seldom kill the bear   they are very much afraid of them and the killing of a White or Grizly bear, is as great a feet as two of their enimey. the fiew of those animals which they chance to kill is found in the leavel open lands and pursued on horses & killed with their Arrows. they are fond of the flesh of this animal and eate imoderately of it when they have a sufficiency to indulge themselves. The men who were complaining of the head ake and cholick yesterday and last night are much better to day. Shabonos Squar gathered a quantity of *fenel* roots which we find very paliatiable and nurushing food. the onion we also find in abundance and boil it with our meat.

Saturday 17th May 1806

rained moderately all the last night and this morning untill, we are wet. the rains unfortunately wet the Crenomuter in the fob of Capt. L. breaches, which has never before been wet since we set out on this expedition. her works were cautiously wiped and made dry by Capt. L. and I think she will receve no injury from this misfortune &c.   we arranged the hunters and horses to each hunter and directed them to turn out in the morning early and continue out untill they killed something. others arranged so as to take care of the hunters horses in their absence. rained moderately all day. at the same time snowed on the mountains which is in to the S. E. of us. no Indians visit us to day which is a singular circumstance as we have not been one day without Indians since we left the long narrows of the Columbia.

the fiew worm days which we have had has melted the snows in the mountains and the river has rose considerably. that icy barier which seperates me from my friends and Country, from all which makes life estimable, is yet white with the snow which is maney feet deep. I frequently consult the nativs on the subject of passing this tremendious barier which now present themselves to our view for [a] great extent. they all appear to agree as to the time those mountains may be passed which is about the middle of *June*. Sergt. Pryor informs me that the snow on the high plains from the river was shoe deep this morning when he came down. At the distance of 18 miles from the river and on the Eastern border of the high Plain the Rocky Mountain commences and presents us with *Winter*   here we have Summer, Spring and winter in the short space of twenty or thirty miles.

Sunday 18th May 1806

The Squar wife to Shabono busied her self gathering the roots of the fenel called by the Snake Indians *Year-pah* [1] for the purpose of drying to eate on the Rocky mountains. those roots are very paliatiable either fresh rosted boiled or dried and are generally between the size of a quill and that of a mans fingar and about the length of the latter. at 3 P M Jo. Field returned from the chase without killing any thing   he complains of being unwell. so[o]n after an old man and a woman arived the man with sore eyes, and the woman with a gripeing and rhumatic effections. I gave the woman a dose of creme of tarter and flour of Sulphur, and the man some eye water. Lapage took a Salmon from an Eagle at a short distance below our camp. this is induces us to believe that the Salmon is in this river and most probably will be here in great numbers in the course of a fiew days.

Monday 19th May 1806

We sent Shabono, Thomson, Potts, Hall & Wizer over to the Villages above to purchase some roots to eate with our pore bear meat, for which purchase we gave them a fiew awls, knitting pins, & arm ban[d]s and directed them to proceed up on this side of the river opposit to the Village and cross in the cano[e] which we are informed is at that place. about 11 oClock 4 men and 8 women came to our camp with Thompson who went to the Village very early this morning. those men applyed for Eye water and the Women had a variety of Complaints tho' the most general complaint was the Rhumitism,   ains in the back and the sore eyes,   they also brought fowd. a very young Child whome th*ey* said had been very sick. I administered eye water to all, two of the women I gave a carthartic, one whose spirets were very low and much hiped [depressed] I gave 30 drops of Lodomem, and to the others I had their backs hips legs thighs & arms well rubed with *Volitile leniment*   all of those pore people thought themselves much benifited by what had been done for them, and at 3 P. M. they all returned to their Villages well satisfied. at 5 P. M. Potts,

1 The yampa or squawroot, *Carum gairdneri.*

Shabono &c. returned from the Village with about 6 bushels of the root the nativs call *cowse* and some bread of the same root. Rubin & Jos. Fields returned with the horse Capt. Lewis rode across the rocky mountains   we had this horse imediately cut with 2 others which we had not before thought proper to castrate. we amused ourselves about an hour this after noon looking at the men run their horses, several of them would be thought swift horses in the atlantic states.

WEDNESDAY 21ST MAY 1806.

as our tent is not sufficient to keep off the rain we are compelled to have some other resort for a security from the repeeted showers which fall. we have a small half circular place made and covered with grass which makes a very secure shelter for us to sleep under. we divided our store of merchindize amongst our party for the purpose of precureing some roots &c. of the nativs   to each mans part amounted to about an awl knitting pin a little paint and some thread & 2 Needles which is but a scanty dependance for roots to take us over those Great snowey Barriers (rocky mountains) which is and will be the cause of our Detention in this neighbourhood probably untill the 10 or 15 of June. they are at this time covered deep with snow. the plains on the high country above us is also covered with snow. we eate the last of our meat for Dinner to day, and our only certain dependance is the roots we can precure from the nativs for the fiew articles we have left   those roots with what game we can precure from the wo[o]ds will probably last us untill the arival of the Salmon. if they should not; we have a horse in store ready to be killed which the indians have offered to us.

THURSDAY 22ND MAY 1806

a fine day   we exposed all our baggage to the sun to air and dry, also our roots which we have precured of the nativs. as the greater part of our men have not had any meat to eate for 2 days, and the roots they complain of not being accustomed to live on them altogether we directed a large coalt which was given to us by a young man with an elegant mare [to be killed]. this coalt was fat and was handsom looking meat. late in the evening we were informed that the horse which Capt L. rode over the rocky mountains and which was cut day before yesterday had his hip out of place since that time, and could not walk. Capt. Lewis examined him and thought he could not recover. at 5 p. m. two young men highly decurated in their way came to our camp and informed us that the fat fish were in great numbers in Lewis's river. Shabonos son a small child is dangerously ill. his jaw and throat is much swelled. we apply a poltice of onions, after giveing him some creem of tarter &c.   this day proved to be fine and fair which afforded us an oppertunety of drying our baggage which had got a little wet.

FRIDAY 23RD MAY 1806

The child is something better this morning than it was last night. we apply a fresh poltice of the wild Onion which we repeeted twice in the course of the day. the swelling does not appear to increas any since yesterday. The 4 Indians who visited us to day informed us that they came from their village on Lewis's river two days ride from this place for the purpose of seeing of us and getting a little eye water   I washed their eyes with some eye water and they all left us at 2 P. M. and returned to their villages on the opposit side of this river.

the hunters informed us that they had hunted with great industry all the country between the river and for some distance above and below without the smallest chance of killing any game. they inform us that the high lands are very cold with snow which has fallen for every day or night for several [days] past. our horses which was cut is like to doe well.

[Lewis]   SATURDAY MAY 24TH 1806.

The child was very wrestless last night; it's jaw and the back of it's neck are much more swolen than they were yesterday tho' his fever has abated considerably. we gave it a doze of creem of tartar and applyed a fresh poltice of onions. William Bratton still continues very unwell; he eats heartily digests his food well, and has recovered his flesh almost perfectly yet is so weak in the loins that he is scarcely able to walk, nor can he set upwright but with the greatest pain. we have tried every remidy which our engenuity could devise, or with which our stock of medicines furnished us, without effect. John Sheilds observed that he had seen men in a similar situation restored by violent sweats. Bratton requested that he might be sweated in the manner proposed by Sheilds to which we consented. Sheilds sunk a circular hole of 3 feet diamiter and four feet deep in the earth. he kindled a large fire in the hole and heated well, after which the fire was taken out a seat placed in the center of the hole for the patient with a board at bottom for his feet to rest on; some hoops of willow poles were bent in an arch crossing each over the hole, on these several blankets were thrown forming a secure and thick orning of about 3 feet high. the patient being striped naked was seated under this orning in the hole and the blankets well secured on every side. the patient was furnished with a vessell of water which he sprinkles on the bottom and sides of the hole and by that means creates as much steam or vapor as he could possibly bear,   in this situation he was kept about 20 minutes after which he was taken out and suddonly plunged in cold water twise and was then immediately returned to the sweat hole where he was continued three quarters of an hour longer then taken out covered up in several blankets and suffered to cool gradually. during the time of his being in the sweat hole, he drank copious draughts of a strong tea of horse mint. Sheilds says that he had previously seen the tea of Sinneca snake root used in stead of the mint which was now employed for the want of the other which is not to be found in this country. this experiment was made yesterday; Bratton feels himself much better and is walking about today and says he is nearly free from pain.

at 11 A. M. a canoe arrived with 3 of the natives one of them the sick man of whom I have before made mention as having lost the power of his limbs. he is a cheif of considerable note among them and they seem extreemly anxious for his recovery. as he complains of no pain in any particular part we conceive it cannot be the rheumatism, nor do we suppose that it can be a parelitic attack or his limbs would have been more deminished. we have supposed that it was some disorder which owed it's origine to a diet of particular roots perhaps and such as we have never before witnessed. while at the village of the broken arm we had recommended a diet of fish or flesh for this man and the cold bath every morning. we had also given him a few dozes of creem of tarter and flour of sulphur to be repeated every 3d day. this poor wretch thinks that he feels himself somewhat better but to me there appears to be no visible alteration. we are at a loss what to do for this unfortunate man. we gave him a few drops of Laudanum and a little portable soup.

4 of our party pased the river and visited the lodge of the *broken Arm* for the purpose of traiding some awls which they had made of the links of [a] small chain belonging to one of their steel traps, for some roots. they returned in the evening having been very successfull, they had obtained a good supply of roots and bread of cows. this day has proved warmer than any of the preceeding since we have arrived here.

[Clark]   Sunday 25h May 1806

rained moderately the greater part of last night and this morning untill 6 A.M.   The child is not so well to day as yesterday. I repeeted the creem of tarter and the onion poltice. I caused a swet to be prepared for the Indn. in the same hole which bratten had been swetted in two days past

One of our men purchased a Bear skin of the nativs which was nearly of a cream coloured white. this skin which was the skin of an animal of the middle size of bears together with the defferent sizes colours &c. of those which have been killed by our hunters give me a stronger evidence of the various coloured bear of this country being one species only, than any I have heretofore had. the poil of these bear were infinately longer finer & thicker than the black bear   their tallons also longer & more blunt as worn by digging roots. the bear here is far from being as passive as the common black bear,   they have atacked and fought our hunters already but not so fiercely as those of the Missouri. There are also some of the common black bear in this neighbourhood tho no[t] so common as the other species. we attempted to swet the sick indian but could not suckceed. he was not able either to set up or be supported in the place prepared for him. I therefore deturmined to inform the nativs that nothing but sefere [severe] swetts would restore this disabled man, and even that doubtfull in his present situation.

                                          Monday 26th May 1806

The child something better this morning tho the swelling yet continue. we still apply the onion poltice. I derected what should be done for the disabled man, gave him a fiew doses of creem of tarter & flour sulphur, and some portable supe and directed that he should be taken home & swetted &c.   one of our men saw a salmon in the river today, and two others eat of salmon at the near

village which was brought from Lewis's river. our canoe finished
and put into the water. it will carry 12 men. the [river] riseing
very fast and snow appear to melt on the mountains.

[Lewis]   TUESDAY MAY 27TH 1806

Early this morning we sent Reubin Feilds in surch of the horse
which the indians had given us to kill. at 10 in the morning he returned with the horse and we killed and butchered him; he was
large and in good order. Hohâstillpilp told us that most of the
horses we saw runing at large in this neighbourhood belonged to
himself and his people, and whenever we were in want of meat he
requested that we would kill any of them we wished; this is a piece
of liberallity which would do honour to such as bo[a]st of civilization; indeed I doubt whether there are not a great number of our
countrymen who would see us fast many days before their compassion would excite them to a similar act of liberallity.

Charbono's son is much better today, tho' the swelling on the side
of his neck I believe will terminate in an ugly imposthume [abscess]
a little below the ear. the indians were so anxious that the sick
Cheif should be sweated under our inspection that they requested
we would make a second atte[m]pt today; accordingly the hole was
somewhat enlarged and his father a very good looking old man,
went into the hole with him and sustained him in a proper position during the operation; we could not make him sweat as co-
piously as we wished. after the operation he complained of considerable pain, we gave him 30 drops of laudanum which soon
composed him and he rested very well. this is at least a strong
mark of parental affection. they all appear extreemly attentive
to this sick man nor do they appear to relax their asciduity towards
him notwithstand[ing] he has been sick and helpless upwards of
three years. the Chopunnish appear to be very attentive and kind
to their aged people and treat their women with more rispect than
the nations of the Missouri.

[Clark]   WEDNESDAY MAY 28TH 1806

We sent Goodrich to the village of the *broken arm* for hair to
stuff saddle pads. Jo. & R. Fields set out this morning to hunt to⋅

wards the mountains. at noon Shabono York and Lapage returned, they had obtained 4 bags of the dried roots of Cowse and some bread. in the evening Collins, Shannon & Colter returned with 8 deer. deer were very abundant they informed us, but there was not many bear. The Sick Chief is much better this morning   he can use his hands and arms and seems much pleased with the prospects of recovering,   he says he feels much better than he has done for a great number of months. I sincerly wish that the swetts may restore him. I have consented to repeet the sweets.

The Chopunnish held a council in the morning of the 12th among themselves in respect to the Subject on which we had spoken to them the day before,[2] the result as we learnt was favourable,   they placed confidence in the information they had recived and resolved to pursue our advice. after this council was over the principal chief or the *broken arm,* took the flour of the roots of Cows and thickened the Soup in the Kittles and baskets of all his people,   this being ended he made a harangue the purpote of which was makeing known the deliberations of their councils and impressing the necessity of unanimity among them, and a strict attention to the resolution which had been agreed on in councell; he concluded by enviting all such men as had resolved to abide by the decree of the councill to come and eat, and requested such as would not be so bound to show themselves by not partakeing of the feast. I was told by one of our men who was present in the house, that there was not a decenting voice on this great national question, but all swallowed their objections if any they had, very cheerfully with their mush. dureing the time of this loud animated harangue of the Chief the women cryed wrung their hands, tore their hair and appeared to be in the utmost distress.

after this cerimoney was over, the Chiefs and considerate men came in a body to where we were seated at a little distance from our tent, and two young men at the instance of the nation presented Capt L. and myself each a fine horse. and informed us that they had listened with attention to what we had said and were resolved to pursue our counsels &c.   that as we had not seen the Black foot Indians and the Menetarees of Fort de Prarie they did not think it safe to venter over to the plains of the Missouri, where they would fondly go provided those nations would not kill them.

[2] See entry for May 11, p. 380.

that when we had established a tradeing house on the Missouri as we had promised they would come over and trade for arms amunition &c. and live about us. that it would give them much pleasure to be at peace with those nations altho' they had shed much of their blood. They said that they were pore but their hearts were good. we might be assured of their sincerety   Some of their brave men would go over with us to the Missouri and bring them the news as we wished, and if we could make a peace between themselves and their enimies on the other side of the mountains their nation would go over to the Missouri in the latter end of the summer. on the subject of one of their chiefs accompanying us to the land of the White men they could not yet determine, but that they would let us know before we left them. that the Snow was yet so deep in the mountains that if we attempted to pass, we would certainly perish, and advised us to remain untill after the next full moon when the snow would disappear on the South hill sides and we would find grass for our horses.

Shabonos child is better this day than he was yesterday. he is free from fever. the imposthume is not so large but seems to be advanceing to meturity.

FRIDAY MAY 30TH 1806

Lapage and Shabono set out early this morning to the Indian Village in order to trade with them for roots; Serjt. Gass was sent this morning to obtain some goats hair to stuff the pads of our Saddles. Shannon and Collins were permited to pass the river in order to trade with the nativs and lay in a store of roots and bread for themselves with their proportion of the merchendize as others had done; on landing on the opposit shore the canoe was driven broad side with the full force of a very strong current against some Standing trees and instantly filled with water and sunk. Potts who was with them is an indifferent swimmer, it was with dificuelty he made the land. they lost three blankets and a Blanket Cappo and their pittance of merchindize. in our bear state of clothing this was a serious loss. all our invalides are on the recovery. we gave the sick Chief a severe *Swet* to day, shortly after which he could move one of his legs and thy's and work his toes pritty well,   the other leg he can move a little; his fingers and arms seem to be almost entirely restored. he seems highly delighted with his recovery. I begin to entertain strong hope of his recovering by these sweats. one of the men brought me to day some onions from the high plains of a different species from those near the borders of the river as they are also from the shive or small onion noticed below the Falls of Columbia. these onions were as large as an nutmeg, they generally grow double or two bulbs connected by the same tissue of radicles; each bulb has two long line[a]r flat solid leaves. this onion is exceedingly crisp and delicately flavoured indeed. I think more sweet and less strong than any I ever tasted, it is not yet perfectly in blume, the parts of the flower are not distinct.

Sunday June 1st 1806

This morning Geo: Drewyer accompanied by Hohâstillpilp set out in serch of two tomahawks of ours which we have understood were in the possession of certain indians resideing at a distance in the plains on the South Side of Flat Head river; one is a pipe tomahawk which Cap L. left at our camp on Musquetor Creek and the other was stolen from me whilst we lay at the forks of this and Chopunnish rivers last fall. Colter and Willard set out this morning on a hunting excurtion towards the quawmash grounds beyond Collins creek. we begin to feel some anxiety with respect to Sergt. Ordway and party who were sent to Lewis's river for salmon; we have receved no intellegence of them since they set out. we desired Drewyer to make some enquiry after the *Twisted hair;* the old man has not been as good as his word with respect to encamping near us, and we fear we shall be at a loss to procure guides to conduct us by the different routs we wish to pursue from Travillers rest to the waters of the Missouri.

Monday June 2nd 1806

McNeal and York were sent on a tradeing voyage over the river this morning. having exhosted all our merchindize we were obliged to have recourse to every Subterfuge in order to prepare in the most ample manner in our power to meet that wretched portion of our journey, the Rocky Mountains, where hungar and Cold in their most rigorous form assail the waried traveller; not any of us have yet forgotten our sufferings in those mountains in September last, I think it probable we never shall. Our traders McNeal and York are furnished with the buttons which Capt L —. and my self cut off of our coats, some eye water and Basilicon which we made for that purpose and some phials of eye water and some tin boxes which Capt L. had brought from Philadelphia. in the evening they returned without about 3 bushels of roots and some bread haveing made a suckcessfull voyage, not much less pleasing to us than the return of a good cargo to an East India merchant.

Drewyer arived this evening with Neeshneparkkeeook [Cut Nose] and Hohashillpilp who had accompanied him to the lodge of the person who had our tomahawks. he obtained both the tomahawks principally by the influence of the former of those Chiefs. the one which had been stolen we prized most as it was the private property of the late Serjt. Floyd and I was desirous of returning it to his friends. The man who had this tomahawk had purchased it from the man who had stolen it, and was himself at the moment of their arival just expireing. his relations were unwilling to give up the tomahawk as they intended to bury it with the deceased owner, but were at length [induced] to do so for the consideration of a handkerchief, two strands of beeds, which drewyer gave them and two horses given by the Chiefs to be Killed agreeable to their custom at the grave of the deceased. a Wife of Neeshneeparkkeeook died some short time sence, himself and her relations sacrificed 28 horses to her.

about noon Sergt. Ordway Frazier and Wiser returned with 17 salmon and some roots of the cows; the distance was so great from whence they brought the fish, that most of them were nearly spoiled. those fish were as fat as any I ever saw; sufficiently so to cook themselves without the addition of Grease or butter; those which were sound were extreemly delicious; their flesh is of a fine rose colour with a small admixture of yellow. our horses are all recovering & I have no hesitation in declareing that I believe that the Indian method of guilding [is] preferable to that practised by ourselves.

TUESDAY JUNE 3RD 1806

Our invalids are all on the recovery; bratten is much stronger and can walk about with considerable ease. the Indian chief appears to be gradually recovering the use of his limbs, and the child is nearly well; the inflomation on his neck continues but the swelling appears to subside. we still continue the application of the onion poltice. To day the Indians dispatched an express over the mountains to Travellers rest or to the neighbourhood of that creek on Clark's river in order to learn from a band of Flat-Heads who inhabit that river and who have probably wintered on Clarks river near the enterance of travellers rest Creek, the occurences which have taken place on the East side of the mountains dureing last winter. this is the band which we first met with on that river. the mountains being practicable for this express we thought it probable that we could also pass, but the Chiefs informs us that several of the Creek's would yet swim our horses, that there was no grass and that the road was extreemly deep and slipery; they inform us that we may pass conveniently in twelve or fourteen days. we have come to a resolution to remove from hence to the quawmash Grounds beyond Colins Creek on the 10th to hunt in that neighbourhood a fiew days, if possible lay in a stock of meat, and then attempt the mountains about the middle of this month. I begin to lose all hope of any dependance on the Salmon as this river will not fall sufficiently to take them before we shall leave it, and as yet I see no appearance of their running near the shore as the indians informed us they would in the course of a fiew days.

Thursday June 5th 1806.

Colter and Bratten were permitted to visit the Indian Village to day for the purpose of tradeing for roots and bréad, they were fortunate and made a good return. We gave the Indian Chief another sweat to-day, continuing it as long as he could bear it,   in the evening he was very languid but still [continued] to improve in the use of his limbs. the Child is recovereing fast. I applied a plaster of sarve [salve] made of the rozen of the long leafed pine, Beaswax and Bears oil mixed, which has subsided the inflomation entirely, the part is considerably swelled and hard. in the evening Reuben Fields, G. Shannon, Labiech, & Collins returned from the chaise and brought with them five deer and a *brown Bear*.

CHAPTER XXIX

In the Bitter Root Mountains

[Clark]

The Sick Chief is much mended, he can bear his weight on his legs and recovers strength. the Child has nearly recovered. *The Cut nose* and ten or 12 came over today to visit us, two of those were of the tribes from the plains of Lewis's river whome we had not before seen; one of those men brought a horse [for] which I gave a tomahawk which I had exchanged for with the chief of the Clahclahlah's Nation below the Great rapids of Columbia, and [a] broken-down horse which was not able to cross the mountains. we also exchanged 2 of our indifferent horses for sound back horses. in the evening several foot races were run by the men of our party and the Indians; after which our party devided and played at prisoners base untill night. after dark the fiddle was played and the party amused themselves in danceing. one of those Indians informed us that we could not cross the mountains untill the full of the next moon; or about the 1st of July. if we attempted it Sooner our horses would be three days without eating, on the top of the Mountns.   this information is disagreeable to us, in as much as it admits of some doubt, as to the time most proper for us to Set out. at all events we Shall Set out at or about the time which the indians Seem to be generally agreed would be the most proper. about the middle of this month.

Tuesday June 10th 1806.

rose early this morning and had all the horses collected except one of Whitehouses horses which could not be found, an Indian promised to find the horse and bring him on to us at the quawmash fields at which place we intend to delay a fiew days for the laying in some meat by which time we calculate that the Snows will have melted more off the mountains and the grass raised to a sufficient hight for our horses to live. we packed up and Set out at 11 A M we set out with the party each man being well mounted and a light load on a 2d horse, besides which we have several supernumary horses in case of accident or the want of provisions, we therefore feel ourselves perfectly equiped for the Mountains. we assended the hills which are very high and about three miles in extent. the pass of Collins Creek was deep and extreemly difficult tho' we passed without sustaining further injury than wetting some of our roots and bread. The Country through which we passed is extreemly fertile and generally free from Stone, is well timbered with several Species of fir, long leafed pine and Larch. the undergrowth is choke cherry near the watercourses, black alder, a large species of red root now in blume, a Growth which resembles the poppaw in it's leaf, and which bears a berry with five valves of a deep purple colour, two species of shoemate, seven bark, perple haw, service berry, Goose berry, wildrose, honey suckle which bears a white berry, and a Species of dwarf pine which grows about 10 or 12 feet high. after we encamped this evening we Sent out our hunters; Collins killed a doe on which we Suped much to our satisfaction. we had not reached the top of the river hills before we were overtaken by a party of 8 Indians who informed me that they were gowing to the quawmash flatts to hunt; their object I belive is the expectation of being fed by us in which however *kind as they have been* we must disappoint them at this moment as it is necessary that we should use all frugallaty as well as employ every exertion to provide meat for our journey. they have encamped with us.

THURSDAY JUNE 12TH 1806.

All our hunters except Gibson returned about noon; none of them had killed any thing except Shields who brought with him two deer. the days are very worm and the Musquetors our old companions have become very troublesome.

The Cutnose informed us on the 10th before we left him that two young Chiefs would overtake us with a view to accompany us to the Falls of the Missouri and probably to the Seat of our Governmt. our camp is agreeably situated in a point of timbered land on the eastern borders of an extensive leavel and butifull prarie which is intersected by several small branches near the bank of one of which our camp is placed. the quawmash is now in blume   at a Short distance it resembles a lake of fine clear water, so complete is this deseption that on first Sight I could have sworn it was water.

[Lewis]   SATURDAY JUNE 14TH 1806.

We had all our articles packed up and made ready for an early departure in the morning. our horses were caught and most of them hubbled and otherwise confined in order that we might not be detained. from hence to traveller's rest we shall make a forsed march; at that place we shal probably remain one or two days to rest ourselves and horses and procure some meat. we have now been detained near five weeks in consequence of the snows; a serious loss of time at this delightfull season for traveling. I am still apprehensive that the snow and the want of food for our horses will prove a serious imbarrassment to us as at least four days journey of our rout in these mountains lies over hights and along a ledge of mountains never intirely destitute of snow. every body seems anxious to be in motion, convinced that we have not now any time to delay if the calculation is to reach the United States this season; this I am detirmined to accomplish if within the compass of human power.

[Clark]   SUNDAY JUNE 15TH 1806.

Collected our horses early with the intention of makeing an early Start. Some hard Showers of rain detained us we took our final departu[r]e from the quawmash fields and proceeded with much dificuelty owing to the Situation of the road which was very sliprey, and it was with great dificulty that the loaded horses Could assend the hills and Mountains   the[y] frequently sliped down both assending and decending those steep hills. the rain seased and sun shown out. after detaining about 2 hours we proceeded on passing over some ruged hills or Spurs of the rocky Mountain, passing the

Creek on which I encamped on the 17th Sept. last. we passed through bad fallen timber and a high Mountain this evening. from the top of this Mountain I had an extensive view of the rocky Mountains to the South and the Columbian plains for [a] great extent   also the SW. Mountains and a range of high Mountains which divides the waters of Lewis's & Clarks rivers and seems to termonate nearly a West cours[e].

MUNDAY 16TH JUNE 1806

Collected our horses early and Set out 7 AM   proceeded on up the Creek through a gladey swompy bottom covered with grass and quawmash and through most intolerable bad fallen timber over a high Mountain on which great quantity of Snow is yet lying premisquissly through the thick wood, and in maney places the banks of snow is 4 feet deep. we no[o]ned it or dined on a small creek in a small open Vally where we found some grass for our horses to eate, altho' serounded by snow   This morning Windsor bursted his rifle near the Muzzle. Vegitation is propotionable backward; the dog tooth Violet is just in blume, the honeysuckle, huckleberry and a small Species of white maple are beginning to put forth their leaves, where they are clear of the Snow,   those appearances in this comparatively low region augers but unfavourably with respect to the practibility of passing the Mountains, however we deturmine to proceed, accordingly after takeing a hasty meal we set out and continued our rout through a thick wood much obstructed with fallen timber, and interupted by maney Steep reveins and hills which wer very high.

the Snow has increased in quantity so much that the great part of our rout this evening was over the Snow which has become sufficiently firm to bear our horses, otherwise it would have been impossible for us to proceed as it lay in emince masses in some places 8 or ten feet deep. We found much dificulty in finding the road, as it was so frequently covered with snow. we arived early in the evening at the place I had killed and left the flesh of a horse for the party in my rear last Septr.   here is a Small glade in which there is some grass, not a Suffecency of [for] our horses, but we thought it adviseable to remain here all night as we apprehended if we proceeded further we should find less grass. The air is pleasant in the course of the day, but becomes very cold before morning notwithstanding the shortness of the night.

TUESDAY JUNE 17TH 1806

We collected our horses and set out early; we found it dificuelt and dangerous to pass the creek in consequence of it's debth and rapidity; we avoided two other passes of the creek, by assending a steep rockey and difficuelt hill. beyond this creek the road assends the mountain to the hight of the main leading ridges, which divides the waters of the Kooskooske and Chopunnish Riv's. This mountain we ascended about 3 miles when we found ourselves invelloped in snow from 8 to 12 feet deep even on the South Side of the mountain. I was in front and could only prosue the derection of the road by the trees which had been peeled by the nativs for the iner bark of which they scraped and eate, as those pealed trees were only to be found scattered promisquisley, I with great difficulty prosued the direction of the road one mile further to the top of the mountain where I found the snow from 12 to 15 feet deep, but fiew trees with the fairest exposure to the Sun; here was Winter with all it's rigors; the air was cold my hands and feet were benumed.

we knew that it would require four days to reach the fish weare at the enterance of Colt Creek, provided we were so fortunate as to be enabled to follow the p[r]oper ridge of the mountains to lead us to that place; of this all of our most expert woodsmen and principal guides were extreemly doubtfull; Short of that point we could not hope for any food for our horses not even under wood itself as the whole was covered many feet deep in snow. if we proceeded and Should git bewildered in those Mountains the certainty was that we Should lose all of our horses and consequently our baggage enstrements perhaps our papers and thus eventually resque the loss of our discoveries which we had already made if we should be so fortunate as to escape with life. the snow bore our horses very well and the traveling was therefore infinately better than the obstruction of rocks and fallen timber which we met with in our passage over last fall when the snow lay on this part of the ridge in detached spop[t]s only.

under these circumstances we conceived it madness in this stage of the expedition to proceed without a guide who could certainly conduct us to the fishwears on the Kooskooske, as our horses could not possibly sustain a journey of more than 4 or 5 days without food. we therefore come to the resolution to return with our horses while they were yet strong and in good order, and indeaver to keep them so untill we could precure an indian to conduct us over the Snowey Mountains, and again to proceed as soon as we could precure such a guide, knowing from the appearance of the snows that if we remained untill it had disolved sufficiently for us to follow the road that we should not be enabled to return to the United States within this season. having come to this resolution, we ordered the party to make a deposit of all the baggage which we had not imediate use for, and also all the roots and bread of Cows which they had except an allowance for a fiew days to enable them to return to some place at which we could subsist by hunting untill we precured a guide. we left our instrements, and I even left the most of my papers believing them safer here than to Wrisk them on horse back over the road, rocks and water which we had passed.

our baggage being laid on Scaffolds and well covered, we began our retragrade march at 1 P. M. haveing remaind. about three hours on this Snowey mountain. we returned by the rout we had advanced to hungary Creek, which we assended about 2 miles and encamped. we had here more grass for our horses than the proceeding evening, yet it was but scant. the party were a good deel dejected, tho' not as much so as I had apprehended they would have been. this is the first time since we have been on this tour that we have ever been compelled to retreat or make a retragrade march.

Wednesday June 18th 1806

We dispatched Drewyer and Shannon to the Chopunnish Indians in the plains beyond the Kooskooske in order to hasten the arrival of the Indians who promised to accompany us, or to precure a guide at all events and rejoin us as soon as possible. We sent by them a riffle [rifle] which we offered as a reward to any of them who would engage to conduct us to Clarks river at the entrance of Travellers rest Creek; we also directed them if they found difficuelty in induceing any of them to accompany us to offer the reward of two other guns to be given them immediately and ten horses at the falls of Missouri.

we had not proceeded far this morning before J. Potts cut his leg very badly with one of the large knives; he cut one of the large veins on the iner side of the leg; Colters horse fell with him in passing hungary creek and himself and horse were driven down the Creek a considerable distance roleing over each other among the rocks. he fortunately escaped with[out] much injurey or the loss of his gun. he lost his blanket. at 1 P. M. we returned to the glade on a branch of hungary creek where we had dined on the 16th instant. here we again halted and dined. after dinner we proceeded on to the near fork of Collins Creek and encamped in a pleasant situation at the upper part of the Meadows about 2 miles above our encampment of the 15 inst.   we sent out several hunters but they returned without having killed any thing. they saw a number of large fish in the creek and shot at them several times without suckcess. we hope by the means of the fish together with what deer and bear we can kill to be enabled to subsist untill our guide arives without the necessaty of returning to the quaw-mash flats. there is great abundance of good food here to sustain our horses. we are in flattering expectations of the arrival of two young chiefs who informed us that they intended to accompany us to the U. States, and Should Set out from their village in 9 nights after we left them [or] on the 19th inst.   if they set out at that time Drewyer & Shannon will meet them, and probably join us on the 20th or 21st   Musquetors Troublesome.

FRIDAY JUNE 20TH 1806

Labiesh & Crusat returned late in the evening with one deer which the former had killed. the hunters assured us that their greatest exertions would not enable them to support us here more than one or two days longer, from the great scercity of game and the dificuelt access of the Country, the under brush being very thick and great quantities of fallen timber. as we shall necessarily be compelled to remain more than two days for the return of Drewyer & Shannon we determine to return in the morning as far as the quawmash flatts, and endeaver to lay in another stock of meat for the Mountains, our former stock now being nearly exhosted as well as what we have killed on our rout.

by returning to the quawmash flatts we shall sooner be informed wheather or not we can procure a guide to conduct us through the

Mountains; Should we fail in precureing one, we are deturmined to wrisk a passage on the following plan immediately, because should we wait much longer, or untill the Snow disolves in such a manner as to enable us to follow the road we cannot expect to reach the U, States this Winter; this is that Capt L. or myself shall take four of our most expert woodsmen with 3 or four of our best horses and proceed two days in advance takeing a plentifull supply of provisions. for this party to follow the road by the mark the indi[a]ns have made in many places with their baggage on the Sides of the trees by rubbing against them, and to blaize the trees with a tomahawk as they proceed. that after proceeding two days in advance of Hungary Creek, two of those men would be sent back to the party who by the time of their return to hungary Creek would have reached that place. the men So returning would be enabled to inform the main party of the probable suckcess of the proceeding party in finding the road and of their probable progress, in order that should it be necessary, the main party by a delay of a day or two a[t] hungary Creek, should give the advance time to make the road through before the main party could overtake them, and thus prevent delay on that part of the rout where no food is to be obtained for our horses. Should it so happen that the advance should not find the road by the marks of the trees after attempting it for two days, the whole of them would return to the main party. in which Case we would bring back our baggage and attempt a passage over the Mountains through the Country of the Shoshones further to the South, by way of the main S Westerly fork of Lewis's river and Madisons or Gallitins river's, where from the information of the Chopunnish, there is a passage where [which] at this season of the year is not obstructed by snow, though the round is very distant and would require at least a month in it's performance. The Shoshones informed us when we first met with them that there was a passage across the Mountains in that quarter but represented the difficuelties arriseing from Steep ruggid high Mountains, and also an extensive and barren plain which was to be passed without game, as infinitely more difficuelt than the rout by which we came.

Saturday June 21st 1806

We collected our horses early and Set out on our return to the flatts. we all felt some mortification in being thus compelled to retrace our Steps through this tedious and difficuelt part of our rout, obstructed with brush and innumerable logs and fallen timber which renders the traveling distressing and even dangerous to our horses. at the pass of Collin's Creek we met two indians who were on their way over the mountains, they had brought with themm the three horses and the Mule which had left us and returned to the quawmash ground. as well as we could understand the indians they informed us they had Seen Geo. Drewyer & Shannon, and that they would not return untill the expiration of two days. the cause why Drewyer & Shannon did not return with these men we are at a loss to account for. we pressed those indians to remain with us and conduct us over the Mountains on the return of Drewyer & Shannon. they consented to remain two nights for us and accordingly deposited their Stores of roots & Bread in the bushes at no great distance and after Dinner returned with us, as far as the little prarie about 2 Miles distance from the Creek,   here they halted with their horses and informed us they would remain untill we overtook them or at least 2 nights. at 7 in the evening we found ourselves once more at our old encampment where we Shall anxiously await the return of Drewyer & Shannon.

MONDAY JUNE 23RD 1806

Apprehensive from Drewyer & Shannons delay that they had met with some difficuelty in precureing a guide, and also that the two indians who had promised to wait two nights for us would set out today, we thought it most adviseable to dispatch Wizer & Frazier to them this morning with a view if possible to detain them a day or two longer; and directed that in the event of their not being able to detain the indians, that Sergt. Gass, Jo. & R. Fields & Wiser should accompany the Indians by whatever rout they might take to travellers rest and blaize the trees well as they proceeded, and wait at that place untill our arival with the party. at 4 P. M. Shannon Drewyer & Whitehouse returned. Shannon & Drewyer brought with them three indians who had consented to accompany us to the falls of the Missouri for the Compensation of 2 guns. one of those men is the brother of the *cutnose* and the other two are the Same who presented Capt L. and myself with a horse on a former occasion at the Lodge of the broken arm, and the two who promised to pursue us in nine nights after we left the river, or on the 19 th inst. Those are all young men of good Charrector and much respected by their nation.

TUESDAY JUNE 24TH 1806

We collected our horses early this morning and set out accompanied by our 3 guides. Colter joined us this morning haveing killed a Bear, which from his discription of it's poverty and distance we did not think proper to send after. We nooned it as usial at Collin's Creek where we found Frazier, solus; the other four men haveing gorn in pursute of the two indians who had set out from Collin's Creek two hours before Fraziers arrival. after dinner we continued our rout to fish Creek   here we found Sargt. Gass, Wiser and the two indian men whome they had prevail'd on to remain at that place untill our arival; Jos. & R. Fields had killed one Small deer only, and of this they had been liberal to the indians insomuch that they had no provisions; they had gorn on to the branch of hungary creek at which we shall noon it tomorrow in order to hunt. we had fine grass for our horses this evening.

WEDNESDAY JUNE 25TH 1806

last evening the indians entertained us with setting the fir trees on fire. they have a great number of dry limbs near their bodies which when Set on fire create a very sudden and emmence blaize from bottom to top of those tall trees.[1] they are a boutifull object in this situation at night. this exhibition remi[n]de[d] me of a display of firewo[r]ks. the nativs told us that their object in Setting those trees on fire was to bring fair weather for our journey. We collected our horses and set out at an early hour this morning. one of our guides complained of being unwell, a Symptom which I did not much like as such complaints with an indian is generally the prelude to his abandoning any enterprize with which he is not well pleased. we left 4 of those indians at our encampment they promised to pursue us in a fiew hours. at 11 A.M. we arrived at the branch of hungary Creek where we found Jo. & R. Fields. they

---

[1] Clearly the highly inflammable Alpine fir, *Abies lasiocarpa*.

had not killed anything. here we halted and dined and our guides overtook us. at this place the squaw collected a parcel of roots of which the Shoshones Eat. it is a small knob root a good deel in flavour and consistency like the Jerusolem artichoke. after dinner we continued our rout to hungary creek and encamped about one and a half miles below our Encampment of the 61th [sic] inst: The indians all continue with us and I beleive are disposed to be faithfull to their engagements. Capt. L. gave the sick indian a small buffalow robe which he brought from the Missouri, this indian having no other Covering except his mockersons and a dressed Elk skin without the hair.

THURSDAY JUNE 26TH 1806

We collected our horses and set out early and proceeded on Down hungary Creek a fiew miles and assended to the summit of the mountain where we deposited our baggage on the 17th inst. found everything safe and as we had left them. the Snow which was 10 feet 10 inches deep on the top of the mountain, had sunk to 7 feet tho' perfectly hard and firm. we made some fire cooked dinner and dined, while our horses stood on snow 7 feet deep at least. after dinner we packed up and proceeded on. the Indians hastened us off and informed us that it was a considerable distance to the place they wished to reach this evening where there was grass for our horses. accordingly we Set out with our guides who led us over and along the Steep Sides of tremendious Mountains entirely covered with Snow except about the roots of the trees where the Snow was partially melted and exposed a small spot of earth.

we assended and decended several steep lofty hights but keeping on the dividing ridge of the Chopunnish & Kooskooske river we passed no Stream of water. late in the evening much to the Satisfaction of ourselves and the Comfort of the horses we arived at the desired Spot and Encamped on the steep side of a Mountain convenient to a good Spring. here we found an abundance of fine grass for our horses. this Situation was the Side of an untimbered mountain with a fair Southern aspect where the snow from appearance had been disolved about 10 days, the grass was young and tender of course and had much the appearance of the Green Swoard. there is a great abundance of [a] Species of beargrass which

grows on every part of those Mountains, its growth is luxuriant and
continues green all winter but the horses will not eate it. Soon
after we had encamped we were overtaken by a Chopunnish man
who had pursued us with a view to accompany Capt Lewis to the
falls of Missouri. we were now informed that the two young men
we met on the 21st and detained several days were going on a party
of pleasure mearly to the *Oat-lash-shoots* or as they call them *Shalees* a band of the *Tush-she-pâh* Nation [Flatheads] who reside on
Clarks river in the neighbourhood of the Mouth of Travelers rest.
I was taken yesterday with a violent pain in my head which has
tormented me ever since most violently.

FRIDAY JUNE 27TH 1806

the road Still continue[d] on the hights of the Dividing ridge
on which we had traveled yesterday for 9 Ms. or to our encampment of the 16th Septr. last. about 1 M. short of the encampment
we halted by the request of the Guides a fiew minits on an ellevated point and smoked a pipe   on this eminance the nativs
have raised a conic mound of Stons of 6 or 8 feet high and erected
a pine pole of 15 feet long. from this place we had an extencive
view of these Stupendeous Mountains principally covered with
snow like that on which we stood; we were entirely serounded by
those mountains from which to one unacquainted with them it
would have Seemed impossible ever to have escaped, in short without the assistance of our guides, I doubt much whether we who had
once passed them could find our way to Travellers rest in their
present situation for the marked trees on which we had placed considerable reliance are much fewer and more difficuelt to find than
we had apprehended. those indians are most admireable pilots; we
find the road wherever the snow has disappeared tho' it be only
for a fiew paces.

after haveing smoked the pipe and contemplating this Scene
Sufficient to have dampened the Sperits of any except such hardy
travellers as we have become, we continued our march and at the
dist[ance] of 3 M. decended a steep Mountain and passed two small
branches of the Chopunnish river just above their fo[r]k, and again
assend the ridge on which we passed. at the distance of 7 M. arived
at our Encampment of 16th Septr. last passed 3 small branches
passed on a dividing ridge rugid and we arived at a Situation very

similar to our situation of last night tho' [as] the ridge was somewhat higher and the snow had not been so long disolved of course
there was but little grass. here we Encamped for the night haveing
traveled 28 Ms. over these mountains without releiving the horses
from their packs or their haveing any food. our Meat being exhosted we issued a point of *Bears Oil* to a mess which with their
boiled roots made an agreeable dish. Jo. Potts leg which had been
much Swelled and inflaimed for several days is much better this
evening and givs him but little pain. we applied the pounded root
& leaves of wild ginger from which he found great relief. My head
has not pained me so much to day as yesterday and last night.

SATURDAY JUNE 28TH 1806

we continued our rout along the dividing ridge over knobs &
through deep hollows passed our encampmt of the 14 Sept. last
near the forks of the road leaving the one on which we had come one
leading to the fishery to our right imediately on the dividing ridge.
at 12 oClock we arived at an untimberd. side of a mountain with a
southern aspect just above the fishery   here we found an abundance of grass for our horses as the guid[e]s had informed us. as
our horses were hungary and much fatiegued and from information no other place where we could obtain grass for them within
the reach of this evening's travel we deturmined to remain at this
place all night haveing come 13 M. only. the water was distant
from our Encampment we therefore melted snow and used the
water. the whole of the rout of this day was over deep Snow. we
find the travelling on the Snow not worse than without it, as [the]
easy passage it givs us over rocks and fallen timber fully compen-
sates for the inconvenience of sliping, certain it is that we travel
considerably faster on the snow than without it. the snow sinks
from 2 to 3 inches with a horse, is course and firm and seems to
be formed of the larger particles of the Snow; the Surface of the
Snow is reather harder in the morning than after the sun shines
on it a fiew hours, but it is not in that situation so dense as to prevent the horses from obtaining good foothold.

SUNDAY JUNE 29TH 1806

We colected our horses and Set out haveing previously dispatched Drewyer & R. Fields to the warm Springs to hunt. we

prosued the hights of the ridge on which we have been passing for several days; it termonated at the distance of 5 Ms. from our encampment, and we decended to & passed the Main branch of Kooskooke 1½ Ms. above the enterance of Glade Creek which falls in on the N. E. side. we bid adew to the Snow. near the River we found a Deer which the hunters had killed and left us. this was a fortunate supply as all our bears oil was now exhosted and we were reduced to our roots alone without salt. beyond this river we assended a steep Mountain about 2 Miles to it's sumit where we found the old road which we had passed on as we went out, comeing in on our right, the road was now much plainer and much beaten. at noon we arived at the quawmash flatts on Vally Creek and halted to graize our horses and dined haveing traveled 12 miles   here is a pretty little plain of about 50 acres plentifully stocked with quawmash and from appearance this forms one of the principal Stages of the indians who pass the mountains on this road. after dinner we continued our march 7 Ms further to the worm Springs where we arrived early in the evening.

Those Worm or Hot Springs are Situated at the base of a hill of no considerable hight, on the N. Side and near the bank of travellers rest Creek which is at that place about 10 yds wide.[2] these Springs issue from the bottom and through the interstices of a grey freestone rock, the rock rises in irregular masy clifts in a circular range, arround the Springs on their lower Side. imediately above the Springs on the creek there is a handsom little quawmash plain of about 10 acres. the principal spring is about the temperature of the Warmest baths used at the Hot Springs in Virginia. in this bath which had been prepared by the Indians by stopping the river with Stone and mud, I bathed and remained in 10 minits   it was with dificuelty I could remain this long and it causd. a profuse swe[a]t. two other bold Springs adjacent to this are much warmer, their heat being so great as to make the hand of a person Smart extreemly when immerced. we think the temperature of those Springs about the Same as that of the hotest of the hot Springs of Virginia. both the Men and the indians amused themselves with the use of the bath this evening. I observe after the indians remaining in the hot bath as long as they could bear it run and plunge themselves into the creek the water of which is

---

[2] The march of seven miles farther has brought him over the Lolo Pass, the last divide of the Bitterroot Mountains and down to Lolo Creek.

now as cold as ice can make it; after remaining here a fiew minits they return again to the worm bath repeeting the transision several times but always ending with the worm bath. saw the tracks of 2 bear footed indians.

MONDAY JUNE 30TH 1806

just as we had prepard. to set out at an early hour, a deer came in to lick at the Springs and one of our hunters killed it; this secured to us our dinner. and we proceeded down the Creek, sometimes in the bottoms and at other times on the tops or along the Steep sides of the ridge to the N. of the Creek. at 1½ M. we passd our encampment of the 12th of Septr. last. we noon'd it at the place we had on the 12 of Septr. last   whiles here Shields killed a deer on the N. fork near the road. after dinner we resumed our march. soon after setting out Shields killed another deer, and we picked up 3 others which G Drewyer had killed along the road. Deer are very abundant in the neighbourhood of travellers rest of boath Species, also some big horn and Elk. a little before Sunset we arrived at our old encampment on the S. side of the Creek a little above its enterance into Clarks river.[3] here we Encamped with a view to remain 2 days in order to rest ourselves and horses and make our final arrangements for Seperation. we found no signs of the Oatlashshots haveing been here lately. the Indians express much concern for them and apprehend that the Minetarries of Fort d[e] Prarie have destroyed them in the course of the last Winter and Spring, and mention the tracts of the bearfooted indians which we saw yesterday as an evidence of their being much distressed. our horses have stood the journey suprisinly well and only want a fiew days rest to restore them.

During the winter at Fort Clatsop Lewis and Clark had decided that when they returned to Traveller's Rest, where they now are, they would divide the party in order to make two essential explorations which they had not made on the westward journey. They now work out the details.

Lewis is to traverse the route to the Great Falls which they are

3 Traveller's Rest, in Bitterroot Valley.

sure is shorter and better than the one they took outbound. He will go up the Hellgate and Blackfoot Rivers, cross the divide, and go down to the Great Falls by way of either Dearborn or Sun River. Then he will explore Marias River, to "ascertain whether any branch . . . lies as far north" as 50°. (This represents the fixed purpose to find a navigable affluent of the Missouri by which the carriage of Canadian furs can be diverted to American ports.) To accompany him he now selects Gass, Drewyer, the two Fields brothers, Frazier, and Werner. Besides these, Thompson, Goodrich, and McNeal will go with him as far as the Great Falls portage, where they will raise the cache, put the equipment in order, and await the detachment of Clark's force that is to join them there.

Clark will take the rest of the party to the forks of the Beaverhead, where the boats were left last fall. After the boats have been put in condition, he will select a detachment to take them to the Great Falls and help those whom Lewis has left there portage the whole outfit round the falls. (These two detachments will then descend the Missouri by boat to the general rendezvous, the mouth of the Yellowstone, picking up Lewis and his small party at the mouth of the Marias.) Clark will take the others overland to the Yellowstone and down it to some point where it appears to become navigable. From that point he will send Sergeant Pryor with the horses to the mouth of the Yellowstone. After making dugouts, he and the others will take them down the Yellowstone to its mouth.

[Lewis]   Wednesday July 2ed 1806.

in the course of the day we had much conversation with the [Nez Percé] indians by signs, our only mode of communicating our ideas. they informed us that they wished to go in surch of the Cotslash-shoots their friends and intended leaving us tomorrow morning, I prevailed on them to go with me as far as the East branch of Clark's River and put me on the road to the Missouri. I gave the Cheif a medal of the small size; he insisted on exchanging names with me according to their custom which was accordingly done and I was called Yo-me-kol-lick which interpreted is *the white bearskin foalded.*[4] in the evening the indians run their horses, and we

4 A tribute — they name him after the grizzly.

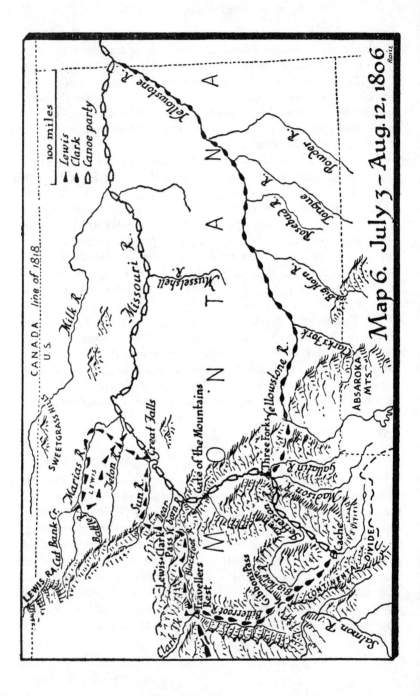

Map 6. July 3 – Aug. 12, 1806

100 miles

Lewis
Clark
Canoe party

CANADA line of 1818
U.S.

LEWIS R. Cut Bank Cr.
SWEETGRASS HILLS
Milk R.
Marias R.
Teton R.
LEWIS
Battle R.
Sun R.
Great Falls
Missouri R.
Musselshell R.
Yellowstone R.
Powder R.
Tongue R.
Rosebud R.
Big Horn R.
Clark's Fork
ABSAROKA MTS.
Three Forks-Yellowstone R.
Gallatin R.
Madison R.
Jefferson R.
Gate of the Mountains
Lewis-Clark Pass (near)
Blackfoot R.
Travellers Rest
Clark Fk.
Bitterroot R.
Gibbons Pass
Big Hole P.
Cache
CONTINENTAL DIVIDE
Salmon R.

M O N T A N A

Ross

had several foot races betwen the natives and our party with various
success. these are a race of hardy strong athletic active men. Goodrich and McNeal are both very unwell with the pox which they
contracted last winter with the Chinnook women   this forms
my inducement principally for taking them to the falls of the
Missouri where during an interval of rest they can use the murcury
freely.

[Clark]   WEDNESDAY JULY 2ND 1806

We gave the second gun to our guides agreeable to our promis,
and to each we gave Powder & ball   I had the greater part of the
meat dried for to subsist my party in the Mountains between the
head of Jeffersons & Clarks rivers where I do not expect to find any
game to kill. had all of our arms put in the most prime order two
of the rifles have unfortunately bursted near the muscle [muzzle],
Shields cut them off and they shute tolerable well   one which is
very short we exchanged with the Indian whoe he had given a
longer gun to induce them to pilot us across the Mountains. we
caused every man to fill his horn with powder & have a sufficiency
of Balls &c.   the last day in passing down Travellers rest Creek
Capt. Lewis fell down the side of a Steep Mountain near 40 feet but
fortunately receved no damage. his hors was near falling on him
but fortunately recovered and they both escaped unhurt.

CHAPTER XXX

Lewis's Short–Cut to the Missouri,
and Exploration of Maria's River

[Lewis] Thursday July 3rd 1806.

All arrangements being now compleated for carrying into effect the several scheemes we had planed for execution on our return, we saddled our horses and set out   I took leave of my worthy friend and companion Capt. Clark and the party that accompanyed him. I could not avoid feeling much concern on this occasion although I hoped this seperation was only momentary. I proceeded down Clark's river [the Bitterroot] seven miles with my party of nine men and five indians. here the Indians recommended our passing the river which was rapid and 150 yds. wide. 2 miles above this place I passed the entrance of the East branch of Clark's River [the Hellgate] which discharges itself by two channels; the water of this river is more terbid than the main stream and is from 90 to 120 yds. wide. as we had no other means of passing the river we busied ourselves collecting dry timber for the purpose of constructing rafts; timber being scarce we found considerable difficulty in procuring as much as made three small rafts. the Indians swam over their horses and drew over their baggage in little basons of deer skins which they constructed in a very few minutes for that purpose. we drove our horses in after them and they followed to the opposite shore. I remained myself with two men who could scarcely swim untill the last; by this time the raft by passing so frequently had fallen a considerable distance down the river to a rapid and difficult part of it crouded with several small Islands and willow bars which were now overflown; with these men I set out on the raft and was soon hurried down with the current a mile and a half before we made shore, on our approach to the shore the raft sunk and I was drawn off the raft by a bush and swam on shore   the two men remained on the raft and fortunately effected a landing at some little distance below. I now joined the party and we proceeded with the indians about 3 Ms. to a small Creek and encamped at sunset. I sent out the hunters who soon returned with three very fine deer of which I gave the indians half.

These people now informed me that the road which they shewed me at no great distance from our Camp would lead us up the East branch of Clark's river and [to] a river they called Cokahlarishkit or the *river of the road to buffaloe* and thence to medicine river and the falls of the Missouri where we wished to go. they alledged that as the road was a well beaten track we could not now miss our way and as they were affraid of meeting with their enimies the Minnetares they could not think of continuing with us any longer, that they wished now to proceed down Clark's river in surch of their friends the Shalees. they informed us that not far from the dividing ridge between the waters of this and the Missouri rivers the roads forked they recommended the left hand as the best rout but said they would both lead us to the falls of the Missouri.[1] I directed the hunters to turn out early in the morning and indeavour to kill some more meat for these poeple whom I was unwilling to leave without giving them a good supply of provision after their having been so obliging as to conduct us through those tremendious mountains. the musquetoes were so excessively troublesome this evening that we were obliged to kindle large fires for our horses these insects torture them in such manner untill they placed themselves in the smoke of the fires that I realy thought they would become frantic.

We saw the fresh track of a horse this evening in the road near our camp which the indians supposed to be a Shale spye. we killed a prarie hen with the short and pointed tail she had a number of young which could just fly.

FRIDAY JULY 4TH 1806.

at half after eleven the hunters returned from the chase unsucessfull. I now ordered the horses saddled smoked a pipe with

[1] The Nez Percés are describing two passes across the Continental Divide, Cadotte's and Lewis and Clark's, and recommending the latter.

these friendly people and at noon bid them adieu. they had cut the meat which I gave them last evening thin and exposed it in the sun to dry informing me that they should leave it in this neighbourhood untill they returned as a store for their homeward journey. it is worthy of remark that these people were about to return by the same pass by which they had conducted us through the difficult part of the Rocky Mountains, altho they were about to decend Clark's river several days journey in surch of the Shale's their relations, a circumstance which to my mind furnishes sufficient evidence that there is not so near or so good a rout to the plains of Columbia by land along that river as that which we came. the several war routs of the Minetarees which fall into this vally of Clark's river concenter at traveller's rest beyond which point they have never yet dared to venture in pursuit of the nations beyond the mountains. these affectionate people our guides betrayed every emmotion of unfeigned regret at seperating from us; they said that they were confidint that the Pahkees, (the appellation they give to the Minetares) would cut us off. the first 5 miles of our rout was through a part of the extensive plain in which we were encamped, we then entered the mountains with the East fork of Clark's river through a narrow confined pass [2] on it's N. side continuing up that river five Ms. further to the entrance of the Cokahlahishkit R. which falls in on the N. E. side, is 60 yds. wide deep and rapid. the banks bold not very high but never overflow. the East fork below its junction with this stream is 100 yds. wide and above it about 90. the water of boath are terbid but the East branch much the most so; their beds are composed of sand and gravel; the East fork possesses a large portion of the former. neither of those streams are navigable in consequence of the rapids and shoals which obstruct their currents. thus far a plain or untimbered country bordered the river which near the junction of these streams spread into a handsome level plain of no great extent; the hills were covered with long leafed pine and fir. I now continued my rout up the N. side of the Cokaplahishkit river through a timbered country for 8 miles and encamped in a handsom bottom on the river where there was an abundance of excellent grass for our horses. the evening was fine, air pleasant and no musquetoes. a

[2] Hell Gate, first called Porte d'Enfer by Canadian trappers because the Blackfeet frequently ambushed the Flatheads and Nez Percés there.

few miles before we encamped I killed a squirrel of the speceis common to the Rocky Mountains and a ground squirrel of a speceis which I had never before seen, I preserved the skins of both of these animals.

For the next five days Lewis's journal consists merely of the courses, bearings, and distances of the trail he is following, plus a few brief, hastily jotted notes. The party come upon fresh tracks which they take to be those of a band of "Pahkees" (Atsina, the Gros Ventres) returning to their own country from a horse-stealing raid. They "are therefore much on our guard both day and night." Lewis recognizes the trail, described by both the Minnetarees and the Nez Percés, that leads to Dearborn River but continues on to another one, also repeatedly described to him, that will lead to Medicine (Sun) River. Following this, on July 7 he crosses "the dividing ridge between the waters of the Columbia and Missouri rivers" by the pass now called Lewis and Clark's. The next day, coming down to the plains, he abandons the well-worn trail in order to hunt, "to procure the necessary skins to make geer and meat for the three men we mean to leave at the falls as none of them are hunters." They are back in the country of abundant game.

[Lewis]   JULY 10TH 1806.

great quantities of prickly pear of two kinds on the plains. the ground is renderd so miry by the rain which fell yesterday that it is excessively fatiegueing to the horses to travel. we came 10 miles and halted for dinner the wind blowing down the river in the fore part of the day was unfavourable to the hunters. they saw several gangs of Elk but they having the wind of them ran off. in the evening the wind set from the West and we fell in with a few elk of which R. Fields and myself killed 3 one of which swam the river and fell on the opposit [side] so we therefore lost it's skin I sent the packhorses on with Sergt. Gass directing them to halt and encamp at the first timber which proved to be about 7 Ms. I retained frazier to assist in skining the Elk. we wer[e] about this time joined by drewer. a large brown bear swam the river near where we were and Drewyer shot and killed it. by the time we butchered the[s]e 2 elk and bar it was near dark   we loaded our horses with the best of the meat and pursued the party and found them encamped as they had been directed in the first timber. we did not reach them until 9 P.M.   they informed us that they had seen a very large bear in the plains which had pursued Sergt. Gass and Thomson some distance but their horses enabled them to keep out of it's reach. they were affraid to fire on the bear least their horses should throw them as they were unaccustomed to the gun. we killed five deer 3 Elk and a bear to day   saw vast herds of buffaloe in the evening below us on the river. we hered them bellowing about us all night. vast assemblages of wolves. saw a large herd of Elk making down the river. passed a considerable rapid in medicine river after dark. the river about a hundred yards wide   is deep and in many parts rappid and today has been much crouded with islands.

JULY 11TH 1806.

I sent the hunters down Medicine river to hunt Elk and proceeded with the party across the plain to the white bear Islands.[3] it is now the season at which the buffaloe begin to coppelate and the bulls keep a tremendious roaring   we could hear them for many miles and there are such numbers of them that there is one continual roar. our horses had not been acquainted with the buffaloe they appeared much allarmed at their appearance and bellowing. when I arrived in sight of the white-bear Islands the missouri bottoms on both sides of the river were crouded with buffaloe   I sincerely beleif that there were not less than 10 thousand buffaloe within a circle of 2 miles arround that place. I directed the hunters to kill some buffaloe as well for the benifit of their skins to enable us to pass the river as for their meat for the men I meant to leave at this place. we unloaded our horses and encamped opposite to the Islands. had some willow sticks collected to make canoes of the hides   by 12 OCk. they killed eleven buffaloe most of them in fine order. the bulls are now generally much fatter than the cows and are fine beef. by 3 in the evening. we

3 Opposite the site of the permanent camp at the end of the portage of last summer.

had brought in a large quantity of fine beef and as many hides as
we wanted for canoes shelters and geer. I then set all hands to prepare two canoes the one we made after the mandan fassion with a
single skin in the form of a bason and the other we constructed of
two skins on a plan of our own.

JULY 12TH. 1806.

We arrose early and resumed our operations in compleating our
canoes which we completed by 10 A. M.   about this time two of
the men whom I had dispatched this morning in quest of the
horses returned with seven of them only. the remaining ten of our
best horses were absent and not to be found. I fear that they are
stolen. I dispatch[ed] two men on horseback in surch of them.
at Noon Werner returned having found three others of the
horses   Sergt. Gass did not return untill 3 P.M. not having
found the horses. he had been about 8 ms. up Medecine river. I
now dispatched Joseph Fields and Drewyer in quest of them the
former returned at dark unsuccessfull and the latter continued
absent all night. at 5 P.M. the wind abated and we transported our
baggage and meat to the opposite shore in our canoes which we
found answered even beyond our expectations. we swam our horses
over also and encamped at sunset. the grass and weeds are much
more luxouriant than they were when I left this place on the 13th
of July 1805.

13TH JULY.

removed above to my old station opposite the upper point of the
white bear island. formed our camp and set Thompson etc at work
to complete the geer for the horses. had the cash [cache] opened
found my bearskins entirely destroyed by the water, the river having risen so high that the water had penitrated. all my specimens
of plants also lost. the Chart of the Missouri fortunately escaped.
opened my trunks and boxes and exposed the articles to dry.
found my papers damp and several articles damp. the stoper had
come out of a phial of laudinum and the contents had run into
the drawer and distroyed a gre[a]t part of my medicine in such
manner that it was past recovery. waited very impatiently for the
return of Drewyer he did not arrive.

14TH JULY

Had the carriage wheels dug up. found them in good order. the iron frame of the boat had not suffered materially. had the meat cut thiner and exposed to dry in the sun. the old cash being too damp to venture to deposit my trunks &c. in I sent them over to the Large island and had them put on a high scaffold among some thick brush and covered with skins. I take this precaution lest some indians may visit the men I leave here before the arrival of the main party and rob them. the hunters killed a couple of wolves, the buffaloe have almost entirely disappeared. saw the bee martin. the wolves are in great numbers howling arround us and loling about in the plains in view at the distance of two or three hundred yards.

TUESDAY JULY 15TH 1806.

Dispatched McNeal early this morning to the lower part of portage in order to learn whether the Cash and white perogue remained untouched or in what state they were. the men employed in drying the meat, dressing deerskins and preparing for the reception of the canoes. at 1 P.M. Drewyer returned without the horses and reported that after a diligent surch of 2 days he had discovered where the horses had passed Dearborn's river at which place there were 15 lodges that had been abandoned about the time our horses were taken; he pursued the tracks of a number of horses from these lodges to the road which we had traveled over the mountains which they struck about 3 ms. South of our encampment of the 7th inst. and had pursued this road Westwardly; I have no doubt but they are a party of the Tushapahs who have been on a buffaloe hunt. his horse being much fatiegued with the ride he had given him and finding that the indians had at least 2 days the start of him thought it best to return. his safe return has releived me from great anxiety. I had already settled it in my mind that a white-bear had killed him and should have set out tomorrow in surch of him, and if I could not find him to continue my rout to Maria's river. I knew that if he met with a bear in the plains even he would attack him. and that if any accedent should happen to seperate him from his horse in that situation the chances in favour of his being killed would be as 9 to 10. I felt so perfectly satisfyed that he had returned in safety that I thought but little of the horses although they were seven of the best I had. this loss great as it is, is not intirely irreparable, or at least dose not defeat my design of exploring Maria's river. I have yet 10 horses remaining, two of the best and two of the worst of which I leave to assist the party in taking the canoes and baggage over the portage and take the remaining 6 with me; these are but indifferent horses most of them but I hope they may answer our purposes. I shall leave three of my intended party, (viz) Gass, Frazier and Werner, and take the two Feildses and Drewyer. by having two spare horses we can releive those we ride. having made this arrangement I gave orders for an early departure in the morning, indeed I should have set out instantly but McNeal road one of the horses which I intend to take and has not yet returned.

a little before dark McNeal returned with his musquet broken off at the breach, and informed me that on his arrival at willow run [*on the portage*] he had approached a white bear within ten feet without discover[ing] him the bear being in the thick brush,   the horse took the allarm and turning short threw him immediately under the bear; this animal raised himself on his hinder feet for battle, and gave him time to recover from his fall which he did in an instant and with his clubbed musquet he struck the bear over the head and cut him with the guard of the gun and broke off the breech,   the bear stunned with the stroke fell to the ground and began to scratch his head with his feet; this gave McNeal time to climb a willow tree which was near at hand and thus fortunately made his escape. the bear waited at the foot of the tree untill late in the evening before he left him, when McNeal ventured down and caught his horse which had by this time strayed off to the distance of 2 Ms. and returned to camp. these bear are a most tremenduous animal; it seems that the hand of providence has been most wonderfully in our favor with rispect to them, or some of us would long since have fallen a sacrifice to their farosity. there seems to be a sertain fatality attatched to the neighbourhood of these falls, for there is always a chapter of accedents prepared for us during our residence at them.

the musquetoes continue to infest us in such manner that we can scarcely exist; for my own part I am confined by them to my bier at least ¾ths of my time. my dog even howls with the torture he experiences from them, they are almost insupportable, they are so numerous that we frequently get them in our thr[o]ats as we breath.

I dispatched a man early this morning to drive up the horses as usual, he returned at 8 A. M. with one of them only. allarmed at this occurrence I dispatched one of my best hands on horseback in surch of them he returned at 10 A.M. with them and I immediately set out. sent Drewyer and R. Fields with the horses to the lower side of Medecine river, and proceeded myself with all our baggage and J. Fields down the missouri to the mouth of Medecine river in our canoe of buffaloe skins   we were compelled to swim the horses above the whitebear island and again across medicine river as the Missouri is of great width below the mouth of that river. having arrived safely below Medicine river we immediately sadled our horses and proceeded down the river to the handsome fall of 47 feet where I halted about 2 hours and took a haisty sketch of these falls; in the mean time we had some meat cooked and took dinner after which we proceeded to the grand falls where we arrived at sunset. on our way we saw two very large bear on the opposite side of the river. as we arrived in sight of the little wood below the falls we saw two other bear enter it; this being the only wood in the neighbourhood we were compelled of course to contend with the bear for possession, and therefore left our horses in a place of security and entered the wood which we surched in vain for the bear, they had fled. here we encamped and the evening having the appearance of rain made our beds and slept under a shelving rock. these falls have abated much of their grandure since I first arrived at them in June 1805, the water being much lower at prese[n]t than it was at that moment, however they are still a sublimely grand object.

I arrose early this morning and made a drawing of the falls. after which we took breakfast and departed. it being my design to

strike Maria's river about the place at which I left it on my return to it's mouth in the beginning of June 1805. I steered my
course through the wide and level plains which have somewhat the
appearance of an ocean, not a tree nor a shrub to be seen. the land
is not fertile, at least far less so, than the plains of the Columbia or
those lower down this river, we killed a buffaloe cow as we
passed throug[h] the plains and took the hump and tonge which
furnish ample rations for four men one day. at 5 P. M. we arrived at *rose* river [the Teton] where I purposed remaining all
night as I could not reach maria's river this evening and unless I
did there would be but little probability of our finding any wood
and very probably no water either. on our arrival at the river we
saw where a wounded and bleading buffaloe had just passed and
concluded it was probable that the indians had been runing them
and were near at hand. the Minnetares of Fort de prarie and the
blackfoot indians rove through this quarter of the country and as
they are a vicious lawless and reather an abandoned set of wretches
I wish to avoid an interview with them if possible. I have no doubt
but they would steel our horses if they have it in their power and
finding us weak should they happen to be numerous wil most
probably attempt to rob us of our arms and baggage; at all events
I am determined to take every possible precaution to avoid them if
possible. I hurried over the river to a thick wood and turned the
horses to graize; sent Drewyer to pursue and kill the wounded
buffaloe in order to determine whether it had been wounded by
the indians or not, and proceeded myself to reconnoitre the adjacent country having sent R. Fields for the same purpose a different rout. I ascended the river hills and by the help of my glass
examined the plains but could make no discovery, in about an
hour I returned to camp, where I met with the others who had been
as unsuccessfull as myself. Drewyer could not find the wounded
buffaloe. J. Fields whom I had left at camp had already roasted
some of the buffaloe meat and we took dinner after which I sent
Drewyer and R. Fields to resume their resurches for the indians;
and set myself down to record the transactions of the day. the bed
of this stream is small gravel and mud; it's banks are low but
never overflow, the hills are about 100 or 150 feet high; it possesses bluffs of earth like the lower part of the Missouri; except
the debth and valocity of it's stream and it is the Missouri in

miniture. from the size of rose river at this place and it's direction I have no doubt but it takes it's source within the first range of the Rocky mountains.

FRIDAY JULY 18TH 1806.

We set out this morning a little before sunrise ascended the river hills and continued our rout as yesterday through the open plains   at about 6 miles we reached the top of an elivated plain which divides the waters of the rose river from those of Maria's river. our course led us nearly parrallel with a creek of Maria's river which takes it's rise in these high plains at the place we passed them; at noon we struck this creek about 6 ms. from its junction with Maria's river where we found some cottonwood timber; here we halted to dine and graize our horses. we passed immence herds of buffaloe on our way in short for about 12 miles it appeared as one herd only the whole plains and vally of this creek being covered with them; saw a number of wolves of both speceis, also Antelopes and some horses. after dinner we proceeded about 5 miles across the plain to Maria's river where we arrived at 6 P. M.   being now convinced that we were above the point to which I had formerly ascended this river and f[e]aring that a fork of this stream might fall in on the North side between this place and the point to which I had ascended it, I directed Drewyer who was with me on my former excurtion, and Joseph Fields to decend the river early in the morning to the place from whence I had returned, and examine whether any stream fell inn or not. I keep a strict lookout every night, I take my tour of watch with the men.

SATURDAY JULY 19TH 1806.

Drewyer and J. Fields set out early this morning in conformity to my instructions last evening. they returned at ½ after 12 OCk. and informed me that the course of the river from hence downwards as far as they were is N. 80. E.   we set out, ascended the river hills having passed the river and proceeded through the open plains up the N. side of the river 20 miles and encamped. at 15 miles we passed a large creek on N. side a little above it's entrance; there is but little running water in this creek at present, it's bed is about 30 yds. wide and appears to come from the broken *Mountains* . so called from their raggid and irregular shape [4] there are three of them extending from east to West almost unconnected, the center mountain terminates in a conic spire and is that which I have called the *tower mountain*   they are destitute of timber. the plains are beautifull and level but the soil is but thin.

SUNDAY JULY 20TH 1806.

We set [out] at sunrise and proceed[ed] through the open plain as yesterday up the North side of the river. the plains are more broken than they were yesterday and a great quanty of small gravel is every where distributed over the surface of the earth which renders travling extreemly painfull to our bearfoot horses. the mineral salts common to the plains of the missouri has been more abundant today than usual. the bluffs of the river are about 200 feet high, steep irregular and formed of earth which readily de-solves with water, slips and precipitates itself into the river as be-fore mentioned frequently of the bluffs of the Missouri below which they resemble in every particular, differing essentially from those of the Missouri above the entrance of this river, they being com-posed of firm red or yellow clay which dose not yield readily to the rains and a large quantity of rock. the soil of the river bottom is fertile and well timbered, I saw some trees today which would make small canoes. from the apparent decent of the country to the North and above the broken mountains I am induced to beleive that the South branch of the Suskashawan receives a part of it's waters from the plain even to the borders of this river and from the brakes [breaks] visible in the plains in a no[r]thern direction think that a branch of that river decending from the rocky mountains passes at no great distance from Maria's river and to the N. E. of the broken mountains.[5] the day has proved excessively warm and we lay by four hours during the heat of it; we traveled 28 miles

4 The Sweetgrass Hills. Lewis's "broken mountains" and "raggid and ir-regular shape" apply with much greater force to the range only a few miles to his left, which has been namd the Lewis Mountains for him.

5 A mistake induced by Lewis's urgent desire to reach the Saskatchewan watershed. The drainage north of his present position is actually that of Milk River.

and encamped as usual in the river bottom on it's N. side. there is scarcely any water at present in the plains and what there is, lies in small pools and is so strongly impregnated with the mineral salts that it is unfit for any purpose except the uce of the buffaloe. those animals appear to prefer this water to that of the river.

MONDAY JULY 21ST 1806.

We set out at sunrise and proceeded a short distance up the North side of the river, we found the ravines which made in on this side were so steep and numerous that we passed the river in doing which the pack horse which carried my instruments missed the ford and wet the instruments. this accident detained us about half an ho[u]r. I took the Instruments out wiped them and dryed their cases. they sustained no material injury. at 2 P. M. we struck a northern branch of Maria's river about 30 yds. wide at the distance of about 8 miles from it's entrance. this stream is closely confined between clifts of freestone rocks the bottom narrow below us and above the rocks confine it on each side; some little timber below but not any above; the water of this stream is nearly clear. from the appearance of this rock and the apparent hight of the bed of the streem I am induced to beleive that there are falls in these rivers somewhere about their junction. being convinced that this stream came from the mountains I determined to pursue it as it will lead me to the most no[r]thern point to which the waters of Maria's river extend which I now fear will not be as far north as I wished and expected. after dinner we set out up the North branch keeping on it's S. side; we pursued it untill dark and not finding any timber halted and made a fire of the dung of the buffaloe. we lay on the south side in a narrow bottom under a Clift. our provision is nearly out, we wounded a buffaloe this eve ning but could not get him.

TUESDAY JULY 22ED 1806.

we continued up the river on it's South side for 17 miles when we halted to graize our horses and eat; there being no wood we were compelled to make our fire with the buffaloe dung which I found answered the purpose very well. we cooked and eat all the meat we had except a small peice of buffaloe meat which was a little tainted. after dinner we passed the river and took our course through a level and beautifull plain on the N. side. the country has now become level, the river bottoms wide and the adjoining plains but little elivated above them; the banks of the river are not usually more than from 3 to four feet yet it dose not appear ever to overflow them. we found no timber untill we had traveled 12 miles further when we arrived at a clump of large cottonwood trees in a beautifull and extensive bottom of the river about 10 miles below the foot of the rocky Mountains where this river enters them; as I could see from hence very distinctly where the river entered the mountains and the bearing of this point being S of West I thought it unnecessary to proceed further and therefore encamped resolving to rest ourselves and horses a couple of days at this place and take the necessary observations.[6]

this plain on which we are is very high; the rocky mountains to the S. W. of us appear but low from their base up yet are partially covered with snow nearly to their bases. there is no timber on those mountains within our view; they are very irregular and broken in their form and seem to be composed principally of clay with but little rock or stone.[7] the river appears to possess at least double the vollume of water which it had where we first arrived on it below; this no doubt proceeds from the avapporation caused by the sun and air and the absorbing of the earth in it's passage through these open plains. I believe that the waters of the Suskashawan apporoach the borders of this river very nearly. I now have lost all hope of the waters of this river ever extending to N. Latitude 50° though I still hope and think it more than probable that both *white earth* river and milk river extend as far north as latd. 50°   we have seen but few buffaloe today no deer and very few Antelopes; gam[e] of every discription is extreemly wild which induces me to beleive that the indians are now, or have been lately in this neighbourhood. we wounded a buffaloe this evening but our horses were so much fatiegued that we were unable to pursue it with success.

6 The expedition's farthest north, and the collapse of Lewis's hope that the Marias watershed would take him north of 49° and afford easy access to the Saskatchewan River. He is on Cut Bank Creek.

7 The Lewis Range, named for the man who is describing it.

WEDNESDAY JULY 23RD 1806.

I dispatched Drewyer an[d] Joseph fields this morning to hunt. I directed Drewyer who went up the river [Cut Bank Creek] to observe it's bearings and the point at which it entered the mountains, this he did and on his return I observed the point at which the river entered to bear S. 50° W. distant about ten miles the river making a considerable bend to the West just above us. Drewyer informed us that there was an indian camp of eleven leather lodges which appeared to have been abandoned about 10 days, the poles only of the lodges remained. we are confident that these are the Minnetares of fort de prarie and suspect that they are probably at this time somewhere on the main branch of Maria's river on the borders of the buffaloe,   under this impression I shall not strike that river on my return untill about the mouth of the North branch.

THURSDAY JULY 24TH 1806.

At 8 A. M. the sun made it's appearance for a few minutes and I took it's altitude but it shortly after clouded up again and continued to rain the ballance of the day   I was therefore unable to complete the observations I wished to take at this place. I determined to remain another day in the hope of it's being fair. the air has become extreemly cold which in addition to the wind and rain renders our situation extreemly unpleasant. several wolves visited our camp today, I fired on and wounded one of them very badly. the small speceis of wolf barks like a dog, they frequently salute us with this note as we pass through the plains.

FRIDAY JULY 25TH 1806.

The weather still continues cold cloudy and rainy, the wind also has blown all day with more than usual violence from the N. W.   late in the evening Drewyer and J. Fields returned the former had killed a fine buck on which we now fared sumptuously. they informed me that it was about 10 miles to the main branch of Maria's River, that the vally formed by the river in that quarter was wide extensive and level with a considerable quantity of timber; here they found some wintering camps of the natives and a great number of others of a more recent date or that had from appearance been evacuated about 6 weeks; we consider ourselves extreemly fortunate in not having met with these people. I determined that if tomorrow continued cloudy to set out as I now begin to be apprehensive that I shall not reach the United States within this season unless I make every exertion in my power which I shall certainly not omit when once I leave this place which I shall do with much reluctance without having obtained the necessary data to establish it's longitude   as if the fates were against me my chronometer from some unknown cause stoped today, when I set her to going she went as usual.

Saturday July 26th 1806.

The mor[n]ing was cloudy and continued to rain as usual, tho' the cloud seemed somewhat thiner I therefore posponed seting out untill 9 A. M. in the hope that it would clear off but finding the contrary result I had the horses caught and we set out biding a lasting adieu to this place which I now call camp *disappointment.* I took my rout through the open plains S. E. 5 ms. passing a small creek at 2 ms. from the mountains when I changed my direction to S. 75 E. for 7 ms. further and struck a principal branch of Maria's river 65 yds. wide, not very deep, I passed this stream to it's south side and continued down it 2 Ms. on the last mentioned course when another branch of nearly the same dignity formed a junction with it, coming from the S. W.   I passed the S. branch just above it's junction and continued down the river which runs a little to the N. of E. 1 ms. and halted to dine and graize our horses. here I found some indian lodges which appeared to have been inhabited last winter in a large and fertile bottom well stocked with cottonwood timber. during our stay at this place R. Fields killed a buck a part of the flesh of which we took with us. after dinner I continued my rout down the river to the North of Ea[s]t about 3 Ms. when the hills puting in close on the S. side I determined to ascend them to the high plain which I did accordingly, keeping the Fieldes with me; Drewyer passed the river and kept down the vally of the river. I had intended to decend this river with it's course to it's junction with the fork which I had ascended and from thence have taken across the country obliquely to rose [Teton] river and decend that stream to it's confluence with Maria's river.

the country through which this portion of Maria's river passes to the fork which I ascended appears much more broken than that above and between this and the mountains. I had scarcely ascended the hills before I discovered to my left at the distance of a mile an assembleage of about 30 horses. I halted and used my spye glass by the help of which I discovered several indians on the top of an eminence just above them who appeared to be looking down towards the river I presumed at Drewyer. about half the horses were saddled. this was a very unpleasant sight, however I resolved to make the best of our situation and to approach them in a friendly manner. I directed J. Fields to display the flag which I had brought for that purpose and advanced slowly toward them,   about this time they discovered us and appeared to run about in a very confused manner as if much allarmed, their attention had been previously so fixed on Drewyer that they did not discover us untill we had began to advance upon them,   some of them decended the hill on which they were and drove their horses within shot of it's summit and again returned to the hight as if to wate our arrival or to defend themselves. I calculated on their number being nearly or quite equal to that of their horses. that our runing would invite pursuit as it would convince them that we were their enimies and our horses were so indifferent that we could not hope to make our escape by flight; added to this Drewyer was seperated from us and I feared that his not being apprized of the indians in the event of our attempting to escape he would most probably fall a sacrefice.

under these considerations I still advanced towards them; when we had arrived within a quarter of a mile of them, one of them mounted his horse and rode full speed towards us, which when I discovered I halted and alighted from my horse; he came within a hundred paces halted looked at us and turned his horse about and returned as briskly to his party as he had advanced; while he halted near us I held out my hand and becconed to him to approach but he paid no attention to my overtures. on his return to his party they all decended the hill and mounted their horses and advanced towards us leaving [other] horses behind them, we also advanced to meet them. I counted eight of them but still supposed that there were others concealed as there were several other horses saddled. I told the two men with me that I apprehended that these were the Minnetares of Fort de Prarie and from their known character I expected that we were to have some difficulty with them;

that if they thought themselves sufficiently strong I was convinced they would attempt to rob us in which case be their numbers what they would I should resist to the last extremity prefering death to that of being deprived of my papers instruments and gun and desired that they would form the same resolution and be allert and on their guard.

when we arrived within a hundred yards of each other the indians except one halted   I directed the two men with me to do the same and advanced singly to meet the indian with whom I shook hands and passed on to those in his rear, as he did also to the two men in my rear; we now all assembled and alighted from our horses; the Indians soon asked to smoke with us, but I told them that the man whom they had seen pass down the river had my pipe and we could not smoke untill he joined us. I requested as they had seen which way he went that they would one of them go with one of my men in surch of him, this they readily concented to and a young man set out with R. Fields in surch of Drewyer. I now asked them by sighns if they were the Minnetares of the North [8] which they answered in the affermative; I asked if there was any cheif among them and they pointed out 3   I did not believe them however I thought it best to please them and gave to one a medal to a second a flag and to the third a handkerchief, with which they appeared well satisfyed. they appeared much agitated with our first interview from which they had scarcely yet recovered, in fact I believe they were more allarmed at this accedental interview than we were. from no more of them appearing I now concluded they were only eight in number and became much better satisfyed with our situation as I was convinced that we could mannage that number should they attempt any hostile measures.

as it was growing late in the evening I proposed that we should remove to the nearest part of the river and encamp together, I told them that I was glad to see them and had a great deel to say to them. we mounted our horses and rode towards the river which was at but a short distance, on our way we were joined by Drewyer Fields and the indian. we decended a very steep bluff about 250 feet high to the river where there was a small bottom of nearly ½

[8] Lewis interprets the sign as designating the Atsina, the Fall Indians or Gros Ventres, who of course were not a Blackfoot tribe, though they were affiliated with the Blackfeet. He appears to have been mistaken, however; they were a group of Piegans, one of the three Blackfoot tribes.

mile in length and about 250 yards wide in the widest part; in this bottom there stand t[h]ree solitary trees near one of which the indians formed a large simicircular camp of dressed buffaloe skins and invited us to partake of their shelter which Drewyer and myself accepted and the Fieldses lay near the fire in front of the she[l]ter. with the assistance of Drewyer I had much conversation with these people in the course of the evening.[9] I learned from them that they were a part of a large band which lay encamped at present near the foot of the rocky mountains on the main branch of Maria's river one ½ days march from our present encampment; [10] that there was a whiteman with their band; that there was another large band of their nation hunting buffaloe near the broken mountains and were on there way to the mouth of Maria's river where they would probably be in the course of a few days. they also informed us that from hence to the establishment where they trade on the Suskasawan river is only 6 days easy march or such as they usually travel with their women and childred[n] which may be estimated at about 150 ms. that from these traders they obtain arm[s] amunition sperituous liquor blankets &c. in exchange for wolves and some beaver skins.

I told these people that I had come a great way from the East up the large river which runs towards the rising sun, that I had been to the great waters where the sun sets and had seen a great many nations all of whom I had invited to come and trade with me on the rivers on this side of the mountains, that I had found most of them at war with their neighbours and had succeeded in restoring peace among them, that I was now on my way home and had left my party at the falls of the missouri with orders to decend that river to the entrance of Maria's river and there wait my arrival and that I had come in surch of them in order to prevail on them to be at peace with their neighbours particularly those on the West side of the mountains and to engage them to come and trade with me when the establishment is made at the entrance of this river to all which they readily gave their assent and declared it to be their wish to be at peace with the Tushepahs whom they said had killed a number of their relations lately and pointed to several of those present who had cut their hair as an evidince of the truth of what they had asserted. I found them extremly fond of smoking and

[9] That is, in sign language.
[10] Probably a lie and probably told as a defensive measure.

plyed them with the pipe untill late at night. I told them that if they intended to do as I wished them they would send some of their young men to their band with an invitation to their chiefs and warriors to bring the whiteman with them and come down and council with me at the entrance of Maria's river and that the ballance of them would accompany me to that place, where I was anxious now to meet my men as I had been absent from them some time and knew that they would be uneasy untill they saw me. that if they would go with me I would give them 10 horses and some tobacco. to this proposition they made no reply, I took the first watch tonight and set up untill half after eleven; the indians by this time were all asleep, I roused up R. Fields and laid down myself; I directed Fields to watch the movements of the indians and if any of them left the camp to awake us all as I apprehended they would attempt to s[t]eal our horses. this being done I feel into a profound sleep and did not wake untill the noise of the men and indians awoke me a little after light in the morning.

Lewis has made a serious error in judgment, one which only remarkably good luck enabled him and his party to survive. The Nez Percés and Flatheads had repeatedly emphasized the hostility and aggressiveness of the Blackfeet and their affiliates the Atsina. It was right to turn over his watch to Reuben Fields — not to have done so would have been an offensive if not indeed a hostile act — and to appear to go to sleep. But he ought to have stayed awake and on the alert. Furthermore, he ought to have foreseen just such an attempt as the Indians made when they saw an opportunity, and he ought so to have impressed the necessity of vigilance on his men that no opportunity could have occurred.

JULY 27TH 1806. SUNDAY.

This morning at daylight the indians got up and crouded around the fire, J. Fields who was on post had carelessly laid his gun down behi[n]d him near where his brother was sleeping, one of the indians the fellow to whom I had given the medal last evening sliped behind him and took his gun and that of his brother unperceived by him, at the same instant two others advanced and seized the guns of Drewyer and myself, J. Fields seeing this

turned about to look for his gun and saw the fellow just runing off
with her and his brother's he called to his brother who instantly
jumped up and pursued the indian with whom they overtook at
the distance of 50 or 60 paces from the camp s[e]ized their guns and
rested them from him and R. Fields as he seized his gun stabed the
indian to the heart with his knife   the fellow ran about 15 steps
and fell dead; of this I did not know untill afterwards, having
recovered their guns they ran back instantly to the camp.

Drewyer who was awake saw the indian take hold of his gun
and instantly jumped up and s[e]ized her and rested her from him
but the indian still retained his pouch,   his jumping up and
crying damn you let go my gun awakened me   I jumped up and
asked what was the matter which I quickly learned when I saw
drewyer in a scuffle with the indian for his gun. I reached to seize
my gun but found her gone, I then drew a pistol from my holster
and terning myself about saw the indian making off with my
gun   I ran at him with my pistol and bid him lay down my gun
which he was in the act of doing when the Fieldses returned and
drew up their guns to shoot him which I forbid as he did not appear to be about to make any resistance or commit any offensive
act, he droped the gun and walked slowly off, I picked her up instantly,   Drewyer having about this time recovered his gun and
pouch asked me if he might not kill the fellow which I also forbid
as the indian did not appear to wish to kill us,   as soon as they
found us all in possession of our arms they ran and indeavored to
drive off all the horses   I now hollowed to the men and told
them to fire on them if they attempted to drive off our horses, they
accordingly pursued the main party who were dr[i]ving the horses
up the river and I pursued the man who had taken my gun who
with another was driving off a part of the horses which were to the
left of the camp. I pursued them so closely that they could not take
twelve of their own horses but continued to drive mine with some
others; at the distance of three hundred paces they entered one of
those steep nitches in the bluff with the horses before them   being nearly out of breath I could pursue no further, I called to
them as I had done several times before that I would shoot them
if they did not give me my horse and raised my gun, one of them
jumped behind a rock and spoke to the other who turned arround
and stoped at the distance of 30 steps from me and I shot him
through the belly,   he fell to his knees and on his wright elbow

from which position he partly raised himself up and fired at me, and turning himself about crawled in behind a rock which was a few feet from him. he overshot me, being bearheaded I felt the wind of his bullet very distinctly.

not having my shotpouch I could not reload my piece and as there were two of them behind good shelters from me I did not think it prudent to rush on them with my pistol which I had discharged I had not the means of reloading untill I reached camp; I therefore returned leasurly towards camp,   on my way I met with Drewyer who having heared the report of the guns had returned in surch of me and left the Fieldes to pursue the indians,   I desired him to haisten to the camp with me and assist in catching as many of the indian horses as were necessary and to call to the Fieldes if he could make them hear to come back that we still had a sufficient number of horses,   this he did but they were too far to hear him. we reached the camp and began to catch the horses and saddle them and put on the packs. the reason I had not my pouch with me was that I had not time to return about 50 yards to camp after geting my gun before I was obliged to pursue the indians or suffer them to collect and drive off all the horses. we had caught and saddled the horses and began to arrange the packs when the Fieldses returned with four of our horses; we left one of our horses and took four of the best of those of the indian's; while the men were preparing the horses I put four sheilds and two bows and quivers of arrows which had been left on the fire, with sundry other articles; they left all their baggage at our mercy. they had but 2 guns and one of them they left   the others were armed with bows and arrows and eyedaggs.[11] the gun we took with us. I also retook the flagg but left the medal about the neck of the dead man that they might be informed who we were. we took some of their buffaloe meat and set out ascending the bluffs by the same rout we had decended last evening leaving the ballance of nine of their horses which we did not want.

the Fieldses told me that three of the indians whom they pursued swam the river one of them on my horse. and that two others ascended the hill and escaped from them with a part of their horses, two I had pursued into the nitch one lay dead near the camp and the eighth we could not account for but suppose that he ran off early in the contest. having ascended the hill we took our course

[11] Short axes: elsewhere, "eye-dogs."

through a beatifull level plain a little to the S. of East. my design was to hasten to the entrance of Maria's river as quick as possible in the hope of meeting with the canoes and party at that place having no doubt but that they [the Indians] would pursue us with a large party and as there was a band near the broken mountains or probably between them and the mouth of that river we might expect them to receive inteligence from us and arrive at that place nearly as soon as we could,   no time was therefore to be lost and we pushed our horses as hard as they would bear. at 8 miles we passed a large branch 40 yds. wide which I called battle river. at 3 P. M. we arrived at rose river about 5 miles above where we had passed it as we went out, having traveled by my estimate compared with our former distances and cou[r]ses about 63 ms.   here we halted an hour and a half took some refreshment and suffered our horses to graize; the day proved warm but the late rains had supplyed the little reservors in the plains with water and had put them in fine order for traveling,   our whole rout so far was as level as a bowling green with but little stone and few prickly pears.

after dinner we pursued the bottoms of rose river but finding[it] inconvenient to pass the river so often we again ascended the hills on the S. W. side and took the open plains; by dark we had traveled about 17 miles further,   we now halted to rest ourselves and horses about 2 hours, we killed a buffaloe cow and took a small quantity of the meat. after refreshing ourselves we again set out by moonlight and traveled leasurely, heavy thunderclouds lowered arround us on every quarter but that from which the moon gave us light. we continued to pass immence herds of buffaloe all night as we had done in the latter part of the day. we traveled untill 2 OCk in the morning having come by my estimate after dark about 20 ms.   we now turned out our horses and laid ourselves down to rest in the plain very much fatiegued as may be readily conceived. my indian horse carried me very well in short much better than my own would have done and leaves me with but little reason to complain of the robery.

JULY 28TH 1806. MONDAY.

The morning proved fair,   I slept sound but fortunately awoke as day appeared, I awaked the men and directed the horses to be saddled, I was so soar from my ride yesterday that I could scarcely stand, and the men complained of being in a similar situation however I encouraged them by telling them that our own lives as well as those of our friends and fellow travellers depended on our exertions at this moment; they were allert soon prepared the horses and we again resumed our march; the men proposed to pass the missouri at the grog spring where rose river approaches it so nearly and pass down on the S. W. side, to this I objected as it would delay us almost all day to reach the point [12] by this circuetous rout and would give the enemy time to surprise and cut off the party at the point if they had arrived there, I told them that we owed much to the safety of our friends and that we must wrisk our lives on this occasion, that I should proceed immediately to the point and if the party had not arrived that I would raft the missouri a small distance above, hide our baggage and march on foot up the river through the timber untill I met the canoes or joined them at the falls; I now told them that it was my determination that if we were attacked in the plains on our way to the point that the bridles of the horses should be tied together and we would stand and defend them, or sell our lives as dear as we could.

we had proceeded about 12 miles on an East course when we found ourselves near the missouri; we heard a report which we took to be that of a gun but we were not certain; still continuing down the N. E. bank of the missouri about 8 miles further, being then within five miles of the grog spring we heared the report of several rifles very distinctly on the river to our right, we quickly repared to this joyfull sound and on arriving at the bank of the river had the unspeakable satisfaction to see our canoes coming down. we hurried down from the bluff on which we were and joined them striped our horses and gave them a final discharge imbarking without loss of time with our baggage. I now learned that they had brought all things safe having sustaned no loss nor met with any accident of importance. Wiser had cut his leg badly with a knife and was unable in consequence to work. we decended the river opposite to our principal cash which we proceeded to open after reconnoitering the adjacent country.

we found that the cash had caved in and most of the articles burried therin were injured; I sustained the loss of two very large bear skins which I much regret; most of the fur and baggage belonging to the men were injured. the gunpowder corn flour poark and salt had sustained but little injury the parched meal was spoiled or nearly so. having no time to air these things which they much wanted we droped down to the point to take in the several articles which had been buried at that place in several small cashes; these we found in good order, and recovered every article except 3 traps belonging to Drewyer which could not be found. here as good fortune would have it Sergt. Gass and Willard who brought the horses from the falls joined us at 1 P. M. I had ordered them to bring down the horses to this place in order to assist them in collecting meat which I direceted them to kill and dry here for our voyage, presuming that they would have arrived with the perogue and canoes at this place several days before my return. having now nothing to detain us we passed over immediately to the island in the entrance of Maria's river to launch the red perogue, but found her so much decayed that it was impossible with the means we had to repare her and therefore mearly took the nails and other ironworks about her which might be of service to us and left her. we now reimbarked on board the white perog[u]e and five small canoes and decended the river about 15 ms. and encamped on the S. W. side near a few cottonwood trees.

Traveling downstream with ease and unexpected speed, the party pass the mouth of the Musselshell on August 1, the mouth of the Milk River on the 4th, and, after a day in which they traveled 83 miles, the Yellowstone on the 7th. The last was the general rendezvous but, finding no game in the vicinity, Clark had moved downstream.

[Lewis]   THURSDAY AUGUST 7TH 1806.

at 4 P. M. we arrived at the entrance of the Yellowstone river. I landed at the point and found that Capt. Clark had been encamped at this place and from appearances had left it about 7 or 8 days. I found a paper on a pole at the point which mearly contained my name in the hand wrighting of Capt. C. we also found the remnant of a note which had been attached to a peace of Elk'shorns in the camp; from this fragment I learned that game was scarce at the point and musquetoes troublesome which were the

reasons given for his going on; I also learnt that he intended halting a few miles below where he intended waiting my arrival. I now
wrote a note directed to Colter and Collins provided they were behind, ordering them to come on without loss of time; this note I
wraped in leather and attatched to the same pole which Capt. C.
had planted at the point; this being done I instantly reimbarked
and decended the river in the hope of reaching Capt. C's camp
before night. about 7 miles below the point on the S. W. shore I
saw some meat that had been lately fleased and hung on a pole; I
directed Sergt. Ordway to go on shore [and] examine the place; on
his return he reported that he saw the tracks of two men which
appeared so resent that he beleived they had been there today, the
fire he found at the plce was blaizing and appeared to have been
mended up afresh or within the course of an hour past. he found
at this place a part of a Chinnook hat which my men recognized as
the hat of Gibson; from these circumstances we concluded that
Capt. C's camp could not be distant and pursued our rout untill
dark with the hope of reaching his camp   in this however we
were disappointed and night coming on compelled us to encamp
on the N. E. shore in the next bottom above our encampment of
the 23rd and 24th of April 1805. as we came too a herd of buffaloe
assembled on the shore of which we killed a fat cow.

FRIDAY AUGUST 8TH 1806.

Beleiving from the recent appearances about the fire which we
past last evening that Capt. Clark could be at no great distance
below I set out early; the wind heard [hard] from the N. E. but by
the force of the oars and currant we traveled at a good rate untill
10 A. M. by which time we reached the center of the beaver bends
about 8 ms. by water and 3 by land above the entrance of White
earth river. not finding Capt. Clark I knew not what calculation
to make with rispect to his halting and therefore determined to
proceed as tho' he was not before me and leave the rest to the
chapter of accedents. at this place I found a good beach for the
purpose of drawing out the perogue and one of the canoes which
wanted corking and repairing. the men with me have not had leasure since we left the West side of the Rocky mountains to dress any
skins or make themselves cloaths and most of them are therefore
extreemly bare. I therefore determined to halt at this place untill

the perog[u]e and canoe could be repared and the men dress skins and make themselves the necessary cloathing. we encamped on the N. E. side of the river; we found the Musquetoes extreemly trouble-some but in this rispect there is but little choise of camps from hence down to St. Louis. from this place to the little Missouri there is an abundance of game I shall therefore when I leave this place travel at my leasure and avail myself of every opportunity to col-lect and dry meat untill I provide a sufficient quantity for our voy-age not knowing what provision Capt. C. has made in this rispect. I formed a camp unloaded the canoes and perogue, had the latter and one of the canoes drawn out to dry, fleased what meat we had collected and hung it on poles in the sun, after which the men busied themselves in dressing skins and making themselves cloaths.

Colter and Collins have not caught up with the party when Lewis resumes his journey on the afternoon of August 10.

MONDAY AUGUST 11TH 1806.

We set out very early this morning. it being my wish to arrive at the birnt hills by noon in order to take the latitude of that place as it is the most northern point of the Missouri, I enformed the party of my design and requested that they would exert themselves to reach the place in time as it would save us the delay of nearly one day; being as anxious to get forward as I was they plyed their oars faithfully and we proceeded rapidly. We saw but little game untill about 9 A.M. when we came up with a buffaloe swiming the river which I shot and killed; leaving the small canoes to dress it and bring on the meat I proceeded. we had gone but little way be-fore I saw a very large grizzly bear and put too in order to kill it, but it took wind of us and ran off. the small canoes overtook us and informed that the flesh of the buffaloe was unfit for uce and that they had therefor left it. half after 11 A.M. we saw a large herd of Elk on the N. E. shore and I directed the men in the small canoes to halt and kill some of them and continued on in the perogue to the birnt hills; when I arrived here it was about 20 minutes after noon and of course the observation for the meridian Altitude was lost.

Jus[t] opposite to the birnt hills there happened to be a herd of

Elk on a thick willow bar and finding that my observation was lost
for the present I determined to land and kill some of them accordingly we put too and I went out with Cruzatte only. we fired on the
Elk I killed one and he wounded another, we reloaded our guns
and took different routs through the thick willows in pursuit of
the Elk; I was in the act of firing on the Elk a second time when
a ball struck my left thye about an inch below my hip joint, missing
the bone it passed through the left thye and cut the thickness of the
bullet across the hinder part of the right thye; the stroke was very
severe; I instantly supposed that Cruzatte had shot me in mistake
for an Elk as I was dressed in brown leather and he cannot see
very well; under this impression I called out to him damn you, you
have shot me, and looked towards the place from whence the ball
had come, seeing nothing I called Cruzatte several times as loud
as I could but received no answer;   I was now preswaded that
it was an indian that had shot me as the report of the gun did not
appear to be more than 40 paces from me and Cruzatte appeared
to be out of hearing of me.

In this situation not knowing how many indians there might be
concealed in the bushes I thought best to make good my retreat to
the perogue, calling out as I ran for the first hundred paces as loud
as I could to Cruzatte to retreat that there were indians hoping to
allarm him in time to make his escape also; I still retained the
charge in my gun which I was about to discharge at the moment the
ball struck me. when I arrived in sight of the perogue I called the
men to their arms to which they flew in an instant, I told them that
I was wounded but I hoped not mortally, by an indian I beleived
and directed them to follow me that I would return & give them
battle and releive Cruzatte if possible who I feared had fallen into
their hands; the men followed me as they were bid and I returned
about a hundred paces when my wounds became so painfull and
my thye so stiff that I could scarcely get on; in short I was compelled to halt and ordered the men to proceed and if they found
themselves overpowered by numbers to retreat in order keeping up
a fire.

I now got back to the perogue as well as I could and prepared
myself with a pistol my rifle and air-gun being determined as a
retreat was impracticable to sell my life as deerly as possible. in
this state of anxiety and suspense I remained about 20 minutes
when the party returned with Cruzatte and reported that there

were no indians nor the appearance of any; Cruzatte seemed much allarmed and declared if he had shot me it was not his intention, that he had shot an Elk in the willows after he left or seperated from me. I asked him whether he did not hear me when I called to him so frequently which he absolutely denied. I do not beleive that the fellow did it intentionally but after finding that he had shot me was anxious to conceal his. knowledge of having done so. the ball had lodged in my breeches which I knew to be the ball of the short rifles such as that he had, and there being no person out with me but him and no indians that we could discover I have no doubt in my own mind of his having shot me. with the assistance of Sergt. Gass I took off my cloaths and 'dressed my wounds myself as well as I could, introducing tents of patent lint into the ball holes,   the wounds blead considerably but I was hapy to find that it had touched neither bone nor artery.

I sent the men to dress the two Elk which Cruzatte and myself had killed which they did in a few minutes and brought the meat to the river. the small canoes came up shortly after with the flesh of one Elk. my wounds being so situated that I could not without infinite pain make an observation I determined to relinquish it and proceeded on. we came within eight miles of our encampment of the 15th of April 1805 and encamped on N. E. side. as it was painfull to me to be removed I slept on board the perogue; the pain I experienced excited a high fever and I had a very uncomfortable night. at 4 P. M. we passed an encampment which had been evacuated this morning by Capt. Clark,   here I found a note from Capt. C. informing me that he had left a letter for me at the entrance of the Yelow stone river, but that Sergt. Pryor who had passed that place since he left it had taken the letter; that Sergt. Pryor having been robed of all his horses had decended the Yelowstone river in skin canoes and had overtaken him at this encampment. this I fear puts an end to our prospects of obtaining the Sioux Cheifs to accompany us as we have not now leasure to send and engage Mr. Heney on this service, or at least he would not have time to engage them to go as early as it is absolutely necessary we should decend the river.[13]

13 They had determined to hire Heney to go in search of Sioux chiefs who would descend the Missouri with them and go on to Washington. The theft of the horses which Pryor was driving frustrated the plan, since the horses were to be exchanged for goods which they could give the Sioux for presents. See below, p. 450.

TUESDAY AUGUST 12TH 1806.

Being anxious to overtake Capt. Clark who from the appearance of his camps could be at no great distance before me, we set out early and proceeded with all possible expedition   at 8 A. M. the bowsman informed me that there was a canoe and a camp he beleived of whitemen on the N.E. shore. I directed the perogue and canoes to come too at this place and found it to be the camp of two hunters from the Illinois by name Joseph Dickson and Forest Hancock.[14] these men informed me that Capt. C. had passed them about noon the day before. they also informed me that they had left the Illinois in the summer [of] 1804 since which time they had been ascended the Missouri, hunting and traping beaver; that they had been robed by the indians and the former wounded last winter by the Tetons of the birnt woods; that they had hitherto been unsuccessfull in their voyage having as yet caught but little beaver, but were still determined to proceed. I gave them a short discription of the Missouri, a list of distances to the most conspicuous streams and remarkable places on the river above and pointed out to them the places where the beaver most abounded. I also gave them a file and a couple of pounds of powder and some lead. these were articles which they assured me they were in great want of. I remained with these men an hour and a half when I took leave of them and proceeded. while I halted with these men Colter and Collins who seperated from us on the 3rd i[n]st rejoined us. they were well no accident having happened. they informed me that after proceeding the first day and not overtaking us that they had concluded that we were behind and had delayed several days in waiting for us and had thus been unable to join us untill the present mome[n]t. my wounds felt very stiff and soar this morning but gave me no considerable pain. there was much less inflamation than I had reason to apprehend there would be. I had last evening applyed a poltice of peruvian barks.

at 1 P. M. I overtook Capt. Clark and party and had the pleasure of finding them all well. as wrighting in my present situation is extreemly painfull to me I shall desist untill I recover and leave to my fri[e]nd Capt. C. the continuation of our journal.

[14] These two trappers are not only the first white men whom the expedition has seen since leaving the Mandan villages in April 1805 — they are also the first to follow the trail which the expedition had blazed.

CHAPTER XXXI

CLARK'S EXPLORATION OF THE YELLOWSTONE

W hile Lewis was making his strenuous reconnaissance of the Marias, Clark had been conducting the other exploration which they had decided was necessary, that of the Yellowstone. His log of this journey, July 3 to August 12, forms Chapter XXXI of the Journals. Since he was entirely on his own, the daily entries are longer than those which he customarily wrote and the chapter runs eighty-nine pages. Though it is an interesting account, nothing of importance happens and the whole chapter is omitted here. The summary that follows is reprinted from Chapter XII of DeVoto, The Course of Empire.

Clark's party started up Bitterroot Valley July 3.[1] He wanted to find the road to the Jefferson River which they had heard about while toiling along the Salmon last year. Shields found it and on July 6 it took them across the Continental Divide by what is now called Gibbon's Pass. (Not far in miles from the Lost Trail Pass by which they had crossed from the Salmon to Bitterroot Valley.) It led on down to Big Hole Valley, where Sacajawea could really be a guide. Holding to her landmarks, on July 8 they reached the place where they had sunk the dugouts in a pond last August 23. There was a furious digging to raise the Cache — after more than six months of abstinence they could chew and smoke tobacco again. Clark embarked most of the party in the boats for the Three Forks, leaving Ordway to take the horses there by land. Downstream by boat was a different matter from the dreadful upstream tug. They

---

[1] Lewis had left Traveller's Rest for the Hellgate River earlier the same day.

made ninety-seven miles the first day and reached the Three Forks on the third.

Here Clark divided his party. Taking eight men, besides Charbonneau, Sacajawea, and her eighteen-month-old child, he struck overland with the herd of forty-nine horses, heading for the Yellowstone. Ordway took the rest of the command down the Missouri in the boats toward the first rendezvous, the Great Falls. Three days brought Ordway to the Gate of the Mountains and three more to the head of the portage, White Bear Island, which he reached on July 19.

Lewis, traveling the direct route from Traveller's Rest, had reached the portage, a week earlier. He had left there all his party except Drewyer and the two Fields brothers, putting Sergeant Gass in command. He had also left horses, and with them to pull last year's truck-frames the job was easy. They raised the caches, transported the whole outfit across the eighteen-mile portage, and got the white pirogue into the water. They took eight days, as against more than a month last year. Lewis was to meet them at the mouth of the Marias, which he was now exploring, and on July 27 Gass started thither with the horses and Ordway headed the boats downstream. The next day, well above the mouth of the Marias, they saw Lewis and his three men who had just reached the Missouri after a hell-for-leather ride, and fired a swivel to welcome them.

Meanwhile Clark's little party had had an interlude of pure enjoyment, the most comfortable traveling of the whole expedition. On July 15 he reached the Yellowstone and saw the majestic mountains through which it flows north from Yellowstone Park. He could find no timber big enough for dugouts and the river was too swift, he decided, for the bullboats he had thought of making. So, looking for better timber, he struck off down the beautiful Yellowstone Valley by pack train. Signal smokes showed that he was being watched and he thought the watchers must be Crows. He found some suitable trees and made two dugouts. They were 28 feet long, 16 or 18 inches deep, 16 to 24 inches wide — in such craft, axe-hewn and hollowed by fire, the great Yellowstone was first navigated by white men. The Crows, honored by all Plains tribes as the most expert horse-thieves, crawled up one night and got half the horses, taking them away over hard and gravelly ground so that their trail could not be followed. The first American horses the Crows ever got.

Clark ordered Sergeant Pryor, with three men, to take the rest of the *remuda* to the rendezvous at the mouth of the Yellowstone and on to the Mandan villages. (They were money; they could be traded to the village tribes for corn and skin-cloathing.) In addition, tying up the expedition's loose ends as he traveled, he gave Pryor a letter to the Northwester who had most impressed the captains, Hugh Heney. Pryor was to take it to the posts on the Assiniboine River, as soon as he could get there from the Mandans. It offered Heney, who had traded with the Teton Sioux, the job of inducing several Sioux chiefs to accompany Lewis and Clark to Washington, to be impressed and pacified. Clark offered the going wage — and, with a look ahead, the job of agent for the Sioux at the post which Lewis had advised the government to establish on the Cheyenne River.

Heney was given, half explicitly, an additional mission: to counteract among his Sioux clients the influence of the British traders from the Minnesota River. And the letter had two further purposes. Clark told Heney that the expedition had accomplished its objective by descending the Columbia to its mouth. He added that there was now in progress an exploration of a northern affluent of the Missouri which it had discovered and named the Marias. By this means the North West Company, and Montreal, would learn at the earliest possible moment that the United States had reached the Pacific, had nailed down its claim to the Columbia country, and had investigated its northern boundary.

This was first-rate policy but it did not get started. On Pryor's second night out, the accomplished Crows managed to steal all the horses he was driving. That left no currency to buy goods to give to Heney for presents to the Sioux, and the letter was never delivered. . . . How well these men had mastered the West is demonstrated by Pryor's action. Unhorsed deep in the wilderness, with his command and commander outdistancing him farther every day, he was entirely assured. He shot buffalo and made two Mandan bullboats. Two, not one. One would have comfortably transported four men and their small outfit, but if it had capsized all the rifles would have been lost. Pryor embarked his detachment in these novel craft and floated off down the Yellowstone, soon mastering their use. They floated up to where Clark was waiting for them on August 8. Pryor reported that bullboats were better for such a river than dugouts.

Clark, however, had taken his party down in his two new dugouts, lashing them together for greater stability, a trick he had
seen used on the middle Missouri. There were no difficulties and
the party lived high on buffalo meat. He ventured to name a southern affluent Clark's Fork. (Not to be confused with the much big-
ger Clark's Fork of the Columbia, the extension of the Blackfoot,
Hellgate, and Bitterroot.) It is a beautiful stream that comes down
from the Absaroka Mountains, passing through a spectacular gorge
that is soon to be ruined by a dam. He carved his name on a rock
formation which he named Pompey's Pillar for Sacajawea's child,
who traveled in his dugout and had become "my boy Pomp." He
passed and identified the mouth of the Big Horn on July 6, and
repeated the Minnetarees' faulty information that it was very long
and headed with the Platte. (Manuel Lisa was to build his post
here a year later and send Colter, who was now with Clark, to
determine whether the Minnetarees were right.) He passed the
Rosebud on July 28, the Tongue on the 29th, and Powder River,
which he seems not to have identified, on the 30th. On August 3,
fatly fed, comfortable, an easy master of the job, he brought the expedition's biggest loop full circle, reaching the Missouri. They
had come to this confluence on the upstream journey April 26 1805.

He summed up — or rather Lewis presently wrote a summary
from Clark's notes. It could be called The Error of the Southwest.
The Yellowstone, said the summary, rose on the border of New
Mexico, whence a short, good road led to the Spanish settlements.
(These unseen settlements were always Santa Fe.) Its source was adjacent to those of the Willamette, the Snake, the Platte, the Bitterroot (!), and the Big Horn. Pirogues would be the best craft for
the Yellowstone but even "batteaux," big boats, could go all the
way to the mountains. (There must have been a lot of water in the
river that year too.) The Big Horn and Clark's Fork must be navigable for a considerable distance. (Entirely wrong.) Besides the
Big Horn, the mouth of Clark's Fork would be a good site for a
trading post, for it would be fairly safe from the Blackfeet. This
last suggestion seems, temporarily, to undercut the promise to the
Snakes, the Nez Percés, and various Columbia River tribes that the
American trade would seek them out. But only temporarily.

The journal says that the Yellowstone has "a considerable fall"
somewhere in the mountains. This statement has been crossed out
and an explicit "No" has been written after it. Both the statement

and the denial are beyond explanation. Clark had talked to no Indians while he was coming down the river. There had been no mention of the tremendous Yellowstone Falls in any of the notes made at the villages or among the Snakes.

At the rendezvous mosquitoes were so numerous and buffalo momentarily so scarce that Clark dropped down the Missouri for some distance, leaving a note on a post for Pryor and Lewis. On August 11 the two trappers, Dixon and Handcock, the first followers, rowed their dugouts round the bend and stopped at Clark's camp. Here was the first news of anything downriver. The peace which the captains had negotiated at the villages had lasted only a little longer than the echoes of the orations: the Mandans and the Minnetarees were fighting the Arikaras. Also the Assiniboins were on the prod: they had killed a Northwester on the Souris, had vaingloriously forbidden his company to go to the villages (which was just talk), and had sent out word that they were going to get Charles MacKenzie.

The next day, August 12, Lewis's party came down the Missouri and, yelling, turned in toward the camp.

Dixon and Handcock came back down the river, having decided to return with the party to the Mandan villages.

[Clark]   WEDNESDAY (FRIDAY) 13TH AUGUST 1806

We Set out at sunrize and proceeded on very well with a Stiff breeze astern the greater part of the day. passed the Little Missouri river at 8 A. M. and arived at the Enterance of Myry river at sun set and encamped on the N E Side haveing came by the assistance of the wind, the current and our oars 86 miles.

THURSDAY (SATURDAY)14TH AUGUST 1806

Set out at Sunrise and proceeded on. when we were opposit the Minetares Grand Village we Saw a number of the Nativs viewing of [us]   we derected the Blunderbuses fired Several times,   Soon after we Came too at a Croud of the nativs on the bank opposit the Village of the Shoe Indians or *Mah-har-has* at which place I saw the principal Chief of the Little Village of the Menitarre & the principal Chief of the *Mah-har-has.* those people were extreamly pleased to See us. the chief of the little Village of the Menetarras cried Most imoderately,   I enquired the cause and was informed it was for the loss of his Son who had been killed latterly by the Blackfoot Indians. after a delay of a fiew minits I proceeded on to the black cats Village on the N.E. side of the Missouri where I intended to Encamp but the Sand blew in Such a manner that we deturmined not to continue on that side but return to the side we had left. here we were visited by all the inhabitants of this village who appeared equally as well pleased to see us as those above. I walked up to the Black Cats village & eate some simnins with him, and Smoked a pipe   this Village I discovered had been rebuilt sin[c]e I left it and much smaller than it was; enquiring into the cause was informed that a quarrel had taken place and (*a number of*) Lodges had removed to the opposd. Side.

I had soon as I landed despatched Shabono to the Minetarras inviting the Chiefs to visit us, & Drewyer down to the lower Village of the Mandans to ask Mr. Jessomme to come and enterpret for us. Mr. Jessomme arived and I spoke to the chief of the Village informing them that we spoke to them as we had done when we were with them last and we now repeeted our invitation to the principal Chiefs of all the Villages to accompany us to the U States &c. &c.   the Black Cat Chief of the Mandans, spoke and informed me that he wished to Visit the United States and his Great Father but was afraid of the *Sioux* who were yet at war with them and had killed several of their men since we had left them, and were on the river below and would certainly kill him if he attempted to go down. I indeavered to do away [with] his objections by informing him that we would not suffer those indians to hurt any of our red children who should think proper to accompany us, and on their return they would be equally protected, and their presents which would be very liberal, with themselves, conveyed to their own Country at the expence of the U. States &c. &c.   the Chief of the *Mah-har-has* told me if I would send with him he would let me have some corn. I directed Sergt Gass & 2 men to accompany him to his Village, they Soon returned loaded with Corn.

THURSDAY AUGUST 15TH 1806 (continued)
MANDANS VILG.

after assembling the Chiefs and Smokeing one pipe, I informed them that I still Spoke the Same words which we had Spoken to them when we first arived in their Country in the fall of 1804. we then envited them to visit their great father the president of the U. States and to hear his own Councils and recieve his gifts from his own hands as also .See the population of a government which can at their pleasure protect and Secure you from all your enimies, and chastize all those who will shut their years to his Councils. we now offer to take you at the expense of our Government and

Send you back to your Country again with a considerable present in Merchendize which you will receive of your great Father.

the Great chief of the Menetaras Spoke, he Said he wished to go down and see his great father very much, but that the Scioux were in the road and would most certainly kill him or any others who should go down   they were bad people and would not listen to any thing which was told them. when he Saw us last we told him that we had made peace with all the nations below,   Since that time the Seioux had killed 8 of their people and Stole a number of their horses. he Said that he had opened his ears and followed our Councils, he had made peace with the Chyennes and rocky Mountains indians, and repieted the same objecctions as mentioned. if the Sieoux were at peace with them and could be depended on he as also other Chiefs of the villages would be glad to go and See their great father, but as they were all afraid of the Sieoux they should not go down &c.

The Black Cat Chief of the Mandans Village on the North Side of the Missouri sent over and requested me to go over to his village. after takeing a Smoke he informed me that as the Scioux were very troublesom and the road to his great father dangerous none of the village would go down with us. I told the Cheifs and wariers of the village who were then present that we were anxious that some of the village Should go and See their great father and hear his good words & receve his *bountifull gifts* &c. and told them to pitch on Some Man on which they could rely on and Send him to see their Great father, they made the same objections which the Chief had done before. a young man offered to go down, and they all agreed for him to go down   the charactor of this young man I knew as a bad one and made an objection as to his age and Chareckter   at this time Gibson who was with me informed me that this young man had Stole his knife and had it then in his possession,   this I informed the Chief and directed him to give up the knife   he delivered the knife with a very faint apology for his haveing it in his possession. I then reproached those people for wishing to send such a man to See and hear the words of so great a man as their great father,   they hung their heads and said nothing for some time when the Cheif spoke and Said that they were afraid to Send any one for fear of their being killed by the Sieux. being informed by one of our enterpreters that the 2d Chief of the Mandans comonly called the little crow intended to accompany us down,   I took Charbono and walked to the Village to see this Chief and talk with him on the subject   he told me he had deturmined to go down, but wished to have a council first with his people which would be in the after part of the day.

Colter one of our men expressed a desire to join Some trappers [*the two Illinois Men we met, & who now came down to us*] who offered to become shearers with [him] and furnish traps &c.   the offer [was] a very advantagious one, to him, his services could be dispenced with from this down and as we were disposed to be of service to any one of our party who had performed their duty as well as Colter had done,   we agreed to allow him the privilage provided no one of the party would ask or expect a Similar permission to which they all agreed that they wished Colter every suckcess and that as we did not wish any of them to Seperate untill we Should arive at St. Louis they would not apply or expect it &c.   great number of the nativs of the different villages came to view us and exchange robes with our men for their Skins   we gave Jo Colter Some Small articles which we did not want and some powder and lead. the party also gave him several articles which will be usefull to him on his expedittion.

This evening Charbono informed me that our back was scercely turned before a war party from the two menetarry villages followed on and attacked and killed the Snake Indians whome we had seen and in the engagement between them and the Snake indians they had lost two men one of which was the Son of the principal Chief of the little village of the Menitarras. that they had also went to war from the Menetarras and killed two Ricaras. he further informed me that a missunderstanding had taken place between the Mandans & Minetarras and had very nearly come to blows about a woman,   the Menitarres at length presented a pipe and a reconsilliation took place between them.

FRIDAY 16TH AUGUST 1806

as our swivel could no longer be Serveceable to us as it could not be fireed on board the largest Perogue, we concluded to make a present of it to the Great Chief of the Menitaras (the One Eye) with a view to ingratiate him more Strongly in our favour   I had the

Swivel Charged and Collected the Chiefs in a circle around it and adressed them with great ceremoney. told them I had listened with much attention to what the One Eye had Said yesterday and beleived that he was sincere & Spoke from his heart. I reproached them very severely for not attending to what had been said to them by us in council in the fall of 1804 and at different times in the winter of 1804 & 5, and told them our backs were scercely turned before a party followed and killed the pore defenceless Snake indians whom we had taken by the hand & told them not to be afraid that you would never them Strike again &c.   also mentioned the ricer[a]s &c. The little cherry old Chief of the Menetarras spoke as follows Viz: "Father we wish to go down with you to See our Great Father, but we know the nations below and are afraid of the Scioux who will be on the river and will kill us on our return home. The Scioux has Stolen our horses and killed 8 of our men Since you left us, and the Ricaras have also Struck us. we Staid at home and listened to what you have told us. we at length went to war against the Scioux and met with Ricaras and killed two of them, they were on their way to strike us. We will attend to your word and not hurt any people   all Shall be Welcom and we Shall do as you direct." The One Eye said his ears would always be open to the word of his great father and Shut against bad council &c   I then [with] a good deel of ceremony made a present of the swivel to the *One Eye* Chief,   and told him when he fired this gun to remember the words of his great father which we had given him. after the council was over the gun was fired & delivered, they chief appeared to be much pleased and conveyed it immediately to his village &c.   we Settled with and discharged colter. we Sent for Mr. Jessomme and told him to use his influence to prevail on one of the Chiefs to accompany us and we would employ him. he informed us soon after that the big white Chief would go if we would take his wife & Son & Jessoms wife & 2 children [which] we wer[e] obliged to agree to do

SATURDAY 17TH OF AUGUST 1806

Settled with Touisant Chabono for his services as an enterpreter the price of a horse and Lodge purchased of him for public Service in all amounting to 500$ 33⅓ cents. derected two of the largest of

the Canoes be fastened together with poles tied across them So as
to make them Study [steady] for the purpose of Conveying the
Indians and enterpreter and their families

we were visited by all the principal Chiefs of the Menetarras to
take their leave of us   at 2 oClock we left our encampment after
takeing leave of Colter who also Set out up the river in company
with Messrs. Dickson & Handcock. we also took our leave of T.
Chabono, his Snake Indian wife and their child who had accompanied us on our rout to the pacific ocean in the capacity of interpreter and interprete[s]s. T. Chabono wished much to accompany us in the said Capacity if we could have provailed [upon] the
Menetarre Chiefs to dec[e]nd the river with us to the U. States, but
as none of those Chiefs of whoes language he was Conversent
would accompany us, his services were no longer of use to the
U. States and he was therefore discharged and paid up. we offered
to convey him down to the Illinois if he chose to go, He declined
proceeding on at present, observing that he had no acquaintance
or prospects of makeing a liveing below, and must continue to live
in the way that he had done. I offered to take his little son a butifull promising child who is 19 months old to which they both
himself & wife wer willing provided the child had been weened.
they observed that in one year the boy would be sufficiently old to
leave his mother & he would then take him to me if I would be so
friendly as to raise the child for him in such a manner as I thought
proper, to which I agreed &c.

we droped down to the *Big White Cheifs* Mandan village ½ a
mile below on the South Side,   all the Indians proceeded on
down by land. and I walked to the lodge of the Cheif whome I
found sorounded by his friends   the men were Setting in a circle
Smokeing and the womin crying. he Sent his baggage with his
wife & son, with the Interpreter Jessomme & his wife and 2 children
to the Canoes provided for them. after Smokeing one pipe, and
distributing some powder & lead which we had given him, he informed me that he was ready and we were accompd. to the Canoes
by all the village   Maney of them Cried out aloud. as I was
about to shake with the Grand Cheifs of all the villages there assembled they requested me to Set one minit longer with them
which I readily agreed to and directed a pipe to be lit. the Cheifs
informed that when we first came to their Country they did not

beleive all we Said   but they were now convinced that every
thing we had told them were true, that they should keep in memory
every thing which we had said to them, and Strictly attend to our
advice, that their young men Should Stay at home and Should no[t]
go again to war against any nation, that if any atacted them they
should defend themselves, that we might depend on what they
said, and requested us to inform their great father. the also requested me to tell the Ricaras to come and see them, not to be
afraid that no harm Should be done them, that they were anxious
to be in peace with them.

The Seeoux they said they had no dependance in and Should kill
them whenever they came into their country to do them harm &c.
I told them that we had always told them to defend themselves, but
not to strike those nations we had taken by the hand, the Sieoux
with whome they were at war we had never seen   on our return
we Should inform their great father of their conduct towards his
faithfull red children and he would take Such Steps as will bring
about a lasting peace between them and his faithfull red children.
I informed them that we should inform the ricaras what they had
requested &c. The Grand Chief of the Minetarres said that the
Great Cheif who was going down with [us] to see their great father
was a[s] well as if he went also, and on his return he would be fully
informed of the words of his great father, and requested us to take
care of this Gt. Chief. we then saluted them with a gun and set out
and proceeded on to *Fort Mandan* where I landed and went to view
the old works   the houses except one in the rear bastion was
burnt by accident, some pickets were standing in front next to the
river.

The mouth of Heart River was passed on August 18.

TUESDAY 19TH OF AUGUST 1806

Capt. Lewis'es wounds are heeling very fast, I am much in hope
of his being able to walk in 8 or 10 days. the wind rose and become
very strong from the S.E. and a great appearance of rain. Jessomme
the Interpreter let me have a piece of a lodge and the Squars
pitched or Stretched it over Some Sticks,   under this piece of

leather I Slept dry, it is the only covering which I have had Sufficient to keep off the rain Since I left the Columbia. it began to rain moderately soon after night.

WEDNESDAY 20TH OF AUGUST 1806

I observe a great alteration in the Current course and appearance of this pt. of the Missouri. in places where there was Sand bars in the fall 1804 at this time the main current passes, and where the current then passed is now a Sand bar. Sand bars which were then naked are now covered with willow several feet high. the enterance of some of the Rivers & creeks changed owing to the mud thrown into them, and a layor of mud over some of the bottoms of 8 inches thick.

[Mouth of Cannonball River passed today.]

THURSDAY 21TE AUGUST 1806

at 8 A.M. Met three frenchmen Comeing up, they proved to be three men from the Ricaras two of them Reeved & Greinyea wintered with us at the mandans in 1804 we Came too, those men informed us that they were on their way to the Mandans, and intended to go down to the Illinois this fall. one of them quit[e] a young lad requested a passage down to the Illinois,   we concented and he got into a Canoe to [ply] an Ore. Those men informd. us that 700 Seeoux had passed the Ricaras on their way to war with the Mandans & Menitarras and that their encampment where the Squaws and children wer, was Some place near the Big Bend of this river below. they also informed us that no trader had arived at the Ricaras this Season, and that they were informed that the Pania or Ricara Chief who went to the United States last Spring was a year, died on his return at Some place near the Sieoux river &c.[1]   those men had nether powder nor lead   we gave them a horn of powder and some balls and after a delay of an hour we parted from the[m].

at half past 11 a.m. we arived in view of the upper Ricara villages, a Great number of womin Collecting wood on the banks,   we Saluted the village with four guns and they returned

[1] The Arikara chief died in Washington in April, 1806.

the Salute by fireing Several guns in the village,   I observed Several very white Lodges on the hill above the Town which the ricaras from the Shore informed me were Chyennes who had just arived. we landed opposit to the 2d Village and were met by the most of the men women and children of each village as also the Chyennes, they all appeared anxious to take us by the hand and much rejoiced to See us return. I was Saluted by the two great Chiefs, whome we had made or given Medals to as we assend[ed] this river in 1804. I Set myself down on the Side of the Bank and the Chiefs & brave men of the Ricaras & Chyennes formed a cercle around me. after takeing a Smoke of Mandan tobacco which the Big white Chief who was seated on my left hand furnished, I in- formed them as I had before informed the Mandans & Menitarras, where we had been, what we had done and said to the different nations in there favour and envited Some of their chiefs to ac- company us down and See their great father and receve from his own mouth his good councils and from his own hands his *bounti- full* gifts &c. telling pretty much the Same which I had told the mandans and menitarras. told them not to be afraid of any nation below that none would hurt them &c.

I also told the ricaras that I was very sorry to here that they were not on friendly terms with their neighbours the Mandans & Menetarras, and had not listened to what we had said to them but had Suffered their young men to join the Sieoux who had killed 8 Mandans &c.   that their young men had Stolen the horses of the Minetarras, in retaliation for those enjories the Mandans & Menetarras had sent out a war party and killed 2 ricaras. how could they expect other nations would be at peace with them when they themselves would not listen to what their great father had told them. I further informed them that the Mandans & Menetaras had opened their ears to what we had said to them but had Staid at home untill they were Struck that they were still disposed to be friendly and on good terms with the ricaras,   they then Saw the great chief of the Mandans by my Side who was on his way to see his great father, and was derected by his nation & the Menetaras & Maharhas, to Smoke in the pipe of peace with you and to tell you not to be afraid to go to their towns, or take the Birds in the plains   that their ears were open to our councils and no harm Should be done to a Ricara.

The Sun being very hot the Chyenne Chief envited us to his Lodge which was pitched in the plain at no great distance from the River. I accepted the invitation and accompanied him to his lodge which was new and much larger than any which I have Seen   it was made of 20 dressed Buffalow Skins in the Same form of the Seeoux and lodges of other nations of this quarter   about this lodges was 20 others several of them nearly the Same Size. I enquired for the ballance of the nation and was informed that they were near at hand and would arive on tomorrow and when all together amounted to 120 Lodges. after Smokeing I gave a medal of the Small size to the Chyenne Chief &c. which appeared to alarm him,   he had a robe and a fleece of fat Buffalow meat brought and gave me with the meadel back and informed me that he knew that the white people were all *medecine* and that he was afraid of the midal or any thing that white people gave to them. I had previously explained the cause of my g[i]veing him the medal & flag, and again told him the use of the medal and the caus[e] of my giveing it to him, and again put it about his neck delivering him up his preasent of a roab & meat, informing him that this was the medecene which his Great father directed me to deliver to all the great chiefs who listened to his word and followed his councils, that he had done so and I should leave the medal with him as a token of his cincerity &c.   he doubled the quantity of meat, and received the medal

in the evening the Great Chief requested that I would walk to his house which I did, he gave me about 2 quarts *(carrots)* of Tobacco, 2 beaver Skins and a trencher of boiled corn & beans to eat (as it is the custom of all the Nations on the Missouri to give Something to every white man who enters their lodge something to eat)   this chief informed me that none of his chiefs wished to go down with us they all wished to see the cheif who went down return first, that the Chyennes were a wild people and were afraid to go. that they Should all listen to what I had said. The interpreter informed me that the cheifs of those villages had no intention of going down   one the cheifs of the village on the island talkd. of going down. I returned to the boat where I found the principal chief of the lower vilege who had cut part of his hair and disfigured himself in Such a manner that I did not know him, he informed me the Seeux had killed his nephew and that [he] Was in tears for him &c.   we deturmined to proceed down to the Island and accordingly took the chief on board and proceeded on down to the Isd. village at which place we arived a little before dark and were met as before by nearly every individual of the Village. The one arm 2d Cheif of this village whome we had expected to accompany us down Spoke to the mandan Cheif in a loud and thretening tone which caused me to be Some what alarmed for the Safty of that cheif,   I inform the Ricaras of this village that the Mandans had opened their ears to and fold. our councils, that this cheif was on his way to see their Great Father the P. of U S. and was under our protection that if any enjorey was done to him by any nation that we Should all die to a man. I at length went to the grand chiefs Lodge by his particular invitation, the Mandan chief Stuck close to me the Chief had prepd. a Supper of boiled young corn, beens & [s]quashes of which he gave me in Wooden bowls   he also gave me near 2 quarts of the Tobacco (*Seed*), & informed me he had always had his ears open to what we had Said, that he was well convinced that the Seeoux was the caus[e] of all the trouble between the Mandans & them.

Friday 22nd August 1806

as I was about to leave the cheifs [*of the Chyennes*] lodge he requested me to Send Some traders to them, that their country was full of beaver and they would then be encouraged to kill beaver, but now they had no use for them as they could get nothing for their skins and did not know well, how to catch beaver. if the white people would come amongst them they would become acquainted and they [*the white people*] would learn them how to take the beaver. I promised the Nation that I would inform their Great father the President of the U States, and he would have them Supplied with goods, and mentioned in what manner they would be Supplied &c. &c.

I am happy to have it in my power to Say that my worthy friend Capt. Lewis is recovering fast, he walked a little to day for the first time. I have discontinud the tent in the hole the ball came out

Tuesday 26th of August 1806

at 8 passed the place the Tetons were encamped at the time they attempted to Stop us in Sept. 1804, and at 9 A.M. passed the enterance of Teton River. Saw Several black tail or Mule deer and Sent out to kill them but they were wild and the humters could not get a Shot at either of them. a fiew miles below the Teton river I observed a buffalow Skin Canoe lying on the S Shore and a Short distance lower a raft which induces me to suspect that the Tetons are not on the Missouri at the big bend as we were informed by the Ricaras, but up the Teton river. at 5 P.M. we landed a[t] Louisells fort on Ceder Island,   this fort is entire and every part appears to be in the same state it was when we passed it in Sept. 1804   we proceeded on about 10 miles lower and encamped on the S. W. Side. as we were now in the country where we were informed the Seioux were assembled we were much on our guard deturmined to put up with no insults from those bands of Seioux, all the arms &c. in perfect order. Capt. L. is still on the mending hand he walks a little. we made *60* miles to day with the wind ahead greater part of the day.

SATURDAY 30TH OF AUGUST 1806.

Capt. Lewis is mending Slowly. I took 3 hunters and walked on the N. E. Shore with a view to kill some fat meet. we had not proceeded far before Saw a large plumb orchd. of the most delicious plumbs,   out of this orchard 2 large Buck Elks ran the hunters killed them. I stoped the canoes and brought in the flesh which was fat and fine. here the party collected as many plumbs as they could eate and Several pecks of which they put by &c.   after a delay of nearly 2 hours we again proceeded on downwards,   I saw Several men on horseback which with the help of a spie glass I found to be Indians on the high hills to the N. E.   we landed on the S. W. side and I sent out two men to a village of Barking Squirels to kill some of those animals [2]   imedeatily after landing about 20 indians was discovered on an eminance a little above us on the opposite Side. one of those men I took to be a french man from his [having] a blanket capoe & a handkerchief around his head. imediately after 80 or 90 Indian men all armed with fusees & Bows & arrows came out of a wood on the opposite bank about ¼ of a mile below us. they fired of[f] their guns as a Salute we re-

[2] Prairie dogs; Clark wanted to add specimens of them to the expedition's collection.

turned the Salute with 2 rounds. we were at a loss to deturmin of what nation those indians were. from their hostile appearance we were apprehensive they were Tetons,   but from the country through which they roved we were willing to believe them either the Yanktons, Pon[c]ars or Mahars either of which nations are well disposed towards the white people. I deturmined to find out who they were without running any risque of the party and in-dians,   and therefore took three french men who could Speak the Mahar Pania and some Seeoux and in a Small canoe I went over to a Sand bar which extended Sufficiently near the opposite shore to converse.

imedeately after I set out 3 young men set out from the opposite Side and swam next me on the Sand bar. I derected the men to Speak to them in the Pania and Mahar Languages first neither of which they could understand   I then derected the man who could speak a fiew words of Seioux to inquire what nation or tribe they belong to   they informed me that they were Tetons and their chief was the black buffalow   this chief I knew very well to be the one we had seen with his band at Teton river which band had attempted to detain us in the fall of 1804 as we assended this river and with whome we wer near comeing to blows. I told those Indians that they had been deef to our councils and ill treated us as we assended this river two years past, that they had abused all the whites who had visited them since. I believed them to be bad people & should not suffer them to cross to the Side on which the party lay, and directed them to return with their band to their camp, that if any of them come near our camp we Should kill them certainly. I lef[t] them on the bear [bar] and returned to th[e] party and examined the arms &c   those indians seeing some corn in the canoe requested some of it which I refused being deturmined to have nothing to do with those people.

Several others swam across one of which understood pania, and as our pania interpreter was a very good one we had it in our power to inform what we wished. I told this man to inform his nation that we had not forgot their treatment to us as we passed up this river &c. that they had treated all the white people who had visited them very badly; robed them of their goods, and had wounded one man whom I had Seen. we viewed them as bad peo-ple and no more traders would be Suffered to come to them, and whenever the white people wished to visit the nations above they would come sufficiently Strong to whip any vilenous party who dare to oppose them and words to the same purpote. I also told them that I was informed that a part of all their bands were going to war against the Mandans &c, and that they would be well whiped as the Mandans & Minitarres &[c] had a plenty of Gúns Powder and ball, and we had given them a cannon to defend themselves. and derected them to return from the Sand bar and inform their chiefs what we had said to them, and to keep away from the river or we Should kill every one of them &c. &c.   those fellows requested to be allowed to come across and make cumerads which we positively refused and I directed them to return imediately which they did and after they had informed the Chiefs &c. as I suppose what we had said to them, they all set out on their return to their camps back of a high hill.   7 of them halted on the top of the hill and blackguarded us, told us to come across and they would kill us all &c of which we took no notice.

we all this time were extreamly anxious for the arival of the 2 fields & Shannon whome we had left behind, and were some what consd. as to their Safty.   to our great joy those men hove in Sight at 6 P. M.   Jo Fields had killed 3 black tail or mule deer.   we then Set out,   as I wished to see what those Indians on the hill would act, we steared across near the opposit Shore,   this notion put them [in] some agitation as to our intentions,   some set out on the direction towards their Camps others walked about on the top of the hill and one man walked down the hill to meet us and invited us to land to which invitation I paid no kind of attention. this man I knew to be the one who had in the fall 1804 accompanied us 2 days and is said to be the friend to the white people. after we passd him he returned on the top of the hill and gave 3 strokes with the gun (*on the earth — this is swearing by the earth*) he had in his hand   this I am informed is a great oath among the indians.

CHAPTER XXXIII

The Home Stretch

[Clark]   Monday 1st of September 1806

At 9 A. M. we passed the enterance of River Quiequur [the Niobrara] which had the Same appearance it had when we passed up water rapid and of a milky white colour   about two miles below the Quicurre,   9 Indians ran down the bank and beckened to us to land, they appeared to be a war party, and I took them to be Tetons and paid no kind of attention to them further than an enquirey to what tribe they belonged,   they did not give me any answer, I prosume they did not understand the man who Spoke to them as he Spoke but little of their language. as one canoe was yet behind we landed in an open commanding Situation out of sight of the indians deturmined to delay untill they came up. about 15 minits after we had landed Several guns were fired by the indians, which we expected was at the three men behind. I calld out 15 men and ran up with a full deturmination to cover them if possible let the number of the indians be what they might. Capt. Lewis hobled up on the bank and formed the remainder of the party in a Situation well calculated to defend themselves and the Canoes &c.

when I had proceeded to the point about 250 yards I discovered the Canoe about 1 mile above & the indians where we had left them. I then walked on the Sand beech and the indians came down to meet me   I gave them my hand and enquired of them what they were Shooting at, they informed me that they were Shooting off their guns at an old Keg which we had thrown out of one of the Canoes and was floating down. those indians informed me they were Yanktons, one of the men with me knew one of the Indians to be the brother of young Durion's wife. finding those indians to be Yanktons I invited them down to the boats to Smoke. when we arived at the Canoes they all eagerly Saluted the Mandan Chief, and we all set and smoked Several pipes. I told them that we took them to be a party of Tetons and the fireing I expected was at the three men in the rear Canoe and I had went up with a full intention to kill them all if they had been tetons & fired on the canoe as we first expected, but finding them Yanktons and good men we were glad to see them and take them by the hand as faithfull Children who had opened their ears to our Councils. one of them Spoke and Said that their nation had opened their years & done as we had directed them ever since we gave the Meadel to their great Chief, and should continue to do as we had told them

we enquired if any of their chiefs had gone down with Mr. Durion, the[y] answered that their great Chief and many of their brave men had gone down, that the white people had built a house near the Mahar village where they traded. we tied a piece of ribon to each mans hair and gave them some corn of which they appeared much pleased. The Mandan chief gave a par of elegant Legins to the principal man of the indian party, which is an indian fashion (to make presents)   the Canoe & 3 men haveing joined us we took our leave of this party telling them to return to their band and listen to our councils which we had before given to them. Their band of 80 Lodges were on plum creek a fiew miles to the north. after we all came together we again proceeded on down to a large Sand bar imediately opposit to the place where we met the Yanktons in council at the Calumet Bluffs and which place we left on the 1st of Sepr. 1804. I observed our old flag Staff or pole Standing as we left it.

Wednesday 3rd September 1806

passed the enterance of redstone River on the N. E. Side at 11 A M. and at half past 4 P. M we Spied two boats & Several men,   our party p[l]eyed their ores and we soon landed on the Side of the Boats   the men of [these] boats Saluted us with their Small arms   I landed & was met by a Mr. James Airs [Aird] from the Mackanaw by way of Prarie Dechien and St. Louis. this Gentleman is of the house of Dickson & Co. of Prarie de Chian who has

a Licence to trade for one year with the Sieoux   he has 2 Batteaux loaded with Merchendize for that purpose. This Gentleman
receved both Capt. Lewis and my self with every mark of friendship he was himself at the time with a chill of the agu on him which
he has had for Several days. our first enquirey was after the President of our country and then our friends and the State of the
politicks of our country &c. and the State [of] Indian affairs to all
of which enquireys Mr. Aires gave us a Satisfactory information as
he had it in his power to have collected in the Illinois which was
not a great deel. soon after we Landed a violent Storm of Thunder
Lightning and rain from the N. W. which was violent with hard
claps of thunder and Sharp Lightning which continued untill
10 P M after which the wind blew hard. I set up late and partook
of the tent of Mr. Aires which was dry.

Mr. Aires unfortunately had his boat Sunk on the 25 of July
last by a violent storm of Wind and hail by which accident he lost
the most of his usefull articles as he informed us. this Gentleman
informed us of maney changes & misfortunes which had taken place
in the Illinois amongst others the loss of Mr. Cady [Pierre]
Choteaus house and furniture by fire. for this misfortune of our
friend Choteaus I feel my self very much concernd &c.   he also
informed us that Genl. Wilkinson was the governor of the Louisiana
and at St. Louis. 300 of the american Troops had been cantuned
on the Missouri a fiew miles above it's mouth,   Some disturbance
with the Spaniards in the Nackatosh [Natchitoches] Country is the
cause of their being called down to that country, the Spaniards had
taken one of the U. States frigates in the Mediteranean,   Two
British Ships of the line had fired on an American Ship in the port
of New York, and killed the Capts. brother. 2 Indians had been
hung in St. Louis for murder and several others in jale. and that
Mr. Burr & Genl Hambleton fought a Duel, the latter was killed
&c. &c.   I am happy to find that my worthy friend Capt. L's is so
well as to walk about with ease to himself &c.   we made *60* Miles
to day   the river much crowded with Sand bars, which are very
differently Situated from what they were when we went up.

THURSDAY 4TH SEPTEMBER 1806.

as we were in want of some tobacco I purposed to Mr. Airs to
furnish us with 4 carrots for which we would Pay the amount to

any Merchant of St. Louis   he very readily agreed to furnish us with tobacco and gave to each man as much as it is necessary for them to use between this and St. Louis, an instance of Generossity for which every man of the party appears to acknowledge. Mr. Airs also insisted on our accepting a barrel of flour.   we gave to this gentleman what corn we could Spear amounting to about 6 bushels,   this corn was well calculated for his purpose as he was about to make his establishment and would have it in his power to hull the corn &c.   the flower was very acceptable to us   we have yet a little flour part of what we carried up from the Illinois as high as Maria's river and buried it there untill our return &c.

at 8 A. M. we took our leave and Set out, and proceeded on very well,   at 11 A. M. passed the Enterance of the big Sieoux River which is low, and at meridian we came too at Floyds Bluff below the Enterance of Floyds river and assended the hill, with Capt. Lewis and Several men,   found the grave had been opened by the nativs and left half covered. we had this grave completely filled up, and returned to the canoes and proceeded on to the Sand bar on which we encamped from the 12th to the 20th of August 1804 near the Mahar Village,   here we came to and derected every wet article put out to dry, all the bedding of the party and Skins being wet. as it was late in the evening we deturmined to continue all night. had issued to each man of the party a cup of flour. a little before night Several Guns were heard below and in a direction towards the Mahar village which induced us to suspect that Mr. McClellin who we was informed was on his way up to trade with the Mahars had arived at the Creek below and that those reports of Guns was some of his party out hunting.

FRIDAY 5TH SEPTEMBER 1806

the report of the guns which was heard must have been the Mahars who most probably have just arrived at their village from hunting the buffalow. this is a season they usialy return to their village to secure their crops of corn Beens punkins &c &c.   proceeded on very well passd the blue Stone bluff at 3 P. M.

SATURDAY 6TH SEPTEMBER 1806.

at the lower point of Pelecan Island a little above the Petite River de Seeoux we met a tradeing boat of Mr. Og. Choteaux [Auguste Chouteau] of St. Louis bound to the River Jacque to

trade with the Yanktons,   this boat was in care of a Mr. Henry
Delorn,   he had exposed all his loading (*to dry*) and sent out
five of his hands to hunt   they soon arived with an Elk. we
purchased a gallon of whiskey of this man (*promised to pay
Choteau who would not receive any pay*) and gave to each man of
the party a dram which is the first spiritious licquor which had
been tasted by any of them since the 4 of July 1805. several of the
party exchanged leather for linen Shirts and beaver for corse hats.
Those men could inform us nothing more than that all the troops
had movd. from the Illinois and that Genl. Wilkinson was prepareing to leave St. Louis. We advised this trader to treat the
Tetons with as much contempt as possible and stated to him where
he would be benefited by such treatment &c &c. and at 1 P. M. set
out   those men gave us 2 Shots from a Swivell they had on the
bow of their boat which we returned in our turn. The Chief & the
Squaws & children are awarey of their journey. Children cry &c.

TUESDAY 9TH SEPTEMBER 1806

   passed the enterance of the great river Platt which is at this time
low the water nearly clear the current turbelant as usial; the Sand
bars which choked up the Missouri and confined the [river] to a
narrow Snagey Chanel are wastd. a way and nothing remains but
a fiew Small remains of the bear [bar] which is covered with drift
wood. below the R. Platt the current of the Missouri becomes evidently more rapid than above and the Snags much more noumerous
and bad to pass   late in the evening we arived at the Bald pated
prarie and encamped imediately opposit our encampment of the
16th and 17th of July 1804. our party appears extreamly anxious
to get on, and every day appears [to] produce new anxieties in them
to get to their country and friends. My worthy friend Cap Lewis
has entirely recovered   his wounds are heeled up and he can
walk and even run nearly as well as ever he could,   the parts are
yet tender &c &c.   the climate is every day preceptably wormer
and air more Sultery than I have experienced for a long time. the
nights are now so worm that I sleep comfortable under a thin
blanket, a fiew days past 2 was not more than sufficient

WEDNESDAY 10TH SEPTEMBER 1806.

   at [blank in MS] P M we met a Mr. Alexander La fass and three
french men from St. Louis in a Small perogue on his way to the

River Platt to trade with the Pania Luup or Wolf Indians. this man was extreemly friendly to us he offered us any thing he had,   we axcepted of a bottle of whisky only which we gave to our party,   Mr. *la frost* informed us that Genl. Wilkinson and all the troops had decended the Mississippi and Mr. Pike [1] and young Mr. Wilkinson had Set out on an expedition up the Arkansaw river or in that direction   after a delay of half an hour we proceedd on about 3 miles and met a large perogue and 7 Men from St. Louis bound to the Mahars for the purpose of trade, this perogue was in Charge of a Mr. La Craw (*Croix*)   we made Some fiew enquiries of this man and again proceeded on through a very bad part of the river crouded with Snags & Sawyers and incamped on a Sand bar about 4 miles above the Grand Nemahar. we find the river in this timbered country narrow and more moveing Sands and a much greater quantity of Sawyers or Snags than above. Great caution and much attention is required to Stear clear of all those dificuelties in this low State of the water.

FRIDAY 12TH OF SEPTEMBER 1806

we Set out at Sunrise the usial hour and proceeded on very well   about 7 miles met 2 perogues from St. Louis one contained the property of Mr. Choteau bound to the panias or River Platt, the other going up trapping as high as the Mahars. here we met one of the french men who had accompanied us as high as the Mandans   he informed us that Mr. McClellan was a fiew miles below   the wind blew a head   soon after we passed those perogues, we Saw a man on Shore who informed us that he was one of Mr. McClellins party and that he was a Short distance below, we took this man on board and proceeded on and Met Mr. McClellin [2] at the St. Michls. Prarie   we came too   here we found Mr. Jo Gravelin the Ricaras enterpreter whome we had Sent down with a Ricaras Chief in the Spring of 1805. and old M. Durion the Sieux enterpreter,   we examined the instructions of those interpreters and found that Gravelin was ordered to the Ricaras with a Speach from the president of the U. States to that nation and some presents which had been given the Ricara Chief who had visited the U. States and unfortunately died at the City

---

[1] Zebulon Pike.
[2] Robert McClelan. Clark had served with him under Wayne.

of Washington, he was instructed to teach the Ricaras agriculture & make every enquirey after Capt. Lewis my self and the party. Mr. Durion was enstructed to accompany Gravelin and through his influence pass him with his presents &[c.] by the tetons bands of Sieux, and to provale on Some of the Principal chiefs of those bands not exceeding six to Visit the Seat of the Government next Spring. he was also enstructed to make every enquirey after us. we made Some Small addition to his instructions by extending the number of Chiefs to 10 or 12 or 3 from each band including the Yanktons &c. Mr. McClellin receved us very politely, and gave us all the news and occurrences which had taken place in the Illinois within his knowledge the evening proveing to be wet and cloudy we concluded to continue all night,

SATURDAY 13TH SEPTEMBER 1806

rose early Mr. McClellen gave each man a Dram and a little after Sunrise we Set out we landed at the Camp of the 5 hunters whome we had Sent a head, they had killed nothing, the wind being too high for us to proceed in Safty through the eme[n]city of Snags which was imediately below we concluded to lye by and Sent on the Small canoes a Short distance to hunt and kill Some meat, I felt my self very unwell and derected a little Chocolate which Mr. McClellin gave us, prepared of which I drank about a pint and found great relief.

SUNDAY 14TH SEPTR 1806

at 2 P. M. a little below the lower [end] of the old Kanzas Village we met three large boats bound to the Yanktons and Mahars the property of Mr. Lacroy, Mr. Aiten & Mr. Coutau all from St. Louis, those young men received us with great friendship and pressed on us Some whisky for our men, Bisquet, Pork and Onions, & part of their Stores, we continued near 2 hours with those boats, makeing every enquirey into the state of our friends and country &c. those men were much affraid of meeting with the Kanzas. we proceeded on to an Island near the middle of the river below our encampment of the 1st of July 1804 and encamped haveing decended only 53 miles to day. our party received a dram and Sung Songs untill 11 oClock at night in the greatest harmoney.

TUESDAY 16TH SEPTEMBER 1806

the Day proved excessively worm and disagreeable, so much so that the men rowed but little,   at 10 A. M. we met a large trade-ing perogue bound for the Panias we continued but a Short time with them. at 11 A. M. we met young Mr. Bobidoux [Robidoux] with a large boat of six ores and 2 canoes,   the licenes of this young man was to trade with the Panias Mahars and ottoes reather an extroardanary a license for [so] young a man and without the Seal of the teritory anexed,   as Genl. Wilkinsons Signeture was not to this instrement we were somewhat doubtfull of it. Mr. Browns Signiture we were not acquainted with without the Teri-torial Seal. we made Some enquireys of this young man and cau-tioned him against prosueing the Steps of his brother in attempting to degrade the American Charector in the eyes of the Indians.

WEDNESDAY 17TH SEPTEMBER 1806

at 11 A. M. we met a Captain McClellin [3] late a Capt. of Artily. of the U States Army assending in a large boat. this gentleman an acquaintance of my friend Capt. Lewis was Somewhat astonished to see us return and appeared rejoiced to meet us. we found him a man of information and from whome we received a partial ac-count of the political State of our country,   we were makeing enquires and exchangeing answers &c. untill near mid night. this Gentleman informed us that we had been long Since given out [up] by the people of the U S Generaly and almost forgotten,   the President of the U. States had yet hopes of us; we received some civilities of Capt. McClellin, he gave us Some Buisquit, Chocolate Sugar & whiskey, for which our party were in want and for which we made a return of a barrel of corn & much obliged to him.

Capt. McClellin informed us that he was on reather a specula-tive expedition to the confines of New Spain, with the view to entroduce a trade with those people. his plan is to proceede up this river to the Enterance of the river platt there to form an establishment from which to trade partially with the Panas & Ottoes, to form an acquaintance with the Panias and provail [on] Some of their principal Chiefs to accompany him to Santa Fee where he will appear in a stile calculated to atract the Spanish

[3] John McClallan.

government in that quarter and through the influence of a hand-some present he expects to be promited to exchange his merchin-dize for Silver & gold of which those people abound. he has a kind of introductory Speach from Govr. Wilkinson to the Panias and Ottoes and a quantity of presents of his own which he purposes distributing to the Panias and ELeatans [4] with a view to gain their protection in the execution of his plans,   if the Spanish Gov-ernmt. favour his plans, he purposes takeing his merchendize on mules & horses which can easily be procured of the panias, to some point convenient to the Spanish Settlements within the Louisiana Teritory to which place the inhabitants of New mexico may meet him for the purpose of trade &c.   Capt. McClellins plan I think a very good one if strictly prosued &c.

THURSDAY 18TH OF SEPTEMBER 1806

our party entirely out of provisions subsisting on poppaws. we divide[d] the buiskit which amounted to nearly one buisket per man, this in addition to the poppaws is to last us down to the Settlement's which is 150 miles   the party appear perfectly con-tented and tell us that they can live very well on the pappaws. we made 52 miles to day only. one of our party J. Potts complains very much of one of his eyes which is burnt by the Sun from ex-poseing his face without a cover from the Sun. Shannon also com-plains of his face & eyes &c.

FRIDAY 19TH OF SEPTR. 1806

we arived at the Enterance of Osage River at dark and encamped on the Spot we had encamped on the 1st & 2nd of June 1804 have-ing came 72 miles. a very singular disorder is takeing place amongst our party that of the Sore eyes. three of the party have their eyes inflamed and Sweled in Such a manner as to render them extreamly painfull, particularly when exposed to the light, the eye ball is much inflaimed and the lid appears burnt with the Sun,   the cause of this complaint of the eye I can't [account] for. from it's sudden appearance I am willing to believe it may be owing to the reflection of the sun on the water.

[4] Ietans: properly the Utes but here probably intended to designate the Co-manches, who were known to roam along the route to Sante Fe.

SATURDAY 20TH SEPTR. 1806

as three of the party was unabled to row from the State of their eyes we found it necessary to leave one of our crafts and divide the men into the other Canoes,   we left the two Canoes lashed together which I had made high up the River Rochejhone,   those Canoes we Set a 'drift and a little after day light we Set out and proceeded on very well. at meridian we passed the enterance of the Gasconnade river below which we met a perogue with 5 french men bound to the Osarge Gd. village. the party being extreemly anxious to get down ply their ores very well,   we saw some cows on the bank which was a joyfull Sight to the party and caused a Shout to be raised for joy at [blank in MS.] P. M we came in Sight of the little french Village called Charriton [La Charette]   the men raised a Shout and Sprung upon their ores and we soon landed opposit to the Village. our party requested to be permited to fire off their Guns which was alowed & they discharged 3 rounds with a harty cheer, which was returned from five tradeing boats which lay opposit the village. we landed and were very politely received by two young Scotch men from Canada one in the employ of Mr. Aird a Mr. [blank space in MS]. and the other Mr. Reed,   all of those boats were bound to the Osage and Ottoes. those two young Scotch gentlemen furnished us with Beef flower and some pork for our men, and gave us a very agreeable supper. as it was like to rain we accepted of a bed in one of their tents. we purchased of a citizen two gallons of Whiskey for our party for which we were obliged to give Eight dollars in Cash, an imposition on the part of the citizen. every person, both French and americans seem to express great pleasure at our return, and acknowledged themselves much astonished in seeing us return. they informed us that we were supposed to have been lost long since, and were entirely given out by every person &c.

Those boats are from Canada in the batteaux form and wide in perpotion to their length. their length about 30 feet and the width 8 feet & pointed bow and stern, flat bottom and rowing six ores only   the Skenackeity form. those Bottoms are prepared for the navigation of this river,   I beleive them to be the best calculated for the navigation of this river of any which I have Seen. they are wide and flat not Subject to the dangers of the roleing Sands, which larger boats are on this river. the American inhabitants express great disgust for the governmt. of this Teritory. from what I can lern it arises from a disapmt. of getting all the Spanish Grants Confirmed.

SUNDAY 21ST SEPTR. 1806

rose early this morning   colected our men several of them had axcepted of the invitation of the citizens and visited their families. at half after 7 A. M we Set out. passed 12 canoes of Kickapoos assending on a hunting expedition. Saw Several persons also stock of different kind on the bank which reviv'd the party very much. at 3 P M we met two large boats assending. at 4 P M we arived in Sight of St. Charles, the party rejoiced at the Sight of this hospita[b]l[e] village plyed thear ores with great dexterity and we Soon arived opposit the Town   this day being Sunday we observed a number of Gentlemen and ladies walking on the bank,   we saluted the Village by three rounds from our blunderbuts and the Small arms of the party,   and landed near the lower part of the town. we were met by great numbers of the inhabitants,   we found them excessively polite. we received invitations from Several of those Gentlemen   Mr. Querie under took to Supply our party with provisions &c.   the inhabitants of this village appear much delighted at our return and seem to vie with each other in their politeness to us all. we came only 48 miles to day. the banks of the river thinly settled &c. (*some Settlements since we went up*)

MONDAY 22ND OF SEPTR. 1806

This morning being very wet and the rain Still continueing hard, and our party being all sheltered in the houses of those hospitable people, we did not [think] proper to proceed on untill after the rain was over, and continued at the house of Mr. Proulx. I took this oppertunity of writeing to my friends in Kentucky &c.   at 10 A M. it seased raining and we colected our party and Set out and proceeded on down to the Contonemt. at Coldwater Creek about 3 miles up the Missouri on it's Southern banks,   at this place we found Colo. Hunt & a Lieut. Peters & one Company of Artillerists   we were kindly received by the Gentlemen of this place. Mrs. Wilkinson the Lady of the Govr. & Genl. we wer sorry to find in delicate health.

we were honored with a Salute of [blank space in MS.] Guns and a harty welcom. at this place there is a publick store kept in which I am informed the U. S have 60000$ worth of indian Goods

TUESDAY 23RD SEPTR. 1806

we rose early took the Chief to the publick store & furnished him with Some clothes &c.   took an early breckfast with Colo. Hunt and Set out   decended to the Mississippi and down that river to St. Louis at which place we arived about 12 oClock. we Suffered the party to fire off their pieces as a Salute to the Town. we were met by all the village and received a harty welcom from it's inhabitants &c. here I found my old acquaintance Majr. W. Christy who had settled in this town in a public line as a Tavern Keeper. he furnished us with store rooms for our baggage and we accepted of the invitation of Mr. Peter Choteau and took a room in his house. we payed a friendly visit to Mr. August Chotau and some of our old friends this evening. as the post had departed from St. Louis Capt. Lewis wrote a note to Mr. Hay in Kahoka [Cahokia] to detain the post at that place untill 12 tomorrow which was reather later than his usial time of leaveing it

WEDNESDAY 24TH OF SEPTEMBER 1806

I sleped but little last night   however we rose early and commenc[e]d wrighting our letters   Capt Lewis wrote one to the presidend and I wrote Govr. Harrison & my friends in Kentucky and Sent of[f] George Drewyer with those letters to Kohoka & delivered them to Mr. Hays &c.   we dined with Mr. Chotoux to day,   and after dinner went to a store and purchased some clothes,   which we gave to a Tayler and derected to be made. Capt. Lewis in opening his trunk found all his papers wet, and some seeds spoiled.

THURSDAY 25TH OF SEPTR. 1806 —

had all of our skins &c. suned and stored away in a storeroom of Mr. Caddy Choteau. payed some visits of form, to the gentlemen of St. Louis. in the evening a dinner & Ball

FRIDAY 25TH [26] OF SEPTR. 1806 —

a fine morning   we commenced wrighting &c.

APPENDIX I

Jefferson's Instructions to Lewis

APPENDIX II

Personnel of the Expedition

APPENDIX III

Itemized List of Specimens and Artifacts Sent to Jefferson from Fort Mandan

INDEX

APPENDIX I

JEFFERSON'S INSTRUCTIONS TO LEWIS

To Meriwether Lewis, esquire, Captain of the 1st regiment of infantry of the United States of America: Your situation as Secretary of the President of the United States has made you acquainted with the objects of my confidential message of Jan. 18, 1803, to the legislature. you have seen the act they passed, which, tho' expressed in general terms, was meant to sanction those objects, and you are appointed to carry them into execution.

Instruments for ascertaining by celestial observations the geography of the country thro' which you will pass, have already been provided. light articles for barter, & presents among the Indians, arms for your attendants, say for from 10 to 12 men, boats, tents, & other travelling apparatus, with ammunition, medicine, surgical instruments & provisions you will have prepared with such aids as the Secretary at War can yield in his department; & from him also you will recieve authority to engage among our troops, by voluntary agreement, the number of attendants above mentioned, over whom you, as their commanding officer are invested with all the powers the laws give in such a case.

As your movements while within the limits of the U. S. will be better directed by occasional communications, adapted to circumstances as they arise, they will not be noticed here. what follows will respect your proceedings after your departure from the U. S.

Your mission has been communicated to the Ministers here from France, Spain & Great Britain, and through them to their governments: and such assurances given them as to it's objects as we trust will satisfy them. the country of Louisiana having been ceded by Spain to France, the passport you have from the Minister of France, the representative of the present sovereign of the country, will be a protection with all it's subjects: And that from the Minister of England will entitle you to the friendly aid of any traders of that allegiance with whom you may happen to meet.

The object of your mission is to explore the Missouri river, & such principal stream of it, as, by it's course & communication with the waters of the Pacific Ocean, may offer the most direct & practicable water communication across this continent, for the purposes of commerce.

Beginning at the mouth of the Missouri, you will take observations of latitude & longitude, at all remarkable points on the river, & especially at the mouths of rivers, at rapids, at islands & other places & objects distinguished by such natural marks & characters of a durable kind, as that they may with certainty be recognized hereafter. the courses of the river between these points of observation may be supplied by the compass, the log-line & by time, corrected by the observations themselves. the variations of the compass too, in different places, should be noticed.

The interesting points of portage between the heads of the Missouri & the water offering the best communication with the Pacific Ocean should also be fixed by observation, & the course of that water to the ocean, in the same manner as that of the Missouri.

Your observations are to be taken with great pains & accuracy, to be entered distinctly, & intelligibly for others as well as yourself, to comprehend all the elements necessary, with the aid of the usual tables, to fix the latitude and longitude of the places at which they were taken, & are to be rendered to the war office, for the purpose of having the calculations made concurrently by proper persons within the U. S.   several copies of these, as well as your other notes, should be made at leisure times & put into the care of the most trustworthy of your attendants, to guard by multiplying them, against the accidental losses to which they will be exposed. a further guard would be that one of these copies be written on the paper of the birch, as less liable to injury from damp than common paper.

The commerce which may be carried on with the people inhabiting the line you will pursue, renders a knolege of these people important. you will therefore endeavor to make yourself acquainted, as far as a diligent pursuit of your journey shall admit,

with the names of the nations & their numbers;
the extent & limits of their possessions;
their relations with other tribes or nations;
their language, traditions, monuments;
their ordinary occupations in agriculture, fishing, hunt-
    ing, war, arts, & the implements for these;
their food, clothing, & domestic accomodations;
the diseases prevalent among them, & the remedies
    they use;
moral & physical circumstances which distinguish them
    from the tribes we know;
peculiarities in their laws, customs & dispositions;
and articles of commerce they may need or furnish, & to
    what extent.

And considering the interest which every nation has in extending
& strengthening the authority of reason & justice among the people
around them, it will be useful to acquire what knolege you can of
the state of morality, religion & information among them, as it may
better enable those who endeavor to civilize & instruct them, to
adapt their measures to the existing notions & practises of those on
whom they are to operate.

Other object worthy of notice will be
    the soil & face of the country, it's growth & vegetable pro-
        ductions; especially those not of the U. S.
    the animals of the country generally, & especially those
        not known in the U. S.
    the remains and accounts of any which may deemed rare
        or extinct;
    the mineral productions of every kind; but more particu-
        larly metals, limestone, pit coal & salpetre; salines &
        mineral waters, noting the temperature of the last, &
        such circumstances as may indicate their character.
    Volcanic appearances.
    climate as characterized by the thermometer, by the
        proportion of rainy, cloudy & clear days, by lightening,
        hail, snow, ice, by the access & recess of frost, by the

winds prevailing at different seasons, the dates at which
particular plants put forth or lose their flowers, or leaf,
times of appearance of particular birds, reptiles or
insects.

Altho' your route will be along the channel of the Missouri, yet
you will endeavor to inform yourself, by inquiry, of the character
& extent of the country watered by it's branches, & especially on it's
southern side. the North river or Rio Bravo which runs into the
gulph of Mexico, and the North river, or Rio colorado, which runs
into the gulph of California, are understood to be the principal
streams heading opposite to the waters of the Missouri, and running
Southwardly. whether the dividing grounds between the Missouri
& them are mountains or flatlands, what are their distance from the
Missouri, the character of the intermediate country, & the people
inhabiting it, are worthy of particular enquiry. The Northern
waters of the Missouri are less to be enquired after, because they
have been ascertained to a considerable degree, and are still in a
course of ascertainment by English traders & travellers. but if you
can learn anything certain of the most Northern source of the
Missisipi, & of it's position relative to the lake of the woods, it will
be interesting to us. some account too of the path of the Canadian
traders from the Missisipi, at the mouth of the Ouisconsin river, to
where it strikes the Missouri and of the soil & rivers in it's course,
is desireable.

In all your intercourse with the natives treat them in the most
friendly & conciliatory manner which their own conduct will admit;
allay all jealousies as to the object of your journey, satisfy them of
it's innocence, make them acquainted with the position, extent, character, peaceable & commercial dispositions of the U. S. of our wish
to be neighborly, friendly & useful to them, & of our dispositions to
a commercial intercourse with them; confer with them on the points
most convenient as mutual emporiums, & the articles of most desireable interchange for them & us. if a few of their influential chiefs,
within practicable distance, wish to visit us, arrange such a visit with
them, and furnish them with authority to call on our officers, on
their entering the U. S. to have them conveyed to this place at public
expence. if any of them should wish to have some of their young
people brought up with us, & taught such arts as may be useful to

them, we will receive, instruct & take care of them. such a mission, whether of influential chiefs, or of young people, would give some security to your own party. carry with you some matter of the kinepox, inform those of them with whom you may be of it' efficacy as a preservative from the small-pox; and instruct & incourage them in the use of it. this may be especially done wherever you winter.

As it is impossible for us to foresee in what manner you will be recieved by those people, whether with hospitality or hostility, so is it impossible to prescribe the exact degree of perseverance with which you are to pursue your journey. we value too much the lives of citizens to offer them to probably destruction. your numbers will be sufficient to secure you against the unauthorised opposition of individuals, or of small parties: but if a superior force, authorised or not authorised, by a nation, should be arrayed against your further passage, & inflexibly determined to arrest it, you must decline it's further pursuit, and return. in the loss of yourselves, we should lose also the information you will have acquired. by returning safely with that, you may enable us to renew the essay with better calculated means. to your own discretion therefore must be left the degree of danger you may risk, & the point at which you should decline, only saying we wish you to err on the side of your safety, & bring back your party safe, even if it be with less information.

As far up the Missouri as the white settlements extend, an intercourse will probably be found to exist between them and the Spanish posts at St. Louis, opposite Cahokia, or Ste. Genevieve opposite Kaskaskia. from still farther up the river, the traders may furnish a conveyance for letters. beyond that you may perhaps be able to engage Indians to bring letters for the government to Cahokia or Kaskaskia, on promising that they shall there receive such special compensation as you shall have stipulated with them. avail yourself of these means to communicate to us, at seasonable intervals, a copy of your journal, notes & observations of every kind, putting into cypher whatever might do injury if betrayed.

Should you reach the Pacific ocean [One full line scratched out, indecipherable. — Thwaites.] inform yourself of the circumstances which may decide whether the furs of those parts may not be collected as advantageously at the head of the Missouri (convenient as is supposed to the waters of the Colorado & Oregon or Columbia) as at Nootka sound or any other point of that coast; & that trade be consequently conducted through the Missouri & U. S. more beneficially than by the circumnavigation now practised.

On your arrival on that coast endeavor to learn if there be any port within your reach frequented by the sea-vessels of any nation, and to send two of your trusty people back by sea, in such way as shall appear practicable, with a copy of your notes. and should you be of opinion that the return of your party by the way they went will be eminently dangerous, then ship the whole, & return by sea by way of Cape Horn or the Cape of good Hope, as you shall be able. as you will be without money, clothes or provisions, you must endeavor to use the credit of the U. S. to obtain them; for which purpose open letters of credit shall be furnished you authorising you to draw on the Executive of the U. S. or any of its officers in any part of the world, on which drafts can be disposed of, and to apply with our recommendations to the Consuls, agents, merchants, or citizens of any nation with which we have intercourse, assuring them in our name that any aids they may furnish you, shall honorably repaid, and on demand. Our consuls Thomas Howes at Batavia in Java, William Buchanan on the isles of France and Bourbon, & John Elmslie at the Cape of good hope will be able to supply your necessities by draughts on us.

Should you find it safe to return by the way you go, after sending two of your party round by sea, or with your whole party, if no conveyance by sea can be found, do so; making such observations on your return as may serve to supply, correct or confirm those made on your outward journey.

In re-entering the U. S. and reaching a place of safety, discharge any of your attendants who may desire & deserve it, procuring for them immediate paiment of all arrears of pay & cloathing which may have incurred since their departure; & assure them that they shall be recommended to the liberality of the legislature for the grant of a soldier's portion of land each, as proposed in my message to Congress & repair yourself with your papers to the seat of government.

To provide, on the accident of your death, against anarchy, dispersion & the consequent danger to your party, and total failure of the enterprise, you are hereby authorised, by any instrument signed & written in your hand, to name the person among them who shall succeed to the command on your decease, & by like instruments to change the nomination from time to time, as further experience of the characters accompanying you shall point out superior fitness; and all the powers & authorities given to yourself are, in the event of your death, transferred to & vested in the successor so named, with further power to him, & his successors in like manner to name each his successor, who, on the death of his predecessor, shall be invested with all the powers & authorities given to yourself.

Given under my hand at the city of Washington, this 20th day of June 1803

Th. Jefferson
Pr. U S. of America

APPENDIX II

THE PERMANENT PARTY

Commanding:
  Meriwether Lewis, Captain 1st U.S. Infantry
  William Clark, Second Lieutenant, U.S. Corps of Artillerists

Sergeants:
  John Ordway
  Nathaniel Pryor
  Charlies Floyd (died August 20 1804)
  Patrick Gass (appointed August 26 1804, in place of Floyd)

Interpreters: [1]
  George Drewyer (properly spelled Drouillard, apparently)
  Touissant Charbonneau

Privates:
  William Bratton
  John Collins
  John Colter
  Peter Cruzatte
  Joseph Fields
  Reuben Fields

[1] This is a special rank, created so that those who held it could be paid at a higher rate than privates or noncoms. (Interpreters were paid $25 per month, sergeants $8, enlisted men $5.) Drewyer's appointment was dated January 1 1804, though he had been engaged the previous November; Charbonneau's was dated April 7 1805, though he had served since November 1804. Cruzatte and Labiche regularly acted as interpreters, but at a private's pay.

Robert Frazier (enlisted October 8 1804; originally with Warfing-
ton's detachment)
George Gibson
Silas Goodrich
Hugh Hall
Thomas P. Howard
Francis Labiche
Baptiste Lepage (enlisted November 2 1804, in place of Newman)
Hugh McNeal
John Newman (dropped from permanent party October 13 1804,
later discharged)
John Potts
Moses B. Reed (deserted August 4 1804; recaptured and later
discharged)
George Shannon
John Shields
John B. Thompson
William Werner
Joseph Whitehouse
Richard Windsor
Peter Wiser

Also: Clark's slave, York; Charbonneau's Shoshone wife, Sacajawea

U.S. SOLDIERS ATTACHED TO EXPEDITION AS FAR
AS THE MANDAN VILLAGE

Corporal Richard Warfington
Privates:
  John Boleye (Boley?)
  John Dame
  Robert Frazier (enlisted in permanent party)
  John Robertson
  Ebenezer Tuttle
  Isaac White

ST. LOUIS BOATMEN

Baptiste Deschamps, "patroon"

Joseph Collin
Charles Hébert
—— Liberté (deserted July 29 1804) [2]
Baptiste LaJeunesse
Etienne Mabbauf
Peter Pinaut
Paul Primaut
Francis Rivet [3]
Peter Roi

There can be little doubt that the above is the roster of Deschamps' party, though it numbers ten, whereas Biddle makes it nine. Perhaps the discrepancy is explained by the assignment of one boatman to Warfington's pirogue. (*Journals*, I, 31.) Conceivably this may also explain the assignment of Rivet to Floyd's mess. On August 21 1806, when the expedition is nearing the Arikara village on its return journey, Clark records meeting "Reeved & Greinyea," who "wintered with us at the Mandans in 1804." (*Journals*, V, 349–50.) Later in the same entry he speaks of them as "Reevey & Grienway." On the authority of Mrs. E. E. Dye, a novelist, Thwaites identifies these men (*Journals*, I, 283) as "François Rivet and Philippe Degie," engagés of the expedition who were "locally celebrated" in Oregon, where they are buried, "as being men who had been with Lewis and Clark." No one named Degie and no one whose name resembles Greinyea or Grienway is mentioned anywhere in the *Journals*. In his entry for the next day, August 22, Clark says that at the Arikara village, "we found a french man by the name of Rokey who was one of our Engagees as high as the Mandans," who asked, and was permitted, to accompany the expedition to St. Louis. There is no other mention of him.

2 The spelling of his name is uncertain. Also, Ordway's journal calls him Jo Barter.
3 Status uncertain. On May 26 1804, when the messes were formed, he was attached to Floyd's, not Deschamps'.

APPENDIX III

ITEMIZED LIST OF SPECIMENS AND ARTIFACTS
SENT TO JEFFERSON FROM FORT MANDAN

(See Clark's entry for April 3 1805)

Box No. 1, contains the following articles i. e.

In package No. 3 & 4 Male & female antelope, with their Skelitons.

No. 7 & 9 the horns of two mule or Black tailed deer. a Mandan bow an quiver of arrows — with some Recara's tobacco seed.

No. 11 a Martin Skin, Containing the tail of a Mule Deer, a weasel and three Squirels from the Rockey mountains.

No. 12, The bones & Skeleton of a Small burrowing wolf of the Praries the Skin being lost by accedent.

No. 99. The Skeliton of the white and Grey *hare.*

Box No. 2, Contains 4 Buffalow *Robes,* and a ear of Mandan Corn.

The large Trunk Contains a male & female *Braro* or burrowing dog of the Praire and the female's *Skeliton.*

a carrote of Ricaras *Tobacco*

a red fox Skin Containing a *Magpie*

No. 14 Minitarras Buffalow robe Containing Some articles of Indian dress.

No. 15 a mandan *robe* containing two burrowing Squirels, a white *weasel* and the Skin of a Loucirvia. also

13 red fox Skins.

1 white Hare Skin &c.

4 horns of the mountain ram

1 Robe representing a battle between the Sioux & Ricaras aga the Minetares and Mandans.

In Box No. 3.

Nos. 1 & 2 the Skins of the Male & female Antelope with their Skeletons. & the Skin of a Yellow *Bear* which I obtained from the *Sieoux*

No. 4. Box. Specimens of plants numbered from 1. to 67.

Specimens of Plants numbered from 1 to 60.

1 Earthen pot Such as the Mandans manufacture and use for culinary purposes.

1 Tin box containing insects mice &c.

a Specimine of the fur of the antilope.

a Specimon of a plant, and a parcel of its roots higly prized by the natives as an efficatious remidy in cases of the bite of the rattle Snake or Mad Dog.

In a large Trunk

Skins of a male and female Braro, or burrowing Dog of the Prarie, with the Skeleton of the female.

1 Skin of the red fox Containing a Magpie

2 Cased Skins of the white hare.

1 Minitarra Buffalow robe Containing Some articles of Indian Dress.

1 Mandan Buffalow robe Containing a dressed Lousirva Skin, and 2 cased Skins of the Burrowing Squirel of the Praries.

13 red fox Skins

4 Horns of the Mountain Ram, or *big horn*.

1 Buffalow robe painted by a mandan man representing a battle fought 8 years Since by the Sioux & Recaras against the mandans, me ni tarras & Ah wah har ways. (Mandans &c. on horseback

Cage No. 6.

Contains a liveing burrowing Squirel of the praries

Cage No. 7.

Contains 4 liveing Magpies

Cage No. 9.

Containing a liveing hen of the Prairie

a large par of Elks horns containing by the frontal bone.

INDEX